Managerial Accounting for the Hospitality Industry

Lea R. Dopson

David K. Hayes

WILEY

John Wiley & Sons, Inc.

For general information on our other products and services, or technical support, please contact our Customer Care Department within the United States at 800-762-2974, outside the United States at 317-572-3993 or fax 317-572-4002.

Wiley also publishes its books in a variety of electronic formats. Some content that appears in print may not be available in electronic books. For more information about Wiley products, visit our web site at http://www.wiley.com.

Library of Congress Cataloging-in-Publication Data:

Dopson, Lea R.
    Managerial accounting for the hospitality industry / Lea R. Dopson,
David K. Hayes.
        p. cm.
    Includes bibliographical references.
    ISBN 978-0-471-72337-0 (cloth/cd)
    1. Hospitality industry—Accounting. 2. Managerial accounting. I.
Hayes, David K. II. Title.
    HF5686.H75D67 2009
    647.94068′1—dc22

                                        2008022802

Printed in the United States of America

10   9   8   7   6   5   4

Contents

Preface   vii

■ **Part I   Accounting Fundamentals   1**

Chapter 1   Hospitality Industry Accounting   3

Unique Aspects of the Hospitality Industry   4
The Purpose of Accounting in the Hospitality Industry   6
Branches of Accounting   7
Why Hospitality Managers Use Managerial Accounting   15
The Uniform System of Accounts   16
Ethics and Hospitality Accounting   18
The Blue Lagoon Water Park Resort: A Case Study   22
Can You Do the Math?   24

Apply What You Have Learned   25
Key Terms and Concepts   26
Test Your Skills   26

Chapter 2   Accounting Fundamentals Review   29

Bookkeeping and Accounting   30
The Accounting Formula   31
Recording Changes to The Accounting Formula   32
Generally Accepted Accounting Principles   43
The Hospitality Business Cycle   54

Apply What You Have Learned   55
Key Terms and Concepts   56
Test Your Skills   56

■ **Part II   Financial Statements   61**

Chapter 3   The Income Statement   63

The Purpose of the Income Statement   64
Income Statement Preparation   70
Income Statement Analysis   86

Apply What You Have Learned   105
Key Terms and Concepts   105
Test Your Skills   106

Chapter 4   The Balance Sheet   112

The Purpose of the Balance Sheet   113
Balance Sheet Formats   119
Balance Sheet Content   120
Components of the Balance Sheet   123
Balance Sheet Analysis   129

Apply What You Have Learned   136
Key Terms and Concepts   136
Test Your Skills   137

Chapter 5   The Statement of Cash Flows   143

Understanding Cash Flows   144
The Purpose of the Statement of Cash Flows   145
Sources and Uses of Funds   147
Creating the Statement of Cash Flows   155
Statement of Cash Flows Analysis   167

Apply What You Have Learned   171
Key Terms and Concepts   171
Test Your Skills   172

Chapter 6   Ratio Analysis   180

Purpose and Value of Ratios   181
Types of Ratios   185
Comparative Analysis of Ratios   225
Ratio Analysis Limitations   226

Apply What You Have Learned   228
Key Terms and Concepts   229
Test Your Skills   230

■ **Part III   Management of Revenue and Expense   237**

Chapter 7   Food and Beverage Pricing   239

Factors Affecting Menu Pricing   240
Assigning Menu Prices   242
Menu Price Analysis   249

Apply What You Have Learned   268
Key Terms and Concepts   268
Test Your Skills   269

Chapter 8   Revenue Management for Hotels   274

Establishing Room Rates   275
Revenue Management   287
Non-Room Revenue   300

Apply What You Have Learned   305
Key Terms and Concepts   306
Test Your Skills   307

Chapter 9   Managerial Accounting for Costs   313

The Concept of Cost   314
Types of Costs   315
Cost/Volume/Profit Analysis   335

Apply What You Have Learned   342
Key Terms and Concepts   343
Test Your Skills   343

■ **Part IV   Accounting Information for Planning   351**

Chapter 10   Forecasting in the Hospitality Industry   353

The Importance of Accurate Forecasts   354
Forecast Methodology   357
Utilizing Trend Lines in Forecasting   374

Apply What You Have Learned   376
Key Terms and Concepts   376
Test Your Skills   377

Chapter 11   Budgeting and Internal Controls   380

The Importance of Budgets   381
Types of Budgets   383

Operations Budget Essentials 387
Developing an Operations Budget 388
Monitoring an Operations Budget 397
Cash Budgeting 406
Managing Budgets through Internal Controls 413

Apply What You Have Learned 418
Key Terms and Concepts 419
Test Your Skills 420

Chapter 12 Capital Investment, Leasing, and Taxation **428**

Capital Budgeting 430
Capital Investment 433
Financing Alternatives 447
Taxation 454

Apply What You Have Learned 461
Key Terms and Concepts 461
Test Your Skills 462

Glossary **469**

About the Authors **489**

Index **491**

Preface

Managerial Accounting for the Hospitality Industry is a book that we the authors were particularly excited and privileged to develop. We view it as an essential book not merely because the topic of managerial accounting is so important, but more critically because the success of hospitality students themselves is so important. In addition to their "people skills," all hospitality professionals must possess "numbers skills." Hospitality is a business, and it has been said that accounting is the language of business. A clear understanding of that language simply must be acquired by all who wish to achieve their business's financial and profit objectives. It is the goal of this book to provide each reader with that crucial understanding.

Together we have over 50 years experience teaching students who wish to make a professional career in the field of hospitality. During those years, at many institutions and at a variety of instructional levels, we have consistently found that the students we teach have had difficulty understanding and applying accounting concepts in general, and managerial accounting concepts specifically. For many students, accounting—the language of business—was perceived as a *foreign language*, and one that they did not easily grasp. Our personal experience, however, as well as our admiration for the abilities of our students, convinced us that the root cause of this situation rests more with the lack of appropriate instructional tools and techniques available to the instructors teaching these students than with the interest or capability of the students themselves.

Alternative managerial accounting texts present accounting as if their hospitality readers wish to be accountants. Most simply do not. We recognize, significantly, that readers first and foremost desire to be hospitality *managers*. As such, they will legitimately want to know precisely how the accounting skills they will acquire by reading this book can help them better do their jobs. This text uses a close examination of the Blue Lagoon Water Park Resort, an extensive and true-to-the-industry case study that permits students to immediately apply what they have learned to the key management decisions made at a full-service resort. Through a myriad of practical hospitality examples such as this that clearly illustrate accounting concepts, this text will show managers exactly how to use accounting information to achieve their professional and personal goals.

To the Student

Learning managerial accounting by reading this book will be fun. That's a promise from us to you. It is an easy promise to keep because working in the hospitality industry is fun. And it is challenging. Learning managerial accounting (accounting used by managers) will be exactly the same: *fun and challenging*. In this book, you will see how hospitality managers actually consider and apply accounting information.

If you work hard and do your best, you will find you do have the ability to master all of the information in this text. When you do, you will have gained an invaluable management tool that will enhance your company's performance and, by doing so, advance your own hospitality career.

To the Instructor

Students who begin to learn managerial accounting, like those students seeking to acquire any new language, will encounter a new vocabulary, unique ways of thinking, and even new ways of applying what they have learned. In many ways, learning accounting, the language of business, is exactly like learning a foreign language.

As any adult who has tried knows well, learning a new language can be hard and the difficulty inherent in learning to *speak* it well is often underestimated by those who are already *fluent* in the language. The result, when applied to managerial accounting, is that knowledgeable and well-intentioned teachers find too many of their students struggle, are left behind, and do not ultimately become fluent in the language.

It was our goal to apply to managerial accounting the best foreign language instructional practices we could identify. As hospitality and culinary professionals, we were quite pleased to find that there are five clearly identifiable (and constant) ingredients in the standardized recipe for extremely successful foreign language instruction. The application of these same learning principles, so effective in teaching students other new languages, helps solve the real instructional dilemma faced by managerial accounting instructors and students in so many hospitality programs. The five key ingredients identified and enthusiastically incorporated in the development of this text are:

1. **An Early Start:** Countries whose students are highly multilingual begin widespread or compulsory education in foreign languages by age eight. This contrasts starkly with the United States, where the majority of students who study a foreign language do not start before age 14. Applying this principle, we sought to develop an accounting text that could be used by students as they first enter their hospitality programs. Freshman in four-year programs, first-year community college students, entry-level culinary arts students, and all those with little to no previous background in accounting will find the book immediately applicable and easy to understand. This is so because, uniquely, the book does not rely on any prerequisite accounting courses to fulfill its educational purpose.

2. **Significant Student Interest:** Some hospitality students see themselves more as *people* persons than *numbers* persons. That's okay. But learning accounting can be just as fun and exciting for people persons as it is for numbers persons. All hospitality students, we believe, are keen to learn about their industry. This book harnesses that student interest by constant reference to how the accounting information they are learning applies *directly* to the fascinating field of hospitality management and the student's own future success.

3. **A Well-Articulated Conceptual Framework:** In the design of any successful instructional program, there are two key questions that must be painstakingly addressed. Simply put, these are:

   ■ What must be taught?
   ■ In what order shall it be taught?

   We were privileged to have the opportunity to access the best teaching practices and experiences of outstanding hospitality practitioners and educators nationally as we carefully constructed the book's content and order of information. Experienced managerial accounting instructors will find all of the core topics they teach have been incorporated and in a manner they will find greatly aids their students' comprehension and retention.

4. **Ample Practice Time:** Language instructors know that one of the best ways for their students to become fluent is to "practice"—a lot! In recognition of this fact, an extensive number of practice problems were developed for this text. Thus, a great number of financial formulas and statements are presented in the text, precisely at the point where they are most meaningful.

   This text goes further, however. In many cases, an accounting problem is of a *conceptual* or *theoretical* nature. Instructors who assign these types of questions will find they require students to critically apply accounting concepts they have learned, as well as their own values and beliefs, to solve important business problems.

5. **Effective Assessment Tools:** The best educational programs carefully and accurately measure student progress. The importance of student assessment goes far beyond the simple assignment of a grade at semester's end. Identification of areas in which students may need further instruction, ease of administration, and exam quality were all factors meticulously incorporated into the extensive assessment tools developed for this book. The importance, to students as well as instructors, of measurement and evaluation examinations, quizzes, and other tools that are perceived as both fair and are error free is critical, and what we strove for during the writing of this book.

It is our belief that the careful and consistent application of these five successful teaching techniques, joined with accurate and up-to-date managerial accounting information, unite to make this text unsurpassed for making students of all abilities fluent in the fascinating and fun-to-learn language known as *Managerial Accounting for the Hospitality Industry*.

Text Content

This is a book about the theory and practice of managerial accounting techniques in the hospitality industry. In the usual introduction to an applied accounting text such as this, the authors will proudly say something along the lines of "this book is not based upon a bunch of ivory tower theories," implying, of course, that the use of theory in teaching is somehow suspect. Typically, they then go on to describe their own book in such terms as "practical, real-world, down-to-earth, and/or realistic." We have found that it is a good idea to be suspect when such qualifiers are used. The famed management consultant Dr. W. Edwards Deming was fond of saying, "No theory, no learning." He was correct.

Deming knew well that the purpose of well-developed theories is to explain, predict, or advise. The content of this book was carefully chosen to achieve these three goals. Thus, it is practical, because practicality enhances learning by allowing students to apply new information (accounting) in a setting interesting and familiar to them (hospitality). But it is also unabashedly theoretical because practical advancements in any endeavor result from carefully examining old theories and improving upon them (which, after all, is why the newest version of the Boeing 747 travels a good bit faster than the Wright brothers' original aircraft). Thus, with the goal of effectively aiding in teaching the theory and the practice of managerial accounting, the authors created a manuscript with 12 chapters, divided among four major parts:

Part I: Accounting Fundamentals

Part I introduces readers to the foundations of managerial accounting and contains the following chapters:

1. *Hospitality Industry Accounting*
2. *Accounting Fundamentals Review*

In this critical underpinning section, readers will learn about the different types of accounting used by those in business, why generally accepted accounting principles (GAAP) are applied, and their own ethical responsibilities related to the reporting of financial information.

Part II: Financial Statements

Part II of the text examines in detail the three most important financial documents utilized by managerial accountants as well as how financial ratios are used to evaluate and analyze these documents. It contains the following four vital chapters:

3. *The Income Statement*
4. *The Balance Sheet*
5. *The Statement of Cash Flows*
6. *Ratio Analysis*

In this section, readers are introduced to the key financial documents they will prepare and analyze. The chapter on ratio analysis teaches them the most up-to-date means of examining the information contained in these critical documents.

Part III: Management of Revenue and Expense
Part III of this text introduces readers to specific activities they will use to manage their revenues and expenses. The chapters included in this section are:
7. *Food and Beverage Pricing*
8. *Revenue Management for Hotels*
9. *Managerial Accounting for Costs*

These chapters teach readers exactly how hospitality professionals use managerial techniques to optimize their revenues and analyze their costs to maximize profitability.

Part IV: Accounting Information for Planning
In the concluding section of the text, readers are given the information needed to plan for the current and future success of their businesses. Chapters included in this section are:
10. *Forecasting in the Hospitality Industry*
11. *Budgeting and Internal Controls*
12. *Capital Investment, Leasing, and Taxation*

This section contains a range of topics and information important to managerial accountants, including forecasting restaurant and hotel revenues. In addition, the various types of budgets used by managerial accountants in hospitality are presented as well as information about the development and monitoring of these budgets. The text concludes with a chapter containing important information about capital budgeting, the computation of rates of investment returns, leasing, and taxation.

Text Features

From a reader's perspective, the features of a textbook often are as important as its content. Thoughtfully designed textbook features make the content presented easy to read, easy to understand, and easy to retain. Readers will find that ***Managerial Accounting for the Hospitality Industry*** is especially reader friendly. The following strategically designed features help readers learn the concepts of managerial accounting:

■ *Overview:* Each chapter begins with a brief narrative overview. This is simply a quick and easy guide to the chapter's contents. Overviews make it easy for readers to see what the chapter is about and what they will learn by reading it.

■ *Chapter Outline:* The chapter outline at the beginning of each chapter shows the listing for each topic in order of their introduction and provides a simple way to quickly find material within the chapter.

■ *Learning Outcomes:* Each chapter utilizes this short feature to explain in short and clear terms (and before any content is presented), exactly what a reader will be able to *do* when they have mastered the chapter's content. This feature makes it easy for readers to see what the chapter is about and the skills they will obtain by reading it.

■ *Go Figure! Exercises:* These exercises provide scenarios that involve stepped out calculations using the formulas presented within each chapter to illustrate the various key accounting principles/concepts.

 *go figure!*

For example, consider the case of T.D. Highwater. Mr. Highwater owns a hotel that, last year, generated $10 million of recorded revenue and $9 million of recorded expenses, resulting in a profit of $1 million. Shondra, Mr. Highwater's hotel manager, is pleased that the profit she generated for the hotel was $1 million. Mr. Highwater, however, reported the $1 million profit on his income tax returns and was required by current tax laws to pay $300,000 of the $1 million in taxes. If you were Mr. Highwater, would you say your "profit" for the year was:

1. $1 million or
2. $700,000?

The answer is $700,000 ($1,000,000 − $300,000 = $700,000) since Mr. Highwater incurred an expense of $300,000 in income taxes paid to the government.

■ *Fun on the Web!:* The importance of the Internet as a learning tool cannot be overlooked in any field of study. The student-friendly *Fun on the Web!* feature identifies useful websites to visit and gives readers specific instructions about what they should do, consider, and learn when they visit each site.

fun on the Web!

The 2002 Sarbanes-Oxley Act became law to help rebuild public confidence in the way corporate America governs its business activities. The Act has far-reaching implications for the tourism, hospitality, and leisure industry. To examine an overview of its provisions, go to:

www.sarbanes-oxley.com/section.php

■ *Apply What You Have Learned:* Each chapter contains a true-to-life mini-case designed to make readers think about how they would personally use the information they have learned to respond to managerial accounting challenges they may encounter in their careers. Thought-provoking questions are included at the end of this feature to assist students in considering the solutions they would implement when addressing the issues raised in the case.

Apply What You Have Learned

Now, just as she was about to graduate, the Club's food and beverage director called Samara into her office to offer her the job of beverage manager. It was an important job, as the Club's beverage department grossed over $500,000 per year. Samara was excited about the opportunity and the pay!

1. Properly accounting for beverage sales is an important part of a beverage manager's job. What are two additional, specific areas of financial accounting that would be important for Samara to understand if she is to succeed in her new job?

■ *Key Terms and Concepts:* As is true with many areas of specialization within hospitality management, managerial accountants certainly speak their own language. Readers often need help in remembering key vocabulary terms and concepts they should have mastered after reading a section of a book. Thus, Key Terms and Concepts are listed at the conclusion of each chapter (and in the order in which they were presented) to provide a valuable study aid. An alphabetical glossary of these terms is available at the end of the text and on the text's web site: www.wiley.com/college/dopson.

■ *Test Your Skills:* This capstone feature consists of accounting "word problems" to be solved using the information and skills learned in the chapter. It is included in each chapter and allows readers the chance to apply and practice, in a variety of hospitality settings, the concepts they have now mastered. Requiring, in nearly all cases, multiple calculations to complete the problem set, this feature also provides valuable opportunities to learn about creative ways hospitality professionals utilize managerial accounting to address operational problems. All "Test Your Skills" problems are designed as Excel spreadsheets and are found on the Student CD included in the back of this book.

Test Your Skills

1. Rosa and Gabriel own two Mexican grills in a large city in Texas. Rosa has primary responsibility for the grill in the suburbs, and Gabriel has primary responsibility for the grill in the downtown area. The menu items and product costs are the same in both grills, but the market in the downtown area demands lower menu prices than that in the suburbs. So, Rosa has set her desired product cost percentage at 28%, and Gabriel's desired product cost percentage is 32% since he can't charge as much as Rosa. Rosa likes to use the product cost percentage method to price menu items, and Gabriel likes to use the factor method. Help both of them determine their selling prices. (Spreadsheet hint: Use the ROUND function for the Factor column to three decimal places.)

■ A *Glossary* of terms at the end of the book helps readers quickly find definitions for key managerial accounting terms and concepts.

■ *Student CD-ROM:* A CD, included with the purchase of each text, introduces students to the important skill of spreadsheet development. A section called *Before You Start: How to Use Spreadsheets* gives students a quick and easy guide to spreadsheet use and development. It includes formulas that students will need to complete the "Test Your Skills" exercises at the end of each chapter of this text. We have intentionally chosen the simplest formulas that have the widest use. There are two versions of these guidelines included on this CD so that both students using Excel 2003 and Excel 2007 will have the information they need to create and work with Excel spreadsheets. Simply click on the link for the version of Excel you are using.

Using the supplied CD, students can immediately see how their answers to "Test your Skills" problems translate into managerial accounting solutions via spreadsheet formula development and manipulation. This CD assists students in understanding the how and why of building spreadsheet solutions for the hospitality managerial accounting problems they will face in the classroom and their careers. The spreadsheets for each of the "Test Your Skills" exercises have also been created in Excel 2003 and Excel 2007 so students can work with the appropriate set of spreadsheets based on the version of Excel they're using.

Instructors will find that the grading of problem sets becomes much easier when, with the aid of the CD, all students use a consistent approach to classroom assignments.

The CD also includes a convenient listing of "Frequently Used Formulas for Managing Operations." This is an easy reference for quickly finding essential accounting formulas presented in the text. "'Fun on the Web!' Sites" contains hyperlinks to those sites referenced throughout the text in which additional information on a variety of vital accounting and management topics can be found.

Instructor and Student Resources

To help instructors effectively manage their time and to enhance student learning opportunities, several significant educational tools have been developed specifically for this text. An Instructor Tools CD-ROM, a Student Study Guide, companion websites for instructors and students and WebCT and Blackboard course materials are all provided to assist instructors and students in the teaching and learning process.

Instructor Tools CD-ROM. As an aid to instructors, an Instructor Tools CD-ROM (ISBN: 978-0-470-25737-1) has been developed for this text. The CD includes:

■ Lecture outlines

■ Suggested answers for "Apply What You Have Learned"

■ Answers to chapter-ending "Test Your Skills" problems

■ A Test Bank including exam questions and answers

■ "Test Your Skills" spreadsheet answers and formulas

■ PowerPoint slides

■ Student Study Guide solutions

Student Study Guide. As an aid to students, a Student Study Guide (ISBN: 978-0-470-14055-0) has been developed for this text. This Student Study Guide can be ordered separately or packaged with the text. Each chapter of the Student Study Guide includes:

■ Study Notes

■ Key Terms and Concepts Review (matching key terms with their definitions)

■ Discussion Questions that enhance student learning of conceptual topics

■ Quiz Yourself—10 point multiple-choice quiz

Companion Website. This segment of Wiley's website, devoted entirely to this book (www.wiley.com/college/dopson), includes very important resources for instructors' use to enhance student learning. These are:

PowerPoint slides. These easy-to-read teaching aids are excellent tools for instructors presenting their lectures via computer or for those who wish to download the slides and present them as overhead transparencies.

Apply What You Have Learned suggested answers. Instructors will be able to access suggested answers to the "Apply What You Have Learned" mini-cases at the end of each chapter within the password-protected instructor's companion website.

Test Your Skills spreadsheet answers and formulas. Instructors will be able to access answers and formulas to the "Test Your Skills" spreadsheet exercises at the end of each chapter saved in both Excel 2003 and Excel 2007 within the password-protected portion of the instructor's companion website.

Test Bank. Instructors utilizing the book's companion website will find a password-protected bank of exam questions that includes each question's correct answer.

Instructor Tools CD-ROM. Instructors can access a password-protected online version of the Instructor Tools CD-ROM on the instructor's companion website. "Frequently Used Formulas for Managing Operations," "'Fun on the Web!' Sites," PowerPoint slides, and the Glossary are also available on the book's student companion website.

In addition, all of the course materials included in the WebCT and Blackboard courses to accompany this text are available on the instructor's companion website.

The guidelines on how to use Excel spreadsheets that are provided on the Student CD are also available on the student's companion site.

WebCT and Blackboard Course Materials. This segment of Wiley's website devoted entirely to this book (www.wiley.com/college/dopson) includes WebCT and Blackboard course materials.

Sample Syllabus. The sample syllabus includes a catalog description, suggested prerequisites, instructional materials, instructional methods, learning outcomes, a sample course schedule, and outcomes assessment.

PowerPoint Presentations. These easy-to-read teaching aids are excellent tools for instructors presenting their lectures and for students who want to download PowerPoint handouts for note taking in class.

Student Study Notes. These study notes follow the instructor lecture outline found in the Instructor Tools CD-ROM, and they provide students an abbreviated content of each chapter to study for exams.

Multiple Choice Quizzes. These 10-point multiple-choice quizzes are the same as those in the Student Study Guide. These can be used in the Assessments tool in WebCT or Blackboard to give students more practice at problem solving and understanding of formulas.

Matching Quizzes. These matching quizzes of "Key Terms and Concepts" are similar to those in the Student Study Guide. However, they are divided into 10-point (or less) quizzes. Students will have to match key terms and concepts with their corresponding definitions. These can be used in the Assessments tool in WebCT or Blackboard to give the students more practice at definitions of terms.

Before You Start: How to Use Excel Spreadsheets. This guide provides the same instructions on how to develop and use Excel spreadsheets in Excel 2003 and Excel 2007 as found on the Student CD. It provides a reference to students who are working on spreadsheets and want to quickly look something up online.

Frequently Used Formulas for Managing Operations. This part of the course is the same as on the Student CD. Students can print the formulas, making them more "mobile" for studying than in the book. Students absolutely love this feature!

Fun on the Web! Sites. This part of the course is the same as on the Student CD. The Fun on the Web! links to sites are readily accessible and all in one place so that students can just click and go.

Test Your Skills Student Spreadsheets. This is a great backup just in case students lose their CDs. These spreadsheets are provided in Excel 2003 and Excel 2007 so that students working with either version of Excel can access and manipulate the appropriate set of spreadsheets.

Sample Instruction for Homework Assignments. These sample instructions include point values for "Test Your Skills" assignments and instructions for submitting completed assignments through WebCT or Blackboard.

For more information on WebCT and Blackboard resources available with this book, visit www.wiley.com/college/dopson and click on the link to *Managerial Accounting for the Hospitality Industry* which will bring you to the companion website for this text. Links to WebCT and Blackboard are provided within the Title Information categories listed on the homepage. Click on the links for WebCT or Blackboard for more information regarding demos and how to adopt WebCT or Blackboard cartridges containing valuable resources for both you and your students to use for this course, or contact your Wiley representative.

Acknowledgments

Managerial Accounting for the Hospitality Industry has been designed to be the most technically accurate, flexible, and reader-friendly teaching resource available on the topic. We would like to acknowledge the many individuals who assisted in its development.

Special appreciation goes to Peggy Richards Hayes, a self-proclaimed non-accountant but also the individual singly most responsible for ensuring that this text would be easy to read, easy to understand, easy to apply, and easy to remember. Her insightful, pointed, and kindly (and sometimes brutally) offered reactions to each originally drafted page of the manuscript will undoubtedly help ensure the success of this effort. Her unwavering confidence that we could "make it clearer to make it better!" and insistence that we do so, ensured the final text met and ultimately exceeded our goals of clarity.

We also wish to thank the Dopson family: Thandi, Loralei, Tutti, Terry, and Laurie for their endless patience and support throughout the process. In addition, we thank Raktida Siri and Nancy Kniatt for all of their efforts in helping with text details and supplemental materials. All are greatly appreciated.

Particular mention is appropriate for those professionals who reviewed the original draft outlines of each chapter, and those readers who carefully reviewed each chapter draft as it was written and re-written. We also want to recognize those hospitality practitioners and instructors who participated in a thorough review of each chapter's final version. For comment, collaboration, and constructive criticism on the manuscript, we thank our reviewers:

Greg Charles, Western Culinary Institute
Stephen M. LeBruto, University of Central Florida
Basak Denizci, University of South Carolina
Michael C. Dalbor, University of Nevada, Las Vegas
Ben K. Goh, Texas Technical University
Ronald Jordan, University of Houston
Hyung-il Jung, University of Central Florida
Sueanne Kubicek, Northern Arizona University
James Mawhinney, Pennsylvania Culinary Institute

Experienced authors know the value of a quality publisher in the development of an outstanding manuscript. We are continually impressed with the high standards exhibited by JoAnna Turtletaub, Wiley Vice President and Publisher and the patient support provided by Rachel Livsey, Senior Editor, Culinary and Hospitality. The effort expended by Rachel to bring this text to full completion was truly prodigious.

Cindy Rhoads, the text's developmental editor, deserves special recognition because of her continual efforts to provide suggestions that strengthened the pedagogical features of the book. She also served as the authors' guide to reviewer input and she scrutinized each word and concept presented in the manuscript. Cindy's efforts helped ensure that this text met the high standards Wiley sets for its own publications and by doing so, helped the authors contribute their very best efforts as well.

We are deeply grateful, as will be the students who read this text, for all of the staff at Wiley for their intellect, patience, and faithfulness in producing this exciting book. It is our desire that all of those reading this text will come to appreciate and justly value the beauty of the new language they will learn to speak by using *Managerial Accounting for the Hospitality Industry*.

Lea R. Dopson, Ed.D.
Denton, TX

David K. Hayes, Ph.D.
Okemos, MI

PART I

Accounting Fundamentals

CHAPTER 1

Hospitality Industry Accounting

OVERVIEW

Hospitality is one of the world's most exciting and rewarding industries. If you choose it for your career, you will select from a wide variety of employers, locations, and daily job activities that can lead to your success and personal satisfaction. In this chapter, you will review some important ways in which the hospitality industry is unique. You will also learn the definition of accounting and how accounting helps managers like you use financial information to make good decisions. As you learn that there are several specialty areas (called branches) within accounting, it will become clear to you and you will understand why knowing about hospitality managerial accounting, the specialty area of accounting examined in this text, will help you improve the operating effectiveness of any restaurant, hotel, club, bar, or institutional facility you manage. Finally, you will learn about some of the important ethical responsibilities you will assume when you apply managerial accounting principles to the hospitality business you are responsible for managing.

CHAPTER OUTLINE

- Unique Aspects of the Hospitality Industry
- The Purpose of Accounting in the Hospitality Industry
- Branches of Accounting
- Why Hospitality Managers Use Managerial Accounting
- The Uniform System of Accounts
- Ethics and Hospitality Accounting
- The Blue Lagoon Water Park Resort: A Case Study
- Can You Do the Math?
- Apply What You Have Learned
- Key Terms and Concepts
- Test Your Skills

LEARNING OUTCOMES

At the conclusion of this chapter, you will be able to:

- ✓ Explain the primary purpose of accounting and each of the five branches of accounting.
- ✓ Explain why managerial accounting in the hospitality industry is different from managerial accounting used in other industries.
- ✓ Recognize the Uniform Systems of Accounts appropriate for the hospitality business you manage.
- ✓ Recognize your ethical responsibilities as a managerial accountant in the hospitality industry.

Unique Aspects of the Hospitality Industry

Whether you are reading this book for a class, to improve your business skills, or simply to better understand managerial accounting, you probably are familiar with the term **hospitality**. Hospitality can be defined as the friendly and charitable reception and entertainment of guests or strangers. Hospitality also refers to a specific segment of the travel and tourism industry. The question of precisely which specific businesses should or should not be included as part of the hospitality segment of travel and tourism is subject to open debate and honest disagreement. As a result, those colleges and universities that offer educational programs in hospitality may elect to call them either Hospitality Management or Culinary, Hotel, and Restaurant Management, or Travel and Tourism Management, or Restaurant Management, or Hotel Management, or Institutional Management or any of a number of other name variations. The difficulty with precise classification is clear when you realize that, for most industry observers, each of the ten following individuals are considered to be hospitality managers:

Hospitality Manager	Job Title
Brenda	Director of food services for a 5,000-student school district
Jorge	Managing director of a 750-room resort hotel
Samantha	Regional manager of a 500-unit quick-service restaurant (QSR) chain with responsibility for the 30 units in her assigned territory
Carl	General manager of a 75-room limited service, all-suite hotel near a city's airport
Karin	Manager of a 400-member country club offering dining services and an 18-hole golf course
Trahill	Director of sales and marketing for a 2,000-room casino hotel
Jack	Food and beverage director for the Student Union of a 30,000-student university
Shay	Dietary services director at a 500-bed hospital
Nuntima	Front office manager at a 350-room full-service hotel
Eddie	Chef/owner of "Chez Edward," an exclusive and upscale 60-seat restaurant

While each of the industry sub-segments these managers work in are very different and can be classified in very different ways (for example, profit versus nonprofit; or corporate versus privately owned), one way to classify them is by their emphasis on either lodging or food and beverage (F&B) services.

The authors recognize the potential over-simplification of such a classification but also believe that it is the emphasis on providing lodging and meals (in a variety of settings) that distinguishes those who are considered to be working in the "hospitality" industry.

When hospitality is defined as the lodging and food services industries, it can include a variety of managers in related fields. These include hotels, restaurants, clubs, resorts, casinos, cruise ships, theme parks; the recreation and leisure market: arenas, stadiums, amphitheaters, civic centers, and other recreational facilities; the convention center market; the education market: colleges, universities, and elementary and secondary school nutrition programs; the business dining market: corporate cafeterias, office complexes, and manufacturing plants; the health-care market: long-term care facilities and hospitals; and the corrections market: juvenile detention centers and prisons.

When all of the different segments of the hospitality industry are included, it is easy to see that there are literally hundreds of specialized management positions available. The number of opportunities offered by the hospitality industry is significant; as are the opportunities for those managers who understand and can utilize their hospitality accounting skills.

With such a diverse hospitality management audience, the challenge of creating a "hospitality managerial accounting" text such as this one is daunting. But as you will discover as you read this book, the authors have worked very hard to assemble a managerial accounting text that can be of maximum help to the widest possible range of hospitality practitioners.

The Purpose of Accounting in the Hospitality Industry

Some hospitality students believe that learning accounting is very difficult. *It will not be difficult for you.* The term "accounting" originated from Middle French (*acompter*), which itself originated from Latin (*ad + compter*) meaning "to count." As a result, you already have years of experience as an accountant (a counter)! A more detailed definition of **accounting** is the process of recording financial transactions, summarizing them, and then accurately reporting them. As a result, a good definition for an **accountant** is simply a person skilled in the recording and reporting of financial transactions.

Just as you learned in elementary school about the rule that says 2 + 2 always equals 4, accountants in business have developed their own specialized rules and procedures that govern counting, recording, and summarizing financial transactions as well as analyzing and reporting them. This book will explain many of the accounting rules and procedures that are frequently utilized by professional hospitality managers.

In the business world, as well as in many other fields, accounting is used to report (account for) an organization's money and other valuable property. Accounting is utilized by all managers in business and especially by those in the hospitality industry. In fact, in almost every hospitality job, accounting is important. Accounting in the hospitality industry is utilized every time a guest purchases food, beverages, or a hotel guest room.

Accounting in business occurs even before a hospitality facility ever opens. This is so because businesspersons estimate their costs before they decide to build their facilities and often seek loans from banks to help them. Those banks will assuredly want to know about the proposed business's estimated financial performance before they decide to lend it money.

Accurate accounting is important to many other individuals in the hospitality industry. The owners of a restaurant or hotel will certainly want to monitor their business's financial condition. These owners may be one or more individuals, partnerships, or small or very large corporations, but they all care about the performance of their investments. Investors in the hospitality industry generally want to put their money in businesses that will conserve or increase their wealth. To monitor whether or not their investments are good ones, investors will always seek out and rely upon accurate financial information. When it is properly done, accounting is simply the process of providing that information.

Accounting is actually quite a large field of study. To understand why accounting plays such a significant role in business, consider just a few examples of the type of basic and important questions the discipline of accounting can readily answer for hospitality managers:

1. What was the total sales level achieved by our business last month?
2. What was our most popular menu item? What was our least popular one?
3. What was the average selling price of our hotel rooms last week? Was that higher or lower than our competitors?

4. Are we more or less profitable this month than last month?
5. What is our company realistically worth if we were to sell it today?

The above are some of the questions hospitality managers can utilize accounting to answer. However, it is important to understand that accounting is not the same as management. Accounting is a tool used by good managers. To understand why you, as a talented hospitality manager, will play a more important decision-making role in your business than will the field of accounting, consider these examples of the type of questions that *cannot* be best answered by using accounting information alone.

1. Our hotel swimming pool currently closes at 10:00 p.m. Would we sell more guest rooms if the pool were to remain open 24 hours per day instead? How many?
2. Should I select Jackie or Samuel as the person assigned to train our new dining room wait staff?
3. Should the size of the fish portion used to make our signature "Blackened Trout" be 8 ounces or 11 ounces?
4. Would our country club members prefer to have an increase in the number of inexpensive, or of higher quality (but more costly) wines, when we create the club's new wine list?
5. Would our new 500-room resort be more successful if it were built in Punta Cana in the Dominican Republic, or is the future of the Riviera Maya near the city of Tulum in Mexico likely to become, in the long term, a more popular tourist destination?

Notice that in each of these questions, the best decision requires that you utilize your own experience and judgment of what is "right" for your guests, your business, your employees, and yourself. As a result, while accounting alone could not make the decisions called for in the questions above, when properly used, it can help you make *better* decisions about these types of issues than those that would be made by managers who do not understand how accounting could help them. The purpose of this book is to teach you how to use accounting techniques as well as your own education, experience, values, and goals to make the very best management decisions possible for yourself and the businesses you are responsible for managing.

Branches of Accounting

Proper accounting includes both recording financial information and also accurately reporting it. Some accountants are skilled at one or both of these processes. Most of those who work as accountants recognize that there are actually very specialized fields or branches of accounting. While some of these branches do overlap, they include:

- Financial accounting
- Cost accounting

- Tax accounting
- Auditing
- Managerial accounting

Most hospitality managers are not accountants, but it is important for them to understand the function of the accounting work performed in each of these branches.

Financial Accounting

Business essentially consists of the buying and selling of goods and services. In the hospitality industry, the items sold by businesses are typically food, beverages, and hotel rooms. Depending upon the specific area within hospitality, however, a wide variety of other products and items such as travel or activities like golf, gaming, and entertainment may be sold to guests. Business accountants who specialize in **financial accounting** are skilled at recording, summarizing, and reporting financial transactions. Financial transactions include **revenue**, the term used to indicate the money you take in, **expense**, the cost of the items required to operate the business, and **profit**, the dollars that remain after all expenses have been paid.

These transactions can be used to develop the following profit-oriented formula:

$$\text{Revenue} - \text{Expenses} = \text{Profit}$$

Financial accounting also includes accounting for **assets**, which are those items owned by the business, and **liabilities**, which are the amounts the business owes to others. Finally, financial accountants record and report information about **owners' equity**, which is the residual claims owners have on their assets, or the amount left over in a business after subtracting its liabilities from its assets.

These transactions can be used to develop the following equation for the balance sheet:

$$\text{Assets} = \text{Liabilities} + \text{Owners' Equity}$$

In this book, you will discover that the work of financial accountants can be extremely helpful to professional hospitality managers. In later chapters, we will examine, in detail, how these accountants do some of the important parts of their jobs.

To understand how financial accounting can help hospitality managers, consider the case of Faye Richards. She is interested in buying her own small pizza shop. The shop would be located in a strip shopping center and would sell primarily pizzas, hot subs, and soft drinks. Some of the many financial considerations Faye would have as she tries to decide if buying the shop is a good idea would be:

1. How much revenue do pizza shops like this typically achieve on an average day?
2. What do pizza shops normally spend to properly staff their stores?

3. How much should I spend on the equipment I need to buy to make the food I will sell?
4. Given the size and location of my store, what is a reasonable price to expect to pay for obtaining insurance for my business?
5. How much money am I likely to make for myself during the first year I own the store?

Faye can get important information from her financial accountant, but she will also need managerial skills and her own intuition and talents to provide answers to some of the other business questions she will face.

Cost Accounting

Cost accounting is the branch of accounting that is concerned with the classification, recording, and reporting of business expenses. Because all businesses seek to control their costs and not waste money, those who operate businesses are very concerned about where they spend their money.

For cost accountants, a **cost**, or expense, is most often defined as "time or resources expended by the business." To understand why cost accounting is so important, consider Mike Edgar, the manager of a private country club. Reporting to Mike, among others, are those individuals responsible for the operation of the club's golf course, pro shop, swimming pools, and food and beverage services. Each of these major areas will expend money to achieve the goals Mike and the club's members set for them.

It is very unlikely that Mike could know, on a daily basis, about all the purchases his staff will make. Mike however, will be responsible to the club's members for the money they have spent. Because this is true, it will be important for Mike to have a reliable system in place that allows him to fully understand what has been purchased, who purchased it, and the reason for the purchase.

Cost accountants determine costs by departments, by business function or area of responsibility, and by the products and services sold by the business. They create systems to classify costs and report them in ways that are most useful to those who need to know about how a business spends its money.

Some of the kinds of questions that cost accountants could help Mike answer include:

1. How much does it cost the club to host one member who is playing golf?
2. What were the total costs of utilities (water, electricity, and natural gas) incurred by the country club last month?
3. Did it cost more this year to fertilize the golf course than it did last year?
4. Are all managers in the country club accounting in the same manner for the cost of the meals eaten during work hours by their staff?
5. Does it cost more money to operate our country club than other clubs of the same size and type?

The work of cost accountants is critical for hospitality managers who seek to fully understand the costs of operating their businesses. As a result, throughout this text, we will utilize many of the techniques that have been developed by these accounting specialists.

Tax Accounting

A **tax** is simply a charge levied by a governmental unit on income, consumption, wealth, or other basis. In the United States, governmental units that can assess taxes include townships, cities, counties, states, and various agencies of the federal government. As a result, nearly all businesses are subject to paying some taxes.

Tax accounting is the branch of accounting that concerns itself with the proper and timely filing of tax payments, forms, or other required documents with the governmental units that assess taxes. Professional tax accounting techniques and practices ensure that businesses properly fulfill their legitimate tax obligations.

In the hospitality industry, managers are required to implement systems that will carefully record any taxes that will be owed by their businesses. Consider, for example, Latisha Brown, the general manager of a 220-room full-service hotel located in her state's capital and very near the airport. The work of tax accountants could help Latisha ensure that she has the systems in place to:

1. Record the **occupancy tax** her hotel must pay. This tax, which is the money paid to a local taxing authority based upon the amount of revenue a hotel achieves when selling its guest rooms, is typically due and payable each month for the room revenue the hotel achieved in the prior month.
2. Maintain records of the total taxable revenue achieved by the hotel and collect all money required to pay the **sales tax** that will be due as a result of realizing those sales.
3. Address specific tax-related questions, such as, "Is the hotel required to collect and pay occupancy tax on those guests who were assessed a no-show charge because they failed to arrive at the hotel when they had a confirmed reservation?"
4. Monitor changing laws to ensure that all **payroll taxes** due on those individuals employed by Latisha are properly recorded and submitted.

As you can see from these very few examples, the work of tax accountants is critically important to hospitality managers. Throughout this text, we will often examine how the specific actions taken by hospitality managers will affect the amount of taxes the businesses they manage must pay.

Auditing

An **audit** is an independent verification of financial records. An **auditor** is the individual or group of individuals that completes the verification. As you have seen, the accurate reporting of financial transactions is important to many different entities including managers, owners, investors, and taxing authorities. The auditing branch of accounting is chiefly concerned with the accuracy and truthfulness of financial reports. It is also concerned with safeguarding the assets of a business from those unscrupulous individuals who would seek to defraud or otherwise take advantage of it.

When financial transactions are not reported truthfully, it is very easy for many individuals to suffer great harm. The total collapse of the Enron Corporation in late 2001, as well as other highly publicized business failures such as Global Crossing and World-Com, demonstrate the importance of auditing. In each of these cases, investors, employees, and other stakeholders lost billions of dollars. In fact, the word "Enron" has now become synonymous with accounting fraud. Enron filed for bankruptcy on December 2, 2001, a consequence of the combination of too much debt and some unusually risky investments. Business failures are not unusual and it is certainly important to note that Enron did not go bankrupt because it violated accounting rules. Rampant violation of standardized accounting rules, however, led Enron's investors, creditors, employees, and others to believe the company was financially sound when, in fact, it was not. If properly performed, the auditing branch of accounting is designed to point out accounting weaknesses and irregularities and thus prevent accounting fraud of this type.

In part because of the potential damage that could be done by unscrupulous corporate managers, in 2002 the United States Congress passed the **Sarbanes-Oxley Act** (**SOX**). Technically known as the Public Company Accounting Reform and Investor Protection Act, this law provides criminal penalties for those found to have committed accounting fraud. Sarbanes-Oxley covers a whole range of corporate governance issues including the regulation of auditors assigned the task of verifying a company's financial health. Ultimately, Congress determined that a company's implementation of proper accounting techniques was not merely good business, it would be the law and violators would be subject to prison terms.

 *fun on the Web!*

The 2002 Sarbanes-Oxley Act became law to help rebuild public confidence in the way corporate America governs its business activities. The Act has far-reaching implications for the tourism, hospitality, and leisure industry. To examine an overview of its provisions, go to:

www.sarbanes-oxley.com/section.php

Not surprisingly, as a result of SOX, the role of auditor and the techniques used in auditing have become increasingly important. Individuals who are directly employed by a company to examine that company's own accounting procedures are called **internal auditors**. They can play a valuable role in assessment because they usually understand the company's business so well. **External auditors** are individuals or firms who are hired specifically to give an independent (external) assessment of a company's compliance with standardized accounting practices.

In the hospitality industry, managers of smaller restaurants, clubs, and lodging facilities most often serve as their own in-house auditors. If the facility they manage is part of a larger company or chain of units, their company may also employ auditors. In larger hotels, the **controller**, who is the person responsible for managing the hotel's accounting processes, may serve as the auditor or, in very large properties, full-time individuals are employed specifically to act as the property's in-house auditors.

As you have learned, auditors not only help ensure honesty in financial reporting, they play an important role in devising the systems and procedures needed to help ensure the protection and safeguarding of business assets. As a result, hospitality managers use auditors and auditing techniques to address many internal questions, a few of which are:

1. Are all purchases we make supported by the presence of a legitimate invoice before we process payment?
2. Are guest adjustments from their bill supported by written documentation explaining why the bill was adjusted?
3. Is all the revenue reported as achieved by the business fully documented and **reconciled** (compared and matched) to deposits ultimately made in the business's bank accounts?
4. Are wages paid to all employees supported by a written and verifiable record of hours worked?

The best auditors help ensure that financial records are accurate as well as assist managers in reducing waste and preventing fraud. In this text, the procedures, techniques, and strategies developed by this important branch of accounting will often be utilized to help you learn to become the best hospitality manager you can be.

Managerial Accounting

Managerial accounting is the basic topic of this book as well as the final branch we will examine. To clearly understand the purpose of managerial accounting, assume that Karen Gomez is the person responsible for providing meals to international travelers on flights from New York to Paris. She manages a large commercial kitchen located near the John F. Kennedy Airport. Karen's clients are the airlines who count on her company to provide those who have chosen to fly with them tasty and nutritious meals at a per-meal price the airline finds affordable.

One of Karen's clients wishes to add a new flight beginning next month. The evening flights will carry an average of 500 travelers, each of whom will be offered one of two in-flight meal choices for dinner. The client would like to provide each flier with a choice of a beef or a chicken entree. To ensure that the maximum number of fliers can receive their first choice, should Karen's company plan to provide each flight with 500 beef and 500 chicken entrees? The answer, most certainly, is no.

To prepare 1,000 meals (500 of each type) would indeed ensure that each traveler would always receive his or her first meal choice, but it would also result in the production of 500 wasted meals (the 500 meals *not* selected) on each flight. Clearly, it would be difficult for Karen to provide the airline with cost-effective per-meal pricing when that many meals would inevitably be wasted. The more cost-effective approach would be to accurately forecast the number of beef and chicken entrees that would likely be selected by each group of passengers, and to then produce that number. The problem, of course, is in knowing the optimum number of each meal type that should be produced. If Karen had carefully and properly recorded previous meal-related transactions (entrees chosen by fliers on previous flights) she would be in a much better position to use managerial accounting to estimate the actual number of each entree type the new passengers would likely select. If she had done so, she would be using managerial accounting. **Managerial accounting** is simply the system of recording and analyzing transactions for the purpose of making management decisions of precisely this kind.

Because you utilize accounting information (historical records in this specific case) to make management decisions, managerial accounting is one of the most exciting of the accounting branches. Its proper use requires skill, insight, experience, and intuition. These are the same characteristics possessed by the best hospitality managers. As a result, excellent hospitality managers most often become excellent managerial accountants.

The branches of accounting we have reviewed and the main purpose of each can be very briefly summarized as shown in Figure 1.1.

Now that you have reviewed the major branches of accounting, it may be easier to understand why it is so important for businesses to employ highly skilled professionals to perform their accounting functions. In the United States, those individuals recognized as highly competent and professional in one or more of the branches of accounting have earned the designation of **Certified Public Accountant (CPA)**.

To become a CPA, a person must meet the requirements of the state or jurisdiction in which they want to practice. These requirements, which vary from state to state, are established by law and administered by each state's Board of Accountancy. Once certified, most CPAs join the American Institute of Certified Public Accountants (AICPA), which is the national, professional organization for all Certified Public Accountants.

FIGURE 1.1 Branches and Purpose of Accounting

Branch	Purpose
1. Financial	Record financial transactions
2. Cost	Identify and control costs
3. Tax	Compute taxes due
4. Auditing	Verify accounting data and procedures
5. Managerial	Make management decisions using accounting information

W fun on the Web!

The AICPA is the national, professional organization for all Certified Public Accountants. Its mission is to provide members with the resources, information, and leadership that enable them to provide valuable services in the highest professional manner to benefit the public as well as employers and clients. You can view the AICPA website at:

www.aicpa.org

When you arrive, click on "About Us," then click on "AICPA Code of Professional Conduct."

Another certification that may be earned is the **Certified Management Accountant (CMA)**. A CMA assists businesses by integrating accounting information into the business decision process. In order to become a CMA, professionals must meet the educational and experience requirements of the designation, and they must complete the CMA examination, which includes the general areas of business analysis, management accounting and reporting, strategic management, and business applications. The certification also requires compliance with ethical standards and practices. The Institute of Management Accountants (IMA) is the organization that grants the CMA certification.

W fun on the Web!

The IMA is a professional organization for Certified Management Accountants. Its mission is to provide a dynamic forum for management accounting and finance professionals to develop and advance their careers through certification, research and practice development, education, networking, and the advocacy of the highest ethical and professional practices. You can view the IMA website at:

www.imanet.org

When you arrive, click on "About IMA."

Those hospitality professionals who work extensively in the areas of accounting and technology often become members of the **Hospitality Financial and Technology Professionals (HFTP)**. HFTP was formed in 1952 and has its headquarters in Austin, Texas. It offers its own certifications for hospitality professionals working in the accounting and technology areas, and it provides a global network for them.

W fun on the Web!

You can view the Hospitality Financial and Technology Professionals (HFTP) website when you go to:

www.hftp.org

When you arrive, click on "About Us" to learn about its goals and the programs offered to its members.

The majority of hospitality managers are *not* likely to become CPAs or even certified members of HFTP. As a practicing hospitality professional, you are most likely interested in learning how using accounting information in the management jobs you will hold can help you make better, more informed decisions. Because that is true, before you start to learn more about managerial accounting, it is important for you to understand exactly *why* you should learn more about it.

Why Hospitality Managers Use Managerial Accounting

Hospitality accounting is not a separate branch of accounting, but it is a very specialized area that focuses on those accounting techniques and practices used in restaurants, hotels, clubs, and other hospitality businesses. If hospitality were very similar to other industries, there would be little reason to create a separate book about, or even to study, managerial accounting for hospitality. It is true that accountants in the hospitality industry follow the same rules as accountants in any other field. The hospitality industry, however, like the people who work in it, is unique. Those who would maintain that any managerial accountant or CPA can be equally effective as one very familiar with the hospitality industry fail to recognize the culture, history, language, and norms that differentiate this exciting field.

To confirm some of the reasons why managerial accounting is a separate field of study, take the hospitality accounting term quiz in Figure 1.2.

As you may have discovered by taking the quiz, those practicing managerial accounting in the hospitality industry have specialized knowledge. That knowledge is the result of learning the intricacies of the restaurant or hotel business and then applying what they know to a financial analysis process. Managers in the hospitality industry have found that it is helpful to standardize some aspects of their own industry segment's accounting procedures. They have done so by creating standardized, or uniform, methods of reporting their financial accounts.

FIGURE 1.2   Hospitality Accounting Term Quiz

Match the hospitality accounting term on the left with its corresponding manager's definition on the right.

Hospitality Term	Manager's Definition (Formula)
1. ADR	**a.** Selling price − product cost
2. Check average	**b.** Cost of goods sold / revenue
3. Occupancy %	**c.** Fixed costs / contribution margin %
4. Sales break-even point	**d.** Rooms sold / rooms available for sale
5. RevPar	**e.** EP weight / AP weight
6. Profit margin	**f.** Total sales / number of guests served
7. Product cost %	**g.** Room revenue / rooms available
8. Product yield %	**h.** Beginning inventory + purchases − ending inventory
9. Contribution margin	**i.** Net income / total sales
10. Cost of goods sold	**j.** Room revenue / rooms sold

Turn to the next page to find out the number of questions you got right, and then read the following test results key.

Test Results Key	
Number Correct	**Rank**
9–10	**Chief Executive Officer (CEO):** Congratulations! You are already a star! With your current knowledge, you can quickly learn to be an exceptional managerial accountant in the hospitality industry.
7–8	**Company Vice President:** You are well on your way to mastering all of the concepts you must understand to become an excellent managerial accountant.
5–6	**District Manager:** Achieving this score means you already have the conceptual skills and understanding you will need to move up rapidly.
3–4	**Unit Manager:** You know more than most. Experience and more practice will help you advance rapidly.
2 or less	**Don't worry!** When you finish learning the material in this book you will get a perfect score!

The Uniform System of Accounts

It is helpful when all managers in a segment of the hospitality industry utilize the same guidelines for recording and computing their financial data. The manner in which operating statistics are compiled and in which revenue (or expense) data is reported can be very significant to the proper interpretation of that data.

Laws exist requiring owners to properly report and pay taxes due, to file certain documents with the government, and to supply accurate business data to various other entities. As a result, many hospitality companies require that their managers use a series of suggested (uniform) accounting procedures created specifically for their own segment of the hospitality industry. These are called a **uniform system of accounts** and simply represent agreed upon methods of recording financial transactions within a specific industry segment. In the hospitality industry, some of the best known of these uniform systems are:

- Uniform System of Accounts for the Lodging Industry
- Uniform System of Accounts for Restaurants
- Uniform System of Financial Reporting for Clubs

Uniform System of Accounts for the Lodging Industry (USALI). The hotel industry was one of the first of the segments within hospitality to encourage its members to standardize their accounting procedures. In the United States, the first uniform system of accounts for the lodging industry was developed in New York in 1925 by members of the Hotel Association of New York City Inc.

The USALI is now developed by the Hospitality Financial and Technology Professionals (HFTP) and the Educational Institute (EI) of the American Hotel & Lodging Association (AH&LA). The USALI gives hoteliers and their accountants a consistent and easily understood "roadmap" to record revenues, expenses, and a hotel's overall financial condition. It is continually updated as those in hotel management stay abreast of the many changes occurring in their industry.

W fun on the Web!

You can purchase a copy of the most current Uniform System of Accounts for the Lodging Industry from the Educational Institute of the American Hotel and Lodging Association. To visit its website, go to:

www.ei-ahla.org

When you arrive, click on "Products" then "Books" to arrive at a location that allows you to browse and review all of their publications (including the Uniform System of Accounts).

Uniform System of Accounts for Restaurants (USAR). The Uniform System of Accounts for Restaurants, prepared for the National Restaurant Association (NRA) by Deloitte and Touche LLP, assists restaurant operators by suggesting a common language for the industry and by giving them an opportunity to compare the results of one restaurant

Answers to the Hospitality quiz:
1. j; 2. f; 3. d; 4. c; 5. g; 6. i; 7. b; 8. e; 9. a; 10. h

to another and one accounting period to another. In addition, it allows those managers using it to compare the financial results of their own operation to industry norms.

W fun on the Web!

You can purchase a copy of the most current Uniform System of Accounts for Restaurants from the National Restaurant Association. To visit its website, go to:

www.restaurant.org

When you arrive, click on "Store."

Uniform System of Financial Reporting for Clubs (USFRC). Club management is another example of an industry segment that requires specialized knowledge and thus, its own uniform system of accounts. The USFRC is a club accounting resource for club managers, officers, and controllers. It is produced through the joint efforts of Hospitality Financial and Technology Professionals (HFTP) and the Club Managers Association of America (CMAA). The USFRC is a financial reporting system geared specifically to member-owned, not-for-profit city and country clubs.

W fun on the Web!

You can actually review the Table of Contents of the Uniform System of Accounts book created for club managers if you visit the Club Managers Association of America website. To do so, go to:

www.cmaa.org

When you arrive, click on "Education" then "Books and Publications" to arrive at a location that allows you to browse and review all of their publications (including the Uniform System of Accounts).

Whenever practical and possible, hospitality managers working in a specific segment of the industry should seek out and then use the uniform system of accounts that has been developed especially for them.

Ethics and Hospitality Accounting

The hospitality industry is one of the most honorable, exciting, and rewarding industries in the world. It will continue to offer its members solid employment opportunities and serve as the backbone of many local economies only if its current managers maintain the integrity of those who have gone before them. Among a variety of responsibilities, this includes preparing and presenting their important financial information in a manner that is both legal and ethical.

Sometimes it may not be clear whether an actual course of action is illegal or simply wrong. Put another way, an activity (including an accounting activity) may be legal, but still the wrong thing to do. As a future hospitality manager, it is important that you are able to make this distinction. **Ethics** refers to the choices of proper conduct made by an individual in his or her relationships with others. Ethical behavior refers to behavior that is considered "right" or the "right thing to do." Consistently choosing ethical behavior over behavior that is not ethical is important to your long-term career achievements. This is so because hospitality managers often will not know what the law may actually require in a given situation. When managerial activities are examined, employers, in many cases, will simply consider whether a manager's actions were intentionally ethical or unethical.

How individuals determine what constitutes ethical behavior can be influenced by their cultural background, religious views, professional training, and their own moral code. It is certainly true that the definition of ethical behavior may vary based upon an individual's own perception of what is ethical. While it may sometimes be difficult to determine precisely what constitutes ethical behavior, the five guidelines in Figure 1.3 can prove to be very useful when you are evaluating the ethical implications of a specific decision or course of action.

An example of the way an individual would actually apply the five ethical guidelines is demonstrated in the following hypothetical situation:

Assume that you are the controller of a large hotel. Along with the food and beverage director, executive chef, director of sales and marketing, and other managers in the hotel, the general manager has assigned you to assist in the planning of your hotel's New Year's Eve gala. The event will require a large amount of wine and champagne. As part of your responsibilities, you conduct a competitive bidding process with the wine purveyors in your area and, based upon quality and price, you concur with the food and beverage Director's recommendation that you place a very large order (in excess of $20,000) with a single purveyor. One week later, you receive a case of very expensive champagne, delivered to your home with a nice note from the purveyor's representative stating how much he appreciated the order and that he is really looking forward to doing business with you in the years ahead. What do you do with the champagne?

Ethical Analysis

Your first thought may be the most obvious one and that is, you drink it. However, it is hopeful that you will first apply the five questions of the ethical decision-making process to your situation.

1. Is it legal?

   From your perspective, it may not be illegal for you to accept a case of champagne. However, there could be liquor laws in your state that prohibit the purveyor from

FIGURE 1.3   Ethical Guidelines

1. Is it legal?

Any course of action that violates written law or company policies and procedures is wrong.

2. Does it hurt anyone?

Is the manager accruing benefits that rightfully belong to the owner of the business? Discounts, rebates, and free products are the property of the business, not the manager.

3. Am I being honest?

Is the activity one that you can comfortably say reflects well on your integrity as a professional, or will the activity actually diminish your reputation?

4. Would I care if it happened to me?

If you owned the business, would you be in favor of your manager behaving in the manner you are considering? If you owned multiple units, would it be good for the business if all of your managers followed the considered course of action?

5. Would I publicize my action?

If you have trouble remembering the other questions, try to remember this one. A quick way to review the ethical merit of a situation is to consider whom you would tell about it. If you are comfortable telling your boss about the considered course of action, it is likely ethical. If you would prefer that your actions go undetected, you are probably on shaky ethical ground. If you wouldn't want your action to be read aloud in a court of law (even if your action is legal), you probably shouldn't do it.

gifting that amount of alcoholic beverage. You must also consider whether or not it is permissible within the guidelines established by the company for which you work. In this case, violation of a stated or written company policy may subject you to disciplinary action or even the termination of your employment.

2. Does it hurt anyone?

When asking this question you have to recognize who the stakeholders are in this particular situation. How might others in your company feel about the gift you received? After all, you probably agreed to work for this hotel at a set salary. If benefits are gained because of decisions you make while on duty, should those benefits accrue to the business or to you? Besides, any gifts received by you will most likely be paid by your business through future price increases.

3. Am I being honest?

Do you really believe that you can remain objective in the purchasing/bid aspect of your job and continue to seek out the best quality for the best price, knowing that one of the purveyors rewarded you handsomely for last year's choice and may be inclined to do so again?

4. Would I care if it happened to me?

If you owned the company you work for, and you knew that one of the managers you had hired was given a gift of this size from a vendor, would you question the objectivity of that manager? Would you like to see all of your managers receive such gifts? Would you be concerned if they did?

5. Would I publicize my action?

Would you choose to keep the champagne in the event that you knew that tomorrow, the morning headlines of your city newspaper were going to read:

"Controller and Food and Beverage Director of Local Hotel Each Receive Case of Champagne After Placing Large Order with Purveyor: Hotel Owners to Investigate"

Your general manager would see it, other employees would see it, all of the other purveyors that you are going to do business with would see it, and even potential future employers would see it.

What are some of the realistic alternatives to keeping the champagne?

1. Return it to the purveyor with a nice note telling them how much you appreciate it but your company policy will not allow you to accept it.
2. Turn the gift over to the general manager to be placed into the normal liquor inventory (assuming that the law will allow it to be used as such).
3. Donate it to the employee Christmas party.

Use the five questions listed in Figure 1.3 to evaluate each of these three courses of action. See the difference? If you are like most managers, each of the three alternatives presented will "pass" the five-question test while the alternative of accepting the champagne for personal use will not.

Just as the ethical nature of a manager's daily actions can be examined, so too can that manager's approach to recording and reporting financial data. Everyone would agree that hospitality managers should follow any laws that regulate the reporting of financial information. Laws do not exist, however, to cover every situation that future managerial accountants will encounter. Society's views of acceptable behavior, as well as specific laws, are constantly changing. Ethical behavior, however, is always important to responsible individuals as well as their organizations. There are rules that must be followed if a manager's financial records are to be trusted and if the interpretations made about that financial data is to be perceived as honest. As you continue through this text, you will see that, in many instances, hospitality managers may be faced with ethical choices about how they report and assess financial data. As well, in your own career, you will likely find many instances in which you are faced with ethical choices about your own managerial decisions. It is important to understand that each management decision you make partially shapes and helps define the type of manager you are as well as the type you are perceived to be by others. In nearly all instances in which a company's financial officers have deceived its investors and owners, there have been instances where lapses in ethical judgments have directly resulted in significant harm to the company's shareholders and employees.

In the following chapters, you will discover exactly how hospitality managers use the information you have already learned, new information (that you will learn) related specifically to the hospitality industry, and their own personal skills to analyze their businesses using managerial accounting techniques for the hospitality industry. As you have seen, however, the hospitality industry is very broad. As a result, some of those managerial accounting techniques that may be of great interest to a hotel manager may be of much less interest, for example, to the manager of a carry-out pizza store. As authors of a managerial accounting text, it is important that we create a book that will serve the widest possible audience. Even so, we realize that the specific interests of a future hotel general manager will vary from that of a student interested, for example, in a career in college and university food services.

The Blue Lagoon Water Park Resort: A Case Study

To study what managers must actually know and do to utilize managerial accounting, we will examine the challenges of the Blue Lagoon Water Park Resort.

Everybody understands swimming pools. You have outdoor swimming pools and indoor swimming pools. So far, that's pretty easy to understand. But, when you combine Disney World, Sea World, Wet 'N Wild, Great Wolf Lodge, and Kalahari Water Park Resort & Convention Center, things start to get more difficult to understand. When does a hotel with an indoor water park reach the status of a hotel water park resort? For Paige Vincent, the challenge of fully understanding the answer to that question was about to begin. She had just been offered (and accepted) the position of general manager of the 50,000-square-foot Blue Lagoon Water Park Resort. An indoor park with 240 guest rooms, the facility was a destination resort that would also be one of the largest hotels in a 200-mile area.

The investment group that owned the park and had hired Paige was impressed with her undergraduate degree in hospitality, her ten years of progressive advancement with a well-known full-service hotel chain, and her five years of multi-unit food service operations experience. A commitment to outstanding guest service was one of Paige's greatest strengths. However, she also knew that she had impressed the park's owners with her knowledge of the financial management skills needed to operate a facility expected to gross in excess of $25,000,000 per year in total revenue with $14,000,000 plus in rooms revenue alone.

The new job paid well but was a big one. In addition to being responsible for 150 full- and part-time employees, as general manager, Paige was responsible for all of the resort's operating units including:

- 240 guest rooms and suites with an average daily rate (ADR) of $200 (including room and park admission fees) and an average hotel occupancy of 80%.
- A 50,000-square-foot water play area with:
  - Four-story water slides (2)
  - Hot tub/whirlpools (3)
  - Kiddie pool play area with two slides
- Adults only lounge area
- Snack bar
- Full service restaurant
- Full service bar and lounge
- Guest activity areas including:
  - Video arcade
  - Retail store
  - Tanning/spa facility
  - Exercise facility
- Employee cafeteria

Paige understood well that it would take all of the managerial accounting skills she possessed, as well as many new ones she would learn, to effectively manage the Blue Lagoon. She was excited about her new position and very anxious to get started.

In addition, Joshua Richards is the owner of Joshua's Restaurant located across the street from the Blue Lagoon Water Park Resort. He offers a simple American-style menu including beef, chicken, pork, and seafood items. He averages approximately $2,540,000 in revenues per year with a 260-seat restaurant (averaging 2.14 turns) and an average selling price per person of $12.50.

In this book, we will use, when practical, the Blue Lagoon Water Park Resort and Joshua's Restaurant as our reference points for managerial accounting activities. As you examine the issues facing Paige Vincent and Joshua Richards, you will actually be examining many of the accounting-related issues you yourself will face as a managerial accountant in your own specialty area.

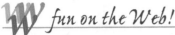

fun on the Web!

If you have not personally visited a major indoor water park, you can take a mini-tour of a facility that is larger than, but similar to the hypothetical one Paige Vincent will be managing in this text. To do so, go to:

www.Kalahariresort.com

This very large park is one of the most popular in the Wisconsin Dells area.

Can You Do the Math?

Some students begin their managerial accounting course concerned that they will have difficulty with the math portion of the course. Answer the following questions and then score yourself to see if you will have difficulty with the math presented in this text.

go figure!

Questions

A. $2 + 2 =$ _____
B. $6 - 2 =$ _____
C. $8 \times 2 =$ _____
D. $16 / 2 =$ _____
E. $(8 + 2) / 2 =$ _____

Answers

A. 4
B. 4
C. 16
D. 8
E. 5

Did you get all the answers correct? OF COURSE YOU DID! The math in this book is no harder than the questions you just answered. Trust us! Because you got all the answers correct, you easily have the math skills you will need to successfully learn the material in this text. That is true because the mastery of managerial accounting is primarily related to knowing *which* numbers to use in a calculation and how to interpret the results of the calculation, not the application of advanced mathematics!

In this text, you will learn about the specific managerial accounting methods, procedures, and strategies used by those managing hospitality businesses. Because you now know that the field of accounting can be specialized by branches as well as by the business in which accountants may work, this book's title *Managerial Accounting for the Hospitality Industry*, should give you a very clear idea about the useful, interesting, and fun things you will learn about accounting in the remaining chapters.

Apply What You Have Learned

Samara Tate couldn't have been happier. As she looked back on the past two years, she realized just how much her hard work had paid off. First, she had been hired as a waitress at the exclusive Sycamore Country Club working in the "Members Only" dining room. Then, as she continued to work part-time at the Club and pursue a degree in hospitality management, she had been promoted to banquet bartender. After one year in that position, she had been promoted to banquet bar supervisor. Her knowledge and strong leadership skills had impressed the Club's managers as much as her personality had impressed the Club's membership.

Now, just as she was about to graduate, the Club's food and beverage director called Samara into her office to offer her the job of beverage manager. It was an important job, as the Club's beverage department grossed over $500,000 per year. Samara was excited about the opportunity and the pay!

1. Properly accounting for beverage sales is an important part of a beverage manager's job. What are two additional, specific areas of financial accounting that would be important for Samara to understand if she is to succeed in her new job?
2. Maintaining accurate records about costs is an important part of nearly every manager's job. Name two hospitality-specific areas of costs that you think would be important for Samara to understand well if she is to excel in her new job.
3. Assume that Samara accepts the beverage manager's position. Identify at least two specific tasks she is likely to be assigned to which she would be required to apply her knowledge of managerial accounting.
4. Do you think Samara could do a good job of managing the Club's entire beverage department without a good understanding of the way managerial accounting information is used by hospitality managers? Why or why not?

Key Terms and Concepts

The following are terms and concepts discussed in the chapter that are important for you to know as a manager. To help you review, please define the following terms.

Hospitality	Sales tax	Hospitality Financial and
Accounting	Payroll taxes	Technology Professionals
Accountant	Audit	(HFTP)
Financial accounting	Auditor	Hospitality accounting
Revenue	Sarbanes-Oxley Act (SOX)	Uniform system of accounts
Expense	Internal auditors	Uniform System of Accounts
Profit	External auditors	for the Lodging Industry
Assets	Controller	(USALI)
Liabilities	Reconcile	Uniform System of Accounts
Owners' equity	Managerial accounting	for Restaurants (USAR)
Cost accounting	Certified Public Accountant	Uniform System of Financial
Cost	(CPA)	Reporting for Clubs
Tax	Certified Management	(USFRC)
Tax accounting	Accountant (CMA)	Ethics
Occupancy tax		

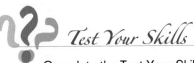

Test Your Skills

Complete the Test Your Skills exercises by placing your answers in the shaded boxes.

1. Match the branch of accounting that would be best used to answer the following questions.

	Question	Branch of Accounting
a.	How should I record transactions associated with cash, payroll, and short-term debt?	
b.	How much does it cost to pay for maintenance for my swimming pool this year?	
c.	What occupancy tax is owed by the hotel this month?	
d.	How should I record transactions associated with revenue, expenses, and profit?	
e.	How much sales tax should we have collected this month?	
f.	Are all food purchases made this month documented with legitimate invoices?	
g.	If I wanted to achieve a profit of $10,000 in the month of April, how many pizzas will I need to sell?	

h.	Are all bonuses paid to managers supported by documented revenue performance measures?	
i.	What were the total costs of salaries and wages incurred by the restaurant this month?	
j.	Would it be more profitable if I made my potato salad by scratch or purchased it pre-prepared?	

2. Richard owns a coffee bean shop that sells gourmet coffee and chocolates. Prepare both weekly and monthly profit formulas so that Richard has a good idea about his current profit situation.

WEEK	REVENUE	EXPENSES	PROFIT / LOSS
1	$956.34	$1,258.75	
2	2,286.45	1,687.54	
3	2,678.91	2,563.87	
4	1,875.23	1,378.95	
Month			

a. In which week did Richard have the most profit?

b. Did Richard show a profit for all four weeks? If not, which week(s) did he experience a loss?

c. As the owner, Richard wanted a profit of $1,000 for the month. Did he reach his goal?

3. Laurie Tenk is a purchasing agent for a restaurant chain. One of her suppliers has been late on deliveries the past two weeks. She has discussed this with the salesperson, and he assures her that the problem will be solved. In an effort to "make things right," the salesperson delivers two cases of hot dogs to her office for "sampling." She plans to have a backyard barbecue this weekend for her neighbors. The free hot dogs would lower her cost of this event considerably.

From an ethical point of view, how should she handle this situation? Explain your decision-making process and defend your answer. Use the five Ethical Guidelines in this chapter as a basis for your answer to explain what should be done with the hot dogs.

a. Is it legal?

b. Does it hurt anyone?

c. Am I being honest?

d. Would I care if it happened to me?

e. Would I publicize my action?

f. What should be done with the two cases of hot dogs?

4. The chief financial officer (CFO) of a publicly-owned restaurant chain notices that the "bonus" for the chief executive officer (CEO) is much higher than anticipated for the year. She suspects that the CEO is committing corporate fraud by embezzling the extra money. She notifies the CEO of this discrepancy, but is told that she has calculated the amount incorrectly.

   a. How would this suspected fraud be legally detected?

   b. What legislation does this fall under?

CHAPTER 2

Accounting Fundamentals Review

OVERVIEW

This chapter is a review of some accounting fundamentals that must be understood before you can begin to actually study managerial accounting. It can be helpful even if you have recently completed one or more introductions to accounting courses. The chapter presents and explains in detail the basic accounting formula, credits and debits, and generally accepted accounting principles (GAAP). The chapter concludes with a brief review of how accounting is used in the hospitality business cycle. When you have successfully finished this chapter, you will have mastered the concepts you must learn to begin your detailed study of managerial accounting for the hospitality industry.

CHAPTER OUTLINE

- Bookkeeping and Accounting
- The Accounting Formula
- Recording Changes to The Accounting Formula
- Generally Accepted Accounting Principles
- The Hospitality Business Cycle
- Apply What You Have Learned
- Key Terms and Concepts
- Test Your Skills

LEARNING OUTCOMES

At the conclusion of this chapter, you will be able to:

✓ Explain the basic accounting formula and how it is modified using debits and credits.
✓ Identify generally accepted accounting principles and state why they exist.
✓ Describe how accounting is used in the hospitality business cycle.

Bookkeeping and Accounting

Many of the records used by accountants to report and analyze financial statements are actually created by bookkeepers. In the hospitality industry, **bookkeepers** of all types perform the critically important task of initially recording financial transactions in a business. For example, the recording of an individual financial transaction such as the sale of a cup of coffee in a restaurant is actually a bookkeeping task completed by a server using the restaurant's cash register. A manager may then record from the cash register the total number of cups of coffee sold in a given time period. These sales, as well as the others achieved by the restaurant will be incorporated into its monthly financial statements to be analyzed by the restaurant's accountants, managers, and owners. Clearly, if the bookkeeping tasks of the servers, bartenders, kitchen staff, and managers of a restaurant, and the front desk, controller, and other staff of a hotel are not properly performed, the resulting financial data generated by these business's accountants will not be accurate and decisions made based upon the numbers supplied are likely to be flawed as well.

As can be seen in Figure 2.1, bookkeeping forms the foundation of accurate financial reporting and analysis. This is so because it is simply impossible to make a meaningful analysis of a hospitality operation's financial standing if the data summarized by the accounting staff was erroneously or carelessly supplied by those performing bookkeeping

FIGURE 2.1   Transaction Recording and Analysis

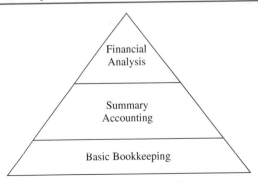

tasks. In addition, hospitality managers will not be able to properly analyze financial information and make correct decisions if the accounting information is inaccurate.

In the hospitality industry, the actual distinctions between bookkeeping and accounting are not always very clear-cut. In addition, because many restaurants and hotels are so small, bookkeeping, accounting, and financial analysis (managerial accounting) may all be done by only one or two individuals. Because that is so, in this text we will not make a significant distinction between bookkeeping and accounting. As a manager, however, it is important that you ensure accurate and timely bookkeeping and accounting methods to produce the financial data you must analyze to make decisions.

The Accounting Formula

Even if you have a basic knowledge of accounting fundamentals, this chapter can still serve as a good accounting review and may also teach you even more about accounting than you previously knew. If you have not completed one or more introductory accounting courses, you will certainly find the information in this chapter to be of great value both as you complete this text and as you progress in your hospitality career. This is so because, in most cases, career advancement in the hospitality industry will mean that you will assume responsibility for increasing numbers of restaurants, hotels, or other operations you are assigned to manage. With increased units, staff, and sales levels typically come increases in the amount of money for which you are held accountable and the complexity of the financial transactions that take place within your area of responsibility. Because that is true, a solid foundation in the basics of accounting will be absolutely necessary for your future career development.

In Chapter 1 you learned that businesses must account for their assets, which are those items they own; their liabilities, which are the amounts the business owes to others; and their owners' equity, which is the residual claims owners have on their assets, or the amount left over in a business after subtracting its liabilities from its assets. An **account** is simply a device used to record increases or decreases in the assets, liabilities, or owners' equity portion of a business. There is a very specific and unchanging relationship between assets, liabilities, and owners' equity. This relationship is expressed in a mathematical formula so precise, clear-cut, and unchanging that it is actually called **The Accounting Formula**. The Accounting Formula states that, for *every* business:

$$\text{Assets} = \text{Liabilities} + \text{Owners' Equity}$$

Using basic algebra, variations of this formula can be developed as presented in Figure 2.2.

Owners' equity accounts include two major sub-categories called permanent accounts and temporary accounts. **Permanent owners' equity accounts** include items such as stock (or owner's investment) and **retained earnings** (accumulated account of profits over the

FIGURE 2.2   Variations of the Accounting Formula

Assets = Liabilities + Owners' Equity

Assets − Liabilities = Owners' Equity

Assets − Owners' Equity = Liabilities

life of the business that have not been distributed as dividends). **Dividends** are money paid out of net income to stockholders as a return on their investment in the company's stocks. **Temporary owners' equity accounts** include revenue and expense accounts. These temporary accounts can increase owners' equity (revenue accounts) or decrease owners' equity (expense accounts). They are used to show changes in the owners' equity account during a single accounting period. At the end of the accounting period, the temporary accounts (revenue and expense) are **closed out** (their balances reduced to zero). The resulting current period's net profit or loss is used to update the balance of the permanent owners' equity account (in retained earnings). The permanent and temporary owners' equity accounts are shown in the following modification of The Accounting Formula:

Assets = Liabilities

+ Permanent Owners' Equity (Stocks + Retained Earnings)

+ Temporary Owners' Equity (Revenue − Expenses)

Two major financial statements, the balance sheet and the income statement, are developed from The Accounting Formula. The **balance sheet** is an accounting summary that closely examines the financial condition, or health, of a business. It does so by reporting the value of a company's total assets, liabilities, and owners' equity on a specified date. The **income statement** reports in detail and for a very specific time period, a business's revenue from all its revenue-producing sources, the expenses required to generate those revenues, and the resulting profits or losses (net income).

Recording Changes to The Accounting Formula

Every time a business makes a financial transaction, it has an affect on (changes) The Accounting Formula you have just learned about. Accountants accurately and skillfully report changes to The Accounting Formula while always ensuring that the formula stays in balance.

Consider Figure 2.3. It is simply a graphic representation of The Accounting Formula.

FIGURE 2.3   Graphic Representation of the Accounting Formula

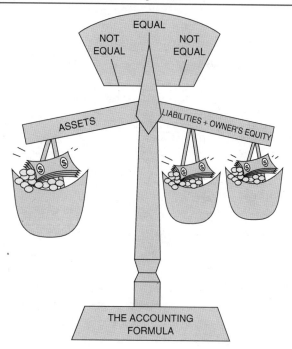

Conceptually, it should be easy for you to see that additions to or subtractions from one of the sides of the scale *must* be counterbalanced with an equal addition to, or subtraction from, the other side of the scale if the formula is to stay in balance. As a result, the scale is to remain in its mandatory "equal" position. It is also possible, of course, to make changes (additions or subtractions) to only one side of the scale. For example, an equal dollar value added to and then subtracted from the asset total would not cause the overall formula to be out of balance. An accounting method that ensures balance of The Accounting Formula is called double entry accounting.

Double Entry Accounting

As you have seen, it is important that a business keeps accurate financial records. To do so, businesses in the United States and many other parts of the world utilize a system called **double entry accounting**. Sometimes called double entry bookkeeping, double entry accounting requires that the person recording a financial transaction make at least two separate accounting entries (changes to its accounts) every time a financial transaction modifies The Accounting Formula of a business.

The double entry accounting system originated in Medieval Europe. According to most historians, the system was first devised and used extensively by Venice (Italy) merchants in the mid-1400s. A double entry system simply means each transaction made is recorded twice instead of once. It is used to catch recording errors and to accurately track the various streams of money in and out of businesses. This is done not only for managers of the business, but because others who need to know about a business's finances must have the information available in a format they understand. Today, 600 years after it originated, the agreed language of accounting is still double entry accounting. For many students, learning this language, (just like learning to speak and understand any foreign language) can be confusing. While it is not the intent of this book to make you completely "fluent" in the language of double entry accounting (doing so would take several courses and several years) it is the intent of the book to give you a basic understanding of how the language is structured and how it is designed to operate.

The Journal and General Ledger

Assume that a hospitality business was created to sell products and services to customers. To do so, it bought raw ingredients; hired staff; purchased land, building, and equipment; created products or services and ultimately sold these to its customers or guests. When it did so, each individual financial transaction it initiated would have an affect on The Accounting Formula and thus should be accurately recorded.

When utilizing the double entry accounting system, each of a business's individual transactions are originally recorded (twice because it is a double entry system!) in the business's unique journal of financial transactions. A **journal**, then, is the written record of a specific business's financial transactions. It would be possible, of course, to maintain two separate journals as a way of double checking the accuracy of the business's financial records. As you will learn, however, maintaining only one journal, and utilizing, for cross-checking purposes, two entries per transaction, is an easier, more accurate and more convenient method than maintaining two completely separate records.

A **journal entry** is made to a specific account when changes to The Accounting Formula are recorded. The up-to-date balances of all a business's individual asset, liability, and owners' equity, (as well as revenue and expense) accounts are maintained in its **general ledger**. Figure 2.4 summarizes the important concepts that accountants must recognize *prior to* learning about how to record changes to The Accounting Formula.

Credits and Debits

You have learned that accountants use a double entry accounting system to record each of a business's financial transactions twice. Doing so helps minimize the chance of making a recording error and helps ensure that The Accounting Formula stays in balance. You have also learned that the asset, liability, and owners' equity portions of The Accounting Formula can be broken down into smaller units called accounts. Thus, for example, the worth of a hotel's assets could be sub-divided into separate accounts that place a specific value on its cash bank balance, furniture, building, and land. Because of their shape, accountants often call these individual accounts **"T" accounts**. Figure 2.5 is an example of a T account.

FIGURE 2.4   Foundational Accounting Concepts

Important concepts for an accountant to remember about maintaining a business's general ledger are:

1. The Accounting Formula, which is the summary of a business's asset, liability, and owners' equity accounts, must stay in balance.
2. The Accounting Formula is affected every time a business makes a financial transaction.
3. Each financial transaction is to be recorded two times in a double entry accounting system; thus minimizing the chance for making an error in recording.
4. The original records of a business's financial transactions are maintained in its journal, and each financial transaction recorded is called a journal entry.
5. The current balances of each of a business's individual asset, liability, and owners' equity accounts are totaled and maintained in its general ledger.

FIGURE 2.5   T Account

Name of Account	
Left (Debit)	**Right (Credit)**

As shown in Figure 2.5, a T account consists of three main parts.

Part 1: The top of the T is used for identifying the name of the account. Thus, for example, a business would likely have a T account for "Cash" to identify that portion of its assets. If appropriate, it would also likely have a T account for "Loan" to identify, for example, that portion of its liabilities. A T account is created whenever an accountant wishes to add additional detail to a portion of The Accounting Formula.

Part 2: The left side of a T account is called the **debit** side. Each journal entry made on the *left* side of a T account is always called a **debit entry**.

Part 3: The right side of a T account is called the **credit** side. Each journal entry made on the *right* side of a T account is always called a **credit entry**.

Note that the T account in Figure 2.5 looks very similar to the scale presented in Figure 2.3. In fact, the manner in which an accountant uses T accounts to make a journal entry can be conceptualized in much the same way as the scale in The Accounting Formula. This is so because of the journal entry principles presented in Figure 2.6.

FIGURE 2.6   Journal Entry Principles

1. To make a complete journal entry, at least two different accounts must be used to record the event (when using double entry accounting).
2. Each journal entry must consist of at least one debit entry and one credit entry.
3. The total of all debit entries in a transaction must always equal the total of all credit entries.
4. When the above principles are followed, The Accounting Formula will always be in balance. If the formula is not in balance, an error has been made in recording one or more journal entries and must be corrected.*

* Sometimes those who are new to double entry accounting can make mistakes because it is easy to forget that a debit is made on the left side of a T account and a credit is made on the right side. It is easy to remember the correct way to make the entries, however, if you just remember that the word "debit" has one less letter in it than does the word "credit"; and it is also true that the word "left" has one less letter than the word "right"! Thus;

Debit = Left
Credit = Right

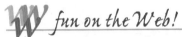

fun on the Web!

Automated accounting systems help reduce accounting errors in many ways (including the rejection of any journal entry that does not result in equal debit and credit entries). To view two of the most popular automated hospitality accounting systems, visit the websites of Peachtree accounting (a product of Sage Software Inc.), and Microsoft Dynamics GP (a Microsoft product). You can see demonstrations of their respective products at:

www.Peachtree.com

and at

www.Microsoft.com/dynamics/gp/default.mspx

Accountants simply create individual T accounts to provide greater detail in financial reporting than could be achieved without them. For example, assume the Regal Plaza hotel had $50,000 in cash in its bank account. Assume also that it owned a $5,000 printer used in its front office. Both of these items are clearly hotel assets, but are very different types of assets, and it is important that each type is accounted for separately.

Similarly, assume the Regal Plaza owed $35,000 per month on its 20-year mortgage (a liability). This is a different type of liability than the taxes owed by the hotel (another liability) and thus, for clarity, it makes sense that they should be recorded in a separate T account.

Within each of the three major components of The Accounting Formula, accountants create individual T accounts to clarify the financial standing of the business. Some of the most commonly created of these individual accounts are:

Asset Accounts	Liability Accounts	Owners' Equity Accounts
Current Assets	Current Liabilities	Permanent Accounts
Cash	Accounts payable	Stock (or owners' investment)
Accounts receivable	Taxes due and payable	Retained earnings
Inventories	Notes payable	
Fixed Assets	Long-term debts payable	Temporary Accounts
Furniture, Fixtures, and Equipment		Revenue accounts
Buildings		Expense accounts
Land		
Accumulated Depreciation (contra asset account)		

As you may have noticed, accumulated depreciation is listed as a contra asset account. **Depreciation** is a method of allocating the cost of a fixed asset over the useful life of the asset. Once fully depreciated, the value of the asset at the end of its useful life is called its **salvage value**. **Accumulated depreciation** is a record and accumulation of all depreciation expense charges that occur over the life of the asset. It is listed as a **contra asset**, from the term *contra*, meaning to deduct, and represents deductions to a fixed asset. Contra assets, like accumulated depreciation, behave *opposite* of all other asset accounts with regard to debits and credits.

While there is some suggested standardization of account names, each individual restaurant and hotel will determine the most appropriate accounts for their own use (see Chapter 4). Virtually all hospitality businesses, however, will create one or more accounts called accounts receivable. **Accounts receivable** (often shortened to AR) represent the amount of money owed to a business *by others* (such as customers) and thus is considered to be one of that business's asset accounts. **Accounts payable** (often shortened to AP) represents the amount of money owed by the business *to others* (such as suppliers), and as a result is considered to be one of that business's liability accounts.

It is easy to understand that, because T accounts are used to record changes to the Accounting Formula, each T account that is used by a business could experience increases or decreases in its balance. For example, funds in bank accounts (an asset T account) can increase or decrease, money owed for refunds to guests (a liability T account) may go up or down, and profits maintained by the hotel's owners (an owners' equity T account) may increase or decrease.

T accounts, as historically utilized by accountants, have common characteristics. For example, an asset account such as "Cash" will typically have a positive balance because the account will reflect some money on hand. As a result, a T account set up to monitor the

FIGURE 2.7 Normal Balances of T Accounts

T Account Type	Normal Balance
Asset	Debit
Liability	Credit
Owners' Equity	
Permanent Accounts (Owners' Equity)	Credit
Temporary Accounts	
Revenue	Credit
Expense	Debit

value of this money will, in most cases, have a debit balance. This is so because additions to the current balance of an asset account such as this one are (simply by tradition) recorded on the left (debit) side of a T account. Reductions in the value of an asset account are recorded (again simply by tradition) on the right (credit) side of its T account. The difference between a T account's total debits and total credits is called the **account balance**. Figure 2.7 indicates the normal or expected balances of the various type T accounts.

Recall that each journal entry made on a T account affects its account balance. Figure 2.8 summarizes the impact of each kind of entry on each of the three major components of The Accounting Formula.

A close examination of Figure 2.8 may also help explain why so many new hospitality managers find it difficult to rapidly "learn" the language of accounting. This is so because Figure 2.8 contains a lot of information for you to remember! Dr. Don St. Hilaire

FIGURE 2.8 Impact of Debit and Credit Entries on The Accounting Formula Components

Accounting Formula Component	Journal Entry	Impact on Balance
Assets	Debit	Increases
	Credit	Decreases
Liabilities	Debit	Decreases
	Credit	Increases
Owners' Equity		
Permanent Accounts (Owners' Equity)	Debit	Decreases
	Credit	Increases
Temporary Accounts		
Revenue	Debit	Decreases
	Credit	Increases
Expense	Debit	Increases
	Credit	Decreases

FIGURE 2.9   Left Hand (Debits) and Right Hand (Credits)

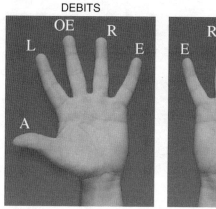
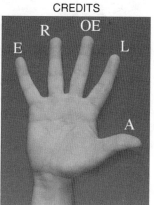

and his students at California State Polytechnic University, Pomona, devised a "trick" that will help make this easier.

Imagine that your left hand represents debits and your right hand represents credits. Your fingers represent the following accounts as shown in Figure 2.9:

Thumb	Assets (A)
Pointer finger	Liabilities (L)
Middle finger	Owners' Equity (OE)
Ring finger	Revenues (R)
Pinky finger	Expenses (E)

Increases ↑ and decreases ↓ in accounts can then be summarized as in Figure 2.10.

Fingers "up" represent increases and fingers "down" represent decreases. So, using the classification of "fingers" in Figure 2.9 and the increases and decreases in accounts shown in Figure 2.10, your hands can be used to remember the impact of debit and credit entries on The Accounting Formula components as in Figure 2.11.

FIGURE 2.10   Increases and Decreases in Accounts

Debits	Credits
↑ Assets	↓ Assets
↓ Liabilities, ↓ Owners' Equity, ↓ Revenues	↑ Liabilities, ↑ Owners' Equity, ↑ Revenues
↑ Expenses	↓ Expenses

FIGURE 2.11 Using Your Hands to Remember Increases and Decreases of Accounts

DEBITS   CREDITS

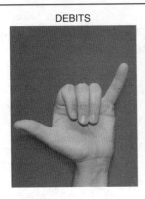
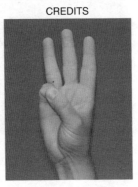

To summarize:

Left Hand – Debits		Right Hand – Credits	
thumb up =	↑ in assets	thumb down =	↓ in assets
pointer finger down =	↓ in liabilities	pointer finger up =	↑ in liabilities
middle finger down =	↓ in owners' equity	middle finger up =	↑ in owners' equity
ring finger down =	↓ in revenue	ring finger up =	↑ in revenue
pinky finger up =	↑ in expenses	pinky finger down =	↓ in expenses

To further see how the use of debits, credits, and double entry accounting affect individual T accounts and thus The Accounting Formula, consider the Stagecoach restaurant. It has just begun its operation with a $1,000,000 check from its owner. The two accounting transactions required to initiate the restaurant's accounting system are:

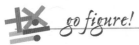 *go figure!*

1. A $1,000,000 debit to "Cash" (↑ Asset)
2. A $1,000,000 credit of the owner's investment (↑ Owners' Equity)

The resulting T accounts are as follows:

Cash

$1,000,000

Owner's Equity

$1,000,000

Upon completion of these initial journal entries, the Stagecoach's Accounting Formula would read as follows:

Assets	= Liabilities	+ Owners' Equity
$1,000,000 =	$0	+ $1,000,000

Now assume that the restaurant's owner established a T account titled "Uniforms," as well as the "Cash" account previously established. The manager then purchases, with cash, $1,000 worth of uniforms for the future dining room staff. This decreases the amount of money in the "Cash" asset account and increases the value of the "Uniforms" asset account. These two accounting transactions are:

 *go figure!*

1. A $1,000 credit to "Cash" (↓ Asset)
2. A $1,000 debit to "Uniforms" (↑ Asset)

The resulting T accounts are as follows:

Cash

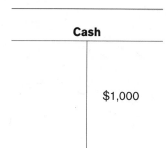

$1,000

Uniforms

$1,000

Now assume that the owner of the Stagecoach purchases a vacant lot adjacent to the restaurant to expand its parking area. The lot is purchased for $50,000 and the owner secures a bank loan to finance the purchase. These two accounting transactions are:

 *go figure!*

1. A $50,000 debit to "Land" (↑ Asset)
2. A $50,000 credit to "Loans Payable" (↑ Liabilities)

The resulting T accounts are as follows:

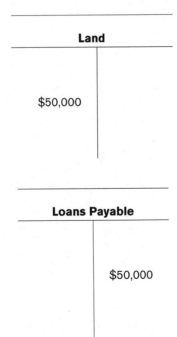

Land

$50,000

Loans Payable

$50,000

The Stagecoach Accounting Formula would now be revised to read:

$1,000,000 Cash + $50,000 Land = $50,000 Loans Payable + $1,000,000 Owners' Equity

Assets   = Liabilities + Owners' Equity

or

$1,050,000 = $1,050,000

At the conclusion of the land purchase, both sides of the equation are still equal (in balance) with each other. Note that the $1,000 debit to uniforms and the $1,000 credit to cash are not included because they are both current assets and cancel each other out.

Two of the most important and frequently used T accounts are revenue and expense accounts. As noted earlier, these two account types belong to the owners' equity portion of the accounting equation and are summarized, and closed out, at the end of each accounting period. Interestingly, hotel managers use a variation of these T accounts when maintaining the **folios** (bills) of their own guests. Guest folios can actually be considered "individual accounts" (accounts for each guest) and as a result, debit and credit entries for these accounts follow most of the same rules as those for all other accounts. Thus, for example, if a guest stays at the Anderson Plaza hotel and, the next morning, has a folio balance (owes the hotel) $100, it requires two (not one) accounting entries to properly record the guest's payment. These two entries would have the effect of reducing (by $100) the account(s) that reflect what guests owe to the hotel, and increasing (by $100) the value of one or more accounts showing what has been paid, by guests, to the hotel.

For some hospitality managers, the principles that accountants use to record financial transactions are easy to understand; other managers may have more difficulty fully comprehending them. All managers, however, can learn the specific recording procedures that are mandated at their own properties. For managerial accountants, the truly important concepts to remember are those of careful and accurate recording (posting) of all financial transactions and the responsibility to ensure that all accounts remain in balance.

Generally Accepted Accounting Principles

Not surprisingly, just as there are a variety of ways to prepare a specific recipe or adequately clean a guest room, there are a variety of methods that could be used to record a business's financial transactions. To utilize a simple example, assume that Mr. and Mrs. Quervo check into a guest room at the Palmer Court hotel at 2:00 a.m. on a Monday morning. They then check out of the hotel at 9:00 a.m. that same morning.

Should the record of the hotel's sale to them be recorded as a sale from Sunday night (because the Quervos checked in very late on "Sunday night"), or should it be recorded as a Monday sale, (because the Quervos were never actually in the hotel on "Sunday")?

Clearly, a reasonable argument could be made that either approach described above is a good one that could reflect an accurate record of the Quervos' stay. It is also clear, however, that if two different hotel controllers each used a different one of the alternatives above they would not be reporting information in exactly the same manner. A reader of their financial reports would need to know, in this case, which of the two methods had been utilized for reporting the hotel's Sunday night sales information.

Because there can be honest differences of opinion about what constitutes the best method of recording a financial transaction and because it is so important that readers of financial statements can immediately depend upon their accuracy, those professionals in the field of accounting have worked hard to develop and consistently follow **generally accepted accounting principles (GAAP)**.

The term "generally accepted accounting principles" has a specific meaning for accountants and auditors. The AICPA (see Chapter 1) Code of Professional Conduct prohibits its members from stating affirmatively that financial statements or other financial data fairly represent a company's financial records unless those records have been prepared in accordance with the generally accepted accounting principles appropriate for the company's industry.

Generally accepted accounting principles are developed by the **Financial Accounting Standards Board (FASB)**. The FASB was created in 1973 and is a private body whose mission is to establish and improve standards of financial accounting and reporting for the guidance and education of the public, including issuers, auditors, and users of financial information. The FASB publishes its recommendations for accounting procedures standardization and these are known as generally accepted accounting principles. As a result of their importance, accountants, auditors, and controllers all utilize GAAP. Because they do, you should understand what these principles are and why they are used.

Specific principles are developed and modified on a continuous basis. There are, however, some principles that are very important and that form the basis for financial accounting procedures in the United States. Regardless of your knowledge of how changes to The Accounting Formula are manually recorded, knowing these principles will help ensure that the accounting in the facility you own or manage is done correctly. Eleven of the most critical generally accepted accounting principles all hospitality managers simply must recognize include:

- Distinct business entity principle
- Going concern principle
- Monetary unit principle
- Time period principle
- Cost principle
- Consistency principle
- Matching principle
- Materiality principle
- Objectivity principle

- Conservatism principle
- Full disclosure principle

The Distinct Business Entity Principle

This **distinct business entity principle** states that a business's financial transactions should be kept completely separate from those of its owners. Essentially, there are three basic types of business ownership in the United States as follows.

> **Corporations:** A corporation, commonly called a **C corporation**, is a legal entity that is separate and distinct from its owners. A corporation is allowed to own assets, can incur its own liabilities, and can sell shares of ownership, among other things. There are variations of corporations including the **Limited Liability Corporation (LLC);** a special form of a corporation that is typically regulated by the state in which it is formed. An LLC limits the potential losses incurred by its owners only to what they have invested in the business. A **Sub S corporation** is another distinctive type of corporation that is granted special status under the tax laws of the United States. These laws are very specific about how and when this type of corporation can be formed and the number of **stockholders** (company owners) it can have.
>
> **Partnerships:** A **partnership** is simply a business entity where two or more individuals agree to share ownership. Under the laws of the United States, its profits are taxed differently than those profits earned by a corporation. Like corporations, there are different types of partnerships, including the **Limited Partnership (LP)** in which one or more general partners manage the business and are liable for its debts and one or more limited partners invest in the business but have limited personal liability for its debts.
>
> **Proprietorships:** A **proprietorship** is a business owned by a single individual. The owner may, or may not, actually manage the business on a day-to-day basis. A sole proprietorship pays personal (but not corporate) income tax on profits made by the business and also has unlimited liability for the debts and other obligations incurred by the business.

It is probably fairly easy for you to see why the personal assets, debts, and expenses of a corporation's stockholders should be kept separate from those of the company in which they own stock, but the distinct business entity accounting principle holds true even for partnerships and proprietorships where the owners may work for, or even manage, the business.

To understand why this is so, consider Soren and Ted. They are equal partners in a family-style restaurant. Because they are equal partners, their profits from the restaurant are to be shared equally. If Soren begins taking food home for his own family from the restaurant, the amount of profit shown by the restaurant will be reduced. Not only will Ted receive (when their profits are split on a 50/50 basis) a smaller amount than he should have, if the restaurant is ever sold, potential buyers might undervalue it because its accounting records would not show that it produced the profit levels it would have delivered if Soren had kept his personal food expenses separate from those of the restaurant's.

The Going Concern Principle

The **going concern principle** simply means that accountants make the assumption that the business will be ongoing (continue to exist) indefinitely and that there is no intention to **liquidate** (sell) all of the assets of the business. The reason this concept is important goes back to The Accounting Formula you learned earlier in this chapter. Recall that, in any business accounting system, the value of a business's assets must equal its liabilities plus its owners' equity. But how do accountants establish the value of a company's assets? To understand this potential accounting dilemma, consider your own favorite piece of jewelry. If someone asked you what it was "worth," how would you reply? Would you set the value of the item at:

1. The amount for which you would sell the item?
2. The cost of replacing the item if it were ever lost or stolen?
3. The price you paid for the item?

Any of these three options could be considered a good way to establish the value of your "asset." Each option would, however, likely place a very different value on the piece of jewelry.

The principle of going concern instructs accountants to ignore Option 1 above because there is no intention of selling the asset. Company assets should be used to create profits, and thus the intention of a business should be to keep, and not sell, such assets. The principle also requires accountants to ignore Option 2 (replacement costs) because, in an ongoing business, there would be no reason to replace, with an identical asset, an asset that the business already owns.

The going concern principle is important because it clearly directs accountants to record the value of a business's assets only at the price paid for them (Option 3). Because the value of some assets could be subjective and even can change over time, it is best to establish a single and consistent method of valuing them. The going concern principle does just that by establishing balance sheet values for assets based upon the price a business paid for them and by using depreciation techniques.

As a result, readers of a financial statement know that asset values represent a business's true cost and not a hypothetical (and perhaps over- or under-inflated) value established by the business's own managers or owners.

The Monetary Unit Principle

The **monetary unit principle** means that to be understandable, financial statements must be prepared in an identifiable monetary unit (specific currency denomination). In the

United States, the U.S. dollar is the monetary unit used for preparing financial statements. Thus, if, for example, a balance sheet prepared for a U.S. company listed the value of its hotel furniture at ten million, the correct interpretation would be $10,000,000 (ten million U.S. dollars).

While at first it might appear obvious that financial statements would be prepared in a currency denomination typically used by the company whose records are being reported, in reality, fulfilling the monetary unit principle can be quite complex. Consider the following two examples from the restaurant and hotel business worlds.

McDonald's

McDonald's operates in over 100 countries. As a result, the revenue they report from customer purchases, as well as the payments they receive from their franchisees for royalty and marketing fees can be submitted in a variety of currency units. Could you have easily named the currency customers use to buy a Big Mac in the ten well-known countries listed in Figure 2.12?

Barceló

Hospitality is an international business; Barceló is an outstanding Spanish hotel company that operates facilities in a variety of foreign countries. In addition, because they service world travelers, many of whom pay with bank cards issued by their own country of origin, currency conversions for Barceló's hotels in the Dominican Republic, Costa Rica, Cuba, Turkey, as well as the United States are extensive. Clearly, however, if Barceló is to issue financial statements that reflect accurately their revenue and profitability, conversion back to one monetary unit is necessary. For Barceló, this unit is the euro.

FIGURE 2.12 Monetary Units of Selected Countries

Country	Monetary Unit
France	Euro
Greece	Drachma
India	Rupee
Ireland	Punt
Poland	Zloty
Russia	Ruble
Spain	Peseta
Sweden	Krona
Turkey	Lira
Vietnam	Dong

W fun on the Web!

To view an interesting site that will show you the current currency conversion rates for many currencies (including the Cambodian riel and the Hungarian forint) go to:

www.oanda.com

Click on "FXConverter" to calculate the conversion rates for over 160 countries

The Time Period Principle

The **time period principle** is important because it requires a business to clearly identify the time period for which its financial transactions are reported. For the owners of a business, it is likely that the most important financial reports they will examine are those that include all of the financial transactions occurring during their **fiscal year**. A fiscal year, which consists of twelve consecutive months, (but not necessarily beginning in January and ending in December like a **calendar year**), would most likely include the business's best, as well as its poorest, periods of financial performance. A fiscal year-end financial report would provide these owners with the information they need to file their taxes and perhaps make other needed financial management decisions.

The amount of time included in any summary of financial information is called an **accounting period**. The managers of a business may be most interested in monthly, weekly, or even daily financial summary reports. These would inform the managers of the business's revenue and expense levels and profitability. The owners of the business would also be interested in such reports. Regardless of the report's readers, however, it is critical that the financial statements clearly state the time period involved.

In some cases, the time period reported in a financial statement is somewhat arbitrary. For example, consider hotels that are open twenty-four hours a day, seven days a week. These businesses never close, however, their managers must still select a point in time (usually between 2:00 a.m. and 5:00 a.m. because that is when hotels process the fewest financial transactions) to end the recording of one business day and begin recording the financial transactions of the next day. In a properly prepared financial summary of any business, the time period principle assures that the reader will be clearly informed of the precise time period included in the summary.

The Cost Principle

The **cost principle**, which supports the principles of going concern and monetary unit, requires accountants to record all business transactions at their cash cost. To illustrate, assume, for example, that a caterer has a client who wants to serve a champagne toast at her wedding. The client requests a certain brand of champagne which the caterer can buy for $12 per bottle, but which will immediately be resold to the guest for $30 per bottle.

The wine wholesaler used by the caterer to provide the champagne may have paid only $10 per bottle for it; the caterer will pay $12 per bottle and the guest pays $30 per bottle. How should the actual value of the wine be established? This principle requires the caterer to value the wine at its own cash cost, or $12 per bottle.

Just as the going concern principle requires accountants to value a business's assets at their purchase price, with few exceptions, it requires businesses to set the value of the items it intends to sell at the price the business actually paid for them.

The Consistency Principle

As you no doubt now realize, there can be real and many times legitimate differences in the way accountants record financial transactions. One of the biggest areas of potential differences involves the decision about how to record revenue and expense. The two choices accountants have in this area are that of selecting an accrual system or a cash system as their basis for reporting revenue and expense. In an **accrual accounting** system, revenue is recorded when it is earned, regardless of when it is collected, and expenses are recorded when they are incurred, regardless of when they are paid.

To illustrate, assume you worked in a job from Monday (the first day of the month), through Friday, (the fifth day of the month), but were paid on the following Monday (the eighth day of the month). Assume also that you use the accrual method of accounting for your own personal income (revenue). Under the rules of accrual accounting, you would report your income as being earned between the first and fifth of the month and not when you were actually paid. Using a similar philosophy, the accrual system instructs accountants to record expenses when they are incurred regardless of when they are paid.

Alternatively, a **cash accounting** system is a method that records revenue as being earned when it is actually received. Likewise, expenditures are recorded when they are actually paid, regardless of when they were incurred. Returning to the previous example, under this system of accounting, you would record your personal income as being earned on the eighth day of the month, which is the day you actually received your paycheck.

The major advantage to using a cash accounting system is its simplicity. If you have a checking account, you already understand how a cash accounting system works. When you make a deposit into your checking account, you add to your cash balance. When you write a check (that is, incur an expense) you subtract from your cash balance. As a result, simply by looking at the current balance in your checking account you will know how much money you have left to spend. Most (but not all) businesses, however, choose to use the accrual accounting system. To understand why they elect to do so, consider two examples, one relating to revenue and the other relating to expense.

Assume that, in a hotel, a guest checks in on the fifteenth day of the month for a thirty-day stay. As agreed upon with the hotel, the guest will pay her total bill upon departure. In this case, the hotel will actually have earned revenue during each of the last fifteen days of the month in which she arrived to occupy her room, as well as the first fifteen days of the following month. If the hotel recorded, as revenue, the total amount paid by the guest upon her departure in the second month, it would have actually understated the revenue it earned in the month the guest arrived and likewise would have overstated the revenue earned in the month the guest departs. For hotels that want to report room revenue when its rooms are actually occupied, this would not be a good reporting system. To avoid this problem, most hotels and restaurants record their revenue when their customers make purchases, rather than when these customers actually pay their bills.

Businesses face a similar reporting issue when they must pay their bills. Consider the case of Kevin Garnett. Kevin owns his own restaurant and wants to have an accurate record of his monthly profits or losses. As a result, Kevin prepares a monthly summary of his revenue and expenses. In his city, one time per year, Kevin must pay the annual property taxes due on his building. The tax amount to be paid is quite large; thus, if Kevin used a cash accounting system and recorded the entire amount of the tax payment in the one month it was paid, it would appear that he had a very poor month (and perhaps even lost money!) during that specific month.

In fact, Kevin's property tax bill is for an entire year's worth of taxes; thus, it would be more reasonable for him to assign 1/12 of the annual tax payment to each of the twelve monthly revenue and expense summaries he prepares. By doing so, Kevin would spread the actual tax bill owed over the twelve months these expenses were actually incurred. The result would be a more accurate reflection of his restaurant's true *monthly* profitability.

The **consistency principle** of accounting states that a business must select and consistently report financial information under the rules of the specific system it elects to use. Thus, if a business uses a cash accounting system, it should use it every time it reports financial data. If it elects to use an accrual system, then that is the manner in which it should consistently report its financial information. Only by following the consistency principle could readers of that business's financial information gain a true understanding of its actual revenue and expense during a specified accounting period.

The Matching Principle

The matching principle applies to those organizations that elect to use an accrual system of accounting. Recall that accrual accounting requires a business's revenue to be reported when earned and its expenses to be recorded when incurred. The **matching principle** is designed to closely match expenses incurred to the actual revenue those expenses helped generate.

To illustrate the way this principle is applied, assume that a hotel purchases new television sets for each of its guest rooms. The televisions are purchased because of management's belief that they will help the hotel generate increased revenue by making the hotel's rooms more attractive to potential guests. As a result, the rooms could be sold more frequently or at a higher rate each time they are sold. Despite the fact that the hotel incurred the expense of acquiring these assets all at one time (when the televisions were purchased) the matching principle requires that the hotel's accountants spread the expense of the televisions over the entire time period in which the televisions will help the hotel generate the additional revenue it seeks.

The depreciation and other accounting rules that financial and tax accountants must utilize to achieve this exact revenue/expense matching can be quite complex and often are dictated by the way in which the tax laws related to a specific business are written and enforced. As an effective hospitality manager, however, it is most important for you to understand that the matching principle is integral to the effective use of an accrual accounting system and therefore must be utilized by you and/or your accountants consistently.

The Materiality Principle

The consistency and matching principles you just learned about require accountants using an accrual system to do their best to match a business's expenses with the time period in which those expenses were incurred. In addition, by using allowable depreciation methods, these principles require accountants to expense the cost of certain long-life assets like furniture and equipment over the time period in which they will help a business generate revenue. The materiality principle, however, allows accountants, under very strict circumstances, to vary from these two important principles.

To understand the reason for the existence of this principle, consider the case of Bess Haley, a hotel front office manager who buys, for $10, a standard stapler that will be used at the front desk. Assume that the stapler has an expected useful life of three years. In this situation, it could be argued that the hotel's accountants should charge, to Bess's departmental expense, $0.28 each month for each of the next 36 months ($10/36 months = $0.28 per month) to properly account for the expense.

The principle of materiality, however, states that, in a case such as this, because the amount of money involved is so small, the hotel's accountants can expense the entire cost of the item in the same month Bess purchased it. Not to do so would cause unnecessary work and in fact, would be unlikely to materially (significantly) affect the outcome of Bess's monthly expense statement. The **materiality principle**, then, means that if an item is deemed to be not significant, then other accounting principles may be ignored if it is not practical to use them. In this case, the accuracy gained by expensing the stapler over its useful life will not likely make a significant difference in the financial reporting of Bess's hotel. A simplified way to remember this principle is this sentence, spoken by one of the author's own accounting professors. He stated that, "because businesses ultimately seek to make a profit, it makes little sense to spend a lot of dollars accounting for a few pennies!"

The amount of money that must be involved before an expense is considered material can vary for each business and thus must be clearly spelled out. The amount of money expended before it is considered "material" should be unmistakably established by the business's owners, carefully applied to the business's records by its accountants, and freely shared with the readers of the business's financial statements.

The Objectivity Principle

While all of the generally accepted accounting principles have great value, it is this one that most ensures readers of a business's financial statements that those documents can be trusted to be reliable. Essentially, the **objectivity principle** states that financial transactions must have a confirmable (objective) basis in fact. That is, there must be a way to verify that a financial transaction actually occurred before it can be recorded in the business's financial records.

To illustrate, assume that a restaurant manager reported that a specific day's total restaurant sales equal $1,000. The objectivity principle states that these sales must have substantiating evidence to prove that they actually occurred. In this example, that evidence could include the individual guest checks used by wait staff to record guest orders, bank card statements showing charges made to guests' cards, or various sales records maintained in an electronic cash register or computer. In each of these cases, there would be objective and verifiable records that substantiate the restaurant manager's assertion that the day's sales actually equaled $1,000.

In a similar manner, expenses must be verifiable before they can be recorded as having been incurred or paid. Examples of methods used to verify the recording and payment of invoices can include delivery slips or original invoices supplied by vendors, cancelled checks or documented **electronic funds transfers** (**EFTs**) showing that funds have been paid or moved electronically from the business to the entity to whom money is owed. Additional types of verifiable expense evidence may include written contracts that show payments are due from the business on a regular basis. Examples of this type of verification include contracts spelling out the terms and length of lease payments or loan repayments.

Recall from Chapter 1 that auditors are accountants who ensure that standards of financial reporting are maintained in a business. As a result, one of an auditor's main tasks is ensuring that businesses report only financial data that have a basis in fact. If businesses were allowed to estimate, rather than directly confirm, their revenue and expenses, the financial summaries produced by them would also be estimates. It follows, then, that these summaries would not precisely reflect the money earned and expenses incurred by the business. Not surprisingly, when significant accounting "scandals" are uncovered by auditors it is usually a violation of this principle (such as a business reporting non-existent revenues or inappropriately documenting its expenses) that generates the scandal.

The Conservatism Principle

Assume that you had a large amount of money and were considering investing in or buying an already operating restaurant or hotel. You want to buy into the business if it is currently profitable, but would be much more hesitant to invest if it is only marginally profitable. Assume also that you were studying the financial records of that business. Which of the two following approaches to reporting its financial performance would you have preferred its accountants had employed when preparing the statements you are reading?

> Approach A: A tendency to overstate (be aggressive) when reporting revenue earned by the business and to be very conservative (low) when reporting the expenses it incurred, or

> Approach B: A tendency to be conservative when reporting revenue earned by the business and realistic when reporting its operating expenses?

If you are like most investors, you probably chose approach B. In fact, the **conservatism principle** requires the accountants of a business to be conservative when reporting its revenue (and thus not to report it until it is actually earned) and realistic when reporting its expense and other liabilities. For example, assume that a restaurant has a signed contract with a private business to serve as host for a retirement party held in honor of one of the business's employees. This accounting principle states that the sales revenue to be achieved during the party is counted only after the party is held. If, however, the restaurant were to purchase additional food and beverages in advance of the party, those expenses would be considered to have been incurred and thus recorded at the time these extra food and beverage products were delivered to the restaurant, even if this were to occur several days or even weeks ahead of the event. In summary, the principle of conservatism requires that accounting for a business should be fair and reasonable. Because accountants are sometimes required to make evaluations or estimates and to select among differing accounting procedures, they should always do so in a way that neither inappropriately overstates (revenue achieved) or understates (expenses or liabilities incurred) when recording a business's financial transactions.

The Full Disclosure Principle

Bookkeeping and accounting most often report financial events that have happened in the past and as result simply need to be recorded. For example, a lunch sale made by an Italian restaurant on Monday will likely be reported by the restaurant's management on Monday night. In a similar manner, a hospital food service director who buys new hot food plate covers on the tenth of the month will likely summarize and report that purchase at the end of the month. As well, a hotel that replaces the individual heating and cooling units in its rooms will, using appropriate depreciation techniques, record this expense over the useful life of the units (a time period that will likely span several years). In each of these cases, when accountants rigorously apply the generally accepted accounting principles you have learned thus far, readers of the financial statements prepared for these businesses can have confidence that all of these transactions described have, in fact, been reported properly. The full disclosure principle, however, requires that accountants do even more.

The **full disclosure principle** requires that any past or even *future* event which could materially affect the financial standing of the business and that cannot be easily discerned from reading the business's financial statements must be separately reported. These reports, prepared in the form of footnotes, must be attached to the financial statements prepared by the business's accountants.

To see why such footnotes may be important, assume that the Italian restaurant in the example above was facing a serious lawsuit resulting from a guest injury that occurred at the restaurant. Assume also that the restaurant's attorneys had advised the restaurant's owners that they would very likely lose the case, and as a result, the restaurant could face significant financial liability. In such a situation, the full disclosure principle would require that the restaurant's accountants identify this future risk to the restaurant's financial standing.

Accountants use full disclosure footnotes to report events that have not happened yet but may, if they do occur, considerably change the conclusions drawn by readers of a business's financial statements. Significant lawsuits are just one example of a future event that must be revealed under the full disclosure principle. Other events that could affect how financial statements are interpreted include changing from a cash to an accrual accounting system, significant tax disputes, modifying depreciation schedules, unusual events that occurred after the financial statements were actually prepared, or any other atypical or non-recurring event that could materially affect the business.

The Hospitality Business Cycle

As you have learned, an accounting period is simply the time frame included in the financial transaction summaries prepared by a business. As a result, hospitality managers can virtually create accounting summaries for any time period of interest to them. Thus, some managers of restaurant businesses, **restaurateurs**, may be most interested in one year summaries of activities, others in monthly summaries, and still others may be most interested in time frames as short as half-hour time blocks during very busy lunch or dinner periods. In a like manner, **hoteliers** managing hotel businesses may be interested in knowing the number of rooms sold last year, last month, or even in the last ten minutes. Regardless of the time frame involved, however, each of these accounting summaries will consist of common components that make up a complete hospitality business cycle.

As can be seen in Figure 2.13, a hospitality business uses its cash (or credit) reserves to purchase products for resale to guests.

The raw materials are processed (meals are produced, and guest rooms are prepared) by workers who create finished products. The sale of these products creates cash or accounts receivables owned by the business. The money resulting from these sales is then used to buy additional products or, if profits are generated, some of it may be retained by the business. Professional accounting records the movement of funds during this business flow or cycle. In each section of the flow chart, transactions are made and recorded. For example, when a

FIGURE 2.13 Hospitality Business Cycle

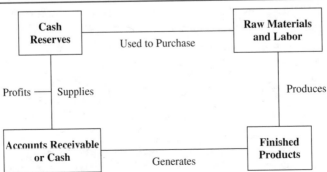

restaurant uses its cash reserves to buy steaks for resale to guests, an accurate record is made of the product purchased and the amount paid for it. Because the double entry accounting method is always used, a record would be made in at least two different restaurant accounts. In this steak example, upon their delivery, there would be an increase in the value of the restaurant's food inventory and a corresponding decrease in the restaurant's cash account (if the restaurant paid cash for the steaks) or an increase in its accounts payables total (if the steaks were purchased on credit). Purchase orders and vendors' invoices make up a large part of the accounting documentation that will be analyzed by hospitality managers in this first segment in the hospitality business cycle.

When the steaks are received, stored properly, and eventually prepared, money will be spent on payroll as well as the other ingredients required to sell the steaks. As a result, payroll records and records related to purchases of equipment, supplies, and other food, in addition to the non-food items needed to operate the restaurant, are important documents in this segment of the hospitality business cycle.

In a similar manner, when products such as the steaks in this example are actually sold to guests, cash receipts and sales records make up the majority of the financial documentation produced. In the hospitality industry, records related to various guest payment forms such as credit, debit, entertainment cards, cash, and checks are important to maintain. Again, the process of recording sales information requires that a minimum of two different restaurant accounts be affected. In this example, accounts affected could be cash and/or accounts receivable, as well as sales revenue. Finally, when profits earned are removed from the business or reinvested in it, extensive and precise documentation is required to keep The Accounting Formula in balance and the operation's books accurate.

In the remaining portions of this book you will learn how talented hospitality managers analyze the data produced in each part of the accounting cycle as they look for areas in which their businesses can be improved. This is done by learning to "read" accounting data and respond to the information it gives you for the betterment of the business you manage. Outstanding hospitality managers use managerial accounting information to improve their businesses, and in the remaining parts of this book you will learn how you can do the same thing.

Apply What You Have Learned

Dave Berger was about to achieve his dream. Having finished culinary school and then completed his hospitality management degree, Dave was ready to seek the financial backing he needed to open what he firmly believed would be his first, and a very successful restaurant. Dave knew food production, was truly creative in the kitchen, and considered himself a real "people person." With his educational background and solid industry experience behind him, Dave knew he had what it took to succeed.

To begin his restaurant project, Dave has scheduled many appointments, including ones with the Small Business Administration (SBA) representative in his local area, the city's largest food distributor, and a tax advisor.

1. Dave is meeting with the SBA to seek the federally backed loan he needs to start his business. In your opinion, how important will be Dave's knowledge and use of GAAP to the lenders who will consider his loan? Why would these entities care about Dave's knowledge in this area?
2. Dave is talking to the food distributor because he wants to establish a delivery line of credit. Doing so would allow Dave to avoid "Cash on Delivery" (COD) requirements the vendor imposes on poor credit risks. How important do you think it will be to this vendor that Dave has a thorough understanding of managerial accounting? Why?
3. Regardless of the business entity Dave selects to operate his business, he will need to file taxes. How do you think his knowledge and use of GAAP will affect the price his accountant will charge to complete his tax filings?

 *Key Terms and Concepts*

The following are terms and concepts discussed in the chapter that are important for you to know as a manager. To help you review, please define the terms below.

Bookkeepers	Salvage value	Proprietorship
Account	Accumulated depreciation	Going concern principle
The Accounting Formula	Contra asset	Liquidate
Permanent owners' equity accounts	Accounts receivable	Monetary unit principle
Retained earnings	Accounts payable	Time period principle
Dividends	Account balance	Fiscal year
Temporary owners' equity accounts	Folios	Calendar year
Closed out	Generally Accepted Accounting Principles (GAAP)	Accounting period
Balance sheet		Cost principle
Income statement	Financial Accounting Standards Board (FASB)	Accrual accounting
Double entry accounting	Distinct business entity principle	Cash accounting
Journal	Corporation (C corporation)	Consistency principle
Journal entry	Limited Liability Corporation (LLC)	Matching principle
General ledger	Sub S corporation	Materiality principle
T accounts	Stockholders	Objectivity principle
Debit	Partnership	Electronic Funds Transfer (EFT)
Debit entry	Limited Partnership (LP)	Conservatism principle
Credit		Full disclosure principle
Credit entry		Restaurateurs
Depreciation		Hoteliers

Test Your Skills

Complete the Test Your Skills exercises by placing your answers in the shaded boxes.

1. Stephanie Martinez opened a Latin Fusion restaurant downtown in a large southern city. She has asked you, her accountant, to complete The Accounting Formulas for some of her first month's transactions. Complete the following Accounting Formulas. (Spreadsheet hint: If you need to record two transactions in one cell, use Alt Enter after the first number to return to the next line within the same cell.)

a. The restaurant started with a $1,200,000 check from its owner, Stephanie.

Assets =	Liabilities +	Owners' Equity	Revenue –	Expenses

b. The restaurant generated revenues of $5,000 on accounts receivable.

Assets =	Liabilities +	Owners' Equity	Revenue –	Expenses

c. Stephanie purchased a $400,000 building with $40,000 cash and a $360,000 mortgage.

Assets =	Liabilities +	Owners' Equity	Revenue –	Expenses

d. Stephanie paid $550 cash for the utilities bill.

Assets =	Liabilities +	Owners' Equity	Revenue –	Expenses

2. Kassi Handover purchased a small café in a northern Texas town with $600,000 of her own money. Help her prepare her T accounts for her first month of operations using the following information.

a. Kassi invested $600,000 cash in the café.

Cash	Owners' Equity

b. Kassi purchased $3,500 in food, all of which is to be paid next month (accounts payable).

Food Inventory	Accounts Payable

c. Kassi generated $10,000 in revenue, all received in cash.

Cash		Revenue	

d. Kassi paid her employees $3,600 this month with payroll checks (cash account).

Cash		Salaries and Wages	

3. Adam Deeds purchased a small roadside motel in April with inheritance money he received from his wealthy aunt. Help him prepare his T accounts for his first month of operations using the information provided.

a. Adam invested $5,000,000 cash in the motel.

Cash		Owners' Equity	

b. Adam purchased a $50,000 point of sale (POS) system with $5,000 cash and $45,000 notes payable.

Cash		POS system		Notes Payable	

c. Adam generated $75,000 in revenues with $52,000 cash and $23,000 accounts receivable.

Cash		Accounts Receivable		Revenues	

d. Adam paid utilities of $750 in cash.

Cash		Utilities Expense	

4. Lisa and Laura are twins who own a seafood restaurant in a coastal town. Lisa likes to report her income statement using accrual accounting, and Laura likes to report her income statement using cash accounting. Given the following information, complete the spreadsheet for March using both accrual accounting for Lisa and cash accounting for Laura.

- The restaurant generated $45,000 in revenue, but only received $30,000.
- Cost of food sold was $14,000, but only 60% was paid to the supplier.
- Salaries and wages were $13,000, but only 50% was paid to employees.
- Utilities expense was $600 and all of it was paid.
- Maintenance expense was $200, but it had been prepaid in January for the quarter.
- Marketing expense was $450 and all of it was paid.
- Rent expense was $6,000 and all of it was paid.

	LISA'S ACCRUAL ACCOUNTING	LAURA'S CASH ACCOUNTING
Revenue		
Expenses:		
Cost of Food Sold		
Salaries and Wages		
Utilities		
Maintenance		
Marketing		
Rent		
Net Profit or (Loss)		

a. Which accounting method, Lisa's accrual accounting or Laura's cash accounting, shows a higher net profit?

b. Which accounting method shows the most accurate amount of money on hand to pay bills?

c. Which accounting method most accurately shows the revenues generated regardless of when they were received?

d. Which accounting method most accurately shows the expenses incurred regardless of when they were paid?

e. Which accounting method most accurately shows actual cash inflows and outflows?

f. Which accounting method shows the most accurate reflection of their restaurant's true profitability?

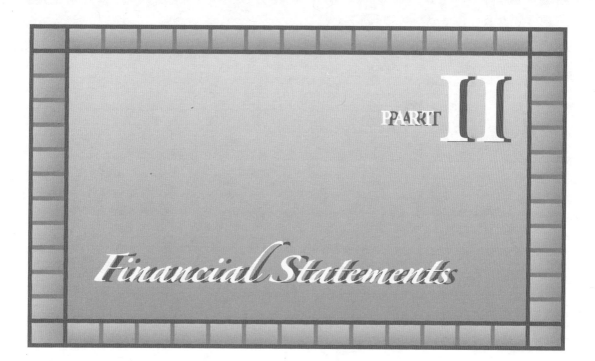

PART II

Financial Statements

CHAPTER 3

The Income Statement

OVERVIEW

Businesses want to be profitable and as a professional hospitality manager or owner, you will want to operate a profitable business. The vehicle businesses use to document and report their profits is called the income statement. In the past, some managers have referred to the income statement as the "Profit and Loss" (P&L) statement and as a result that name for it is still used by some in the hospitality industry. In this book we will simply refer to the document by its shortened name: the Income Statement.

A business's revenue minus its expenses equals its profits. The income statement reports in detail and for a very specific time period, a business's revenue from all its revenue-producing sources, the expenses required to generate those revenues, and the resulting profits or losses (net income).

In this chapter you will learn why the income statement is so important to all those who will typically review and analyze it. You will also see why it is so critical for the manager who is actually operating the business to be able to read and correctly analyze and interpret the income statement. Perhaps most important, in this chapter you will learn how managers read and analyze their income statements to learn as much as possible about the current and future profitability of their businesses.

CHAPTER OUTLINE

- The Purpose of the Income Statement
- Income Statement Preparation
- Income Statement Analysis
- Apply What You Have Learned
- Key Terms and Concepts
- Test Your Skills

LEARNING OUTCOMES

At the conclusion of this chapter, you will be able to:

✓ State the purpose of regularly preparing an income statement for a hospitality business.
✓ Explain the way managers and accountants actually prepare an income statement.
✓ Analyze an income statement to improve the operation of your own business.

The Purpose of the Income Statement

When you manage a hospitality facility, you will receive **revenue**, the term used to indicate the money you take in, and you will incur **expenses**, the cost of the items required to operate the business. The dollars that remain after all expenses have been paid represent your **profit**. For the purposes of this book, the authors will use the following terms interchangeably: revenues and sales; expenses and (in most cases) costs; profit and income.

The following is the basic profit formula used in the hospitality industry and it is also the format followed when preparing the income statement.

$$\text{Revenue} - \text{Expenses} = \text{Profit}$$

To illustrate the formula, consider Paige Vincent, the general manager of the Blue Lagoon Water Park. Paige's water park will generate revenue from a variety of sources. These revenue sources include:

Room sales (including water park admission)
In-room sales of movies and games
Telephone toll charges
Meeting room rentals

Gift shop sales
Restaurant
Lounge/Bar
Snack bar
Video/arcade games

In addition to generating revenue, Paige will, of course, generate expenses and incur costs as she operates each of these major revenue centers. Her goal should be to generate a profit in each of the revenue centers she manages. In fact, many hospitality managers call each individual revenue generating segment within their business a **profit center**.

The revenue − expense = profit formula holds even in what is not typically considered a for-profit segment of the hospitality industry. For example, consider the situation of Hector Bentevina. Hector is the manager of the Blue Lagoon's employee cafeteria. Hector supplies no-cost (to the employees) meals to the park's large group of service workers and managerial staff. In this situation, the water park clearly does not have immediate "profit" as its primary motive in operating the cafeteria. In fact, in many **business dining** situations, food is provided as a service to the company's employees either as a no-cost (to the employee) benefit or at a greatly reduced price. In some cases, executive dining rooms may even be operated for the convenience of management. Thus, it is common in many situations to operate a **cost center** that generates costs but no revenue. In cases such as these, management's goal may be to maintain or achieve a predetermined cost for operating the center. Whether they are operating a profit center or a cost center, however, hospitality managers must know as much as they can about how their revenues and expenses are generated if they are to maximize their revenues and control their costs. Thus, if Paige is to operate the most successful water park she possibly can, she must fully understand the revenue and expense generation in all of her profit (and cost) centers.

Managers are not the only ones interested in a business's revenue, expenses, and profits. All **stakeholders** who are affected by a business's profitability will care greatly about the effective operation of a hospitality business. These stakeholders may include:

■ Owners
■ Investors
■ Lenders
■ Creditors
■ Managers

Truly, the owners, managers, and employees of a hospitality business all benefit most when that business is successful. As a result, when an accurate income statement is used to provide information, the business's owners, lenders, investors, and managers can all make better decisions about how best to develop and operate it.

Owners

The owners of a business typically have the greatest interest in its success. In many companies, however, the owners do not actively participate in the management of the business. For example, in the case of Paige Vincent and the Blue Lagoon Water Park, Paige serves as the general manager (GM) of the park. She is employed by Synergy Promotions, the park's owners. These owners represent themselves and the park's investors and lenders. As a result, Synergy Promotions employs Paige and sets general policies, procedures, and goals for her. Actual day-to-day operations of the park are left to Paige and her management team. In many cases, owners of a business would be unable to exercise close control because they are physically removed from the business. By evaluating the data in the Blue Lagoon's income statement, those responsible for managing Synergy Promotions will better be able to determine the effectiveness of the manager they have selected and the progress made toward goal achievement.

Investors

Investors supply funds to restaurants and hotels to earn money on their investment. These earnings generally include periodic cash payments from profits generated by the business, plus any property **appreciation** (increase in value) achieved during the period of the investment. Restaurants, hotels, and many other hospitality businesses are inherently risky investments because they require specialized management expertise, can be significantly subject to economic upturns and downturns, and are often not easy to sell rapidly. This may be especially true if the business is not operating profitably.

Before individuals, corporations, or other financial entities elect to invest in a business, they will want to know that their investment is a good one. Earnings achieved by an investment are typically expressed as a percentage of money earned to money invested. Thus, one way to evaluate the quality or strength of an investment is to measure the return on investment it generates. **Return on investment (ROI)** is simply a ratio of the money made compared to the money invested. ROI is computed as:

$$\frac{\text{Money earned on funds invested}}{\text{Funds invested}} = \text{ROI}$$

This ratio of earnings achieved to investment is critical to determining investment quality.

go figure!

To illustrate, consider Gerry Tuskey. Gerry is considering investing $100,000 in the Blue Lagoon Water Park. If Gerry is convinced that, on an annual basis, earnings of $15,000 would be achieved for each $100,000 invested, the projected ROI would be computed as

$$\frac{\$15,000}{\$100,000} = 15\% \text{ ROI}$$

If, however, Gerry, upon analyzing the Blue Lagoon s income statement, determined that the money likely to be earned was only 5,000; the resulting ROI would be computed as follows:

$$\frac{\$5,000}{\$100,000} = 5\% \text{ ROI}$$

As a general rule, the higher the ROI sought by an investor, the more risky is the investment. It is also true that different investors, with different investment goals, will evaluate and choose from a variety of investment options. All of the choices they make, however, should be designed to help them reach their investment (ROI) objectives.

W fun on the Web!

Investors can choose from a variety of investment options, such as stocks, bonds, metals, and others, each with its own historic record of returns. A partnership of the National Urban League, Hispanic College Fund Inc., and the Investment Company Institute Education Foundation (as well as other entities) regularly publishes summaries of the ROI achieved by these different investment options. To see them, go to:

www.ici.org/i4s/bro_i4s_expectations.html

Computing the amount of money that is (or may be) earned on invested funds requires a careful reading of a business's income statement. This is so because the income statement is the source of the information required to compute ROI. Without analyzing the information found on the income statement, it is not possible to evaluate an investment's overall attractiveness. For this reason, any informed investor or potential investor in a business will require that the business regularly produce and supply an accurate and timely income statement. In most cases, this means the production of an income statement no less than 12 or 13 times (depending upon the length of a business's accounting period) per year, as well as a fiscal year (see Chapter 2) income statement that summarizes the revenue, expense, and net income data for the company's full operating year.

W fun on the Web!

Many restaurant companies have devoted a section of their websites to communicating with their investors. They do so by having an "Investor Relations" tab on their sites. To view two examples of these, check out the websites of Texas Roadhouse Restaurants and/or Benihana. You can do so by going to:

www.texasroadhouse.com

and

www.benihana.com

When you arrive, click on the "Investor Relations" tab to see the most recent financial communication to the investors in these restaurant companies.

Lenders

Most hotel or restaurant acquisitions are financed with both **debt** (funds lent to a business) and **equity** (funds supplied by its investors or owners). Those who lend money to a business, in most cases, do so with the intent that the money will be repaid. Lenders to businesses in the hospitality industry include banks, insurance companies, pension funds, and other similar capital sources. Lenders may or may not actually own a part of the business in which they invest, but they do agree to provide funds for its construction and/or operation.

In actuality, there are essentially two types of entities that lend money to hospitality businesses. The first of these are lenders who simply agree to fund or finance a business. Typically, this is done by granting the business a loan that must be repaid under the specific **terms** or conditions of the loan. It is important to understand that lenders to a business have first claim to the profits generated by the business. As a result, lenders will be repaid before a business is permitted to distribute profits to its investors. Because this is so, the ROI requirements of lenders are typically lower than those of investors.

Unlike investors who do not actually know what their final ROI will be until the business they invest in summarizes its operational revenue and expenses in an income statement, lenders will typically establish the ROI they require before they make a loan. Thus, for example, a bank may elect to lend a business such as the Blue Lagoon Water Park $1,000,000. The terms of the loan might include the fact that the loan must be repaid, along with 8% **interest**. This interest rate would represent the ROI sought by the bank's managers for their bank's money.

Additional loan terms would likely include information about how much is to be repaid each month, when the payments are to be made, and any fees the lender charges the business for initiating the loan and supplying the funds. Like investors, lenders seek greater returns (higher interest rates) when they perceive the risks of a business not repaying its loan are high. Alternatively, when a lender believes the risk of **default** (nonpayment) of a loan is low, interest rates charged for the use of the lender's funds will be lower also. To determine a business's ability to meet the repayment terms of loans offered to it, a lender will want to carefully review the income statements generated by that business.

Creditors

A **creditor** is a company to whom a business owes money, such as a vendor. For example, when Isabella Rosetta, the food and beverage director at the Blue Lagoon, must purchase food from a vendor, that vendor is likely to extend her credit. As a result, the food ordered by Isabella would be delivered and an **invoice** detailing the purchases made by the Blue Lagoon as well as the cost of the food items purchased would also be delivered. The expectation of the vendor, of course, is that the Blue Lagoon would pay the vendor for the delivered food according to the credit terms established by the vendor. Until that payment is made, however, the creditor has, for all practical purposes, made a "loan" to the Blue Lagoon equal to the dollar value of the food products delivered.

It is important to understand that a business's vendors must also be profitable. Therefore, it is not surprising to learn that vendors will charge higher prices to those businesses they perceive as having a high risk of invoice nonpayment. Customers with lower risk of nonpayment will often be charged lower prices. As a result, vendors are very interested in the creditworthiness of their customers. Over the long run, a company's **creditworthiness**, or the ability to pay bills promptly, is a result of its profitability. As we have seen, profitability is measured, in large part, by the information contained in the income statement. As a result, information from the income statement can be of great interest to many of the vendors utilized by a business and may be required before the vendor grants credit to the business.

Managers

Many hospitality managers consider the income statement to be a reflection of their managerial ability. This is so for a variety of reasons. The income statement details how profitable an operation has been within a designated time period. Excellent managers tend to operate more profitable facilities than do poorer managers. Thus, in some cases, operational performance as measured by the income statement's results is used to establish managers' raises, compute their bonuses, and in many companies, even determine promotional opportunities. Because that is true, it is critical that these managers be able to read and understand their income statements.

Owners, investors, lenders, and managers are not the only ones interested in the results of a business's income statement. Employees are also important stakeholders in a business. While employees do not typically view the actual income statement of their employer, the information the income statement contains will make a large impact on the potential stability of their employment. Certainly, if a business is profitable, employees' jobs are more secure than if the business is struggling. Similarly, if a business is profitable, employee wages are more likely to rise, expansion of the business may create additional job opportunities, and employers may have the ability to provide employees with benefit programs that satisfy their needs as well as those of the business.

For Paige Vincent and all of the other stakeholders in the Blue Lagoon Water Park, understanding how to read and interpret her operational results as reported on the income statement begins with an understanding of how that income statement is actually prepared.

Income Statement Preparation

Either because of your own company policy, lender requirements, or simply because it is good to do so, you will regularly find yourself involved with the preparation or evaluation of income statements. The detail with which these are prepared may vary based upon a variety of factors including the industry in which the business is operated, the sales volume achieved by the operation, the number of units for which income is reported, and the specific desires of the business's owners.

In very small hospitality operations, the owner or managers of the business may be responsible for the preparation of the income statement. In larger restaurant operations, and especially those in the quick-service restaurant (QSR) industry that includes the greatest number of burger, chicken, pizza, coffee, sandwich, and other specialty quick-service-style take-out units, the manager may simply submit financial data about a store to a centralized accounting office. That office would then prepare the unit's income statement. In very large restaurants and in many hotels, the income statement may be prepared by professionals who work onsite.

In all cases, however, as a manager working in the hospitality industry, you must understand the income statement format utilized, as well as how revenue, expenses, and profits are reported.

It is important to realize that, as the hospitality business changes, so too must the accounting systems that record its business transactions change. Changes are routine and are to be expected as the hospitality industry continues to evolve and its managers seek to better record their activities and account for their revenues, expenses, and profits. They will change the format and physical layout (but not the fundamental purpose) of an income statement.

Format

An income statement is designed to identify revenues, expenses, and profits. It is important to understand that an income statement is a summary of financial information for a defined accounting period. Thus, hypothetically, and in its very simplest structure, such a statement could, for example, take the form of Figure 3.1.

In the hospitality industry the physical layout of the actual income statements for different types of businesses will be somewhat different. For example, a restaurant that serves alcohol would want to identify, on its income statement, the revenue generation and costs associated with serving drinks. In a family-style pancake restaurant that serves only food and nonalcoholic beverages, the income statement would not, of course, include a section for alcoholic beverages. In a similar manner, at a limited service hotel that generates its revenue only from room sales, telephone toll calls, and the sale of in-room movies, the income statement would reflect those revenue (profit) centers. In a full-service resort hotel such as the Blue Lagoon, multiple food and beverage outlets and diverse retail profit centers would be included on the income statement.

Consider the case of Joshua Richards. Joshua owns his own restaurant which is located across the street from the Blue Lagoon. His income statement for this year is presented in Figure 3.2. The restaurant income statement, using the Uniform System of Accounts for

FIGURE 3.1   Summary of Financial Information

BLUE LAGOON WATER PARK RESORT
Income Statement
For the Period: January 1 through January 31, 2010

Revenues	$2,100,150
Expenses	$1,937,976
Income (Loss*) Before Income Taxes	$ 162,174

* When an operation's revenue exceeds its expenses, the amount of the profits (revenue – expenses) is simply presented on the statement as shown in Figure 3.1. However, negative numbers (losses) on an income statement are designated one of three ways:

1. By a minus ("–") sign in front of the number. Thus for example, a $1,000 loss would be presented on the statement as –$1,000.
2. By brackets "( )" around the number. Thus for example, a $1,000 loss would be presented on the statement as ($1,000).
3. By the use of the color red (rather than black) to designate the loss amount. Thus for example, a $1,000 loss would be presented on the statement as the figure "$1,000," but the number would be printed in red. This approach gives rise to the slang phrase to **operate in the red** to indicate a business that is not making a profit. In a similar vein, to **operate in the black** would indicate the business is profitable.

Restaurants (USAR), shows sales and cost of sales related to food and beverage and any other expenses related to the functioning of the restaurant.

The USAR can better be understood by dividing it into three sections: gross profit, operating expenses, and nonoperating expenses. Referring to Figure 3.2, the gross profit section consists of Sales through Total Gross Profit, the operating expenses section covers Operating Expenses through Operating Income, and the nonoperating expenses section includes Interest through Net Income. These three sections are arranged on the income statement *from most controllable to least controllable* by the food service manager. The **gross profit section** consists of food and beverage sales and costs that can and should be controlled by the manager on a daily basis. The **operating expenses section** is also under the control of the manager but more so on a weekly or monthly basis (with the exception of wages, which can be controlled daily). Consider the Repairs and Maintenance category. Although repairs will be needed when equipment breaks down, maintenance is typically scheduled on a monthly basis. The manager can control, to some extent, how employees use the equipment, but he or she cannot control or predict the breakdown of equipment when it occurs. The third section of the USAR is the **nonoperating expenses section**. It is this section that is least controllable by the food service manager. Interest paid to creditors for short-term or long-term debt is due regardless of the ability of the manager to control operations.

Furthermore, taxes are controlled by the government; to paraphrase Benjamin Franklin, the only sure things in life are death and taxes. So, the food service manager has little control over the amount of money "Uncle Sam" gets every year. Knowing the three sections of

FIGURE 3.2 Restaurant Income Statement

JOSHUA'S RESTAURANT
Income Statement
For the Year Ended December 31, 2010

SALES:

Food	2,058,376
Beverage	482,830
Total Sales	**2,541,206**

COST OF SALES:

Food	767,443
Beverage	96,566
Total Cost of Sales	**864,009**

GROSS PROFIT:

Food	1,290,933
Beverage	386,264
Total Gross Profit	**1,677,197**

OPERATING EXPENSES:

Salaries and Wages	714,079
Employee Benefits	111,813
Direct Operating Expenses	132,143
Music and Entertainment	7,624
Marketing	63,530
Utility Services	88,942
Repairs and Maintenance	35,577
Administrative and General	71,154
Occupancy	120,000
Depreciation	55,907
Total Operating Expenses	**1,400,769**
Operating Income	**276,428**
Interest	84,889
Income Before Income Taxes	**191,539**
Income Taxes	76,616
Net Income	**114,923**

Prepared using USAR

the income statement allows you to focus on those things over which you have the most control as a manager.

Note also, the differences in presentation format between the restaurant income statement, and Figures 3.3 and 3.4; the January income statements for the Blue Lagoon Resort (hotel format). Figures 3.3 and 3.4 show two alternative formats for a hotel income statement using the Uniform System of Accounts for the Lodging Industry (USALI).

FIGURE 3.3   Hotel Income Statement – Vertical Format

BLUE LAGOON WATER PARK RESORT
Income Statement
For the Period: January 1 through January 31, 2010

Total Revenue	**2,100,150**
Rooms – Revenue	**1,200,000**
Payroll and Related Expenses	247,200
Other Expenses	105,900
Department Income	846,900
Food – Revenue	**600,000**
Cost of Sales	178,200
Payroll and Related Expenses	182,400
Other Expenses	44,400
Department Income	195,000
Beverage – Revenue	**240,000**
Cost of Sales	37,620
Payroll and Related Expenses	44,580
Other Expenses	16,800
Department Income	141,000
Telecommunications – Revenue	**6,000**
Cost of Sales	14,100
Payroll and Related Expenses	4,500
Other Expenses	2,400
Department Income	−15,000
Other Operated Departments – Revenue	**45,000**
Cost of Sales	6,600
Payroll and Related Expenses	15,000
Other Expenses	5,400
Department Income	18,000
Rentals and Other Income – Revenue	**9,150**
Cost of Sales	1,320
Payroll and Related Expenses	4,080
Other Expenses	900
Department Income	2,850
Total Operated Department Income	**1,188,750**
Undistributed Operating Expenses	
Administrative and General	113,100
Information Systems	29,700
Human Resources	48,600
Security	23,100
Franchise Fees	0
Transportation	27,900

(Continued)

FIGURE 3.3   *(Continued)*

Marketing	129,360
Property Operations and Maintenance	99,750
Utility Costs	89,250
Total Undistributed Operating Expenses	**560,760**
Gross Operating Profit	**627,990**
Rent, Property Taxes, and Insurance	146,700
Depreciation and Amortization	105,000
Net Operating Income	**376,290**
Interest	106,000
Income Before Income Taxes	**270,290**
Income Taxes	108,116
Net Income	**162,174**

Prepared using USALI

The USALI can better be understood by dividing it into three sections: operated department income, undistributed operating expenses, and nonoperating expenses. Referring to Figures 3.3 and 3.4, the **operated department income section** consists of separate profit centers as department income. As you can see in these particular statements, department income is generated by rooms, food, beverage, telecommunications, other departments, and rental and other income. Each of these departments report revenues, expenses, and income generated by the department. The **undistributed operating expenses section** covers Undistributed Operating Expenses through Gross Operating Profit. This section includes expenses that cannot truly be assigned to one specific department, and are thus not distributed to the departments. Examples of these expenses are security, transportation, and franchise fees. The **nonoperating expenses section** includes Rent, Property Taxes, and Insurance through Net Income. This section includes items such as rent, depreciation, interest, and income taxes, and is least controllable by the hotel manager.

It is important to note here that depreciation expense (see Chapter 2) in all forms of the income statement serves a very specific purpose. Depreciation is subtracted from the income statement primarily to lower income, thus lower taxes. The portion of assets depreciated each year is considered "tax deductible" because it is subtracted on the income statement before taxes are calculated.

Figure 3.3 shows the operated department income vertically and Figure 3.4 shows the operated department income horizontally. Either format used by individual hotels is a matter of preference.

FIGURE 3.4   Hotel Income Statement – Horizontal Format

BLUE LAGOON WATER PARK RESORT
Income Statement
For the Period: January 1 through January 31, 2010

	Net Revenue	Cost of Sales	Payroll and Related Expenses	Other Expenses	Income (Loss)
Operated Departments					
Rooms	1,200,000	0	247,200	105,900	846,900
Food	600,000	178,200	182,400	44,400	195,000
Beverage	240,000	37,620	44,580	16,800	141,000
Telecommunications	6,000	14,100	4,500	2,400	(15,000)
Other Operated Departments	45,000	6,600	15,000	5,400	18,000
Rentals and Other Income	9,150	1,320	4,080	900	2,850
Total Operated Departments	2,100,150	237,840	497,760	175,800	1,188,750
Undistributed Operating Expenses					
Administrative and General			76,800	36,300	113,100
Information Systems			12,000	17,700	29,700
Human Resources			43,800	4,800	48,600
Security			16,620	6,480	23,100
Franchise Fees			0	0	0
Transportation			4,200	23,700	27,900
Marketing			64,320	65,040	129,360
Property Operations and Maintenance			24,300	75,450	99,750
Utility Costs			0	89,250	89,250
Total Undistributed Operating Expenses			242,040	318,720	560,760
Gross Operating Profit	2,100,150	237,840	739,800	494,520	627,990
Rent, Property Taxes, and Insurance					146,700
Depreciation and Amortization					105,000
Net Operating Income					376,290
Interest					106,000
Income Before Income Taxes					270,290
Income Taxes					108,116
Net Income					162,174

Prepared using USALI

In the remaining portions of this chapter, we will often use data from the Blue Lagoon and other hospitality operations to learn more about collecting and analyzing revenue and expense data, as well as operational profits. We'll be referring to these sample income statements later when we illustrate the various formulas in this chapter.

While the layout of a business's income statement will vary somewhat based upon the Uniform System of Accounts applicable to its industry segment, there are basic commonalities among income statements that you should know about and understand. In general, the process of preparing an income statement for a business consists of the following three steps:

1. Identification of accounting period
2. Documentation of revenue data
3. Documentation of expense data

Accounting Period

In Chapter 2 you learned that the period of time (the specific number of days and dates) included in a summary of financial information is called an accounting period. These accounting periods are established by management and should make sense for the business to which they are applied. For many businesses, the accounting periods established coincide with the calendar months of the year. Thus, for example, at the Blue Lagoon Water Park, 12 monthly income statements are produced, each consisting of the data produced during its respective month.

Many (but not all) businesses choose this alternative because it eases the company's ability to file annual tax returns, most of which are due based upon the calendar year. In some cases, businesses prefer to create income statements that are 28 days long. When they do so, it is because these managers seek to create perfectly "equal" accounting periods. Thus, in this system, each period is equal in length, and has the same number of Mondays, Tuesdays, Wednesdays, and so forth. This helps the manager compare performance from one period to the next without having to compensate for "extra days" in any one period. Additional advantages of the 28-day approach will be clear when you learn more about the analysis of income statements.

Businesses may also elect to create income statements bi-monthly, quarterly, or even annually. Figure 3.5 summarizes the most popular lengths of time used by hospitality managers and accountants when they create income statements.

In some cases, the managers of a business who choose to utilize longer accounting periods may also be interested in "mini" income statements that detail specially selected revenue and expense categories on a shorter-term basis. These may take the form of weekly, daily, or even hourly financial summary reports. In all but the most unusual circumstances, however, these documents would lack the specific and accurate revenue and (especially) the expense data required to produce an income statement which meets the standards considered necessary for incorporating generally accepted accounting principles.

FIGURE 3.5 Common Income Statement Accounting Periods

Accounting Period	Number of Days Included
Month	Varies
Quarter	Varies
Annual	365 days (except leap year)
28-day	28 days
Weekly	7 days
Daily	1 day

Regardless of the income statement time period chosen by management, it is important that this period be clearly indicated at the top of the prepared income statement document. This is done to ensure that the document's readers know, *before* they begin reading, exactly when the financial period which is being reported upon actually began and ended.

Figure 3.3 is an example of the income statement title heading used at the Blue Lagoon Water Park. It is easy to see from this figure that the Blue Lagoon's management has elected to create monthly income statements based upon a calendar month.

Revenue Data

After the inclusion of the document's title and the clear identification of the dates included, the first portion of the income statement details the revenue data to be reported during the identified accounting period. On some businesses' income statements the terms, "sales," "revenue," or a combination (i.e., "sales revenue") may be used; but in all cases the term used should represent the revenue generated during the accounting period by that business's normal business activity.

In many businesses, revenue listed on the income statement will come from more than one source. Managers of these businesses will likely want to know the relative contribution of each source. In Figure 3.3, the Blue Lagoon shows that it generates revenue from six distinct sources: rooms, food, beverage, telecommunications, other operated departments, and rentals and other income.

In a large resort hotel, there might literally be dozens of actual sources of revenue. Thus, they are frequently listed by managers using the procedures recommended by the Uniform System of Accounts for the Lodging Industry (USALI). Currently, the USALI suggests that managerial accountants in the hotel industry use one or more of the following categories to record their hotel's revenues:

- Rooms
- Food
- Beverage
- Telecommunications
- Garage and Parking
- Golf Course

- Golf Pro Shop
- Guest Laundry
- Health Center
- Swimming Pool
- Tennis
- Tennis Pro Shop
- Other Operated Departments
- Rentals and Other Income

Of course, hotels with special revenue-generating features may wish to add additional revenue reporting sections to record that special-feature revenue on their income statements. It is also important to understand that a large resort may have multiple restaurant and bar outlets, several types of retail stores, and many in-room amenities options such as telephone toll charges, purchases from mini-bars, pay-per-view movies, and laundry services. Additional revenue sources could include services such as those for valet parking, activities such as video arcade revenue and spa services, as well as the rental of motorized and un-motorized sports equipment. Regardless of its source, all revenue should be clearly reported on the income statement.

On the other extreme, a hospitality operation may simply have one source of revenues. This could be the case, for example, in a retail bakery shop that sold only high-quality, fresh baked breads. Even in this situation, however, the bakery's owner may want to create sub-categories of revenues to better understand exactly where the bakery's revenue is generated. For example, these might include sub-sections based upon the style of bread produced, (i.e., French, Italian, Sourdough, and the like), the type of flavorings used, (i.e., cheeses, seeds, herbs, etc.), or even the size of loaf (1/2 loaf, 1 pound, 2 pound, etc.).

As a manager in the hospitality industry, it will be an important part of your job to ensure that the revenue sources identified on the income statements for which you are responsible include all of the revenue that is to be reported and that this revenue is grouped in such a way as to be meaningful to the statement's readers. It is for this reason that many operators adopt the income statement format utilized by the uniform systems of accounts for their specific industry segment.

Expense Data

As shown in Figure 3.1, following the title, accounting period, and revenue of the income statement is the section reserved for identifying the expenses incurred by the business.

There are two major issues with which managerial accountants must concern themselves when they consider the expense data included on their income statements. As a result, before we examine actual expense categories utilized on an income statement, these issues must be well-understood. The issues are the **timing** and the **classification** or placement of the expense.

Expense Timing

Just as Paige Vincent must ensure that all of the revenue generated by the Blue Lagoon Water Park in a specific period is accounted for, so too must she make sure that all of the related expenses incurred by the resort have been included in the preparation of her income statement. That is, Paige must make sure that she has included all of the January period's expenses required to generate the revenue reported on the January income statement. Not to do so would understate expenses and, (because of the formula used to compute profits) overstate profit. Alternatively, to intentionally (or even unintentionally) overstate expenses and thus include some expenses that were not, in fact, truly incurred, would have the effect of understating profits.

Recall from Chapter 2 that accrual accounting requires a business's revenue to be reported when earned and its expenses to be recorded when incurred. This matching principle is designed to closely tie expenses of a business to the actual revenues those expenses helped the business generate. While matching expenses to revenue might, at first examination, seem to be a very simple process, in actuality managerial accountants are continually called upon to make important decisions when they determine the appropriateness of which specific expenses to include on an income statement.

Decisions made about how best to match revenues to expenses can be complex and even open to honest difference of opinion among hospitality managers. These decisions will be established by generally accepted accounting principles, by company policy, by property-specific policy, or in some cases, the best decision that can be made by the person(s) preparing the income statement. To see why this is so, consider a sampling of some of the decisions Paige and the managerial accountants working with her must make when they establish the expenses incurred by the Blue Lagoon during the January accounting period for which they are now preparing an income statement. Note that the following six scenarios are only examples of the types of questions Paige may encounter, and thus, you are not expected to know the answers to these. Paige would have to gather and analyze more information than is provided in this chapter to formulate decisions based on these questions.

1. Paige pays local property taxes on the Blue Lagoon twice per year. One half of the bill is due in February and the remaining balance is due (six months later) in August. For the January portion of the property tax expense, should she enter:
   - 1/12 of the annual bill?
   - 31/365 of the annual bill?
   - "$0.00," because she did not pay property tax in the month of January?
2. In the month of January, the Blue Lagoon spent $10,000 on produce purchased from a local vendor. The resort also received an **invoice credit** (refund) in January for $200 for some produce delivered to the kitchen in late December of the previous year (and thus the original cost of the products was included in the cost of December food purchased), but which was later found to be of inferior quality. The result of a

subsequent discussion between Paige's food and beverage director and the vendor was a decision by the vendor to issue the $200 credit. For January, should Paige's produce expense be computed as:

- $10,000?
- $10,000 − $200 = $9,800?

3. The Blue Lagoon pays its employees every two weeks. On January 17 it paid its employees for the time period December 29 through January 11. Because the entire two-week period was paid in January, should Paige count the entire cost of the payroll as a January expense, or only 11/14 of the payroll (to reflect the 11 actual days in January for which the workers were paid?

4. On January 2, Paige paid the entire premium for the resort's annual liquor liability insurance policy. The premium cost was in excess of $10,000. Should Paige attribute this entire expense to the month of January, or only 1/12 of the entire amount?

5. On January 22, the housekeeping department purchased 12 rubber vacuum cleaner drive belts. The total cost of the belts was less than $20. It is expected that this supply of belts will last the hotel for three months. Should the cost of the belts:

- Be charged entirely as a January expense?
- Be expensed in the month they are actually installed on the vacuums?
- Be expensed as they (the new belts) break and thus must be replaced?

6. On the twentieth day of each month, Paige receives the resort's monthly water bill. The bill received in the month is for water used in the prior month. As a result, on January 20, Paige receives December's water usage bill. Should this be considered a "January" expense, or should Paige delay the production of her property's income statement until February 20 (at which time she would be able to include the actual charges for January's water usage)?

Recall that the consistency principle of accounting requires managers to be uniform in decision making. That is, if an expense is treated in a specific manner in one instance, it should be treated in an identical manner in all subsequent situations. Additional factors that may influence decisions regarding the recording of expenses include rules and regulations enforced by taxing authorities and other governmental agencies.

Expense Classification

Most managers want to be able to use their income statements to help them better manage their operations. To ensure that the income statement is as helpful as possible, these managers ensure that expenses are carefully and consistently classified by those who are preparing the statements. To see why this is so important, carefully consider the operated departments' payroll expense summaries that are generated by the Blue Lagoon's managerial accountants in Figure 3.6.

FIGURE 3.6   Operated Departments' Payroll and Related Expense Summaries

Option 1 (With no detailed classification)

BLUE LAGOON WATER PARK RESORT
Operated Departments' Total Payroll and Related Expenses: January 2010

Payroll and Related Expenses	$497,760

Option 2 (With department-specific detailed classification)

BLUE LAGOON WATER PARK RESORT
Operated Departments' Total Payroll and Related Expenses: January 2010

Department	
Rooms	$247,200
Food	182,400
Beverage	44,580
Telecommunications	4,500
Other Operated Departments	15,000
Rentals and Other Income	4,080
Total Operated Departments	$497,760

The payroll summaries presented in Options 1 and 2 are both accurate because they present the same data. It is easy to see, however, that the data as presented in Option 2 will very likely provide the Blue Lagoon's management team with better information about how payroll dollars are actually being utilized in the operated departments of the resort.

Expense classification is the process of carefully considering how a business's expenses will be detailed for reporting purposes. Earlier in this chapter you learned that many managers consider each individual revenue-generating segment within their overall business to be its own profit center. As a result these managers may seek to place (assign) to each department or profit center the expense that center utilized to generate its revenue. These managers concern themselves not merely with the proper timing of expenses; they are equally concerned about the placement of the expense as well.

In some cases, the proper placement of an expense is very straightforward. For example, the purchase of a case of Chardonnay used during a wedding reception will clearly be classified as a beverage expense in the beverage department's portion of an income statement. In a similar manner, the purchase and use of electronic key cards created for guest use can easily be classified as a front desk expense within the overall expense reporting of a hotel. Chlorine purchased for use in a swimming pool can easily be considered an expense in the maintenance and operation portion of a water park's total operating expenses.

In a small operation, costs may be easy to classify. In a larger operation with multiple profit centers, operating expenses may be harder to classify. Consider, for example, the costs related to advertising and marketing the Blue Lagoon. In this case, each dollar spent on promotion will likely have some impact on each of the resort's profit centers. It would likely be difficult to determine, however, the proportional amount of the advertising cost that should be pro-rated to each of the resort's rooms, food, beverage, or retail sales outlets. In a similar manner, items such as property taxes may also be difficult to assign to a specific department or profit center. Even payroll costs in a resort such as the Blue Lagoon can be difficult to classify. For example, it is easy to see that a front desk agent's payroll costs should be assigned to the hotel's rooms department. It is less easy to determine how the chef's payroll costs should be allocated between the resort's restaurant and the cocktail lounge, where recipes and production procedures for appetizers and snack items are developed. Even more difficult to pro-rate accurately would be an item such as the salary of the resort's general manager.

In the hotel industry, when an expense is easily attributable to one department, it is classified as a **departmental cost**. This type of cost is sometimes referred to as a **direct operating expense**. As you learned earlier in this chapter, when the expense cannot truly be assigned to one specific area within an operation, it is classified as an **undistributed operating expense**. The current version of the USALI, for example, suggests that the following categories be considered as undistributed operating expenses:

Administrative and General
Information Systems
Human Resources
Security
Franchise Fees
Transportation
Marketing
Property Operations and Maintenance
Utility Costs

As you have learned, it is important that managerial accountants understand the issues related to timing and classification of their expenses when preparing income statements. While it is not, in most cases, a legal requirement that a hospitality operation use a specific method for timing and classifying expenses, many restaurateurs and hoteliers use, or advise their accountants to use, the uniform system of accounts (see Chapter 3) established for their own segment of the hospitality industry. It is important to understand that the uniform systems of accounts for any segment of the hospitality industry are constantly evolving as new accounting challenges are encountered. Thus, it is not unusual to encounter two managerial accountants who utilize the uniform systems slightly differently to best address the issues of their own businesses. In the remainder of this text, we will, in most cases, utilize these uniform systems to present and illustrate the information you will learn.

FIGURE 3.7   Income Statement with Revenue Schedules Identified

BLUE LAGOON WATER PARK RESORT
Income Statement
For the Period: January 1 through January 31, 2010

Revenues:

Rooms (Schedule 1)	$1,200,000	
Food (Schedule 2)	$ 600,000	
Beverage (Schedule 3)	$ 240,000	
Telecommunications (Schedule 4)	$ 6,000	
Other Operated Departments (Schedule 5)	$ 45,000	
Rentals and Other Income (Schedule 6)	$ 9,150	
Total Revenues		$2,100,150
Expenses		$1,937,976
Income (Loss) Before Income Taxes		$ 162,174

Schedules

Thus far we have concerned ourselves with the examination of income statement summaries. In addition to summaries, managerial accountants may use one or more departmental **schedules** to provide statement readers with more in-depth information about important areas of revenues and expenses. These schedules provide the reader detail where the statement preparer feels it is useful to do so. As a result, the revenue or expense portion of an income statement could consist of only one line or several sources. As shown in Figure 3.7, it may consist of a summary with reference to one or more departmental schedules that will provide additional detail.

In the previous chapter, you learned about the Uniform System of Accounts for Restaurants (USAR), the lodging industry (USALI), and clubs (USFRC). The methods managerial accountants in those industries use to create appropriate schedules are important areas addressed by these uniform systems. It is essential to recognize, however, that managers should always strive to use the specific methods of reporting that best maximize and clarify the information provided to the statement's readers. Information about how much revenue and costs a business generates is critical to many of a statement's readers, thus it should be presented clearly, honestly, and in keeping with generally accepted accounting principles (see Chapter 2). Not to do so is not only dishonest and unethical; in some situations it may also be illegal!

It is important to realize that schedules should be created to help readers better understand the income statement they are reading. To see how that is done, consider the information in Figure 3.8, a portion of the rooms department schedule for the Blue Lagoon. After reviewing the data, it should be easy for you to see that the Blue Lagoon's management will simply know and understand more about the specific sources of the

FIGURE 3.8   Rooms Department Revenue Schedule

BLUE LAGOON WATER PARK RESORT
Schedule 1: Rooms Department Revenue
For the Period: January 1 through January 31, 2010

Rooms Revenue:

Transient Leisure	$ 600,000
Group Leisure	$ 390,000
Transient Package	$ 150,000
Group Package	$ 60,000
Total	$1,200,000

---

resort's revenues if they examine the schedule in Figure 3.8 than if the only rooms revenue information available for examination was that which was listed in Figure 3.3.

Note that, in this case, the management of the Blue Lagoon has elected to tell readers of its income statement about the relative revenues provided by those guests who are transient (individual) leisure travelers, group leisure travelers, transient guests who purchased a specially packaged collection of goods and services (a **package**), and those individual guests who purchased their package as part of a larger group.

Hotels of various types will provide readers of their financial statements the most information if they create schedules geared for their specific operation. Thus, for example, a hotel located near an airport may determine that it is best to create revenue schedules that identify corporate versus leisure travelers. An all-suite hotel property may determine that it is best to create revenue schedules based upon those guests who are transient versus those who are considered extended stay guests. Because it is important for those in charge of marketing to direct their marketing efforts to specific guest types, many rooms managers in the industry frequently use one or more of the following segments to classify guests and thus the revenues they generate:

    Transient (Individual)
            Corporate
            Leisure
            Discount
            Package
            Long-term stay
    Group
            Corporate
            Leisure
            Discount
            Package
            Association

Tour bus
Airline crew
Social, Military, Education, Religious, Fraternal (**SMERF**)
Other

As a manager working in the hotel industry, you can assist your property the most by ensuring the rooms revenue schedules you help create or interpret are geared as specifically as possible to your own property. In the food and beverage revenue area, revenue schedules may be created based upon the sales achieved by individual restaurants and bars within the hotel, guest types, or even hours of operation. The purpose of each revenue or expense schedule created, however, should be that of enhancing and clarifying readers' understanding of the income statement.

Because your entire career may take you into many segments of the hospitality industry, it is more critical for you to understand the principles behind the preparation of an income statement than the current format of any specific business's income statement. In this text, we will present several formats, each of which may be useful if you follow the principles of income statement preparation presented in Figure 3.9.

fun on the Web!

Several software developers produce products that can help managerial accountants prepare their own income statements. One of the most popular is Intuit. To view their product offerings, go to:

www.intuit.com

When you arrive, click on "Business Management" to review QuickBooks; an inexpensive accounting product that can easily be utilized by smaller restaurants and lodging facilities.

FIGURE 3.9   Principles of Income Statement Preparation

A properly prepared income statement:

1. Clearly identifies the business whose revenues and expenses are being summarized.
2. Plainly states the specific accounting period for which the statement has been prepared.
3. Includes a summary, in the most informative (detailed) manner practical, of all the revenue generated by the business during the accounting period.
4. Summarizes all accounting period expenses utilized by the business to generate the stated revenue.
5. Utilizes a logical and consistent system to classify expenses.
6. Provides additional clarity via the use of schedules where appropriate.
7. Incorporates the use of a uniform system of accounts if applicable.

Income Statement Analysis

Income statements summarize data. Managers analyze that data because they rely on their income statements to help them better understand and thus better manage, their business. As you read the following questions, consider why the answers to these would be of interest to the resort's owners, investors, lenders, and managers.

- What was the resort's total revenue for the period?
- How much profit was made during the period?
- Was more or less money made than was made in the same period last year?
- Did the resort make the amount of profit it was expected to make? If not, why not?
- In what areas of the resort were costs higher (or lower) than expected?
- Which areas of the resort require extra attention from management to ensure that they are operating according to management's plan?
- Did the resort's operational performance meet the financial expectations of its owners and managers? If not, in which departments or areas did it fall short? In which departments or areas did it exceed expectations?

Depending on their roles, the owners, investors, lenders, and managers may place different importance on the answers to these questions. You as a manager, however, will be primarily interested in the revenues, expenses, and profits over which you will have primary control.

Because the income statement is naturally divided into three main parts, it is those same three parts that make up the areas of analysis important to managers. Because you now understand how an income statement is developed, in the next sections of this text, you will learn about how managers use the income statement to examine and evaluate:

Revenue
Expenses
Profit

Revenue Analysis

Managers are concerned about revenue levels in a business because it is one very important measure of guest satisfaction. In most cases, expenses for a business will go up continually. Employees will get raises, in most cases products and services used by the business will tend to increase (not decrease) in price, and items such as taxes and insurance tend to cost a business more each year than they did the year before. In the face of these types of rising costs, you must normally increase your revenue levels if you hope to maintain or increase the amount of profit made by your business.

If the owners and managers of a restaurant seek to increase revenue, they must do so by:

1. Increasing the number of guests served, and/or
2. Increasing the average amount spent by each guest.

If a manager determines that his revenue has declined from previous periods, it may be that fewer people are coming to his restaurant, or those who do come are spending less each time they frequent the business.

In the hotel business, if management seeks to increase its rooms revenue, it must do so by:

1. Increasing the number of rooms sold, and/or
2. Increasing the average daily rate (ADR) for the rooms it sells.

If revenue has declined from previous periods, it will be that fewer rooms have been sold, or that those rooms sold were sold at a lower ADR.

A careful analysis of revenue in a restaurant or hotel involves more than simply identifying the total amount of sales. Consider Lars and Cheryl, two hotel managers, who each state that the sales in their respective hotels last month were $200,000. The two hotels would appear to be "equal" until you realize that Lars' hotel has 300 rooms and Cheryl's has 150. Now the $200,000 revenue generation takes on new meaning and the hotels do not appear nearly as equal. In a similar manner, consider Tamara, a restaurateur, who states that sales in her sub shop this February were $50,000. The revenue number by itself is helpful, but it would be more helpful to compare the $50,000 sales to the sales volume she achieved the prior February. Consider the information in Figure 3.10 and you will easily see that a revenue performance of $50,000 could be viewed quite differently based upon the restaurant's prior performance.

In most cases, managers are concerned about the sources and total amount of sales or revenue their businesses have achieved, but they should also be interested in the changes (increases or decreases) to revenue experienced by their businesses. Increases in revenue, for example, may be tied to increased numbers of guests served, expansion of products and services sold, an increase in the number of hours the business is operated, or changes in the prices charged. Declines in revenue could indicate reduced numbers of guests served, reduced spending on the part of each guest served, or any number of a variety of other explanations that should be known by management.

FIGURE 3.10   Revenue Comparisons

Tamara's Sub Shop Restaurant
Revenue for February

	Revenue Last February	Revenue This February	Conclusion
1.	$50,000	$50,000	Equal sales
2.	$75,000	$50,000	Declining sales
3.	$25,000	$50,000	Increasing sales

Managerial accountants must be very careful when analyzing changes in revenues. In some cases, revenues may have appeared to increase (or decrease) when in fact they have not. Consider, for example, the case of Priscilla Hanley. Priscilla manages a sports bar in a college town. Saturday is her most popular night. Sales on that night are much higher than any other night. If Priscilla were to compare, for example, the sales revenue she achieved this September to that achieved in September last year, it may be important for her to first compare the number of Saturdays in the two months. If, for example, this year the month contained five Saturdays and last year it contained only four, it might appear that her sales revenue had increased significantly. In fact, the majority of the increase may have been due to the differences in the number of Saturdays included in each of the respective months. Additional factors that managerial accountants often consider when making a complete evaluation of revenue increases include:

- The number of days included in the accounting period
- Changes in the number of high- or low-volume days included in the accounting period
- Differences in date placement of significant holidays (i.e., month or day of week)
- Changes in selling prices
- Variations in operational hours

Expense Analysis

While most managers are very interested in the sales levels achieved by their businesses, they are equally interested in the expenses incurred. This is so because management's primary responsibility is to deliver a quality product or service to the guest, at a price mutually agreeable to both parties. In addition, the quality must be such that the consumer, or end user of the product or service, feels that excellent value was received for the money spent on the transaction. When this level of service is achieved, the business will prosper. If management focuses on reducing expenses more than servicing guests, problems will certainly surface.

It is important to remember that guests cause businesses to incur costs. You do not want to get yourself in the mindset of reducing costs to the point where it is thought that "low" costs are good and "high" costs are bad. A restaurant with $5,000,000 in revenue per year will undoubtedly have higher expenses than the same size restaurant with $200,000 in revenue per year. The reason is quite clear. The food products, labor, and equipment needed to sell $5,000,000 worth of food are likely to be much greater than that required to produce a smaller amount of revenue. Remember, if there are fewer guests, there are likely to be fewer costs, but fewer profits as well! As an effective manager, the real question to be considered is not whether costs are high or low. The question is whether costs are too high or too low, given management's view of the value it hopes to deliver to the guest and the goals of the operation's owners. Managers can eliminate nearly all costs by closing the operation's doors. Obviously, however, when you close the doors to expense, you close the doors to profits. Expenses, then, must be incurred, and they must be managed in a way that allows the operation to achieve its desired profit levels.

Profit (Loss) Analysis

Managers want to operate profitable businesses because a profitable business is generally one that consistently provides excellent products and services at prices guests feel represent a good value for their money. In the hospitality industry, profit may easily be considered the reward for providing outstanding products and service. As a result, many managers feel that it is the third (profit) section of the income statement that is the most important of all. Profit can be considered, to a large degree, the ultimate measure of the ability of hospitality professionals to plan and operate a successful business.

Earlier in this chapter, you learned that the dollars which remain after all expenses have been paid represent the "profit" made by your business. Despite that fairly clear definition, profit is often viewed very differently by different readers of the income statement. To understand a significant reason why this is so, it is important for managers to understand the many factors that affect profit.

For example, consider the case of T.D. Highwater. Mr. Highwater owns a hotel that, last year, generated $10 million of recorded revenue and $9 million of recorded expenses, resulting in a profit of $1 million. Shondra, Mr. Highwater's hotel manager, is pleased that the profit she generated for the hotel was $1 million. Mr. Highwater, however, reported the $1 million profit on his income tax returns and was required by current tax laws to pay $300,000 of the $1 million in taxes. If you were Mr. Highwater, would you say your "profit" for the year was:

1. $1 million or
2. $700,000?

The answer is $700,000 ($1,000,000 − $300,000 = $700,000) since Mr. Highwater incurred an expense of $300,000 in income taxes paid to the government.

As this example suggests, the amount of money (profit) earned by a business can reasonably be considered to be affected by factors not directly related to the day-to-day operation of the business. Because that is so, the profit section of an income statement most often will not be labeled as "profit" but rather will seek to tell the reader those factors that have, and have not, been included in the computation of net income which are shown on the statement.

As shown in Figure 3.3, income statements for hotels using the USALI currently recommend specifying gross operating profit before such items as rent, depreciation, interest, and income taxes. The USAR (Figure 3.2) recommends indicating income levels before and after interest as well as income taxes. The critical point for you to remember is that the word "profit" may have different meanings to different statement readers. As a result, it is important to clearly understand the factors that have and have not been included in the profit section of any income statement you are preparing or reading.

Net income, or profit, is sometimes known as the **bottom line**, simply because it is often the "bottom-most" line on an income statement. In a properly prepared income statement, it represents the difference between all recorded revenue transactions and all recorded expense transactions. Interestingly, for most hospitality managers, the bottom line is *not* the most important number on the income statements they will generate. This is so because experienced managers know that they do not control all of the factors that can affect unit profits. In the example of Mr. Highwater's hotel, it is very unlikely that Shondra would have any control over the income taxes required to be paid by Mr. Highwater. Thus, she is most likely to be interested in the hotel's profits *before* taxes, while Mr. Highwater, quite understandably, may be more interested in profits that remain *after* he has paid his taxes. As a result of issues such as these, many hospitality managers (as opposed to the business's owners) may concern themselves most about income that remains after subtracting the expenses they can actually control.

Vertical Analysis

When managers review their income statements, they will do more than simply read the numbers achieved by the unit. To help managers carefully evaluate the revenues, expenses, and profit produced by their businesses, they can use a **vertical analysis** approach, which compares all items on the income statement to revenues using percentages. In this approach, an operation's total revenue figure takes a value of 100%.

For example, when a hotel's accountant reports the costs of the hotel's food department, these are commonly expressed as a percentage of total hotel revenue. This can be seen when you review the vertical income statement for the Blue Lagoon Water Park Resort presented in Figure 3.11.

go figure!

When analyzing the Blue Lagoon Water Park Resort income statement as presented in Figure 3.11, managerial accountants would compute the food cost (food cost of sales) as a percentage of total revenue.

Thus:

$$\frac{\text{Food Costs (Food Cost of Sales)}}{\text{Total Revenue}} = \text{Food Cost \%}$$

or

$$\frac{\$\ 178,200}{\$2,100,150} = 8.5\%$$

FIGURE 3.11   Vertical Analysis of a Hotel Income Statement

BLUE LAGOON WATER PARK RESORT
Income Statement
For the Period: January 1 through January 31, 2010

	Dollars	%
Total Revenue	**2,100,150**	**100.0**
Rooms – Revenue	**1,200,000**	**57.1**
Payroll and Related Expenses	247,200	11.8
Other Expenses	105,900	5.0
Department Income	846,900	40.3
Food – Revenue	**600,000**	**28.6**
Cost of Sales	178,200	8.5
Payroll and Related Expenses	182,400	8.7
Other Expenses	44,400	2.1
Department Income	195,000	9.3
Beverage – Revenue	**240,000**	**11.4**
Cost of Sales	37,620	1.8
Payroll and Related Expenses	44,580	2.1
Other Expenses	16,800	0.8
Department Income	141,000	6.7
Telecommunications – Revenue	**6,000**	**0.3**
Cost of Sales	14,100	0.7
Payroll and Related Expenses	4,500	0.2
Other Expenses	2,400	0.1
Department Income	−15,000	−0.7
Other Operated Departments – Revenue	**45,000**	**2.1**
Cost of Sales	6,600	0.3
Payroll and Related Expenses	15,000	0.7
Other Expenses	5,400	0.3
Department Income	18,000	0.9
Rentals and Other Income – Revenue	**9,150**	**0.4**
Cost of Sales	1,320	0.1
Payroll and Related Expenses	4,080	0.2
Other Expenses	900	0.0
Department Income	2,850	0.1
Total Operated Department Income	**1,188,750**	**56.6**

(Continued)

FIGURE 3.11 (*Continued*)

Undistributed Operating Expenses		
Administrative and General	113,100	5.4
Information Systems	29,700	1.4
Human Resources	48,600	2.3
Security	23,100	1.1
Franchise Fees	0	0.0
Transportation	27,900	1.3
Marketing	129,360	6.2
Property Operations and Maintenance	99,750	4.7
Utility Costs	89,250	4.2
Total Undistributed Operating Expenses	**560,760**	**26.7**
Gross Operating Profit	**627,990**	**29.9**
Rent, Property Taxes, and Insurance	146,700	7.0
Depreciation and Amortization	105,000	5.0
Net Operating Income	**376,290**	**17.9**
Interest	106,000	5.0
Income Before Income Taxes	**270,290**	**12.9**
Income Taxes	108,116	5.1
Net Income	**162,174**	**7.7**

Prepared using USALI

When utilizing vertical analysis, individual sources of revenue and the operation's expenses are expressed as a fraction of total revenues. Thus each percentage computed is a percent of a "common" number. As a result, vertical analysis is also sometimes referred to as **common-size analysis**.

For some new hospitality managers, however, this term can be somewhat misleading. This is so because, while restaurants and hotels are both hospitality operations, they are very different types of operations. As a result, it is not surprising that some of the vertical analysis format procedures utilized in the preparation of income statements for restaurants and hotels (as well as some other industry segments) are similar, while other aspects may vary somewhat.

Consider again the case of Joshua Richards. Joshua owns his own restaurant which is located across the street from the Blue Lagoon. When using a vertical analysis approach, managers express values on their income statement as a percentage of revenues. In Joshua's restaurant, the vertical analysis of the income statement would be presented as shown in Figure 3.12.

FIGURE 3.12   Vertical Analysis of a Restaurant Income Statement

JOSHUA'S RESTAURANT
Income Statement
For the Year Ended December 31, 2010

	Dollars	%
SALES:		
Food	$2,058,376	81.0%
Beverage	482,830	19.0
Total Sales	**$2,541,206**	**100.0**
COST OF SALES:		
Food	767,443	37.3
Beverage	96,566	20.0
Total Cost of Sales	**$ 864,009**	**34.0**
GROSS PROFIT:		
Food	1,290,933	62.7
Beverage	386,264	80.0
Total Gross Profit	**$1,677,197**	**66.0**
OPERATING EXPENSES:		
Salaries and Wages	714,079	28.1
Employee Benefits	111,813	4.4
Direct Operating Expenses	132,143	5.2
Music and Entertainment	7,624	0.3
Marketing	63,530	2.5
Utility Services	88,942	3.5
Repairs and Maintenance	35,577	1.4
Administrative and General	71,154	2.8
Occupancy	120,000	4.7
Depreciation	55,907	2.2
Total Operating Expenses	**$1,400,769**	**55.1**
Operating Income	**$ 276,428**	**10.9**
Interest	84,889	3.3
Income Before Income Taxes	**$ 191,539**	**7.5**
Income Taxes	76,616	3.0
Net Income	**$ 114,923**	**4.5**

Prepared using USAR

Note that each revenue and expense category in Joshua's Restaurant Income Statement in Figure 3.12 is represented in terms of both its whole dollar amount and its percentage of total sales. *All ratios are calculated as a percentage of total sales **except** the following:*

■ Food costs are divided by food sales.
■ Beverage costs are divided by beverage sales.

- Food gross profit is divided by food sales.
- Beverage gross profit is divided by beverage sales.

Food and beverage items use their respective food and beverage sales as the denominator so that these items can be evaluated separately from total sales. Since food costs and beverage costs are the most controllable items on the restaurant income statement, Joshua needs to separate these sales and costs out of the aggregate and evaluate these items more carefully.

go figure!

When analyzing Joshua's income statement as presented in Figure 3.12, managerial accountants would compute his food cost percentage as a percentage of "food" sales, rather than "total" sales.
Thus:

$$\frac{\text{Food Costs}}{\text{Food Sales}} = \text{Food Cost \%}$$

or

$$\frac{\$767,443}{\$2,058,376} = 37.3\%$$

As you may have noticed, food cost % for hotels is calculated by dividing food costs by *total* sales (revenue), whereas food cost % for restaurants is calculated by dividing food costs by *food* sales. Therefore, the authors of this text prefer the term "vertical analysis" to the term "common-size" analysis because the denominator is not always "common" among different industry segments.

As a general rule, however, all items of the hotel income statement are divided by total revenues. All items on the restaurant income statement are divided by total revenues with the exception of food and beverage costs and gross profit as noted earlier.

Vertical analysis may be used to compare a unit's percentages with industry averages, budgeted performance, other units in a corporation, or percentages from prior periods.

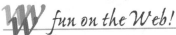

fun on the Web!

A useful publication for comparing a restaurant's percentages with industry averages is the *Restaurant Industry Operations Report* published by the National Restaurant Association. To purchase a copy of this annual report, go to:

www.restaurant.org

When you arrive, click on "Store" to see the most recent version of this helpful analytical tool for income statement average percentages.

For most owners, perhaps no figure is more important to analyze and compare than the **profit margin**. This percentage is the most telling indicator of a manager's overall effectiveness at generating revenues and controlling costs in line with forecasted results.

 *go figure!*

As can be seen in Figure 3.12, profits for Joshua's Restaurant refer to the net income figure at the bottom of his income statement. Joshua's net income for this year was $114,923 and his total sales for this year were $2,541,206. His profit percentage using the profit margin formula is as follows:

$$\frac{\text{Net Income}}{\text{Total Sales}} = \text{Profit margin}$$

$$\text{or}$$

$$\frac{\$114,923}{\$2,541,206} = 4.5\%$$

In both the USAR and USALI, an important objective is that of **responsibility accounting** for each separate department. That is, it is important for upper management to know how each department is performing. When it does, individual department managers can be held responsible for their own efforts and results.

Recall that, in most cases, increases in expenses are a good (not bad!) thing. Expenses should increase when increased revenues require management to provide more products or labor to make the sale. In fact, if expenses are reduced too much (for example by choosing lower cost but inferior ingredients when making food for sale or providing too few front desk agents during a busy check-in period) the effect on revenue can be both negative and significant. As a result, managers analyzing the expense portion of an income statement should be most concerned about the relationship between revenue and expense (vertical analysis) and less concerned about the total dollar amount of expense.

As a professional hospitality manager, you can do even more to analyze expenses. This is so because excellent hospitality managers learn to be very creative in compiling and analyzing information related to their expenses. Consider the information presented in Figure 3.13.

Note that this schedule, created as an important supplement to the income statement prepared for Joshua's Restaurant (see Figure 3.2), expresses each direct operating expense as a percentage of total direct operating expenses. This is a form of vertical analysis because the common denominator for all expense % calculations is total direct operating expenses. Thus, for example, the $40,964 expended for laundry and linen comprises 31.0% of all direct operating expenses.

FIGURE 3.13   Vertical Analysis – Direct Operating Expenses Schedule

JOSHUA'S RESTAURANT
Direct Operating Expenses Schedule
For the Year Ended December 31, 2010

Type of Expense	Expense in $	% of Direct Operating Expenses	Notes
Uniforms	13,408	10.2	
Laundry and Linen	40,964	31.0	
China and Glassware	22,475	17.0	Expense is higher than budgeted because china shelf collapsed on March 22.
Silverware	3,854	2.9	
Kitchen Utensils	9,150	6.9	
Kitchen Fuel	2,542	1.9	
Cleaning Supplies	10,571	8.0	
Paper Supplies	2,675	2.0	
Bar Expenses	5,413	4.1	
Menus and Wine Lists	6,670	5.1	Expense is lower than budgeted because the new wine supplier agreed to print the wine lists free of charge.
Exterminating	1,803	1.4	
Flowers and Decorations	9,014	6.8	
Licenses	3,604	2.7	
Total Direct Operating Expenses	132,143	100.00	

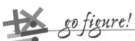 *go figure!*

The formula utilized to compute the percentage in this example is:

$$\frac{\text{Specific Expense}}{\text{Total Expenses}} = \text{Specific Expense \%}$$

or

$$\frac{\text{Laundry and Linen Expense}}{\text{Total Direct Operating Expenses}} = \text{Laundry and Linen Expense \%}$$

or

$$\frac{\$40,964}{\$132,143} = 31.0\%$$

Note also in Figure 3.13 that the manager for Joshua's has inserted a "Notes" section that gives the reader of the income statement even more information about the "whys" behind the numbers included in this specific schedule (i.e., the collapse of the china shelf on March 22 would certainly lead to higher china costs). In this case, the shelving collapse information is an important "why" that helps explain variation from previously expected results.

Learning to identify the significant whys behind the numbers presented in an income statement is not a task learned in weeks or even months. In fact, the best managers working in the hospitality industry seek to improve their skills in this area each year.

Horizontal Analysis

Managers can utilize **horizontal analysis** (also called **comparative analysis**) to evaluate the dollars or percentage change in revenues, expenses, or profits experienced by a business. A horizontal analysis of income statements requires at least two different sets of data. Often the two sets of data evaluated for a business are its current period results and the results of some prior period. Alternative comparisons, however, are often made. As a consequence, managers who use horizontal analysis to evaluate their income statements may be concerned with comparisons such as their:

- Current period results vs. prior period results
- Current period results vs. budgeted (planned) results
- Current period results vs. the results of similar business units
- Current period results vs. industry averages

Determining Variance

The *dollar change* or **variance** shows changes from previously experienced levels, and will give you an indication of whether your numbers are improving, declining, or staying the same. To see how a horizontal comparison is actually computed, consider the total sales in 2009 (last year) and 2010 (this year) at Joshua's Restaurant as reported in Figure 3.14.

 *go figure!*

To calculate the variance, Joshua would use the following formula:

> **Sales This Year − Sales Last Year = Variance**
>
> or
>
> **$2,541,206 − $2,306,110 = $235,096**

FIGURE 3.14 Comparative Analysis of a Restaurant Income Statement

JOSHUA'S RESTAURANT
Income Statements
For the Years Ended December 31, 2009 and 2010

	2009	2010	$ Change	% Change
SALES:				
Food	$1,891,011	$2,058,376	167,365	8.9
Beverage	415,099	482,830	67,731	16.3
Total Sales	**$2,306,110**	**$2,541,206**	**235,096**	**10.2**
COST OF SALES:				
Food	712,587	767,443	54,856	7.7
Beverage	94,550	96,566	2,016	2.1
Total Cost of Sales	**$ 807,137**	**$ 864,009**	**56,872**	**7.0**
GROSS PROFIT:				
Food	1,178,424	1,290,933	112,509	9.5
Beverage	320,549	386,264	65,715	20.5
Total Gross Profit	**$1,498,973**	**$1,677,197**	**178,224**	**11.9**
OPERATING EXPENSES:				
Salaries and Wages	641,099	714,079	72,980	11.4
Employee Benefits	99,163	111,813	12,650	12.8
Direct Operating Expenses	122,224	132,143	9,919	8.1
Music and Entertainment	2,306	7,624	5,318	230.6
Marketing	43,816	63,530	19,714	45.0
Utility Services	73,796	88,942	15,146	20.5
Repairs and Maintenance	34,592	35,577	985	2.8
Administrative and General	66,877	71,154	4,277	6.4
Occupancy	120,000	120,000	0	0.0
Depreciation	41,510	55,907	14,397	34.7
Total Operating Expenses	**$1,245,383**	**$1,400,769**	**155,386**	**12.5**
Operating Income	**$ 253,590**	**$ 276,428**	**22,838**	**9.0**
Interest	86,750	84,889	(1,861)	(2.1)
Income Before Income Taxes	**$ 166,840**	**$ 191,539**	**24,699**	**14.8**
Income Taxes	65,068	76,616	11,548	17.7
Net Income	**$ 101,772**	**$ 114,923**	**13,151**	**12.9**

Prepared using USAR

Effective managers are also interested in computing the **percentage variance**, or percentage change, from one time period to the next. Thus, Joshua's sales percentage variance is determined as follows:

$$\frac{(\text{Sales This Year} - \text{Sales Last Year})}{\text{Sales Last Year}} = \textbf{Percentage Variance}$$

or

$$\frac{(\$2,541,206 - \$2,306,110)}{\$2,306,110} = 10.2\%$$

Of course, an alternative and shorter formula for computing the percentage variance is as follows:

$$\frac{\text{Variance}}{\text{Sales Last Year}} = \textbf{Percentage Variance}$$

or

$$\frac{\$235,096}{\$2,306,110} = 10.2\%$$

Another way to compute the percentage variance is to use a math shortcut, as follows:

$$\left(\frac{\text{Sales This Year}}{\text{Sales Last Year}}\right) - 1 = \textbf{Percentage Variance}$$

or

$$\left(\frac{\$2,541,206}{\$2,306,110}\right) - 1 = 10.2\%$$

Of course, *all dollar variances and percentage variances of expenses on the income statement can be calculated in the same way*. Understanding how to read the expense portion of an income statement and to compute variations from expected results or prior period results as well as variation from budget are important first steps in analyzing the expenditures of a business.

When computing the percentage change between two sets of data, it can sometimes be confusing to identify the numerator (top number) and the denominator (bottom number) that should be used in the percentage calculation. If that is true in your case, Figure 3.15 can be helpful to you until you have made enough percentage change calculations to easily remember the proper procedure.

Figure 3.16 shows the departmental schedule of expenses for the Property Operations and Maintenance department of the Blue Lagoon. You can see that the actual Property Operations and Maintenance expense for the Blue Lagoon for January was $99,750. Thus

FIGURE 3.15   Percentage Change Computation Help Box

The dollar differences between identical categories listed on two different income statements is easy to compute and is always the numerator in any percentage change (variation) calculation. The denominator, however, varies.

When computing % change or variation in data from:	Use as the Denominator
Current Period to Prior Period	Prior Period's number
Current Period to Budget (Plan)	Budget (Plan) number
Current Period to Similar Business Unit	Similar Business Unit's number
Current Period to Industry Average	Industry Average number

the dollar amount spent in this area is known. The question for the managers responsible for that department, however, is simply this: "Were our expenses too high?" Stated another way, the comparative income statement helps managers analyze their expenses and take corrective action if it is needed.

The managers responsible for this area would like to know as much as possible about where their money was spent. One way to do this is to compare the amount spent to the amount that was budgeted to be spent. In Chapter 11 of this text you will learn how managerial accountants develop budgets. Once budgets have been developed, they can be utilized to measure the difference or variation between the amount that was budgeted to be spent and the amount that was actually spent.

There are two basic formulas used by managers to compare actual expenditures to budgeted expenditures. These are:

1. Variation (in dollars) from budget
2. Percent of variation from budget

To compute the variation (in dollars) from budget, simply subtract the budgeted amount of expense from the amount actually spent.

go figure!

Thus, for example, (from Figure 3.16) in the area of *computer equipment*, the variation (in dollars) from budget for the Blue Lagoon's Property Operations and Maintenance department would be computed as:

> **Actual Expense − Budgeted Expense = Variance**
>
> or
>
> **$1,695 − $1,200 = $495**

FIGURE 3.16 Comparative Analysis – Property Operations and Maintenance Schedule

BLUE LAGOON WATER PARK RESORT
Property Operations and Maintenance Schedule
For the Period: January 1 through January 31, 2010

	Budget	Actual	Difference $	Difference %
Payroll and Related Expenses				
Chief Engineer	$ 4,800	$4,711	(89)	(1.9)
Engineer Assistants	12,060	12,089	29	0.2
Benefit Allocation	6,840	7,500	660	9.6
Total Payroll and Related Expenses	**$23,700**	**$24,300**	**600**	**2.5**
Other Expenses				
Computer Equipment	$ 1,200	$ 1,695	495	41.3
Equipment Rental	3,900	4,200	300	7.7
Electrical & Mech. Equipment	9,000	8,490	(510)	(5.7)
Elevators	2,520	2,520	0	0.0
Elevator Repairs	420	840	420	100.0
Engineering Supplies	1,350	1,050	(300)	(22.2)
Floor Covering	600	0	(600)	(100.0)
Furniture	9,000	11,460	2,460	27.3
Grounds	3,000	3,360	360	12.0
HVAC (heating/ventilation & air conditioning)	9,000	8,550	(450)	(5.0)
Kitchen Equipment	300	534	234	78.0
Laundry Equipment	450	336	(114)	(25.3)
Light Bulbs	900	900	0	0.0
Maintenance Contracts	4,200	3,948	(252)	(6.0)
Operating Supplies	480	477	(3)	(0.6)
Painting & Decorating	1,500	852	(648)	(43.2)
Parking Lot	1,800	2,568	768	42.7
Pest Control	1,200	1,290	90	7.5
Plants & Interior	885	888	3	0.3
Plumbing & Heating	4,500	5,340	840	18.7
Refrigeration & A/C	5,460	5,880	420	7.7
Signage Repair	300	0	(300)	(100.0)
Snow Removal	6,000	5,910	(90)	(1.5)
Travel & Entertainment	1,200	570	(630)	(52.5)
Telecommunications	600	528	(72)	(12.0)
Trash Removal	1,800	1,680	(120)	(6.7)
Uniforms	1,650	1,584	(66)	(4.0)
Total Other Expenses	**$73,215**	**$75,450**	**2,235**	**3.1**
Total Property Operations and Maintenance	**$96,915**	**$99,750**	**2,835**	**2.9**

Some managers prefer to express variations from budget in percentage terms. Thus, the percentage variance for computer equipment is determined as follows:

$$\frac{(\text{Actual Expense} - \text{Budgeted Expense})}{\text{Budgeted Expense}} = \text{Percentage Variance}$$

or

$$\frac{(\$1,695 - \$1,200)}{\$1,200} = 41.3\%$$

Of course, an alternative and shorter formula for computing the percentage variance is as follows:

$$\frac{\text{Variance}}{\text{Budgeted Expense}} = \text{Percentage Variance}$$

or

$$\frac{\$495}{\$1,200} = 41.3\%$$

Another way to compute the percentage variance is to use a math shortcut as follows:

$$\left(\frac{\text{Actual Expense}}{\text{Budgeted Expense}}\right) - 1 = \text{Percentage Variance}$$

or

$$\left(\frac{\$1,695}{\$1,200}\right) - 1 = 41.3\%$$

It is easy to see that the computer equipment expense is "over" budget by $495. How do we know if this variance is too much? This overage represents a relatively large percentage increase of 41.3%. Most managers would consider a 41.3% variation from budget to be very significant and well worth investigating to determine the corrective action required.

On the other hand, as shown in Figure 3.16, the total property operations and maintenance expenses are $2,835 over budget, but the percentage variance is only 2.9% ((99,750 − 96,915)/96,915 = 2.9). Does this represent an area of concern? In general, the larger the budgeted number, the smaller the percentage of variance from budget that will command significant management attention. In this case, a 2.9% variation in budget represents $2,835 and may in fact command the manager's immediate attention and corrective action if applicable.

If our budget was accurate, and we are within reasonable limits of our budget, we are said to be **in-line** or in compliance with our budget. If, as management, we decided that plus (more than) or minus (less than) a designated percentage (such as 10%) of budget in each category would be considered in-line or acceptable, we are in-line with regard to expenses.

Many operators use the concept of "significant" variation to determine whether a problem exists. In this case, a significant variation is any variation in expected costs that management feels is a cause for concern. This variation can be caused by costs that were either higher or lower than the amount originally budgeted or planned for.

As also shown in Figure 3.14, net income (profit) can be expressed on the income statement simply as a number ($114,923 in this example) or by using a form of either vertical analysis, horizontal analysis, or both. Not surprisingly, managers seeking to make net income comparisons to budget or prior periods, either in terms of dollar differences or percentage differences, will utilize the same mathematical formulas used to make revenue and expense comparisons.

go figure!

This is a skill you have already learned, as you can see from the following formulas based on the data in Figure 3.14!

Net Income This Year − Net Income Last Year = Variance

or

$114,923 − $101,772 = $13,151

Joshua's net income percentage variance is determined as follows:

$$\frac{\text{(Net Income This Year − Net Income Last Year)}}{\text{Net Income Last Year}} = \textbf{Percentage Variance}$$

or

$$\frac{(\$114,923 - \$101,772)}{\$101,772} = 12.9\%$$

Of course, an alternative and shorter formula for computing the percentage variance is as follows:

$$\frac{\text{Variance}}{\text{Net Income Last Year}} = \textbf{Percentage Variance}$$

or

$$\frac{\$13,151}{\$101,772} = 12.9\%$$

Another way to compute the percentage variance is to use a math shortcut, as follows:

$$\left(\frac{\text{Net Income This Year}}{\text{Net Income Last Year}}\right) - 1 = \text{Percentage Variance}$$

or

$$\left(\frac{\$114{,}923}{\$101{,}772}\right) - 1 = 12.9\%$$

Professional restaurateurs and hoteliers have developed specialized methods of analyzing their revenues, expenses, and profits. These techniques have been developed to help determine expenses based on sales volume. Typically, as sales volume increases, the expenses required to support those sales also increase. For example, a restaurateur whose steak house operation is experiencing an increase in sales would expect to see increases in steak purchases. In a similar manner, the hotelier whose property is increasing its occupancy percentage will very likely see increases in expenses related to in-room guest amenities such as soap, shampoos, mouthwash, coffee cups, and in-room coffee supplies. In future chapters of this text you will learn about the most important and commonly utilized of these hospitality-specific expense analysis techniques. Each of them, however, depends upon the accurate revenue and expense information contained in a carefully prepared and timely income statement.

Each business that stays in operation will periodically assemble and evaluate a **balance sheet**. Also known as the statement of financial condition, the balance sheet is a summary of a business's assets, liabilities, and owners' equity. You will recall these familiar terms from the Accounting Formula you learned about in Chapter 2 (Assets = Liabilities + Owners' Equity).

Interestingly, most financial accounting texts and many managerial accounting texts introduce their readers to the concept of the balance sheet before they fully understand the income statement. The authors of this text believe that a study of the balance sheet is best undertaken by managers who first have learned about and understand income statements well. This is so because some managers who operate profitable businesses will nonetheless find that sometimes the owners of these businesses elect to sell or close them. Alternatively, other hoteliers and restaurateurs may find that the businesses they manage produce only a marginal profit (or may even lose money!) but these businesses continue to be operated year after year. An understanding of the effect of the income statement on the balance sheet will help you make sense of this seemingly illogical situation. Because you already understand income statements as well as how these important financial summaries are prepared and analyzed, you are now ready to begin your study of Chapter 4 of this text, The Balance Sheet. In doing so, you will begin to learn how managerial accountants and business owners use the information found on the balance sheet to even better understand and manage their businesses.

Lezinah Ncube has just taken a new job as regional manager of a limited-service hotel chain. Her region includes six hotels, with each hotel consisting of approximately 100 rooms. Each hotel also offers a small amount of meeting space and provides its overnight guests with a complimentary breakfast. Prior to this job, Lezinah served as a district manager for a national pizza company, where she was responsible for the supervision of ten stores.

At the end of her first month's work, Lezinah receives seven income statements; one for each individual hotel, as well as one consolidated income statement summarizing the overall financial performance of her six properties. Lezinah's supervisor has asked her to comment on the financial results achieved by her region.

1. What specific differences will exist between the monthly income statements Lezinah must now analyze and those she likely reviewed in her previous food service job?
2. In food service, restaurateurs evaluating revenue levels are concerned about guest counts and check averages. Hoteliers are concerned about occupancy levels and average daily rates. Explain the similarities between these two sets of concepts, and their affect upon the revenue section of her income statements.
3. Lezinah was very good at P&L analysis in her previous job, but is a bit nervous about the same task in her new position because she has never reviewed a hotel income statement. As her good friend, list and explain for her six specific characteristics of hotel income statements that are identical to those of restaurants, and thus would strongly suggest that her analysis skills as a restaurateur would likely carry over into her new career as a hotelier.

Key Terms and Concepts

The following are terms and concepts discussed in the chapter that are important for you as a manager. To help you review, please define the terms below.

Revenue	Interest	Operated department income
Expenses	Default	section (USALI)
Profit	Creditor	Undistributed operating
Profit center	Invoice	expenses section (USALI)
Business dining	Creditworthiness	Nonoperating expenses
Cost center	Operate in the red	section (USALI)
Stakeholders	Operate in the black	Timing
Appreciation	Gross profit section (USAR)	Classification
Return on investment (ROI)	Operating expenses section	Invoice credit
Debt	(USAR)	Expense classification
Equity	Nonoperating expenses	Departmental cost
Terms	section (USAR)	Direct operating expense

Undistributed operating expense	Vertical analysis	Variance
Schedules	Common-size analysis	Percentage variance
Package	Profit margin	In-line
SMERF	Responsibility accounting	Balance sheet
Bottom line	Horizontal analysis	
	Comparative analysis	

 *Test Your Skills*

Complete the Test Your Skills exercises by placing your answers in the shaded boxes.

1. Nicole Englezakis manages a South African restaurant in a large southern city. The owner wants to know how well Nicole did this year at generating sales, controlling expenses, and providing a profit. Complete Nicole's P&L using vertical analysis.

Nicole's P&L				
	Last Year	**%**	**This Year**	**%**
SALES:				
Food	$3,706,381		$3,746,245	
Beverage	$647,555		1,255,358	
Total Sales				
COST OF SALES:				
Food	1,282,656		1,611,630	
Beverage	145,607		162,231	
Total Cost of Sales				
GROSS PROFIT:				
Food	2,423,725		2,134,615	
Beverage	501,948		1,093,127	
Total Gross Profit				
OPERATING EXPENSES:				
Salaries and Wages	1,230,910		1,256,779	
Employee Benefits	190,394		196,790	
Direct Operating Expenses	234,670		232,571	
Music and Entertainment	4,427		13,418	
Marketing	84,126		111,813	
Utility Services	141,688		156,538	
Repairs and Maintenance	66,416		62,616	

Administrative and General	128,403		125,230	
Occupancy	230,400		211,200	
Depreciation	79,699		98,397	
Total Operating Expenses				
Operating Income				
Interest	166,560		149,405	
Income Before Income Taxes				
Income Taxes	147,192		245,194	
Net Income				

a. When comparing this year to last year, was Nicole's marketing expense in dollars higher or lower?

b. Was Nicole's marketing expense % higher or lower this year?

c. Do you think that her marketing expense this year positively or negatively contributed to her revenues? Why?

d. When comparing this year to last year, was Nicole's salaries and wages expense in dollars higher or lower?

e. Was Nicole's salaries and wages expense % higher or lower this year?

f. Do you think that her salaries and wages expense this year positively or negatively contributed to her net income? Why?

g. The owner promised Nicole that he would give her a raise if she increased profit margin by at least 2%. Should Nicole receive a raise? Why or why not?

2. Terry Ray manages a hotel in an urban Midwestern city. He wants to use vertical analysis in order to evaluate his income statement (P&L). Complete the spreadsheet to help him evaluate his effectiveness as a manager.

Terry's P&L		
Total Revenue	**5,100,350**	
Rooms – Revenue	**3,000,000**	
Payroll and Related Expenses	535,600	
Other Expenses	229,450	
Department Income		
Food – Revenue	**1,400,000**	
Cost of Sales	386,100	
Payroll and Related Expenses	395,200	
Other Expenses	96,200	
Department Income		

Beverage–Revenue	**560,000**	
Cost of Sales	81,510	
Payroll and Related Expenses	96,590	
Other Expenses	36,400	
Department Income		
Telecommunications–Revenue	**14,000**	
Cost of Sales	30,550	
Payroll and Related Expenses	9,750	
Other Expenses	5,200	
Department Income		
Other Operated Departments–Revenue	**105,000**	
Cost of Sales	14,300	
Payroll and Related Expenses	32,500	
Other Expenses	11,700	
Department Income		
Rentals and Other Income–Revenue	**21,350**	
Cost of Sales	2,860	
Payroll and Related Expenses	8,840	
Other Expenses	1,950	
Department Income		
Total Operated Department Income		
Undistributed Operating Expenses		
Administrative and General	245,050	
Information Systems	64,350	
Human Resources	105,300	
Security	50,050	
Franchise Fees	0	
Transportation	60,450	
Marketing	280,280	
Property Operations and Maintenance	216,125	
Utility Costs	193,375	
Total Undistributed Operating Expenses		
Gross Operating Profit		
Rent, Property Taxes, and Insurance	317,850	
Depreciation and Amortization	227,500	
Net Operating Income		
Interest	136,500	
Income Before Income Taxes		
Income Taxes	491,528	
Net Income		

a. The owner gave Terry a goal of 65% total operated department income. Did Terry perform better or worse than this goal? By how much?

b. The owner also gave Terry a goal of 22% total undistributed operating expenses. Did Terry perform better or worse than this goal? By how much?

c. Finally, the owner gave Terry a goal of 20% profit margin for the year. Did Terry perform better or worse than this goal? By how much?

d. If you answered that Terry did not meet his goal in question c, what could he do to get his P&L in line with the owner's goals?

3. Laurie Llamos manages a Mexican restaurant in a rural Texas town. She wants to develop a comparative (horizontal) income statement so that she can compare the differences in her revenues, expenses, and profit from this year to last year. Complete the following comparative income statement.

Laurie's Comparative Income Statement				
			Difference	
	Last Year	**This Year**	**$**	**%**
SALES:				
Food	3,025,618	3,499,239		
Beverage	622,649	772,528		
Total Sales				
COST OF SALES:				
Food	997,622	1,151,165		
Beverage	132,370	144,849		
Total Cost of Sales				
GROSS PROFIT:				
Food				
Beverage				
Total Gross Profit				
OPERATING EXPENSES:				
Salaries and Wages	897,539	1,071,119		
Employee Benefits	138,828	167,720		
Direct Operating Expenses	171,114	198,215		
Music and Entertainment	3,228	11,436		
Marketing	61,342	95,295		
Utility Services	103,314	133,413		
Repairs and Maintenance	48,429	53,366		

Administrative and General	93,628	106,731		
Occupancy	168,000	180,000		
Depreciation	58,114	83,861		
Total Operating Expenses				
Operating Income				
Interest	121;450	127,334		
Income Before Income Taxes				
Income Taxes	261,315	313,850		
Net Income				

a. Laurie's goal was to increase her total sales by 15%. Did she achieve this goal?

b. One of Laurie's plans to increase traffic into her restaurant and thus increase her sales was to hire a mariachi band to play at regular intervals during the meal service. This affected her music and entertainment expense. What was the % difference in music and entertainment, and do you think this had a positive or negative effect on sales?

c. Laurie also wanted to increase her net income by 10%. Did she achieve this goal?

4. Haroun Jackson is the chief engineer of a large hotel in New England. Her general manager has asked her to complete her Property Operations and Maintenance Expense Schedule to determine the detailed costs for her department. Help Haroun complete her schedule.

Haroun's Property Operations and Maintenance Expense Schedule

Type of Expense	Expense	% of Property Operations and Maintenance Expenses
Payroll and Related Expenses		
Chief Engineer	8,637	
Engineer Assistants	22,163	
Benefit Allocation	13,750	
Total Payroll		
Other Expenses		
Computer Equipment	3,108	
Equipment Rental	7,700	
Electrical & Mechanical Equipment	15,565	
Elevators	4,620	
Elevator Repairs	1,540	
Engineering Supplies	1,925	
Floor Covering	5,058	

Furniture	21,010	
Grounds	6,160	
HVAC	15,675	
Kitchen Equipment	979	
Laundry Equipment	616	
Light Bulbs	1,650	
Maintenance Contracts	7,238	
Operating Supplies	875	
Painting & Decorating	1,562	
Parking Lot	4,708	
Pest Control	2,365	
Plants & Interior	1,628	
Plumbing & Heating	9,790	
Refrigeration & A/C	10,780	
Signage Repair	5,881	
Snow Removal	10,835	
Travel & Entertainment	1,045	
Telecommunications	968	
Trash Removal	3,080	
Uniforms	2,904	
Total Other Expenses		
Total Property Operations and Maintenance		

a. What was Haroun's largest single expense as a percentage of total property operations and maintenance?

b. What was Haroun's smallest single expense as a percentage of total property operations and maintenance?

c. Haroun purchased new furniture for her hotel lobby, but does not anticipate any furniture purchases next period. How might this affect her overall total property operations and maintenance expense next period?

CHAPTER 4

The Balance Sheet

OVERVIEW

In this chapter you will learn about the balance sheet. As a hospitality manager, the ability to read and understand a balance sheet is second in importance only to that of the income statement. As you learned, while the income statement provides a summary of a business's operational results over a defined period of time (for example a month or a year), the balance sheet reflects the overall financial condition of a business on the specific day it is prepared. Thus it can be considered a point-in-time "snapshot" of a business's value.

In Chapter 2 you learned that The Accounting Formula is stated as *Assets = Liabilities + Owners' Equity*. The purpose of a balance sheet is to tell its readers as much as possible about each of these three accounting formula components. Thus it provides great detail about the precise nature and condition of a business's assets, liabilities, and owners' equity.

In this chapter you will learn why owners, investors, lenders, and managers all must know how to read and understand a balance sheet. You will also learn how accountants prepare a balance sheet and, most important, how managerial accountants evaluate the information contained in a balance sheet using vertical and horizontal analysis techniques.

CHAPTER OUTLINE

- ■ The Purpose of the Balance Sheet
- ■ Balance Sheet Formats
- ■ Balance Sheet Content
- ■ Components of the Balance Sheet
- ■ Balance Sheet Analysis
- ■ Apply What You Have Learned
- ■ Key Terms and Concepts
- ■ Test Your Skills

LEARNING OUTCOMES

At the conclusion of this chapter, you will be able to:

- ✓ State the purpose of regularly preparing a balance sheet for a hospitality business.
- ✓ Explain the way managers and accountants actually prepare a balance sheet.
- ✓ Analyze a balance sheet to better understand the financial condition of your own business.

The Purpose of the Balance Sheet

Business owners prepare balance sheets to better understand the value of a business and how well its assets have been utilized to produce wealth for the business's owners.

go figure!

To see why this is important, consider the case of John Calvin. John is the sole owner of a popular restaurant that, last year, grossed $1,000,000 in revenue and generated $100,000 in after tax profit. Louise Schneider, who is one of his competitors, also grossed $1,000,000 in revenue and generated $100,000 in profit in the restaurant she owns. Thus, if you were simply to evaluate last year's income statements for each of these restaurateurs, you might conclude that their businesses were "equal" in value because they each produced a $100,000 profit.

In fact, however, a closer look at The Accounting Formula (see Chapter 2) for each of the two businesses reveals the following:

John's Accounting Formula

Assets = Liabilities + Owners' Equity
or
$2,000,000 = $500,000 + $1,500,000

Louise's Accounting Formula

Assets = Liabilities + Owners' Equity
or
$2,000,000 = $1,500,000 + $500,000

Assume that you are one of these restaurants' owners seeking to sell your business for $2,000,000. As you can see, John "owes" less ($500,000) of his restaurant's value to others than does Louise ($1,500,000). Put a different way, if each of these owners sold their operations for $2,000,000, John would, after paying all of the restaurant's debts, receive $1,500,000 ($2,000,000 assets − $500,000 liabilities = $1,500,000) while Louise would receive only $500,000 ($2,000,000 assets − $1,500,000 liabilities = $500,000).

Clearly, these two businesses are different in ways that are important to their owners and these differences can be identified only by a study of their balance sheets. In fact, the type of information contained on a business's balance sheet (and there is really quite a lot of it!) is of critical importance to several different groups including:

Owners
Investors
Lenders
Creditors
Managers

Owners

The balance sheet, prepared at the end of each defined accounting period, lets the owners of the business know about the amount of that business which they actually "own." To illustrate, assume that you purchased a new $25,000 automobile and borrowed all of the money to do so from your local bank. You would, when you picked up the car from the dealership, technically "own" it. That is, the keys are in your possession and you may drive the car to any place you choose at any time you choose. The bank, however, can also be considered an owner since you could not sell the car to another without first paying off the bank's lien against the car. A **lien** is the legal right to hold another's property to satisfy a debt. In this example, your bank's lien against your car is similar to a business's liabilities. These liabilities must be subtracted from the value of the business before its owners can determine the amount of their own equity (free and clear ownership). The balance sheet is designed to show the amount of a business owner's free and clear ownership.

Investors

In most cases, investors seek to maximize the return on investment (ROI) (see Chapter 1) they receive. When a business's balance sheet from one accounting period is compared to its balance sheet covering another time period, investors can measure their return on investment.

 *go figure!*

For example, assume that you invest $50,000 in a restaurant. Assume also that, exactly one year later, your share of the owners' equity in the restaurant is $60,000 (based upon the balance sheet for the restaurant). Using the ROI formula presented in Chapter 1, your ROI for the year would be computed as:

$$\frac{\text{Money Earned on Funds Invested}}{\text{Funds Invested}} = \text{ROI}$$

or

$$\frac{\$10,000}{\$50,000} = 20.0\%$$

Investors simply must have the information contained in a balance sheet if they are to accurately compute their annual returns on investment.

Lenders

Lenders are most concerned about a business's ability to repay its debts. It is easy to see why.

 *go figure!*

Consider two similar hotels, one owned by Ezat, and one by Arlene. Both of these properties have outstanding long-term mortgages totaling $8,000,000. Both hotel owners would like to borrow an additional $1,000,000 from their local bank to refurbish their guest rooms. Both hotels have $60,000 monthly mortgage payments and both show (on the income statement) an after-tax profit of $120,000 per year.

The Accounting Formula (as shown on its balance sheet), for Ezat's hotel is as follows:

$$\text{Assets} = \text{Liabilities} \qquad\qquad + \text{Owners' Equity}$$

or

$$\$11,000,000 = (\$8,000,000 \text{ mortgage} + \$2,880,000 \text{ other liabilities}) + \$120,000$$

Note that Ezat has total liabilities of $10,880,000 (an $8,000,000 mortgage plus $2,880,000 of other liabilities) and owners' equity of $120,000. Put another way, if, for an extended period of time, Ezat's hotel did not actually make a profit, and he elected to use his owners' equity account to fund his monthly mortgage payments, he could make two such payments ($120,000/$60,000 = 2) before that account was depleted.

The Accounting Formula (as shown on its balance sheet), for Arlene's hotel is as follows:

$$\text{Assets} = \text{Liabilities} + \text{Owners' Equity}$$

or

$$\$11,000,000 = \$8,000,000 + \$3,000,000$$

Note that Arlene has total liabilities of only $8,000,000 (her mortgage) and owners' equity of $3,000,000. Put another way, if, for an extended period of time, Arlene's hotel did not make a profit, she could use her owners' equity to make up to 50 mortgage payments ($3,000,000/$60,000 = 50) before her owners' equity account was depleted.

If you were the banker considering a new $1,000,000 loan to give to each of these hotels, you are likely to feel much better about Arlene's ability to withstand a prolonged economic downturn or the construction of a nearby (and directly competitive) hotel than you would Ezat's ability to continue his payments in the face of the same economic pressures. Lenders are interested in a debtor's ability to repay, and it is because of situations such as that of Arlene and Ezat that lenders read the balance sheet of a business in an effort to better understand the financial strength (and thus the repayment ability) of that business.

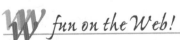 *fun on the Web!*

Although there are many lenders to the hospitality industry, Ashford Hospitality Trust (AHT) is one of the most widely known. AHT is a real estate investment trust that invests in hospitality industry companies by lending them money for hotel investments, mortgages, and other types of loans. To learn more about Ashford Hospitality Trust, go to:

www.ahtreit.com/overview.html

Creditors

Business creditors, much like lenders, are concerned about repayment. For example, when a food supplier agrees to sell food to a restaurant on a credit basis, it does so with the expectation that the restaurant will ultimately be able to pay its bill. In a similar manner, if a hotel places an order for a telephone system (most of which cost in excess of $100,000), the telephone vendor who agrees to ship the system on credit is counting on the fact that the hotel has the ability to pay for it. In both of these cases, it would not be unreasonable for these vendors to ask to see their customers' respective balance sheets before a decision was made regarding the wisdom of extending credit to them. The balance sheet is the financial document that most accurately indicates the long-term ability of a business to repay a vendor who has extended credit to that business.

 *fun on the Web!*

One of the most widely used vendors for the food service industry is Sysco Corporation. It provides food and nonfood supplies to hospitality operations in the United States and Canada. In your career as a hospitality manager, you will most likely encounter Sysco Corporation as one of your creditors. To find out more about Sysco Corporation, go to:

www.sysco.com

Managers

Managers most often are more interested in the information found on the income statement than that found on the balance sheet. However, there are a variety of important reasons why they too must be able to read and analyze their own balance sheets to determine items such as the current financial balances of cash, accounts receivable, inventories, and accounts payable, and other accounts that have a direct impact on operations.

For example, the balance sheet indicates the amount of cash on hand at the end of an accounting period. In Chapter 5 (The Statement of Cash Flows) you will learn more about the extremely vital role cash plays in the operation of a business. It is clear, however, those who operate a business must consistently have sufficient cash on hand to pay their employees, their vendors, and the taxes owed by the business. The balance sheet indicates to management the amount of cash available to them on the day the balance sheet is prepared.

In addition, as you learned in Chapter 2, accounts receivable refers to the amount of money owed to a business by its customers. Thus, managers must be able to read a balance sheet to determine the total amount of accounts receivable owed to the business on the date it is prepared. While in most restaurants guests pay for their food and beverages on the day they are purchased, it is not uncommon for some restaurants to extend credit to special customers. As a result, a restaurant's accounts receivable may be substantial. In the hotel business, a very significant amount of a property's sales may be made on a credit basis. This can be true whether the guests involved are individuals or belong to a larger organization to which the hotel has extended credit.

To understand some of the many reasons why a hotel would elect to extend credit to a guest organization, consider the case of Roy Oliver, President of Oliver Construction, a mid-sized road construction firm. Roy's company has been awarded the state contract to construct two miles of new highway near a hotel. The job is a big one and will last many months. It will also involve the use of dozens of workers, each of whom will require Monday through Thursday night lodging near the worksite. Since the lodging of its workers will be an expense of Oliver Construction, its managers face the alternatives of either (1) allowing each worker to stay at a hotel of their own choosing and then reimbursing each individual worker for his or her night's lodging, or (2) negotiate with a single hotel to place all of the business at one hotel property, and then request that the hotel bill the company directly for all lodging expenses.

It is in the best interest of both the hotel and the guest to select the second alternative. The bookkeeping of the construction company will be simplified if it can purchase rooms on credit, and the company will also likely be able to negotiate a better nightly rate from the hotel because it will be able to guarantee a predetermined number of room nights needed on a regular basis. The hotel benefits from simplified billing as well as a guaranteed sales level. Finally, it is highly likely that other hotels who desire the business from Oliver Construction will be competing for that business, in part, by granting credit to Roy's company.

It is important to remember that, even if the income statement indicates your business is very profitable, excessively large amounts of accounts receivable (which are not identified on your income statement) could be a tell-tale sign that:

- Too much credit has been extended.
- Credit collection efforts may need to be reviewed and improved if necessary.
- Cash reserves could become insufficient to meet the short-term needs of your business.

Limitations of the Balance Sheet

The balance sheet is important to its readers because it reveals, at a fixed point in time, the amount of **wealth** that a company possesses. In this case, wealth is simply defined as the current value of all a company's assets minus all of the company's obligations. While it might seem that establishing the value of a company's assets and liabilities would be a very straightforward process, accountants do not always agree about how to do it. To understand why differences of opinion can exist, consider the case of the Waldorf Astoria. Owned by the Hilton Hotels company, the Waldorf is one of the Historic Hotels of America (as designated by the National Trust for Historic Preservation). If you were asked to place a value on that asset for Hilton you might consider:

An historical approach: In this situation, you would likely value the hotel at the price the Hilton Hotels corporation paid for the property when they bought it.

A current (replacement) value approach: In this situation, you would likely value the property at the amount of money that would be required to replace the hotel.

A future value approach: In this situation, you would likely value the property at the amount of money (income) it could, in the future, earn for the shareholders of the Hilton Hotels company.

While each of the three approaches could make sense with specific assets, in fact, no single approach to valuing assets is used by accountants in the preparation of the balance sheet. As a result, knowledgeable readers of a balance sheet recognize that accountants utilize a variety of evaluation approaches, each of which may make the most sense for specific asset types based upon circumstances and available information.

It is also important to note that balance sheets have been criticized because of the company assets they do *not* value. To understand why, consider the fact that, of all the assets listed on the balance sheet, none take into account the relative value, or worth, of a restaurant or hotel's staff, including its managers.

Many companies are fond of saying that "Our people (staff) are our most important asset," yet the value of experienced, well-trained staff members is not quantified on the balance sheet. To further clarify this important concept, consider the case of Ahmed. He owns his own hotel and is contemplating a $1,000 expenditure for his Marketing and Sales department. His alternatives are spending the $1,000 to replace an aging computer used by one of his sales managers, or using the same $1,000 to send the entire five-person marketing and sales team to a one-day training class on the advanced usage of Microsoft Excel, the spreadsheet software used in his property for producing sales contracts and guest invoices.

If Ahmed decides to purchase the computer, the value of his assets (Property and Equipment) on the balance sheet will increase, while if he elects to "invest" in his staff via the training program, no such balance sheet increase will occur. Yet, in this case, it well could be that the training class, rather than a single upgraded computer, will make a much greater difference in the effectiveness, efficiency, accuracy, and "worth" (future profitability) of the hotel's marketing and sales department. Thus, as an astute hospitality management accountant, you must recognize both the value and limitations of balance sheets when you review them.

Balance Sheet Formats

You have learned that a balance sheet represents an accountant's systematic method of documenting the value of a business's assets, liabilities, and owners' equity on a specific date. In this section, you will learn about the actual layout (format) of balance sheets and their content as well as when and precisely how managerial accountants prepare them.

There are two basic methods accountants use to display the information on a balance sheet. When using the **account format** those preparing the balance sheet list the assets of a company on the left side of the report and the liabilities and owners' equity accounts on

FIGURE 4.1 Account Format Balance Sheet

BLUE LAGOON WATER PARK RESORT
Balance Sheet
December 31, 2010

Assets		Liabilities and Owners' Equity	
Current Assets		Current Liabilities	
Cash	2,314,750	Accounts Payable	1,438,100
Marketable Securities	3,309,600	Notes Payable	1,319,900
Net Receivables	1,053,950	Other Current Liabilities	1,264,600
Inventories	1,497,200	Total Current Liabilities	4,022,600
Total Current Assets	8,175,500		
		Long-Term Liabilities	
Investments	5,023,500	Long-Term Debt	14,577,400
Property and Equipment		Total Liabilities	18,600,000
Land	7,712,550		
Building	22,290,500	Owners' Equity	
Furnishings and Equipment	7,289,000	Common Stock	3,000,000
Less Accumulated Depreciation	4,668,900	Paid in Capital	18,775,100
Net Property and Equipment	32,623,150	Retained Earnings	6,116,850
Other Assets	669,800	Total Owners' Equity	27,891,950
Total Assets	46,491,950	Total Liabilities and Owners' Equity	46,491,950

the right side. Figure 4.1 is an example of a balance sheet for the Blue Lagoon Water Park Resort, prepared using the account format.

When using the **report format** those preparing the balance sheet list the assets of a company first and then the liabilities and owners' equity accounts (vertically), and present the totals in such a manner as to prove to the reader that assets equal liabilities plus owners' equity. Figure 4.2 is an example of the Blue Lagoon Water Park Resort's balance sheet prepared using the report format.

Note that, in both type formats, the date on which the balance sheet was prepared is clearly identified. Just as the income statement you learned about in the last chapter must plainly state the accounting period over which it is prepared, the balance sheet must plainly state its preparation date.

Balance Sheet Content

As you already know, The Accounting Formula is stated as *Assets = Liabilities + Owners' Equity*, and the purpose of a balance sheet is to tell its readers as much as possible about each of these three Accounting Formula components. This is an easy formula to memorize,

FIGURE 4.2 Report Format Balance Sheet

BLUE LAGOON WATER PARK RESORT
Balance Sheet
December 31, 2010

Assets

Current Assets		
Cash	2,314,750	
Marketable Securities	3,309,600	
Net Receivables	1,053,950	
Inventories	1,497,200	
Total Current Assets		8,175,500
Investments		5,023,500
Property and Equipment		
Land	7,712,550	
Building	22,290,500	
Furnishings and Equipment	7,289,000	
Less Accumulated Depreciation	4,668,900	
Net Property and Equipment		32,623,150
Other Assets		669,800
Total Assets		46,491,950

Liabilities and Owners' Equity

Current Liabilities		
Accounts Payable	1,438,100	
Notes Payable	1,319,900	
Other Current Liabilities	1,264,600	
Total Current Liabilities		4,022,600
Long-Term Liabilities		
Long-Term Debt		14,577,400
Total Liabilities		18,600,000
Owners' Equity		
Common Stock	3,000,000	
Paid in Capital	18,775,100	
Retained Earnings	6,116,850	
Total Owners' Equity		27,891,950
Total Liabilities and Owners' Equity		46,491,950

but it is also important for you to understand what it really means. More specifically, you need to understand *why* a balance sheet balances.

Why a Balance Sheet Balances—Dr. Dopson's Stuff Theory

Dr. Lea Dopson, a hospitality managerial accounting professor, is one of the authors of this book. She has developed "Dr. Dopson's Stuff Theory" to explain to her students and to you why a balance sheet balances.

Imagine that you were asked to develop a balance sheet representing the "stuff" in your life. You are asked to list all the stuff (assets) that you have and how you got your stuff (liabilities and owners' equity). Your balance sheet might look something like Figure 4.3.

Dr. Dopson's Stuff Theory is simple. For all the stuff (assets) you have in your life, you got it from either (1) borrowing money that you have to repay such as through credit cards or loans (liabilities), or (2) acquiring the stuff through others such as your parents, siblings, or friends (investors' equity) or paying for the stuff yourself through money you earned (retained earnings equity—explained in detail later in this chapter). Of course, this simple example doesn't take into account the depreciation on your stuff. One important thing to remember is that you are reporting your stuff and how you *got* (past tense) your stuff. In this sense, the list of your stuff *balances* with how you got it. This is why a balance sheet balances!

This same concept applies to businesses when preparing their balance sheets. For example, a business might purchase a building (asset) and pay for it with a loan from a bank (liability). Or, the business might purchase furniture (asset) and pay for it with money from an investor (owners' equity). In this way, all assets (stuff) must equal liabilities plus owners' equity (how they got their stuff). Now that you understand the "why" of the balance sheet, let us turn to the "what" or components of the balance sheet.

FIGURE 4.3 Dr. Dopson's Stuff Theory

Your Stuff	How You <u>Got</u> Your Stuff	
Assets =	**Liabilities +**	**Owners' Equity**
Television		Hand-me-down from sister (investor)
Car	Car loan	
Computer	Credit card	
Clothes	Credit card	
Food		Income (money you earned)
Couch and chair	Credit card	
Kitchen knives	Credit card	
School books		Money from parents (investors)
Bed		Bed from home your parents bought you when you were 15 (investors)
Toiletries		Income (money you earned)

Components of the Balance Sheet

The balance sheet is often subdivided into components under the broad headings of Assets, Liabilities, and Owners' Equity. These sub-classifications have been created by accountants to make information more easily accessible to readers of the balance sheet and to allow for more rapid identification of specific types of information for decision making. While there can be variation based upon the needs of a specific business, your ability to read and analyze a balance sheet will improve greatly if you understand the most common of these asset, liability, and owners' equity sub-classifications.

Assets

Current Assets

Current assets are those which may reasonably be expected to be sold or turned into cash within one year (or one operating season). Current assets are typically listed on the balance sheet in order of their **liquidity**, which is defined as the ease in which current assets can be converted to cash in a short period of time (less than 12 months). Figure 4.4 lists the most common types of current assets in order of liquidity that you would typically encounter when you read a balance sheet.

For purposes of preparing a balance sheet, the term **cash** refers to the cash held in cash banks (for example, those used by cashiers in a restaurant), money held in checking or savings accounts, electronic fund transfers from payment card companies (such as MasterCard, American Express, Visa, and the like), and **certificates of deposit (CDs)**, which are financial instruments with a fixed term and interest rate. CDs serve businesses in the same way that interest bearing savings accounts serve individuals.

Marketable securities include those investments such as stocks and bonds that can readily be bought and sold and thus are easily converted to cash. If the intent of management is to hold (not sell) a particular stock or bond for an extended period of time, it would not be listed as a current asset, but rather it would be recorded on the balance sheet as an investment (discussed later in this section). Marketable securities are stocks and bonds the business purchases from *other* companies. These are not to be confused with a company's stocks that are listed on its balance sheet as owners' equity.

FIGURE 4.4   Order of Liquidity of Current Assets

Current assets, typically listed on the balance sheet in order of their liquidity, include:

Cash
Marketable securities
Accounts receivable (net receivables)
Inventories
Prepaid expenses

Accounts receivable represent the amount of money owed to a business *by others* (such as customers). **Net receivables** (the term *net* means that something has been subtracted out) are those monies owed to the business after subtracting any amounts that may not be collectable (**doubtful accounts**). For example, consider the case of Andrew Rice. Andrew is the general manager of the Oakridge Resort. Last December his hotel hosted a holiday party for the Hayman Company. The company was extended credit of $5,000 for their event and as a result did not pay their bill upon the completion of the party. It is now six months later and repeated attempts to contact the company for payment have been unsuccessful. In fact, the Hayman Company cannot be reached because it is no longer in business. In such a case, it is "doubtful" that the money owed to the hotel will ever be collected. Thus, Andrew should subtract the amount owed by the Hayman Company from the total amount owed to the hotel when he computes his final accounts receivable number, or net receivables.

In the hospitality industry, **inventories** will include the value of the food, beverages, and supplies used by a restaurant, as well as sheets, towels, and the in-room replacement items (hangers, blow dryers, coffee makers, and the like), used by a hotel. In most hospitality industry situations, the value of an inventory item will equal the amount the business paid for it. Thus, when computing the value of its inventory, a business would assign a case of Johnny Walker Scotch the same value as it paid for it. In those unique situations where the current value of an item is significantly different than the price a business paid for it (for example in the case of extremely rare wines that may have been held in a restaurant's wine cellar for many years and thus have appreciated greatly in value) then, because of the conservatism principle of accounting, the lower of the original cost or the current value should be the item's inventory value.

Prepaid expenses are best understood as items that will be used within a year's time, but which must be completely paid for at the time of purchase. Typical hospitality examples include annual insurance policies as well as local tax assessments and some long-term service contracts.

The order of liquidity for current assets is easily explained. Cash is listed first because it is already cash. Marketable securities are less liquid than cash, but can be readily sold for cash. Net receivables can be collected from others (customers), but not as easily as converting marketable securities to cash. Inventories must be made ready for sale to customers (as in the case of ingredients for food) and the money must be collected. There is no guarantee that payment for all inventories will be collected in full, and thus some may end up being reported as receivables. Finally, prepaid expenses are the least liquid current asset because once paid, refunds for this money are very difficult (if not impossible) to receive.

go figure!

To better illustrate prepaid expenses, assume that a tavern purchases a one-year liquor liability policy that costs $12,000. The policy is paid for, in its entirety, on January 1. Thus a one-time payment of $12,000 is made.

If the tavern owner were to prepare a balance sheet on February 1, the prepaid expense for liquor liability insurance would be valued at $11,000. This is so because the

$12,000 policy covers a 12-month period, thus the amount "used up" is $1,000 per month.

> **$12,000/12 months = $1,000 per month**

On February 1, the remaining "prepaid" amount of the insurance would be $11,000.

> **$12,000 per year – $1,000 used in January = $11,000 prepaid insurance remaining**

Those prepaid expenses that will be of value or benefit to the business for more than one year (for example a three-year prepaid insurance policy) should be listed on the balance sheet as "Other Assets."

Noncurrent (Fixed) Assets

Noncurrent (fixed) assets consist of those assets which management intends to keep for a period longer than one year. Although many variations exist, these typically include investments, property and equipment (land, building, furnishings and equipment, less accumulated depreciation or amortization), and other assets as can be see in Figure 4.1 and Figure 4.2.

Included in this group are **investments** made by the business. If an asset is considered an investment, it is management's intent to retain the asset for a period of time longer than one year, unlike marketable securities, which can be readily sold and converted to cash within one year. Investments are typically one of three types:

- *Securities* (stocks and bonds) acquired for a specific purpose such as a restaurant company that purchases a significant amount of stock in a smaller company with the intent of influencing the operations of the smaller company.
- Assets owned by a business but not currently used by it. An example would be vacant land owned by a restaurant company that is going to build (but has not yet built) a restaurant on the site.
- Special funds that have a specific purpose. The most common of these is a **sinking fund**, in which monies are reserved and invested for use in the future. This makes sense, for example, in the case of a business, such as a hotel, which must reserve the significant amount of money needed to renovate the property every six or seven years.

Investments are valued on the balance sheet at their fair market value. **Fair market value** is most often defined as the price at which an item would change hands between a buyer and a seller without any compulsion to buy or sell, and with both having reasonable knowledge of the relevant facts. Not surprisingly, it can sometimes be difficult to accurately determine fair market value for an item without actually selling it!

Property and equipment, which includes land, building, furnishings and equipment, usually make up a significant portion of the total value of a hospitality business and are another form of noncurrent asset. These are listed on the balance sheet at their original cost less their accumulated depreciation (see Chapter 2). To better understand this, consider the case of Charlene. She purchased a restaurant which had a property and equipment value of $1,000,000. During the time she has owned the restaurant, and following the rules of depreciation appropriate for her business, she has been permitted to reduce their value by $400,000 to reflect wear and tear on these assets over their estimated useful life. This "noncash" depreciation expense has, of course, resulted in a reduction over time of her annual taxable income.

As a second result of depreciating her assets, the value of the property and equipment on her balance sheet is now $600,000 ($1,000,000 purchase price − $400,000 accumulated depreciation = $600,000 remaining value).

Other assets are a noncurrent asset group that includes items that are mostly intangible. This includes the value of **goodwill** (the difference between the purchase price of an item and its fair market value). Goodwill is an asset that is **amortized** (systematically reduced in value) over the period of time in which it will be of benefit to the business. Other items in this category may include the cash surrender value of life insurance policies taken out on certain company executives, deferred charges such as loan fees that are amortized over the life of the loan, and restricted cash that is set aside for a specific (restricted) purpose. In the hospitality industry, initial franchisee fees paid to secure a specific franchise agreement will be listed under other assets and amortized over the life of the franchise agreement. Thus, for example, if $50,000 is paid to secure a hotel franchise and the life of the agreement is five years, the matching principle of accounting would dictate that the franchise agreement be listed as an "Other Asset" and then be amortized over the five-year term of the agreement.

It is easy to see that the methods of depreciation and amortization used by a business have a significant effect on how it reports the value of its assets. For this reason, the techniques of depreciation and amortization used by a business should be prepared and shown in the Notes to Financial Statements that should be attached to the balance sheet.

As previously noted it can be difficult to accurately assess the value of a business's assets. Figure 4.5 summarizes the approach to evaluation typically used by hospitality accountants when they seek to establish the value of a company's assets.

FIGURE 4.5   Methods of Determining Asset Worth

Asset Type	Worth Established By
Cash	Current value
Marketable securities	Fair market value or amortized cost
Accounts receivable	Estimated future value
Inventories	The lesser of current value or price paid
Investments	Fair market value or amortized cost
Property and equipment	Price paid adjusted for allowed depreciation

Because the methods used to evaluate the worth of a business's assets vary by asset type, it is not surprising that some accountants believe that summing these items is a process much like adding apples to oranges. Historically, however, these variously arrived at values are indeed summed together to estimate the total worth of a company's assets. Because this is true, balance sheet readers need to be aware of these differences when evaluating a company's financial position. As a result, savvy balance sheet analysts (and you will become one when you complete this chapter!) are very careful when relying on the balance sheet to communicate a company's noncash asset values.

Liabilities

Liabilities can be classified as either current or long-term. **Current liabilities** are defined as those obligations of the business that will be repaid within a year. In most cases this involves payment from the cash assets of the business. The most important sub-classifications of current liabilities include notes payable, income taxes payable, and accounts payable. In the hospitality industry, current liabilities typically consist of payables resulting from the purchase of food, beverages, products, services, and labor. Current period payments utilized for the reduction of long-term debt are also considered a current liability.

Interestingly, guests' prepaid deposits (such as those required by a hotel that reserves a ballroom for a wedding to be held several months in the future) are also listed as a current liability (because these monies are held by the business but have not been earned at the time the hotel accepts the deposit). Dividends that have been declared but not yet paid and income taxes that are due but not yet paid will also be included in this liability classification.

Long-term liabilities are those obligations of the business that will not be completely paid within the current year. Typical examples include long-term debt, mortgages, lease obligations, and deferred income taxes resulting from the depreciation methodology used by the business.

Owners' Equity

While the liabilities section of the balance sheet identifies nonowner (external) claims against the business's assets, the owners' equity portion identifies the asset claims of the business's owners. In Chapter 2 you learned that ownership of a company can take a variety of forms. For corporations, **common stock** is the balance sheet entry that represents the number of shares of stock issued (owned) multiplied by the value of each share. Thus, for example, if a company has issued 1,000,000 shares of common stock and each share has a **par value** (the value of the stock recorded in the company's books) of $25, the total value of the company's outstanding capital stock recorded on the balance sheet would be $25,000,000 (1,000,000 × $25 = $25,000,000).

It is important to understand that common stock is valued at its historical cost regardless of its current selling price. Initially, most companies designate a stated or par value for the stock they issue and as each share is sold, an amount equal to the par value is reported in the common stock section of the balance sheet. Any differences between the selling price and par value are reported in the **paid in capital** portion of the balance sheet. For example, if a company initially issues stock with a par value of $25 but sells its shares for $30 (because that is their fair market value) $25 for each share sold would be reported as common stock and the remaining $5 per share would be recorded as additional paid in capital or (in some balance sheet formats) "paid in capital in excess of par."

Some companies also issue **preferred stock** that will pay its stockholders (owners) a fixed dividend. When more than one type of stock is issued by a company, the value of each type should be listed separately on the balance sheet.

As you learned earlier in Chapter 2, retained earnings are the final entry on the owners' equity portion of the balance sheet. **Retained earnings** refer simply to the accumulated amount of profits over the life of the business that have not been distributed as dividends. Thus these "earnings" have been "retained" (not spent). If no profits have been retained, the value of this entry is "zero." If net losses have occurred, the entry amount in this section may actually be a negative number.

When a company is organized as a sole proprietorship, the balance sheet reflects that single ownership. As a result, owners' equity is recorded, for example, as shown in Figure 4.6.

When a partnership operates the business, each partner's share is listed on the balance sheet. Thus, for example, if a company was owned by four partners with various proportions of ownership, the owners' equity portion of the balance sheet would list them as shown in Figure 4.7.

Just as you learned that the true value of assets may be difficult to determine, in a similar manner it can be difficult to accurately place a true value on ownership in a hospitality business. To illustrate, assume that Norma Jean owns a profitable, independent, Italian-style restaurant with balance sheet values of $1,000,000 in assets, $400,000 in liabilities, and thus an owners' equity entry of $600,000. It would appear that the "value" of her ownership is $600,000. Assume also, however, that a national competitor such as

FIGURE 4.6   Owners' Equity: Sole Proprietorship

Owner's Equity	
"Shane Carter": Capital	$450,000

FIGURE 4.7   Owners' Equity: Partnership

Owners' Equity	
Mathers, Marshal: Capital	$150,000
Jackson, Curt: Capital	$100,000
Young, Andre: Capital	$ 75,000
Jones, Russ: Capital	$ 75,000
	$400,000

Olive Garden is considering opening a restaurant across the street from Norma Jean's business. It is easy to see that the impact of that potential event could have a significant effect on the true "value" of Norma Jean's restaurant because it could materially affect the price she might receive if she attempted to sell her business. Because that is so, it is easy to see why many bankers and investors are extremely cautious when committing funds to hospitality operations. It is also why you may need to carefully take into consideration non-balance-sheet circumstances when evaluating a company's financial position, even when you are utilizing accurate data that is taken directly from the company's balance sheet and the footnotes that are intended to assist in further explaining the information it contains.

fun on the Web!

Understanding how to read financial statements is an important part of every restaurant manager's job. There are a variety of common-sense resources available that can help make this complex area easily understandable. To see one of the best, go to:

www.barnesandnoble.com

When you arrive, enter "Raymond Schmidgall" in the author search line to view a copy of his book *Restaurant Financial Basics*, published by John Wiley & Sons.

Balance Sheet Analysis

After the balance sheet has been prepared, managerial accountants use a variety of methods to analyze the information it contains. Three of the most common types of analysis are:

- Vertical (common-size) analysis
- Horizontal (comparative) analysis
- Ratio analysis

In the remaining portions of this chapter, vertical and horizontal analysis of the balance sheet will be explained. In Chapter 6 (Ratio Analysis), you will learn about the ratio analysis methods used to analyze balance sheets, as well as those ratio analysis methods used to analyze income statements (examined in Chapter 3) and statements of cash flows (to be examined in Chapter 5).

Vertical Analysis of Balance Sheets

In Chapter 3 you learned that income statements can be analyzed using vertical and horizontal techniques. In very similar ways, the balance sheet can be reviewed using these same techniques. Recall that, when using a vertical analysis approach, managers express values as a percentage of a total. When using vertical analysis on a balance sheet, the business's Total Assets take on a value of 100%. Total Liabilities and Owners' Equity also take a value of 100%. This can easily be seen in Figure 4.8, where Total Assets equals $46,491,950 (100%), and Total Liabilities and Owners' Equity equals $46,491,950 (100%).

When utilizing vertical analysis, individual asset categories are expressed as a percentage (fraction) of Total Assets. Individual liability and owners' equity classifications are expressed as a percentage of Total Liabilities and Owners' Equity. Thus, each percentage computed is a percent of a "common" number, which is why this type analysis is sometimes referred to as common-size analysis.

As with vertical analysis of the income statement (Chapter 3), vertical analysis of the balance sheet may be used to compare a unit's percentages with industry averages, other units in a corporation, or percentages from prior periods.

Horizontal Analysis of Balance Sheets

A second popular method of evaluating balance sheet information is the horizontal analysis method. As was true with the income statement (Chapter 3), a horizontal analysis of a balance sheet requires at least two different sets of data. Often the two sets of data evaluated for a business are its current period results and the results of some prior period. It is because of this "comparison" approach that the horizontal analysis technique is also called a comparative analysis. Managers who use horizontal analysis to evaluate the balance sheet may be concerned with comparisons such as their:

- Current period results vs. prior period results
- Current period results vs. budgeted (planned) results
- Current period results vs. the results of similar business units
- Current period results vs. industry averages

Figure 4.9 illustrates a horizontal (comparative) analysis of the Blue Lagoon Water Park Resort's balance sheet. In this analysis, comparisons are made between the balance sheet values shown in 2009 (last year) and those in 2010 (this year).

Determining Variance

The *dollar change* or variance shows changes from previously experienced levels, and will give you an indication of whether your numbers are improving, declining, or staying the same. To see how a horizontal comparison is actually computed, consider the cash account at the Blue Lagoon Water Park Resort reported in Figure 4.9.

FIGURE 4.8   Vertical (Common-Size) Balance Sheet Analysis

BLUE LAGOON WATER PARK RESORT
Balance Sheet
December 31, 2010

	$	%
Assets		
Current Assets		
Cash	2,314,750	5.0
Marketable Securities	3,309,600	7.1
Net Receivables	1,053,950	2.3
Inventories	1,497,200	3.2
Total Current Assets	8,175,500	17.6
Investments	5,023,500	10.8
Property and Equipment		
Land	7,712,550	16.6
Building	22,290,500	47.9
Furnishings and Equipment	7,289,000	15.7
Less Accumulated Depreciation	4,668,900	10.0
Net Property and Equipment	32,623,150	70.2
Other Assets	669,800	1.4
Total Assets	46,491,950	100.0
Liabilities and Owners' Equity		
Current Liabilities		
Accounts Payable	1,438,100	3.1
Notes Payable	1,319,900	2.8
Other Current Liabilities	1,264,600	2.7
Total Current Liabilities	4,022,600	8.6
Long-Term Liabilities		
Long-Term Debt	14,577,400	31.4
Total Liabilities	18,600,000	40.0
Owners' Equity		
Common Stock	3,000,000	6.4
Paid in Capital	18,775,100	40.4
Retained Earnings	6,116,850	13.2
Total Owners' Equity	27,891,950	60.0
Total Liabilities and Owners' Equity	46,491,950	100.0

FIGURE 4.9   Horizontal (Comparative) Balance Sheet Analysis

BLUE LAGOON WATER PARK RESORT
Balance Sheets
December 31, 2009 and 2010

	2009	2010	$ Change	% Change
Assets				
Current Assets				
Cash	2,370,800	2,314,750	(56,050)	(2.4)
Marketable Securities	4,109,600	3,309,600	(800,000)	(19.5)
Net Receivables	1,655,300	1,053,950	(601,350)	(36.3)
Inventories	897,200	1,497,200	600,000	66.9
Total Current Assets	9,032,900	8,175,500	(857,400)	(9.5)
Investments	4,223,500	5,023,500	800,000	18.9
Property and Equipment				
Land	7,712,550	7,712,550	0	0.0
Building	22,290,500	22,290,500	0	0.0
Furnishings and Equipment	5,063,655	7,289,000	2,225,345	43.9
Less Accumulated Depreciation	3,408,900	4,668,900	1,260,000	37.0
Net Property and Equipment	31,657,805	32,623,150	965,345	3.0
Other Assets	588,800	669,800	81,000	13.8
Total Assets	45,503,005	46,491,950	988,945	2.2
Liabilities and Owners' Equity				
Current Liabilities				
Accounts Payable	2,038,100	1,438,100	(600,000)	(29.4)
Notes Payable	2,104,255	1,319,900	(784,355)	(37.3)
Other Current Liabilities	1,814,600	1,264,600	(550,000)	(30.3)
Total Current Liabilities	5,956,955	4,022,600	(1,934,355)	(32.5)
Long-Term Liabilities				
Long-Term Debt	13,821,750	14,577,400	755,650	5.5
Total Liabilities	19,778,705	18,600,000	(1,178,705)	(6.0)
Owners' Equity				
Common Stock	2,925,000	3,000,000	75,000	2.6
Paid in Capital	17,850,100	18,775,100	925,000	5.2
Retained Earnings	4,949,200	6,116,850	1,167,650	23.6
Total Owners' Equity	25,724,300	27,891,950	2,167,650	8.4
Total Liabilities and Owners' Equity	45,503,005	46,491,950	988,945	2.2

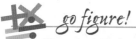 *go figure!*

To calculate the variance in cash, you would use the following formula:

> **Cash This Year − Cash Last Year = Variance**
>
> or
>
> **$2,314,750 − $2,370,800 = ($56,050)**

Effective managers are also interested in computing the percentage variance, or percentage change, from one time period to the next. Thus, the cash percentage variance is determined as follows:

$$\frac{(\text{Cash This Year} - \text{Cash Last Year})}{\text{Cash Last Year}} = \text{Percentage Variance}$$

or

$$\frac{(\$2,314,750 - \$2,370,800)}{\$2,370,800} = (2.4\%)$$

Of course, an alternative and shorter formula for computing the percentage variance is as follows:

$$\frac{\text{Variance}}{\text{Cash Last Year}} = \text{Percentage Variance}$$

or

$$\frac{(\$56,050)}{\$2,370,800} = (2.4\%)$$

Another way to compute the percentage variance is to use a math shortcut, as follows:

$$\left(\frac{\text{Cash This Year}}{\text{Cash Last Year}}\right) - 1 = \text{Percentage Variance}$$

or

$$\left(\frac{\$2,314,750}{\$2,370,800}\right) - 1 = (2.4\%)$$

FIGURE 4.10 Percentage Change Computation Help Box

The dollar differences between identical categories listed on two different balance sheets is easy to compute and is always the numerator in any percentage change (variation) calculation. The denominator, however, varies.

When computing % change or variation in data from:	Use as the Denominator:
Current Period to Prior Period	Prior Period's number
Current Period to Budget (Plan)	Budget (Plan) number
Current Period to Similar Business Unit	Similar Business Unit's number
Current Period to Industry Average	Industry Average number

Of course, *all dollar variances and percentage variances on the balance sheet can be calculated in the same way*. Understanding how to read the balance sheet and to compute variations from expected results or prior period results as well as variation from budget are important first steps in analyzing the balance sheet of a business.

When computing the percentage change between two sets of data, it can sometimes be confusing to identify the numerator (top number) and the denominator (bottom number) that should be used in the percentage calculation. If that is true in your case, Figure 4.10 can be helpful to you until you have made enough percentage change calculations to easily remember the proper procedure.

The importance of horizontal analysis calculations becomes more apparent when you consider that managerial accountants reviewing financial data are often concerned about *both* dollar change and percentage change because a dollar change may at first appear large, but when compared to its base figure, represent a very small percentage change. To illustrate, consider the "Other Assets" and "Total Assets" sections of Figure 4.9. The percentage change in Other Assets is 13.8%, which reflects a dollar change of $81,000. However, the percentage change in "Total Assets" is actually smaller at 2.2%, but represents a much larger dollar change of $988,945. Therefore, managers must be careful to accurately interpret the horizontal analysis when reporting dollar and percentage changes on the balance sheet.

Inflation Accounting

The second reason for computing percentage change in the preparation of balance sheets (as well as other financial documents) will be readily apparent to anyone who has ever talked to a parent, grandparent, or other individual about living in "the good old days." Such conversations will typically include hearing comments such as:

■ "When I was your age, I made $1 per hour and was glad to get the job!"
■ "When I bought my first car, gas was only 50 cents a gallon! Today gas prices are outrageous!"

■ "I would never pay $8 for a hamburger; when I was your age I paid $1.50 for a burger at a nice restaurant and it tasted just as good as the over-priced burgers they sell today!"

The individuals making statements such as these are right of course. They are right because the value of money simply changes over time. In 1976 a gallon of gasoline cost drivers about 50 cents a gallon. However, 1976 was over 30 years ago, and as economists (as well as managerial accountants) know well, if you don't adjust for **inflation** (the tendency for prices and costs to increase) just about *everything* is more expensive today than it was 30 years ago.

Because of the potential effects of inflation and **deflation** (the tendency for prices and costs to decrease), managerial accountants must know how to properly consider them when comparing financial data from two different time periods. For example, if the balance sheet shows that your company had $250,000 in cash in the bank three years ago and today you also have $250,000 cash in the bank, do you have as much cash in the bank today as you did three years ago? While the answer might appear obvious because the actual amount is the same, the **purchasing power** (amount of goods and services that can be bought) of that money is likely diminished due to the effects of inflation. That simply means that the $250,000 you have today is probably worth "less" than the same $250,000 you had three years ago. Because financial information is often compared from one period to the next, this potential "change" in dollar values can, if not evaluated properly, cause mistakes in your analysis and conclusions.

Fortunately, managerial accountants have developed special comparison techniques that do allow them to compare financial data from very different time periods by first adjusting for known inflation or deflation rates. Accounting for inflation (sometimes called **current dollar accounting**) can be very complex, and while an in-depth discussion of all its intricacies are beyond the scope of this text, as a managerial accountant you can easily understand the major issues addressed by inflation accounting and (in Chapter 12) learn basic techniques that will help you address these issues.

 *fun on the Web!*

Understanding how inflation accounting affects the valuation of a business is a concept that is more popular internationally than it is in the United States. One reason for this may be the importance of inflation and deflation to the relative values of currencies issued by governments. Hospitality managers who will work internationally must understand inflation accounting principles very well. One text that does a good job explaining the importance of accurately assigning the proper value to financial reporting data can be found at:

www.amazon.com

When you arrive, enter "John S. Hughes" in the author search line to view a copy of his book *Financial Accounting: A Valuation Emphasis*, published by John Wiley & Sons.

Because you have successfully completed this chapter, you have now learned how businesses record their profitability (on the income statement) as well as their financial wealth (on the balance sheet). In Chapter 5, you will discover how companies monitor and thus manage the cash that is generated by their businesses. It is often said in the hospitality business that "cash is king." In the coming chapter you will learn precisely why that is so true!

Apply What You Have Learned

Charlotte Lebioda grew up in the hotel business. Her parents owned and operated a 100-room limited-service hotel for 20 years. When Charlotte graduated from hospitality school, her parents retired, turning the business over to Charlotte.

Her hotel has an appraised value of $3,000,000 and total mortgage debt of $1,000,000, and her initial equity was $2,000,000.

The franchisor with which Charlotte's property is associated has approached her to see if she wants her to develop a second property to be located ten miles from the original hotel. The franchisor is proposing a 100-room property, which can be built at a cost of $4,000,000. In addition, the franchisor has indicated that a special financing arrangement has been put in place that allows existing franchisees to obtain 100% financing if their current properties score in the top 10% of the franchisor's annual inspection program. Charlotte's property qualifies for the special financing offer.

1. Develop The Accounting Formula for Charlotte's hotel as it exists prior to constructing the new hotel.
2. Develop The Accounting Formula for Charlotte's two properties, as it would exist if she built the new hotel.
3. Assume you were advising Charlotte. What would you tell her about the impact of the new hotel on the assets, liabilities, and owners' equity portions of her new Accounting Formula? What do you believe are the key factors Charlotte should consider before agreeing to build the new property?

Key Terms and Concepts

The following are terms and concepts discussed in the chapter that are important for you to know as a manager. To help you review, please define the following terms.

Lien	Current assets	Doubtful accounts
Wealth	Liquidity	Inventories
Account format	Cash	Prepaid expenses
(balance sheet)	Certificates of deposit (CDs)	Noncurrent (fixed) assets
Report format	Marketable securities	Investments
(balance sheet)	Net receivables	Securities

Sinking fund	Current liabilities	Retained earnings
Fair market value	Long-term liabilities	Inflation
Property and equipment	Common stock	Deflation
Other assets	Par value	Purchasing power
Goodwill	Paid in capital	Current dollar accounting
Amortized	Preferred stock	

Test Your Skills

Complete the Test Your Skills exercises by placing your answers in the shaded boxes.

1. Kwan's boss has asked him to evaluate his current assets on his balance sheet. However, Kwan is not exactly sure what his current assets are. Help Kwan by examining his balance sheet accounts and answering the following questions.

Balance Sheet Accounts

Investments	373,256	Paid in Capital	486,486
Other Current Liabilities	73,954	Accumulated Depreciation	203,144
Building	627,998	Inventories	51,818
Accounts Payable	213,659	Common Stock	133,421
Long-Term Debt	395,315	Prepaid Expenses	15,000
Cash	85,976	Retained Earnings	477,500
Furnishings and Equipment	308,334	Land	309,080
Notes Payable	47,858	Net Receivables	40,000
Marketable Securities	196,154	Other Assets	23,721

Using the balance sheet accounts:

a. Identify the current assets.

b. List them in the order of liquidity.

c. Calculate Total Current Assets.

d. Explain to Kwan why each current asset is listed in its particular order of liquidity.

Current Asset Accounts (In Order)	Dollar Amounts
Total Current Assets	

2. Aidan Norton owns Aidan's Lodge in a rural Midwestern town. His accountant is out with the flu, and Aidan has to develop his balance sheet without his accountant's help. Using the following balance sheet accounts, help Aidan complete his balance sheet.

Balance Sheet Accounts

Investments	1,275,000	Paid in Capital	3,000,000
Other Current Liabilities	1,590,000	Accumulated Depreciation	1,185,000
Building	3,250,000	Inventories	380,000
Accounts Payable	1,460,000	Common Stock	750,000
Long-Term Debt	1,800,000	Retained Earnings	2,865,000
Cash	587,500	Land	1,957,500
Furnishings and Equipment	1,850,000	Net Receivables	2,675,000
Notes Payable	335,000	Other Assets	170,000
Marketable Securities	840,000		

AIDAN'S LODGE			
Balance Sheet December 31, 20XX			
Assets		**Liabilities and Owners' Equity**	
Current Assets		Current Liabilities	
		Total Current Liabilities	
Total Current Assets			
		Long-Term Liabilities	
Property and Equipment		Total Liabilities	
		Owners' Equity	
Net Property and Equipment			
		Total Owners' Equity	
Total Assets		**Total Liabilities and Owners' Equity**	

3. Rachel owns a franchise restaurant of a large restaurant chain in New England. Help her calculate a vertical analysis of her balance sheet.

RACHEL'S RESTAURANT
Balance Sheet December 31, 20XX

	$	%
Assets		
Current Assets		
Cash	57,317	
Marketable Securities	130,769	
Net Receivables	80,000	
Inventories	34,545	
Total Current Assets		
Investments	248,837	
Property and Equipment		
Land	206,053	
Building	418,665	
Furnishings and Equipment	205,556	
Less Accumulated Depreciation	135,429	
Net Property and Equipment		
Other Assets	15,814	
Total Assets		
Liabilities and Owners' Equity		
Current Liabilities		
Accounts Payable	142,439	
Notes Payable	31,905	
Other Current Liabilities	147,907	
Total Current Liabilities		

Long-Term Liabilities		
Long-Term Debt	218,272	
Total Liabilities		
Owners' Equity		
Common Stock	78,947	
Paid in Capital	324,324	
Retained Earnings	318,333	
Total Owners' Equity		
Total Liabilities and Owners' Equity		

Rachel has been asked by her regional manager to compare her balance sheet percentages with the averages of the chain. Select percentages of the chain follow:

Select Chain Percentages (Vertical Analysis)

Cash	6.70%
Inventories	1.30%
Accounts Payable	10.50%
Notes Payable	1.10%

a. Compare Rachel's Cash % with the chain's %. Is it higher or lower? What might this mean?

b. Compare Rachel's Inventories % with the chain's %. Is it higher or lower? What might this mean?

c. Compare Rachel's Accounts Payable % with the chain's %. Is it higher or lower? What might this mean?

d. Compare Rachel's Notes Payable % with the chain's %. Is it higher or lower? What might this mean?

4. Rachel's regional manager (from Question 3) has asked Rachel to calculate a horizontal analysis of her balance sheet. Help Rachel calculate her horizontal analysis.

RACHEL'S RESTAURANT
Balance Sheet December 31, 20XX

	Last Year	This Year	$ Change	% Change
Assets				
Current Assets				
Cash	63,049	57,317		
Marketable Securities	104,615	130,769		
Net Receivables	64,000	80,000		
Inventories	48,363	34,545		
Total Current Assets				
Investments	323,488	248,837		
Property and Equipment				
Land	206,053	206,053		
Building	418,665	418,665		
Furnishings and Equipment	267,223	205,556		
Less Accumulated Depreciation	142,710	135,429		
Net Property and Equipment				
Other Assets	12,651	15,814		
Total Assets				
Liabilities and Owners' Equity				
Current Liabilities				
Accounts Payable	253,354	142,439		
Notes Payable	38,286	31,905		
Other Current Liabilities	192,279	147,907		
Total Current Liabilities				
Long-Term Liabilities				
Long-Term Debt	102,560	218,272		
Total Liabilities				

Owners' Equity				
Common Stock	102,631	78,947		
Paid in Capital	421,621	324,324		
Retained Earnings	254,666	318,333		
Total Owners' Equity				
Total Liabilities and Owners' Equity				

a. Rachel's regional manager told her to try to decrease her accounts receivable this year. Did she do this?

b. Rachel's regional manager told her to try to reduce her inventories this year to be more in line with the chain's average inventories. Did she do this?

c. Rachel's regional manager told her to pay more of her accounts payable this year. Did she do this?

d. Rachel's regional manager told her to pay off more of her total current liabilities this year. Did she do this?

e. Based on her ability to achieve the goals outlined in Questions a through d, do you think Rachel did a good job overall?

CHAPTER 5

The Statement of Cash Flows

In business, it is often said that "cash is king." Those who make this statement are actually making reference to the absolutely critical role that *cash* and *cash management* will play in the successful operation of your business. Those businesses that routinely generate cash in excess of their immediate needs for it are said to have a "positive cash flow." That is, more cash is flowing into the business than is being removed from it. Those businesses that do not generate enough cash to support their operations are said to have a "negative cash flow."

In this chapter you will learn about the Statement of Cash Flows (SCF). The SCF is a report that tells its readers about increases (inflows) and decreases (outflows) of cash of a business during a specific accounting period.

Typically, businesses accumulate cash (by making sales), spend cash (for necessary expenses), may invest their excess cash, or they can use it to pay down any debt the business may have. In some cases, excess cash generated by the business will be returned to its owners in the form of profits or dividends.

The SCF examines the cash flows resulting from a business's operating, investing, and financing activities, and in this chapter you will learn about the sources and uses of funds that affect cash availability. As well, you will learn how managers actually create an SCF. Finally, you will discover how hospitality managers read, analyze, and utilize the important information that is contained in an SCF.

CHAPTER OUTLINE

- Understanding Cash Flows
- The Purpose of the Statement of Cash Flows
- Sources and Uses of Funds
- Creating the Statement of Cash Flows
- Statement of Cash Flows Analysis
- Apply What You Have Learned
- Key Terms and Concepts
- Test Your Skills

LEARNING OUTCOMES

At the conclusion of this chapter, you will be able to:

✓ State the reason cash flows are critical to the operation of a successful business.
✓ Identify sources and uses of funds to assist in the creation of a statement of cash flows.
✓ Create a statement of cash flows using an income statement and two balance sheets.
✓ Analyze a statement of cash flows to better manage the cash flows of your own business.

Understanding Cash Flows

If you manage your own living expenses budget, then you already have a basic understanding of cash flows. Assume for example, that you have income from a variety of sources. These sources may include money paid to you from a job you perform, income from parents or other family members intended to help you with school or living expenses, and interest you may earn on savings accounts held in your name. In addition, you are most likely to have living and school expenses that must be paid. You already know that you must have enough money on hand to pay your bills as they become due, but you will also find that if you do not have sufficient cash to pay your bills, it will cost you *more* to pay those bills than it otherwise would have.

go figure!

To illustrate, consider the case of Lauren and Trahile. Both are college students attending State University. Each lives off campus. Each will receive $10,000 during the semester to pay for their books, tuition, and needed school supplies. All of Lauren's money is deposited in the bank at the beginning of the semester. Trahile will receive his money in four equal, monthly installments of $2,500 each. Each will receive the same amount of money in the semester and it should be enough to pay for their school expenses. Assume that, on September 5 of their senior year in college, each must buy their books, pay their tuition, and purchase their supplies. For Lauren, cash payments to others (her cash outflows), are as follows:

Books	$ 500
Tuition	$8,000
Supplies	$ 750
Total Payments Due	$9,250

Lauren will easily pay all of her bills with the money that is in her savings account.

Since Trahile has only $2,500 in his account (because the balance of his money will be paid in equal installments over the course of the semester), he cannot fully pay the bills due. Because this is true, he will likely find that:

1. He cannot pay cash for everything, and if he pays for his books via credit card, his bank will charge him interest on the "borrowed" funds until they are repaid.
2. He will not be able to completely pay his tuition, which may result in penalties or interest due on the unpaid amount, or he may be forced to take out an interest accruing student loan to pay the full amount.
3. He may choose to buy only part of the supplies he needs, thus conserving cash but putting him at a disadvantage when it comes to competing with the other students in his classes.

The point to remember is that Trahile will face decisions, challenges, and additional expenses in paying his bills that Lauren simply will not face. Clearly, having access to cash at the right time (versus having the right amount of cash) is important to individuals. As you will learn in this chapter, it is also critically important to businesses.

The Purpose of the Statement of Cash Flows

For many years, businesses that issued income statements (see Chapter 3) and balance sheets (see Chapter 4) to those outside the company were encouraged to also supply a document called the **statement of changes in financial position**, or funds statement. The intent of this statement was to indicate how cash inflows and outflows affected the business during a specific accounting period.

In 1961, the American Institute of Certified Public Accountants (AICPA) officially recommended that a funds statement be included with the income statement and balance sheet in annual reports to shareholders. In 1971 the Accounting Principles Board (APB) officially made the funds statement one of the three primary financial documents required in annual reports to shareholders. In late 1987, the Financial Accounting Standards Board (FASB) called for a statement of cash flows to replace the more general funds statement. The **Statement of Cash Flows (SCF)** shows all sources and uses of funds from operating, investing, and financing activities of a business. Additionally, the FASB, in an effort to help investors and creditors better predict future cash flows, specified a universal SCF format that is still used today.

W fun on the Web!

The mission of the Financial Accounting Standards Board is to establish and improve standards of financial accounting and reporting for the guidance and education of the public, including issuers, auditors, and users of financial information. To stay up to date with their activities, periodically visit their website at:

www.fasb.org

The reason the FASB ultimately required the statement of cash flows can be easily understood if you consider the case of Rolando Gamez. Rolando owns and operates three nationally franchised coffee shops in his town. On a monthly basis, Rolondo and his accountant prepare an individual income statement for each coffee shop, as well as a **consolidated income statement** that combines the revenue, expense, and profit information from each individual coffee shop into one (consolidated) income statement. As well, each month they prepare an updated balance sheet for Rolondo's business. Because you learned about income statements and balance sheets earlier in this text, you realize that Rolando can discover much about his business by carefully studying these two financial statements. What he could not learn from studying them, however, is:

- How can current assets have decreased if I made a profit in the accounting period?
- Do I have cash available for investments like stocks and bonds?
- Do I have cash available for the expansion of my business or will I need to borrow money?
- If I take money out of my business in the form of profits paid to me, will the business have enough remaining cash to meet its operational needs?
- How can I take out cash if the business is losing money?

As you can see there are a variety of questions Rolando would like answered that simply cannot be answered only with the information found in his income statement or balance sheet.

The cash inflows and outflows of a business are of significant importance to a business's owners, investors, lenders, creditors, and managers. The presentation of accurate information about cash flows should enable investors in a business to:

1. Predict the amount of cash that can be distributed via profit payouts or dividend distributions.
2. Evaluate the possible risk associated with a business.

In Chapter 4 you learned that liquidity refers to the ease in which a current asset can be converted to cash. Thus, liquidity can also be considered as "nearness to cash." In a similar manner, **solvency** refers to the ability of a business to pay its debts as they become due. Because most debts incurred by a business are repaid in cash, solvency is an important measure of a firm's likelihood to remain a going concern, (a business that generates enough cash to stay in business). If a business is not considered by lenders and investors to be a going concern, that business will likely find that its ability to borrow money is severely diminished. If it can borrow money, it will find that the money it does borrow will come with the increased costs that reflect the higher risk associated with lending money to a business that does not consistently demonstrate a strong positive cash flow. This is so because, when cash flows are not positive, investors will demand higher return on investment (ROI) levels to compensate for the greater risk they are taking, and lenders will seek higher interest rates to compensate themselves for that same higher risk level.

The SCF prepared by Rolando will report the movement of cash into and out of his business in a given time period. As you learned in Chapter 4, cash on a balance sheet is considered to be a current asset. **Cash**, in this case, refers to currency, checks on hand, and deposits in banks. It is important to understand that cash is not synonymous with the term "revenue" or "sales." To illustrate, assume that you traveled by plane to Nashville, Tennessee, to attend the Country Music Association Awards held in the Grand Ole Opry theater adjacent to the 3,000+ room Opryland Hotel. If you stayed two nights at that Gaylord Hotel's property and paid for your room with a credit card, the hotel would have made a sale (created revenue), but the hotel would not have an immediate increase in its cash position. It will not actually increase its cash position until your bank deposits the money you owed to the Opryland Hotel into the hotel's bank account. This is a process that typically takes several days. As a result, the hotel would have increased revenues, but not cash, on the day of your departure from the property.

In addition to understanding the nature of cash, you should also know that **cash equivalents** are short-term, temporary investments such as treasury bills, certificates of deposit, or commercial paper that can be quickly and easily converted to cash. In our coffee shops example, Rolondo will use cash to pay his bills, repay loans, and make investments, allowing him to provide the goods and services desired by his customers. The SCF is designed to report his business's **sources and uses of funds** (inflows and outflows of money affecting the cash position) as well as his beginning and ending cash and cash equivalents balances for each accounting period.

Sources and Uses of Funds

One tool that can be used to help you identify money inflows and outflows of a hospitality business is to calculate its sources and uses of funds from its balance sheets from last period to this period. Sources represent inflows and uses represent outflows of funds for the hospitality business.

FIGURE 5.1 Sources and Uses of Funds for Assets

Assets	Increases	Decreases
Current Assets		
Cash	Use	Source
Marketable Securities	Use	Source
Net Receivables	Use	Source
Inventories	Use	Source
Prepaid Expenses	Use	Source
Investments	Use	Source
Property and Equipment		
Land	Use	Source
Building	Use	Source
Furnishings and Equipment	Use	Source
Accumulated Depreciation	Source	Use
Other Assets	Use	Source

When comparing assets from last period's balance sheet to this period's balance sheet, decreases in assets represent sources of funds and increases in assets represent uses of funds as shown in Figure 5.1. As you will notice, accumulated depreciation behaves in an opposite manner to the other assets. This is because depreciation is a contra asset account (see Chapter 2).

To explain why this is so, consider the direct effect of increasing or decreasing each asset account using the examples below.

Asset	Source or Use	Example
Decrease in Cash	Source	Cash on the balance sheet represents an account in the bank. When you withdraw money from the bank (decrease the cash account), you have a source of funds. You literally have the cash in hand to spend!
Increase in Cash	Use	Cash on the balance sheet represents an account in the bank. When you deposit the cash into your bank account (increase in the cash account), you do not have the money in your hand to spend. In effect, the bank is "using" your money, so it is a use of funds.
Decrease in Marketable Securities	Source	Marketable securities are stocks and bonds you own from other companies that you will keep for a short term (less than a year). If you sell these securities, you receive money from the sale, which is a source of funds. This decreases the amount of securities you own.

Asset	Source or Use	Example
Increase in Marketable Securities	Use	Marketable securities are stocks and bonds you own from other companies that you will keep for a short term (less than a year). If you buy these securities, you pay money for the purchase, which is a use of funds. This increases the amount of securities you own.
Decrease in Net Receivables	Source	Accounts receivable represents money that guests owe you for products or services that you have provided. If they pay you what they owe, this decreases accounts receivable and provides a source of funds for you.
Increase in Net Receivables	Use	Accounts receivable represents money that guests owe you for products or services that you have provided. If accounts receivable increases, then that means that more people owe you money. Since you have provided products or services without being paid, this is a use of funds for you.
Decrease in Inventories	Source	If you sell your inventory (e.g., food products) to your guests and they pay you for it, then it is a source of funds. Selling the food decreases your inventory.
Increase in Inventories	Use	If you buy more inventories (e.g., food products) from your suppliers, then it is a use of funds. Buying the food increases your inventory.
Decrease in Prepaid Expenses	Source	Prepaid expenses are items that will be used within a year's time, but which must be completely paid for at the time of purchase. As the prepaid expense is amortized throughout the year, it decreases. Since it was prepaid, it is a source of funds.
Increase in Prepaid Expenses	Use	Prepaid expenses are items that will be used within a year's time, but which must be completely paid for at the time of purchase. If prepaid expenses increase, that means that an item was paid in advance, thus it is a use of funds.
Decrease in Investments	Source	Investments are stocks and bonds you own from other companies that you will keep for the long term (more than a year). If you sell these securities, you receive money from the sale, which is a source of funds. This decreases the amount of securities you own.

Asset	Source or Use	Example
Increase in Investments	Use	Investments are stocks and bonds you own from other companies that you will keep for the long term (more than a year). If you buy these securities, you pay money for the purchase, which is a use of funds. This increases the amount of securities you own.
Decrease in Property and Equipment	Source	If you sell property or equipment, then it is a source of funds. Selling the property or equipment decreases this account.
Increase in Property and Equipment	Use	If you buy property or equipment, then it is a use of funds. Buying the property or equipment increases this account.
Increase in Accumulated Depreciation	Source	Depreciation is subtracted on the income statement to lower income, and thus, lower taxes. If you increase the amount of depreciation that you subtract, you decrease your taxes, thus providing a source of funds.
Decrease in Accumulated Depreciation	Use	Depreciation is subtracted on the income statement to lower income, and thus, lower taxes. If you decrease the amount of depreciation that you subtract, you increase your taxes, thus providing a use of funds.
Decrease in Other Assets	Source	An example of another asset is restricted cash, which is cash deposited in a separate account for a restricted purpose, such as retiring long-term debt. When you withdraw money from the bank account (decrease the restricted cash account), you have a source of funds. You literally have the cash in hand to spend!
Increase in Other Assets	Use	An example of another asset is restricted cash, which is cash deposited in a separate account for a restricted purpose, such as retiring long-term debt. When you deposit cash into your bank account (increase in the restricted cash account), you do not have the money in your hand to spend. In effect, the bank is "using" your money, so it is a use of funds.

Alternatively, increases in liabilities and owners' equity represent sources of funds and decreases in liabilities and owners' equity represent uses of funds as shown in Figure 5.2.

To explain why this is so, consider the direct effect of increasing or decreasing each liability and owners' equity account using the following examples.

FIGURE 5.2   Sources and Uses of Funds for Liabilities and Owners' Equity

Liabilities and Owners' Equity	Increases	Decreases
Current Liabilities		
Accounts Payable	Source	Use
Notes Payable	Source	Use
Other Current Liabilities	Source	Use
Long-Term Liabilities		
Long-Term Debt	Source	Use
Owners' Equity		
Common Stock	Source	Use
Paid in Capital	Source	Use
Retained Earnings	Source	Use

Liabilities and Owners' Equity	Source or Use	Example
Increase in Accounts Payable	Source	Accounts payable represents money that you owe to your suppliers for products or services that you have received. If accounts payable increases, you have been provided products or services without having paid for them. So, this is a source of funds for you.
Decrease in Accounts Payable	Use	Accounts payable represents money that you owe to your suppliers for products or services that you have received. If you pay what you owe, this decreases accounts payable and provides a use of funds for you.
Increase in Notes Payable	Source	Notes payable are short-term loans (less than a year). If you increase notes payable by borrowing money, this is a source of funds for you.
Decrease in Notes Payable	Use	Notes payable are short-term loans (less than a year). If you decrease notes payable by paying back money you borrowed, this is a use of funds for you.
Increase in Other Current Liabilities	Source	An example of other current liabilities is accrued wages. Accrued wages are wages that you owe to your employees for work they have already done. (They may have not been paid yet due to the timing of work and the date of the balance sheet.) If you have benefited from their work, but have not paid them yet, this is a source of funds for you.

Liabilities and Owners' Equity	Source or Use	Example
Decrease in Other Current Liabilities	Use	An example of other current liabilities is accrued wages. Accrued wages are wages that you owe to your employees for work they have already done. (They may have not been paid yet due to the timing of work and the date of the balance sheet.) If you have paid them for their work, thus decreasing other current liabilities, then it is a use of funds for you.
Increase in Long-Term Debt	Source	Long-term debt includes long-term loans (more than a year). If you increase long-term debt by borrowing money, this is a source of funds for you.
Decrease in Long-Term Debt	Use	Long-term debt includes long-term loans (more than a year). If you decrease long-term debt by paying back the money you owe, this is a use of funds for you.
Increase in Capital Stock (Common Stock + Paid in Capital)	Source	Common stock and paid in capital represent your company stocks you have sold to stockholders. If you sell these stocks, you receive money from the sale, which is a source of funds. This increases the amount of issued stocks on your balance sheet.
Decrease in Capital Stock (Common Stock + Paid in Capital)	Use	Common stock and paid in capital represent your company stocks you have sold to stockholders. If you buy back these stocks (also called treasury stock), you pay money for them, which is a use of funds.
Increase in Retained Earnings	Source	Retained earnings represent the accumulated account of profits over the life of the business that have not been distributed as dividends. If your retained earnings increases, that means you have increased your net income for the year, thus providing a source of funds.
Decrease in Retained Earnings	Use	Retained earnings represent the accumulated account of profits over the life of the business that have not been distributed as dividends. If your retained earnings decreases, that may mean you may have experienced a loss in net income for the year, thus providing a use of funds.

FIGURE 5.3   Trick for Remembering Sources and Uses of Funds

Sources	Uses
↓ Assets*	↑ Assets*
↑ Liabilities	↓ Liabilities
↑ Owners' Equity	↓ Owners' Equity

* Remember that depreciation is a contra asset account and behaves
the opposite of all other assets, so ↑ in depreciation is a source
and ↓ of depreciation is a use.

Now that you understand the "why" behind sources and uses of funds, you may begin to see a pattern emerging. Specifically, assets all behave the same (with the exception of depreciation), liabilities all behave the same, and owners' equity accounts all behave the same. Figure 5.3 shows you a trick to help you remember all of this! Up arrows represent "increases" and down arrows represent "decreases." Assets in each column have opposite arrows from liabilities and owners' equity. Also, arrows in the left column are opposite of those in the right column. If you can remember only one, you can remember all the rest. For example, if you sell a piece of equipment, then the asset arrow is down, and it is a source of funds. Once you have that arrow correct, then you can remember the directions of the other arrows. Be careful, though! If you get your one example backwards, then *all* of the others are wrong! Memorize Figure 5.3; it will help you immensely!

Now, let's turn to an example of sources and uses of funds with numbers. The 2009 and 2010 balance sheets of the Blue Lagoon Water Park Resort are shown in Figure 5.4. Follow the steps below to calculate Sources and Uses of Funds for Blue Lagoon.

1. Draw the chart shown in Figure 5.3 to help you identify sources and uses of funds.
2. Draw up arrows ↑ and down arrows ↓ next to the balance sheets to indicate increases and decreases in the accounts from 2009 to 2010.
3. Calculate the difference in each account from 2009 to 2010.
4. Place the difference in each account under the appropriate Sources or Uses column. Do *not* calculate subtotals and totals.
5. Add the numbers in the Sources column and then add the numbers in the Uses column.
6. The totals in each column should equal each other. If they do, you have identified the correct sources and uses of funds, and you are finished!
7. If the totals in each column do *not* equal each other, calculate the difference between the columns and divide by 2. This is the amount of your mistake.

Now that you fully understand sources and uses of funds, we will turn our attention to creating the statement of cash flows.

FIGURE 5.4   Sources and Uses of Funds for Blue Lagoon Water Park Resort

BLUE LAGOON WATER PARK RESORT
Balance Sheets
December 31, 2009 and 2010

	2009	2010		Sources	Uses
Assets					
Current Assets					
Cash	2,370,800	2,314,750	↓	56,050	
Marketable Securities	4,109,600	3,309,600	↓	800,000	
Net Receivables	1,655,300	1,053,950	↓	601,350	
Inventories	897,200	1,497,200	↑		600,000
Total Current Assets	9,032,900	8,175,500			
Investments	4,223,500	5,023,500	↑		800,000
Property and Equipment					
Land	7,712,550	7,712,550	-		
Building	22,290,500	22,290,500	-		
Furnishings and Equipment	5,063,655	7,289,000	↑		2,225,345
Less Accumulated Depreciation	3,408,900	4,668,900	↑	1,260,000	
Net Property and Equipment	31,657,805	32,623,150			
Other Assets	588,800	669,800	↑		81,000
Total Assets	45,503,005	46,491,950			
Liabilities and Owners' Equity					
Current Liabilities					
Accounts Payable	2,038,100	1,438,100	↓		600,000
Notes Payable	2,104,255	1,319,900	↓		784,355
Other Current Liabilities	1,814,600	1,264,600	↓		550,000
Total Current Liabilities	5,956,955	4,022,600			
Long-Term Liabilities					
Long-Term Debt	13,821,750	14,577,400	↑	755,650	
Total Liabilities	19,778,705	18,600,000			
Owners' Equity					
Common Stock	2,925,000	3,000,000	↑	75,000	
Paid in Capital	17,850,100	18,775,100	↑	925,000	
Retained Earnings	4,949,200	6,116,850	↑	1,167,650	
Total Owners' Equity	25,724,300	27,891,950			
Total Liabilities and Owners' Equity	45,503,005	46,491,950			
Total Sources and Uses of Funds				**5,640,700**	**5,640,700**

Creating the Statement of Cash Flows

The statement of cash flows should be prepared just as often as you prepare your income statement and balance sheet. In order to build a statement of cash flows, you will need the following:

- Income statement for this year, including a statement of retained earnings
- Balance sheet from last year
- Balance sheet from this year

A Condensed Income Statement and Statement of Retained Earnings for the Blue Lagoon Water Park Resort for the year 2010 is shown in Figure 5.10. A **condensed income statement** for a hotel reports the revenues, expenses, and profits in a summary format, absent of specific departmental and undistributed expense details. Departmental and undistributed expenses are reported only as a summary of cost of sales, payroll and related expenses, and other expenses. The condensed income statement is sufficient for the purposes of preparing a statement of cash flows. In addition, a **statement of retained earnings** reports the changes in retained earnings (accumulated account of profits over the life of the business that have not been distributed as dividends) from last year to this year. From Figure 5.10, you can see that the statement of retained earnings is calculated as follows:

Retained Earnings, December 31, 2009	$4,949,200
Net Income for 2010	+ 1,946,090
Subtotal	= 6,895,290
Cash Dividends Paid in 2010	− 778,440
Retained Earnings, December 31, 2010	=$6,116,850

You will also need last year's balance sheet and this year's balance sheet to report the changes in balance sheet accounts from one year to the next. This will show you the sources and uses of funds that will affect the cash changes you will report on the statement of cash flows. Figure 5.11 shows the Blue Lagoon Water Park Resort's 2009 and 2010 balance sheets (with sources and uses of funds) as were calculated earlier in this chapter.

The format of an SCF consists of the following:

- Cash flow from operating activities
- Cash flow from investing activities
- Cash flow from financing activities
- Net changes in cash
- Supplementary schedules

Figure 5.5 is an example of the standard format used to prepare a statement of cash flows.

FIGURE 5.5 Statement of Cash Flows Format

Cash Provided (inflow) or Used (outflow) by:	
Operating activities	$XXX
Investing activities	$XXX
Financing activities	$XXX
Net increase (decrease) in cash	$XXX
Cash at beginning of the accounting period	$XXX
Cash at the end of the accounting period	$XXX
Supplementary Schedule of Noncash Investing and Financing Activities	$XXX
Supplementary Disclosure of Cash Flow Information	
Cash paid during the year for:	
Interest	$XXX
Income taxes	$XXX

Cash Flow from Operating Activities

Cash flow from operating activities is the result of all of the transactions and events that normally make up a business's day-to-day activities. These include cash generated from selling goods or providing services, as well as income from items such as interest and dividends. Operating activities will also include your cash payments for items such as inventory, payroll, taxes, interest, utilities, and rent. The net amount of cash provided (or used) by operating activities is a key figure on a statement of cash flows because it shows cash flows that managers can control the most.

To better understand this first of the three SCF classifications, recall Paige Vincent, the manager of the Blue Lagoon Water Park Resort who was introduced in Chapter 1. Paige's operation will have cash inflows from the following operating activities:

- Sales of rooms, food, beverages, and resort services
- Interest income from money held in bank accounts
- Dividend income (if any)
- Income from all other noninvestment or financing activities (for example money received to settle a lawsuit or for an insurance settlement)

Of course, Paige will incur operating activity expenses that cause cash to flow out of her business. These will include cash outflows for:

- Food, beverages, and rooms-related supplies and materials purchased from the hotel's vendors for resale to guests

■ Salaries, wages, and taxes for employees

■ Items such as rent, utilities, insurance, and other related costs of operating the business

■ Taxes, duties, fines, fees, and penalties imposed by government entities

■ All other payments not defined as investing or financing activities (for example, money paid to settle a lawsuit and cash contributions to charities)

Figure 5.6 summarizes the cash inflows and outflows associated with operating activities.

The first step in creating a statement of cash flows is to develop a summary of cash inflows and outflows resulting from operating activities. As you can see from Figure 5.6, you will need information provided on the income statement including sales, expenses, and thus, net income.

There are two methods that are used in calculating and reporting the amount of cash flow from operating activities on the statement of cash flows. These are the indirect method and the direct method. Although both produce identical results, the indirect method is more popular because it more *easily* reconciles the difference between net income and the net cash flow provided by operations. An easier method (when the results are the same) is nearly always a better accounting approach to use than a harder one, so the indirect method is the one you will now learn.

When using the indirect method, you start with the figure for net income (taken from your income statement) and then adjust this amount up or down to account for any income statement entries that do not actually provide or use cash. Unfortunately, this is a bit more complex than it would at first seem. In Chapter 2, the significant advantages of using an accrual accounting system for developing an income statement were carefully explained. As you may recall, in an accrual accounting system, revenue is recorded when it is earned, regardless of when it is collected, and expenses are recorded when they are incurred, regardless of when they are paid. Therefore, the accrual income statement must be converted to a cash basis in order to report cash flow from operating activities.

FIGURE 5.6   Operating Activities – Cash Inflows and Outflows Summary

Cash Inflows

■ Sales of products and services (including accounts receivable)

■ Interest and dividend income*

■ Income from all other noninvestment or financing activities

Cash Outflows

■ Expenses related to the sales of products and services (including inventories and accounts payable)

■ Other operating and nonoperating expenses

■ All other payments not defined as investing or financing activities

---

* Note: While many in business feel that cash inflows from interest or dividends would be better considered as investing or financing activities, the FASB classifies them as operating activities (which means you must also!).

Although there may be several items on the income statement that may need to be adjusted from an accrual basis to a cash basis, the two most common are

■ Depreciation, and
■ Gains/losses from a sale of investments/equipment.

Depreciation is a method of allocating the cost of a fixed asset over the useful life of the asset (see Chapter 2). More important, however, depreciation is subtracted from the income statement primarily to lower income, and thus lower taxes. The portion of assets depreciated each year is considered "tax deductible" because it is subtracted on the income statement before taxes are calculated (see Chapter 3). Because this is so, net income is "artificially" lowered by subtracting depreciation. Specifically, no one is writing a check to "depreciation" and no money is actually being spent. Therefore, the cash is still there! In order to adjust net income to reflect actual cash, then, depreciation must be added back as shown in Figure 5.12.

In order to calculate cash flow from operating activities, net income also needs to be adjusted for gains/losses from a sale of investments/equipment. A gain on a sale of an investment/equipment occurs when the original cost of the investment/equipment is lower than the price at which it is sold at a later date. Conversely, a loss on a sale of an investment/equipment occurs when the original cost of the investment/equipment is higher than the price at which it is sold at a later date.

go figure!

Assume Archie McNally had, for $150,000, purchased some land to expand his business. Five years later he sold the land for $100,000. The difference between the purchase price and the selling price is $50,000 ($150,000 − $100,000).

Purchase Price	$150,000
Selling Price	− $100,000
Loss on Sale	= $ 50,000

Archie lost money on the deal. Therefore, he can subtract the loss of $50,000 from his income statement to reduce his taxes. However, just like depreciation, he did not write a check for "loss" to anyone, and therefore, his cash is still there! In order to adjust net income to reflect actual cash on his statement of cash flows, the $50,000 loss would be added back. In addition, the $100,000 of land that he sold would be shown on the investing activity portion of the statement of cash flows. Alternatively, a gain on the sale would result in an addition to his income statement. A gain, then, would have to be subtracted from net income on the statement of cash flows.

The remaining adjustments to net income when calculating cash flow from operating activities come from the sources and uses of funds that you calculated from your balance sheets. *Sources of funds are shown as a positive number on the statement of cash flows and uses of funds are shown as a negative number on the statement of cash flows.*

In general, the sources and uses of funds you need for cash flow from operating activities will come from your current assets and current liabilities since these typically represent current activities. The exceptions to this are marketable securities, which belongs in investing activities, and notes payable (short-term debt), which belongs in financing activities.

Cash Flow from Investing Activities

An investment (see Chapter 4) can be understood simply as the acquisition of an asset for the purpose of increasing future financial return or benefits. **Cash flow from investing activities** summarizes this part of a business's action. A business's investing activities include those transactions and events involving the purchase and sale of marketable securities, investments, land, buildings, equipment, and other assets not generally purchased for resale.

Thus, for example, if Paige Vincent elected to purchase land adjacent to the Blue Lagoon Water Park Resort for the purpose of expanding the size of the resort's parking lot, the cash inflows and outflows associated with that purchase would be accounted for as an investment activity. This is true because, in this situation, Paige is buying an item (land) that is not intended to be re-sold to guests but rather that is intended to improve the long-term financial performance of the resort. Thus, while the purchase may be critical to the continued success of her business, it is a purchase that is not recorded in her cash flow from operating activities. Investing activities are not classified as operating activities because, if you are a hospitality manager, your investing activities are considered to have less of a direct relationship to the central, ongoing operation of your business than will your sale of hotel rooms, food, beverages, or the other services you will provide your guests.

Figure 5.7 summarizes the most common examples of cash inflows and outflows related to the investing activities of a business.

The cash flow from investing activities comes from the sources and uses of funds that you calculated from your balance sheets. *Sources of funds are shown as a positive number on*

FIGURE 5.7 Investing Activities – Cash Inflows and Outflows Summary

Cash Inflows
- The sale of marketable securities (short-term investments) owned by the business
- The sale of long-term investments
- The sale of property, buildings, furnishings, equipment, and other assets
- Income from all other nonoperating or financing activities

Cash Outflows
- The purchase of marketable securities (short-term investments)
- The purchase of long-term investments
- The purchase of property, buildings, furnishings, equipment, and other assets
- All other payments not defined as operating or financing activities

the statement of cash flows and uses of funds are shown as a negative number on the statement of cash flows.

In general, the sources and uses of funds you need for cash flow from investing activities will come from your long-term assets (investments, property and equipment, and other assets). The exception to this is marketable securities, which is a current asset that belongs in investing activities.

Cash Flow from Financing Activities

The third and final of the three cash inflow and outflow activity summaries that make up a complete SCF relates to the financing activities of a business. **Cash flow from financing activities** refers to a variety of actions including:

- Obtaining resources (funds) from the owners of a business (e.g., by selling company stocks)
- Providing owners with a return of their original investment amount (e.g., payment of dividends)
- Borrowing money
- Repaying borrowed money

When a business corporation sells portions of ownership in itself via the issuance of stock, declares a stock dividend (payment to stockholders based upon the number of stock shares they own), re-purchases its own stock, borrows money, or pays back money, it is engaging in a financing activity.

It is important to remember that, even though repayments of loans are considered a financing activity, interest paid and interest received are classified as operating activities (as part of the income statement). Thus, for example, if Paige Vincent sought to purchase the parcel of land she desired for her parking lot expansion by taking out a loan to buy it, cash payments made to reduce the **principal** (the amount borrowed) of the loan would be considered cash flow related to a financing activity, while any interest paid to secure the loan would be considered an operating expense. Loans, notes, and mortgages are all examples of financing activities that affect cash flows.

Figure 5.8 summarizes the most common examples of cash inflows and outflows related to the financing activities of a business.

The cash flow from financing activities comes from the sources and uses of funds that you calculated from your balance sheets. *Sources of funds are shown as a positive number on the statement of cash flows and uses of funds are shown as a negative number on the statement of cash flows.*

In general, the sources and uses of funds you need for cash flow from financing activities will come from your long-term debt and equity. The exception to this is notes payable (short-term debt), which is a current liability that belongs in financing activities. Also, dividends paid must be recorded here because that is a cash outflow from net income.

FIGURE 5.8   Financing Activities–Cash Inflows and Outflows Summary

Cash Inflows
■ Funds obtained from short-term borrowing
■ Funds obtained from long-term borrowing
■ Proceeds from the issuance (sale) of stock
■ Income from all other nonoperating or investment activities

Cash Outflows
■ Repayment of loans (short-term and long-term loans)
■ Re-purchase of issued stock
■ Dividend payments to stockholders
■ All other payments not defined as operating or investing activities

FIGURE 5.9   General Additions and Subtractions to the Statement of Cash Flows

Operating Activities
Net income
+/– Depreciation
+/– Losses/gains from the sale of investments/equipment
+/– Current assets (except marketable securities)
+/– Current liabilities (except notes payable)
Investing Activities
+/– Marketable securities
+/– Investments
+/– Property and equipment
+/– Other assets
Financing Activities
+/– Notes payable
+/– Long-term debt
+/– Common stocks and paid in capital
+/– Dividends paid

In general, additions and subtractions to the statement of cash flows are shown in Figure 5.9. This is easy to remember if you think in terms of the balance sheet. With the exceptions noted, operating activities are developed using current assets and current liabilities, investing activities are developed using long-term assets, and financing activities are developed using long-term debt and owners' equity.

Net Changes in Cash

Net changes in cash represent all cash inflows minus cash outflows from operating, investing, and financing activities. It is, in effect, the total net change when combining all three activities. This net change in cash must equal the difference between the cash account at the beginning of the accounting period and the cash account at the end of the accounting period. If the net change does not equal the difference between the beginning and ending cash balances, then the statement of cash flows was not prepared properly. In other words, this section of the statement of cash flows can be used to check your math!

go figure!

For example, assume Rolando (from earlier in this chapter) prepared his statement of cash flows, which resulted in the following:

Cash Flow from Operating Activities	($150,000)
Cash Flow from Investing Activities	$100,000
Cash Flow from Financing Activities	+ $ 25,000
Net decrease in cash	= ($ 25,000)
Cash at the beginning of the period	$625,000
Cash at the end of the period	$600,000

Notice that his net decrease in cash ($25,000) equals the difference between his cash at the beginning and the ending of the period,

$$\$625{,}000 - \$600{,}000 = \$25{,}000$$

Supplementary Schedules

Supplementary schedules to the statement of cash flows include additional information reporting noncash investing and financing activities and cash paid for interest and income taxes.

Businesses can, of course, increase their assets and/or decrease their liabilities without utilizing cash. Consider, for example, the owners of a piece of land that Rolando seeks to buy for a new coffee shop told him that they would be willing to exchange the piece of land for shares of his stock. If he were to accept the offer (valued at $100,000), his balance sheet would, of course, change (with an increase in the asset portion of the balance sheet titled "Land," and a corresponding increase in the Owners' Equity portion of the balance sheet), but the cash position of his business would not have changed because this would have been a **noncash transaction**. Any noncash investing and financing transactions undertaken by a company should be reported in a Supplementary Schedule of Noncash Investing and Finance Activities that is attached as a supplement to the SCF.

Following is an example of a noncash investing and financing activities schedule that would explain the exchange of Rolando's stock for title to the land he plans to use for his new coffee shop.

Supplementary Schedule of Noncash Investing and Financing Activities	
Stock exchange for land (for new coffee shop)	$100,000

Also included in the statement of cash flows (and required by the FASB) is the Supplementary Disclosure of Cash Flow Information, which reports cash paid during the year for interest and income taxes.

Now that you better understand cash flows, and when you recall that all financial reports should be prepared with the purpose of informing their readers to the greatest possible degree, it is easy to understand that a complete SCF should include:

■ A summary of cash inflows and outflows resulting from operating activities
■ A summary of cash inflows and outflows resulting from investing activities
■ A summary of cash inflows and outflows resulting from financing activities
■ Net changes in cash from the beginning to the ending of the accounting period
■ A supplementary schedule of noncash investing and financing activities (if applicable)
■ A supplementary disclosure of cash flow information

Using this format, let's turn to the example of the Blue Lagoon Water Park Resort. Figure 5.10 shows the Condensed Income Statement and Statement of Retained Earnings, Figure 5.11 shows the 2009 and 2010 Balance Sheets (with Sources and Uses of Funds), and Figure 5.12 shows the Statement of Cash Flows.

FIGURE 5.10 Condensed Income Statement and Statement of Retained Earnings

BLUE LAGOON WATER PARK RESORT
Condensed Income Statement and Statement of Retained Earnings
For the Period: January 1 through December 31, 2010

Income Statement	
Revenue	**25,201,800**
Cost of Sales	2,854,080
Payroll and Related Expenses	8,877,600
Other Expenses	5,934,240
Gross Operating Profit	**7,535,880**
Rent, Property Taxes, and Insurance	1,760,400
Depreciation and Amortization	1,260,000
Net Operating Income	**4,515,480**
Interest	1,272,000
Income Before Income Taxes	**3,243,480**
Income Taxes	1,297,390
Net Income	**1,946,090**
Statement of Retained Earnings	
Retained Earnings, December 31, 2009	4,949,200
Net Income for 2010	1,946,090
Subtotal	6,895,290
Cash Dividends Paid in 2010	778,440
Retained Earnings, December 31, 2010	6,116,850

FIGURE 5.11 Balance Sheets (with Sources and Uses of Funds)

BLUE LAGOON WATER PARK RESORT
Balance Sheets
December 31, 2009 and 2010

	2009	2010		Sources	Uses
Assets					
Current Assets					
Cash	2,370,800	2,314,750	↓	56,050	
Marketable Securities	4,109,600	3,309,600	↓	800,000	
Net Receivables	1,655,300	1,053,950	↓	601,350	
Inventories	897,200	1,497,200	↑		600,000
Total Current Assets	9,032,900	8,175,500			
Investments	4,223,500	5,023,500	↑		800,000
Property and Equipment					
Land	7,712,550	7,712,550	-		
Building	22,290,500	22,290,500	-		
Furnishings and Equipment	5,063,655	7,289,000	↑		2,225,345
Less Accumulated Depreciation	3,408,900	4,668,900	↑	1,260,000	
Net Property and Equipment	31,657,805	32,623,150			
Other Assets	588,800	669,800	↑		81,000
Total Assets	45,503,005	46,491,950			
Liabilities and Owners' Equity					
Current Liabilities					
Accounts Payable	2,038,100	1,438,100	↓		600,000
Notes Payable	2,104,255	1,319,900	↓		784,355
Other Current Liabilities	1,814,600	1,264,600	↓		550,000
Total Current Liabilities	5,956,955	4,022,600			
Long-Term Liabilities					
Long-Term Debt	13,821,750	14,577,400	↑	755,650	
Total Liabilities	19,778,705	18,600,000			
Owners' Equity					
Common Stock	2,925,000	3,000,000	↑	75,000	
Paid in Capital	17,850,100	18,775,100	↑	925,000	
Retained Earnings	4,949,200	6,116,850	↑	1,167,650	
Total Owners' Equity	25,724,300	27,891,950			
Total Liabilities and Owners' Equity	45,503,005	46,491,950			
Total Sources and Uses of Funds				5,640,700	5,640,700

FIGURE 5.12   Statement of Cash Flows

BLUE LAGOON WATER PARK RESORT
Statement of Cash Flows
December 31, 2010

Net Cash Flow from Operating Activities

Net Income		1,946,090
Adjustments to reconcile net income to net cash flow from operating activities		
Depreciation	1,260,000	
Decrease in Net Receivables	601,350	
Increase in Inventories	(600,000)	
Decrease in Accounts Payable	(600,000)	
Decrease in Other Current Liabilities	(550,000)	111,350
Net Cash Flow from Operating Activities		2,057,440

Net Cash Flow from Investing Activities

Decrease in Marketable Securities	800,000	
Increase in Investments	(800,000)	
Increase in Furnishings and Equipment	(2,225,345)	
Increase in Other Assets	(81,000)	
Net Cash Flow from Investing Activities		(2,306,345)

Net Cash Flow from Financing Activities

Decrease in Notes Payable	(784,355)	
Increase in Long-Term Debt	755,650	
Increase in Capital Stock		
(Common Stock + Paid in Capital)	1,000,000	
Dividends Paid	(778,440)	
Net Cash Flow from Financing Activities		192,855

Net decrease in cash during 2010		(56,050)
Cash at the beginning of 2010		2,370,800
Cash at the end of 2010		2,314,750

Supplementary Disclosure of Cash Flow Information

Cash paid during the year for		
Interest	1,272,000	
Income Taxes	1,297,390	

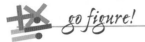

Building the Blue Lagoon Water Park Resort Statement of Cash Flows

Net Cash Flow from Operating Activities

- Net income of $1,946,090 is transferred from the bottom of the income statement to the top of the statement of cash flows.
- Depreciation of $1,260,000 from the income statement is added.
- Net receivables of $601,350 as a source of funds is added.
- Inventories of $600,000 as a use of funds is subtracted.
- Accounts payable of $600,000 as a use of funds is subtracted.
- Other current liabilities of $550,000 as a use of funds is subtracted.
- Items from depreciation to other current liabilities are added together to equal $111,350 (adjustments to net income).
- Net income and adjustments to net income are added together to result in $2,057,440 in net cash flow from operating activities.

Net Cash Flow from Investing Activities

- Marketable securities of $800,000 as a source of funds is added.
- Investments of $800,000 as a use of funds is subtracted.
- Furnishings and equipment of $2,225,345 as a use of funds is subtracted.
- Other assets of $81,000 as a use of funds is subtracted.
- All items from marketable securities to other assets are added to result in ($2,306,345) in net cash flow from investing activities.

Net Cash Flow from Financing Activities

- Notes payable of $784,335 as a use of funds is subtracted.
- Long-term debt of $755,650 as a source of funds is added.
- Capital stock of $1,000,000 as a source of funds is added.
- Dividends paid of $778,400 as a use of funds is subtracted.
- All items from notes payable to dividends paid are added to result in $192,855 in net cash flow from financing activities.

Net Changes in Cash

- Net decrease in cash during 2010 of ($56,050) is calculated by adding net cash flow from operating activities, net cash flow from investing activities, and net cash flow from financing activities. $2,057,440 + ($2,306,345) + $192,855 = ($56,050).
- Cash at the beginning of 2010 of $2,370,800 is transferred from the cash account of the 2009 balance sheet (ending balance of 2009 becomes beginning balance of 2010).

- Cash at the end of 2010 of $2,314,750 is transferred from the cash account of the 2010 balance sheet.
- Notice that cash at the beginning of 2010 minus cash at the end of 2010 equals the net decrease in cash during 2010. $2,370,800 − $2,314,750 = $56,050 decrease or ($56,050). This shows that the statement of cash flows was calculated correctly. This is your math check!

Schedule of Noncash Investing and Financing Activities

- The Blue Lagoon Water Park Resort did not have any noncash investing and financing activities. This part of the statement of cash flows is not required unless noncash transactions occur.

Supplementary Disclosure of Cash Flow Information

- Cash paid during the year for interest of $1,272,000 is transferred from the income statement.
- Cash paid during the year for income taxes of $1,297,390 is transferred from the income statement.

Statement of Cash Flows Analysis

The SCF is a document that is not analyzed nearly as much as the income statement or balance sheet. Part of the reason for this is that the SCF is a relatively newcomer to the managerial accounting world (it has only been required by the FASB since 1988). Also, many managers' jobs are more concerned with operations (income statement) and the effective use of assets (balance sheet) than cash management as cash management is often the job of the operation's owner, **Chief Financial Officer** (CFO), controller, or accountant. Despite the lesser analysis of the SCF, it is clear that the ability of a business to generate cash from its core business operations is an important indicator of its financial health and the risk that investors take when they invest in it.

One way to analyze a statement of cash flows is to first look at the sources and uses of funds identified by comparing last year's balance sheet with this year's balance sheet. By matching "like" dollar amounts of sources and uses of funds, you can surmise how funds were spent based on how funds were generated. For example, by looking at Figure 5.11, you can make some comparisons of the sources and uses of funds of the Blue Lagoon Water Park Resort as shown in Figure 5.13.

Without any information other than the numbers, you can look at the matching or near-matching amounts to make some assumptions about cash flow. The Blue Lagoon might have sold short-term marketable securities to purchase long-term investments, collected accounts receivable to pay accounts payable; sold stock and used cash available from depreciation (remember it is added back to cash flows) to pay for more furnishings and equipment; borrowed long-term debt to pay off higher interest, short-term debt (notes payable); used money placed back into the business (net income minus dividends paid,

FIGURE 5.13 Comparison of Sources and Uses of Funds for the Blue Lagoon Water Park Resort

Source	Amount	Use	Amount
Marketable securities	$800,000	Investments	$800,000
Net receivables	$601,350	Accounts payable	$600,000
Capital stock (Common stock + paid in capital) AND depreciation	$1,000,000 + $1,260,000 = $2,260,000	Furnishings and equipment	$2,225,345
Long-term debt	$755,650	Notes payable	$784,355
Retained earnings (as increase in net income − dividends)	$1,167,650	Inventories AND Other current liabilities	$600,000 + $550,000 = $1,150,000

FIGURE 5.14 Cash Flow Summary Comparisons for the Blue Lagoon Water Park Resort

	Last Year	This Year	$ Change	% Change
Net Cash Flow From				
Operating activities	1,831,120	2,057,440	226,320	12.4%
Investing activities	(3,075,130)	(2,306,345)	768,785	25.0%
Financing activities	167,010	192,855	25,845	15.5%
Change in Cash	(1,077,000)	(56,050)	1,020,950	94.8%

shown as an increase in retained earnings) to pay for inventories and pay off other current liabilities. Of course, in order to truly analyze these inflows and outflows of cash, you will need to confirm your assumptions with the CFO or owner.

Another method of analyzing the statement of cash flows is to compare operating, investing, and financing activities from last year to this year. Consider, for example, the Blue Lagoon Water Park Resort cash flow summary comparisons for the last two years as shown in Figure 5.14.

The *dollar change* or variance shows changes from previously experienced levels, and will give you an indication of whether your numbers are improving, declining, or staying the same. To see how this is computed, consider investing activities last year and investing activities this year as reported in Figure 5.14.

 *go figure!*

To calculate the variance in investing activities, you would use the following formula:

Investing Activities This Year − Investing Activities Last Year = Variance

or

($2,306,345) − ($3,075,130) = $768,785

Effective managers are also interested in computing the percentage change, or percentage variance, from one time period to the next. Thus, Blue Lagoon's percentage variance for investing activities is determined as follows:

$$\frac{(\text{Investing Activities This Year} - \text{Investing Activities Last Year})}{\text{Investing Activities Last Year}} = \text{Percentage Variance}$$

or

$$\frac{(\$2,306,345) - (\$3,075,130)}{|\$3,075,130|} = 25.0\%$$

Of course, an alternative and shorter formula for computing the percentage variance is as follows:

$$\frac{\text{Variance}}{\text{Investing Activities Last Year}} = \text{Percentage Variance}$$

or

$$\frac{\$768,785}{|\$3,075,130|} = 25.0\%$$

Of course, all dollar variances and percentage variances in the cash flow summary comparisons can be calculated in the same way. Notice that when dealing with a negative number for last year, the absolute value (positive) of the number is used in the denominator. When dealing with positive numbers, use positive numbers. From Figure 5.14, you can see that the Blue Lagoon's cash flow has improved in operating activities by 12.4%, investing activities by 25.0%, and financing activities by 15.5%. Also, net change in cash was 94.8% compared to last year.

While present cash flows in a business are certainly no absolute guarantee of future cash flows, it is a good indication of how well managers of the company are generating cash flows. Of course, in addition to knowing how much (and when) cash is generated, investors also want to know how management is using the cash it accumulates. For example, assume that you as a manager generate $1,000,000 in positive cash flows. You may, for example, elect to use all or part of this cash to:

- Pay dividends to your investors
- Retire some of the company's long-term debt
- Buy additional land for new development
- Give managers bonuses
- Give employees raises

■ Invest in new equipment
■ Leave the money in your company's bank account

Thus, it is not merely how much cash is generated, but the ultimate use of the cash that should also be communicated by your future statements of cash flows.

Because management's ultimate use of cash is often equally as important as how much cash is actually available to spend, for many investors and managers, a business's free cash flow is an important measure of its economic health. **Free cash flow** is simply the amount of cash a business generates from its operating activities *minus* the amount of cash it must spend on its investment activities and capital expenditures. Thus, free cash flow is considered a good measure of a company's ability to pay its debts, ensure its growth, and pay (if applicable) its investors in the form of dividends.

 *go figure!*

If you have ever received a paycheck, you already understand the concept of free cash flow. To illustrate, consider Jeff and Nancy. They both have jobs in which they generate income, and they both have house and car payments (debts). The following illustrates the free cash flow that Jeff and Nancy have after their payments.

Jeff	
Income	$5,000
Payments	$4,000
Free Cash Flow	$1,000
Nancy	
Income	$4,000
Payments	$1,500
Free Cash Flow	$2,500

Clearly, despite her lower gross cash flow (income), Nancy has a better free cash flow. In business terms, Nancy's company would be better able to withstand a sales downturn or similar short-term financial difficulty than would Jeff's.

A company with a positive free cash flow can grow and invest its excess cash in its own expansion or alternative investments. If a company has a negative free cash flow it will need to supplement its cash from other sources. This would entail borrowing funds or seeking additional investors. Clearly, a company with a consistent negative free cash flow simply must turn that situation around or face the ultimate closing of the business.

The formula for free cash flow is:

	Net cash provided from operating activities
Less	**Cash used to acquire property and equipment**
Equals	**Free Cash Flow**

Now that you fully understand the income statement (Chapter 3), balance sheet (Chapter 4), and the statement of cash flows, you are ready to begin the process of collectively analyzing these documents to better understand your business. It is so important that you learn how to do it that analysis of financial statements is the topic of the next chapter.

Apply What You Have Learned

Mary Margaret Glenn knew the going would be tough the first couple of years. She was now finding out exactly how tough. After five years of working for others, Mary and her former college roommate had pooled their resources and purchased a small building not far from the college campus. In it, they served gourmet coffees and specialty pastries. Business was good, when "good" was defined as consistently increasing weekly sales levels and strong profit margins.

Unfortunately, during the recently completed campus Spring Break, their sales volume fell significantly (about 80%). As Mary's roommate pointed out, however, the expenses did not fall. Rent, insurance, utilities, and lease payments were just a few of the operation's expenses that did not take a break during Spring Break. As a result, cash was tight. The operation would make its bi-weekly payroll, but not by much. Fortunately, the students had returned, and so had revenues. But it had been a narrow escape—too narrow, thought Mary.

1. What are some specific operations-related activities you could suggest to Mary to avoid a cash flow crisis the next time her business volume reduces dramatically?
2. What are some specific investment-related activities you could suggest to Mary to avoid a cash flow crisis the next time her business volume reduces dramatically?
3. What are some specific finance-related activities you could suggest to Mary to avoid a cash flow crisis the next time her business volume reduces dramatically? Which of all your suggestions do you believe you would implement if you found yourself in Mary and her roommate's situation? Why?

Key Terms and Concepts

The following are terms and concepts discussed in the chapter that are important for you to know as a manager. To help you review, please define the following terms.

Statement of changes in
financial position

Statement of cash flows
(SCF)

Consolidated income
statement

Solvency

Cash

Cash equivalents

Sources and uses of funds

Condensed income
statement

Statement of retained
earnings

Cash flow from operating
activities

Cash flow from investing
activities

Cash flow from financing
activities

Principal (loan)

Net changes in cash

Supplementary schedules

Noncash transaction

Chief Financial Officer (CFO)

Free cash flow

 *Test Your Skills*

Complete the Test Your Skills exercises by placing your answers in the shaded boxes.

1. Marvin Pearson is the managerial accountant for Highway Subs, a chain of sandwich shops located at major Interstate highway exits. He is about to begin work on a statement of cash flows for his organization and needs a quick refresher. Help him out by labeling each of the following items as a Source or Use of funds. Place an "**S**" before the statements identifying a source of funds, and a "**U**" for those statements identifying a use of funds.

a.		Increase in cash
b.		Decrease in marketable securities
c.		Decrease in net receivables
d.		Increase in inventories
e.		Increase in property and equipment
f.		Decrease in common stock
g.		Decrease in cash
h.		Increase in retained earnings
i.		Increase in notes payable
j.		Decrease in inventories
k.		Increase in common stock
l.		Decrease in accounts payable
m.		Decrease in long-term debt
n.		Increase in marketable securities
o.		Decrease in property and equipment
p.		Increase in long-term debt
q.		Decrease in notes payable
r.		Increase in accounts payable
s.		Increase in net receivables
t.		Increase in depreciation

2. The Fred Proffet Company has been in the contract food service management business for many years. Their clients chose the Proffet Company for its creativity and attention to detail. Allisha McKay is the person who prepares the summary of sources and uses of funds for the Proffet Company. Help her do that by using the balance sheets that

follow to calculate the company's sources and uses of funds, and answer the questions that follow.

THE FRED PROFFET COMPANY
Balance Sheets
December 31, 2011 and 2012

	2011	2012	↑↓	Sources	Uses
Assets					
Current Assets					
Cash	336,000	350,000			
Marketable Securities	1,240,000	1,200,000			
Net Receivables	1,520,000	1,550,000			
Inventories	844,000	830,000			
Total Current Assets	3,940,000	3,930,000			
Property and Equipment	1,200,000	1,500,000			
Less Accumulated Depreciation	420,000	525,000			
Net Property and Equipment	780,000	975,000			
Total Assets	4,720,000	4,905,000			
Liabilities and Owners' Equity					
Current Liabilities					
Accounts Payable	584,000	565,000			
Notes Payable	134,000	90,000			
Other Current Liabilities	636,000	300,000			
Total Current Liabilities	1,354,000	955,000			
Long-Term Liabilities					
Long-Term Debt	720,000	1,100,000			
Total Liabilities	2,074,000	2,055,000			
Owners' Equity					
Common Stock	300,000	320,000			
Paid in Capital	1,200,000	1,280,000			
Retained Earnings	1,146,000	1,250,000			
Total Owners' Equity	2,646,000	2,850,000			
Total Liabilities and Owner's Equity	4,720,000	4,905,000			
Total Sources and Uses of Funds					

a. Did the change in Cash reflect a Source or a Use of funds? What was the amount of that change?

b. Did the change in Net Receivables reflect a Source or a Use of funds? What was the amount of that change?

c. Did the change in Notes Payable reflect a Source or a Use of funds? What was the amount of that change?

d. Did the change in Retained Earnings reflect a Source or a Use of funds? What was the amount of that change?

e. What was the total amount of Sources and Uses of Funds?

3. Now that Allisha McKay (see Question 2 above) has compiled the sources and uses of funds information she needs, she is ready to prepare The Fred Proffet Company's Statement of Cash Flows for the Year Ended 2012. Help her complete the company's Statement of Cash Flows by using the information taken from the following Condensed Income Statement and Statement of Retained Earnings for 2012, and the 2011 and 2012 Balance Sheets in Question 2. Then, answer the questions that follow:

THE FRED PROFFET COMPANY
Condensed Income Statement and Statement of Retained Earnings
For the Period: January 1 through December 31, 2012

Income Statement	
Sales	$5,200,000
Cost of Sales	1,560,000
Gross Profit	3,640,000
Operating Expenses (excluding depreciation)	2,860,000
Depreciation	105,000
Operating Income	675,000
Interest	242,000
Income Before Income Taxes	433,000
Income Taxes (40%)	173,000
Net Income	260,000
Statement of Retained Earnings	
Retained Earnings, December 31, 2011	1,146,000
Net Income for 2012	260,000
Subtotal	1,406,000
Cash Dividends Paid in 2012	156,000
Retained Earnings, December 31, 2012	1,250,000

THE FRED PROFFET COMPANY
Statement of Cash Flows
December 31, 2012

Net Cash Flow from Operating Activities

Net Income

Adjustments to reconcile net income to net
cash flows from operating activities

    Depreciation

    Increase in Net Receivables

    Decrease in Inventories

    Decrease in Accounts Payable

    Decrease in Other Current Liabilities

Net Cash Flow from Operating Activities

Net Cash Flow from Investing Activities

    Decrease in Marketable Securities

    Increase in Property and Equipment

Net Cash Flow from Investing Activities

Net Cash Flow from Financing Activities

    Decrease in Notes Payable

    Increase in Long-Term Debt

    Increase in Capital Stock
        (Common Stock + Paid in Capital)

    Dividends Paid

Net Cash Flow from Financing Activities

Net Increase in Cash during 2012

Cash at the beginning of 2012

Cash at the end of 2012

**Supplementary Disclosure of Cash Flow
Information**

Cash paid during the year for

    Interest

    Income Taxes

   a. What is Allisha's proper entry for "Net Cash Flow from Operating Activities"?

   b. What is Allisha's proper entry for "Net Cash Flow from Investing Activities"?

   c. What is Allisha's proper entry for "Net Cash Flow from Financing Activities"?

   d. What is Allisha's proper entry for "Net Increase in Cash during 2012"?

   e. Since all changes in cash are accounted for in the Statement of Cash Flows, what is the purpose of the "Supplementary Disclosure of Cash Flow Information" portion of the statement?

4. Victor Ortega is the owner of a very successful small company that operates a carry-out pizza parlor. He also prepares his own financial statements. His task today is the completion of his 2011 Statement of Cash Flows. Using the following Condensed Income Statement and Statement of Retained Earnings for 2011, as well as his 2010 and 2011 Balance Sheets, help Victor complete his Statement of Cash Flows for Year Ending 2011. Then, answer the questions that follow:

ORTEGA'S PIZZA
Condensed Income Statement and Statement of Retained Earnings
For the Period: January 1 through December 31, 2011

Income Statement	
Sales	$700,000
Cost of Sales	210,000
Gross Profit	490,000
Operating Expenses (excluding depreciation)	388,000
Depreciation	14,000
Operating Income	88,000
Interest	30,000
Income Before Income Taxes	58,000
Income Taxes (40%)	23,000
Net Income	35,000
Statement of Retained Earnings	
Retained Earnings, December 31, 2010	50,000
Net Income for 2011	35,000
Subtotal	85,000
Cash Dividends Paid in 2011	20,000
Retained Earnings, December 31, 2011	65,000

ORTEGA'S PIZZA
Balance Sheets
December 31, 2010 and 2011

	2010	2011	↑↓	Sources	Uses
Assets					
Current Assets					
Cash	42,000	30,000			
Marketable Securities	85,000	91,000			
Net Receivables	93,000	80,000			
Inventories	58,000	67,000			
Total Current Assets	278,000	268,000			
Property and Equipment	965,000	915,000			
Less Accumulated Depreciation	40,000	30,000			
Net Property and Equipment	925,000	885,000			
Total Assets	1,203,000	1,153,000			
Liabilities and Owners' Equity					
Current Liabilities					
Accounts Payable	40,000	45,000			
Notes Payable	125,000	150,000			
Accrued Wages	38,000	23,000			
Total Current Liabilities	203,000	218,000			
Long-Term Liabilities					
Long-Term Debt	500,000	300,000			
Total Liabilities	703,000	518,000			
Owners' Equity					
Common Stock	75,000	95,000			
Paid in Capital	375,000	475,000			
Retained Earnings	50,000	65,000			
Total Owners' Equity	500,000	635,000			
Total Liabilities and Owners' Equity	1,203,000	1,153,000			
Total Sources and Uses of Funds					

ORTEGA'S PIZZA
Statement of Cash Flows
December 31, 2011

Net Cash Flow from Operating Activities
  Net Income

  Adjustments to reconcile net income to net
  cash flows from operating activities
    Depreciation
    Decrease in Net Receivables
    Increase in Inventories
    Increase in Accounts Payable
    Decrease in Accrued Wages
  Net Cash Flow from Operating Activities

Net Cash Flow from Investing Activities
    Increase in Marketable Securities
    Decrease in Property and Equipment
  Net Cash Flow from Investing Activities

Net Cash Flow from Financing Activities
    Increase in Notes Payable
    Decrease in Long-Term Debt
    Increase in Capital Stock
      (Common Stock + Paid in Capital)
    Dividends Paid
  Net Cash Flow from Financing Activities

Net Decrease in Cash during 2011
Cash at the beginning of 2011
Cash at the end of 2011

Supplementary Disclosure of Cash Flow
Information
Cash paid during the year for
  Interest
  Income Taxes

a. Did the change in "Inventories" reflect a Source or a Use of funds? What was the amount of that change?

b. Did the change in "Long-Term Debt" reflect a Source or a Use of funds? What was the amount of that change?

c. What is Victor's proper entry for "Net Cash Flow from Operating Activities"?

d. What is Victor's proper entry for "Net Cash Flow from Investing Activities"?

e. What is Victor's proper entry for "Net Cash Flow from Financing Activities"?

CHAPTER 6

Ratio Analysis

OVERVIEW

A ratio can be defined simply as the relationship between one number and another. As you will learn when you read this chapter, it is often the case that knowing the relationship between two numbers is a lot more valuable than knowing the value of either (or both) of the individual numbers you use when you create the ratio.

Mathematically, you get a ratio anytime you divide one number by another number. In this chapter you will learn why managerial accountants in the hospitality industry use ratios developed from numbers found on their income statements, balance sheets, and statements of cash flows, as well as other operating data, to create ratios that really help them better understand and manage their businesses. You will also learn about the five main types of ratios most commonly used by accountants in any business. These are:

■ Liquidity Ratios
■ Solvency Ratios
■ Activity Ratios
■ Profitability Ratios
■ Investor Ratios

In addition, you will learn about some ratios that have been developed especially for use by managers in the hospitality industry.

■ Hospitality-Specific Ratios

Ratio analysis is used to analyze profitability and it is also used to examine, in detail, the asset, liability, and owners' equity positions of a business. In this chapter you will learn how to compute and analyze the ratios used to evaluate each of these three major components of the basic Accounting Formula.

CHAPTER OUTLINE

- ■ Purpose and Value of Ratios
- ■ Types of Ratios
- ■ Comparative Analysis of Ratios
- ■ Ratio Analysis Limitations
- ■ Apply What You Have Learned
- ■ Key Terms and Concepts
- ■ Test Your Skills

LEARNING OUTCOMES

At the conclusion of this chapter, you will be able to:

✓ State the purpose and value of calculating and using ratios to analyze the health of a hospitality business.
✓ Distinguish between liquidity, solvency, activity, profitability, investor, and hospitality-specific ratios.
✓ Compute and analyze the most common ratios used in the hospitality industry.

Purpose and Value of Ratios

Ratios are important in a variety of fields. This is especially true in the hospitality industry. If you are a hospitality manager with a foodservice background, you already know about the importance of ratios.

go figure!

For example, to cook regular white rice, you use a ratio of two cups water to one cup of rice.

Two Cups of Water : One Cup of White Rice
or
2:1

For wild rice, however, experienced cooks know the ratio is different. To prepare wild rice, the proper ratio is

Four Cups of Water : One Cup of Wild Rice

or

4:1

If you are the supervisor of a banquet crew, you may know that, in your own facility, providing proper service to 500 wedding guests eating a served meal requires a banquet staff consisting of one banquet server per 10 guests to be served, or:

One Server : Ten Served Guests

or

1:10

For a wedding buffet (because these guests serve themselves) the proper ratio to provide excellent service is likely to be different. It may be:

One Server : Twenty Self-Serve Guests

or

1:20

Just as cooks, bakers, and service managers use time tested ratios to properly prepare and serve food, managerial accountants and investors monitor a company's performance by using financial ratios.

Before you learn to compute and evaluate a variety of ratios, however, you should understand an important relationship between certain ratios and their resulting percentages. You know that a ratio is created when you divide one number by another. A special relationship (a **percentage**) results when the numerator (top number) used in your division is a *part* of the denominator (bottom number).

In fraction form, a percentage is expressed as the part, or a portion of 100. Thus, 10 percent is written as 10 "over" 100 (10/100). In its common form, the "%" sign is used to express the percentage. If we say 10%, then we mean "10 out of each 100." Instead of using the % sign, the decimal form uses the (.) or decimal point to express the percent relationship. Thus, 10% is expressed as 0.10 in decimal form. The numbers to the right of the decimal point express the percentage.

Each of these three methods of expressing percentages is used in the hospitality industry, and to be successful you must develop a clear understanding of how each percentage is computed. Once that is known, you can express the percentage in any form that is required or that is useful to you. To determine what percent one number is of another number, divide the number that is the part by the number that is the whole.

 *go figure!*

For example, assume that 840 guests were served during a banquet at your hotel, and 420 of them asked for coffee with their meal. To find what percent (what ratio) of your guests ordered coffee, divide the part (420) by the whole (840) as follows:

$$\frac{\text{Part}}{\text{Whole}} = \text{Percent}$$

or

$$\frac{420}{840} = 50\% \text{ or } 0.50$$

Thus, 50% (common form) or 0.50 (decimal form) represents the proportion of people at the banquet who ordered coffee.

Many people become confused when converting from one form of percent to another. If that is a problem, remember the following conversion rules:

1. To convert from common form to decimal form, move the decimal two places to the left, that is, 50.00% = 0.50.
2. To convert from decimal form to common form, move the decimal two places to the right, that is, 0.50 = 50.00%.

In the remaining portions of this chapter you will learn about many different types of ratios. Some of these will be percentage ratios and others will not.

Value of Ratios to Stakeholders

As you learned in Chapter 3, all stakeholders who are affected by a business's profitability will care greatly about the effective operation of a hospitality business. These stakeholders may include:

■ Owners
■ Investors

- Lenders
- Creditors
- Managers

Each of these stakeholders, though, may have different points of view of the relative value of each of the ratios calculated for a hospitality business. This is so because owners and investors are primarily interested in their return on investment (ROI), while lenders and creditors are mostly concerned with their debt being repaid. At times these differing goals of stakeholders can be especially troublesome to managers who have to please their constituencies. One of the main reasons for this conflict lies within the concept of financial leverage.

Financial leverage is most easily defined as the use of debt to be reinvested to generate a higher return on investment (ROI) than the cost of debt (interest).

 *go figure!*

To illustrate, assume a hospitality manager:

Borrows $10,000 to be repaid at 10% interest
Reinvests *the same* $10,000 in an investment that gains 12% ROI
And thus, creates a surplus of 2% gain

In this case, borrowing $10,000 and reinvesting the same $10,000 at a higher rate of return earns a net gain of 2% after the debt is repaid. The manager, in this case, has leveraged debt to secure a gain.

Because of financial leverage, owners and investors generally like to see debt on a company's balance sheet because if it is reinvested well, it will provide more of a return on the money they have invested. Conversely, lenders and creditors generally do not like to see too much debt on a company's balance sheet because the more debt a company has, the less likely it will be able to generate enough money to pay off its debt. So, how can a manager who must manage this debt please both investors and lenders? The answer is not always clear, but it usually depends on the immediate or future financial goals of the business. The main thing for you to remember is that placing a value (good or bad) on ratios is not always easy or even desirable because of the differing points of view stakeholders may have at any given time.

Many managers feel that ratios are most useful when they compare a company's actual performance to a previous time period, competitor company results, industry averages, or budgeted (planned for) results. In this chapter you will learn about the most commonly used ratios. You will also learn that, when a ratio is compared to a standard or goal, the resulting differences (if differences exist) can tell you much about the financial performance (health) of the company you are evaluating.

Types of Ratios

Over time, accountants have developed a variety of ratios they believe to be helpful in analyzing a business. The most common way to classify these ratios is by the information they provide the user, thus managerial accountants working in the hospitality industry refer to:

- Liquidity Ratios
- Solvency Ratios
- Activity Ratios
- Profitability Ratios
- Investor Ratios
- Hospitality-Specific Ratios

In this chapter you will learn about the purpose of (and formulas for) these types of ratios and you will learn how to use them to analyze your business. Most numbers for these ratios can be found on a company's income statement, balance sheet, and statement of cash flows. To calculate the majority of ratios in this chapter, we will use the statements from the Blue Lagoon Water Park Resort as can be found in Figures 6.1, 6.2, 6.3, and 6.4.

In addition, some managers use averages in the denominators of some ratios to smooth out excessive fluctuations from one period to the next. With the exception of inventory turnover, the ratios in this chapter will not use averages in the denominators.

FIGURE 6.1   Condensed Income Statement

BLUE LAGOON WATER PARK RESORT
Condensed Income Statement
For the Period: January 1 through December 31, 2010

Income Statement	
Revenue	**25,201,800**
Cost of Sales	2,854,080
Payroll and Related Expenses	8,877,600
Other Expenses	5,934,240
Gross Operating Profit	**7,535,880**
Rent, Property Taxes, and Insurance	1,760,400
Depreciation and Amortization	1,260,000
Net Operating Income	**4,515,480**
Interest	1,272,000
Income Before Income Taxes	**3,243,480**
Income Taxes	1,297,390
Net Income	**1,946,090**

FIGURE 6.2   Balance Sheet

BLUE LAGOON WATER PARK RESORT
Balance Sheet
December 31, 2010

Assets

Current Assets		
Cash	2,314,750	
Marketable Securities	3,309,600	
Net Receivables	1,053,950	
Inventories	1,497,200	
Total Current Assets		8,175,500
Investments		5,023,500
Property and Equipment		
Land	7,712,550	
Building	22,290,500	
Furnishings and Equipment	7,289,000	
Less Accumulated Depreciation	4,668,900	
Net Property and Equipment		32,623,150
Other Assets		669,800
Total Assets		46,491,950

Liabilities and Owners' Equity

Current Liabilities		
Accounts Payable	1,438,100	
Notes Payable	1,319,900	
Other Current Liabilities	1,264,600	
Total Current Liabilities		4,022,600
Long-Term Liabilities		
Long-Term Debt		14,577,400
Total Liabilities		18,600,000
Owners' Equity		
Common Stock	3,000,000	
Paid in Capital	18,775,100	
Retained Earnings	6,116,850	
Total Owners' Equity		27,891,950
Total Liabilities and Owners' Equity		46,491,950

FIGURE 6.3   Statement of Cash Flows

BLUE LAGOON WATER PARK RESORT
Statement of Cash Flows
December 31, 2010

Net Cash Flow from Operating Activities

Net Income		1,946,090
Adjustments to reconcile net income to net cash flow from operating activities		
Depreciation	1,260,000	
Decrease in Net Receivables	601,350	
Increase in Inventories	(600,000)	
Decrease in Accounts Payable	(600,000)	
Decrease in Other Current Liabilities	(550,000)	111,350
Net Cash Flow from Operating Activities		2,057,440

Net Cash Flow from Investing Activities

Decrease in Marketable Securities	800,000	
Increase in Investments	(800,000)	
Increase in Furnishings and Equipment	(2,225,345)	
Increase in Other Assets	(81,000)	
Net Cash Flow from Investing Activities		(2,306,345)

Net Cash Flow from Financing Activities

Decrease in Notes Payable	(784,355)	
Increase in Long-Term Debt	755,650	
Increase in Capital Stock (Common Stock + Paid in Capital)	1,000,000	
Dividends Paid	(778,440)	
Net Cash Flow from Financing Activities		192,855

Net decrease in cash during 2010	(56,050)
Cash at the beginning of 2010	2,370,800
Cash at the end of 2010	2,314,750

Supplementary Disclosure of Cash Flow Information

Cash paid during the year for

Interest	1,272,000
Income Taxes	1,297,390

FIGURE 6.4 Statement of Retained Earnings and Investor Information

BLUE LAGOON WATER PARK RESORT
December 31, 2010

Statement of Retained Earnings

Retained Earnings, December 31, 2009	$4,949,200
Net Income for 2010	1,946,090
Subtotal	6,895,290
Cash Dividends Paid in 2010	778,440
Retained Earnings, December 31, 2010	$6,116,850

Investor Information

Dividends paid to common shareholders	$ 778,440
Common shares outstanding	1,000,000
Market price per share	$25.00
Earnings per share	$1.95
Dividends per share	$0.78

Liquidity Ratios

In Chapter 4 you learned that liquidity was defined as the ease at which current assets can be converted to cash in a short period of time (less than 12 months). **Liquidity ratios** have been developed to assess just how readily current assets could be converted to cash, as well as how much current liabilities those current assets could pay. That is important, of course, when you realize that one company may have very few current assets to convert to cash (for current liabilities payment), but it may also have very little current liabilities. Alternatively, another company may have many current assets that can quickly be converted to cash, but it may also have so many current liabilities that they exceed the cash that is actually available to pay them.

In this section we will examine three widely used liquidity ratios and working capital. These are:

- Current Ratio
- Quick (Acid-Test) Ratio
- Operating Cash Flows to Current Liabilities Ratio
- Working Capital

Current Ratio

One of the most frequently computed liquidity ratios is the **current ratio**.

 *go figure!*

A summary of the important facts you should know about the current ratio follows:

Current Ratio	
Definition	Current ratio shows the firm's ability to cover its current liabilities with its current assets.
Sources of Data	
Numerator	Balance sheet
Denominator	Balance sheet
Formula	$\dfrac{\text{Current assets}}{\text{Current liabilities}}$
Example	$\dfrac{\$8,175,500}{\$4,022,600} = 2.03 \text{ times}$

The Blue Lagoon Water Park Resort has $2.03 in readily available current assets to pay each $1.00 of its current obligations.

The higher the current ratio, the more current assets a business has available to cover its current liabilities. Current ratios can be interpreted in the following manner:

When current ratios are:

Less than 1: The business may have a difficult time paying its short-term debt obligations because of a shortage of current assets.

Equal to 1: The business has an equal amount of current assets and current liabilities.

Greater than 1: The business has more current assets than current liabilities and should be in a good position to pay its bills as they come due.

It might seem that it would be desirable for every hospitality business to have a high current ratio (because then the business could easily pay all of its current liabilities). That is not always the case. While potential creditors would certainly like to see a business in a position to readily pay all of its short-term debts, investors may be more interested in the financial leverage provided by short-term debts. Also, it is possible that the current ratio is high because of significant amounts of accounts receivable. That situation may mean that the business's credit policies (or its accounts receivable collection efforts) may need to be re-evaluated and improved. Some unscrupulous managers even attempt to add "window dressing" to the current ratios they compute by valuing their unsold inventories higher than they should (for example, by overstating the worth of unsold wines in their wine cellars to artificially inflate inventory values). In such cases, the current ratios do not reflect the use of "real" dollars.

The current ratio is so important to a hospitality business that lenders will frequently require that any business seeking a loan maintain a minimum current ratio during the life of any loan it is granted.

Quick (Acid-Test) Ratio

Another extremely useful liquidity ratio is called the **quick ratio**. The quick ratio is also known as the **acid-test ratio**.

 *go figure!*

A summary of the important facts you should know about the quick ratio follows:

	Quick (Acid-Test) Ratio
Definition	Quick ratio shows the firm's ability to cover its current liabilities with its *most liquid* current assets.
Sources of Data	
Numerator	Balance sheet
Denominator	Balance sheet
Formula	$$\dfrac{\text{Cash} + \text{marketable securities} + \text{accounts receivable}}{\text{Current liabilities}}$$ or $$\dfrac{\text{Current assets} - (\text{inventories} + \text{prepaid expenses})}{\text{Current liabilities}}$$
Example	$\dfrac{\$6,678,300}{\$4,022,600} = 1.66 \text{ times}$

The Blue Lagoon has $1.66 in "quickly" convertible current assets, for each $1.00 of current liabilities.

As you can see, the main difference between the current ratio formula and the quick ratio formula is the inclusion (or exclusion) of inventories and prepaid expenses. The computation for the current ratio includes inventories and prepaid expenses, while the computation for the quick ratio does not. This is because the purpose of the quick ratio is primarily to identify the relative value of a business's cash (and *quickly* convertible to cash) current assets. Specifically, cash is already cash, marketable securities can easily be sold to produce cash, and accounts receivable can be collected to provide cash. On the other hand, inventories must be sold to customers (in the case of fine wine, for example, this could take several months) and prepaid expenses are difficult (if not impossible) to recoup from entities (like insurance companies) once paid.

In some hospitality businesses, current ratio and quick ratio computations will yield very similar results. In those businesses such as limited service hotels, where the amount of product held in inventory is very small (consisting primarily of in-room guest amenities) the current and quick ratios computed will be very similar. Alternatively, in an upscale restaurant with an extensive and expensive wine list, the dollar value of inventories may be quite significant, and thus, the differences between that operation's current and quick ratio may also be significant.

Investors and creditors view quick ratios in a manner similar to that of current ratios. That is, investors tend to prefer lower values for quick ratios, while creditors prefer higher ratios. As a result, hospitality managers actually operating the business must be aware of the needs and requirements of both groups.

Operating Cash Flows to Current Liabilities Ratio

The third liquidity ratio to be examined is the **operating cash flows to current liabilities ratio**. This ratio relies on the operating cash flow portion of the overall statement of cash flows for its computation. It utilizes information from the balance sheet and the statement of cash flows you learned about in Chapters 4 and 5.

 *go figure!*

A summary of the important facts you should know about the cash flows to current liabilities ratio follows:

Operating Cash Flows to Current Liabilities Ratio	
Definition	Operating cash flows to current liabilities ratio shows the firm's ability to cover its current liabilities with its operating cash flows.
Sources of Data	
Numerator	Statement of cash flows
Denominator	Balance sheet
Formula	$\dfrac{\text{Operating cash flows}}{\text{Current liabilities}}$
Example	$\dfrac{\$2,057,440}{\$4,022,600} = 51.1\%$

The Blue Lagoon can cover 51.1% of its current liabilities with its operating cash flows.

The operating cash flows to current liabilities ratio seeks to provide an answer to the question, "What portion of our current liabilities can be paid with the cash generated by our own operations?" Clearly, if a business cannot generate enough money (cash) from its own operations activity to pay its short-term debts, it will need to seek additional money through investing or financing activities. If, however, a business can generate enough of its own cash to pay its short-term debts, it will not be forced to raise or borrow additional funds.

Although the Blue Lagoon's ratio is only 51.1%, this may not be of undo concern since its current and quick ratios are both relatively strong. However, investors and creditors would probably like to see this number as a higher percentage. In general, investors and creditors view the operating cash flows to current liabilities ratio in a manner similar to that of the current and quick (acid-test) ratios.

Working Capital

A measure that is related to the current and quick ratios is **working capital**. Although not a true ratio because it does not require that one number be divided by another number, it is a measure that many lenders require.

 *go figure!*

A summary of the important facts you should know about working capital follows:

Working Capital	
Definition	Working capital is the difference between current assets and current liabilities.
Sources of Data	
Numerator	Balance sheet
Denominator	Balance sheet
Formula	Current assets − Current liabilities
Example	$8,175,500 − $4,022,600 = $4,152,900

The Blue Lagoon has $4,152,900 in working capital.

Although working capital can be calculated for all hospitality businesses, new businesses are usually required by lenders to obtain a target working capital to maintain start-up loans. This is because lenders want to be sure that new businesses will have enough resources to pay current obligations, especially during the uncertainty and risk of the first year of operations.

Because of financial leverage, investors tend to prefer lower values for liquidity ratios, while creditors prefer higher values. As a result, it will be your responsibility as a professional hospitality manager to understand liquidity ratios well, and to balance the legitimate needs of both these groups.

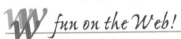 *fun on the Web!*

One of the advantages of understanding managerial accounting is that you can use your knowledge for your own personal wealth accumulation and investment purposes. To see how information you now know about liquidity ratios can help you better manage your own money, go to:

www.beginnersinvest.about.com

When you arrive, enter the words "liquidity ratios" in the search field.

Solvency Ratios

You have learned that liquidity ratios address the ability of a business to pay its short-term debt. **Solvency ratios** help managers evaluate a company's ability to pay long-term debt. Solvency ratios are important because they provide lenders and owners information about a business's ability to withstand operating losses incurred by the business. Losses incurred by a business may be short term, as for example when a new competitor initially opens a business, or when road construction or repair in front of a restaurant or hotel results in decreased traffic and reduced revenue. Operating losses can also be longer term, as for example when hurricane Katrina (2005) closed dozens of New Orleans restaurants, many of which were closed for an extended period of time.

Few people actually go into business thinking they will lose money, yet inevitably, some hospitality businesses do lose money. Because that is so, solvency ratios will continue to be important management tools for evaluating the long-term viability of businesses that must endure short-term operating losses. As a rule, those businesses with higher solvency ratio values are better able to withstand losses than are those businesses with lower solvency ratio values. In this section you will learn about the following five solvency ratios:

- Solvency Ratio
- Debt to Equity Ratio
- Debt to Assets Ratio
- Operating Cash Flows to Total Liabilities Ratio
- Times Interest Earned Ratio

Solvency Ratio

In Chapter 2, you learned that the basic accounting formula is:

$$\textbf{Assets} = \textbf{Liabilities} + \textbf{Owners' Equity}$$

A business is considered **solvent** when its assets are greater than its liabilities. The **solvency ratio** is simply a comparison of a business's total assets to its total liabilities.

 *go figure!*

A summary of the important facts you should know about the solvency ratio follows:

Solvency Ratio	
Definition	Solvency ratio shows the firm's ability to cover its total liabilities with its total assets.
Sources of Data	
Numerator	Balance sheet
Denominator	Balance sheet
Formula	$\dfrac{\text{Total assets}}{\text{Total liabilities}}$
Example	$\dfrac{\$46,491,950}{\$18,600,000} = 2.50 \text{ times}$

The Blue Lagoon has $2.50 of total assets to every $1.00 of total liabilities.

To better understand this ratio, consider that this is really a comparison between what a company "owns" (its assets) and what it "owes" those who do not own the company (liabilities). A ratio of "1.00" would mean that assets equal liabilities. Values over 1.00 indicate that a company owns more than it owes, while values less than 1.00 indicate a company owes more than it owns.

Creditors and lenders prefer to do business with companies that have a high solvency ratio (between 1.5 and 2.00) because it means these companies are likely to be able to repay their debts. Investors, on the other hand, generally prefer a lower solvency ratio, which may indicate that the company uses more debts as financial leverage.

Debt to Equity Ratio

The **debt to equity ratio** is a measure used by managerial accountants to evaluate the relationship between investments that have been made by the business's lenders and investments that have been made by the business's owners.

 *go figure!*

A summary of the important facts you should know about the debt to equity ratio follows:

Debt to Equity Ratio	
Definition	Debt to equity ratio compares total liabilities to owners' equity.
Sources of Data	
Numerator	Balance sheet
Denominator	Balance sheet
Formula	$\dfrac{\text{Total liabilities}}{\text{Total owners' equity}}$
Example	$\dfrac{\$18,600,000}{\$27,891,950} = 0.67$

The Blue Lagoon has $0.67 of total liabilities to every $1.00 of total owners' equity.

From a lender's perspective, the higher the lender's own investment (relative to the actual investment of the business's owners) the riskier is the investment and the less interested they will be in loaning money. Most restaurants and hotels are considered to be fairly risky investments, and lenders are cautious when considering loaning money to them. The result is that lenders usually look favorably on projects that yield relatively low (less than 1.00) ratios of this type. All other things being equal, a company that can generate and retain earnings (as part of owners' equity) will be able to reduce this ratio, thus reducing risk to potential lenders. Owners, not surprisingly, often seek to maximize their financial leverage and create total liabilities to total equity ratios in excess of 1.00.

Debt to Assets Ratio

The **debt to assets ratio** is simply a comparison of a business's total liabilities to its total assets.

 *go figure!*

A summary of the important facts you should know about the debt to assets ratio follows:

Debt to Assets Ratio	
Definition	Debt to assets ratio shows the percentage of assets financed through debt.
Sources of Data	
Numerator	Balance sheet
Denominator	Balance sheet
Formula	$\dfrac{\text{Total liabilities}}{\text{Total assets}}$
Example	$\dfrac{\$18,600,000}{\$46,491,950} = 0.40 \text{ or } 40\%$

The Blue Lagoon has a 40% debt to assets ratio, which means that 40% of its assets are financed through debt.

Specifically, the debt to assets ratio shows the percentage investment in company assets that has been made by the business's lenders. As with the other solvency ratios, more debt will be favored by investors because of financial leverage and less debt will be favored by lenders to ensure re-payment of loans.

Operating Cash Flows to Total Liabilities Ratio

The **operating cash flows to total liabilities ratio** utilizes information from the balance sheet and the statement of cash flows to compare the cash generated by operating activities to the amount of total liabilities it has incurred.

 *go figure!*

A summary of the important facts you should know about the operating cash flows to total liabilities ratio follows:

Operating Cash Flows to Total Liabilities Ratio	
Definition	Operating cash flows to total liabilities ratio shows the firm's ability to cover its total liabilities with its operating cash flows.
Sources of Data	
Numerator	Statement of cash flows
Denominator	Balance sheet
Formula	$\dfrac{\text{Operating cash flows}}{\text{Total liabilities}}$
Example	$\dfrac{\$2,057,440}{\$18,600,000} = 0.11 \text{ times}$

The Blue Lagoon can cover its total liabilities 0.11 times (less than one time) with its operating cash flows.

This ratio is particularly useful because it looks at cash flow over a period of time, and then compares that cash flow to the company's liability level. In nearly all cases, both owners and lenders would like to see this ratio kept as high as possible because a high ratio indicates a strong ability to repay debt from the business's normal business operations. This is a relatively low ratio for the Blue Lagoon and should be examined carefully by managers for possible areas of improvement.

Times Interest Earned Ratio

The **times interest earned ratio** compares interest expense to earnings before interest and taxes. **Earnings before interest and taxes (EBIT)** are labeled as net operating income on the USALI.

 *go figure!*

A summary of the important facts you should know about the times interest earned ratio follows:

Times Interest Earned Ratio	
Definition	Times interest earned shows the firm's ability to cover interest expenses with earnings before interest and taxes.
Sources of Data	
Numerator	Income statement
Denominator	Income statement
Formula	$$\dfrac{\text{Earnings before interest and taxes (EBIT)}}{\text{Interest expense}}$$
Example	$\dfrac{\$4,515,480}{\$1,272,000} = 3.55 \text{ times}$

The Blue Lagoon can cover its interest expense 3.55 times with its net operating income (earnings before interest and taxes).

This ratio indicates the strength a company has to repay the interest on its debts. The higher this ratio, the greater the number of "times" the company could repay its interest expense with its earnings before interest and taxes. In the opinion of many experts, when this ratio is less than two, it indicates a real weakness in a company's ability to meet its interest payment obligations. As it approaches four or more, it indicates sufficient strength on the part of the business to make its interest payments in a timely manner. Ratios as high as five or more, however, may indicate that the company is underleveraged, that is, its ability to borrow money (and repay it!) may be an underutilized financing activity of the business.

Activity Ratios

The purpose of computing **activity ratios** is to assess management's ability to effectively utilize the company's assets. Activity ratios measure the "activity" of a company's selected assets. They do so by creating ratios that measure the number of times these assets *turn over* (are replaced), thus assessing management's *efficiency* in handling inventories and long-term assets. As a result, these ratios are also known as **turnover ratios** or **efficiency ratios**.

In the restaurant business, for example, the efficient turnover of inventories is a critical management task. This is so because a large amount of the inventory (food and beverages) in most restaurants is subject to spoilage or reduced product quality if too much inventory is kept on hand.

In this section you will learn about the following activity ratios:

- Inventory Turnover
- Property and Equipment (Fixed Asset) Turnover
- Total Asset Turnover

Inventory Turnover

Inventory turnover refers to the number of times the total value of inventory has been purchased and replaced in an accounting period. Each time the cycle is completed once, you are said to have "turned" the inventory. For example, if you usually keep $100 worth of oranges on hand at any given time and your monthly usage of oranges is $500, you would have replaced (turned) your orange inventory five times in the month. Although inventory turnover can be computed for all types of inventories in all types of businesses, the examples used in this section will be based on a restaurant's food and beverage inventories.

To calculate **food inventory turnover** and **beverage inventory turnover ratios**, we will use the Condensed Food and Beverage Department Schedule shown in Figure 6.5.

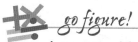 *go figure!*

A summary of the important facts you should know about food and beverage turnover ratios follows:

Food Inventory Turnover Ratio	
Definition	Food inventory turnover shows the speed (number of times) that food inventory is replaced (turned) during a year.
Sources of Data	
Numerator	Income statement
Denominator	Balance sheet
Formula	$\dfrac{\text{Cost of food consumed}}{\text{Average food inventory*}}$
Example	$\dfrac{\$2,190,400}{(\$120,000 + \$90,000)/2} = 20.9$ times
*(Beginning food inventory + ending food inventory)/2	

Beverage Inventory Turnover Ratio	
Definition	Beverage inventory turnover shows the speed (number of times) that beverage inventory is replaced (turned) during a year.
Sources of Data	
Numerator	Income statement
Denominator	Balance sheet
Formula	$\dfrac{\text{Cost of beverage consumed}}{\text{Average beverage inventory}^*}$
Example	$\dfrac{\$451,440}{(\$60,000 + \$45,000)/2} = 8.6 \text{ times}$
*(Beginning beverage inventory + ending beverage inventory)/2	

The Blue Lagoon has a food inventory turnover ratio of 20.9 times and a beverage inventory turnover ratio of 8.6 times.

FIGURE 6.5 Condensed Food and Beverage Department Schedule

BLUE LAGOON WATER PARK RESORT
Condensed Food and Beverage Department Schedule
For the Period: January 1 through December 31, 2010

	Food	Beverage
Sales	7,200,000	2,880,000
Cost of sales		
Beginning inventory	120,000	60,000
+Purchases	2,160,400	436,440
−Ending inventory	90,000	45,000
=Cost of goods consumed*	2,190,400	451,440
−Employee meals	52,000	0
=Cost of goods sold*	2,138,400	451,440
Gross profit	5,061,600	2,428,560
Operating expenses		
Payroll and related expenses	2,188,800	534,960
Other expenses	532,800	201,600
Total expenses	2,721,600	736,560
Department income	2,340,000	1,692,000

* The topics of cost of goods sold and cost of goods consumed will be explained later in this chapter in the Hospitality-Specific Ratios section.

The obvious question is, "Are the Blue Lagoon food and beverage turnover ratios good or bad?" The answer to this question is relative to the **target turnover ratios** (desired turnover ratios) for the Blue Lagoon.

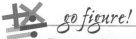 *go figure!*

For example, assume the Blue Lagoon food and beverage manager desires to turn over food inventory 26 times per year. This means that food inventory will be replaced every two weeks (52 weeks per year/26 times = 2 weeks). The following shows situations in which actual food inventory turnover is above and below the Blue Lagoon target of 26 times.

Blue Lagoon food inventory turnover:

Actual turnover (low)	20.9 times
Target turnover	26.0 times
Actual turnover (high)	32.0 times

A low turnover (20.9 times) might have occurred because sales were less than expected, thus causing food to move slower out of inventory (bad). It could also mean that the food and beverage manager decided to buy more inventory each time (thus, making purchases fewer times) because of discount prices due to larger (bulk) purchases (good).

A high turnover (32.0 times) might have occurred because sales were higher than expected, thus causing food to move faster out of inventory (good). It could also mean that significant wastage, pilferage, and spoilage might have occurred causing food to move out of inventory faster, but *not* due to higher sales (bad).

For some quick-service restaurants, inventory turnovers of 150 or more per year are common. In restaurants that stock large amounts of expensive (and often slow selling) wines, inventory turnover rates for these products may well be much less than ten times per year. In general, restaurant industry professionals usually set a target of relatively high food inventory turnover rates. It simply makes sense that if an average 5% profit margin is made on the sale of a food inventory item, we would like to sell (turn) that item as many times per year as possible. If the item was sold from inventory only once a year, one 5% profit would result. If the item turned 10 times, a 5% profit on each of the 10 sales would result. For this reason, inventory turnover is a carefully monitored ratio in the restaurant industry.

Property and Equipment (Fixed Asset) Turnover

The **property and equipment (fixed asset) turnover ratio** is, as its name implies, concerned with fixed asset usage. **Fixed assets** consist of the property, building(s), and equipment actually owned by the business.

go figure!

A summary of the important facts you should know about the property and equipment (fixed asset) turnover ratio follows:

Property and Equipment (Fixed Asset) Turnover Ratio	
Definition	Property and equipment turnover ratio shows management's ability to effectively use net property and equipment to generate revenues.
Sources of Data	
Numerator	Income statement
Denominator	Balance sheet
Formula	$\dfrac{\text{Total revenue}}{\text{Net property and equipment}}$
Example	$\dfrac{\$25,201,800}{\$32,623,150} = 0.77 \text{ times}$

For the Blue Lagoon, each $1.00 of net property and equipment generates $0.77 of revenue.

A simple example will explain how to interpret this ratio. Assume that you had an old fryer in your kitchen that you used only to make French fries. This fryer generates $50,000 worth of revenue from French fries sales per year. You buy a new fryer that makes twice the French fries the old fryer did; therefore, it generates $100,000 of French fries revenues per year. The new fryer, then, would have a fixed asset turnover ratio two times higher than that of the old fryer (assuming the fryers have approximately the same value). As you can see, the new fryer is more effective at generating revenues than the old fryer.

One thing to note is that the term "net" in any calculation generally means that something has been subtracted. When calculating the net property and equipment turnover ratio, "net" refers to the subtraction of accumulated depreciation. Because of this, you must be careful in interpreting this ratio. The more aged property and equipment you have, the more accumulated depreciation is subtracted from the denominator. This causes the denominator to be lower and the ratio to be higher. Thus, an excessive amount of old equipment would make the ratio higher and deceivingly better.

In the restaurant business (and especially in a situation where fixed assets are minimal because the restaurant is leased rather than owned) this ratio could be four times or more. In the hotel business, (where fixed assets are high) the ratio could vary from less than one time to a high of two or three times per year. Creditors, owners, and managers like to see this ratio as high as possible because it measures how effectively net fixed assets are used to generate revenue.

Total Asset Turnover

The **total asset turnover ratio** is concerned with total asset usage. Total assets consist of the current and fixed assets owned by the business.

 *go figure!*

A summary of the important facts you should know about the total asset turnover ratio follows:

Total Asset Turnover Ratio	
Definition	Total asset turnover shows management's ability to effectively use total assets to generate revenues.
Sources of Data	
Numerator	Income statement
Denominator	Balance sheet
Formula	$\dfrac{\text{Total revenue}}{\text{Total assets}}$
Example	$\dfrac{\$25,201,800}{\$46,491,950} = 0.54$ times

For the Blue Lagoon, each $1.00 of total assets generates $0.54 of revenue.

The difference between the total asset turnover ratio and the fixed asset turnover ratio is that current assets and fixed assets are both included in the denominator (total assets). As is the case with the property and equipment turnover ratio, restaurants may have higher ratios than hotels because hotels typically have more fixed assets (thus making the denominator larger and the ratio smaller). Creditors, owners, and managers like to see this ratio as high as possible because it measures how effectively total assets are used to generate revenue.

It is important, however, to understand that this ratio does not look at the profitability of a business, but rather only the revenue. Thus, a business with a total asset turnover could do a good job generating sales, but still not make a profit. The analysis of this ratio is an excellent example of why wise managerial accountants will always look at a variety of ratios when doing a thorough analysis of a business and the effectiveness of its management. Thus, we will now turn to the analysis of profitability ratios, which measure management's effectiveness at providing a profit for the hospitality business.

Profitability Ratios

In the final analysis, it is the job of management to generate profits for the company's owners, and **profitability ratios** measure how well management has accomplished this task. They will help you better understand the bottom line, or actual profitability, of companies you manage or analyze. It is important to realize that a company's profitability cannot be properly measured solely by evaluating the amount of money it returns to the company's owners. This is so because profits must also be evaluated in terms of the size of investment in the business that has been made by the company's owners. Clearly, the higher the investment made by the company's owners, the greater will be their profit expectations.

There are a variety of profitability ratios managerial accountants use to analyze a company's profitability. In this section, you will learn about the following ratios:

- Profit Margin
- Gross Operating Profit Margin (Operating Efficiency)
- Return on Assets
- Return on Owners' Equity

Profit Margin

Profit margin is the term managerial accountants use to describe the ability of management to provide a profit for the company's owners. This straightforward ratio simply compares the amount of net income generated by a business to the revenue it generated in the same time period.

 **go figure!**

A summary of the important facts you should know about profit margin follows:

Profit Margin	
Definition	Profit margin shows management's ability to generate sales, control expenses, and provide a profit.
Sources of Data	
Numerator	Income statement
Denominator	Income statement
Formula	$\dfrac{\text{Net income}}{\text{Total revenue}}$
Example	$\dfrac{\$1,946,090}{\$25,201,800} = 7.7\%$

The Blue Lagoon has a 7.7% profit margin, which means that it makes $0.077 profit for every $1.00 of revenues it generates.

While it would be possible, and even helpful, to compare the profit margin percentage achieved to a variety of standards such as the hospitality business's prior year performance, its budgeted performance, or an industry average, professional managerial accountants know that the computation of profit margin is merely the first step in a complete analysis of a business's ability to generate profits for its owners. Because of this, most managerial accountants also compute one or more of the additional profitability ratios that you will learn about next.

Gross Operating Profit Margin

The **gross operating profit margin** is also known as the **operating efficiency ratio.** In the opinion of most managerial accountants, it is a better measure of actual management effectiveness than is profit margin.

go figure!

A summary of the important facts you should know about gross operating profit margin follows:

Gross Operating Profit Margin (Operating Efficiency Ratio)	
Definition	Gross operating profit margin shows management's ability to generate sales, control expenses, and provide a gross operating profit.
Sources of Data	
Numerator	Income statement
Denominator	Income statement
Formula	$\dfrac{\text{Gross operating profit}}{\text{Total revenue}}$
Example	$\dfrac{\$7,535,880}{\$25,201,800} = 29.9\%$

The Blue Lagoon has a 29.9% gross operating profit margin, which means that it makes $0.299 gross operating profit for every $1.00 of revenues it generates.

The value of the gross operating profit margin is that it measures management effectiveness by computing a profitability ratio that *excludes* those nonoperating expenses and fixed charges that cannot be directly controlled by management. Nonoperating expenses include items such as management fees set by a property's owners. Fixed charges include items such as property and income taxes, insurance, occupation costs (rent or mortgage), interest, and depreciation. It is for this reason that operating managers tend to be more interested in their achieved gross operating profit margins (which they can control) than with their profit margins (which they only partially control). Thus, the gross operating profit margin tends to be a better indicator of management performance than the profit margin.

Return on Assets

The next profitability ratio we will examine relates profits to assets. When investors provide funds or secure assets for a business, they certainly hope that the money they have provided will, at some point, be returned to them. They also seek profits. The original investment and profits paid back to owners are called **returns**. When developing profitability ratios, managerial accountants want to examine the size of an investor's return. **Return on assets (ROA)** is one such ratio.

go figure!

A summary of the important facts you should know about the return on assets ratio follows:

	Return on Assets Ratio
Definition	Return on assets shows the firm's ability to use total assets to generate net income.
Sources of Data	
Numerator	Income statement
Denominator	Balance sheet
Formula	$\dfrac{\text{Net income}}{\text{Total assets}}$
Example	$\dfrac{\$1,946,090}{\$46,491,950} = 4.2\%$

The Blue Lagoon has a 4.2% return on assets ratio, which means that it makes $0.042 of net income for every $1.00 of total assets it has.

The importance of this ratio is easy to understand if you analyze it using a comparison of two companies.

go figure!

For example, assume that two different hotels generate a net income of $100,000 per year. If, however, the owners of Hotel A commit assets of $5,000,000 to operate their property, and the owners of Hotel B commit assets valued at $10,000,000, the rate of return (relative to the value of their assets) for these two ownership groups is very different.

Hotel A

$$\frac{\$100,000}{\$5,000,000} = .02 \text{ or } 2\% \text{ return on assets}$$

Hotel B

$$\frac{\$100,000}{\$10,000,000} = .01 \text{ or } 1\% \text{ return on assets}$$

Thus, the return on assets ratio relates investment size to the size of the investor's return.

Not surprisingly, investors seek high rates of return on assets. Like nearly all investments, however, when returns in the restaurant or hotel business are perceived to be higher, the risks associated with those investments tend to be higher also. Lower rates of return are generally (but not always) associated with lower risk. Of course, because ROA is dependent upon net income achieved through operations (the numerator in the equation), rates of return on assets can be low simply because the business using the assets has a low net income (maybe due to high depreciation or interest expenses that have been subtracted). A low ROA also could be the result of excess assets (the dominator in the equation). It is for these reasons that managerial accountants carefully review the ROA achieved in a business and compare it to industry averages, the business owner's own investment goals, and other valid benchmarks.

Return on Owners' Equity

The **return on equity (ROE)** is a ratio developed to evaluate the rate of return on the personal funds actually invested by the owners (and/or shareholders) of the business.

 *go figure!*

A summary of the important facts you should know about the return on equity ratio follows:

	Return on Equity Ratio
Definition	Return on equity shows the firm's ability to use owners' equity to generate net income.
Sources of Data	
Numerator	Income statement
Denominator	Balance sheet
Formula	$\dfrac{\text{Net income}}{\text{Total owners' equity}}$
Example	$\dfrac{\$1,946,090}{\$27,891,950} = 7.0\%$

The Blue Lagoon has a 7.0% return on equity ratio, which means that it makes $0.07 of net income for every $1 of owners' equity it has.

The ways in which investors' rates of return are computed can vary. Some managerial accountants believe returns based on pre-tax income are most informative, while others compute rates of return after all taxes have been paid. Both methods have value. An "after taxes" return on owners' equity is usually computed because it is only the after tax income that is available to corporations for a dividend return to shareholders. Even for individual business owners, the greatest interest is in determining the total amount they have personally invested and the total amount (after taxes) that investment will actually **yield** (return back to them).

Realize that if owners knew there was no risk of losing their initial cash contributions investments, they would always seek to maximize the size of their return on owners' equity. It is equally important to remember, however, that in the business world, increased returns are typically associated with increased investment risk. Thus most experienced investors seek to achieve their own balance between the risk they are willing to assume and the investment returns they seek to achieve.

Investor Ratios

Investor ratios assess the performance of earnings and stocks of a company. Investors are interested in these ratios because they can be used to choose new stocks to buy and to monitor stocks they already own. Investors are typically interested in two types of returns they may receive from their stock investments: money that is earned from the sale of stocks at higher prices than originally bought, and money that can be earned through the distribution of dividends.

Although investors use many different ratios to make decisions on investments, those you will learn about in this section are:

- Earnings per Share
- Price/Earnings Ratio
- Dividend Payout Ratio
- Dividend Yield Ratio

Earnings per Share

Earnings per share (EPS) is a ratio of most interest to those who buy and sell stocks in publicly traded companies, as well as to those managers who operate these companies.

 *go figure!*

A summary of the important facts you should know about earnings per share follows:

Earnings Per Share	
Definition	Earnings per share compares net income to common shares.
Sources of Data	
Numerator	Income statement
Denominator	Statement of retained earnings and investor information
Formula	$$\frac{\text{Net income}}{\text{Total number of common shares outstanding}}$$
Example	$$\frac{\$1,946,090}{1,000,000} = \$1.95$$

The Blue Lagoon has $1.95 earnings per share ratio, which means that it generates $1.95 of net income for every common share it has outstanding.

Potential investors can monitor the selling price of a company's stock each day simply by going online and entering the company's stock symbol into one of the many free programs that provide information to investors. By law, companies must regularly report (file information about) they net income and the total number of shares of stock they has issued. Those who manage publicly traded companies know that many investors compute and analyze earnings per share as a measure of managers' total effectiveness. It is important to recognize, however, that this ratio is strongly affected by both the amount of money a company earns and the number of shares of stock its board of directors elects to issue to the public.

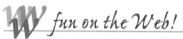 *fun on the Web!*

Many stock price monitoring programs are available on the Web at no charge. One of the easiest to use can be found at:

www.excite.com

When you arrive, click on "Find Symbol" (left center of the page) to discover the symbol used by the company whose stock price and other financial information you wish to review.

Price/Earnings Ratio

In the previous examination of earnings per share, we discovered that each share of stock of the Blue Lagoon earned $1.95 for its owner. We did not examine, however, what the value of such a stock would be. For investors, the question of a stock's "value" is assessed, in part, by computing its **price/earnings (P/E) ratio**. The price/earnings ratio compares market price per share to earnings per share.

 *go figure!*

A summary of the important facts you should know about price/earnings ratio follows:

Price/Earnings (P/E) Ratio	
Definition	Price/earnings ratio shows the perception of the firm in the market about future earnings growth of the company.
Sources of Data	
Numerator	Statement of retained earnings and investor information
Denominator	Statement of retained earnings and investor information
Formula	$\dfrac{\text{Market price per share}}{\text{Earnings per share}}$
Example	$\dfrac{\$25.00}{\$1.95} = 12.8$ times

The Blue Lagoon has a P/E ratio of 12.8 times.

Note that neither the numerator nor denominator of this ratio is located directly on the company's financial statements although, as you have learned, the calculation for earnings per share does use information from the income statement. The numbers of the P/E ratio for the Blue Lagoon, however, can be found on the statement of retained earnings and investor information in Figure 6.4.

Investors of the Blue Lagoon would discover that they must pay 12.8 times the annual earnings per share of this company for each share they wish to purchase. In general, the P/E ratio shows the perception of the Blue Lagoon in the market about future earnings growth. It is a perception because the numerator, the market price of the stock, is determined by the value that stockholders perceive the company's shares are worth. Thus, a P/E ratio of 12.8 would generally show a higher perceived value of future earnings growth of the firm than a lower P/E ratio.

Price/earnings ratios for hospitality industry stocks vary greatly. The question of whether a specific P/E ratio is a "good" one or a "bad" one is dependent upon the goals of the investor as well as that specific investor's view of the company's profitability and growth potential. It is important to understand that each time a company's publicly issued stock changes hands; the seller believes it is in his or her best interest not to own the stock, while the buyer equally believes it is in his or her best interest to own it. As a result, stock values can vary greatly and are influenced by a variety of factors; only one of which is the perceived potential earnings growth of the company.

Dividend Payout Ratio

The **dividend payout ratio** compares dividends to be paid to stockholders with earnings per share. This ratio is determined annually by the company's board of directors based on the desired amount to pay stockholders (dividends) and the amount to be reinvested (retained) in the company.

 *go figure!*

A summary of the important facts you should know about dividend payout ratio follows:

Dividend Payout Ratio	
Definition	Dividend payout ratio shows the percentage of net income that is to be paid out in dividends.
Sources of Data	
Numerator	Statement of retained earnings and investor information
Denominator	Statement of retained earnings and investor information
Formula	$\dfrac{\text{Dividend per share}}{\text{Earnings per share}}$
Example	$\dfrac{\$0.78}{\$1.95} = 40\%$

The Blue Lagoon has a dividend payout ratio of 40%, which means that 40% of net income will be paid to stockholders as dividends.

In general, well-established companies will pay a higher percentage of net income in dividends than higher growth companies. This is because high growth companies tend to reinvest net income to purchase more assets. Furthermore, once a company has a history of paying out dividends, then it generally continues this policy so that stock prices remain stable in the market. If the company suddenly decreases the amount of dividends paid, then the stock price may fall.

Dividend Yield Ratio

Dividend yield ratio compares the dividends per share to the market price per share.

 *go figure!*

A summary of the important facts you should know about dividend yield ratio follows:

Dividend Yield Ratio	
Definition	Dividend yield ratio show the stockholders' return on investment paid in dividends.
Sources of Data	
Numerator	Statement of retained earnings and investor information
Denominator	Statement of retained earnings and investor information
Formula	$\dfrac{\text{Dividend per share}}{\text{Market price per share}}$
Example	$\dfrac{\$0.78}{\$25.00} = 3.1\%$

The Blue Lagoon has a dividend yield ratio of 3.1%, which means that stockholders can expect to be paid 3.1% of the stock price as dividends.

The dividend yield ratio can be used by investors who wish to find stocks that will supplement their income with dividends. A high dividend yield would provide a cash flow to the stockholder through dividend payments. Generally, a stock with a high dividend yield indicates that the stock's company is stable and not reinvesting (retaining) its earnings because it is distributing them as dividends. A company with a low dividend yield typically indicates a high prospect for future growth since net income is being reinvested in the business and not being distributed as dividends.

Thus far we have examined financial ratios that could be used in virtually any business. There are, however, some ratios that were created specifically for those managers and managerial accountants working in the hospitality industry. In the next section, you will examine these ratios.

Hospitality-Specific Ratios

Hoteliers have developed specialized ratios for their work as have restaurateurs. If you are an experienced hospitality professional, or have taken other courses in hospitality management, you are very likely familiar with many of these ratios. There are literally dozens of valuable ratios used in the hospitality industry. It is even likely that, during your career, you will create your own unique ratios that will help you better manage your own operations! In this section, several ratios that are most frequently used by hotel and restaurant managers will be explained. The numbers used to create these ratios are often found on daily, weekly, monthly, or annual operating reports that managers design to fit their operational needs.

Hotel Ratios

Hoteliers have developed specialized ratios to help them better understand and manage their businesses. Although hotel managers use a variety of ratios to analyze their businesses, some ratios are designed to analyze information related particularly to rooms.

The hotel-specific ratios you will learn in this section are:

- Occupancy Percentage
- Average Daily Rate (ADR)
- Revenue per Available Room (RevPAR)
- Revenue per Available Customer (RevPAC)
- Cost per Occupied Room (CPOR)

Occupancy Percentage

Hotel managers and owners are interested in the **occupancy percentage** (percentage of rooms sold in relation to rooms available for sale) they achieve during a given accounting period because occupancy percentage is one measure of a hotel's effectiveness in selling rooms.

 *go figure!*

Using the information provided in Chapter 1, you know that the Blue Lagoon Water Park Resort has 240 guestrooms and suites. Assuming all rooms are available for sale and the resort operates 365 days in a year, the Blue Lagoon would have

> 240 rooms x 365 days = 87,600 rooms available for sale per year

If the Blue Lagoon actually sold 70,080 rooms in 2010, then the occupancy percentage would be calculated as follows:

$$\frac{\text{Rooms Sold}}{\text{Rooms Available for Sale}} = \text{Occupancy \%}$$

or

$$\frac{70,080}{87,600} = 80\%$$

This means that, on average, 192 out of 240 rooms (192/240 = 80%) were sold each day in 2010.

Of course, this represents an average, so some days would have a higher or lower number of rooms sold. In addition, this calculation is based on the assumption that all rooms in the hotel were available for sale during the year. However, this assumption does not always hold. Most hotels, if they are maintaining facility standards, will have rooms, floors, or entire wings at various times of the year that are **out of order** (**OOO**), meaning that repairs, renovation, or construction is being done and the rooms are not sellable. When calculating occupancy percentage, then, adjustments (subtractions) should be made to the denominator to account for rooms that are out of order.

Hoteliers often calculate variations on the occupancy percentage formula to analyze different kinds of information regarding occupancy. Complimentary occupancy (percentage of rooms provided on a **complimentary** (**comp**) basis or free of charge), average occupancy per room (average number of guests occupying each room), and multiple occupancy (percentage of rooms occupied by two or more people) are all variations of room occupancy that a hotelier may be interested in knowing. You will learn more about variations such as these in Chapter 8.

Occupancy percentage is a ratio that can be used to compare a hotel's performance to previous accounting periods, to forecasted or budgeted results, to similar hotels, and to published industry averages or standards. Industry averages and other hotel statistics are readily available through companies such as **Smith Travel Research** (**STR**). While a complete discussion of how hoteliers utilize (STR) **Star Reports** is beyond the scope of this chapter, it is important to recognize that Smith Travel Research, founded in 1985 by Randy Smith, is a compiler and distributor of hotel industry data. As an independent third party, STR collects and distributes summaries of hotel financial and operational data related to historic performance. Each week STR collects performance data on over 23,000 hotels representing more than 2.8 million rooms. This data is provided by hotel chain headquarters, management companies, owners, and independent hotels. The data is audited for accuracy and checked for adherence to STR reporting guidelines.

fun on the Web!

To investigate the statistics supplied for the lodging industry, go to the Smith Travel Research (STR) site at:

www.smithtravelresearch.com

When you arrive, search for your geographic location under "Find Local Market Data."

Average Daily Rate

Hoteliers are interested in the **average daily rate (ADR)** they achieve during an accounting period. ADR is the amount, on average, for which a hotel sells its rooms.

go figure!

Assuming that the total number of rooms sold at the Blue Lagoon Water Park Resort for the year was 70,080 and total rooms revenue was $14,016,000, the ADR is computed as follows:

$$\frac{\text{Total Rooms Revenue}}{\text{Total Number of Rooms Sold}} = \text{Average Daily Rate (ADR)}$$

or

$$\frac{\$14,016,000}{70,080} = \$200$$

This confirms the information provided in Chapter 1 that the Blue Lagoon Water Park Resort has an ADR of $200 including room and park admission fees.

ADR is one measure of a hotel's effectiveness in selling its rooms at a favorable rate. Most hotels, however, will offer their guests the choice of several different **room types**. These room types may include standard sized rooms, upgraded rooms such as parlor or whirlpool suites, connecting rooms or very large suites. Each specific room type will likely sell at a different nightly rate. When a hotel reports its total nightly revenue, however, its overall *average* daily rate is computed.

Revenue per Available Room

Experienced hoteliers know that high occupancy percentages can be achieved by selling rooms inexpensively, and that high ADRs can be achieved at the sacrifice of significantly lowered occupancy percentages. Thus, hoteliers have developed a measure of performance that *combines* occupancy percentage and ADR to compute **revenue per available room (RevPAR)**.

go figure!

Using the information about the Blue Lagoon Water Park Resort provided in the previous two sections, RevPAR is computed as follows:

Occupancy % x ADR = RevPAR

or

80% x $200 = $160

Another way to calculate RevPAR is:

$$\frac{\text{Total Rooms Revenue}}{\text{Rooms Available for Sale}} = \text{Revenue per Available Room (RevPAR)}$$

or

$$\frac{\$14,016,000}{87,600} = \$160$$

Thus, the Blue Lagoon has a RevPAR of $160.

RevPAR is useful when a comparison of occupancy percentages or ADRs alone is not meaningful.

go figure!

For example, a regional manager who wants to compare the performance of two hotels in her region on the basis of occupancy percentages and ADRs might have the following information:

Hotel A has an occupancy % of 80% and an ADR of $120.
Hotel B has an occupancy % of 60% and an ADR of $180.

Which hotel is performing better? The only real meaningful comparison she could make would be on the basis of RevPAR:

Hotel A has a RevPAR of 80% x $120 = $96
Hotel B has a RevPAR of 60% x $180 = $108

Therefore, Hotel B would have a higher RevPAR and thus, better overall performance based on occupancy percentage *and* ADR.

Revenue per Available Customer

Hotel managers are interested in the **revenue per available customer (RevPAC)** (revenues generated by each customer) because guests spend money on many products in a hotel in addition to rooms.

go figure!

The total revenue figure for the Blue Lagoon Water Park Resort provided in Figure 6.1 is $25,201,800. Assuming all revenues reflect guest expenditures, this amount represents all revenues generated by areas in the resort including rooms, park admission, restaurants, lounges, snack bar, video arcade, retail store, tanning/spa facility, and exercise facility (see Chapter 1). Also, assuming an average of three guests (family) per room sold, the total number of guests for the year would be 210,240 (3 guests × 70,080 rooms sold = 210,240 guests).

Using this information for the Blue Lagoon, RevPAC is computed as follows:

$$\frac{\text{Total Revenue from Hotel Guests}}{\text{Total Number of Guests}} = \text{RevPAC}$$

or

$$\frac{\$25,201,800}{210,240} = \$119.87$$

Thus, each guest (including children) on average is spending $119.87 in the resort.

RevPAC is an especially helpful ratio when comparing two groups of guests proposing to stay at a property. If a hotel manager wishes to maximize the amount of total revenues generated by guests throughout the property, then groups that generate a high RevPAC will be preferable to book than groups that generate a lower RevPAC.

Cost per Occupied Room

In the hotel business, **cost per occupied room (CPOR)** is a ratio that compares specific costs in relation to the number of occupied rooms. CPOR is a ratio computed for a variety of costs such as guest amenities, housekeeping, laundry, in-room entertainment, security, and a variety of other costs.

go figure!

Assuming housekeeping costs (excluding payroll) for the Blue Lagoon Water Park Resort in 2010 is $1,016,640 and number of rooms sold (occupied) is 70,080, the CPOR for housekeeping costs is as follows:

$$\frac{\text{Cost Under Examination}}{\text{Rooms Occupied}} = \text{Cost per Occupied Room}$$

or

$$\frac{\$1,016,640}{70,080} = \$14.51$$

Thus, housekeeping costs per occupied room for the Blue Lagoon are $14.51.

CPOR can be used to compare one type of cost in a hotel to other hotels within a chain, a company, a region of the country, or to any other standard that may be deemed appropriate by the hotel's managers or owners.

Now that you have learned some of the ratios hotels use to evaluate performance, we will turn our attention to common ratios that restaurateurs use to evaluate their activities.

Restaurant Ratios

Most restaurants buy and sell highly perishable goods (food). The restaurant industry is noted for fairly small profit margins, thus managers in this industry must carefully control their costs if they are to maintain their restaurants' profitability.

The restaurant-specific ratios you will learn in this section are:

- Cost of Food Sold (Cost of Sales: Food)
- Cost of Beverage Sold (Cost of Sales: Beverage)
- Food Cost Percentage
- Beverage Cost Percentage
- Labor Cost Percentage
- Average Sales per Guest (Check Average)
- Seat Turnover

Consider the case of Joshua Richards from Chapter 3. Joshua owns his own restaurant which is located across the street from the Blue Lagoon Water Park Resort. His income statement for this year is presented in Figure 6.6. Joshua's income statement information will be used to calculate the ratios in this section.

Cost of Food Sold (Cost of Sales: Food)

Cost of food sold (cost of sales: food) is simply the dollar amount of all food expenses incurred during the accounting period. **Cost of goods sold** is a general term for cost of any products sold. For restaurants, cost of goods sold as referenced in the inventory turnover section of this chapter refers to cost of food sold and cost of beverage sold.

FIGURE 6.6 Restaurant Income Statement

JOSHUA'S RESTAURANT
Income Statement
For the Year Ended December 31, 2010

SALES:	
Food	2,058,376
Beverage	482,830
Total Sales	**$2,541,206**
COST OF SALES:	
Food	767,443
Beverage	96,566
Total Cost of Sales	**$864,009**
GROSS PROFIT:	
Food	1,290,933
Beverage	386,264
Total Gross Profit	**$1,677,197**
OPERATING EXPENSES:	
Salaries and Wages	714,079
Employee Benefits	111,813
Direct Operating Expenses	132,143
Music and Entertainment	7,624
Marketing	63,530
Utility Services	88,942
Repairs and Maintenance	35,577
Administrative and General	71,154
Occupancy	120,000
Depreciation	55,907
Total Operating Expenses	**$1,400,769**
Operating Income	**276,428**
Interest	84,889
Income Before Income Taxes	**191,539**
Income Taxes	76,616
Net Income	**$114,923**

Prepared using USAR

The formula for cost of food sold follows:

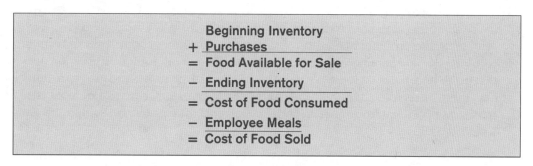

Beginning Inventory
\+ Purchases
\= Food Available for Sale
\− Ending Inventory
\= Cost of Food Consumed
\− Employee Meals
\= Cost of Food Sold

To fully understand the cost of food sold formula and ultimately analyze it properly, you must first understand that **beginning inventory** is the dollar value of all food on hand at the beginning of the accounting period. Some foodservice managers refer to the value of this inventory by its synonymous term, **opening inventory.** Beginning inventory is determined by completing an actual count and valuation of the products on hand.

Purchases, as used in this formula, are the sum costs of all food purchased during the accounting period. It is determined by adding all properly tabulated invoices for food purchased during the accounting period. **Food available for sale** is the sum of the beginning inventory plus the value of all purchases. It represents the value of all food that was available for sale during the accounting period.

Ending inventory refers to the dollar value of all food on hand at the end of the accounting period. Some foodservice managers refer to the value of this inventory by its synonym, **closing inventory**. It also is determined by completing a physical inventory.

The **cost of food consumed** is the actual dollar value of all food used, or consumed, by the operation. Again, it is important to note that this is not merely the value of all food sold, but rather the value of all food no longer in the establishment. This includes the value of any meals eaten by employees and also food that is lost due to wastage, pilferage, and spoilage. **Cost of goods consumed** is a general term for cost of any products consumed. For restaurants, cost of goods consumed as referenced in the inventory turnover section of this chapter refers to cost of food consumed and cost of beverage consumed. It is this number that is used in the numerator of the Inventory Turnover Ratio you learned about earlier in this chapter.

Employee meals are a labor-related, not food-related expense. Free or reduced-cost employee meals are an employee benefit in much the same manner as is medical insurance or paid vacation. Therefore, the cost of this benefit, if provided, should be accounted for in the Employee Benefits line item of the Operating Expenses section of the income statement (see Chapter 3). Since this expense belongs under Employee Benefits, it is omitted (subtracted) from cost of food consumed to yield the cost of food sold (cost of sales) on the income statement. As a result, the final cost of food sold value is actually the cost of food consumed minus the cost of employee-related meals.

Some operators prefer slightly different variations on the basic cost of food sold formula, depending on the unique aspects of their units. One variation of the formula is used when food or beverage products are transferred from one foodservice unit to another. **Transfers out** are items that have been transferred out of one unit to another, and **transfers in** are items that have been transferred in to one unit from another.

This variation should be used when, for example, an operator seeks to compute one cost for a bar and another for the bar's companion restaurant. In this situation, it is likely that fruits, juices, vegetables, and similar items for drink garnishes and mixes are transferred out of the kitchen to the bar, while wine, sherry, and similar items for cooking may be transferred from the bar to the kitchen. The formula for cost of food sold in this situation would be as follows:

	Beginning Inventory
+	**Purchases**
=	**Food Available for Sale**
−	**Ending Inventory**
=	**Cost of Food Consumed**
−	**Value of Transfers Out**
+	**Value of Transfers In**
−	**Employee Meals**
=	**Cost of Food Sold**

go figure!

For Joshua's Restaurant, the Cost of Food Sold (Cost of Sales: Food) would be calculated as follows:

	Beginning Inventory	**$51,400**
+	**Purchases**	771,000
=	**Food Available for Sale**	822,400
−	**Ending Inventory**	53,750
=	**Cost of Food Consumed**	**$768,650**
−	**Value of Transfers Out**	11,992
+	**Value of Transfers In**	25,785
−	**Employee Meals**	15,000
=	**Cost of Food Sold**	**$767,443**

Thus, the cost of food sold for Joshua's is $767,443.

Cost of Beverage Sold (Cost of Sales: Beverage)

Cost of beverage sold (cost of sales: beverage) is simply the dollar amount of all beverage expenses incurred during the accounting period.

The cost of beverage sold is calculated the same way as cost of food sold except that the products are alcoholic beverages (beer, wine, and spirits). In addition, employee meals are not subtracted because employees are not drinking alcoholic beverages (you hope!) as part of their employee benefits.

The computation of cost of beverage sold is as follows:

> **Beginning Inventory**
> **+ Purchases**
> **= Beverage Available for Sale**
>
> **− Ending Inventory**
> **= Cost of Beverage Sold**

If transfers to the kitchen (wine and sherry) and transfers from the kitchen (fruits, juices, and vegetables) occur, then transfers out are beverage items that have been transferred out of the bar to the kitchen, and transfers in are food items that have been transferred from the kitchen to the bar.

The cost of beverage sold formula is amended for transfers as follows:

> **Beginning Inventory**
> **+ Purchases**
> **= Beverage Available for Sale**
>
> **− Ending Inventory**
> **− Value of Transfers Out**
>
> **+ Value of Transfers In**
> **= Cost of Beverage Sold**

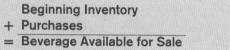

go figure!

For Joshua's Restaurant, the Cost of Beverage Sold (Cost of Sales: Beverage) would be calculated as follows:

	Beginning Inventory	$11,520
+	**Purchases**	112,589
=	**Beverage Available for Sale**	124,109
−	**Ending Inventory**	13,750
−	**Value of Transfers Out**	25,785
+	**Value of Transfers In**	11,992
=	**Cost of Beverage Sold**	$96,566

Thus, the cost of beverage sold for Joshua's is $96,566.

Notice that the transfers out of food in the cost of food calculation are the same as transfers in to beverage in the cost of beverage calculation, and transfers in to food are the same as transfers out to beverage. This is because food and beverages are being transferred between the units. Calculating transfers between food and beverage results in an accurate reflection of the actual costs being incurred in each area.

As a managerial accountant, it is important for you to know exactly which formula or variation of it is in use when analyzing your cost of food sold or cost of beverage sold. The variations on the basic formulas, while slight, can make big differences in the interpretation of your cost information.

It is also critical that, in all cases, accurate beginning and ending inventory figures be maintained if an operation's true food and beverage cost data are to be computed. It is important to note that ending inventory for one accounting period becomes beginning inventory for the next period. For example, if inventories are taken monthly, an operation's January 31 ending inventory amount will become the February 1 beginning inventory figure (thus a physical inventory need only be taken one time per accounting period, not twice).

Food Cost Percentage

A restaurant's food cost percentage is the ratio of the restaurant's cost of food sold (cost of sales: food) and its food revenue (sales). Thus, **food cost percentage** represents the portion of food sales that was spent on food expenses.

 *go figure!*

Using Joshua's Restaurant in Figure 6.6, the calculation for food cost percentage is:

$$\frac{\text{Cost of Food Sold}}{\text{Food Sales}} = \text{Food Cost \%}$$

or

$$\frac{\$767,443}{\$2,058,376} = 37.3\ \%$$

Thus, the food cost % for Joshua's is 37.3%.

For many restaurants, the food cost percentage, its management, and its control are the single most important keys to profitability.

Beverage Cost Percentage

A restaurant's beverage cost percentage is the ratio of the restaurant's cost of beverage sold (cost of sales: beverage) and its beverage revenue (sales). Thus, **beverage cost percentage** represents the portion of beverage sales that was spent on beverage expenses.

 *go figure!*

Using Joshua's Restaurant in Figure 6.6, the calculation for beverage cost percentage is:

$$\frac{\text{Cost of Beverages Sold}}{\text{Beverage Sales}} = \text{Beverage Cost \%}$$

or

$$\frac{\$96,566}{\$482,830} = 20.0\%$$

Thus, the beverage cost percentage for Joshua's is 20.0%.

For most restaurants, the beverage cost percentage, its management, and its control are extremely important because alcoholic beverages represent an expensive cost and a serious security problem. As some restaurateurs are known to say, alcoholic beverages have a way of "growing legs and walking out the back door" because they are at high risk for being stolen by "thirsty" employees.

Labor Cost Percentage

For most restaurants, labor is second only to food as their highest expense, and in many cases, labor cost represents the highest expense. As a result, restaurateurs are very interested in the **labor cost percentage**, which is the portion of total sales that was spent on labor expenses. Labor costs include salaries and wages and other labor-related expenses such as employee benefits.

 *go figure!*

Using Joshua's Restaurant in Figure 6.6, the calculation for labor cost percentage is:

$$\frac{\text{Cost of Labor}}{\text{Total Sales}} = \text{Labor Cost \%}$$

or

$$\frac{\$825,892^*}{\$2,541,206} = 32.5\%$$

*Cost of labor is calculated by adding salaries and wages to employee benefits or $714,079 + $111,813 = $825,892.

Thus, the labor cost % for Joshua's is 32.5%.

To compute this ratio, data for both the numerator and denominator are taken from the restaurant's income statement. Some managers calculate labor cost by adding together all labor-related costs as was done for Joshua's (salaries and wages and employee benefits), and others only include salaries and wages in the cost of labor. These differences are a matter of choice and usually depend on the kinds of labor costs the manager wishes to analyze.

Increasing total sales (the denominator) will help decrease the labor cost percentage even as total dollars spent on labor increases, assuming some of the labor costs represent fixed expenses such as salaries. It is important to understand that it is typically *not* in the best interest of restaurant operators to reduce the total amount they spend on labor. In most foodservice situations, managers *want* to serve more guests, and that typically requires additional staff.

The labor cost percentage is important because it helps managers relate the amount of products they sell to the cost of the staff needed to sell them. Controlling and evaluating labor cost will be an important part of your job as a hospitality manager. In fact, many managers feel it is more important to control labor costs than product costs because, for many of them, labor and labor-related costs comprise a larger portion of their operating budgets than do the food and beverage products they sell. This is because labor costs have become progressively higher due to continual increases in the minimum wage and other labor-related costs such as insurance for employees.

Average Sales per Guest (Check Average)

Restaurateurs who record both their revenue and the number of guests they serve have the information they need to compute an average sales per guest ratio. **Average sales per guest** is the average amount of money spent per customer during a given accounting period. Average sales per guest is also commonly known as **check average.**

go figure!

Assuming Joshua's Restaurant in Figure 6.6 served 203,300 guests during the year, the calculation for average sales per guest is:

$$\frac{\text{Total Sales}}{\text{Number of Guests Served}} = \text{Average Sales per Guest (Check Average)}$$

or

$$\frac{\$2,541,206}{203,300} = \$12.50$$

Thus, the average sales per guest for Joshua's is $12.50, meaning that each guest spent, on average, $12.50 when dining at his restaurant.

Most **point of sale (POS) systems** (computer systems used for tracking sales data) are programmed to tell you the amount of revenue you have generated in a selected time period, the number of guests you have served, and the average sales per guest. If the operation does not have a POS system in place, the revenue generated may be determined by a cash register, and the number of guests served may be determined by an actual guest head count, by a count of the number of plates or trays issued, or by adding the number of individuals listed on the guest checks used by service staff. This measure of "sales per guest" is an important one because it carries information needed to monitor menu item popularity, estimate staffing requirements, and even determine purchasing procedures. It is also a very commonly reported financial statistic used by those who evaluate restaurant chains because it allows the financial analyst to measure the chain's effectiveness in increasing sales to its current guests, rather than to increase sales simply by opening additional restaurants.

Check average is a ratio that can be used to compare a restaurant's performance to previous accounting periods, to forecasted or budgeted results, to similar restaurants, and to published industry averages or standards. As was noted in Chapter 3, industry averages and other restaurant statistics are readily available through publications such as the *Restaurant Industry Operations Report* published by the National Restaurant Association.

Seat Turnover

Knowledgeable restaurant managers know that keeping their dining room tables full of guests who stay for a long enough time to eat their meal comfortably, but a short enough time to allow the table to be used for other diners, is a real key to their operation's profitability. To evaluate the restaurant's effectiveness in "turning tables" the seat turnover ratio is a popular one. **Seat turnover** measures the number of times seats change from the current diner to the next diner in a given accounting period.

 *go figure!*

Assuming Joshua's Restaurant in Figure 6.6 had 260 seats and served 203,300 guests (**covers**) during the year, the calculation for seat turnover is:

$$\frac{\text{Covers Served}}{\text{Number of Seats} \times \text{Number of Operating Days in Period}} = \text{Seat Turnover}$$

or

$$\frac{203,300}{260 \times 365} = \frac{203,300}{94,900} = 2.14 \text{ turns}$$

Thus, the seat turnover for Joshua's is 2.14 times, meaning that each seat changed from the current diner to the next diner, on average, 2.14 times per day.

FIGURE 6.7 Ratio Summary

Liquidity Ratios: To assess the ability to pay short-term debts
Current
Quick
Operating Cash Flows to Current Liabilities
Working Capital

Solvency Ratios: To assess the ability to pay long-term debts
Solvency
Debt to Equity
Debt to Assets
Operating Cash Flows to Total Liabilities
Times Interest Earned

Activity Ratios: To assess the ability to effectively utilize assets
Inventory Turnover
Property and Equipment Turnover
Total Asset Turnover

Profitability Ratios: To assess the ability to create a return for owners
Profit Margin
Gross Operating Profit Margin
Return on Assets
Return on Equity

Investor Ratios: To assess the performance of earnings and stocks
Earnings per Share
Price/Earnings
Dividend Payout
Dividend Yield

Hospitality-Specific Ratios: To assess the performance of hospitality operations
Hotel Ratios
   Occupancy Percentage
   Average Daily Rate (ADR)
   Revenue per Available Room (RevPAR)
   Revenue per Available Customer (RevPAC)
   Cost per Occupied Room (CPOR)
Restaurant Ratios
   Cost of Food Sold (Cost of Sales: Food)
   Cost of Beverage Sold (Cost of Sales: Beverage)
   Food Cost Percentage
   Beverage Cost Percentage
   Labor Cost Percentage
   Average Sales per Guest (Check Average)
   Seat Turnover

Interestingly, this ratio does not use information from the income statement, the balance sheet, or the statement of cash flows. Rather, it is one of the many financial ratios used by managers in the hospitality industry for which the data is generated completely internally. In the case of seat turnover, information about the number of covers (guests) served comes from the POS system, or a physical tally of guests. The number of seats in the restaurant is the result of a physical count also, and finally, the number of operating days in the accounting period is simply taken from the operating calendar.

The interpretation of this ratio must be carefully undertaken because its value is so greatly determined by the "covers served" that comprises this ratio's numerator. In some restaurants, this number is easily determined. In others, however, management must make decisions about the definition of a cover. In many cases, it must answer questions such as:

■ Is a guest who accompanies another diner but does not eat considered a cover?
■ Must a cover purchase a minimum number of menu items or dollar value of items to be considered a cover?
■ Should the definition of a cover change from breakfast, lunch, and dinner?

Regardless of the decisions made on these issues, managers want to see this ratio as high as reasonably possible because the seat turnover ratio is an important indication of a restaurant's ability to effectively utilize its "seats" to sell it products.

As a managerial accountant, you will select, calculate, and analyze the financial ratios that you decide are important to your own segment of the industry and to the profitable operation of your own business. In this chapter, you have learned about a variety of ratios used by managerial accountants. Figure 6.7 is a summary of these ratios.

Comparative Analysis of Ratios

Like many other types of financial data, a company's financial ratios are often compared to previous accounting periods, to forecasted or budgeted results, or to published industry averages or standards. To better understand the value of such comparisons, consider the Blue Lagoon Water Park Resort. Figure 6.8 details the occupancy percentage achieved by the Blue Lagoon in the past three years.

From the data in Figure 6.8, it might seem simple to conclude that the managers of the Blue Lagoon are not doing as good a job selling hotel rooms this year as they have in the past. Consider, however, the data presented in Figure 6.9, which compares the occupancy % of the Blue Lagoon and the city in which it is located.

FIGURE 6.8 The Blue Lagoon Occupancy Percentage

	Occupancy Percentage		
	2008	**2009**	**2010**
Blue Lagoon	82.0%	80.4%	80.0%

FIGURE 6.9   City-Wide and the Blue Lagoon Occupancy Percentage

	Occupancy Percentage		
	2008	**2009**	**2010**
City-Wide	81.0%	79.1%	77.0%
Blue Lagoon	82.0%	80.4%	80.0%

From this data it is clear to see that, while the Blue Lagoon's occupancy has indeed declined along with that of the city, the decline at the Blue Lagoon is less severe than that of the average hotel in the city (2-point decline over the three years for the Blue Lagoon versus a 4-point city-wide decline). In fact, where two years ago the Blue Lagoon outperformed the city by only one occupancy point, it now outperforms the city by three occupancy points. Clearly, the data in Figure 6.9 paints a different picture of the Blue Lagoon's revenue-generating performance than does the data in Figure 6.8. This example demonstrates that financial ratios may not depict as clear a measure by themselves as when they are compared to those of previous accounting periods, budgeted results, industry averages, or similar properties.

In addition, ratios computed by managerial accountants typically show *what* is happening, but rarely do they show *why* it is happening. That is the job of the manager. It is for this reason that ratio analysis must be carefully undertaken. Now that you understand ratios and how they interrelate, with additional managerial experience, you will be able to utilize them effectively!

fun on the Web!

Many investors and managers like to compare the operating ratios of their own companies to those of industry averages or standards. These industry averages are available on several free sites including Standard and Poor's "Industry Surveys" and Reuters "Investor." You can access these free sites at:

www.yahoo.com

These industry comparisons can help you answer the question, "Is this company's performance better, worse, or the same as that of its direct competitors?"

Ratio Analysis Limitations

Any serious discussion of financial ratios must include an examination of the weaknesses inherent in an over-dependency on them. One weakness, as has been illustrated in this chapter, is that ratios, by themselves, may be less meaningful unless compared to those of previous accounting periods, budgeted results, industry averages, or similar properties. Another limitation is that financial ratios do not measure a company's **intellectual capital**

assets such as brand name, potential for growth, and intellectual or human capital when assessing a company's true worth.

As you have learned in this chapter, the computation of most ratios involves the use of numbers found on the balance sheet or income statement. Many would maintain that, in today's economy, intellectual assets such as customer lists, current customer contracts, growth potential, patents, and brand awareness (all of whose values are not listed on these financial statements), are undervalued, under-recognized, and underreported. Figure 6.10 shows a list of some of the intellectual capital assets that should be analyzed in addition to financial ratios to assess the health and worth of a company.

To better understand why the recognition of intellectual capital assets is so important, consider a hospitality company who decides to purchase new communication devices for all of its managers. These devices would appear on the balance sheet as company assets. The company's investment in training its managers how to use the devices, (an excellent investment in the company's future!) is, however, considered an operating expense (and thus results in a short-term reduction in profitability). Most company executives, who wish to show maximum financial efficiency in the shortest possible time frame (as measured by traditional ratio analysis), do not wish to show reduced company profitability. Thus, current accounting procedures, in this example, provide an incentive to buy the devices but a disincentive to train employees to use them! As a result, current accounting procedures can actually serve to discourage management from investing in the human capital so vital to success in the hospitality industry.

In the future, it is likely that hospitality companies will create methods to account for the value of their client lists, brand names, and employee skills because all of these nontraditional intellectual capital assets, as well as others, contribute significantly to the actual value of a hospitality company. Perhaps *you* will be one of the industry leaders that develop an appropriate procedure for accurately assessing the value of these important intellectual assets in the future!

FIGURE 6.10   Intellectual Capital Assets

- Documented management systems
- Documented processes
- Brand names
- Patents
- Management contracts
- Recipe files
- Employee service contracts
- Standardized and proprietary training programs
- Customer lists
- Customer contracts (in effect)
- Supplier discount contracts
- Organizational structure
- Organizational culture

W fun on the Web!

Many managers feel that business ratios are the guiding stars by which they steer their companys' course. The ratios provide targets and standards; and they direct management toward the best long-term strategies as well as the smartest short-term solutions. These managers also believe ratio *analysis* is too important a task to leave exclusively to accountants!

One author who presents this position very well is Ciaran Walsh. Walsh's book can be found at:

www.amazon.com

When you arrive, enter "Ciaran Walsh" in the book search line to view a copy of *Key Management Ratios: Master the Management Metrics that Drive and Control Your Business*, Third Edition.

 *pply What You Have Learned*

Andrea Hayman knows her business, but she often wonders if anyone else really does. Andrea owns and operates a successful catering company. Each catered event she manages is unique. Her company enjoys an excellent reputation because of Andrea's attention to detail and total commitment to customer service.

In a good month, Andrea and her staff of 25 employees will serve over 10,000 lunch and dinner meals. Sales last year exceeded $2,500,000. Andrea's company was simply the one that people always called when a large specialty party or event needed to be executed extremely well.

The biggest catered event Andrea held last month involved a political fundraiser for the Governor. Her company served 3,500 people for dinner at the Fairgrounds, and Andrea's team performed flawlessly. Although she was confident that she knew how to operate her business, she wondered about her profitability. Were her food production people and bartenders as cost conscious as they should be? Were her servers truly efficient? Were her profits "reasonable"? These were legitimate questions, and Andrea wanted solid answers.

1. Identify and write out one specific food, one beverage, one labor, and two profitability ratios you believe would be critical for Andrea to compute and monitor if she wants to effectively analyze her business success.
2. What would be your reply to Andrea if she asked you how often each of the five ratios you have suggested should be computed? Why?

3. How could comparative ratio analysis help address Andrea's concerns? What are some data sources Andrea could turn to as she sought answers to her business effectiveness questions?

Key Terms and Concepts

The following are terms and concepts discussed in the chapter that are important for you to know as a manager. To help you review, please define the following terms.

Percentage	Property and equipment (fixed asset) turnover ratio	Cost per occupied room (CPOR)
Financial leverage		
Liquidity ratios	Fixed assets	Cost of food sold (cost of sales: food)
Current ratio	Total asset turnover ratio	
Quick ratio	Profitability ratios	Cost of goods sold
Acid-test ratio	Profit margin	Beginning inventory
Operating cash flows to current liabilities ratio	Gross operating profit margin	Opening inventory
	Operating efficiency ratio	Purchases
Working capital	Returns	Food available for sale
Solvency ratios (as a group of ratios)	Return on assets (ROA)	Ending inventory
	Return on equity (ROE)	Closing inventory
Solvent	Yield (investment)	Cost of food consumed
Solvency ratio (as a single ratio)	Investor ratios	Cost of goods consumed
	Earnings per share (EPS)	Employee meals
Debt to equity ratio	Price/earnings (PE) ratio	Transfers out
Debt to assets ratio	Dividend payout ratio	Transfers in
Operating cash flows to total liabilities ratio	Dividend yield ratio	Cost of beverage sold (cost of sales: beverage)
	Occupancy percentage	
Times interest earned ratio	Out of order (OOO)	Food cost percentage
Earnings before interest and taxes (EBIT)	Complimentary (comp)	Beverage cost percentage
	Smith Travel Research (STR)	Labor cost percentage
Activity ratios	Star Reports	Average sales per guest
Turnover ratios	Average daily rate (ADR)	Check average
Efficiency ratios	Room types	Point of sale (POS) systems
Inventory turnover	Revenue per available room (RevPAR)	Seat turnover
Food inventory turnover		Covers
Beverage inventory turnover	Revenue per available customer (RevPAC)	Intellectual capital assets
Target turnover ratios		

 *Test Your Skills*

Complete the Test Your Skills exercises by placing your answers in the shaded boxes

1. Blue owns Blue's Bistro. He thinks he has performed well in 2011 and he is trying to analyze the Bistro's performance for the year, but he needs your help!

Following are Blue's condensed income statement, and statement of retained earnings and investor information for 2010 and 2011.

BLUE'S BISTRO
Condensed Income Statement and
Statement of Retained Earnings and Investor Information
For the Periods Ending December 31, 2010 and 2011

	2010	2011
Income Statement		
Sales	552,500	742,205
Cost of Sales	227,075	259,800
Gross Profit	325,425	482,405
Operating Expenses (excluding depreciation)	160,225	280,275
Depreciation	60,000	59,000
Operating Income (EBIT)	105,200	143,130
Interest	34,000	15,863
Income Before Income Taxes	71,200	127,267
Income Taxes (40%)	28,480	50,907
Net Income	42,720	76,360
Statement of Retained Earnings and Investor Information		
Retained Earnings		
Retained Earnings, Beginning	154,480	177,200
Net Income	42,720	76,360
Subtotal	197,200	253,560
Cash Dividends Paid	20,000	50,000
Retained Earnings, Ending	177,200	203,560
Investor Information		
Market Price per Share	$10.00	$65.00
Earnings per Share	$ 1.42	$ 6.07

Following are the 2010 and 2011 balance sheets for Blue's Bistro.

BLUE'S BISTRO
Balance Sheets
December 31, 2010 and 2011

	2010	2011
Assets		
Current Assets		
Cash	42,000	30,000
Marketable Securities	93,000	80,000
Net Receivables	138,000	152,000
Inventories	5,000	6,000
Total Current Assets	278,000	268,000
Property and Equipment	1,200,000	1,091,760
Less Accumulated Depreciation	200,000	141,000
Net Property and Equipment	1,000,000	950,760
Total Assets	1,278,000	1,218,760
Liabilities and Owners' Equity		
Current Liabilities		
Accounts Payable	107,000	45,000
Notes Payable	15,000	59,000
Accrued Wages	38,000	23,000
Total Current Liabilities	160,000	127,000
Long-Term Liabilities		
Long-Term Debt	340,800	138,200
Total Liabilities	500,800	265,200
Owners' Equity		
Capital Stock	600,000	750,000
Retained Earnings	177,200	203,560
Total Owners' Equity	777,200	953,560
Total Liabilities and Owners' Equity	1,278,000	1,218,760

Using Blue's Bistro income statements and balance sheets, analyze the health of Blue's Bistro by calculating the following ratios. Round to the hundredth's place (i.e., 12.34% or 12.34 times).

	Blue's Bistro 2010	Blue's Bistro 2011
Current Ratio		
Quick Ratio		
Inventory Turnover (Assume inventories were $6,000 for 2009)		
Property and Equipment Turnover		
Times Interest Earned		
Debt to Assets		
Profit Margin		
Return on Assets		
Return on Equity		
Price per Earnings Ratio		

2. The Food and Beverage department at the Fox Hills Country Club is an important part of the Club's overall profit structure. February food sales were $310,450 and beverage sales were $49,875. Because they represent such significant costs, Frankie Watson, the Club's Food and Beverage Director, keeps a careful watch on her food and beverage cost percentages. Using the following information for February that Frankie has recorded, help her calculate the answers to the questions that follow.

Given:

Beginning Food Inventory	$ 5,410
Food Purchases	$72,385
Ending Inventory	$ 5,772
Transfers "Out of Kitchen"	$ 922
Transfers "Into Kitchen"	$ 1,346
Employee Meals	$ 1,622

Calculate the following:

Beginning Inventory	
Purchases	
Food Available for Sale	
Ending Inventory	
Cost of Food Consumed	
Transfers Out	
Transfers In	
Employee Meals	
Cost of Food Sold	

Food Sales	
Food Cost %	

Given:

Beginning Beverage Inventory	$ 1,099
Beverage Purchases	$12,588
Ending Beverage Inventory	$ 1,244
Transfers "Out of Bar"	$ 1,346
Transfers "Into Bar"	$ 922

Calculate the following:

Beginning Inventory	
Purchases	
Beverage Available for Sale	
Ending Inventory	
Transfers Out	
Transfers In	
Cost of Beverage Sold	

Beverage Sales	
Beverage Cost %	

a. What was the amount of Frankie's Cost of Food Consumed in the month of February?

b. What was the amount of Frankie's Cost of Food Sold in the month of February?

c. What was Frankie's Food Cost % in the month of February?

d. What was the amount of Frankie's Cost of Beverage Sold in the month of February?

e. What was Frankie's Beverage Cost % in the month of February?

3. Elaine Ware owns her own nonfranchised full-service hotel. Her competition is intense, so Elaine very carefully monitors the financial performance of her property. Ratios are essential to the management decisions she makes. Use the following information to calculate Elaine's operating ratios. The figures are based on one day's operation.

Hotel	
Total Rooms	225
Rooms Available for Sale	200
Rooms Occupied and Sold	140

Number of Guests	308
Housekeeping Costs	$ 2,170
Rooms Revenue	$17,500
Total Revenue from Hotel Guests	$53,900
Restaurant	
Total Food Sales	$ 2,700
Total Beverage Sales	$ 900
Total Sales	$ 3,600
Number of Guests (Covers) Sold	180
Number of Seats in the Restaurant	150
Labor Cost	$ 1,260
Food:	
Beginning Inventory	$ 5,000
Purchases	$ 500
Ending Inventory	$ 4,565
Transfers Out	$ 200
Transfers In	$ 100
Employee Meals	$ 25
Beverage:	
Beginning Inventory	$ 7,000
Purchases	$ 250
Ending Inventory	$ 7,188
Transfers Out	$ 100
Transfer In	$ 200

Calculate the following:

Hotel
a. Occupancy Percentage
b. Average Daily Rate (ADR)
c. RevPAR
d. RevPAC
e. Housekeeping CPOR

Restaurant
f. Check Average
g. Seat Turnover
h. Cost of Food Sold
i. Food Cost Percentage
j. Cost of Beverage Sold
k. Beverage Cost Percentage
l. Labor Cost Percentage

4. Tina Bell has just gotten a call from her stockbroker, and he is strongly suggesting that she buy 1,000 shares of Moonbean Coffee House stock. He wants her to buy today; however, Tina wants to analyze the value of the stock on her own first.

Tina has the following information about Moonbean stock:

Net Income	$1,200,000
Total Number of Common Shares Outstanding	750,000
Market Price per Share	$26.60
Dividends per Share	$0.80

Given this information, help Tina calculate the following investor ratios:

a. Earnings per Share	
b. Price per Earnings	
c. Dividend Payout Ratio	
d. Dividend Yield Ratio	

e. Based upon the dividend payout ratio only, what would you expect this company's view to be regarding reinvesting earnings back into the business versus paying them out in stockholder dividends?

f. Would you advise Tina to buy this stock? What additional information might you seek in order to help her make a good decision? Explain your answer.

PART III

Management of Revenue and Expense

CHAPTER 7

Food and Beverage Pricing

This chapter is the first in the three-chapter section on the management of revenue and expense. It explains how foodservice professionals establish selling prices for the items they serve their guests. As a professional hospitality manager, properly pricing the products you sell will be crucial to your own success as well as to the profitability of your business.

In this chapter, you will learn about the important relationship between the costs of the products you will sell and the prices you must charge your guests. If your prices are too low, your profits may be too low also. If you charge too much for your items, however, guests may not buy enough of them to ensure that you will make a profit. Not surprisingly, foodservice managers have different opinions on how to best price the items they sell. Because this is true, you will learn about factors affecting menu prices as well as several pricing approaches and techniques. In addition you will examine methods used to evaluate the wisdom and effectiveness of the pricing strategy you actually have chosen to use in your business.

CHAPTER OUTLINE

- ■ Factors Affecting Menu Pricing
- ■ Assigning Menu Prices
- ■ Menu Price Analysis
- ■ Apply What You Have Learned
- ■ Key Terms and Concepts
- ■ Test Your Skills

LEARNING OUTCOMES

At the conclusion of this chapter, you will be able to:

✓ Identify the factors that affect a foodservice operation's menu pricing strategy.
✓ Utilize the product cost percentage and contribution margin methods of menu pricing.
✓ Utilize matrix analysis and goal value analysis to evaluate menu pricing strategies.

Factors Affecting Menu Pricing

Perhaps no area of hospitality management is less well understood than the area of pricing food and beverage products. This is not surprising when you consider the many and varied factors that can play a part in the pricing decision. Some of the most common factors affecting menu prices include one or more of the following:

Factors Influencing Menu Price

1. Local Competition
2. Service Levels
3. Guest Type
4. Product Quality
5. Portion Size
6. Ambiance
7. Meal Period
8. Location
9. Sales Mix

Local Competition The price a competitor charges for his or her product can be useful information in helping you arrive at your own selling price. It should not, however, be the overriding or determining factor in your pricing decision. Successful foodservice operators spend their time focusing on building guest value in their own operation and not in attempting to mimic the efforts of the competition. In fact, in the consumers' mind, higher prices are often associated with higher quality products.

Service Levels Guests expect to pay more for the same product when service levels are higher. As the personal level of service increases, costs increase and thus prices must also be increased. In the hospitality industry, those companies that have been able to survive and thrive over the years have done so because of their uncompromising commitment to high levels of guest service. This trend will continue.

Guest Type Some guests are simply less price sensitive than others. All guests, however, want value for their money. A thorough analysis of who your guests are and what they value most is critical to the success of any restaurant's pricing strategy.

Product Quality Effective restaurateurs generally choose from a variety of quality levels when selecting the items they will sell their guests, and consequently, establishing the prices for which these items sell. To be successful, you should select the quality level that best represents your guests' anticipated desire as well as your own operational goals, and then you must price your products accordingly.

Portion Size Portion size plays a large role in determining menu pricing. Great chefs know that people "eat with their eyes first!" However, every menu item should be analyzed with an eye toward determining if the quantity being served is the "proper" quantity. You would, of course, like to serve this proper amount, but no more than that. The effect of portion size on menu price is significant, and it will be your job to establish and maintain strict control over proper portion size.

Ambiance If people ate only because they were hungry, few restaurants would be open today. Fun, companionship, time limitations, adventure, and variety are just a few reasons diners cite for eating out rather than eating at home. However, excellent product quality with outstanding service goes much farther over the long run than do clever restaurant designs. Ambiance may draw guests to a location the first time. When this is true, prices may be somewhat higher if the quality of products and ambiance also support the price structure.

Meal Period In some cases, diners expect to pay more for an item served in the evening than for that same item served at a lunch period. Sometimes this is the result of a smaller "luncheon" portion size, but in other cases the portion size, as well as service levels, may be the same in the evening as earlier in the day. Managers must exercise caution in this area. Guests should clearly understand why a menu item's price changes with the time of day. If this cannot be answered to the guest's satisfaction, it may not be wise to implement a time-sensitive pricing structure.

Location Location can be a major factor in determining price. It used to be said of restaurants that success was due to three things: location, location, location! There is, of course, no discounting the value of a prime restaurant location, and location alone can influence price. It does not, however, guarantee success. A location can be good for business or bad for business. If it is good, menu prices may reflect that fact. If a location is indeed bad, menu prices may need to be lower to attract a sufficient clientele to ensure the operation's total revenue requirements.

Sales Mix Sales mix, by far, most heavily influences a manager's menu pricing decisions. **Sales mix** refers to the frequency with which specific menu items are selected by guests. As experienced managers know, some menu items sell better than others simply because they are more popular. As well, some items cost more to produce than others. Understanding the importance of sales mix is critical when you are setting menu item prices.

W fun on the Web!

Look up the following site to evaluate restaurants' pricing strategies based on reviewers' perceptions of service levels, guest type, product quality, ambiance, location, and much more!

www.zagat.com

First, choose a city. Then click on your specific restaurant criteria or just click on "Most Popular." Then click on any restaurant for a review that includes a features list, reviewers' ratings, prices, and much more. Look at several restaurant reviews. Evaluate whether you think the menu prices and the features/review are a "good fit" in your opinion.

Assigning Menu Prices

When examined closely, it is easy to see that there should be a clear and direct relationship between a restaurant's profits and its menu prices. Menu item pricing is related to revenue, costs (expenses), and profits by virtue of the following basic formula that you learned in Chapter 1:

> **Revenue x Expense = Profit**

When foodservice operators find that their profits are too low, they frequently question whether prices (which affect revenues) are too low. It is important to understand, however, that revenue and price are not synonymous terms. Revenue refers to the amount spent by *all* guests, while price refers to the amount charged to *one* guest. Thus, total revenue is generated by the following formula:

> **Price x Number Sold = Total Revenue**

FIGURE 7.1 Alternative Results of Price Increases

Old Price	New Price	Number Served	Total Revenue	Revenue Result
$1.00		200	$200.00	
	$1.25	250	$312.50	Increase
	$1.25	200	$250.00	Increase
	$1.25	160	$200.00	No Change
	$1.25	150	$187.50	Decrease

From this formula, it can be seen that there are actually two components of total revenue. While price is one component, the other is the number of items sold and, thus, guests served. The economic laws of **supply and demand** state that, for most products purchased by consumers, as the price of an item increases, the number of those items sold will generally decrease. Conversely, as the price of an item decreases, the number of those items sold will generally increase. For this reason, experienced restaurateurs know that price increases must be evaluated based on their impact on total revenue and not on price alone.

To illustrate the relationship of pricing to total revenue, assume that you own a quick-service restaurant chain. You are considering raising the price of small drinks from $1.00 to $1.25. Figure 7.1 illustrates the possible effects of this price increase on total revenue in a single unit.

Note especially that, in at least one alternative result, increasing the price has the effect of actually decreasing total revenue. Experienced foodservice managers know that increasing prices without giving added value can result in higher prices but, frequently, lower revenues because of reduced guest counts. This is true because guests demand a good price/value relationship when making a purchase. The **price/value relationship** simply reflects guests' view of how much value they are receiving for the price they are paying.

 *go figure!*

Assume that Sofia wants to raise the price of cheesecake sold in her downtown delicatessen. The cheesecakes currently sell for $2.00 a slice. She sells 100 servings per day. If she raises the price by 50 cents, how can she compute the number of slices that must be sold to keep her revenue constant? Sofia can use the following computations.

> **Current Number Sold × Current Price = Current Revenue**
>
> or
>
> **100 × $2.00 = $200.00**

To calculate the number of newly priced cheesecakes that must be sold to maintain Sofia's current revenue, she makes the following computation:

$$\frac{\text{Current Revenue}}{\text{New Price}} = \text{Number That Must Be Sold}$$

or

$$\frac{\$200.00}{\$2.50} = 80 \text{ must be sold}$$

Thus, in this example, if Sofia sells more than 80 pieces of cheesecake per day, her revenue will increase. If she sells less than 80 pieces, however, her total revenue will decrease. The actual results she achieves will depend largely on the price/value relationship her customers perceive regarding the higher priced cheesecake.

Marketing Approaches to Pricing

For a restaurateur, the prices of the items sold on their menu can represent a variety of concepts. For example, when Ruth Chris, the famous New Orleans steakhouse restaurant group sets the price for a steak on its menu, it seeks to tell its customers, "Come here for quality!" When Wendy's selects items for its 99-cent menu, it seeks to tell customers "Come here for value!" As these two examples demonstrate, price can be a valuable guest communications tool. As a result, some restaurateurs view menu pricing as primarily a product marketing function.

In a sales approach to marketing, the goal is to *maximize volume* (number of covers sold). Many quick-service restaurants use the sales approach to expand volume and as a result, increase customer counts. Increased customer counts should result in maximized total operational revenues. This approach works best when service levels are limited, the products sold are easily produced, and the cost of providing the product can reliably and consistently be controlled.

Other managers, usually in full-service restaurants, use the marketing philosophy of *maintaining your current competitive position* relative to the other restaurants in your market that target the same customers as you. Using this approach, restaurateurs try to stay within a fairly narrow range of menu prices that are similar to their immediate competitors. Restaurateurs utilizing this approach feel that guests are primarily price conscious and will not pay "more" for the menu items at their restaurants than they would pay at competitive restaurants.

Cost Approaches to Pricing

Another approach, which the authors believe is a good way to examine menu pricing, is to view it primarily from a *cost approach to pricing*, which is the focus of this chapter.

There are a variety of methods used by restaurateurs to set prices. The best of these methods consider an operation's costs and profit goals when determining menu prices. Currently, the two most popular pricing systems are those that are based upon:

■ Food cost percentage
■ Item contribution margin

Food Cost Percentage

Recall that in Chapter 6, you learned that the formula for computing food cost percentage for a restaurant is as follows:

$$\frac{\text{Cost of Food Sold}}{\text{Food Sales}} = \text{Food Cost \%}$$

This formula can be worded somewhat differently for a single menu item without changing its accuracy. Consider that:

$$\frac{\text{Item Food Cost}}{\text{Selling Price}} = \text{Item Food Cost \%}$$

The principles of algebra allow you to rearrange the formula as follows:

$$\frac{\text{Item Food Cost}}{\text{Item Food Cost \%}} = \text{Selling Price}$$

This method of pricing is based on the idea that food cost should be a predetermined percentage of selling price.

 go figure!

If you have a menu item that costs $1.50 to produce, and your desired food cost percentage for that item is 40%, the following formula is used to determine what the item's menu price should be:

$$\frac{\text{Item Food Cost}}{\text{Item Food Cost \%}} = \text{Selling Price}$$

or

$$\frac{\$1.50}{0.40} = \$3.75$$

Thus, in this example, the recommended selling price, given a $1.50 item food cost, is $3.75.

If the item is sold for $3.75, then a 40% food cost should be achieved for that item. A check on your work can also be done using the item food cost percentage formula:

$$\frac{\text{Item Food Cost}}{\text{Selling Price}} = \text{Item Food Cost \%}$$

or

$$\frac{\$1.50}{\$3.75} = 40\%$$

When you use a predetermined food cost percentage to price menu items, you are stating the belief that food cost in relation to selling price is of vital importance.

Experienced foodservice managers know that a second formula for arriving at appropriate selling prices based on predetermined food cost percentage goals can be employed. This method uses a cost factor or multiplier that can be assigned to each desired food cost percentage.

For example, if you were attempting to price a product and achieve a food cost of 40%, the factor would be calculated using the following formula:

$$\frac{1.00}{\text{Desired Item Food Cost \%}} = \text{Pricing Factor}$$

or

$$\frac{1.00}{0.40} = 2.5$$

Figure 7.2 details a factor table for desired item food cost percentages from 20% to 45%.

FIGURE 7.2 Pricing-Factor Table

Desired Food Cost %	Factor
20	5.000
23	4.348
25	4.000
28	3.571
30	3.333
33 $\frac{1}{3}$	3.000
35	2.857
38	2.632
40	2.500
43	2.326
45	2.222

go figure!

A factor, when multiplied by the item's cost, will result in a selling price that yields the desired item food cost percentage. For example, the pricing factor of 2.5 multiplied by an item food cost of $1.50 will yield a selling price that is based on a 40% item food cost. The computation would be as follows:

> **Pricing Factor x Item Food Cost = Selling Price**
>
> or
>
> **2.5 x 1.50 = $3.75**

As can be seen, these two different methods of arriving at the proposed selling price yield the same results. One formula simply relies on division, while the other relies on multiplication. The decision about which formula to use is completely up to you. With either approach, the selling price will be determined with a goal of achieving a given food cost percentage for each item.

Item Contribution Margin

Some foodservice managers prefer an approach to menu pricing that is focused, not on food cost percentage, but rather on an **item contribution margin**. Item contribution margin is defined as the amount that remains after the food cost of a menu item is subtracted from that item's selling price. Item contribution margin is the money left over (after subtracting the cost of food from selling price) that "contributes" to paying for labor and other expenses *and* providing a profit. Some restaurateurs refer to item contribution margin as **item gross profit margin** (selling price minus item food cost). This term is sometimes used because it employs the same calculation as gross profit margin on the income statement (food sales minus food cost).

go figure!

If an item sells for $3.75 and the food cost for this item is $1.50, the item contribution margin would be computed as follows:

> **Selling Price – Item Food Cost = Item Contribution Margin**
>
> or
>
> **$3.75 – $1.50 = $2.25**

The principles of algebra allow you to rearrange the formula to determine selling price. For example, when the item food cost is $1.50 and the *desired* item contribution margin is $2.25, the selling price is calculated as follows:

> **Item Food Cost + Desired Item Contribution Margin = Selling Price**
>
> or
>
> **$1.50 + $2.25 = $3.75**

Establishing menu price, with this method, is a matter of combining item food cost with a predetermined (desired) item contribution margin. Management's role here is to determine the desired contribution margin for each menu item. When using this approach, you would likely establish different contribution margins for various menu items or groups of items. For example, in a cafeteria where items are priced separately, entrées might be priced with an item contribution margin of $2.50 each, desserts with an item contribution margin of $1.25, and drinks, perhaps, with an item contribution margin of $0.75. Those managers who rely on the contribution margin approach to pricing do so in the belief that the average contribution margin per item is a more important consideration in pricing decisions than food cost percentage.

Food Cost Percentage versus Item Contribution Margin

Much has been written about the advantages of using both of the approaches to menu pricing about which you have just learned. Indeed, there are even additional methods that can be used for determining menu prices, but these specialized pricing approaches are beyond the scope of this text. For example, some large foodservice organizations have established highly complex computer-driven formulas for determining appropriate menu prices. For the average managerial accountant, however, understanding the use of food cost percentage, item contribution margin, or a combination of both will suffice when attempting to arrive at appropriate pricing decisions.

While the debate over the "best" method of pricing menu items is likely to continue for some time, you should remember to view pricing as an important process with an end goal of establishing a good price/value relationship in the mind of your guest while achieving profits for your operation. For these reasons, it is important that the menu not be priced so low that no profit is possible or so high that you will not be able to sell a sufficient number of items to make a profit. In the final analysis, it is your guest's perception of an item's price/value relationship that will eventually determine what your sales and profits will be on that item.

 *fun on the Web!*

Jack E. Miller was a National Restaurant Association (NRA) board member, a well-known hospitality educator, and former Director of the Hospitality program at St. Louis Community College. A colleague of the authors prior to his death, Jack's book, *Menu Pricing and Strategy*, is the most complete examination of menu pricing theories we have seen. A dedicated and down-to-earth hospitality practitioner, Jack's insight into the foodservice menu and the importance of pricing it correctly has helped thousands of restaurateurs, and it can help you, too. To obtain a copy of the book, go to

www.barnesandnoble.com

When you arrive, enter "Jack Miller" in the author search line to view a copy of the fourth edition of his book, *Menu Pricing and Strategy*, published by John Wiley & Sons.

Menu Price Analysis

Many methods have been proposed as being the best way to analyze the profitability of a menu and its pricing structure. The one you choose to use, however, should simply seek to answer the question, "How does the sale of this menu item contribute to the overall success of my operation?" It is unfortunate, in many ways, that the discussion of menu analysis typically leads one to elaborate mathematical formulas and computations. This is, of course, just one component of the analysis of a menu. It is not, however, nor should it ever be, the only component.

Consider the case of Danny, who operates a successful family restaurant called "The Mark Twain," in rural Tennessee. The restaurant has been in his family for three generations. One item on the menu is mustard greens with scrambled eggs. It does not sell often, but both mustard greens and eggs are ingredients in other, more popular items. Why does Danny keep the item in a prominent spot on the menu? The answer is simple and has little to do with money. The menu item was Danny's grandfather's favorite. As a thank you to his grandfather, who started the business and inspired Danny to become service and guest oriented, the menu item survives every menu reprint.

Menu analysis, then, is about more than just numbers. It involves marketing, imaging, sociology, psychology, and many times, the manager's emotions. Remember that guests respond not just to weighty financial analyses, but rather to menu design, the description of the menu item, the placement of items on the menu, their price, and their current popularity. While the financial analysis of a menu is indeed done "by the numbers," you must realize that financial analysis, however properly undertaken, is just one part, albeit an important part, of the total menu analysis picture.

FIGURE 7.3   Three Methods of Menu Analysis

Type of Analysis	Variables Considered	Method	Desired Result
1. Food cost %	**a.** Food cost % **b.** Popularity	Matrix Analysis	Minimize overall food cost %
2. Contribution margin	**a.** Contribution margin **b.** Popularity	Matrix Analysis	Maximize contribution margin
3. Goal value	**a.** Food cost % **b.** Contribution margin % **c.** Popularity **d.** Selling price **e.** Variable cost %	Goal Value Analysis	Achieve predetermined profit % goals

If you investigate the menu analysis methods that have been widely used, you will find that each seeks to perform the analysis using one or more of the following important operational variables with which you are already familiar:

- Food cost percentage
- Popularity (sales mix)
- Contribution margin
- Selling price
- Variable costs

The most popular systems of menu analysis, shown in Figure 7.3, will be reviewed because they represent the three major philosophical approaches to menu analysis.

Consider the case of Isabella, the food and beverage director for the Blue Lagoon Water Park Resort. One of her foodservice outlets is a full-service steak and seafood restaurant. At this restaurant, Isabella sells seven items in the entrée section of her menu. The items and information related to their cost, selling price, contribution margin, and popularity are presented in Figure 7.4, Isabella's Menu Analysis Worksheet. The information in Figure 7.4 will be used to illustrate the matrix analysis of food cost percentage and contribution margin, and goal value analysis in this section of the chapter. Before learning these types of analyses, however, it will be helpful for you to understand how the numbers in the worksheet are calculated.

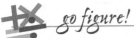 *go figure!*

The numbers in the rows of the table in Figure 7.4 are calculated as follows:

Individual Menu Item Rows:

> # Sold and Selling Price can be obtained from a POS system.
> Total Sales = # Sold × Selling Price
> Item Food Cost can be obtained from a standardized recipe cost sheet.

FIGURE 7.4 Isabella's Menu Analysis Worksheet

Date: 1/1 – 1/7

Menu Item	# Sold	Selling Price	Total Sales	Item Food Cost	Total Food Cost	Item Contribution Margin	Total Contribution Margin	Food Cost %
Strip Steak	73	$17.95	$1,310.35	$8.08	$ 589.84	$9.87	$720.51	45
Coconut Shrimp	121	16.95	2,050.95	5.09	615.89	11.86	1,435.06	30
Grilled Tuna	105	17.95	1,884.75	7.18	753.90	10.77	1,130.85	40
Chicken Breast	140	13.95	1,953.00	3.07	429.80	10.88	1,523.20	22
Lobster Stir-Fry	51	21.95	1,119.45	11.19	570.69	10.76	548.76	51
Scallops & Pasta	85	14.95	1,270.75	3.59	305.15	11.36	965.60	24
Beef Medallions	125	15.95	1,993.75	5.90	737.50	10.05	1,256.25	37
Total	**700**		**11,583.00**		**4,002.77**		**7,580.23**	
Average / Weighted Average	**100**	**16.55**	**1,654.71**	**5.72**	**571.82**	**10.83**	**1,082.89**	**35**

Total Food Cost = # Sold × Item Food Cost
Item Contribution Margin = Selling Price − Item Food Cost
Total Contribution Margin = # Sold × Item Contribution Margin
Food Cost % = Total Food Cost / Total Sales *or* Item Food Cost / Selling Price

Total Row:

The totals in the # Sold, Total Sales, Total Food Cost, and Total Contribution Margin columns are calculated by simply adding the numbers in those columns.

Average/Weighted Average Row:

Do the weighted average calculations *in the following order*:

Average/ Weighted Average	Calculation
Average # Sold	700 Total # Sold / 7 menu items = 100
Average Total Sales	11,583.00 Total Sales / 7 menu items = 1,654.71
Weighted Average Selling Price	1,654.71 Average Total Sales / 100 Average # Sold = 16.55
Average Total Food Cost	4,002.77 Total Food Cost / 7 menu items = 571.82
Weighted Average Item Food Cost	571.82 Average Total Food Cost / 100 Average # Sold = 5.72
Average Total Contribution Margin (CM)	7,580.23 Total CM / 7 menu items = 1,082.89
Weighted Average Item Contribution Margin (CM)	1,082.89 Average Total CM/ 100 Average # Sold = 10.83
Weighted Average Food Cost %	571.82 Average Total Food Cost/ 1,654.71 Average Total Sales = 35%

Now that you know how to calculate the numbers in the worksheet, you are ready to learn about matrix analysis of food cost percentage and contribution margin, and goal value analysis.

Matrix Analysis

The **matrix analysis** mentioned in Figure 7.3 is essentially just an easy method used to make comparisons among menu items. A matrix allows menu items to be placed into categories based on their unique characteristics such as food cost percentage, popularity, and contribution margin. Each approach to matrix analysis has its proponents and detractors, but an understanding of each will help you as you attempt to develop your own philosophy of menu analysis.

Food Cost Percentage

Matrix analysis that focuses on food cost percentage is the oldest and most traditional method used. Too frequently dismissed today as "old thinking," it is important for you to understand that, until the mid-1980s, it was overwhelmingly the single most popular method of evaluating the effectiveness of menu pricing decisions made by management.

When analyzing a menu using the food cost percentage method, you are seeking menu items that have the effect of *minimizing your overall food cost percentage*. The rationale for this is that a lowered food cost percentage leaves more of the sales dollar to be spent for other operational expenses. A criticism of the food cost percentage approach is that items that have a higher food cost percentage may be removed from the menu in favor of items that have a lower food cost percentage but, may also contribute fewer dollars to overall profit because the overall contribution margin of the menu may suffer.

To analyze Isabella's menu using the food cost percentage method, she must segregate her items based on the following two variables:

- Popularity (number sold)
- Food cost percentage

 *go figure!*

To determine average popularity (number sold) of her menu items, Isabella divides the total number of items sold by the number of items on her menu. In this case, the computation is:

$$\frac{\text{Total Number Sold}}{\text{Number of Menu Items}} = \text{Average Number Sold}$$

or

$$\frac{700}{7} = 100$$

To determine her average item food cost percentage, she divides average total food cost by average total sales. The computation is:

$$\frac{\text{Average Total Food Cost}}{\text{Average Total Sales}} = \text{Weighted Average Food Cost Percentage}$$

or

$$\frac{\$571.82}{\$1,654.71} = 35\%$$

Since she has an average popularity of 100 covers sold per menu item, any item which sold more than 100 times during this week's accounting period would be considered *high* in popularity, while any item selling less than 100 times would be considered *low* in popularity. Similarly, since her overall average food cost is 35%, she determines that any individual menu item with a food cost percentage above 35% will be considered *high* in food cost percentage, while any menu item with a food cost below 35% will be considered *low*.

The food cost percentage matrix to analyze these variables follows:

		Popularity	
		Low	**High**
Food Cost %	**High**	Square 1 High Food Cost %, Low Popularity	Square 2 High Food Cost %, High Popularity
	Low	Square 3 Low Food Cost %, Low Popularity	Square 4 Low Food Cost %, High Popularity

Based on the number sold and food cost percentage data in Figure 7.4, Isabella can classify her menu items in the following manner:

Square	Characteristics	Menu Item
1	High food cost %, low popularity	Strip Steak (45%, 73) Lobster Stir-Fry (51%, 51)
2	High food cost %, high popularity	Grilled Tuna (40%, 105) Beef Medallions (37%, 125)
3	Low food cost %, low popularity	Scallops & Pasta (24%, 85)
4	Low food cost %, high popularity	Coconut Shrimp (30%, 121) Chicken Breast (22%, 140)

Or, when placed in the proper squares, the menu items are classified as follows:

		Popularity 100	
		Low	**High**
Food Cost 35%	**High**	Square 1 Strip Steak Lobster Stir-Fry	Square 2 Grilled Tuna Beef Medallions
	Low	Square 3 Scallops & Pasta	Square 4 Coconut Shrimp Chicken Breast

Note that each menu item inhabits one, and only one, square. Using the food cost percentage method of menu analysis, Isabella would like as many menu items as possible to fall within square 4. Both coconut shrimp and chicken breast have below-average food cost percentages and above-average popularity. When developing a menu that seeks to minimize food cost percentage, items in the fourth square are highly desirable. They should be well promoted and have high menu visibility. Isabella should promote them to her guests and take care not to develop and attempt to sell menu items that are similar enough in nature that they could detract from the sales of these items.

The characteristics of the menu items that fall into each of the four matrix squares are unique and, thus, should be managed differently. Because of this, each of the menu items that fall in the individual squares requires a special marketing strategy, depending on their square location. These strategies can be summarized as shown in Figure 7.5.

FIGURE 7.5 Analysis of Food Cost Matrix Results

Square	Characteristics	Problem	Marketing Strategy
1	High food cost %, low popularity	Marginal due to both high food cost and lack of sales	**a.** Remove item from the menu. **b.** Consider current food trends to determine if the item itself is unpopular, or if its method of preparation is unpopular. **c.** Survey guests to determine current wants regarding this item. **d.** If this is a high contribution margin item, consider reducing price and/or portion size.
2	High food cost %, high popularity	Marginal due to high food cost	**a.** Increase price. **b.** Reduce prominence on the menu. **c.** Reduce portion size. **d.** Combine the sale of this item with one that has a lower cost and thus provides a lower overall food cost %.
3	Low food cost %, low popularity	Marginal due to lack of sales	**a.** Relocate item on the menu for greater visibility. **b.** Take off the regular menu and run as a special. **c.** Reduce menu price. **d.** Eliminate other unpopular menu items in order to increase demand for this one.
4	Low food cost %, high popularity	None	**a.** Promote well. **b.** Increase visibility on the menu.

It can be quite effective to use the food cost percentage method of menu evaluation. It is fast, logical, and time tested. Remember that if you achieve too high a food cost percentage, you run the risk that not enough money will remain to generate a profit on your sales. Again, however, you should be cautioned against promoting low-cost items with low selling prices at the expense of higher food percentage items with higher prices that may contribute greater gross profits.

 *go figure!*

Most foodservice operators would say it is better to achieve a 20% food cost than a 40% food cost.

Consider, however, that a chicken dish that sells for $5.00 and cost you just $1.00 to produce yields a 20% item food cost ($1.00 / $5.00 = 20%). In this case, there are $4.00 ($5.00–$1.00 = $4.00) remaining to pay for the labor and other expenses of serving this guest.

Compare that scenario to one where the same guest buys a steak for $10.00 that you can produce for $4.00. Your food cost percentage would be 40% ($4.00 / $10.00 = 40%). In this case, however, there are $6.00 ($10.00–$4.00 = $6.00) remaining to pay for the labor and other expenses of serving this guest!

It is because of conflicting situations such as these that some operators prefer to analyze their menus using the contribution margin matrix.

Contribution Margin

When analyzing a menu using the contribution margin approach (also widely known as **menu engineering**), the operator seeks to produce a menu that *maximizes the menu's overall contribution margin.* Recall that each menu item will have its own contribution margin, defined as the amount that remains after the food cost of the menu item is subtracted from the item's selling price. Contribution margin, then, is the amount that you will have available to pay for your labor and other expenses and to keep for your profit.

A common, and legitimate, criticism of the contribution margin approach to menu analysis is that it tends to favor high-priced menu items over low-priced ones, since higher priced menu items, in general, tend to have the highest contribution margins. Over the long term, this can result in sales techniques and menu placement decisions that tend to put in the guest's mind a higher check average than the operation may warrant or desire.

To analyze Isabella's menu using the contribution margin method, she must segregate her items based on the following two variables:

■ Popularity (number sold)
■ Contribution margin

go figure!

In Figure 7.4, to determine average popularity (number sold) of her menu items, Isabella divides the total number of items sold by the number of items on her menu. In this case, the computation is:

$$\frac{\text{Total \# Sold}}{\text{Number of Menu Items}} = \text{Average \# Sold}$$

or

$$\frac{700}{7} = 100$$

To determine her weighted average item contribution margin, she divides average total contribution margin by average number sold. The computation is:

$$\frac{\text{Average Total Contribution Margin}}{\text{Average \# Sold}} = \text{Weighted Average Item Contribution Margin}$$

or

$$\frac{1,082.89}{100} = \$10.83$$

To develop the contribution margin matrix, managers proceed along much the same lines as with the food cost percentage matrix. In this case, average item popularity is 100 and (weighted) average item contribution margin is $10.83.

The contribution margin matrix to analyze these variables follows.

		Popularity	
		Low	**High**
Contribution Margin	**High**	Square 1 Bleh ✓ High Contribution Margin, Low Popularity	Square 2 High Contribution Margin, High Popularity
	Low	Square 3 Low Contribution Margin, Low Popularity	Square 4 Low Contribution Margin, High Popularity

raise price
Could be great

Great ↑

Based on the number sold and contribution margin data in Figure 7.4, Isabella can classify her menu items in the following manner:

Square	Characteristics	Menu Item
1	High contribution margin, Low popularity	Scallops & Pasta ($11.36, 85)
2	High contribution margin, High popularity	Coconut Shrimp ($11.86, 121) Chicken Breast ($10.88, 140)
3	Low contribution margin, Low popularity	Strip Steak ($9.87, 73) Lobster Stir-Fry ($10.76, 51)
4	Low contribution margin, High popularity	Grilled Tuna ($10.77, 105) Beef Medallions ($10.05, 125)

Or, when placed in the proper squares, the menu items are classified as follows:

		Popularity 100	
		Low	High
Contribution Margin $10.83	High	Square 1 Scallops & Pasta	Square 2 Coconut Shrimp Chicken Breast
	Low	Square 3 Strip Steak Lobster Stir-Fry	Square 4 Grilled Tuna Beef Medallions

Again, each menu item finds itself in one, and only one, matrix square. Using the contribution margin method of menu analysis, Isabella would like as many of her menu items as possible to fall within square 2, that is, high contribution margin and high popularity. From this analysis, Isabella knows that both coconut shrimp and chicken breast yield a higher than average contribution margin. In addition, these items sell very well. For these reasons, Isabella would seek to give high menu visibility to items with high contribution margin and high popularity when using the contribution margin approach.

Each of the menu items that fall in the four squares requires a special marketing strategy, depending on its location. These strategies can be summarized in Figure 7.6.

The selection of either food cost percentage or contribution margin as a menu analysis technique is really an attempt by the foodservice operator to answer the following questions:

■ Are my menu items priced correctly?
■ Are the individual menu items selling well enough to warrant keeping them on the menu?
■ Is the overall profit margin on my menu items satisfactory?

FIGURE 7.6 Analysis of Contribution Margin Matrix Results

Square	Characteristics	Problem	Marketing Strategy
1	High contribution margin, Low popularity	Marginal due to lack of sales	**a.** Relocate on menu for greater visibility. **b.** Consider reducing selling price.
2	High contribution margin, High popularity	None	**a.** Promote well. **b.** Increase prominence on the menu.
3	Low contribution margin, Low popularity	Marginal due to both low contribution margin and lack of sales	**a.** Remove from menu. **b.** Consider offering as a special occasionally, but at a higher menu price.
4	Low contribution margin, High popularity	Marginal due to low contribution margin	**a.** Increase price. **b.** Reduce prominence on the menu. **c.** Consider reducing portion size.

Because of the limitations of matrix analysis, some sophisticated observers feel that neither the matrix food cost nor the matrix contribution margin approach is tremendously effective in analyzing menus. They argue that this is the case because the axes on the matrix are determined by the average food cost percentage, contribution margin, or sales level (popularity). When this is done, some menu items will *always* fall into the less desirable categories. This is so because, in matrix analysis, high food cost percentage, for instance, really means food cost percentage *above* the average. Obviously, then, some items *must* fall below the average regardless of their role in operational profitability. Eliminating the poorest items only shifts other items into undesirable categories. To illustrate this drawback to matrix analysis, consider the following example.

go figure!

Assume that one of Isabella's competitors, Joshua Richards, who owns Joshua's Restaurant across the street from the Blue Lagoon Water Park Resort, sells only four items, as follows:

Joshua's #1 Menu

Item	Number Sold
Beef	70
Chicken	60
Pork	15
Seafood	55

(handwritten notes in right margin):
High Pop.
210 – Dry Rub Ribs
242 – BBQ Ribs
160 – Mesquite Chick
195 – ½ Roast Chicken

Total	**200**
Average sold	**50 (200 / 4)**

Joshua may elect to remove the pork item, since its sales range is below the average of 50 items sold. If Joshua adds turkey to the menu and removes the pork, he could get the following results:

Joshua's #2 Menu

Item	Number Sold
Beef	65
Chicken	55
Turkey	50
Seafood	30
Total	**200**
Average sold	**50 (200 / 4)**

As can be seen, the turkey item drew sales away from the beef, chicken, and seafood dishes and did not increase the total number of menu items sold. In this case, it is now the seafood item that falls below the menu average. Should it be removed because its sales are below average? Clearly, this might not be wise. Removing the seafood item might serve only to draw sales *from* the remaining items to the seafood replacement item, placing a new item in the "below average" category. Obviously, the same type of result can occur when you use a matrix to analyze food cost percentage or contribution margin. As someone once stated, half of us are always below average in everything. Thus, a matrix analysis approach *forces* some items to be below average. It is simple to use, but with that simplicity comes a lack of utility. How, then, can an operator answer complex questions related to price, sales volume, and overall profit margin? One answer is to avoid the overly simplistic matrix analysis and employ all, or even part, of a more effective method of menu analysis called goal value analysis.

Goal Value Analysis

Goal value analysis was introduced by Dr. David Hayes and Dr. Lynn Huffman in an article titled "Menu Pricing: A Better Approach," published by the respected hospitality journal *The Cornell Quarterly*, in 1985. Ten years later, at the height of what was known as the **value pricing** (extremely low pricing strategies used to drive significant increases in guest counts) debate, goal value analysis proved its effectiveness in a second article based on its methodology, which was also published in *The Cornell Quarterly* (1995). Goal value analysis is a highly advanced approach to menu analysis that is more complex, but more useful, than is matrix analysis.

Essentially, **goal value analysis** is a menu pricing and analysis system that compares goals of the foodservice operation to performance of individual menu items. It uses the power of an algebraic formula to replace less sophisticated menu averaging techniques. The advantages of goal value analysis are many, including ease of use, accuracy, and the ability to simultaneously consider more variables than is possible with two-dimensional matrix analysis. Mastering its capability can truly help you create menus that are effective, popular, and, most important, profitable.

Perhaps the most accurate criticism of both the food cost percentage and contribution margin approaches to menu analysis relate to the actual costs of food and beverages. In years past, food and beverage products were the single largest cost borne by a restaurant. Today, the cost of labor is likely to *exceed* that of food and beverages in many restaurants. In such a situation, how logical is it to utilize a menu analysis system that:

- Is based upon food costs or contribution margin alone?
- Ignores labor costs?

Actually, the authors believe it is somewhat surprising that more restaurateurs are not clamoring for a more modern menu evaluation technique. We suspect, however, as more restaurateurs focus on their cost of labor (and other expenses), more sophisticated menu evaluation techniques will become commonplace. As well, these more sophisticated techniques require sophisticated managers, hospitality instructors, and students.

Goal value analysis was the pioneering effort in advanced menu analysis because it evaluates each menu item's food cost percentage, contribution margin, popularity, and, *unlike* the two previous analysis methods introduced, includes the analysis of the menu item's nonfood variable and fixed costs as well as its selling price. The total dollar amount of **fixed costs** does not vary with sales volume, while the total dollar amount of **variable costs** changes as volume changes. An example of a fixed cost is manager salaries, and an example of a variable cost is hourly wages. You will learn more about fixed and variable costs in Chapter 9.

Returning to the data in Figure 7.4, we see that Isabella has an overall food cost percentage of 35%. In addition, she served 700 guests at an entrée check average of $16.55. If we knew about Isabella's overall fixed and variable costs, we would know more about the profitability of each of Isabella's menu items. One difficulty, of course, resides in the assignment of nonfood variable costs to individual menu items. *The majority of nonfood variable costs assigned to menu items is labor cost.*

For example, the strip steak on her menu is likely purchased precut and vacuum-sealed. Its preparation simply requires opening the steak package, in-cooler aging it for a day or two, seasoning the steak when it is ordered by the guest, and then placing it on a broiler. The lobster stir-fry, on the other hand, is a complex dish that requires cooking and shelling the lobster, cleaning and trimming the vegetables, then preparing the item when ordered by quickly cooking the lobster, vegetables, and a sauce in a wok. Thus, the *variable* labor cost of preparing the two dishes is very different. It is assumed that Isabella responds to these differing costs by charging more for a more labor-intensive dish and less for one that is less labor intensive. Other dishes require essentially the same amount of labor to prepare; thus, their variable labor costs figure less significantly in the establishment of price. Because that is true, for analysis purposes, most operators find it convenient to assign nonfood variable costs to individual menu items based on the overall restaurant's nonfood variable costs. For example, if labor and other variable costs are 30% of total sales for the restaurant, all menu items may be assigned that same variable cost percentage.

For the purpose of her goal value analysis, Isabella determines her total variable costs. These are all the costs that vary with her sales volume, excluding the cost of the food itself. She computes those variable costs from her income statement and finds that they account for 30% of her total sales. Using this information, Isabella assigns a variable cost of 30% of selling price to each menu item.

Having compiled the information in Figure 7.4, Isabella can use the algebraic goal value formula to create a specific goal value for her entire menu, and then use the same formula to compute the goal value of each individual menu item. Menu items that achieve goal values higher than that of the overall menu goal value will contribute greater than average profit percentages. As the goal value for an item increases, so, too, does its profitability. The overall menu goal value can be used as a "target" in this way, assuming that Isabella's average food cost percentage, average number of items sold per menu item, average selling price (check average), and average variable cost percentage all meet the overall profitability goals of her restaurant.

The goal value formula is as follows:

$$A \times B \times C \times D = \text{Goal Value}$$

where

$$A = 1.00 - \text{Food Cost \%}$$

$$B = \text{Item Popularity (Number Sold)}$$

$$C = \text{Selling Price}$$

$$D = 1.00 - (\text{Variable Cost \%} + \text{Food Cost \%})$$

The entire equation, then, is as follows:

$$(1.00 - \text{Food Cost \%}) \times (\text{Number Sold}) \times (\text{Selling Price})$$
$$\times [1.00 - (\text{Variable Cost \%} + \text{Food Cost \%})]$$

Note that *A* in the preceding formula is actually the contribution margin *percentage* of a menu item and that *D* is the amount available to fund fixed costs and provide for a profit after all variable costs are covered.

 *go figure!*

Using 30% for variable cost % and the average/ weighted average numbers from Figure 7.4 for # sold (100), selling price ($16.55), and food cost % (35%), Isabella calculates the formula to compute the goal value of her *total menu* as follows:

A	×B	×C	×D	= Goal Value
(1.00 − 0.35)	×100	×$16.55	×[1.00 − (0.30 + 0.35)]	= Goal Value
			or	
0.65	×100	×$16.55	×0.35	= 376.5

According to this formula, any menu item whose goal value equals or exceeds 376.5 will achieve profitability that equals or exceeds that of Isabella's overall menu.

The computed goal value is neither a percentage nor a dollar figure because it is really a numerical target or score. Figure 7.7 details the goal value data Isabella needs to complete a goal value analysis on each of her seven menu items.

Figure 7.8 details the results of Isabella's goal value analysis. Note that she has calculated the goal values of her menu items and ranked them in order of highest to lowest goal value. She has also inserted her overall menu goal value in the appropriate rank order.

Note that the grilled tuna falls slightly below the profitability of the entire menu, while the strip steak and lobster stir-fry fall substantially below the overall goal value score. Should these two items be replaced? The answer, most likely, is no *if* Isabella is satisfied with her current target food cost percentage, profit margin, check average, and guest count. Every menu will have items that are more (and less) profitable than others. In fact, many operators develop and promote items called loss leaders. A **loss leader** is a menu item that is priced very low, sometimes even below total costs, for the purpose of drawing large numbers of guests to the operation. If, for example, Isabella has the only operation in town that serves outstanding lobster stir-fry, that item may, in fact, contribute to the overall

FIGURE 7.7   Isabella's Goal Value Analysis Data

Item	Food Cost % (in decimal form)	Number Sold	Selling Price	Variable Cost % (in decimal form)
Strip Steak	0.45	73	$17.95	0.30
Coconut Shrimp	0.30	121	16.95	0.30
Grilled Tuna	0.40	105	17.95	0.30
Chicken Breast	0.22	140	13.95	0.30
Lobster Stir-Fry	0.51	51	21.95	0.30
Scallops & Pasta	0.24	85	14.95	0.30
Beef Medallions	0.37	125	15.95	0.30

FIGURE 7.8   Goal Value Analysis Results

Rank	Item	Food Cost %	Number Sold	Selling Price	Variable Cost %	Goal Value
1	Chicken Breast	0.22	140	$13.95	0.30	731.2
2	Coconut Shrimp	0.30	121	16.95	0.30	574.3
3	Scallops & Pasta	0.24	85	14.95	0.30	444.3
4	Beef Medallions	0.37	125	15.95	0.30	414.5
	Overall menu (Goal Value)	*0.35*	*100*	*$16.55*	*0.30*	*376.5*
5	Grilled Tuna	0.40	105	17.95	0.30	339.3
6	Strip Steak	0.45	73	17.95	0.30	180.2
7	Lobster Stir-Fry	0.51	51	21.95	0.30	104.2

success of the operation by drawing people who will buy it, while their fellow diners may order items that are more profitable.

The accuracy of goal value analysis is well documented. Used properly, it is a convenient way for management to make decisions regarding required profitability, sales volume, and pricing. Because all of the values needed for the goal value formula are readily available, management need not concern itself with puzzling through endless decisions about item replacement.

Items that do not achieve the targeted goal value tend to be deficient in one or more of the key areas of food cost percentage, popularity, selling price, or variable cost percentage. In theory, all menu items have the potential of reaching the goal value.

 *go figure!*

For example, examine the goal value analysis results for the item, strip steak:

$$
\begin{array}{cccccc}
& A & \times B & \times C & \times D & = \text{Goal Value} \\
\text{Strip Steak} & (1 - 0.45) & \times 73 & \times 17.95 & \times [1 - (0.30 + 0.45)] & = \text{Goal Value} \\
& 0.55 & \times 73 & \times 17.95 & \times 0.25 & = 180.2
\end{array}
$$

This item did not meet the goal value target. Why? There can be several answers. One is that the item's 45% food cost is too high. This can be addressed by reducing portion size or changing the item's recipe since both of these actions have the effect of reducing the food cost percentage and, thus, increasing the A value. A second approach to improving the goal value score of the strip steak is to work on improving the B value, that is, the number of times the item is sold. This may be done through merchandising or, since it is one of the more expensive items on the menu, incentives to service staff for upselling this item. Variable *C*, menu price, while certainly in line with the rest of the menu, can also be adjusted upward; however, you must remember that adjustments upward in *C* may well result in declines in the number of items sold (*B* value)! Increases in the menu price, however, will also have the effect of *decreasing* the food cost percentage and the variable cost percentage of the menu item (and increasing the contribution margin). Finally, the *D* value can be improved by decreasing labor and other non-food variable costs. An easy way to determine the effects of changes made to goal values is to use an Excel spreadsheet. Once you put the formulas in a spreadsheet, it is then easy to see how changes made to food costs, number of items, selling prices, and variable costs affect the goal values.

Obviously, the changes you undertake as a result of any type of menu analysis are varied and can be complex. As you gain experience in knowing the tastes and behaviors of your guests, however, your skill in menu-related decision making will quickly improve. Sophisticated users of the goal value analysis system can, as suggested by Lendal Kotschevar, Ph.D. and Marcel Escoffier in their book, *Management by Menu*, modify the formula to increase its accuracy and usefulness even more. In the area of variable costs, a menu item might be assigned a low, medium, or high variable cost. If overall variable costs equal 30%, for example, management may choose to assign a variable cost of 25% to those items with very low labor costs attached to them, 30% to others with average labor costs, and 35% to others with even higher labor costs. This adjustment affects only the *D* variable of the goal value formula and can be accommodated quite easily.

Goal value analysis will also allow you to make better decisions more quickly. This is especially true if you know a bit of algebra and realize that anytime you determine a desired goal value *and* when any three of the four variables contained in the formula are known, you can solve for the fourth unknown variable by using goal value as the numerator and placing the known variables in the denominator. Figure 7.9 shows you how to solve for each unknown variable in the goal value formula.

 *go figure!*

To illustrate how the information in Figure 7.9 can be used, return to the information in Figure 7.8 and assume that, in Isabella's case, she feels the 12-ounce strip steak she is offering may be too large for her typical guest and that is why its popularity (*B* value) is low. Thus, Isabella elects to take three actions:

1. She reduces the portion size of the item from 12 ounces to 9 ounces, resulting in a reduction in her food cost from $8.08 to $6.10.
2. Because she knows her guests will likely be hesitant to pay the same price for a smaller steak, she also *reduces* the selling price of this item by $1 to $16.95. She feels that this will keep the strip steak from losing any popularity resulting from the reduction in portion size. Her new food cost percentage for this item is 36% ($6.10 / $16.95 = 36%).
3. Since the labor required to prepare this menu item is so low, she assigns a below-average 25% variable cost to its *D* value.

Isabella now knows three of the goal value variables for this item and can solve for the fourth. Isabella knows her *A* value (1.00−0.36), her *C* value ($16.95), and her *D* value [1.00−(0.25 + 0.36)]. The question she would ask is this, "Given this newly structured menu item, how many must be sold to make the item achieve the targeted goal value?" The answer requires solving the goal value equation for *B*, the number sold. From Figure 7.9, recall that, if *B* is the unknown variable, it can be computed by using the following formula:

$$\frac{\text{Goal Value}}{A \times C \times D} = B$$

In this case,

$$\frac{376.5}{(1.00 - 0.36) \times \$16.95 \times [1.00 - (0.25 + 0.36)]} = B$$

Thus,

$$89 = B$$

According to the formula, 89 servings of strip steak would have to be sold to achieve Isabella's target goal value.

FIGURE 7.9 Solving for Goal Value Unknowns

Known Variables	Unknown Variable	Method to Find Unknown
A, B, C, D	**Goal Value (GV)**	$A \times B \times C \times D$
B, C, D, GV	**A**	$\dfrac{GV}{B \times C \times D}$
A, C, D, GV	**B**	$\dfrac{GV}{A \times C \times D}$
A, B, D, GV	**C**	$\dfrac{GV}{A \times B \times D}$
A, B, C, GV	**D**	$\dfrac{GV}{A \times B \times C}$

Again, goal value analysis is a very useful estimation tool for management. You can use it to establish a desired food cost percentage, target popularity figure, selling price, or variable cost percentage.

Goal value analysis is becoming increasingly linked to breakeven analysis because of their mathematical similarities (see Chapter 9). In addition to the ability to analyze multiple cost variables simultaneously, goal value analysis is valuable because it is not, as is matrix analysis, dependent on *past* operational performance to establish profitability. It can be used by management to establish *future* menu targets.

 *go figure!*

To illustrate, assume that Isabella wishes to achieve a greater profit margin and a $17.00 entrée average selling price for next year. She plans to achieve this through a reduction in her overall food cost to 33% and her other variable costs to 29%. Her overall menu goal value formula for next year, assuming no reduction or increase in guest counts, would be as follows:

A	x B	x C	x D	= Goal Value
(1.00 − 0.33)	x 100	x $17.00	x [1.00 − (0.29 + 0.33)]	= Goal Value
		or		
0.67	x 100	x $17.00	x 0.38	= 432.8

Thus, each item on next year's menu should be evaluated with the new goal value in mind. It is important to remember, however, that Isabella's actual profitability will be heavily influenced by sales mix. Thus, all pricing, portion size, and menu placement decisions become critical. Note that Isabella can examine each of her menu items and determine whether she wishes to change any of the items' characteristics in order to meet her goals. It is at this point that she must remember, however, that a purely quantitative approach to menu analysis is neither practical nor desirable. Menu analysis and pricing decisions are always a matter of experience, skill, and educated predicting because it is difficult to know in advance how changing any one menu item may affect the sales mix of the remaining items. In the final analysis, regardless of the techniques utilized, establishing food costs and then assigning reasonable menu prices based on these costs is a critical role for foodservice managers serving as their own managerial accountants.

fun on the Web!

A solid understanding of food and beverage cost control is critical to the success of every foodservice manager. As well, managerial accountants must understand food and beverage costs and their control if they are to analyze a foodservice operation's financial performance. To obtain a copy of a popular book on cost controls, go to

www.amazon.com

When you arrive, enter "Lea Dopson" in the author search line to view a copy of the most recent edition of *Food and Beverage Cost Control*, published by John Wiley & Sons. This book has been on the market for more than fifteen years and is one of the best-selling and most up-to-date explanations of this important area of hospitality management.

Apply What You Have Learned

Jessica Castillo had always been interested in food and cooking. After culinary school and several extensive apprentice stints with some of the best chefs in New York and a spectacular year in London, Jessica felt she was ready to open her own restaurant.

Creativity and customer focus were Jessica's strengths, as was a firm conviction that she didn't want her dining room filled only with "rich people." She wanted to make the types of foods she served available to as wide an audience as possible. Jessica wanted to serve a diverse group of customers, but she also knew she had to make a reasonable profit if she wanted to stay in business.

Menu pricing had always puzzled Jessica. In her few years in the hospitality industry, Jessica had already seen several cases of restaurateurs who planned for a 25% or 30% food cost, priced their menu accordingly, and yet failed to generate the profits they needed to stay open. She was keenly aware that many fine dining establishments such as the one she wished to open frequently encountered that very fate.

1. Assume that Jessica asked you for your input on her menu-pricing quandary. Draft a short paragraph describing your philosophy of the relationship between "menu price" and "profits."
2. Consider the type of operation Jessica plans to open. Identify five factors that you believe will have a significant impact on the prices Jessica should charge for her menu items.
3. Consider the industry segment in which Jessica's restaurant will operate. What role do you believe her competitors' pricing should play in influencing her own menu prices? Do you think the same situation would exist in other segments of the restaurant industry? Be prepared to explain your answer.

Key Terms and Concepts

The following are terms and concepts discussed in the chapter that are important for you to know as a manager. To help you review, please define the following terms.

Sales mix	Item gross profit margin	Goal value analysis
Supply and demand	Matrix analysis	Fixed costs
Price/value relationship	Menu engineering	Variable costs
Item contribution margin	Value pricing	Loss leader

 *Test Your Skills*

Complete the Test Your Skills exercises below by placing your answers in the shaded boxes.

1. Rosa and Gabriel own two Mexican grills in a large city in Texas. Rosa has primary responsibility for the grill in the suburbs, and Gabriel has primary responsibility for the grill in the downtown area. The menu items and product costs are the same in both grills, but the market in the downtown area demands lower menu prices than that in the suburbs. So, Rosa has set her desired product cost percentage at 28%, and Gabriel's desired product cost percentage is 32% since he can't charge as much as Rosa. Rosa likes to use the product cost percentage method to price menu items, and Gabriel likes to use the factor method. Help both of them determine their selling prices.

Rosa and Gabriel's Mexican Grill (Suburb–Rosa)

Desired Product Cost Percentage: 28%

Product Cost Percentage Method

Item	Cost of Product	Desired Product Cost Percentage	Selling Price
Steak Fajitas	$4.50		
Chicken Fajitas	4.00		
Carne Asada	4.25		
Cheese Enchiladas	2.00		
Beef Enchiladas	2.50		
Enchiladas Verde	2.00		
Chili Rellenos	2.75		
Tacos	0.30		
Bean Chalupas	0.25		
Tortilla Soup	0.30		

Rosa and Gabriel's Mexican Grill (Downtown – Gabriel)

Desired Product Cost Percentage: 32%

Factor Method

Item	Cost of Product	Factor	Selling Price
Steak Fajitas	$4.50		
Chicken Fajitas	4.00		
Carne Asada	4.25		
Cheese Enchiladas	2.00		
Beef Enchiladas	2.50		
Enchiladas Verde	2.00		
Chili Rellenos	2.75		
Tacos	0.30		
Bean Chalupas	0.25		
Tortilla Soup	0.30		

2. David Ward operates a successful BBQ Rib restaurant. His entrée menu has eight items. Following are last week's sales and cost data for all eight items. Using this data, complete David's menu analysis worksheet.

David's Menu Analysis Worksheet

Menu Item	Number Sold	Selling Price	Total Sales	Item Cost	Total Cost	Item Contribution Margin	Total Contribution Margin	Food Cost %
Dry-Rubbed Ribs	210	$11.95		$4.10				
BBQ Ribs	242	9.95		4.25				
Salmon Grill	51	14.95		6.45				
Brisket	88	8.95		2.85				
Sausage Links	103	6.95		1.45				
Cowboy Combo	145	9.95		4.20				
1/2 Roast Chicken	185	8.95		3.10				
Mesquite Chicken	160	6.95		1.75				
Total								
Weighted Average								

3A. Utilizing the data from David's menu analysis worksheet in question 2, create a food cost percentage matrix and place each menu item in its appropriate box.

Food Cost Percentage Matrix

	Low Popularity (Below___Sold)	High Popularity (Above___ Sold)
High Food Cost % **(Above___%)**		
Low Food Cost % **(Below___%)**		

   a. Using this type analysis, which items are David's "best"?

   b. Using this type analysis, which items might David consider removing from his menu?

   c. What is one strength of this type menu analysis system?

   d. What is one weakness of this type menu analysis system?

   e. What marketing strategies might David use for items that fall in square 2?

3B. Utilizing the data from David's menu analysis worksheet in question 2, create a contribution margin matrix and place each menu item in its appropriate box.

Contribution Margin Matrix

	Low Popularity (Below_____Sold)	High Popularity (Above_____Sold)
High Contribution Margin **(Above $_____)**		
Low Contribution Margin **(Below $_____)**		

   a. Using this type analysis, which items are David's "best"?

   b. Using this type analysis, which items might David consider removing from his menu?

   c. What is one strength of this type menu analysis system?

   d. What is one weakness of this type menu analysis system?

   e. What marketing strategies might David use for items that fall in Square 1?

4. Sissy LaRoussa has studied both the food cost percentage and contribution margin matrix methods of menu analysis and believes they rely too heavily on the cost of food for their conclusions. Sissy operates a "Quick Wok" outlet in her local mall's food court. She serves hot and tasty Asian cuisine to the mall shoppers. In her operation, both labor costs and occupation costs (her lease) exceed food costs on her monthly income statement. From that income statement, she knows that her nonfood variable cost (primarily her labor cost as well as a percentage sales fee assessed by the mall's owners) averages 35% of her menu selling price. She wants to use goal value analysis to determine which, if any, of her menu items are failing to perform well for her. Utilizing last week's sales data presented in the following chart, calculate the goal value for each item.

Then sort (in descending rank order) by goal value. Be sure to include the *Overall Menu Goals* in the appropriate rank order. (Spreadsheet hint: Review "Before You Start: How to Use Spreadsheets" on your CD-ROM before you attempt this problem in Excel. In order for the table to sort correctly, you must put the ENTIRE goal value formula in each cell of the Goal Value column.)

Sissy's Quick Wok

Item	Food Cost %	Number Sold	Selling Price	Variable Cost %	Goal Value
Beef and Broccoli	0.25	773	$4.99	0.35	
Sweet and Sour Pork	0.18	321	3.99	0.35	
General Tao's Chicken	0.20	640	4.99	0.35	
Vegetable Stir-Fry	0.11	440	4.49	0.35	
3-Item Combo	0.41	310	6.99	0.35	
Coconut Shrimp	0.24	485	5.99	0.35	
Asian Ribs	0.30	145	6.99	0.35	
Overall Menu Goals	*0.25*	*445*	*5.50*	*0.35*	

a. Using this type analysis, which item would be considered Sissy's most profitable item?

b. What is the primary cause of that item's high goal value?

c. Using this type analysis, which item would be considered Sissy's least profitable item?

d. What is the primary cause of that item's lower goal value?

e. Based on the results of the goal value analysis, identify specific actions you would recommend Sissy take to improve the profitability of her menu items that do not meet her goals.

CHAPTER 8

Revenue Management for Hotels

OVERVIEW

Just as properly pricing menus is critical to the success of restaurant managers, effectively establishing and managing a hotel's room rate structure is essential to the success of hoteliers and to the profitability of the hotels they operate. In this chapter, you will learn how hoteliers decide what they will charge for the hotel rooms and the other products they sell. You will discover that hotels typically offer their guests a variety of room rates depending upon the specific characteristics of the rooms sold and the guests to whom the rooms are sold.

While the greatest majority of revenue generated by hotels is the result of guest room sales, hotels also generate non-guest room sales. In this chapter, you will discover these non-room revenue sources and why hoteliers must consider them carefully if they are to maximize sales and thus help ensure their hotels' profitability.

CHAPTER OUTLINE

- Establishing Room Rates
- Revenue Management
- Non-Room Revenue
- Apply What You Have Learned
- Key Terms and Concepts
- Test Your Skills

LEARNING OUTCOMES

At the conclusion of this chapter, you will be able to:

✓ Utilize alternative methods when establishing a hotel's room rate structure.
✓ Apply revenue management and analysis techniques to the administration of a hotel's room rate structure.
✓ Recognize the importance to a hotel of properly managing and controlling its non-room revenue.

Establishing Room Rates

Any serious exploration of hotel room rates and their management must include basic information about room rate economics. Interestingly, the fundamental rules of supply and demand (see Chapter 7) related to hotel rooms are largely based upon the time frame examined. In the short term, the law of demand is most important. **Room rate economics** recognizes that, when the supply of hotel rooms is held constant, an increase in demand for those rooms will result in an increase in their selling price. Conversely, when supply is held constant, a decrease in demand leads to a decreased selling price. Understanding the law of demand is critical because, unlike managers in other industries, hoteliers cannot increase their inventory levels of rooms (supply) in response to increases in demand. Hotel rooms simply cannot be designed, financed, and built on demand! You must come to fully understand the critical importance of this basic concept if you are to be the successful manager of a hotel's revenue generation activities.

Hotel managers must also understand that their own inventory of rooms is highly perishable. If a hotel does not sell room 101 on Monday night, it will never again be able to sell that room on that night, and the potential revenue that would be generated from the sale is lost forever. In a hotel, unsold inventory vanishes forever.

Since information about supply is readily known, and since forecast data helps to estimate demand, you can learn to accurately gauge the relationship between guest room supply and demand. Using this information, you can determine the best rates to be assigned to each of your rooms. A **rack rate** is the price at which a hotel sells its rooms when no discounts of any kind are offered to the guests. Rack rates, however, will vary based upon the type of room sold. Figure 8.1 lists the rack rates that are associated with Paige Vincent's Blue Lagoon Water Park Resort based on her **room mix** (the variety of room types) in her hotel.

Note that, in this example, rack rates vary by bed type (kings at this hotel are less expensive than doubles), by amenities (suites are likely to have features not found in standard rooms), by location (park-view rooms are more expensive than rooms that have less desirable views), and by size (parlor suites cost more than non-parlor suites and

FIGURE 8.1   Blue Lagoon Water Park
Rack Rates Based on Room Types

Room Type	Rack Rate
Standard King	$145
Standard Double	$151
Family King Suite	$173
Family Double Suite	$183
Park-View King Suite	$207
Park-View Double Suite	$217
Double Parlor Suite	$255
Triple-Double Suite	$269

triple-double suites are more expensive than regular double suites). Some larger hotels may have dozens of different room types, each with its unique rack rate. Even the smallest of hotels, however, will likely have several room types and, therefore, multiple rack rates.

Some hotels have very strong seasonal demand. For example, a hotel near a ski resort with a high occupancy during the ski season may experience a lower occupancy in the off-season and will likely respond by varying its rack rates. These hotels, then, will have a **seasonal rate** that is offered during that hotel's highest volume season which is higher or lower than the standard rack rate. In some cases, it makes sense for hoteliers to create **special event rates**. Sometimes referred to as "super" or "premium" rack, these rates are used when a hotel is assured of very high demand levels. Examples include rates for rooms during Mardi Gras (New Orleans hoteliers) and on New Year's Eve (New York City hoteliers).

Hotels often negotiate special rates for selected guests. In most cases, these negotiated rates will vary by room type. In addition to rack and negotiated rates, hotels typically offer **corporate rates, government rates**, and **group rates**. Each of these rates would be offered to members of these respective groups.

Some hotels have great success "packaging" the guest rooms they sell with other hotel services or local area attractions. When a hotel creates a package, the **package rate** charged must be sufficient to ensure that all costs associated with the package have been considered. This is so because the package rate allows a guest to pay one price for all of the features and amenities included in the package.

Just as a hotel's revenue managers can create a variety of rates, they can also create discounts at various percentage or dollar levels for each rate type we have examined. The result is that a hotel, with multiple room types and multiple rate plans, may have literally *hundreds* of rate types programmed into its property management system. A **property management system (PMS)** is a computer system used to manage guest bookings, online reservations, check-in/check-out, and guest purchases of amenities offered by the hotel. In addition, the use of one or more authorized **fade rates**, a reduced rate authorized for use when a guest seeking a reservation is hesitant to make the reservation because the price is perceived as too high, can result in even more room rates to be managed.

Given the number of room types found in a typical hotel and the number of rate types associated with each room, you can now appreciate the complexity of forming and managing a hotel's room rates. Add to that challenge the fact that each rate type can be discounted or increased by any number of percentage points and at various times of the year or in response to specific special events. Because of these reasons, the true intricacies of the rate development process become apparent.

The Hubbart Room Rate Formula

Hoteliers want to maximize their profits and thus collect the highest rate possible for their rooms. However, the rate cannot be so high that it discourages guests from staying at the hotel. Similarly, the rate cannot be so low that it prevents the hotel from making a profit. Thus, the room rate charged should not result from a mere "guess" about its appropriateness but, ideally, would evolve from a rational examination of guest demand (because it is the most significant factor impacting room rates) *and* a hotel's costs of operation. Mathematically, such a rate should be easy to compute with specific and accurate assumptions, and not surprisingly, such a formula has been developed.

Recognized by hoteliers worldwide, this formula for determining room rates was developed in the mid-1950s by the national hotel accounting firms of Horwath & Horwath and Harris Kerr Forster. The model was named in honor of Roy Hubbart, a Chicago hotelier and a major advocate of a "Hubbart" formula–style approach to room pricing.

Essentially, the **Hubbart formula** is used to determine what a hotel's average daily rate (ADR) *should* be to reach the hotel owner's financial goals. To compute the Hubbart formula, specific financial and operational assumptions are determined. These include dollar amounts for property construction (or purchase), the total cost of the hotel's operations, the number of rooms to be sold, and the owner's desired ROI on the hotel's land, property, and equipment.

The Hubbart formula is a "bottom-up" approach to determining the appropriate ADR for a hotel, based on its desired net income. It is considered bottom up because it literally requires you to completely reverse the income statement from the bottom up. Figure 8.2 shows the comparison between the normal format of the income statement and the bottom-up format for the Hubbart formula. Not only are the accounts reversed, but the calculations of addition and subtraction are reversed as well.

Using the bottom-up approach, you start by calculating the desired net income based on the owner's desired return on investment (ROI) and work your way up the income statement by adding back estimated taxes, nonoperating expenses, and undistributed operating expenses and then subtracting out estimated operated departments income (excluding rooms). The result will be the estimated operated department income for rooms.

Then, you can separate the estimated operated department income for rooms into rooms revenue and rooms expenses. Once rooms expenses are subtracted out, rooms revenue will remain. This revenue can then be split again to determine number of rooms to be sold and, finally, ADR. The resulting ADR is the average price that should be charged for your rooms in order to achieve the owner's desired net income (ROI).

FIGURE 8.2 Comparison of Normal and Bottom-Up Formats

Normal Format for the Income Statement	Bottom-Up Format for the Hubbart Formula
Operated Department Income (Rooms)	Net Income
+ Operated Departments Income (Excluding Rooms)	+ Taxes
− Undistributed Operating Expenses	+ Nonoperating Expenses
− Nonoperating Expenses	+ Undistributed Operating Expenses
− Taxes	− Operated Departments Income (Excluding Rooms)
= Net Income	= Operated Department Income (Rooms)

To illustrate the Hubbart formula, we will use the Blue Lagoon Water Park Resort's Income Statement as shown in Figure 8.3. We will assume for the sake of calculating this formula that we *do not* know the operated department income for rooms, rooms revenues, or rooms expenses. Remember, the point of using the Hubbart formula is to *predict* rooms revenue, and subsequently, ADR.

 *go figure!*

The steps required to compute the Hubbart formula in this example are:

1. **Calculate the hotel's target before-tax net income**. Multiply the required rate of return (ROI) of the owner's investment, and then adjust the answer for before-tax net income.

   Assume an investor considers paying $16,217,417 for the 240-room hotel at the Blue Lagoon and desires a 12% return on the investment.

   > $16,217,417 × 0.12 = $1,946,090 ROI (hotel's target net income)

   Calculate before-tax net income. Divide the after-tax net income (owner's ROI) by 1.00 minus the tax rate.

   > $$\frac{\text{After-Tax Net Income (ROI)}}{1.00 - \text{Tax Rate}} = \text{Before-Tax Net Income}$$
   >
   > or, assuming a tax rate of 40%
   >
   > $$\frac{\$1,946,090}{1.00 - 0.40} = \$3,243,483.30 \sim \$3,243,480 \text{ (rounded down)}$$

In order to be consistent with the Income Before Taxes number in Figure 8.3, we will round the before-tax net income down to $3,243,480. Normally, you wouldn't round this number down (the IRS would not like that!), but in order for the Blue Lagoon statements to work nicely for the entire book, the rounded-down number works better.

2. **Calculate estimated nonoperating expenses**. Calculate estimates of nonoperating expenses including rent, property taxes, and insurance plus depreciation and amortization plus interest expense.

In this example, the total nonoperating expenses are as follows:

Rent, Property Taxes, and Insurance	1,760,400
Depreciation and Amortization	1,260,000
Interest Expense	1,272,000
Total Nonoperating Expenses	**$4,292,400**

3. **Calculate estimated undistributed operating expenses**. Calculate estimates of undistributed operating expenses including administrative and general, information systems, human resources, security, franchise fees, transportation, marketing, property operations and maintenance, and utility costs.

In this example, the total undistributed operating expenses are as follows:

Administrative and General	1,357,200
Information Systems	388,800
Human Resources	583,200
Security	277,200
Franchise Fees	0
Transportation	334,800
Marketing	1,552,320
Property Operations and Maintenance	1,197,000
Utility Costs	1,071,000
Total Undistributed Operating Expenses	**$6,761,520**

4. **Calculate estimated operated departments income excluding rooms**. Calculate estimates of revenues minus expenses to determine estimated income for all non-rooms departments. These include income from food, beverage, telecommunications, other operated departments, and rentals and other income.

In this example, estimated operating departments income excluding rooms is as follows:

Food	2,340,000
Beverage	2,076,000
Telecommunications	−180,000
Other Operated Departments	216,000
Rentals and Other Income	34,200
Total Operated Departments Income Excluding Rooms	**$4,486,200**

5. **Calculate the operated department income for rooms**. Using the results from steps 2 through 4: *add* the owner's desired ROI (adjusted for before-tax net

FIGURE 8.3 Income Statement

BLUE LAGOON WATER PARK RESORT
Income Statement
For the Period: January 1 through December 31, 2010

	Net Revenue	Cost of Sales	Payroll and Related Expenses	Other Expenses	Income (Loss)
Operated Departments					
Rooms	?	?	?	?	?
Food	7,200,000	2,138,400	2,188,800	532,800	2,340,000
Beverage	3,264,000	451,440	534,960	201,600	2,076,000
Telecommunications	72,000	169,200	54,000	28,800	-180,000
Other Operated Departments	540,000	79,200	180,000	64,800	216,000
Rentals and Other Income	109,800	15,840	48,960	10,800	34,200
Total Operated Departments	25,201,800	2,854,080	5,973,120	2,077,200	**14,297,400**
Undistributed Operating Expenses					
Administrative and General			921,600	435,600	1,357,200
Information Systems			144,000	244,800	388,800
Human Resources			525,600	57,600	583,200
Security			199,440	77,760	277,200
Franchise Fees			0	0	0
Transportation			50,400	284,400	334,800
Marketing			771,840	780,480	1,552,320
Property Operations and Maintenance			291,600	905,400	1,197,000
Utility Costs			0	1,071,000	1,071,000
Total Undistributed Operating Expenses			2,904,480	3,857,040	**6,761,520**
Gross Operating Profit	25,201,800	2,854,080	8,877,600	5,934,240	**7,535,880**
Rent, Property Taxes, and Insurance					1,760,400
Depreciation and Amortization					1,260,000
Net Operating Income					**4,515,480**
Interest					1,272,000
Income Before Income Taxes					**3,243,480**
Income Taxes					1,297,390
Net Income					**1,946,090**

income), *add* total nonoperating expenses, *add* total undistributed operating expenses, *subtract* total operated departments income excluding rooms (see Figure 8.2).

In this example, estimated operated department income for rooms is as follows:

Before-Tax Net Income	$3,243,480
Total Nonoperating Expenses	+4,292,400
Total Undistributed Operating Expenses	+6,761,520
Total Operated Departments Income Excluding Rooms	−4,486,200
Operated Department Income for Rooms	**$9,811,200**

6. ***Calculate the estimated rooms department revenues based on estimated occupancy***. Add estimated operated department income for rooms (from step 5) to estimated rooms expenses based on estimated occupancy to determine estimated rooms department revenues.

From historical data, the rooms manager has calculated that payroll and related expenses and other expenses for rooms is $60 per room. Also, the manager has determined that the hotel has an average occupancy % of 80%, and the hotel has 240 rooms (see Chapter 1).

Calculate the estimated number of rooms to be sold in the year:

240 rooms x 365 days in a year x 0.80 occupancy = 70,080 rooms

Calculate the estimated rooms expenses based on $60 per room:

70,080 rooms x $60 = $4,204,800

Calculate the estimated rooms department revenues:

Operated Department Income for Rooms	9,811,200
Estimated Rooms Expenses	+4,204,800
Estimated Rooms Department Revenues	**$14,016,000**

7. ***Calculate the hotel's required ADR***. Divide the estimated rooms department revenues (from step 6) by the estimated number of rooms to be sold (from step 6):

$$\frac{\text{Estimated Rooms Department Revenues}}{\text{Estimated Number of Rooms to be Sold}} = \text{Hotel's Required ADR}$$

or

$$\frac{\$14,016,000}{70,080} = \$200$$

Thus, the ADR that should be charged for the Blue Lagoon's rooms in order to achieve the owner's desired net income (ROI) is $200.

A summary of the Hubbart formula calculations for the Blue Lagoon Water Park Resort is shown in Figure 8.4.

The seven steps required to compute the Hubbart formula are summarized in Figure 8.5.

The Hubbart formula is useful because it requires managerial accountants and hoteliers to consider the hotel owner's realistic investment goals and the costs of operating the hotel before determining the room rate. It has been criticized for relying on assumptions about the reasonableness of an owner's desired ROI and the need to know expenses that are affected by the quality of the hotel's management. Another criticism that is also frequently voiced is that the formula requires the room rate to compensate for operating losses incurred by other areas (such as from telecommunications).

In the authors' opinions, however, the formula's primary shortcoming relates to identifying the number of rooms forecasted to be sold. Based upon room rate economics principles we have examined, the number of rooms sold is dependent, to a significant degree, on the rate charged for the rooms. However, the Hubbart formula requires that the number of rooms sold be estimated *prior* to knowing the rate at which they would

FIGURE 8.4 Summary of Hubbart Formula Calculations for the Blue Lagoon

Steps 1–5:

Bottom-Up Format for the Hubbart Formula	**Calculations**
Before-Tax Net Income	$ 3,243,480
+ Nonoperating Expenses	+4,292,400
+ Undistributed Operating Expenses	+6,761,520
− Operated Departments Income (Excluding Rooms)	−4,486,200
= Operated Department Income (Rooms)	**$9,811,200**

Step 6:

240 rooms × 365 days in a year × 0.80 occupancy = 70,080 rooms
70,080 rooms × 60 expense per room = 4,204,800 estimated rooms expenses

Operated Department Income for Rooms	9,811,200
Estimated Rooms Expenses	+4,204,800
Estimated Rooms Department Revenues	**$14,016,000**

Step 7:

$$\frac{\$14,016,000}{70,080} = \$200$$

FIGURE 8.5   Computation of the Hubbart Room Rate Formula

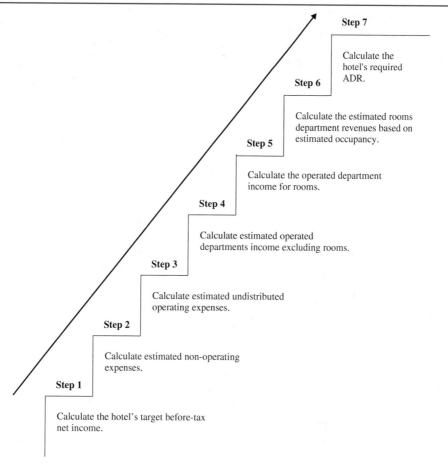

Step 7
Calculate the hotel's required ADR.

Step 6
Calculate the estimated rooms department revenues based on estimated occupancy.

Step 5
Calculate the operated department income for rooms.

Step 4
Calculate estimated operated departments income excluding rooms.

Step 3
Calculate estimated undistributed operating expenses.

Step 2
Calculate estimated non-operating expenses.

Step 1
Calculate the hotel's target before-tax net income.

sell. Despite its limitations, the Hubbart formula remains an important way to view the necessity of developing a room rate that:

■ Provides an adequate return to the hotel's owner(s)
■ Recovers the hotel's nonoperating expenses
■ Considers the hotel's undistributed operating expenses
■ Accounts for all the hotel's non-room operated departments income (or loss)
■ Results in a definite and justifiable overall ADR goal

The $1.00 per $1,000 Rule

There are alternative ways that hoteliers have historically determined room rate. One of the most interesting applies the **$1.00 per $1,000 rule**. Essentially, the rule states that, for every $1,000 invested in a hotel, the property should charge $1.00 in ADR.

Few would argue that the "cost" of items such as the land and labor required to build a hotel in New York City is the same as that of a town in rural Indiana. However, advocates defend the $1.00 per $1,000 rule of thumb because areas in which building or purchase costs are higher tend to be the areas where ADRs can also be higher. A recent analysis of this rule, published in the *Cornell Hotel and Restaurant Administration Quarterly* (August 2003) confirms that this conventional wisdom or "rule of thumb" has stayed remarkably accurate for many types of hotels. The analysis, conducted by John W. O'Neill, a professor at Pennsylvania State University, surveyed 327 hotels over 12 years and confirms that the key attributes that drive how closely a hotel's valuation fits the $1.00 per $1,000 standard are the number of guest rooms, occupancy levels, ADR, and age of the facility. The dollar-per-thousand rule is most accurate for hotels that have high occupancies (around 70%), high ADRs for their area of operation, and are newly built. On the other hand, large, old properties frequently fail to achieve the dollar-per-thousand standard. On average, the ratio for the entire 327 hotels examined in his study was $1 of ADR for every $800 in room value (a bit short of the $1.00 per $1,000 convention).

Despite some limitations, the $1.00 per $1,000 rule does reflect the tendency for hotel buyers to discuss hotel selling prices in terms of a hotel's **average cost per key**, which is simply the average purchase price of a hotel's guest room expressed in thousands of dollars. For example, a 200-room hotel offered for sale at $12,000,000 is selling at a cost per key of $60,000 ($12,000,000/200 rooms = $60,000). Cost per key is also frequently called **average cost per room**.

To illustrate this rule's use, assume that an investor is considering the purchase of a 120-room limited-service hotel for $6,000,000.

The $1.00 per $1,000 rule would be computed by using the following two formulas.

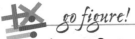

go figure!

Average Cost per Room is calculated as follows:

$$\frac{\text{Purchase Price}}{\text{Number of Rooms}} = \text{Average Cost per Room}$$

or

$$\frac{\$6,000,000}{120} = \$50,000$$

Then, ADR is calculated as follows:

$$\frac{\text{Average Cost per Room}}{\$1,000} = \text{ADR}$$

or

$$\frac{\$50,000}{\$1,000} = \$50$$

Since the rate is so closely tied to occupancy level, most proponents also believe a relatively high (approximately 70%) occupancy assumption and appropriate management is required for the formula to be useful. Also, the computed rate should be increased proportionately if occupancy is forecasted to fall below 70%. The rate can be decreased proportionately if the hotel's occupancy percentage is forecasted to exceed the 70% level.

It is important to recognize that the rate computed using the $1.00 per $1,000 rule does *not* become the hotel's rack rate. Instead, it is the overall ADR that the hotel must achieve when it sells all of its various rooms at all of their respective rates. In this example, the hotel may establish a rack rate of, for example, $89.00 per night. However, the hotel's revenue managers would seek an ADR of $50.00 after all rate discounts. Few (if any) sophisticated investors would use the $1.00 per $1,000 rule *exclusively* to evaluate the feasibility of a hotel purchase. However, even with its limitations, it has remained a helpful, short-hand way to evaluate hotel purchase prices and potential ADRs.

Alternative Room Rate Methodologies

Additional historical methods of rate determination include those based upon the square footage of guest rooms (assuming that a hotel's larger rooms should sell for more than its smaller rooms), and rates determined by various "ideal" sales levels of the different hotel room types available to be sold. These include rates derived from selling the hotel's least expensive rooms first, selling the hotel's most expensive rooms first, and pricing schemes considering an equal sale of higher- and lower-priced rooms. Additional rate structures have been proposed that focus on single versus double occupied rooms.

However, today's hotel room rate structures have been changed, and changed forever, by the advent of the Internet as the most popular method used for selling hotel rooms.

Web-Influenced Room Rate Methodologies

Every hotelier understands that properly pricing their rooms is critical to attracting first-time and repeat business. However, close examination of many pricing tactics would reveal that they often use one or more of the following nontraditional, non-cost methods to establish rates:

- **Competitive Pricing**. Charge what the competition charges.
- **Follow the Leader Pricing**. Charge what the dominant hotel in the area charges.
- **Prestige Pricing**. Charge the highest rate in the area and justify it with better product and/or service levels.
- **Discount Pricing**. Reduce rates below that of the likely competitors.

All of these pricing strategies appear upon first examination, to be "seat of the pants" approaches because they reflect supply, demand, and the psychological aspects of consumer behavior without considering a hotel's cost structure. Closer examination, however, reveals that they are also the logical strategies for a simple but vitally important observation. That observation is:

With the advent of the Internet, the world of hotel room rate determination as known by previous generations of hoteliers is gone forever.

Of course, hotel investors and managerial accountants will continue to use traditional accounting formulas to determine whether they believe specific hotels are (or are not) a wise investment. Determining the proper room rates to charge in a hotel, however, is more complex and even more important than it has ever been. Managerial accountants who do not understand this are perceived by those in hotel operations as hopelessly out of touch with the "real world" in which these managers must navigate. The reasons for the significant changes that have taken place in room rate-setting "rules" are very straightforward. They are:

- The consumer's use of the Internet
- The competition's use of the Internet

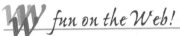 *fun on the Web!*

To better understand today's rate determination realities, consider a consumer-friendly website such as:

www.sidestep.com

Here users can for free, and within seconds, compare alternative room rates for *all* of the hotels in their desired travel area. Any traveler with access to the Internet can compare the room rates offered by one hotel to the rates offered by all of its competitors. The evaluation will contrast the prices of well-known hotel brands and franchises as well as independents. Guests can then book their rooms online as rapidly increasing numbers of travelers choose to do.

Hoteliers involved with the financial management of today's hotels determine room rates based upon the realities of a challenging environment that was simply unknown to previous generations of hoteliers. As a result of the Internet, consumers can easily compare prices, but so can a hotel's major competitors. Gone are the times when night auditors or others on the front office staff conducted the nightly **call-around** to ask other hotels' night auditors what their hotels were charging for rooms and then used that information (often of questionable accuracy) to make decisions about what their own hotel's rate offerings should be.

While the call-around was standard practice as late as the early 2000s, consider modern hoteliers utilizing one of the many websites similar to www.Travelaxe.com and others that allow them to easily:

- Select competitive hotels whose rates are to be monitored
- Obtain real-time room rates offered by these hotels on any number of travel websites advertising the rates
- Search the rates and sites as frequently as desired

- Perform rate comparisons by specific check-in and check-out dates
- Assess rate comparisons based upon room type
- Assess rate comparisons based upon date of guest arrival

For hoteliers who believe they are too busy to closely monitor their competitors' rate information, companies such as RateGain (www.rategain.com) will, for a price, create daily, weekly, or on-demand competitor reports and e-mail the hotelier whenever a designated competitor's rates rise or fall below pre-selected thresholds.

When guests and competitors can discover rates online, the dynamics of rate-setting change, and as a result rates are often set *independently* of traditional construction or operating cost considerations. Guests care very little how much it "costs" a hotel to provide its rooms. They care about the lodging value they receive. As a result, a hotel's rates are heavily influenced by the laws of supply and demand. To illustrate, assume that, on a given Saturday, all similar hotels in your market area offer guest rooms in the range of $100 to $150 per night. In this situation, it would be difficult for your single hotel of the same type to command a rate of $250 per night even if its operating costs justify this rate. If the revenue manager of your hotel placed a $250 per night rate on the hotel's website, it is unlikely that any but, perhaps, the most brand-loyal of consumers would select the property. This would be less important if the Internet were not the major source of traveler information related to hotel room prices. In fact, however, it is. Even senior citizens, one of the last demographic groups to "log on," are now using the Internet in ever-larger numbers. Future generations of travelers will grow up without knowing anything except the Internet as a source of travel-pricing information, and the impact of that fact is tremendously significant.

It is also important to fully understand that the rate at which a hotel first sells its rooms to guests may not be the rate those guests will ultimately pay. This is so because, in the past, if a traveler called a hotel directly, was quoted the rack rate and then booked the reservation, it would have been perceived by the hotel to be a successful sale. Today, however, that same guest can make the hotel reservation and, every day until their date of arrival, can go online to shop for an even lower price for the same room. If a lower rate were to be found, the guest could re-contact the hotel, cancel the original reservation, and secure the new, lower rate. In addition, the consumer would likely feel frustrated that the hotel did not offer its lower rate initially!

Despite the advent of the Internet, modern hotel pricing techniques cannot involve purely subjective approaches. Instead, they must be highly sophisticated and use logical reactions to available real-world information and resulting supply and demand forces. If managerial accountants are to truly assist hoteliers in maximizing property RevPARs, (see Chapter 6), they must understand the importance of the Internet as well as the importance of yield management.

Revenue Management

Revenue management, also called **yield management**, is a set of techniques and procedures that use hotel-specific data to manipulate occupancy, ADR, or both for the purpose of maximizing the revenue yield achieved by a hotel. **Yield** is a term used to describe the percentage of total potential revenue that is actually realized. **Revenue managers** are individuals responsible for making decisions regarding the pricing and selling of guest rooms in order to maximize yield. Yield management, first coined by the airline industry, is now used less commonly in the hotel industry than is the term revenue management, but its basic philosophy and the actual techniques originally employed to implement it are important concepts for you to understand.

go figure!

For example, consider a property that has the potential of generating $50,000 with a fully booked hotel, but only generates revenues of $30,000 on a given Saturday. The hotel's yield would be calculated as follows:

$$\frac{\text{Total Realized Revenue}}{\text{Total Potential Revenue}} = \text{Yield}$$

or

$$\frac{\$30,000}{\$50,000} = 60\%$$

Because revenue is a product of both price and number sold, yield in the hotel industry is a product of ADR and occupancy. Hoteliers know that when demand for rooms is high, rates can also be high. Alternatively, when occupancy levels (demand for rooms) are relatively low, room rates may also be lower. Recall from Chapter 6 that RevPAR is a combination of ADR and occupancy % and is calculated using the following formula:

$$\text{ADR} \times \text{Occupancy\%} = \text{RevPAR}$$

Essentially, then, to increase yield simply means to increase the hotel's RevPAR. Therefore, any change (decrease or increase) in either or both of the factors comprising RevPAR will change the yield of the hotel's revenue.

To truly understand revenue (yield) management in a hotel setting, assume that you would like to have a guest room near Times Square in New York City on New Year's Eve so you can easily join the crowds counting down the old year and ringing in the New Year. You are told that, because demand for rooms near Times Square on December 31 is so heavy, available rooms on that date have been assigned a special event rate and will cost twice as much as usual. Would you book the room?

The interaction between consumers and the business transactions they desire is affected by strong demand, supply shortage, or both. In the hotel industry, revenue management can be viewed quite simply as the application of specific tactics that predict (forecast) consumer behavior and effectively price highly perishable products (rooms) to maximize RevPAR.

Retailers that can easily carry inventory to the next day such as those who sell carpet, lumber, and computer supplies have difficulty employing revenue management because customers do not readily accept significant price variation in their products. Interestingly, those that are perceived by customers to be easily able to increase inventory (supply)—think bread, milk, and restaurant meals—do not generally use revenue management tactics even though they may sell a perishable commodity.

Because hotel rooms are highly perishable, the goal of revenue management is to consistently maintain the highest possible revenue from a given amount of inventory. It is important to remember that revenue management techniques are used during periods of low, as well as high, demand. For example, if a hotel is usually booked solid in October of each year, there is little reason to offer a discount to a group wanting rooms at that time, unless the group is willing to purchase enough additional hotel services to justify the discount. In this case, effective revenue managers would seek to sell all of their rooms at a rate as close to the rack rate as is possible. Revenue managers should be implementing revenue management procedures at their hotels if:

- Demand for their rooms varies by day of week, time of month, or season.
- Demand varies in response to local special events.
- Their demand variance is predictable.
- They have never turned away a customer willing to pay a higher price for a room because available inventory had been previously sold to another guest at a lower price.
- Their hotel serves guests who are value conscious as well as those who can afford to spend more for the sake of convenience, status, or other motivating factors.
- They have, or can create, clearly discernable differences in service or product levels that can be easily explained to guests.
- Their property is willing to commit the resources necessary to properly train staff prior to implementation of revenue management.
- They seek to maximize RevPAR.

Although the actual revenue management techniques used by hoteliers vary by property, in their simplest form, all these techniques are employed to:

- Forecast demand
- Eliminate discounts in high demand periods
- Increase discounts during low demand periods
- Implement "Special Event" rates during periods of extremely heavy demand

Sophisticated mathematical programs that help hoteliers manage revenues are built into most property management systems (PMS) used in the industry today. Using information gleaned from the hotel's historical sales data, revenue management features in a PMS can:

- Recommend room rates that will optimize the number of rooms sold
- Recommend room rates that will optimize sales revenue

■ Recommend special room restrictions (for example, minimum length of stay requirements) that serve to optimize the total revenue generated by the hotel during a specific time period

■ Identify special high consumer demand dates that deserve special management attention to pricing

To further illustrate the importance of a modern PMS system, consider the Memorial Day holiday. Observed on the last Monday of May, it is a "slow" day for many business hotels. For Indianapolis, Indiana hoteliers housing Indianapolis 500 race fans, however, the day is huge, as are the few days before and after. For this reason, a modern PMS system in an Indianapolis hotel should:

1. Identify all future dates affected by the Memorial Day race
2. Adjust rates on those dates to reflect the demand for any remaining rooms to be sold
3. Establish (or recommend) minimum length of stay requirements
4. Identify "pay in advance" policies (if applicable) that should be put in place

PMS systems can "remember" more important dates than can an individual hotelier or revenue manager. However, it is a hotelier's skill and experience that is most critical to the revenue maximization process. To illustrate this, consider the case of the corporate traveler who stays at her favorite hotel nearly every Tuesday and Wednesday night. On a particular Tuesday she arrives and is told by the new revenue manager that her usual, discounted corporate rate of $99 cannot be honored on that night because the hotel forecasts a sell-out. The rate she must pay is $149. In this case, the hotel's new revenue manager is aggressively managing yield and, perhaps appropriately, has eliminated corporate rate discounts on this day. When, however, the guest complains that she is a loyal customer who has always been willing to pay their assigned rate (even when the hotel was not busy), she is told by the front desk agent, "There's nothing I can do." Should the hotel manager be surprised when that guest leaves and never returns? The answer is no. Recall that the goal of a talented revenue manager is to increase RevPAR, not only on a daily basis, but on a long-term basis as well. In the long term, offending loyal guests by incompetently managing yield benefits neither guest nor hotel.

In the final analysis, revenue management is a helpful concept in that it prevents those who price hotel rooms from over-emphasizing occupancy percentage or ADR. Since the advent of revenue management, the individuals at a hotel who are responsible for rooms pricing decisions have been evaluated based upon both the hotel's occupancy percentage and the ADR it achieves (RevPAR). To better understand how these individuals are evaluated, it is first important to understand the concept of competitive set.

In the hotel industry, a **competitive set (comp set)** simply consists of those hotels with whom a specific hotel competes and to which it compares its own operating performance. Thus, a full-service hotel's comp set would include full-service hotels, while a budget hotel's comp set would consist of other, competitive budget hotels.

To fully evaluate RevPar changes, hoteliers look to the relative performance of their comp set. They do so to better understand the room rate economics that affected their own

FIGURE 8.6   The Blue Lagoon's Room Statistics for Last Night

Room Revenue	$38,400
Total Rooms in Hotel	240
Out-of-Order (OOO) Rooms	5
Complimentary (Comp) Rooms Occupied	3
On-Change Rooms*	7
Rooms Sold	192

* **On-change rooms** are rooms that are vacant but not yet cleaned.

property during a specific time period, as well as how the hotel's management responded to the supply and demand challenges they faced during that period. The importance of comp set data is readily apparent. Consider again Paige Vincent from the Blue Lagoon. Paige's hotel averages a RevPAR of $160 ($200 ADR × 80% occupancy = $160 RevPAR). That performance might seem very good, but if you knew that the average RevPAR of the hotels in Paige's comp set was $170, the $160 performance she achieved does not appear as strong. Alternatively, if the average RevPAR of Paige's comp set was $150, Paige's $160 RevPAR appears to be very good.

Increasingly, however, sophisticated hoteliers are even realizing the shortcomings of an over-emphasis on RevPAR. To better understand why this is so, it is important to take a closer look at its two fundamental components, occupancy percentage and ADR.

Occupancy Percentage

It might seem that the occupancy percentage for a hotel would be a straightforward calculation. Consider, however, Paige Vincent, general manager of the Blue Lagoon Water Park Resort. As you may recall, the hotel at the Blue Lagoon has 240 guest rooms (Chapter 1). On a day last week, the room revenue statistics report generated from Paige's property management system produced the information contained in Figure 8.6.

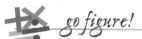 *go figure!*

From the data in this report, it is clear that the hotel's total room revenue for the day was $38,400, however, what is less clear is exactly how Paige should compute her occupancy percentage. Should she:

1. Include only sold rooms in her computation? If so, her formula would be:

$$\frac{\text{Rooms Sold}}{\text{Total Rooms in Hotel}} = \text{Occupancy \%}$$

or

$$\frac{192}{240} = 80.0\%$$

2. Include complimentary rooms as well as sold rooms in her computation? If so, her formula would be:

$$\frac{\text{Rooms Sold} + \text{Comp Rooms Occupied}}{\text{Total Rooms in Hotel}} = \text{Occupancy \%}$$

or

$$\frac{192 + 3}{240} = 81.3\%$$

3. Subtract non-sellable out-of-order rooms from her rooms available count? If so, her formula would be:

$$\frac{\text{Rooms Sold}}{\text{Total Rooms in Hotel} - \text{OOO Rooms}} = \text{Occupancy \%}$$

or

$$\frac{192}{240 - 5} = 81.7\%$$

4. Subtract non-sellable on-change rooms from her rooms available count? If so, her formula would be:

$$\frac{\text{Rooms Sold}}{\text{Total Rooms in Hotel} - \text{On-Change Rooms}} = \text{Occupancy \%}$$

or

$$\frac{192}{240 - 7} = 82.4\%$$

A case could be made for each of these alternative occupancy percentage calculations available to Paige. In fact, as you can easily see, there can even be variations and combinations of the four approaches presented. Each has its advocates. The point for you to remember, however, is that managerial accountants who will be utilizing occupancy percentage as a useful comparison and analysis statistic simply must ensure that they fully understand the way the occupancy percentage is calculated in their own property.

ADR

Just as occupancy percentage is a critical component of RevPAR, average daily rate (ADR) is equally critical. Given the previous discussion on the variety of formulas that can be used to calculate occupancy percentage, it should not be surprising that variations of the formulas for ADR are also used. Generally, hotel managers calculate ADR using one of the two following formulas:

$$\frac{\text{Total Rooms Revenue}}{\text{Total Number of Rooms Sold}} = \text{ADR}$$

or

$$\frac{\text{Total Rooms Revenue}}{\text{Total Number of Rooms Occupied}} = \text{ADR}$$

Notice that the only difference in the two formulas are the words *sold* and *occupied*. In fact, while both of these ADR formulas are commonly used, and a case can be made for their accuracy, in today's hotel industry neither of these may accurately reflect ADR.

 *go figure!*

To understand why, again consider the case of Paige Vincent. Utilizing her data in Figure 8.6 and the "rooms sold" approach to ADR computation, her ADR for the night would be:

$$\frac{\text{Total Rooms Revenue}}{\text{Total Number of Rooms Sold}} = \text{ADR}$$

or

$$\frac{\$38,400}{192} = \$200$$

Utilizing the data in Figure 8.6 and the "rooms occupied" approach to ADR computation, which adds comp rooms to sold rooms, her ADR for the night would be:

$$\frac{\text{Total Rooms Revenue}}{\text{Total Number of Rooms Occupied}} = \text{ADR}$$

or

$$\frac{\$38,400}{192 + 3} = \$196.92$$

Despite the slight differences in these two ADR computations, neither is as useful to the hotel's owners and to Paige as the computation of her net ADR yield, which will be explained in the next section.

Net ADR Yield

Net ADR yield is the percentage of ADR actually received by a hotel *after* subtracting the cost of fees and assessments associated with the room's sale. This statistic was first introduced in the second edition of *Hotel Operations Management*, by David K. Hayes and Jack D. Ninemeier, published in 2006. For a single room it is computed as:

$$\frac{\text{Room Rate} - \text{Reservation Generation Fees}}{\text{Room Rate Paid}} = \text{Net ADR Yield}$$

To really understand net ADR yield, you must first understand how hotel rooms were sold in the past as well as how they are sold in today's competitive marketing environment. In the distant past, hotels clearly preferred that guests arrive with a previously made reservation. In fact, those guests who arrived without one were often viewed with some amount of suspicion. Of course, if the hotel had vacant rooms, the front office agent would quote a rate (often higher than that quoted to other guests) to the non-reserved guest and the room would be sold.

Today, most hotel guests already have a room reservation prior to arrival, and the **reservation distribution channels** (sources of reservations) used to make their reservations will charge the hotel widely varying fees for making them. As a result, given today's hotel rooms marketing systems, a walk-in guest is among the hotel's most prized and most profitable!

When a guest makes a reservation via the Internet, no less than three reservation-generation fees are typically charged to the hotel, including fees from:

- **Internet Travel Sites**—websites for booking travel to end users (Expedia.com, Travelocity.com, Priceline.com, etc.)
- **Global Distribution System (GDS)**—system that books and sells rooms for multiple companies
- **Central Reservation System (CRS)**—system used by companies to centrally book reservations

Consider the information in Figure 8.7. As you can see, the hotel pays "zero" reservation fees on a walk-in reservation and pays several fees for the reservation made by the Internet user.

If the reservation is made by a travel agent, additional fees are charged. Historically, these fees have been accounted for as a hotel expense, and thus the full ADR (not the ADR minus reservation generation fees) has been used to compute RevPAR. Unfortunately, with increased usage of high-priced distribution channels, a room's selling price (quoted) and the ADR the hotel actually *receives* can be radically different.

FIGURE 8.7   Walk-In versus Internet User Fees Charged to Hotel

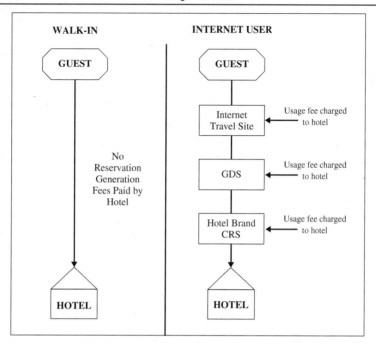

go figure!

Consider again, the case of the Blue Lagoon. Assume that a guest paid $200 for a room night and total reservation fees of $80 were charged to the hotel. The net ADR yield for the room night is as follows:

$$\frac{\text{Room Rate} - \text{Reservation Generation Fees}}{\text{Room Rate Paid}} = \text{Net ADR Yield}$$

or

$$\frac{\$200 - \$80}{\$200} = 60\%$$

Clearly, in cases such as this, it is the ADR *after* the cost of reservation generation fees ($200 − $80 = $120) that should be most important to hoteliers and their attempts to increase RevPAR. Sophisticated hoteliers understand that all revenue dollars are *not* created equally. A $200 room sold on a distribution channel that results in a high net ADR yield is simply more profitable than the same rate sold on a distribution channel that results in a significantly lower net ADR yield. If net ADR yield is not used, hotel owners and managers run the risk of significantly over-inflated RevPARs accompanied by significantly reduced profits as well. In summary, it is accurate to state that one of today's most popular distribution channels (the Internet) can also be one of the least desirable (profitable) channels for hotels.

𝒲 *fun on the Web!*

The management of E-distribution channels has become so important to hotel profitability and such an important area of specialization, that a separate industry association has been developed for those who work in this important area of revenue management. The Hotel Electronic Distribution Network Association (HEDNA) is growing. You can learn more about it at:

www.hedna.org

Flow-Through

Flow-through is a concept that, while not directly connected to rooms pricing, is extremely helpful to understanding the pricing philosophy that is best used by a specific hotel. **Flow-through** is a measure of the ability of a hotel to convert increased revenue dollars to increased gross operating profit dollars. To fully understand flow-through, consider again the case of the Blue Lagoon Water Park Resort. Simplified income statements detailing revenue and expenses for January 2010 and for the same month of the prior year are presented in Figure 8.8.

go figure!

From Figure 8.8, the Blue Lagoon's flow-through for January 2010 is calculated as the change in gross operating profit (GOP) from the prior year divided by the change in total revenues from the prior year as follows:

$$\frac{\text{GOP This Year} - \text{GOP Last Year}}{\text{Total Revenues This Year} - \text{Total Revenues Last Year}} = \text{Flow-Through}$$

or

$$\frac{\$627,990 - \$519,940}{\$2,100,150 - \$1,952,850} = 73.4\%$$

Gross operating profit (GOP) is, in effect, total hotel revenue less those expenses that are considered directly controllable by management. Flow-through was created by managerial accountants to measure the ability of a hotel to convert increases in revenue directly to increases in GOP.

FIGURE 8.8   Vertical Income Statements

BLUE LAGOON WATER PARK RESORT
Vertical Income Statements
For the Months Ended January 31, 2009 and 2010

	Last Year (2009)	%	This Year (2010)	%
Revenue				
Rooms	1,105,000	56.6%	1,200,000	57.1%
Non-Rooms	847,850	43.4%	900,150	42.9%
Total Revenue	**1,952,850**	100.0%	**2,100,150**	100.0%
Operated Department Expenses				
Rooms	335,890	17.2%	353,100	16.8%
Non-Rooms	537,034	27.5%	558,300	26.6%
Total Operated Department Expenses	**872,924**	44.7%	**911,400**	43.4%
Total Operated Department Income	**1,079,926**	55.3%	**1,188,750**	56.6%
Total Undistributed Operating Expenses	**559,986**	28.7%	**560,760**	26.7%
Gross Operating Profit	**519,940**	26.6%	**627,990**	29.9%
Rent, Property Taxes, and Insurance	146,700	7.5%	146,700	7.0%
Depreciation and Amortization	105,000	5.4%	105,000	5.0%
Net Operating Income	**268,240**	13.7%	**376,290**	17.9%
Interest	106,000	5.4%	106,000	5.0%
Income Before Income Taxes	**162,240**	8.3%	**270,290**	12.9%
Income Taxes	64,896	3.3%	108,116	5.1%
Net Income	**97,344**	5.0%	**162,174**	7.7%

In this example, 73.4% (73.4 cents of every additional revenue dollar) has been converted to gross operating profits. For most hotels, incremental revenue increases return disproportionably high profit levels because variable costs (costs that change in relation to volume) are so low. Note that, for the Blue Lagoon, an increase in revenues of 7.5% [($2,100,150/$1,952,850) − 1 = 7.5%] over the prior year resulted in significant gross operating profit increases of 73.4% related to that additional revenue.

Flow-through is computed to help managers identify the impact of increases in revenue on profitability. When it is high (over 50%), it usually reflects efficiency on the part of management in converting additional revenues into additional profits. For most hotels, flow-throughs that are less than 50% may indicate inefficiency in converting additional revenues into additional profits. Understanding the flow-through characteristic of a specific hotel helps management better understand the importance of incremental levels of revenue and thus the importance of utilizing truly effective revenue management techniques.

GOPPAR

While GOPPAR is not really a new concept, it has recently been touted as an alternative to the RevPAR analysis method of evaluating the effectiveness of a hotel's revenue generation ability. **Gross operating profit per available room (GOPPAR)** is simply defined as a hotel's total revenue minus its management's controllable expenses per available room. Thus, for example, the costs of a hotel's lawn care services, utility bills, and even food and beverage expenses are considered when computing GOPPAR. These same expenses are not, of course, considered when computing RevPAR. In fact, in most cases, those managers directly responsible for revenue generation do not control the majority of costs used to compute GOPPAR. How then, did it become popular to suggest GOPPAR, a term more familiar to managerial accountants than hotel revenue managers, as a method of evaluating the decision making of those revenue managers?

For a simple example of why this is so, consider a hotel with 500 rooms that elects to launch a major television advertising campaign in its local market. Assume also that the campaign costs $100,000 per month, and that it increases RevPAR by $1.00. Based on RevPAR alone, this would seem to be a wise decision since RevPAR has increased. However, would the campaign really be deemed successful? Most observers would say "no." The $1.00 increase in RevPAR yields a rooms revenue increase of $15,000 per month (500 rooms x 30 days x $1.00 RevPAR increase = $15,000). Despite the fact that RevPAR certainly did increase, the amount of money spent by the hotel ($100,000) to increase RevPAR exceeded, by far, the actual amount of the revenue increase of $15,000! Clearly, the short-term effect on hotel profitability of spending $100,000 per month to increase revenues by $15,000 per month will be a negative one.

Thus, while it is one of the most recognized of the performance measures in the hospitality industry, there are still some pitfalls to be aware of when analyzing a hotel's performance based solely on RevPAR. For example, in those cases where room revenue accounts for only 50 to 60% of total revenue (as is the case in large convention hotels with extensive meeting rooms and food and beverage revenues), RevPAR represents only half of the hotel's revenues and neglects to consider all other sources of incremental revenues.

It is for shortcomings such as these that hoteliers now consider an analysis of a hotel's GOPPAR to be of such importance. As you may remember, gross operating profit (GOP) is total hotel revenue less those expenses that are considered directly controllable by management.

go figure!

Using the Blue Lagoon Water Park Resort January 2010 income statement in Figure 8.8, total rooms available to be sold are 7,440 (240 rooms × 31 days = 7,440) and GOPPAR is calculated as follows:

$$\frac{\text{Gross Operating Profit}}{\text{Total Rooms Available to Be Sold}} = \text{GOPPAR}$$

or

$$\frac{\$627,990}{7,440} = \$84.41$$

Many industry professionals feel that GOPPAR, because it reflects the gross operating profits (not revenue) of a hotel, actually provides a clearer indication of overall performance than does RevPAR. RevPAR indicates the performance of a hotel in terms of rooms inventory sales and marketing, however, it provides no indication of how much money the hotel actually is, or should be, making. GOPPAR takes into consideration the cost containment and management control of the hotel and must be considered in any effective rooms pricing strategy. The difficulty is *not* that RevPAR is a poor measurement, but rather it is the fact that RevPAR should not be the *only* measurement of a hotel's revenue managers' effectiveness.

In conclusion, the actual pricing of a hotel's rooms is a very complex process. The reasons for this complexity are easier to understand when you realize that experienced hoteliers establishing their hotels' room rates must consider the real cost of providing the room as well as a variety of other factors impacting price including:

- Room rate economics
- Market supply and demand
- RevPAR
- Web-influenced marketing activities
- Revenue management strategies
- Net ADR yield
- Flow-through rates
- GOPPAR

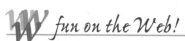

fun on the Web!

Few topics are of more importance to hoteliers than pricing their products. There are a number of good resources within the hospitality industry that will be of help, but a general examination of pricing and pricing theory is also useful. You will find an excellent treatment of pricing philosophy in the fourth edition of *The Strategy and Tactics of*

Pricing: A Guide to Growing More Profitably, by Thomas Nagle and John Hogan. To obtain a copy of the book, go to

www.barnesandnoble.com

When you arrive, enter "Thomas Nagle" in the author search line to view a copy of his book.

Non-Room Revenue

Non-room revenue is important to the managers of both limited-service and full-service hotels. It is common for limited-service hotels to generate 5 to 20% of their total revenue from non-room sources. In full-service hotels, the non-rooms revenue generated may range from 20 to 50% of total revenue. Historically, non-room revenue has been listed on a hotel's income statement as attributed to one of the following categories:

- Food
- Beverage
- Telecommunications
- Garage and parking
- Golf course
- Golf pro shop
- Guest laundry
- Health center
- Swimming pool
- Tennis
- Tennis pro shop
- Other operated departments
- Rentals and other income

Of course, not every hotel will create revenues in every non-room revenue area. For example, a hotel that operates a golf course will collect greens fees from golfers using the course, and report these as income attributed to the golf department. A hotel without a golf course would not generate greens fees. Because of the unique nature of individual hotel properties, approaches to the pricing of non-room revenue items are quite varied and must always be adapted to the specific nature and characteristics of the hotel seeking to maximize these revenues.

Food and Beverage Revenue

Food and beverage revenues typically make up the largest portion of a hotel's non-room revenue. For those less familiar with the hotel business, it might seem that the pricing of a hotel's food and beverage products would be identical to that of a restaurant. It is not identical, and in many cases, it is not even similar. To understand why, it is important to understand that a restaurant manager wants to financially support the *restaurant* itself through sales. In a properly managed hotel food and beverage (F&B) department, the department head wants to financially support the *hotel* through sales. The philosophical and practical differences between these two approaches are immense. For example, in many hotels, complementary breakfast is served to all overnight guests. The food and beverage department in such a property may be reimbursed for the "cost" of providing the breakfast, but the actual "sales" value of the breakfast, including a profit, would not likely be transferred. Similarly, if a large group of rooms could be sold by the sales department only if the value of meals served to the group are significantly discounted, or even provided on a complementary basis, for example, a no-charge "Welcome Reception" for the group, it may well be in the best interest of the hotel to do what is necessary to secure the group rooms sale, even at a significant cost to the F&B department.

The cost of providing food and beverages in guest rooms (room service) is another excellent example of the way hotel food service operations differ from their restaurant counterparts. Many full-service hotels offer high quality room service. Significant planning by room service managers is required to determine how quality goals can be attained when food must be transported over long distances involving relatively long time periods between the plating of the food and its service to guests. In many cases, room service is provided to guests at a "loss," but significantly enhances the overall guest experience and thus helps the hotel achieve higher room rates.

The extent of banquet operations is yet another way that hotel F&B operations differ from most restaurants. Many hotels generate significant revenue from the sale of food and beverages at group functions. In fact, in many full-service hotels, the main focus of the F&B department is on banquets and in-house catered events, and not on its public restaurants and bars. In banquets, as in room service, attention to detail is absolutely critical and impacts the cost of delivering quality products.

The amount of profit generated by a traditional restaurant is relatively easy to calculate. All revenue is generated from the sale of food and/or beverage products in the restaurant. In addition, all expenses usually will be clearly identified in the accounting records of the establishment. By contrast, the process of assigning revenues and expenses applicable to the F&B department in a hotel is more difficult. Consider, for example, a holiday weekend package plan that includes one night's stay, dinner, and breakfast and is sold to guests for one price. How should the revenue generated from the guests be split between room revenue and the F&B department? Consider applicable expenses also. How much, if any, of the salary paid to the hotel's general manager, controller, and other staff specialists along with other expenses including utilities, landscaping, and marketing, should be allocated between departments (including F&B) within the hotel? It is, then, difficult to compare the profitability of a restaurant directly with that of its F&B counterpart in a lodging property.

With proper pricing structures, hotel F&B departments can be profitable, but they face significant challenges to profitability. For example, traditional restaurants are open at the times when the majority of their guests want to be served. By contrast, a hotel restaurant will most likely remain open for three meal periods daily to serve hotel guests. In addition, restaurants may close for a day or more during weather emergencies, while hotel restaurants will likely remain open to provide food services to its guests. As a result, payroll-related costs in hotel F&B departments tend to be higher than their restaurant counterparts.

Many of the differences between hotel and restaurant food services relate primarily to the fact that, for nonconvention hotels, offering F&B services is not the primary business purpose of the hotel. Instead, food service is often viewed as an amenity to attract guests and to provide food and beverage alternatives to increase the hotel's revenues from the guest base established by guest room sales. To some extent, then, the role of the F&B department is, appropriately, secondary to that of those departments that sell and service guest rooms. Experienced managerial accountants understand this and resist the temptation to aggressively and expensively seek to market the F&B operation to non-hotel guests living in the local area.

In addition to the restaurants and lounges found in hotels, for those hotels with liquor licenses (many limited-service hotels do not have them), income statements will be prepared that include revenue and expense detail in one or more of the following categories:

- Room service
- Banquets
- Breakfast
- Lunch
- Dinner
- Meeting room rental
- Meeting room set-up and décor
- Audio and visual (A/V) equipment rental
- Service charges

Service charges are properly reported as F&B income because, unlike a tip, a service charge is a mandatory addition to a guest's food and beverage bill. Typical service charge rates in full-service hotels range from 15 to 25% of the guest's total pre-tax food and beverage charges. Service charges are collected from the guest by the hotel and distributed in the manner deemed best by the hotel. In the usual case, not all service charges collected are or even should be distributed to the specific employees who have serviced the guests paying the service charge. As a result, the portion of the hotel's mandatory service charge that is not returned to employees is often considered a direct contribution toward F&B profits.

Telecommunications Revenue

In the not-so-distant past, in-room telephone toll charges contributed a significant amount of money to a hotel's annual revenue. Today, however, the advent of cell telephones, and the reputation for excessive charges that has plagued hotels have lead to significant declines in this revenue source. For many hotel brands, mandatory free local telephone calls have reduced revenues for their operators and at the same time have pressured full-service competitors to reduce or even eliminate their own local telephone charges.

While most hotels still do charge for long-distance calls, the advent of the Internet and **Voice Over Internet Protocol** (VOIP), which allows for "free" long-distance calls via computer, have reduced and will continue to reduce even this source of hotel revenue. As a result, for most hoteliers, focus on the telephone department has shifted from a "pricing" concern to a "cost" accounting and management concern. This is so because, when guests make telephone calls outside the hotel, it is in the best interest of the hotel to route those calls in a way that minimizes the hotel's cost. For example, if a registered guest directly dials a person in another state from his or her hotel room, it is the hotel that will actually be billed for the call. The hotel would want to identify a telephone vendor that will ensure its cost of providing the call to be as low as possible while still assuring that guests have quality long-distance service.

In regard to revenue generation and collection, when a call is made, the hotel will, depending on the distance and length of the call, add a charge to the guest's folio to offset the cost of that call. The procedure for doing so involves programming the hotel's **call accounting system**, to generate telephone toll charges based upon:

- Time of day
- Call length
- Call distance (local or long distance)
- Use or non-use of international service providers (carriers)

Note that these cost factors are the same factors that will ultimately affect the hotel's own monthly telephone bill. As a result, all of these should indeed be considered when establishing appropriate in-room guest telephone charges.

A hotel's management must carefully consider and ultimately determine which of the telephone calls made by guests will be billed to them, as well as the rates at which those calls will be billed. An effective call accounting system, when **interfaced** (electronically connected) with the hotel's property management system will post these charges directly to the guest's folio and provide the documentation (call date, time, and number that was called) required to justify the collection of these charges when the guest checks out. It is important to understand that, while telephone revenue, as a percentage of total hotel revenue, has been declining significantly in recent years, a properly managed call accounting system is still a vital part of the hotel's revenue generation program. This is so because any telephone revenue that goes uncollected due to an improperly managed call accounting system is damaging to a hotel's bottom line.

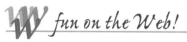 *fun on the Web!*

For an overview of the many features and capabilities provided by today's telephone systems, review the site of one of the industry's leading providers at:

www.mitel.com

When you arrive at the Mitel site, click on "Solutions," and then "Hospitality."

Other Operated Departments Revenue

The revenue generating departments operated by a hotel are as varied as hotels themselves. The following non-exhaustive list includes hotel departments and services that you are very likely to encounter during your hotel career.

- Pay-per-view movies
- Pay-per-play in-room games
- In-room safes
- Internet access charges
- Gift shop sales
- Vending revenue
- Coat check fees
- Resort activities fees
- Parking charges

While an in-depth examination of, for example, the proper procedures for establishing vending machine prices or parking charges requires a knowledge of those areas greater than can be provided in this text, most hoteliers will encounter and need to fully understand the following "other" revenue generating areas or departments:

- Pay-per-view movies
- Pay-per-play in-room games
- In-room safes
- Internet access charges
- Miscellaneous other income

Pay-per-View Movies. Pay-per-view movie systems have long been a popular feature offered to hotel guests. Essentially, these systems offer guests the opportunity to view movies that are currently, or that have just recently finished, showing in movie theaters. In addition, most pay-per-view providers offer a variety of adult-oriented movies. The demand for these current and popular movies can be quite strong. Guests pay the hotel a set fee for viewing the movies. Then, at month's end, the movie provider charges the hotel based on the number of movies viewed, as well as for any equipment charges included in the hotel's pay-per-view contract.

Pay-per-Play In-Room Games. Guests are increasingly offered the chance to play "video" games on the television screens in their rooms. The games are typically accessed in the same manner as pay-per-view movies. While these game services are very similar to pay-per-view movies (they are pay-per-play), the significant difference is the requirement for an in-room joystick, mouse, or keyboard to actually play the game. Pay-per-play games' growing popularity is unquestionable and may, for some hotels, someday exceed that of movies.

In-Room Safes. Recently hotels have begun offering in-room safes for guests' use. These safes are electronic (battery driven) and can be opened only by the guest and the hotel's own staff. Charges, if any, for the use of the safe are typically posted to the guest's folio. Individual per-night charges for these safes are typically nominal, but can be significant if each room is equipped with one. Also, in most states, if the hotel is to provide in-room safes under the control of the guest, the hotel must also offer, and publicize the fact that it offers, a safe at "no-charge" where guests can keep their valuables during their stay. Hoteliers interested in providing in-room safes for a fee are well advised to consult their property's attorney prior to implementation of the service.

Internet Access Charges. The ability of hotels to profitably harness the Internet on a pay-to-connect basis in a guest's room or elsewhere on the hotel's property is an increasingly demanded service. This is especially the case when the guest's own portable (laptop) personal computer is used to make the connection. Some hotels profitably charge for Internet usage, and, for those that do, their interface to the PMS (to allow for the posting of guest charges) must be programmed, maintained, and controlled. This process becomes more difficult when you recognize that, increasingly, hotels are turning away from hard-wired Internet connections that limit a guest's mobility when using the Internet. As a result, pricing and collecting for supplying guests' **Wi-Fi** (short for *Wireless Fidelity*) access and **hot spots** (a Wi-Fi area that allows for high-speed wireless Internet access) has become a somewhat vexing problem for hoteliers as well as their managerial accountants!

Miscellaneous Other Income. Hotels can generate small amounts of income from a variety of sources including the sale of postage stamps, minor charges for copies, and faxing guest documents. Perhaps the largest source of miscellaneous "Other Income" typically reported by hotels, however, is that related to guest **no-show charges.** Guests are assessed no-show charges when they have a guaranteed reservation and neither cancel the reservation nor show up at the hotel on their expected date of arrival. Where no-show policies are in place, they should, of course, be carefully explained to guests at the time reservations are made.

In this, and the preceding chapter, you encountered a variety of factors that affect the pricing of hospitality products and services. In all cases, the actual cost of providing these items is of critical importance to proper pricing. In the following chapter, you will learn how managerial accountants actually determine the true cost of providing the products and services sold in their operations.

Apply What You Have Learned

Bill O'Leary could see both sides of the issue. As the general manager of the 500-unit Plazamar Hotel, he knew how important it was to remember that both members of his room revenue management team now sitting across his desk shared the same goals.

What Elizabeth Sipes was asking for, he knew, seemed reasonable to her. As director of sales and marketing, Elizabeth had worked hard to secure a chance to bid on the annual meeting of the State Dental Association. While the normal ADR achieved by the Plazamar was $150 per night, Elizabeth wanted to bid the rooms for the dental meeting (350 rooms per night for three nights) at $99 per night. At that proposed rate, she was convinced the hotel would win the bid. And if only 150 rooms remained to be sold on those three nights, the hotel could increase the rates of its remaining rooms and thus maximize its RevPAR. At a bid rate higher than $99 per night, she warned, the State Dental Association would likely elect to go to the Altoona Hotel, the Plazamar's biggest competitor.

"Let them have the dentists," said Tony Baltimore, the hotel's front office manager. "The Altoona only has 400 rooms. If they sell out, we'll take their overflow. With our normal 65% occupancy and all of their overflow, we'll sell out anyway. And we can get $150 per night or more for all 500 of our rooms. That's how you maximize RevPAR."

1. Assume you are Bill. Whose argument makes most sense to you? Why?
2. Assume the Plazamar is a full-service hotel. What impact would non-rooms revenue have on Bill's decision?
3. Based upon this scenario, assess the rooms revenue management decision-making process in place at the Plazamar. Do you believe it is working well? Why?

Key Terms and Concepts

The following are terms and concepts discussed in the chapter that are important for you to know as a manager. To help you review, please define the terms below.

Room rate economics
Rack rate
Room mix
Seasonal rate
Special event rate
Corporate rate
Government rate
Group rate
Package rate
Property management
   system (PMS)
Fade rate
Hubbart formula
$1.00 per $1,000 rule
Cost per key
Average cost per room
Competitive pricing

Follow the leader pricing
Prestige pricing
Discount pricing
Call around
Revenue management
Yield management
Yield
Revenue manager
Competitive set (comp set)
On-change rooms
Net ADR yield
Reservation distribution
   channels
Internet Travel Sites
Global Distribution System
   (GDS)

Central Reservation System
   (CRS)
Flow-through
Gross Operating Profit Per
   Available Room
   (GOPPAR)
Non-room revenue
Service charge
Voice Over Internet Protocol
   (VOIP)
Call accounting system
Interfaced
Wi-Fi
Hot spot
No-show charges

 *Test Your Skills*

Complete the Test Your Skills exercises by placing your answers in the shaded text boxes.

1. Jerry Dickson has been approached by the franchise sales representative of a major hotel chain. The sales representative is trying to interest Jerry in building one of the franchise brand's full-service hotels. The hotel will cost $8,000,000 to build and will consist of 200 rooms. Mortgage payments on the hotel will be $750,000 per year and other nonoperating expenses will be $250,000 per year.

    At an assumed 60% occupancy level, the rooms manager has calculated that payroll and related expenses and other expenses for rooms is $45 per room, and undistributed operating expenses related to operating the hotel are $1,000,000.

    The hotel is projected to make an operating income of $125,000 per year from the F&B department and $50,000 from all other non-rooms departments.

    Jerry is interested in the project if he can achieve a 12% return on the investment, assuming a 40% tax rate.

    a. Utilizing the Hubbart room rate formula, what is the room rate required for Jerry to meet his 12% investment target?

    b. Assume Jerry decided that, due to the potentially risky nature of this venture, he required a 15% (not 12%) return on his investment. What is the room rate required for Jerry to meet this more aggressive investment target?

    c. Assume the occupancy rate estimated to be achieved by the franchise sales representative was 70% and this number was utilized to compute the Hubbart rate (rather than Jerry's more conservative 60%). What would the sales representative tell Jerry his ADR would have to be to achieve Jerry's 15% investment goals?

    d. Assume instead, that the food and beverage operating income is estimated at $75,000 per year rather than $125,000. Using the 15% desired investment return and a 70% occupancy rate, what new room rate would allow Jerry to meet his investment goals?

    (Spreadsheet hint: Calculate question a. above first and type the answer for ADR in the cell provided at the bottom of the spreadsheet. For items b., c., and d., change only the numbers that are required in each question, and all the other numbers in the spreadsheet will change accordingly. Then, type the answers for ADR (as you go) in the cells provided at the bottom of the spreadsheet.)

Step 1. Calculate the hotel's target before-tax net income.

Owner's investment	
ROI	
After-Tax Net Income	

After-Tax Net Income	
Tax	
Before-Tax Net Income	

Step 2. Calculate estimated nonoperating expenses.

Mortgage	
Other Nonoperating Expenses	
Total Nonoperating Expenses	

Step 3. Calculate estimated undistributed operating expenses.

Undistributed Operating Expenses	

Step 4. Calculate estimated operated departments income excluding rooms.

F & B Operating Income	
Other Non-Rooms Income	
Total Non-Rooms Operating Income	

Step 5. Calculate the operated department income for rooms.

Before-Tax Net Income	
Nonoperating Expenses	
Undistributed Operating Expenses	
Total Non-Rooms Operating Income	
Rooms Operated Department Income	

Step 6. Calculate the estimated rooms department revenues based on estimated occupancy.

Rooms	
Days in Period	
Occupancy %	
Total Rooms	

Total Rooms	
Expense per Room	
Total Room Expenses	

Rooms Operated Department Income	
Total Room Expenses	
Rooms Revenue	

Step 7. Calculate the hotel's required ADR.

Rooms Revenue	
Total Rooms	
ADR	

1a.	ADR with 12% ROI	
1b.	ADR with 15% ROI	
1c.	ADR with 15% ROI and 70% Occ%	
1d.	ADR with 15% ROI and 70% Occ% and $75,000 F&B Operating Income	

2. Jerielle Pelley is the front office manager at the 125-room Best Stay Inn. Her general manager has asked her to prepare a Net ADR Yield report for the hotel's prior month room sales. The manager has asked Jerielle to address several specific issues in the summary she is to prepare. Using the information provided below, help Jerielle calculate the answers she needs to complete her report.

   The reservation generation fees that must be paid by the hotel include the following:

   ■ The hotel is assessed a $28.00 fee on each room sold by its third-party Internet sites.

   ■ The franchisor assesses an $8.00 fee on each room sold through its CRS.

   ■ The hotel pays a $15.00 travel agent commission on each room sold by travel agents.

   Calculate the net ADR yield percentages for the following distribution channels:

Distribution Channel	Room Rate	Fees	Net ADR Yield
Third-Party Internet Sales	$167.95		
Franchisor-Delivered Sales	$165.90		
Travel Agent Sales	$151.50		
Walk-Ins	$149.95		

    a. What is the net ADR yield on rooms delivered via the hotel's third-party Internet partners?

    b. What is the net ADR yield on rooms delivered via the hotel's franchisor?

    c. What is the net ADR yield on rooms delivered via travel agents?

    d. What is the net ADR yield on rooms sold to walk-ins?

3. Thandi and Darla each own large 250-room limited-service hotels near the busy city international airport. The following chart details the result of their most recent room sales for a five-day period.

Day	Thandi's Hotel 250 rooms				Darla's Hotel 250 rooms			
	Rooms Sold	ADR	Occ %	RevPAR	Rooms Sold	ADR	Occ %	RevPAR
Monday	205	$117.21	82.0%		158		63.2%	$62.64
Tuesday	230	135.45	92.0%	124.61	249	89.53	99.6%	89.17
Wednesday	226	131.25	90.4%	118.65	230	91.14		83.85
Thursday	228	132.22		120.58	248	92.15	99.2%	91.41
Friday	195		78.0%	89.86	138	101.51		56.03
Five-Day Total		126.80					81.8%	76.62

    a. What was Thandi's RevPar on Monday?

    b. What was Darla's ADR on Monday?

    c. What was Darla's occupancy % on Wednesday?

    d. What was Thandi's occupancy % on Thursday?

    e. What was Thandi's ADR on Friday?

    f. What was Darla's occupancy % on Friday?

    g. How many rooms did Thandi sell during the five days?

    h. What was Thandi's occupancy % for the five days?

    i. What was Thandi's five-day RevPAR total?

    j. How many rooms did Darla sell during the five days?

    k. What was Darla's ADR for the five-day period?

    l. Did Thandi or Darla have a higher RevPAR during this five-day period? What do you think was the reason for this difference?

4. The Carlton Hotel had a good October. Sales were up over the previous October. That's good, but Santi Phita, the hotel's general manager, wants to know more about how the hotel performed with regard to flow-through. Using the following income statement, answer his questions.

THE CARLTON HOTEL
Income Statements
For October 2009 and 2010

	October Last Year 2009	%	October This Year 2010	%
Revenue				
Rooms	430,000	78.90%	465,000	79.76%
Non-Rooms	115,000	21.10%	118,000	20.24%
Total Revenue		100.00%		100.00%
Operated Department Expenses				
Rooms	87,000	15.96%	97,500	16.72%
Non-Rooms	127,500	23.39%	123,000	21.10%
Total Operated Department Expenses	**214,500**	39.36%	**220,500**	37.82%
Total Operated Department Income	**330,500**	60.64%	**362,500**	62.18%
Total Undistributed Operating Expenses	**168,500**	30.92%	**177,950**	30.52%
Gross Operating Profit				
Rent, Property Taxes, and Insurance	14,210	2.61%	15,100	2.59%
Depreciation and Amortization	10,925	2.00%	11,500	1.97%
Net Operating Income	**136,865**	25.11%	**157,950**	27.09%
Interest	9,800	1.80%	10,100	1.73%
Income Before Income Taxes	**127,065**	23.31%	**147,850**	25.36%
Income Taxes	64,896	11.91%	67,104	11.51%
Net Income	**62,169**	11.41%	**80,746**	13.85%
Flow-Through				

a. What were the total revenues in October 2009 and October 2010?

b. What was the GOP in dollars in October 2009 and October 2010?

c. What was the percentage of GOP to total revenues in October 2009 and October 2010?

d. What was the flow-through percentage achieved by Santi's hotel? What is your assessment of that percentage?

CHAPTER **9**

Managerial Accounting

for Costs

As you learned in Chapter 1, a cost, or expense, is most often defined as "time or resources expended by the business." A more simple explanation of cost is simply the amount of money needed to do, buy, or make something. If you think about it, these activities describe exactly why most hospitality companies are in business. They do, buy, or make things that are then sold to their guests. This chapter will teach you how to recognize the different types or categories of costs that managerial accountants consider when they analyze the total costs incurred by a hospitality business. The most important of these various types include fixed, variable, step, mixed, direct, indirect, controllable, and non-controllable costs.

Perhaps the most important cost concept restaurateurs or hoteliers must understand, however, is that, in nearly all cases, as the number of items they sell to their guests increases, the total costs associated with providing those items typically declines and, as a result, their profits will increase. Analyzing this relationship between the cost of items sold, the number of items sold (volume of sales), and profitability is called cost/volume/profit (CVP) analysis. The more popular term for this rather complex concept is the "breakeven" analysis. In this chapter you will learn how to use information from your own business to perform a breakeven analysis. In the process you will discover just how important it is that you understand this concept well and that you can readily apply it to help you better manage your own business.

CHAPTER OUTLINE

- The Concept of Cost
- Types of Costs
- Cost/Volume/Profit Analysis
- Apply What You Have Learned
- Key Terms and Concepts
- Test Your Skills

LEARNING OUTCOMES

At the conclusion of this chapter, you will be able to:

✓ Identify the concept of a business cost.
✓ Differentiate between the different types of business costs.
✓ Perform (when costs are known) a cost/volume/profit analysis.

The Concept of Cost

In the two previous chapters you learned about the importance of knowing your costs before establishing menu prices as well as before determining the selling prices of hotel guest rooms. The word *cost* is a popular one in business. In the hospitality industry you can, among other things:

- Control costs
- Determine costs
- Cover costs
- Cut costs
- Measure rising costs
- Eliminate costs
- Estimate costs
- Budget for costs
- Forecast costs

Given all the possible approaches to examining costs, perhaps the easiest way to understand them is to consider their impact on a business's profit. Recall that the basic profit formula was presented in Chapter 1 as follows:

$$\text{Revenue} - \text{Expenses} = \text{Profit}$$

Throughout this chapter, the term cost will be used interchangeably with the term expense. Expressed in another way, and substituting the word costs for expenses, the formula becomes:

$$\text{Revenue} = \text{Profit} + \text{Costs}$$

As you can see, at any specific level of revenue, the lower a business's costs, the greater are its profits. This is true in both the restaurant and hotel industries and is why understanding and controlling costs are so important to successful hospitality managers.

When you consider how businesses operate, it is easy to see why all costs cannot be viewed in the same manner. For example, consider Paige Vincent's Blue Lagoon Water Park Resort. Paige has a monthly mortgage payment she must make regardless of the number of people who visit her park. If Paige knew in advance the average amount she collected from each of the water park's visitors, it would be easy for her to compute the number of total visitors required to meet her monthly mortgage obligation. However, people do not come to Paige's resort so she can pay her mortgage. They come to enjoy the services and facilities her business has to offer. As a result, as the number of people visiting the pool areas of her resort increases, the number of freshly laundered towels she must provide these guests also increases. Paige knows that her "cost of mortgage" will remain regardless of the number of park attendees. Her "cost of providing fresh towels," however, will vary based upon the number of people coming to the park. Thus, while Paige recognizes that her mortgage and towels represent business costs, she also realizes that they are very different types of cost. In fact, there are a variety of useful ways in which hospitality managers and managerial accountants can view costs and thus can better understand and operate their own businesses.

Types of Costs

Not all costs are the same. As a result, cost accountants have identified several useful ways to classify business costs. Among the most important of these are:

- Fixed and variable costs
- Mixed costs
- Step costs
- Direct and indirect (overhead) costs
- Controllable and non-controllable costs
- Other costs
  - Joint costs
  - Incremental costs
  - Standard costs
  - Sunk costs
  - Opportunity costs

In this chapter, you will learn about all of these types of costs. Before examining these classifications of cost, however, it is good for you to recognize that not all business costs can be objectively measured. In fact, in some cases, cost can be a somewhat subjective matter. To illustrate, consider that, in many cases, identifying a cost in the hospitality business can be as simple as reviewing an invoice for purchased meats or produce. For example, the food and beverage director at a Country Club who orders and is delivered $5,000 worth of strip steak for use at a golf outing knows exactly what the steaks "cost." The invoice states the amount. In other cases, however, "cost" is more subjective. Consider the salary of the person at the Country Club who will prepare and send the bill for the golf outing to the individual who will pay for it. The cost of "talking with customers regarding invoice questions" is an example of an activity performed inside many hospitality companies and one for which a clear-cut cost cannot be so easily assigned. Some customers will have invoice questions. Others will not. How then can the real cost of "talking with customers regarding invoice questions" be assigned?

Cost accountants facing such issues can assign each hospitality employee's time to different activities performed inside a company. Many will use surveys to have the workers themselves assign their time to the different activities such as food preparation, guest service, and clean-up. An accountant can then determine the total cost spent on each activity by summing up the percentage of each worker's time and pay that is spent on that activity. This process is called **activity-based costing** and it seeks to assign objective costs to somewhat subjective items such as the payment for various types of labor as well as the even more subjective management tasks involved with planning, organizing, directing, and controlling a hospitality business.

It should be easy for you to understand how allocating costs to various areas of a business can permit its managers to total up and then examine those costs to make good decisions. If upper management believes that too little money is spent in one area (for example, dining room servers in a restaurant) more cost can be allocated to that area. If too much is being spent (for example, for utilities) then action can be taken to correct and control the costs in that area. Using activity-based costing to examine expenses and thus better manage a business is called **activity-based management** and it is just one example of how fully understanding costs can help you make better decisions and operate a more successful business.

Fixed and Variable Costs

As a manager, some of the costs you incur will stay the same each month. For example, if you elect to buy a building for a restaurant and cocktail lounge you operate, your mortgage payment may likely be arranged in a way that requires you to pay the same dollar amount each month. If you operate a hotel and seek to provide music in the lobby for your guests, the amount you will pay for the piped-in music will also be the same each month for the life of the contract you sign with the music provider you select. As a final example, if you elect to lease, rather than purchase, a new dishwasher for your catering business, the monthly amount of the lease payment you must make will likely be at a set dollar value. In each of these examples, the cost involved is the same (fixed) each month. For that reason they are called fixed costs. A **fixed cost** is one that remains constant despite increases or decreases in sales volume (number of guests served or number of rooms sold). Other typical examples of fixed costs include payments for insurance policies, property taxes, and management salaries.

The relationship between sales volume and fixed costs is shown in Figure 9.1, where the cost in dollars is displayed on the *y* (vertical) axis, and sales volume is shown on the *x* (horizontal) axis. Note that the cost is the same regardless of sales volume.

In some cases, the amount hospitality managers must pay for an expense will not be fixed but will vary based on the success of their business. For example, if you own a nightclub, the expenses you incur for paper cocktail napkins used in the cocktail area of your club will increase as the number of guests you serve increases, and they will decrease as the number of guests you serve decreases. In a hotel you manage, each sold guest room will increase the cleaning labor costs, shampoo, soaps, in-room coffee, and the other costs associated with actually selling the room. In the restaurant business, each steak you sell requires that you purchase a steak to replace it. The more steaks you sell, the higher your own steak cost will become because your steak cost will increase when your steak sales increase and decrease when your steak sales decrease. Thus, in this example, your steak costs will *vary* with volume. As a result, some managerial accountants would classify them as

FIGURE 9.1   Fixed Cost Graph

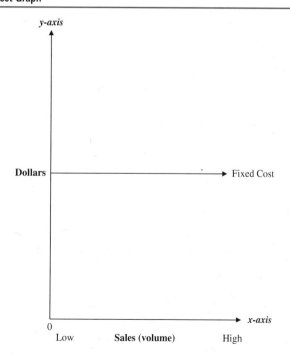

FIGURE 9.2 Variable Cost Graph

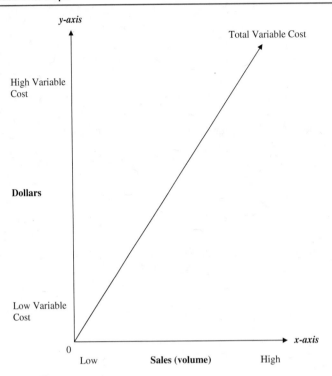

variable costs. A **variable cost** is one that increases as sales volume increases and decreases as sales volume decreases. The relationship between sales volume and variable cost is shown in Figure 9.2, where the cost in dollars is displayed on the *y* (vertical) axis, and sales volume is shown on the *x* (horizontal) axis.

As was stated previously, variable costs increase as sales volume (number of guests) increases.

go figure!

To illustrate, consider Maureen's Bountiful Burgers, a midsize, freestanding restaurant outside a shopping mall, where Maureen features upscale gourmet burgers. If it costs $2.00 of ingredients to make a gourmet burger and 50 guests order burgers, then the total variable food cost is as follows:

Variable Cost per Guest (VC/Guest) × Number of Guests = Total Variable Cost
or
$2.00 × 50 = $100

If the total variable cost and the number of guests are known, VC/Guest can be determined. Using basic algebra, a variation of the total variable cost formula can be computed as follows:

$$\frac{\text{Total Variable Cost}}{\text{Number of Guests}} = \text{VC/Guest}$$

or

$$\frac{\$100}{50} = \$2.00$$

Good managers seek to decrease their fixed costs to their lowest practical levels while still satisfying the needs of the business and its customers. Those same good managers, however, know that *increases* in variable costs are usually very good! For example, would you prefer to be the owner of a restaurant that incurred "zero" steak expense last week (because zero steaks were sold), or the owner of a restaurant that had to incur the expense of buying 500 steaks this week to replace the 500 that were sold last week? You would prefer, of course, to have to purchase extra steaks and incur extra variable costs because that would mean you sold more steaks and increased sales!

Mixed Costs

It is clear that some business costs are fixed and that some vary with sales volume (variable costs). Still other types of cost contain a mixture of both fixed and variable characteristics. Costs of this type are known as semi-fixed, semi-variable, or **mixed costs**. All three of these names imply that costs of this type are neither completely fixed nor completely variable. In this text, these types of cost will be referred to as mixed costs, because that term best explains their true nature.

In order to fully understand mixed costs, it is helpful to see how the variable and mixed portions are depicted on a mixed cost graph as in Figure 9.3. The x axis represents sales volume and the y axis represents costs in terms of dollars. The total mixed cost line is a combination of fixed and variable costs. As you can see, the mixed cost line starts at the point where fixed costs meet the y axis. This is because fixed costs remain the same regardless of sales volume, and thus, must be paid even if no sales occur. The variable cost line, then, sits on top of the fixed cost line, and each guest served or each room sold generates a portion of the variable cost (VC/guest). Because of this, the total mixed cost line includes a combination of the fixed costs and variable costs needed to generate total sales.

In a hotel, the cost associated with a telephone system is an excellent example of a mixed cost. That is, the hotel will pay a monthly fee for the purchase price repayment, or

FIGURE 9.3 Mixed Cost Graph

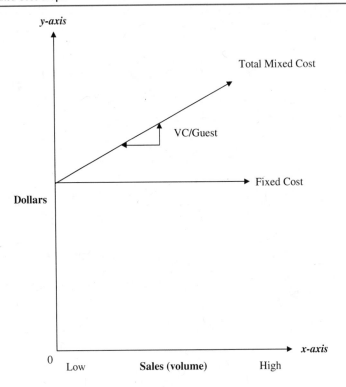

lease, of the actual phone system, including the call accounting interface, music on-hold feature, message waiting service, and other basic telecommunication options selected by the hotel. The monthly fee to be paid represents a fixed cost because it will be the same amount whether the occupancy percentage in the hotel is very low or very high. Increased occupancy, however, is likely to result in increased telephone usage by guests. Because, like your own cell phone bill, hotels pay their monthly telephone bills or access fees based upon the number of calls made and the length of those calls, a hotel's local and long-distance bill will increase as additional hotel guests result in additional telephone calls made.

 *go figure!*

The best way to understand a mixed cost is to understand the mixed cost formula. To illustrate, assume a hotel pays $4,000 per month to lease its telephone system. Assume also that you know (from historical records) that the average guest staying at the hotel makes one local and one long-distance telephone call. The cost, to the hotel, of each call averages $0.50 in access fees, or a total of $1.00 per guest. Assume also that, in a specific month, the hotel anticipates 7,500 guests. Using the following formula for mixed costs, the hotel's telephone bill for the month could be estimated as:

$$\text{Fixed Cost} + \text{Variable Cost} = \text{Total Mixed Cost}$$

or

$$\text{Fixed Cost} + (\text{Variable Cost per Guest} \times \text{Number of Guests}) = \text{Total Mixed Cost}$$

or

$$\$4,000 + (\$1.00 \times 7,500) = \$11,500$$

Separating Mixed Costs into Variable and Fixed Components

As you have already learned, mixed costs include both variable and fixed cost components. A mixed cost can be divided into its fixed and variable components in order for management to effectively control the variable cost portion. It is this variable cost that is the most controllable in the short term.

Several methods can be used to split mixed costs into their fixed and variable components. The most common methods are high/low, scatter diagrams, and regression analysis. Although regression analysis and scatter diagrams provide more precise results, the high/low method is easier to calculate and gives you a good estimate of the variable and fixed components of a mixed cost. Thus, for its practical usability, the high/low method is the one you will learn in this section.

To illustrate the high/low method, consider Joshua's Restaurant, which is located across the street from the Blue Lagoon Water Park Resort. Joshua's costs, including his number of guests served, from his income statements for October, November, and December are shown in Figure 9.4.

FIGURE 9.4   Joshua's Restaurant Costs for October, November, and December

	October	November	December
NUMBER OF GUESTS	**10,000**	**17,000**	**21,000**
Food Cost	35,000	59,500	73,500
Beverage Cost	4,000	6,800	8,400
Salaries and Wages	23,960	27,460	29,460
Employee Benefits	5,125	5,265	5,345
Direct Operating Expenses	6,056	8,156	9,356
Music and Entertainment	1,070	1,070	1,070
Marketing	2,912	3,262	3,462
Utility Services	4,077	5,477	6,277
Repairs and Maintenance	1,630	1,840	1,960
Administrative and General	5,570	5,570	5,570
Occupancy	10,000	10,000	10,000
Depreciation	3,400	3,400	3,400
Interest	7,200	7,200	7,200
Total Costs	**110,000**	**145,000**	**165,000**

go figure!

To demonstrate how the high/low method separates a mixed cost into its variable and fixed components, we will use Joshua's *marketing expense* from Figure 9.4. The high/low method uses the three following steps:

1. *Determine variable cost per guest for the mixed cost.*
   Choose a high volume month (December) and a low volume month (October) that represents *normal* operations. Then, use the following formula to separate out variable cost per guest for the mixed cost:

> **High Cost — Low Cost**
> ————————————————
> **High # of Guests — Low # of Guests**
>
> **= Variable Cost per Guest (VC/Guest)**
>
> or
>
> $$\frac{\$3,462 - \$2,912}{21,000 - 10,000} = \$0.05$$

2. *Determine total variable costs for the mixed cost.*
   Multiply variable cost per guest by either the high or low volume (number of guests) as follows:

> **VC/Guest × Number of Guests = Total Variable Cost**
>
> or
>
> **$0.05 × 10,000 = $500**

3. *Determine the fixed costs portion of the mixed cost.*
   Subtract total variable cost from the mixed cost (at the high volume or low volume you chose in step 2 low volume at 10,000 guests was chosen in this example) to determine the fixed cost portion as follows.

> **Mixed Cost — Total Variable Cost = Fixed Cost**
>
> or
>
> **$2,912 — $500 = $2,412**

Thus, Joshua's mixed marketing expense can be shown with its variable and fixed components as follows:

> Fixed Cost + Variable Cost = Total Mixed Cost
>
> or
>
> Fixed Cost + (Variable Cost per Guest × Number of Guests)
> = Total Mixed Cost
>
> or
>
> *At 10,000 guests served:*
>
> $2,412 + ($0.05 × 10,000) = $2,912

Now that you understand the high/low method for separating mixed costs into variable and fixed components, you are ready to separate *all* of Joshua's costs into their variable and fixed components. In order to determine his variable costs and fixed costs components for his restaurant, Joshua can use the following steps.

1. **Identify all costs as being variable, fixed, or mixed.**
   Joshua's true variable costs are food cost and beverage cost. These costs will vary directly with the number of guests served.
   Joshua's true fixed costs are music and entertainment, administrative and general, occupancy, depreciation, and interest. These are easy to identify, since they are the same every month.
   Joshua's mixed costs are salaries and wages, employee benefits, direct operating expenses, marketing, utility services, and repairs and maintenance. These costs have characteristics of both variable and fixed costs.
2. **Determine variable cost per guest for *each* variable cost.**
   Using Joshua's food cost as an example, variable cost per guest is $35,000/ 10,000 guests = $3.50.
3. **Determine *each* fixed cost.**
   The best way to identify fixed costs is that they are the same each month.
4. **Determine the variable cost and fixed cost portions of *each* mixed cost.**
   Use the high/low method to separate mixed costs into their variable and fixed components as was done with Joshua's marketing expense earlier.

Figure 9.5 shows the variable cost per guest and fixed costs for Joshua's Restaurant.

 *go figure!*

As can be seen in Figure 9.5, Joshua's total variable cost per guest is $5.00 and his total fixed costs are $60,000. Joshua's total costs for October ($110,000), November ($145,000), and December ($165,000) include variable, fixed, and mixed costs. It is important to point out that *total* costs are mixed costs, and thus can be treated as such. Therefore, by substituting Total Cost for Total Mixed Cost in the Total Mixed Cost formula, Joshua's Total Costs can be calculated as follows:

Fixed Costs + Variable Costs = Total Costs

or

Fixed Costs + (Variable Cost per Guest × Number of Guests) = Total Costs

or

At 10,000 guests served:

$60,000 + ($5.00 × 10,000) = $110,000

At 17,000 guests served:

$60,000 + ($5.00 × 17,000) = $145,000

At 21,000 guests served:

$60,000 + ($5.00 × 21,000) = $165,000

As you will notice, total fixed costs and total variable costs per guest are the same for all levels of number of guests served. This is because the total cost equation represents a straight line as shown in Figure 9.6.

FIGURE 9.5   Joshua's Restaurant Variable Costs per Guest and Fixed Costs

	October	November	December	Variable Cost per Guest	Fixed Costs
NUMBER OF GUESTS	10,000	17,000	21,000		
Food Cost	35,000	59,500	73,500	3.50	0
Beverage Cost	4,000	6,800	8,400	0.40	0
Salaries and Wages	23,960	27,460	29,460	0.50	18,960
Employee Benefits	5,125	5,265	5,345	0.02	4,925
Direct Operating Expenses	6,056	8,156	9,356	0.30	3,056
Music and Entertainment	1,070	1,070	1,070	0	1,070
Marketing	2,912	3,262	3,462	0.05	2,412
Utility Services	4,077	5,477	6,277	0.20	2,077
Repairs and Maintenance	1,630	1,840	1,960	0.03	1,330
Administrative and General	5,570	5,570	5,570	0	5,570
Occupancy	10,000	10,000	10,000	0	10,000
Depreciation	3,400	3,400	3,400	0	3,400
Interest	7,200	7,200	7,200	0	7,200
Total Costs	**110,000**	**145,000**	**165,000**	**$5.00**	**$60,000**

FIGURE 9.6   Total Cost Graph

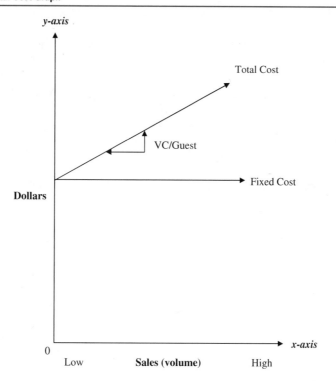

 *go figure!*

As you may remember from high school algebra, the equation for a line is $y = a + bx$. The equation for a line applies to the Total Cost line, where "a" is the y intercept (fixed costs), "b" is the slope of the line (VC/Guest), "x" is the independent variable (Number of Guests or Sales Volume), and "y" is the dependent variable (Total Cost). The *total cost equation* can be summarized as follows for Joshua's Restaurant:

Total Cost Equation

$$y = a + bx$$

or

Total Costs = Fixed Costs + (Variable Cost per Guest × Number of Guests)

or

At any number of guests served at Joshua's Restaurant:

Total Costs = $60,000 + ($5.00 × Number of Guests)

Thus, assuming that in a *normal* month variable costs per guest and fixed costs remain the same for Joshua's Restaurant, total costs in any month can be estimated by using the total cost equation. All Joshua must do is insert the anticipated number of guests into the equation to estimate total costs for any month. For example, if Joshua expects the month of June to have 18,000 guests, he can estimate his total costs as follows:

> **Total Costs = Fixed Costs + (Variable Cost per Guest × Number of Guests)**
>
> or
>
> *At 18,000 guests served:*
>
> **$150,000 = $60,000 + ($5.00 × 18,000)**

Effective managers know they should not categorize fixed, variable, or mixed costs in terms of being either "good" or "bad." Some costs are, by their very nature, related to sales volume. Others are not. It is important to remember that the goal of management is not to reduce, but to *increase* total variable costs in direct relation to increases in total sales volume. Costs are required if you are to service your guests. As long as the total cost of servicing guests is less than the amount you receive from them, expanding the number of guests served will not only increase costs, it will increase profits as well.

Step Costs

Because they are in the service industries, restaurant and hotel managers often find that, in addition to considering their costs as fixed, variable, or mixed, it is also helpful to understand step costs. A **step cost** is a cost that increases as a range of activity increases or as a capacity limit is reached. That is, instead of increasing in a linear fashion like variable costs as seen in Figure 9.2, step cost increases look more like a staircase (hence the name "step" costs).

It is easy to understand step costs. Consider, for example, the restaurant manager who has determined that one well-trained server can effectively provide excellent service for a range of 1 to 30 of the restaurant's guests. If, however, 40 guests are anticipated, a second server must be scheduled. In reality, the restaurant manager does not need a "full" server, in fact, a 1/3 server would be sufficient! As Figure 9.7 demonstrates, however, servers come in "ones." Each additional server added increases the restaurant's costs in a nonlinear (step-like) fashion.

There are a variety of costs that can be considered step costs. One of the most important is the cost of managers and supervisors. For example, one housekeeping supervisor may be able to direct the work activities of eight hotel room attendants. When nine or more room attendants are scheduled to work, additional supervisors must be added, and these additional staff members will increase the hotel's payroll in a "step" fashion.

FIGURE 9.7   Step Costs

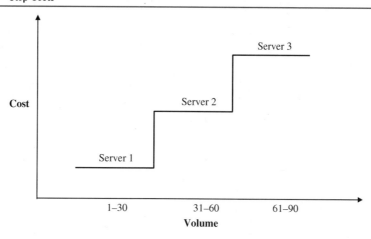

Direct and Indirect (Overhead) Costs

One of the reasons managers carefully consider costs is for the purpose of assigning them to specific operating areas within their businesses. For example, at the Blue Lagoon Water Park Resort, the cost of providing guests' rooms with shampoo, conditioners, and soaps is designated as a housekeeping department cost within the rooms division of the hotel. In a similar manner, the cost of liquor products purchased for use in the hotel's lounge is a cost that would be assigned to the beverage area within the food and beverage department. When a cost can be directly attributed to a specific area or profit center within a business, it is known as a **direct cost**. Direct costs usually (but not always) increase with increases in sales volume. The most common direct costs in a restaurant are those related to the food and beverages it sells. On a restaurant's income statement, these expenses are usually identified as "cost of sales" (see Chapter 3).

An **indirect cost** is one that is not easily assigned to a specific operating unit or department. Consider the position of the controller in a hotel. That person is responsible for the cash control and financial systems for the entire property and all of its operating departments. The cost of employing the controller and his or her staff is considered an indirect cost because it is not easily attributable to any specific department in the hotel.

In the hotel industry, indirect costs are more often known as undistributed expenses and nonoperating expenses (see Chapter 3). Typically, undistributed expenses include administrative and general, information systems, human resources, security, franchise fees, transportation, marketing, property operations and maintenance, and utility expenses. Other indirect costs include nonoperating expenses such as rent and other facility occupation costs, property taxes, insurance, depreciation, amortization, interest, and income taxes.

Indirect costs are also known as **overhead costs**. When there is more than one profit center, management typically will use a **cost allocation** system to assign portions of the overhead costs among the various centers. To illustrate both overhead and cost allocation,

FIGURE 9.8   Harley Hotels Operations Administration

Position	Salary	Related Expense	Total
Director of Operations	$125,000	$ 75,000	$200,000
Corporate Sales Director	$ 90,000	$ 60,000	$150,000
Total	**$215,000**	**$135,000**	**$350,000**

FIGURE 9.9   Harley Hotels Managed Properties

Hotel	Location	Rooms	Annual Revenues
Bitmore	Denver	300	$15,250,000
Los Cobo	Santa Fe	200	$ 8,500,000
The Drake	Dallas	225	$11,750,000
Greenwood	Miami	250	$10,500,000
Sandstone	Las Vegas	525	$22,000,000
Total		**1,500**	**$68,000,000**

consider the case of the Denver-based Harley Hotel Company. This company manages, but does not own hotels. It earns its income by providing hotel owners with the systems and management staff required to successfully operate their hotel properties. The company has five management contracts. The Harley Hotel company employs a director of operations who works directly with each hotel's general manager, as well as a corporate sales director who works with each property's director of sales and marketing. The salary and related costs of each position are found in Figure 9.8.

The five hotels operated by the Harley company, their location, their number of rooms, and their annual revenues are found in Figure 9.9.

 *go figure!*

Assume that you are the individual responsible for making cost allocation decisions for the Harley Hotel Company. How would you assign the costs related to your company employing the director of operations and the corporate sales director?

Certainly, one approach would be to assign each hotel an equal amount of this corporate overhead. If such an approach were used, the allocation to each hotel would be computed as:

$$\frac{\text{Total Overhead}}{\text{Number of Profit Centers}} = \text{Overhead Allocation per Profit Center}$$

or

$$\frac{\$350,000}{5} = \$70,000 \text{ per hotel}$$

Another approach would be to assign overhead costs on the basis of each hotel's size. The logic to such an approach is simply that a larger hotel (the 525-room Sandstone) would likely require more attention from the corporate office than would a smaller property (the 200-room Los Cobo). Utilizing such an approach, the overhead costs would be allocated in the same percentage ratio as each hotel's size as shown in Figure 9.10.

Note that, under this plan, overhead allocation charges, rather than being equal, range from a low of $46,550 (Los Cobo) to a high of $122,500 (Sandstone). Clearly, this approach yields very different results than does one that allocates the company's overhead costs based upon the number of hotels managed ($70,000 per hotel).

Yet, another approach that could be taken to allocate the Harley's overhead costs, and one that is commonly used by restaurant and hotel companies, is that of allocation based on sales revenue achieved by the profit center. Using this approach, the data for the Harley Company would result in the allocation charges shown in Figure 9.11.

Note that for each different allocation approach utilized, the resulting charges to the individual hotels are also different. The alternatives presented here are not the only ones that could be used by the Harley's managerial accountants to assign costs. Considering the time actually spent at each property and/or the recognition of differences in direct costs (for example, because the company is based in Denver, the travel costs for Harley staff are likely to be much higher for trips to the Greenwood in Miami than for trips to the Bitmore in Denver) could reasonably be considered as cost allocation guides. Alternative methods of overhead cost allocation to the five individual hotel profit centers could include

FIGURE 9.10   Overhead Allocation Based on Number of Rooms

Hotel	Rooms	% of Total Rooms	$ of Overhead Charge
Bitmore	300	20.0	$ 70,000
Los Cobo	200	13.3	46,550
The Drake	225	15.0	52,500
Greenwood	250	16.7	58,450
Sandstone	525	35.0	122,500
Total	**1,500**	**100.0**	**$350,000**

FIGURE 9.11   Overhead Allocation Based on Annual Revenues

Hotel	Annual Revenues	% of Total Revenues	$ of Overhead Charges
Bitmore	$15,250,000	22.4	$ 78,400
Los Cobo	$ 8,500,000	12.5	43,750
The Drake	$11,750,000	17.3	60,550
Greenwood	$10,500,000	15.4	53,900
Sandstone	$22,000,000	32.4	113,400
Total	**$68,000,000**	**100.0**	**$350,000**

the number of staff employed by each hotel, the profit levels it achieves or any number of other allocation approaches that seek to fairly and rationally allocate the company's overhead costs.

Controllable and Non-Controllable Costs

While it is useful, in many cases, to consider costs in terms of their being fixed, variable, mixed, step, direct, or indirect, it is also useful to consider some costs in terms of their being controllable or non-controllable. **Controllable costs** are those costs over which a manager has primary control, and **non-controllable costs** are those costs which a manager cannot control in the short term.

In most businesses, managers will only be held responsible for the profits remaining after subtracting the expenses they can directly control. In a hotel, examples of controllable costs are operating department expenses and undistributed operating expenses. This is also a reason why income statements most often will clearly indicate net income before and after the subtraction of management's non-controllable expenses such as rent and other facility occupation costs, property taxes, insurance, depreciation, amortization, interest, and income taxes. In the short run, most of these type costs cannot be directly controlled by a manager. Of course, all costs can, in the long run, be somewhat controlled by the owners of a business because they can elect to continue, close, or expand their operations. Onsite managers and their supervisors make a distinction, however, between controllable and non-controllable costs to indicate those items for which managers can be held directly responsible and those items for which the business's owners are most responsible.

To illustrate, consider the case of Steve, the operator of a neighborhood tavern/sandwich shop. Most of Steve's revenue comes from the sale of beer, sandwiches, and his special pizza. Steve is, of course, free to decide on a weekly or monthly basis the amount he will spend on advertising. Advertising expense, then, is under Steve's direct control and, thus, would be considered a controllable cost. Some of his expenses, however, are not under his control. Taxes on product sales are a familiar form of a non-controllable cost. The state in which Steve operates charges a tax on all alcoholic beverage sales. As the state in which he operates increases the liquor tax, Steve is forced to pay more. In this situation, the alcoholic beverage tax would be considered a non-controllable cost, that is, a cost beyond Steve's immediate control.

As an additional example, assume, for a moment, that you own a quick-service unit that sells take-out chicken. Your store is part of a nationwide chain of such stores. Each month, your store is charged a $500 advertising and promotion fee by the regional headquarters' office. The $500 is used to purchase television advertising time for your company. This $500 charge, as long as you own the franchise, is a non-controllable operating cost.

In every one of these cases, the hospitality manager food service operator will find that even the best control systems will not affect the specific non-controllable cost. As a result, experienced managers focus their attention on managing controllable rather than non-controllable costs.

 *fun on the Web!*

Some hospitality costs are not as controllable as you might think. If your restaurant or hotel plays background music, hosts live bands or Karaoke nights, or even allows DJs to set up in the dining room or ballrooms, your facility will be required to pay artists royalties for the music your guests hear. Although the decision to play music at all is controllable, the royalty costs associated with playing that music are non-controllable. The following groups represent those who produce music. Go to their websites to see how and why you will interact with them.

www.ascap.com—ASCAP is a membership association of over 200,000 U.S. composers, songwriters, lyricists, and music publishers of every kind of music. Through agreements with affiliated international societies, ASCAP also represents hundreds of thousands of music creators worldwide. ASCAP was created by and is controlled by composers, songwriters, and music publishers, with a Board of Directors elected by and from the membership.

www.bmi.com—BMI is an American performing rights organization that represents more than 300,000 songwriters, composers, and music publishers in all genres of music. The non-profit-making company, founded in 1939, collects license fees on behalf of those American artists it represents, as well as artists from around the world who chose BMI for representation in the United States. BMI collects license fees for the public performances of its repertoire of more than 6.5 million compositions.

www.sesac.com—SESAC was founded in 1930, making it the second-oldest performing rights organization in the United States. SESAC's repertory, once limited to European and gospel music, has diversified to include today's most popular music, including R&B, hip-hop, dance, rock classics, country, Latino, Contemporary Christian, jazz, and the television and film music of Hollywood.

Other Cost Types

You have learned about the most common classifications of costs, but there are additional classifications that managerial accountants often find helpful. Some of these may already be familiar to you. You are likely to encounter one or more of the others during your hospitality career, so having a basic understanding of them will be very useful. Considering these costs can help managers make better decisions about the operation of their businesses.

Joint Costs

Closely related to overhead and cost allocation issues is the concept of a **joint cost**. A joint cost is one that should be allocated to two (or more) departments or profit centers. For example, a hotel's Executive Chef will typically be responsible for the food preparation activities of the hotel's restaurant(s) as well as the banquet department, yet these two areas are most often considered separate profit centers within the food and beverage department. In this case, the Executive Chef's salary would have to be considered a joint or shared cost of each area.

Most direct costs are not joint costs, while many indirect costs are considered joint costs. As with overhead costs, one difficulty associated with the assigning of joint costs is the determination of a logical basis for the cost allocation. Commonly used joint cost allocation criteria include guests served, hours worked or wages paid (for staffing related joint costs), sales revenue generated, or hours of operation.

Incremental Costs

For many hospitality managers, the computation of incremental costs is very important. Incremental is a variation of the word "increment" which means "to increase." **Incremental costs** can best be understood as the increased cost of "each additional unit," or even more simply, the cost of "one more." To illustrate, assume that you and two friends will be driving to Florida for a one-week vacation. You compute the cost of gas for the trip to be $200. A third individual approaches you to ask if they also can ride along. Your car easily holds four, thus you agree to allow this individual to go with you. What additional cost have you incurred by adding "one more" friend to the trip? The answer is that the incremental expense (cost of one more) you will incur in this case is very small. It is likely to be only the additional gas your car would use to carry one additional person.

For an example from the hotel industry, consider the costs incurred by a hotel to sell a single sleeping room to a single traveler. Typical costs would include those related to making the reservation, checking in the guest, providing hot water, heat, and power to the room, and room cleaning. At check-out, costs of re-supplying the room with soaps, shampoos, fresh linen, towels, and other consumed in-room guest amenities would also be incurred. In addition, an allocation for a reasonable portion of the hotel's fixed expenses would be assigned.

Now, assume that the managers of a specific hotel knew that the cost of providing this single sleeping room to a single traveler was $40. The direct question related to incremental costs is this: "How much more does it cost to sell the same sleeping room if it is occupied by two guests, rather than one?" The answer can be complex. For example, the cost of making the reservation would not likely change whether one or two guests occupy the room. Alternatively, however, the cost of providing fresh towels to the room at the time it is cleaned may well double. Other guest-influenced costs such as those related to hot water or electrical usage may increase slightly. Because this is so, many hotels do not charge for each additional person occupying a room.

Now that you understand incremental costs in the hotel industry are considered relatively small, consider a hotel resort in the Dominican Republic. It sells its rooms on an all-inclusive plan, which means that guests are free to consume as many food and beverage products as they wish during the entire length of their stay. For this resort, the additional costs incurred when adding "one more" occupant to a specific sleeping room will be significant indeed, and the pricing of its rooms must account for the number of occupants.

Restaurants too are concerned about incremental costs. Consider the case of a pizza company that offers "free" delivery service to customers in an apartment complex near its store. The store's managers know that the total cost of providing the pizza to their customers must include the cost of the pizza itself, as well as the expense incurred delivering the pizza. Both of these costs can be computed rather easily. If, however, the driver can be carefully scheduled in such a manner that two, rather than one, pizzas are delivered in a single trip to the complex, the cost of delivery will not double. In fact, the incremental cost of delivering the second pizza during the same delivery will be small indeed because it would include only the driver's additional delivery time and not the cost of transportation to and from the complex.

Pizza delivery is an excellent illustration of why managerial accountants concern themselves with the computation of incremental costs. They do so because, in a great number of situations, the fixed costs required to deliver a guest service or product are such that the cost of serving "one more" at the same time can be relatively small, and as a result, profits made on the sale to "one more" will be relatively large.

Standard Costs

Managerial accountants, as well as knowledgeable hospitality managers in all industry segments, can read their income statements and find out what their costs *are*. The best hospitality managers, however, want to know what their costs *should be*. It is important to bear in mind that management's primary responsibility is not to eliminate costs; it is to incur costs appropriate for the quality of products and services delivered to guests. When they do, the business will prosper. If management focuses on reducing costs more than servicing guests properly, problems will certainly surface.

Guests cause businesses to incur costs. Managers must resist the temptation to think that "low" costs are good and "high" costs are bad. A restaurant with $5,000,000 in revenue per year will undoubtedly have higher costs than the same size restaurant with $200,000 in revenue per year. The reason is quite clear. The food products, labor, and equipment needed to sell $5,000,000 worth of food is much greater than that required to produce a smaller amount of revenue. Remember, if there are fewer guests, there are likely to be fewer costs, but fewer profits as well! Because that is true, managers seek to understand their **standard costs**, which are simply defined as the costs that *should* be incurred given a specific level of volume.

Standard costs can be established for nearly all business expenses from insurance premiums to plate garnishes. For those with experience in the food service industry, understanding standard costs is easy because they already understand standardized recipes. Just as a standardized recipe seeks to describe exactly how a dish should be cooked and served, a standardized cost seeks to describe how much it should cost to prepare and serve the dish. If the variation from the standard cost is significant, it should be of concern to management.

To illustrate, assume that a restaurant manager established $10.00 as the standard cost of preparing and serving a rib-eye steak. The steak sells for $25.00. If, at the end of the month, the manager finds that the actual cost of preparing and serving each steak is $15.00, profits will suffer. Clearly, in a case such as this, the manager would want to investigate the reasons for the difference between the item's standard cost and its actual cost.

In a similar manner, however, if the manager found, at month's end, the actual cost of providing the steak was $6.00, long-term profits are also likely to suffer. This is so because, at $6.00 cost per steak sold, it is unlikely the restaurant is actually giving its guest the perceived "rib-eye" value intended by management. When costs are significantly below the standard established for them, reduced quality of products served or service levels are often the cause. Thus, experienced managers know that significant variations either above or below standard costs should be carefully investigated.

As an effective manager, the question to be considered is *not* whether costs are high or low. The question is whether costs incurred are at or very near the standard established for them. Managers can eliminate nearly all costs by closing the operation's doors. Obviously, however, when the door to expense is closed, the door to profits closes as well. Expenses, then, must be known in advance (a standard must be established), costs will be incurred, and these costs must then be monitored in a manner that allows the operation to correct significant variations from their standard costs.

Sunk Costs

A **sunk cost** is one that has already been incurred and whose amount cannot now be altered. Because it relates to a past decision, information about a sunk cost must actually be disregarded when considering a future decision. Sunk costs are most often identified and considered when making decisions about the replacement or acquisition of assets.

To illustrate, assume that you are in charge of real estate acquisition for a large chain restaurant. You are considering the purchase of two different pieces of land on which to build a new unit. Neither piece of land is located near your office, so you will need to take flights to examine the sites. The cost of visiting the closest site is $2,000 and the cost of visiting the second is $4,000. After you have concluded your trips, both the $2,000 and the $4,000 must be considered sunk costs. That is, they are costs about which you can now do nothing. They were necessary expenses in the decision-making process about which piece of land would be the best. These costs should not now, however, be among the factors you consider when determining which of the two sites would make the best location for your new restaurant.

Opportunity Costs

In some respects an opportunity cost is not an expense at all. In fact, it is the opposite of an expense because it is the cost of not electing to take a course of action. Specifically, an **opportunity cost** is the cost of foregoing the next best alternative when making a decision. For example, suppose you have two choices, A and B, both having potential benefits or returns for you. If you choose A, then you lose the potential benefits from choosing B (opportunity cost).

Consider a restaurant manager who has some extra cash on hand for the month. He could choose to use his money to buy food inventory that will sit in his storeroom until it is sold, or he could choose to invest the money. If he chooses to buy the excess inventory, then the opportunity cost is the amount of money he would have made if he had invested it in an interest bearing account.

For a personal example, assume that you have $10,000 to invest. You can put the money in your savings account at your bank and earn 5% interest or $500 per year ($10,000 × 0.05 = $500). Alternatively, you can invest the money in a certificate of deposit (CD) at your bank and earn 7%, or $700 ($10,000 × 0.07 = $700) per year. The cost, to you, of choosing to put your money in the savings account rather than the CD is $200 ($700 − $500 = $200). Opportunity costs are often computed when organizations must choose between several similar, but not completely equal, courses of action.

Cost/Volume/Profit Analysis

Experienced managerial accountants know that, for most hospitality businesses, some accounting periods are simply more profitable than others. This is so because most businesses experience "busy" periods and "slow" periods. For example, a ski resort may experience tremendous sales volume during the ski season, but have a greatly reduced volume, or may even close, during the summer. Similarly, a country club manager working in the midwestern part of the United States may find that revenue from greens fees, golf outings, and even food and beverage sales are very high in the summer months, but the golf course will likely be closed for several months in the winter.

Hoteliers in many cities also frequently experience varying levels of sales volume. For those hotels that cater to business travelers, the periods around the major holidays result in reduced business travel and as a result, reduced hotel room revenue. Those hotels that cater to family-oriented leisure travelers will find their busiest months to be the summer when school has traditionally been out of session and families take their vacations. Even year-round travel destinations such as Cancun and Florida's coastline experience spikes in volume during special events such as college spring break.

Because you now have a good understanding of costs and percentages, you know that, for most hospitality businesses, costs as a percentage of sales are reduced when sales are high, and increase when sales volume is lower. The result, in most cases, is greater profits during high volume periods and lesser profits in lower volume periods. This relationship between volume, costs, and profits is easier to understand when you examine it as shown graphically in Figure 9.12.

The *x* (horizontal) axis represents sales volume. In a restaurant, this is the number of covers (guests) served, or dollar volume of sales. In a hotel, it is the number of rooms sold. The *y* (vertical) axis represents the costs associated with generating the sales.

The Total Revenues line starts at 0 because if no guests are served or no rooms are sold, no revenue dollars are generated. The Total Costs line starts farther up the *y* axis because fixed costs are incurred even if no covers are sold. The point at which the two lines cross is called the **breakeven point**. At the breakeven point, operational expenses are exactly equal to sales revenue. Stated in another way, when sales volume in a business equals the sum of its total fixed and variable costs, its breakeven point has been reached. Below the breakeven point, costs are higher than revenues, so losses occur. Above the breakeven point, revenues exceed the sum of the fixed and variable costs required to make the sales, so profits are generated.

FIGURE 9.12 Cost/Volume/Profit Relationship

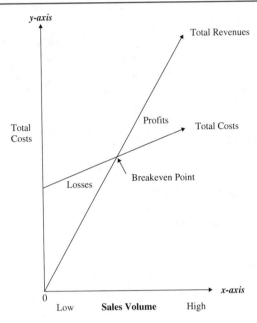

Computation of Cost/Volume/Profit Analysis

Most managers would like to know the breakeven point of their businesses on a daily, weekly, or monthly basis. In effect, by determining the breakeven point, the manager is answering the question, "How much sales volume must I generate before I begin to make a profit?" Beyond the breakeven point, the manager will want to answer another question: "How much sales dollars and volume must I generate to make my *target* profit level?" To answer these questions, you must conduct a cost/volume/profit analysis. A **cost/volume/profit (CVP) analysis** predicts the sales dollars and volume required to achieve a breakeven point or desired profit based on known costs.

Before a CVP analysis can be conducted, a contribution margin income statement must be developed. A **contribution margin income statement** simply shows P&L items in terms of sales, variable costs, contribution margin, fixed costs, and profit. As you may remember from Chapter 7, item contribution margin for menu items was defined as the amount that remains after the food cost of a menu item is subtracted from that item's selling price. Similarly, the **contribution margin** for the overall operation is defined as the dollar amount, after subtracting variable costs from total sales, that *contributes* to covering fixed costs and providing for a profit.

To illustrate, consider again the case of Joshua, who owns Joshua's Restaurant located across the street from the Blue Lagoon Water Park Resort. In the Mixed Cost section of this chapter, Joshua used the high/low method to separate his mixed costs into their variable and fixed components. As was illustrated in Figure 9.5, Joshua served 10,000 guests in October and his variable cost per guest was $5.00, resulting in total variable costs of $50,000 ($5.00

× 10,000 guests = $50,000). In addition, his fixed costs were $60,000. If we assume that his sales per guest (check average) was $12.50, then his total sales were $125,000 ($12.50 × 10,000 guests = $125,000). Based on this information, Joshua has converted his P&L statement to a contribution margin income statement as shown in Figure 9.13.

 *go figure!*

As you can see in Figure 9.13, the contribution margin calculation for Joshua's is as follows:

> **Total Sales — Variable Costs = Contribution Margin**
>
> or
>
> **$125,000 — $50,000 = $75,000**

Joshua can also view his contribution margin income statement in terms of per-guest and percentage sales, variable costs, and contribution margin as shown in Figure 9.14.

Notice the boxed information in Figure 9.14 includes per-guest and percent calculations. These include selling price, (SP), variable costs (VC), and contribution margin (CM). Note also that fixed costs are not calculated as per unit or as a percentage of sales. This is because fixed costs do not vary with sales volume increases.

FIGURE 9.13 Joshua's Contribution Margin Income Statement for October

Total Sales	$125,000	Sales Per Guest	$12.50
Variable Costs	50,000	Guests Served	10,000
Contribution Margin	75,000		
Fixed Costs	60,000		
Before-Tax Profit	15,000		
Taxes (40%)	6,000		
After-Tax Profit	$9,000		

FIGURE 9.14 Joshua's Contribution Margin Income Statement with Per-Guest and Percent Calculations

		Per Guest		Percent
Total Sales	$125,000	SP	$12.50	100%
Variable Costs	50,000	−VC	5.00	40
Contribution Margin	75,000	CM	7.50	60
Fixed Costs	60,000			
Before-Tax Profit	15,000	Guests served =10,000		
Taxes (40%)	6,000			
After-Tax Profit	9,000			

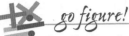

go figure!

To calculate these numbers, the following steps apply:

Step 1. Divide total sales, variable costs, and contribution margin by the number of guests to get per-guest values. Then, calculate CM/guest.

SP/guest $= \$125,000/10,000$ guests $= \$12.50$
VC/guest $= \$50,000/10,000$ guests $= \$5.00$
CM/guest $= \$75,000/10,000$ guests $= \$7.50$

> **SP/guest − VC/guest = CM/guest**
>
> or
>
> **$12.50 − $5.00 = $7.50**

Step 2. Divide VC/guest by SP/guest, and CM/guest by SP/guest to get percentage values. Then, calculate CM%.

SP% $\qquad\qquad\quad = 100\%$
VC% $= \$5.00/\$12.50 = 40\%$
CM% $= \$7.50/\$12.50 = 60\%$

> **SP% − VC% = CM%**
>
> or
>
> **100% − 40% = 60%**

Once Joshua's P&L statement has been converted to a contribution margin income statement and per-guest values and percentages have been calculated, he can proceed to determine his operational breakeven point and sales required to achieve his desired profit. He wants to do this based both on dollar sales and on the number of guests required to do so.

go figure!

To determine the dollar sales required to break even, Joshua uses the following formula:

> $$\frac{\text{Fixed Costs}}{\text{Contribution Margin \%}} = \text{Breakeven Point in Sales Dollars}$$
>
> or
>
> $$\frac{\$60,000}{0.60} = \$100,000$$

Thus, Joshua must generate $100,000 in sales per month *before* he begins to make a profit. At a sales volume of less than $100,000, he would be operating at a loss.

In terms of the number of guests that must be served in order to break even, Joshua uses the following formula:

$$\frac{\text{Fixed Costs}}{\text{Contribution Margin per Guest}} = \text{Breakeven Point in Guests Served}$$

or

$$\frac{\$60,000}{\$7.50} = 8,000 \text{ Guests}$$

Now, assume that Joshua has decided that in July he will plan for $12,000 in after-tax profits. To determine sales dollars and covers needed to achieve his after-tax profit goal, Joshua uses the following formula:

$$\frac{\text{Fixed Costs} + \text{Before-Tax Profit}}{\text{Contribution Margin \%}} = \text{Sales Dollars to Achieve After-Tax Profit}$$

Joshua knows that his after-tax-profit goal is $12,000, but the preceding formula calls for *before-tax profit*. To convert his after-tax profit to before-tax profit, Joshua must compute the following:

$$\frac{\text{After-Tax Profit}}{1 - \text{Tax Rate}} = \text{Before-Tax Profit}$$

or

$$\frac{\$12,000}{1 - 0.40} = \$20,000$$

Now that Joshua knows his before-tax profit goal is $20,000, he can calculate his sales dollars to achieve his desired after-tax profit as follows:

$$\frac{\text{Fixed Costs} + \text{Before-Tax Profit}}{\text{Contribution Margin \%}} = \text{Sales Dollars to Achieve Desired After-Tax Profit}$$

or

$$\frac{\$60,000 + \$20,000}{0.60} = \$133,333.33$$

Thus, Joshua must generate $133,333.33 in sales in July to achieve his desired after-tax profit of $12,000. In terms of calculating the number of guests that must be served in order to make his profit, Joshua uses the following formula:

$$\frac{\text{Fixed Costs} + \text{Before-Tax Profit}}{\text{Contribution Margin per Guest}} = \text{Number of Guests to Achieve Desired After-Tax Profit}$$

or

$$\frac{\$60,000 + \$20,000}{\$7.50} = 10,666.67 \text{ Guests, round up to 10,667 Guests}$$

Notice that the number of guests was rounded up from 10,666.67 to 10,667. You *must always* round the number of guests *up* because (1) a guest (person) does not exist as a fraction, and (2) it is better to slightly overstate the number of guests to achieve breakeven or desired profits than to understate the number and risk a loss or reduce profit. It is better to be safe than sorry!

Also note that once you round the number of guests up to 10,667, you should adjust the total sales dollars to reflect this. Thus, 10,667 × $12.50 = $133,337.50 sales dollars to achieve the desired after-tax profit is more accurate than $133,333.33 you calculated using CM%. The variation in these two sales dollar levels is due to rounding. This difference is minimal and may not warrant adjustment unless an exact sales dollar amount is required based on number of guests.

When calculating sales and guests (or rooms) to achieve breakeven and desired after-tax profits, you can easily remember which formulas to use if you know the following:

1. Contribution margin % is used to calculate sales *dollars*.
2. Contribution margin per *guest* (or *room*) is used to calculate sales volume in *guests* (or *rooms*).

Once you fully understand these CVP analysis concepts, you can predict any sales level for breakeven or after-tax profits based on your selling price, fixed costs, variable costs, and contribution margin. You can also make changes in your selling prices and costs to improve your ability to break even and achieve desired profit levels.

Margin of Safety

Margin of safety shows how close a projected amount of sales will be to breakeven, and thus, how close an operation will be to incurring a loss. Margin of safety calculates the difference between projected sales and breakeven sales.

To illustrate this, consider again Joshua's Restaurant. His breakeven point in sales dollars is $100,000 and his breakeven point in guests served is 8,000. Assume that in August, he anticipates that he will sell 9,000 covers (guests). His sales per guest (check average) is $12.50. His margin of safety is calculated in Figure 9.15.

Thus, Joshua's margin of safety for the month of August is $12,500 and 1,000 guests. If he divides these numbers by 31 days in the month, his margin of safety per day is $403.23 and 32.26 (32) guests.

FIGURE 9.15 Joshua's Margin of Safety for August

	Sales $	Guests
Projected Sales	112,500	9,000
Breakeven Sales	−100,000	−8,000
Margin of Safety	12,500	1,000
Margin of Safety per Day (31 Days)	403.23	32.26 ∼ 32

This means that if sales drop by more than $12,500 or 1,000 guests from anticipated levels in the month of August, Joshua runs the risk of going below breakeven and incurring a loss. This also means that if sales drop by more than $403.23 or 32 guests (roughly eight four-top tables) from anticipated levels per day in August, he runs the risk of going below breakeven and incurring a loss. Joshua must decide if this margin of safety is "safe" enough for his restaurant. If he feels that he will be coming too close to breakeven (and possibly a loss), he may want to increase his marketing efforts for August so that he can increase his anticipated number of guests served.

Notice that the number of guests per day was rounded *down* from 32.26 to 32. You *must always* round the number of guests for margin of safety *down* because (1) a guest (person) does not exist as a fraction, and (2) it is better to slightly understate the number of guests as a safety margin than to overstate the number and thus, your safety net. It is better to be safe than sorry!

Also note that once you round the number of guests down to 32, you should adjust the margin of safety dollars to reflect this. Thus, 32 × $12.50 = $400 margin of safety per day is more accurate than $402.23 that you calculated. The variation in these two sales dollar levels is due to rounding. This difference is minimal and may not warrant adjustment unless an exact sales dollar amount is required based on number of guests.

Minimum Sales Point

All managers should know how to compute a breakeven point. Food service managers must also know how to compute a minimum sales point. A **minimum sales point (MSP)** is simply defined as the dollar sales volume required to justify staying open for a given period of time. Hotel managers do not typically compute MSPs because, except for seasonal hotels, their operations must be open every day of the week even if only a very few guests are staying in the hotel on any specific day or during any specific time period.

The information necessary to compute an MSP is as follows:

- Food cost %
- Minimum payroll cost for the time period
- Variable cost %

Fixed costs are eliminated from the calculation because, even if the volume of sales equals zero, fixed costs still exist and must be paid.

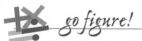 *go figure!*

Consider the situation of Adrian, who is trying to determine whether he should close his steakhouse at 10:00 p.m. or 11:00 p.m. Adrian wants to compute the sales volume necessary to justify staying open the additional hour. He can make this calculation because he knows that his food cost equals 40%, his minimum labor cost to stay open for the extra hour equals $150, and his other variable costs (taken from his P&L

statement) equal 30%. In calculating MSP, his food cost % + variable cost % is called his **minimum operating cost**. Adrian applies the MSP formula as follows:

$$\frac{\text{Minimum Labor Cost}}{1 - \text{Minimum Operating Cost}} = \text{MSP}$$

or

$$\frac{\text{Minimum Labor Cost}}{1 - (\text{Food Cost \%} + \text{Variable Cost \%})} = \text{MSP}$$

or

$$\frac{\$150}{1 - (0.40 + 0.30)} = \$500$$

If Adrian can achieve a sales volume of $500 in the 10:00 p.m. to 11:00 p.m. time period, he should stay open. If this level of sales is not feasible, he should consider closing the operation at 10:00 p.m.

Adrian can use MSP to determine the hours his operation is most profitable. Of course, some operators may not have the authority to close the operation, even when remaining open is not particularly profitable. Corporate policy, contractual hours, promotion of a new unit, competition, and other factors must all be taken into account before the decision is made to modify operational hours.

Apply What You Have Learned

"I think I can buy it at a great price," said Dan Flood. He was talking about the Watershed Restaurant. The property was for sale and Dan was meeting with Loralei Glenn, his friend and an experienced restaurant manager. "It's losing about 7 cents on each dollar sale now," continued Dan, "but I know we can turn that around."

Loralei considered Dan's proposal that they form a partnership, acquire the restaurant, and share in the profits they planned to make. She knew that, before it was possible to share profits, they would actually have to make a profit. That meant, to go from losing 7 cents per dollar to making money, they would have to increase sales, reduce costs, or both. She mentioned that to Dan.

"Well," he replied, "I'm not sure we need to increase the sales at all. If we buy at the right price, I think we just need to reduce our costs. You can do that!"

Assume that the restaurant's sales volume last year was approximately $1,400,000, and thus its loss for the year was about $98,000.

1. If Dan and Loralei decide to buy the restaurant, some fixed costs would be incurred. List at least five important fixed costs that would be directly affected by the purchase decisions Dan would make regarding the acquisition of the property.

2. If Dan and Loralei operate the restaurant, some variable costs would be incurred. List at least five important variable costs that would be directly affected by the operating decisions Loralei will make as she manages the restaurant.

3. Consider the decisions Dan and Loralei will make if they choose to acquire the restaurant. While clearly both are important, whose decisions do you think are the most important to ensuring the future profitability of the Watershed? Why do you think so?

Key Terms and Concepts

The following are terms and concepts discussed in the chapter that are important for you to know as a manager. To help you review, please define the following terms.

Activity-based costing	Cost allocation	Cost/volume/profit (CVP)
Activity-based management	Controllable cost	analysis
Fixed cost	Non-controllable cost	Contribution margin income
Variable cost	Joint cost	statement
Mixed cost	Incremental cost	Contribution margin
Step cost	Standard cost	Margin of safety
Direct cost	Sunk cost	Minimum sales point (MSP)
Indirect cost	Opportunity cost	Minimum operating cost
Overhead cost	Breakeven point	

Test Your Skills

Complete the Test Your Skills exercises by placing your answers in the shaded boxes.

1. Tutti's Sandwich Shop has the following information regarding costs at various levels of monthly sales. Help Tutti separate her costs into fixed costs and variable costs so that she can predict and evaluate costs at varying levels of guests served.

	January	February	March
Monthly Sales in Guests Served	**10,000**	**16,000**	**20,000**
Cost of Sales (Food Cost)	10,500	16,800	21,000
Salaries, Wages, and Benefits	15,000	15,600	16,000
Telephone	12,750	16,350	18,750
Rent on Building	2,400	2,400	2,400
Depreciation on Equipment	600	600	600
Utilities	1,000	1,300	1,500
Maintenance and Repairs	500	740	900
Administrative Costs	2,600	2,600	2,600

Item	Variable Cost per Guest	Fixed Costs
Cost of Sales (Food Cost)		
Salaries, Wages, and Benefits		
Telephone		
Rent on Building		
Depreciation on Equipment		
Utilities		
Maintenance and Repairs		
Administrative Costs		
Total		

a. Develop a total cost equation for Tutti that she can use at any volume of sales.

Total Costs =	Fixed Costs +	(Variable Cost per Guest ×	Number of Guests)
Total Costs =			**X**

b. Determine if Tutti is controlling her costs in April as well as she did in January, February, and March. She sold sandwiches to 30,000 guests in April. Calculate her expected costs based on her actual number of guests.
Expected costs based on the total cost equation:

Total Costs =	Fixed Costs +	(Variable Cost per Guest ×	Number of Guests)

c. Her actual total costs in April were $81,500. Were her actual costs in April higher or lower than expected based on her total cost equation, and was this a favorable or unfavorable variance?

Were actual costs higher or lower than expected?	
Were actual costs favorable or unfavorable?	

2. Big Tex is a true Texan. When he opened his hotel on the plains of West Texas, he named it the Screaming Saloon Inn. He now provides you with the following information about his property.

- The inn has 200 rooms, and averages 95% rooms available for sale throughout the year.
- Average Daily Rate (ADR) = $60
- Variable Costs = 40% of sales
- Fixed Costs = $604,800 per year
- Desired Profit = $650,000 per year (after taxes)
- Tax Rate = 36%
  (Spreadsheet hint: Use the ROUNDUP function in the cells indicated throughout the problem to round up rooms.)

a. Big Tex has asked you to help him calculate the following.
(Spreadsheet hint: Do not calculate SP Percentage. You must type in 100 for SP Percentage in order for the grid to calculate properly.)

	Per Unit (Room)	Percentage
SP		
VC		
CM		

Total fixed costs

Desired after-tax profit

Tax rate

Before-tax profit

Rooms available for sale per year

b. Calculate the rooms sold, occupancy %, and sales dollars he will need to break even.

Breakeven point in rooms sold

Occupancy %

Breakeven point in sales dollars

c. Calculate the rooms sold, occupancy %, and sales dollars he will need to achieve his desired profit.

Rooms sold to achieve
desired after-tax profit

[   ]   Rounded up =   [   ]

Occupancy %

[   ]

Sales dollars to achieve
desired after-tax profit

[   ]

Big Tex decides to hire a new manager to help him out around the hotel, and he will pay her $40,000 per year.

d. Calculate the rooms sold, occupancy %, and sales dollars he will need to break even after he hires the new manager.

Total fixed costs

[   ]

Breakeven point in rooms
sold

[   ]   Rounded up =   [   ]

Occupancy %

[   ]

Breakeven point in sales
dollars

[   ]

---

e. Calculate the rooms sold, occupancy %, and sales dollars he will need to achieve his desired profit after he hires the new manager.

Rooms sold to achieve
desired after-tax profit

[   ]   Rounded up =   [   ]

Occupancy %

[   ]

Sales dollars to achieve
desired after-tax profit

[   ]

---

f. If occupancy % averages 70% after he hires the new manager, what is his margin of safety?

	Sales $	**Rooms**
Projected Sales		
Breakeven Sales		
Margin of Safety		

Big Tex wants his new manager (the same one mentioned in part d. above) to oversee a proposed hotel gift shop. The small gift shop will increase his ADR by 1%, his variable costs by 5%, and his fixed costs by $24,000.

g. Calculate the following to reflect the addition of the gift shop. (Spreadsheet hint: Do not calculate SP Percentage. You must type in 100 for SP Percentage in order for the grid to calculate properly.)

	Per Unit (Room)	**Percentage**
SP		
VC		
CM		

Total fixed costs

h. Calculate the rooms sold, occupancy %, and sales dollars he will need to break even if he opens the gift shop.

Breakeven point in rooms sold   Rounded up =

Occupancy %

Breakeven point in sales dollars

i. Calculate the rooms sold, occupancy %, and sales dollars he will need to achieve his desired profit if he opens the gift shop.

Rooms sold to achieve desired after-tax profit   Rounded up =

Occupancy %

Sales dollars to achieve desired after-tax profit

j. If Big Tex has an average occupancy of 70%, will he be able to hire his new manager and still achieve his desired profit? Why or why not? Base your answer on occupancy %.

k. If Big Tex has an average occupancy of 70%, will he be able to hire his new manager, open his proposed gift shop, and still achieve his desired profit? Why or why not? Base your answer on occupancy %.

3. Fixed costs, variable costs, mixed costs, step costs, direct costs, indirect costs, joint costs, incremental costs, standard costs, sunk costs, opportunity costs ... if Raj Patel heard his dad talk about any more kinds of costs, he thought he would go crazy. His dad was the company owner and accountant. Raj had just taken his first property manager's job in his father's 10-unit hotel company. "The most important costs," said his dad, "are those you can control."

That really doesn't make any sense, thought Raj, all costs are controllable, just close the hotel and all the costs are gone! Raj thought that was a pretty funny way to look at costs, but his dad ... not so much! Raj really did know that his job was to keep his assigned property operating at a high level of profit and to do so he would need to be seriously concerned about the costs he could control. Help Raj identify his controllable costs by placing a "C" before those costs typically controlled by a property general manager and an "N" before those that a property manager would likely not control.

a.		Room maintenance costs
b.		Hotel mortgage
c.		Grounds maintenance services
d.		Supervisor salaries
e.		Cost of pool chemicals
f.		Complimentary breakfast costs
g.		Staff uniform costs
h.		Franchise fees
i.		Employee meal costs
j.		Property taxes
k.		Electronic key card costs
l.		Staff training
m.		Interest expense
n.		Internet advertising
o.		Income taxes
p.		Office supplies
q.		In-room guest amenities
r.		Insurance costs
s.		Electrical usage
t.		Assistant manager's bonus

4. Cindy Liverly is the Corporate Director of Marketing for the Rhodes hotel chain. Rhodes operates upscale properties in five major cities. Each property contributes to the cost of employing the Corporate Director of Marketing as well as the newly appointed Corporate Revenue Manager. The question for Cindy is how to fairly allocate the costs of operating the Corporate Marketing department.

One of the hotel general managers thinks the fairest way to do so is by having each property pay an equal share of the costs. Another feels the costs should be allocated based upon a property's size. Yet another general manager feels that rooms sold, not size, should dictate the proportion to be paid. Cindy's boss has even asked her to investigate allocation based upon the profits made by each hotel. Using the information below, help Cindy with her cost-allocation decision by answering the questions that follow.

Corporate Marketing Expense			
Position	Salary	Office and Travel Expense	Total Costs
Corporate Marketing Director	$165,000	$75,000	$240,000
Corporate Revenue Manager	$110,000	$60,000	$170,000
Total Cost	**$275,000**	**$135,000**	**$410,000**

Property	# of Rooms in Property	Annual Occupancy	Net Income
Denver	425	70.2%	$1,085,875
Dallas	510	68.6%	$1,518,984
Orlando	820	64.9%	$1,532,416
Atlanta	466	71.1%	$1,932,222
New York	371	79.4%	$2,353,513

a. What is the allocation amount for each hotel if the allocation is made on the basis of an "equal" per-property cost allocation?

Total Cost	Number of Properties	Cost per Property

b. What is the allocation amount for each hotel if the allocation is made on the basis of property size?

Property	# of Rooms in Property	% of Total	Cost per Property
Denver	425		
Dallas	510		
Orlando	820		
Atlanta	466		
New York	371		
Total	2,592		

c. What is the allocation amount for each hotel if the allocation is made on the basis of number of rooms sold per year?

Property	# of Rooms in Property	Annual Occupancy	# of Rooms Sold	% of Total	Cost per Property
Denver	425	70.2%			
Dallas	510	68.6%			
Orlando	820	64.9%			
Atlanta	466	71.1%			
New York	371	79.4%			
Total					

d. What is the allocation amount for each hotel if the allocation is made on the basis of net income earned?

Property	Net Income	% of Total	Cost per Property
Denver	$1,085,875		
Dallas	$1,518,984		
Orlando	$1,532,416		
Atlanta	$1,932,222		
New York	$2,353,513		
Total	$8,423,010		

e. If you were the general manager at the Orlando property, which cost allocation method would you prefer? Why?

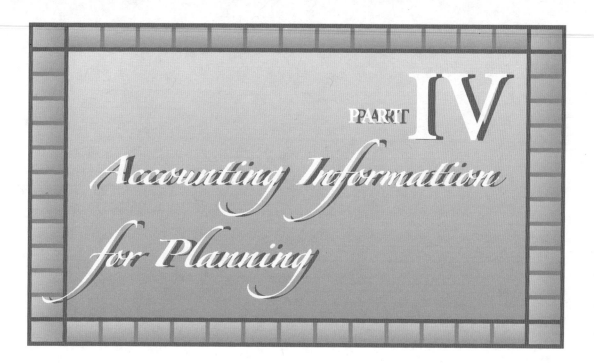

PART **IV**

Accounting Information for Planning

CHAPTER 10

Forecasting in the Hospitality Industry

OVERVIEW

Hospitality managers working in restaurants and hotels simply must be able to accurately predict the number of guests they will serve as well as when those guests will arrive. If they cannot, guest service levels or profits will surely suffer. In this chapter you will learn how hospitality managers forecast business revenues so they can carefully plan to maximize guest satisfaction.

It has been said that average managers know what *has* happened in their operations in the past and good managers know what *is* currently happening in their operations. However, the very best managers also know what *will* happen in the future. While it may not be possible for managerial accountants to predict their future business volume with 100% accuracy, it is possible to create and utilize management tools that will become very accurate in estimating future revenues, expense requirements, and staffing needs.

The advantages of maintaining accurate sales forecasts are many but include greater efficiency in scheduling the employees needed to service anticipated guests, greater accuracy in estimating food production requirements, improved levels of inventory maintained (because demand for products will be better known), and greater effectiveness in developing and maintaining purchasing systems.

In the restaurant business, an understanding of anticipated sales, in terms of either revenue dollars, guest counts, or both, will help you have the right number of workers, with the right amounts of product available, at the right time. For hoteliers, knowing the anticipated demand for guest rooms and other hotel services also allows for the proper scheduling of employees; however, it does even more. Because hotel room rates (unlike a restaurant's menu prices) are often adjusted monthly, weekly, or daily to reflect the immediate demand for rooms, a good understanding of how to forecast room occupancy rates allows hoteliers the ability to maximize RevPAR through the effective pricing of rooms and the elimination of room discounts during periods of high room demand.

In this chapter, you will learn how managerial accountants can accurately forecast revenues as well as how they utilize this information to maximize profit and increase operational efficiency.

CHAPTER OUTLINE

- The Importance of Accurate Forecasts
- Forecast Methodology
- Utilizing Trend Lines in Forecasting
- Apply What You Have Learned
- Key Terms and Concepts
- Test Your Skills

LEARNING OUTCOMES

At the conclusion of this chapter, you will be able to:

✓ Identify reasons why accurate revenue forecasts are important.
✓ Forecast restaurant and hotel revenues.
✓ Utilize trend lines in the forecasting process.

The Importance of Accurate Forecasts

One of the first questions restaurateurs and hoteliers must ask themselves is very simple: "How many guests will we serve today? This week? This year?" The correct answers to questions such as these are critical, since these guests will provide the revenue from which basic operating expenses will be paid. Clearly, if too few guests are served, total revenue may be insufficient to cover expenses, even if costs are well managed. In addition, purchasing decisions regarding the kind and quantity of food or beverage to buy, the number of rooms to clean, or the supplies to have on hand are dependent on knowing the number of guests who will be coming to consume those products.

Labor required to serve the guests is also determined based on the manager's "best guess" of the projected number of customers to be served and what these guests will buy. Forecasts of future revenues are normally based on a careful recording of previous sales, since what has happened in the past in an operation is usually the best predictor of what will happen in that same operation in the future. Finally, operating, cash, and capital budgets (see Chapter 11) cannot be prepared unless an operator knows the amount of revenue upon which these bugets should be based.

In the hospitality industry, there are a variety of ways of counting or defining sales. In its simplest case, *sales* are the dollar amount of revenue collected during some predetermined time period. The time period may be an hour, shift, day, week, month, or year. When used in this manner, sales and revenue are interchangeable terms. It is important, however, to remember that a distinction is made in the hospitality industry between sales (revenue) and sales volume, which is the number of units sold. In many areas of the hospitality industry, for example, in college and university dormitory food service, it is customary that no cash actually changes hands during a particular meal period. Of course, the manager of such a facility still created sales and would be interested in sales volume, that is, how much food was actually consumed by the students on that day. This is critical information because, as we have seen, a manager must be prepared to answer the question, "How many individuals did I serve today, and how many should I expect tomorrow?"

In addition to the importance of accurate sales records for purchasing and staffing, sales records are valuable to the operator when developing labor standards. Consider, for example, a large restaurant with 400 seats. If an individual server can serve 25 guests at lunch, you would need 400/25, or 8, servers per lunch shift if you assumed each seat would be utilized during the lunch period. If management keeps no accurate sales histories or forecasts, too few or too many servers could possibly be scheduled on any given lunch period. With accurate sales records, a sales history can be developed for each food service outlet you operate, and better decisions will be reached with regard to planning for each unit's operation. In a similar manner, knowing the number of hotel rooms to be sold allows hoteliers to staff appropriate numbers of room attendants, laundry workers, front desk staff, and food and beverage employees. Because operating costs are typically well-known, the identification of sales levels naturally leads to improved identification of estimated expenses.

Managers utilizing forecasts and forecast data understand some basic truths about forecasts. These include:

1. **Forecasts involve the future.**

   By their vary nature, forecasts deal with the future. As most observers would agree, the ability of managers to perfectly foresee the future is limited at best. Despite that fact, managers can make forecasts that, if not perfect, are highly accurate. For example, forecasts that are made for the far distant future may be continually modified (and they should be) because it tends to be true that, as the time period forecasted draws nearer, the accuracy of management forecasts increase as well.

Thus, managers can make long-term forecasts and simply modify them as more precise short-term forecast data become available.

2. **Forecasts rely on historical data.**

While experienced managers realize that what has happened in the past is typically an excellent indicator of what will happen in the future, historical data does not, by itself, tell what will happen, but rather it tells what has happened. In some cases, historical information may be missing because the needed records have been deleted, lost, or misfiled. Also, the accuracy of historical data that does exist may sometimes be questionable. In other cases, unusual events (for example, extraordinarily high or low sales results) may serve to make historical data misleading. For these reasons, managers utilize historical data, but then carefully add their own estimates and predictions about how that data will vary or be repeated in the future.

3. **Forecasts are best utilized as a "guide."**

When properly utilized, the fact that forecasts are not perfect is not truly a detriment. For example, few hotel managers forecasting a specific night's sale of 100 rooms (in a 200-room hotel) would instruct the housekeeping department to clean only 100 rooms that night. In fact, in this example, the manager may well instruct the housekeeping department to provide a minimum of 125 rooms (the forecast plus a 25% increase in forecast) in order to ensure the number of guests arriving can in fact be accommodated. In a similar manner, the restaurateur who forecasts 300 diners on a Saturday night will likely schedule staff and purchase products to serve 300 "plus" diners.

In some organizations, it is important to recognize that there can sometimes be "political" aspects to forecasting. Pressure to "look good" to owners, company shareholders, and others can cause forecasts to be inflated even if they are unrealistic. Alternatively, forecasts that are set unrealistically low make it "easy" for managers to achieve them and thereby "look good" to their own bosses.

In still other cases, executives may believe that setting "unreachable" forecast goals will serve as a positive motivator for those responsible for meeting the forecasts. While the wisdom of this approach is questionable, it should serve to remind effective managers that their own forecasts should be accurate, be based upon the best information available, and be free from unwarranted influence or bias. When forecasts have these characteristics, they can indeed serve as useful managerial guides.

To better understand how restaurateurs and hoteliers prepare and utilize effective forecasting techniques, in the remaining portions of this chapter you will learn:

- How restaurateurs forecast sales volume
- How hoteliers forecast sales volume
- How to utilize trend lines to predict future revenues

Forecast Methodology

If only historical data was used to predict future data, forecasting (at least for operations that are already open) would seem to be simple. For example, if a restaurant served 200 guests last Saturday, then perhaps "200" would be the best forecast of how many guests will be served next Saturday. In reality, variation from historical data averages and norms can and does occur. In fact, if you managed the restaurant mentioned in this example, it is most likely that you would not serve *exactly* 200 guests next Saturday. To do so would certainly be possible, but it would also be statistically improbable! In fact, in most cases such as this, variations from revenue forecasts are likely to occur.

When a variation does occur, experienced managers know that some of it can be predicted. Assume that a restaurant has been, for the past several months, experiencing a 10% increase in sales this year when compared to the same period last year. This **trend**, or directional movement of data over time, of increased sales may be very likely to continue. If it does, it would be identified at the end of the year as a major contributor to the restaurant's revenue variation from last year's level.

Several types of trends may occur that can help a hospitality manager forecast revenues. A **seasonal trend**, or a data pattern change due to seasonal fluctuations, can be fairly accurately predicted because it will happen every year. For example, a ski resort manager knows that she will sell more of the resort's sleeping rooms during ski season than during the summer (non-ski) season. **Cyclical trends** tend to be longer than a period of one year and might occur due to a product's life cycle, such as the downturn of revenues after the "new" wears off of a trendy concept. Cyclical trends are variations from normal trends but are ones that are hard to predict because, while they exist in the historical data, they do not do so at regular intervals (like seasonal trends).

Finally there can simply be **random variation**. This variation appears to occur on a totally unpredictable basis. Upon closer examination, however, some random events can be identified. For example, consider the hotelier who operates a 1,000-room property. On a particular day, this manager is informed that the TV set in room 901 has stopped working and must be replaced. The replacement cost is $500. The $500 expense may appear, at first, to be a random one as no one would know when that specific TV set would stop working. Assume, however, that this hotel manager kept good historic cost records. Assume also that, for the past two years, each month, on average, a total of two TV sets owned by the hotel ceased working in its guest rooms. Is this expense random? Most managers would say no. They would say that because, while the particular room in which the expense will be incurred is in fact random, the expense itself is, based upon historical records, quite predictable. The ultimate goal you should set for yourself as a professional hospitality manager responsible for forecasting sales revenues, expenses, or both is to better understand, and thus actually be able to predict, as much of this random variation as possible.

Forecasting Restaurant Revenues

For operating restaurants, accurate sales histories are essential for forecasting future sales. A **sales history** is simply the systematic recording of all sales achieved during a predetermined time period. A sales history is the foundation of an accurate sales forecast. When you predict the number of guests you will serve and the revenues they will generate in a given future time period, you have created a **sales forecast**.

Before you can develop a sales history, however, it is necessary for you to think about the definition of sales that is most helpful to you and your understanding of how the facility you manage functions. The simplest type of sales history records revenue only. The sales history format shown in Figure 10.1 is typical for recording sales revenue on a weekly basis. In this example, sales have been recorded by Noel, the manager of the End-Zone Café, an on-campus coffee shop.

Notice that, in this most basic of cases, a manager would determine daily sales either from the POS system, from sales revenue recorded on the cash register, or from adding the information recorded on the operation's guest checks. That number would then be transfered, on a daily basis, to the sales history by entering the amount of daily sales in the column titled "Daily Sales."

"Sales to Date" is the cumulative total of sales reported in the unit. Thus, sales to date is the number you get when you add today's sales to the sales of all prior days in the reporting period. Sales to date on Tuesday is computed by adding Tuesday's sales to those of the prior day ($1,851.90 + $1,974.37 = $3,826.27). The sales to date column is a running total of the sales achieved by Noel's operation for the week. Should Noel prefer it, the sales period could, of course, be defined in blocks other than one week. Common alternatives are meal periods, days, weeks, two-week periods, four-week (28-day) periods, months, quarters (three-month periods), or any other unit of time that is helpful to the manager.

Some hospitality managers do not have the ability to consider sales in terms of revenue generated. Figure 10.2, the sales history for the Cary Quad Dormitory at State University, is the type of sales history used when no cash sales are typically reported. Notice that, in

FIGURE 10.1 End-Zone Sales History, October 1–7, 20XX

Sales Period	Date	Daily Sales	Sales to Date
Monday	10/1	$1,851.90	$ 1,851.90
Tuesday	10/2	$1,974.37	3,826.27
Wednesday	10/3	$2,004.22	5,830.49
Thursday	10/4	$1,976.01	7,806.50
Friday	10/5	$1,856.54	9,663.04
Saturday	10/6	$2,428.22	12,091.26
Sunday	10/7	$2,241.70	14,332.96
Week Total			**$14,332.96**

FIGURE 10.2   Cary Quad Dorm Sales History

	Guests Served			
Serving Period	**Monday**	**Tuesday**	**Wednesday**	**Total**
7–9 a.m.	216	208	223	647
9–11 a.m.	105	107	115	327
11–1 p.m.	420	425	438	1,283
3–5 p.m.	170	175	164	509
5–7 p.m.	490	480	493	1,463
Total	**1,401**	**1,395**	**1,433**	**4,229**

this case, the manager is interested in recording sales based on serving periods rather than some alternative time frame such as a 24-hour (one-day) period. In this case, the number of students served, not revenue, is of most importance. This non-revenue sales history approach is often used in such settings as extended care facilities, nursing homes, college dormitories, correctional facilities, hospitals, summer camps, all-inclusive hotel resorts, or any other situation where knowledge of the number of actual guests served during a given period is critical for planning purposes.

Given the data in Figure 10.2, the implications for staffing service personnel at the dorm should be evident as is two of the reasons for maintaining sales histories. If this Monday is indicative of most Mondays, more service personnel are needed from 7:00 to 9:00 a.m. than from 9:00 to 11:00 a.m. The reason is obvious. Fewer students eat between 9:00 and 11:00 a.m. (105) than between 7:00 and 9:00 a.m. (216). Notice that, as a knowledgeable manager, if you were operating this dorm, you would likely either reduce staff during the slower service period or shift those workers to some other necessary task. The labor savings achieved would be significant. Secondly, notice that you might decide not to produce as many menu items for consumption during the 9:00 to 11:00 a.m. period because most students have already eaten breakfast. In that way, you could make more efficient use of both labor and food products. As you can see, from a labor and food production standpoint, it is simply easier to manage well when you know the answer to the question, "How many guests will I serve?"

Earlier you learned that, for most restaurant operations, sales revenue consists of the number of guests served as well as how much each of those guests spend. Sales histories can be developed to track the number of guests served as well as to compute average sales per guest, a term commonly known as check average (see Chapter 6). Recall that the formula for average sales per guest is:

$$\frac{\text{Total Sales}}{\text{Number of Guests Served}} = \text{Average Sales per Guest (Check Average)}$$

FIGURE 10.3   Blue Lagoon Bar Sales History

	Sales	Guests Served	Weighted Average Sales Per Guest
Saturday	$4,000	500	$ 8.00
Sunday	$1,600	100	$16.00
Two-day (weighted) average	**$5,600**	**600**	**$ 9.33**

Maintaining histories of average sales per guest is valuable if they are recorded as weighted averages. The reason why can be seen easily by analyzing the data in Figure 10.3. It records sales made in the cocktail lounge of the Blue Lagoon Water Park Resort. Hiroshi Yamamoto, the bar manager, wishes to record the number of people he served as well as his check average for last weekend.

It might be logical to think that Hiroshi could use a **simple average**, or the value arrived at by adding the quantities in a series and dividing that sum by the number of items in the series, to calculate his average sales per guest. If he used a simple average, he would add the $8.00 average sales per guest achieved on Saturday to the $16.00 average sales per guest achieved on Sunday and divide by 2, which would equal $12.00 [($8.00 + $16.00)/2 = $12.00]. *It is important to understand that this would not be correct.* In fact, the **weighted average sales per guest**, or the value arrived at by dividing the total amount guests spend by the total number of guests served, should be used. The weighted average sales per guest for the Blue Lagoon Bar, then, is $9.33 ($5,600/600 = $9.33). Obviously, the difference of $2.67 ($12.00 − $9.33 = $2.67) per guest is significant, especially when hundreds of guests are expected! Thus, a weighted average is a much better predictive managerial tool for Hiroshi to use than a simple average.

A basic sales history consists of revenues generated, number of guests served, and average sales per guest. Some managers, however, use their POS system to develop detailed sales histories that record even more detailed information, such as the number of a particular menu item served, the number of guests served in a specific meal period, or the method of meal delivery (e.g., drive-through versus counter sales). The important concept to remember is that managers have the power to determine the best sales history to maintain based upon that information's ability to assist in predicting future sales.

In most cases, sales histories should be kept for a period of at least two years. This allows managers to have a good sense of what has happened in their business in the recent past as well as the most recent time periods. Of course, managers of new operations or those operations that have recently undergone a major concept change will not have the advantage of reviewing meaningful sales histories. If you find yourself advising managers in such a situation, it is imperative that you encourage them to begin to build and maintain sales histories as soon as possible so they will have good sales history information on which to base their future revenue forecasts.

FIGURE 10.4   Caribbean Corner Sales History

Month	Sales Last Year	Sales This Year	Variance	Percentage Variance
January	$ 72,500	$ 75,000	$ 2,500	3.4%
February	60,000	64,250	4,250	7.1%
March	50,500	57,500	7,000	13.9%
1st Quarter Total	**$183,000**	**$196,750**	**$13,750**	**7.5%**

Forecasting Future Revenues

To learn how managers use sales histories to forecast future sales, consider the case of Monica Rivera. Monica is the manager of The Caribbean Corner, a snack bar in the Blue Lagoon Water Park Resort. Her guests consist of parents who seek quick and healthy snacks for themselves and their children during visits to the park. Her menu consists mainly of fresh tropical fruits and blended juice drinks. Monica has done a good job in maintaining sales histories in the two years she has managed the "Corner." She records the sales dollars she achieves on a daily basis, as well as the number of guests frequenting the Corner. Sales data for the first three months of the year are recorded in Figure 10.4.

 *go figure!*

As can easily be seen, first-quarter sales for Monica's operation have increased from the previous year. She computes the dollar variance for the quarter as follows:

> Sales This Year − Sales Last Year = Variance
>
> or
>
> $196,750 − $183,000 = $13,750

She computes the percentage variance for the quarter as follows:

> $$\frac{\text{Variance}}{\text{Sales Last Year}} = \text{Percentage Variance}$$
>
> or
>
> $$\frac{\$13,750}{\$183,000} = 0.075 \text{ or } 7.5\%$$

Another way to compute the percentage variance is to use a math shortcut, as follows:

$$\left(\frac{\text{Sales This Year}}{\text{Sales Last Year}}\right) - 1 = \text{Percentage Variance}$$

or

$$\left(\frac{\$196,750}{\$183,000}\right) - 1 = 0.075 \text{ or } 7.5\%$$

Of course, there could be a variety of reasons for her increase. For example, Monica may have extended her hours of operation to attract more guests. She may have increased the size of her portions and held her prices constant, thus creating more value for her guests. She may have raised her prices, but kept the snack and drink portions the same size. It is important to understand that sales histories do not record the reasons for increases or decreases in revenue. Knowing those is the job of the operation's manager.

Using all of her knowledge about her own operation and her guests, Monica would like to predict the revenue level she will experience in the next three months of this year. Her sales forecast will be most helpful as she plans for next quarter's anticipated expenses, staffing levels, and potential profits.

The first question Monica must address is how to interpret the amount her sales have actually increased. Revenue increases range from a low in January of 3.4%, to a high in March of 13.9%. The overall quarter average of 7.5% is the figure that Monica elects to use as she predicts her revenue for the next quarter of this year. She feels it is neither too conservative, as would be the case if she used the January percentage increase, nor too aggressive, as would be the case if she used the March figure.

If Monica were to use the 7.5% average increase from the first quarter of this year to predict her sales for the second quarter of this year, a planning sheet for the next quarter of this year could be developed as presented in Figure 10.5.

FIGURE 10.5   Caribbean Corner Second-Quarter Sales Forecast

Month	Sales Last Year	% Increase Estimate	Increase Amount	Sales Forecast
April	$ 68,500	7.5%	$ 5,138	$ 73,638
May	72,000	7.5%	5,400	77,400
June	77,000	7.5%	5,775	82,775
2nd Quarter Total	**$217,500**	**7.5%**	**$16,313**	**$233,813**

FIGURE 10.6 Caribbean Corner First-Quarter Guest Count History

Month	Guests Last Year	Guests This Year	Variance	Percentage Variance
January	13,700	14,200	+ 500	3.6%
February	14,500	15,250	+ 750	5.2%
March	15,500	16,900	+1,400	9.0%
1st Quarter Total	**43,700**	**46,350**	**+2,650**	**6.1%**

go figure!

For the second-quarter total, the sales forecast is calculated as follows:

Sales Last Year + (Sales Last Year × % Increase Estimate) = Sales Forecast

or

$217,500 + ($217,500 × 0.075) = $233,813

An alternative way to compute the sales forecast is to use a math shortcut, as follows:

Sales Last Year × (1 + % Increase Estimate) = Sales Forecast

or

$217,500 × (1 + 0.075) = $233,813

In this example, Monica is using the increases she has experienced in the past quarter to predict increases she may experience in the next quarter. Monthly sales figures from previous periods plus percent increase estimates based on those histories give Monica a good idea of the revenue levels she may achieve in April, May, and June of this year. Clearly, Monica will have a better idea of the sales dollars she may achieve than managers who did not have the advantage of sales histories to help guide their planning.

Forecasting Future Guest Counts

Using the same techniques employed in estimating increases in sales, the noncash operator or any manager interested in guest counts can estimate increases or decreases in the number of guests served. Figure 10.6 shows how Monica, the manager of the Blue Lagoon Water Park Resort's Caribbean Corner, used a guest count history to determine the percentage of guest count increases achieved in her facility in the first quarter of this year.

If Monica were to use the 6.1% average increase from the first quarter of this year to predict her guest count for the second quarter of this year, a planning sheet could be

FIGURE 10.7   Caribbean Corner Second-Quarter Guest Count Forecast

Month	Guests Last Year	% Increase Estimate	Guest Count Increase Estimate	Guest Count Forecast
April	12,620	6.1%	+770	13,390
May	13,120	6.1%	+800	13,920
June	13,241	6.1%	+808	14,049
2nd Quarter Total	**38,981**	**6.1%**	**+2,378**	**41,359**

developed as presented in Figure 10.7. It is important to note that Monica is not required to use the same percentage increase estimate for each month. Indeed, any forecasted increase management feels is appropriate can be used to predict future sales.

 *go figure!*

For the second-quarter total, guest count forecast is calculated as follows:

> **Guest Count Last Year + (Guest Count Last Year × % Increase Estimate)**
> **= Guest Count Forecast**
>
> or
>
> 38,981 + (38,981 × 0.061) = 41,359

This process can be simplified by using a math shortcut, as follows:

> **Guest Count Last Year × (1.00 + % Increase Estimate) = Guest Count Forecast**
>
> or
>
> 38,981 × (1.00 + 0.061) = 41,359

Forecasting Future Average Sales per Guest

Average sales per guest (check average) is simply the amount of money an average guest spends during a visit. The same formula is used to forecast average sales per guest as was used in forecasting total revenue and guest counts. Therefore, using data taken from an operation's sales history, the following formula is employed:

> **Last Year's Average Sales per Guest + Estimated Increase in Sales per Guest**
> **= Sales per Guest Forecast**

FIGURE 10.8   Caribbean Corner Second-Quarter Sales per Guest Forecast

Month	Sales Forecast	Guest Count Forecast	Average Sales per Guest Forecast
April	$ 73,638	13,390	$5.50
May	77,400	13,920	5.56
June	82,775	14,049	5.89
2nd Quarter Total	**$233,813**	**41,359**	**$5.65**

Alternatively, you can compute average sales per guest using the data collected from sales forecasts divided by the data collected from guest count forecasts. To compute Monica's sales per guest forecast, the data from Figures 10.5 and 10.7 can be combined as shown in Figure 10.8.

 *go figure!*

For the second-quarter total, the average sales per guest forecast is determined as follows:

$$\frac{\text{Sales Forecast}}{\text{Guest Count Forecast}} = \text{Average Sales per Guest Forecast}$$

or

$$\frac{\$233,813}{41,359} = \$5.65$$

It is important to note that sales histories, regardless of how well they have been developed and maintained, are not, when used alone, sufficient to accurately predict future sales. The operation's managers must have knowledge of potential price changes, new competitors, facility renovations, and improved selling programs to name just a few of the many factors that must be considered when predicting future revenues. There is no question, however, that managers must develop and monitor, daily, a sales history report appropriate for their own operation. These are easily developed and will serve as the cornerstone of other management systems that must be designed. When added to the knowledge of the unique factors that can impact their operations, managers maintaining accurate sales histories can answer two important questions: "How many people are coming to the operation tomorrow?" and "How much is each person likely to buy?"

Forecasting Hotel Revenues

Accurate and useful forecasts are even more important to hotels than they are to restaurants. This is so because, unlike restaurateurs, hoteliers are most often held accountable not only for controlling costs, but also for the short-term management of revenues via revenue management and other RevPAR maximization techniques. In addition, hotel room rates (unlike most restaurant menu prices) are likely to be adjusted daily, weekly, and monthly based upon a hotel's forecast of future demand for its hotel rooms.

The hotel business, as experienced hoteliers know, can be quite unpredictable at times. As a result, forecasts that are 100% accurate are rare. Forecasts that are consistently or significantly in error, however, will ultimately result in significant financial or operational difficulty for a hotel. This is true whether the forecasts are too high or too low. Forecasts that are implausibly too high:

- Cause unrealistic expectations by the hotel's owners
- Increase feelings of frustration by affected staff when forecasted volume levels are not attained
- Produce budgeting/spending errors by overstating anticipated revenues
- Result in impractical and overly aggressive room rate determinations. When forecasts are excessively high, room rates may be set too high (see Chapter 8).

Alternatively, forecasts that are consistently and unrealistically too low:

- Lead management to believe it is actually performing at higher levels of room sales
- Undermine the credibility of the forecaster(s) because of the suspicion that actual forecast variation is due to **low-balling** (intentionally underestimating) the forecasts
- Result in impractical and under-aggressive room rate determinations (rates too *low*)

With experience, those responsible for forecasting demand for a hotel's rooms can produce room forecasts that will be within 1 to 5% of actual hotel room revenues. To increase accuracy, most hotels produce an extended forecast of one year or more, but then alter those forecasts monthly as new data becomes available. In this manner, while forecasts that are many months away may be modified only slightly each month, a hotel's 30-, 60-, and even 90-day forecasts will become increasingly accurate. It is important to understand that accurate demand forecasts are not an end, but rather, as you learned in Chapter 8, a means of improving the effectiveness of establishing room rates. Experienced hoteliers actually produce not one, but a variety of related forecasts including occupancy forecasts, demand forecasts, and revenue forecasts. **Demand forecasts** predict periods in which demand will be generally high or low based on expected fluctuations in occupancy. Types of hotel forecasts can be found in Figure 10.9.

While restaurateurs rely primarily on historical (and in some cases predictive future data), to estimate revenues and guests to be served, hoteliers must rely on a combination of historical, current, and future data to accurately forecast and manage room demand.

FIGURE 10.9 Hotel Forecast Types

Forecast Type	Purpose/Characteristics
Occupancy Forecast	■ Helps improve employee scheduling ■ Shows guest arrival and departure patterns ■ Forecasts at least 2, 7, 14, 21, and 30 days out ■ Produces daily and weekly occupancy percentages ■ Never exceeds 100%
Demand Forecast	■ Identifies periods of 100% or more occupancy demand for rooms ■ Identifies periods of very low demand ■ Forecasts 30, 60, and 90 days out ■ Produces at least weekly occupancy percentages ■ Used to help establish room rate selling strategies
Revenue Forecast	■ Helps manage the hotel's cash flows ■ Matches revenue forecasts to pre-established budgets ■ Forecasts 30 days out or more ■ Produces at least monthly forecasted revenues ■ Estimates RevPAR

It is important to understand these data-related terms well. Historical data, of course, refers to events that have happened in the past. Current data is related to events that are entered into a hotel's property management system (PMS) but have yet to occur (for example, a reservation entered into the PMS on Thursday for the following Friday night). Accurate current data reflects confirmed (but as of yet not historic) information about the demand for hotel rooms. Future data is that information which is related to events that have yet to occur. It will not currently be found in the hotel's PMS database; for example, large numbers of reservations anticipated to be made because of the announcement of an extremely popular special event to be held two years from now near the hotel. While this future (reservation) data and demand for rooms is somewhat unknown, it can be estimated.

It is important to know that hoteliers create occupancy forecasts in a manner similar to how they compute actual occupancy percentage. That is:

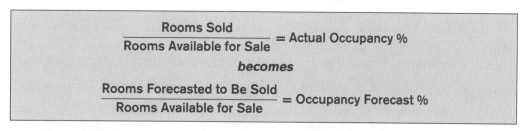

$$\frac{\text{Rooms Sold}}{\text{Rooms Available for Sale}} = \text{Actual Occupancy \%}$$

becomes

$$\frac{\text{Rooms Forecasted to Be Sold}}{\text{Rooms Available for Sale}} = \text{Occupancy Forecast \%}$$

Increasingly, PMSs are designed to include forecasting programs or components. While PMSs may well provide hoteliers the historical and current data necessary to make better decisions, it is the ultimate responsibility of the hotel's managers to make, and act on, their own forecasts. This is so because, while PMS forecasting modules may indeed "guide" them, local property managers themselves will ultimately make the best occupancy forecasts for their own hotels because they:

- Best understand the unique property features affecting demand for their own hotels
- Know about special city-wide events in the area that affect demand
- Have an understanding of the demand for competitive hotel properties in the area
- Can factor in the opening or closing of competitive hotels in the area
- Can include factors such as weather, road construction, and seasonality in their demand assessments
- Can adjust forecasts very quickly when faced with significant demand-affecting events (i.e., power outages and airport or highway closings)

For the best hoteliers, and the managerial accountants who assist them, a thorough understanding of the use of historical, current, and future data is essential to the development of accurate revenue forecasts.

Historical Data

As is true for restaurateurs, one of the best ways for existing hotels to predict future room demand is by examining historical demand. Using historical data held in the PMS, managers can establish a hotel's previously experienced guest reservation, arrival, and departure patterns. Despite its valuable assistance, however, the PMS is not the most crucial component in a hotel's forecasting efforts. The most crucial role is played by the hotel's managers. It is, quite literally, their job to "see" the future of demand for the hotel's guest rooms and services. Thus, managers combine their own skills and experience with relevant historical (and other) data when creating usable demand forecasts. In order to create these forecasts, you must first understand the following terms:

- **Stayover.** A guest who is not scheduled to check out of the hotel on the day his or her room status is assessed. That is, the guest will be staying and using the room(s) for at least one more day.
- **No-Show.** A guest who makes a room reservation but fails to cancel the reservation (or arrive at the hotel) on the date of the reservation.
- **Early Departure.** A guest who checks out of the hotel *before* his or her originally scheduled check-out date.
- **Overstay.** A guest who checks out of the hotel *after* his or her originally scheduled check-out date.

To best understand exactly how hoteliers use their hotel's data to help make demand forecasts, a thorough understanding of the forecasted room demand computation is required. Figure 10.10 shows the method used to compute a single day's occupancy forecast for a 300-room hotel.

FIGURE 10.10   Occupancy Forecast, Monday, January 1

Date: January 1	Day: Monday	
Total rooms available		300
− Out-of-order rooms		0
Net Availability		**300**

Stayovers		40
+ Reservations (Arrivals)		150
Rooms Sold or Reserved		**190**
Forecasted Adjustments:		
− No-shows		15
− Early departures		5
+ Overstays		10
Total Forecast Sold or Reserved After Adjustments		**180**

$$\frac{\text{Total Forecast After Adjustments}}{\text{Net Availability}} = \text{Occupancy Forecast} \qquad \frac{180}{300} = 60\%$$

Of course, in an actual hotel setting, room usage and availability would be forecast by individual room type, as well as for the total number of hotel rooms available. For purposes of examining the forecast process, however, it is enough to understand that the procedures and steps are the same when forecasting room type availability and/or total room availability. It is also important to understand that much of the data in Figure 10.10 is maintained by the PMS. That is, the number of hotel rooms available, the number of out-of-order rooms, the number of stayovers, and the number of reservations currently booked are all data that resides in the PMS. Data for the three forecast adjustments (no-shows, early departures, and overstays), however, describe events that will occur in the future, and thus "real" data on them does not exist. These numbers must be forecast by managers after carefully tracking the hotel's historical data related to them.

Using Current and Future Data

Historical data in the PMS is very valuable because room demand often follows fairly predictable patterns. For example, in most business hotels, room demand for Sunday night will be less than that of Tuesday nights. That historical pattern will hold true, and very accurate demand forecasts can be made using historical data, *unless* current data and estimates of future data dictate otherwise. It is also important to understand that the use of historical data alone is, most often, a very poor way in which to forecast room demand. Current and future data must also be assessed. To understand why, consider the historical room usage and current data in Figure 10.11 for a Saturday night at a 300-room hotel.

FIGURE 10.11   Historical Room Usage and Current Data, Saturday Analysis

TOTAL HOTEL ROOMS = 300
REPORT RUN DATE: MONDAY, 7:00 A.M.

Historical Data	Actual Rooms Sold	Occupancy %
Actual rooms sold last Saturday	195	65%
Average rooms sold last four Saturdays	205	68%
Average rooms sold on Saturdays in the last quarter	188	63%
Average rooms sold on Saturday, year to date	199	66%
Saturday rooms sold one year ago	202	67%
Saturday rooms sold two years ago	185	62%
Average	**196**	**65%**
Current data (on-the-books)	**260**	**87%**

In this situation, based only upon an average of historical data, the hotel's managers could be very tempted to estimate demand for the coming Saturday night at approximately 196 rooms, or 65% occupancy (196 rooms/300 rooms = 65%). However, a close examination of current data reveals that 260 rooms have already been reserved, and with five days remaining until Saturday (today is Monday), additional reservations could be made. Therefore, using *current* data, 260 rooms "on-the-books" and an 87% occupancy will produce a more accurate forecast than that which would be obtained only by using historical data. **On-the-books** is the term hoteliers use to describe current data and it is used in reference to guest reservations. The term originated in the days when hotel reservation data was stored in a bound reservations book, rather than in a software program.

Future data is the final type of information needed to assist hoteliers in accurately forecasting demand. In fact, most hoteliers agree that a manager's ability to accurately assess this information is the most critical determiner of an accurate demand forecast. It is one of the most difficult, yet also one of the most exciting aspects of hotel management.

The importance of future data in forecasting can be demonstrated easily by examining a few real-life situations routinely faced by hoteliers. Consider, for example, that you are the manager in charge of estimating demand (and as a result, establishing room rates) in the following scenarios. Suggested responses (in italics) follow each scenario:

■ A 400-room airport hotel in the northeastern part of the United States usually discounts heavily (sometimes as much as 50% off the rack rate) on Sunday night because, historically, it sells an average of 100 rooms on that night. At noon on Sunday, January 1, the property has 105 reservations on the books. The weather forecast is for heavy snowstorms of the type that have, in the past, significantly delayed flights or closed the airport. On nights such as these, the hotel has experienced a sell-out as airlines seek housing for their stranded passengers and delayed flight crews. Should the hotel managers immediately revise their demand forecast and eliminate the heavy discounts on the rooms remaining to be sold on this Sunday night?

Most talented hoteliers would say, "Yes." The value of the hotel rooms will increase dramatically in the face of a complete airport shut down. The hotel's revenue managers should monitor the weather and make "future" data predictions based upon their own experience, intuition, and information from the Weather Channel! In this scenario, discounts would likely be reduced or eliminated to take advantage of anticipated "future" data.

■ A mid-sized city in a western state is the home of a large university. That university plays football on Saturdays in the fall and the result has been, in the past, a sell-out situation in the city. This is due to the fact that the visiting team's students and fans fill the area's hotel rooms. For the past several years, no hotels in the area have offered discounts on rooms for football Saturdays. The new football schedule for next year has just been released. The university has placed an in-state rival on the schedule. The new opponent school is a much smaller university and is located only 20 minutes away from the city. Traditionally, that school's fan base for its basketball team has been huge, but their football program, because it has not been as strong, draws few fans.

On non-football Saturdays in the fall, a hotel located near the campus football stadium offers a "family package" that includes a room, reduced prices on dinner in the hotel's dining room, and tickets to the local zoo. The program is advertised to local families via a posting on the city Convention and Visitor's Bureau (CVB) website. Should the date the university plays the new opponent be included on the "family package" list of available dates?

Most talented hoteliers would say, "Yes." Even though there is a football game, the prospect of it causing a city-wide sell-out is not strong. While it would be important to monitor the booking activity for that date, all signs point to reduced demand, which will necessitate some discounting on the part of the hotel. The best hoteliers, in anticipation of reduced demand, will take immediate decisive action (even action not usually taken) as they place their "bet" on future room demand patterns.

■ Typically, the 500-room Tower Hotel, attached to the convention center of a large southern state capitol, achieves 60% occupancy on Friday and Saturday nights. It does so by heavily promoting a "weekend getaway package" to local city residents. The package includes rooms offered at 30% off rack rate. The hotel's manager learns from the local CVB that the city has been selected to host, in three years, the International Hospitality Educator's Association convention. This will be the first time the group has met in this city, thus no historical data exists related to their stay in this specific city.

The convention's meetings will all be held at the convention center on the third weekend in July. It is anticipated that the Tower Hotel will be, because of its proximity to the convention center, a very desirable location for attendees. Rooms will most likely sell at rack rate. Should the manager designate the weekend of the educator's convention as one in which the "weekend getaway package" will *not* be offered?

Most talented hoteliers would say, "Yes." They would eliminate the "weekend getaway package" because the educators will likely fill the hotel. This decision would be made despite the fact that:

— *There is no historical data in the PMS related to the educator's convention*
— *The PMS shows that not a single current reservation exists at this time for the date on which the convention will be held.*
— *The date in question is three years away!*

As can be seen from just these few examples, if hoteliers are to make accurate forecasts and properly price their rooms, historical, current, and future data must all be carefully considered. This is so because occupancy forecasting is not simply a matter of identifying the number of hotel rooms that may be sold, but rather it is a multifaceted process that consists of four essential activities that include:

- Generating the demand forecast
- Establishing a room rate strategy
- Monitoring reservation activity reports
- Modifying room rate pricing strategies (if warranted)

For hoteliers (unlike restaurateurs), pricing decisions naturally follow forecast development. Whether based upon building costs, amenities offered, operating expenses, room size, or other factors, the development of the hotel's initial, target ADR is important. What is vastly more important, however, is managing the hotel's room rate in a manner that maximizes RevPar or GOPPAR (see Chapter 9). Thus, accurate demand forecasts will profoundly affect a professional hotelier's room pricing decisions.

As a final hotel forecasting illustration, and one that clearly reveals the importance of forecasting in today's web-driven room reservation environment, assume the revenue manager in a 500-room hotel property forecasts that on a particular Sunday, which is only two weeks away, the hotel's likely occupancy will be 25% or less. In the recent past, there might be little that a revenue manager, with such short notice, could do to directly address this situation. The changing (reducing) of room prices, or increasing of discounts offered for that day meant little when the majority of a hotel's room pricing information was distributed to buyers via various print media (brochures, print ads placed in industry publications, newspapers) and therefore could not rapidly be changed. As a result, despite the fact that the revenue manager might be convinced that the price of the hotel's rooms would affect the number sold (i.e., reducing room rates could result in increased room sales), there was no way to quickly and effectively reach travelers or travel buyers with this reduced room rate information. The consequence would be that only those guests already intending to contact the hotel (typically by calling the hotel directly) could be apprised of the reduced rates. While the number of those potential guests who would be willing buyers at the reduced rates would likely be high, most of the hotel's actual arriving guests (because they preferred the hotel already) would have been willing to buy at the hotel's original (and non-discounted) printed and published rates.

Today, the Internet has changed the world of hotel sales completely, and radically. Currently, revenue managers can (and do) publish room rate changes instantaneously. In fact, with immediate (within 60 seconds) updating of web-based pricing and the ability to contact the hotel's frequent travel program members and other guests via e-mail, an aggressive revenue manager could, within a period of only minutes, initiate and publish reduced room rates on literally thousands of websites. They could also contact, via e-mail, all of those guests (perhaps the ones who had stayed on previous Sunday nights) whom the revenue manager feels might respond to a reduction in the room rates offered on that night. The final selling result may well be significant increases in the hotel's RevPAR on that date. The important point for managerial accountants to remember is that only by creating an accurate forecast can a hotel know when room demand is strong or weak enough to dictate significant changes in pricing strategies and thus affect the procedures and tactics designed to help a hotel achieve its RevPAR and revenue per occupied room (RevPOR) goals.

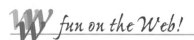 *fun on the Web!*

Forecasting hotel room demand and establishing room rates based upon the forecasts developed is a complex, as well as fascinating, topic of study. One of the best treatments of this topic is found in the newly published book, *Professional Front Office Management* by Robert Woods and colleagues, which can be found at

www.amazon.com

When you arrive, enter *Professional Front Office Management* in the search line to view a copy of this book.

Utilizing Trend Lines in Forecasting

Sophisticated business forecasters in many fields have found that the application of advanced mathematical models can often result in forecasts that are much more accurate than those derived from approaches which do not utilize such advanced formulas.

Fortunately, such formulas exist in somewhat basic forms and are easy for most managers to use. One such popular formula produces a **trend line**, which is a graphical representation of trends in data that you can use to make predictions about the future. For the purpose of this chapter, a trend line will be used to forecast future sales. This analysis is also called a regression analysis. A **regression analysis** estimates an activity (dependent variable—forecasted sales in this case) based on other known activities (independent variables—past sales in this case). By using a regression analysis, you can extend a trend line in a chart beyond the actual known data for the purpose of predicting future (unknown) data values.

Consider again the Blue Lagoon Water Park Resort. Paige, the general manager, has collected the annual sales data for fiscal years 2004 to 2010 as shown in Figure 10.12.

By using Excel (see Before You Start: How to Use Spreadsheets on the student CD-ROM), Paige has created the line graph in Figure 10.13 for the fiscal years 2004 to 2010 using the data in Figure 10.12.

Now that her data is in a chart, Paige can create a trend line (future prediction) using the resort's **baseline data** (known data). Before she begins using a trend line for forecasting, however, she must remember that the revenue projections she makes are only as meaningful as her baseline data. She, as well as all managers creating trend lines, must ensure that:

- There is enough data to show a meaningful trend. Insufficient baseline data will likely skew results.
- The data is entered into the spreadsheet from earliest (oldest) to most recent (newest).

FIGURE 10.12   Blue Lagoon Sales Data in Millions

Fiscal Year	Sales in Millions of Dollars
FY 2004	18.4
FY 2005	21.4
FY 2006	20.3
FY 2007	19.6
FY 2008	22.7
FY 2009	23.7
FY 2010	25.2

FIGURE 10.13   Line Graph of Sales Data for the Blue Lagoon, Years 2004–2010

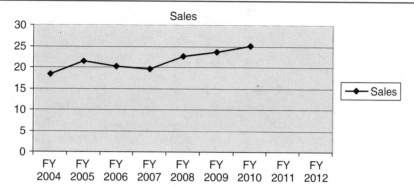

- No data is missing. If data is unavailable for a period, she must enter an estimate.
- All periods are for comparable amounts of time, such as weeks, months, or, as is the case in this example, fiscal years.

If all of the above items are satisfactory, Paige can create a trend line to predict her future sales levels in 2011 and 2012 using Excel (see Before You Start: How to Use Spreadsheets on the student CD-ROM). Figure 10.14 displays the trend line Paige has created.

As you can see, with the use of the trend line, Paige can estimate sales for 2011 and 2012 based on her past sales data.

With the use of trend lines and other sophisticated forecasting techniques, Paige (and you!) can improve future revenue forecasts. This is so because a properly created trend line forecast is a powerful management tool.

FIGURE 10.14   Line Graph and Trend Line of Sales Data for the Blue Lagoon, Years 2004–2012

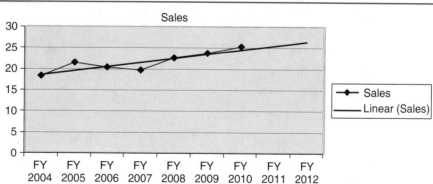

Apply What You Have Learned

It had been an exhausting two weeks, but JoAnna Turtlet was very pleased with the way her hotel staff had performed. From tornado watch, to warning, to the too close for comfort sighting of a tornado that had missed her full-service hotel by only two miles, her team was understandably nervous during the storm. Still, they had performed flawlessly.

Ultimately, the staff had gotten through the ordeal and proceeded to do a great job housing the many individuals whose homes were damaged by the winds, as well as the disaster relief officials who came to the area to help. Now, thanks to a great effort on the part of her sales staff, the hotel had been awarded the Federal Emergency Management Agency (FEMA) contract to house its federal aid workers, as well as a large number of Red Cross volunteers.

Beginning immediately, FEMA estimates it will need 110 of the hotel's 200 rooms for a period of at least four months. The impact on the hotel's business during that time period will be immense, ensuring a virtual sell-out every night. This nearly 100% occupancy will definitely be a change from the average 65% occupancy JoAnna had forecasted for these months.

1. Identify three areas within the hotel's housekeeping department that would be directly affected by the new contract and thus, the new sales forecast.
2. Identify three areas within the food and beverage department that would likely be affected by the new contract and thus, the new sales forecast.
3. Assume that FEMA is billed monthly by the hotel and pays its bills within (but rarely before) 90 days. What affect will this contract have on JoAnna's current cash accounts? What would you advise her to do?

Key Terms and Concepts

The following are terms and concepts discussed in the chapter that are important for you to know as a manager. To help you review, please define the following terms.

Trend
Seasonal trend
Cyclical trend
Random variation
Sales history
Sales forecast
Simple average

Weighted average sales per
　guest
Low-balling
Demand forecast
Stayover
No-show
Early departure

Overstay
On-the-books
Trend line
Regression analysis
Baseline data

 Test Your Skills

Complete the Test Your Skills exercises by placing your answers in the shaded boxes.

1. "I'm telling you the average is about $18.00," said Maya Stafford, the head server at the Mountain Grill. Maya and Raktida were talking about the check average achieved by the Grill on the previous two nights. "Look," continued Maya, "on Saturday night the check average was about $22.00. People drink on Saturday night. On Sunday, it was about $14.00 because they don't drink as much. $22.00 plus $14.00 is $36.00. $36.00 divided by 2 equals $18.00. Say, didn't you tell me you went to restaurant management school? Didn't you learn anything there?!"

   Raktida, the new dining room supervisor (and an honor hospitality school graduate) was unconvinced by Maya's logic. While Maya was a great server, Raktida thought she was dead wrong—by at least $2.00! To find out who is right, complete the Mountain Grill's sales history record below, and then answer the questions following it.

Mountain Grill Two-Day Sales History			
	Sales	Guests Served	Average Sales Per Guest (Check Average)
Saturday		280	
Sunday	$1,450		
Two-Day Total and (Weighted) Average	$7,700	385	

   a. What were the Grill's total sales on Saturday night?
   b. What was the Grill's check average on Saturday night?
   c. What were the Grill's guests served on Sunday night?
   d. What was the Grill's check average on Sunday night?
   e. What was the Grill's two-day check average?
   f. Who was right, Maya or Raktida?
   g. Based on your answer in question f., what was her error in logic as she mentally computed the combined days' check average?

2. Mikel Nordsem is the front office manager at the Plaza Hotel. The hotel has 850 rooms and its market consists primarily of business travelers. Mikel has determined to do a better job forecasting the number of rooms he will sell and occupancy % he will have each day. With a better forecast, he reasons, he can have the appropriate number of staff on hand to quickly serve all the guests who arrive.

Complete the following forecast, and then answer Mikel's important questions.

Date: May 1	Day: Wednesday	
Total rooms available		850
Out-of-order rooms		10
Net Availability		
Stayovers		104
Reservations (Arrivals)		376
Rooms Sold or Reserved		
Forecasted Adjustments:		
No-shows		25
Early departures		12
Overstays		15
Total Forecast Sold or Reserved After Adjustments		
Occupancy Forecast		

a. What is Mikel's net availability for rooms on May 1?

b. How many rooms sold or reserved will Mikel have?

c. After he makes adjustments for no-shows, early departures, and overstays, what will be Mikel's total forecast in rooms?

d. Based on his calculations, what is Mikel's occupancy forecast for May 1?

3. Tina Bonina owns and operates the Cancun Amigos Mexican Cantina. Business is good and getting better. In fact, based on her carefully maintained sales histories, Tina predicts her sales will increase the next quarter by 6.2%. Complete her first-quarter forecast below, and then answer the questions that are important to Tina.

Cancun Amigos Cantina First-Quarter Sales Forecast				
Month	**Sales Last Year**	**% Increase Estimate**	**Increase Amount**	**Sales Forecast**
January	$145,231.00	6.2%		
February	126,337.00	6.2%		
March	164,285.00	6.2%		
1st Quarter Total		6.2%		

   a. What is Tina's sales forecast for January?

   b. What is Tina's sales forecast for February?

   c. What is Tina's sales forecast for March?

   d. What is the total dollar amount of sales the Cantina has been forecasted to achieve in the first quarter?

4. Trisha Hanes purchased Casa del Sol, an 85-room full-service hotel on the Pacific coast in Nicaragua, in 2006. She felt then she was ahead of her time when she made the purchase and now she is convinced of it. As more tourists discover the San Juan Del Sur area and its low-cost vacation benefits, Trisha's business is booming.

   Now as she begins 2010, she wants to secure a bank loan to double the size of her property, and she needs to project her sales forward for three years to meet the bank's loan submission requirements. Help her predict her sales for each of the coming three years using trend line analysis.

Casa del Sol Sales Data in Millions

Fiscal Year	Sales in Millions
FY 2007	$18.4
FY 2008	21.4
FY 2009	22.4
FY 2010*	25.3
FY 2011	forecasted
FY 2012	forecasted
FY 2013	forecasted

* Estimate

   a. Create a line graph of sales for the Casa del Sol for FY 2007 through FY 2010.

   b. Add a trend line (through 2013) to Trisha's sales line graph.

   c. If you were a bank, would you give Trisha the loan? Why or why not?

CHAPTER **11**

Budgeting and Internal Controls

In most operations, the manager is responsible for preparing and maintaining a budget. The budget, or financial plan, simply details the expectations of an operation's owners and managers for a specific period of time. In this chapter you will learn about the variety of ways hospitality managers utilize budgets and the budgeting process to better operate their businesses. In fact, as you will discover, managers most often prepare not one, but several types of budgets. You will learn about the various types of budgets most hospitality operators prepare and why they develop them.

Of all the many budgets that can be produced, the operations budget is the one that is often foremost in the minds of those who actually manage hospitality businesses. This is so because these budgets contain important information about the controllable costs that are frequently used to determine a manager's actual skill and effectiveness. When managers meet budget expectations, they are often rewarded. When their operational budgets are not met, financial and other incentives may be reduced or even eliminated.

As experienced managers know, one important result of creating a budget is the potential to later make comparisons between budgeted and actual financial performance. In this chapter, you will learn how managers analyze their actual financial performance and compare it to the results they had originally planned or budgeted. You will also learn how you can use this information to make changes to your operational procedures or to future budgets. This will ensure that your operation has the very best chance of achieving the goals stated in your financial plan. Furthermore, you will discover that a budget should not be considered a static document. It can be modified and fine-tuned to ensure that you indeed have an excellent chance of accurately planning what will happen in the future of your business.

A second type of budget that is of critical importance to many hospitality managers is the cash budget. It is this budget that allows managers to ensure that the operation's cash on hand, which is used to pay the normal operating costs of the business, is sufficient to cover those expenses.

Finally, you will learn about some of the pitfalls and solutions to controlling the actual outcomes of careful budgeting. An effective control system will have five fundamental characteristics, which are management's concern for assets, accurate data collection and comparison to written standards, separation of responsibilities, cost effectiveness, and regular external review.

CHAPTER OUTLINE

- The Importance of Budgets
- Types of Budgets
- Operations Budget Essentials
- Developing an Operations Budget
- Monitoring an Operations Budget
- Cash Budgeting
- Managing Budgets through Internal Controls
- Apply What You Have Learned
- Key Terms and Concepts
- Test Your Skills

LEARNING OUTCOMES

At the conclusion of this chapter, you will be able to:

✓ Identify the purposes for the various types of budgets used in the hospitality industry.
✓ Create an operations budget and monitor its effectiveness.
✓ Create a cash budget.
✓ Identify the characteristics of a successful internal control program.

The Importance of Budgets

Just as the income statement tells a managerial accountant about past performance, the **budget**, or financial plan, is developed to help you achieve your future goals. In effect, the budget tells you what must be done if predetermined profit and cost objectives are to be met.

To prepare the budget and stay within it assures your predetermined profit levels. Without such a plan, you must guess about how much to spend and how much sales you should anticipate. Effective managers build their budgets, monitor them closely, modify them when necessary, and achieve their desired results. Budgeting can also cause conflicts. This is true, for example, when a hotel's food and beverage department and housekeeping department both seek dollars budgeted for new equipment. The top needs are for either a new kitchen range or a new commercial washing machine. Obviously, the food and beverage manager and the housekeeping manager may hold different points of view on where these funds can best be spent!

While each organization may approach budgeting from its own perspectives and within its own guidelines, a budget is generally produced by:

1. Establishing realistic financial goals for the organization
2. Developing a budget (financial plan) to achieve the goals
3. Comparing actual operating results with planned results
4. Taking corrective action, if needed, to modify operational procedures and/or modify the financial plan

The advantages of preparing and using a budget are summarized in Figure 11.1.

Budgeting is best done by the entire management team, for it is only through participation in the process that the whole organization will feel compelled to support the

---

FIGURE 11.1 Advantages of Preparing and Using a Budget

1. It is an excellent means of analyzing alternative courses of action and allows management to examine these alternatives prior to adopting a particular one.
2. It requires managers to examine the facts regarding what is necessary to achieve desired profit levels.
3. It provides managers defined standards used to develop and enforce appropriate cost control systems.
4. It allows managers to anticipate and prepare for future business conditions.
5. It helps managers periodically carry out a self-evaluation of the organization and its progress toward its financial objectives.
6. It provides a communication channel whereby the organization's objectives are passed along to its various constituencies, including owners, investors, managers, and staff.
7. It encourages department managers who have participated in the preparation of the budget to establish their own operating objectives and evaluation techniques and tools.
8. It provides managers with reasonable estimates of future expense levels and thus serves as an important aid in determining appropriate selling prices.
9. It identifies time periods in which operational cash flows may need to be augmented.
10. It communicates to owners and investors the realistic financial performance expectations of management.

---

budget's implementation. In large organizations, a variety of individuals will be involved in the budgeting process. The **Chief Executive Officer (CEO)**, the highest ranking officer in charge of the overall management of a company, is ultimately responsible for the company's financial performance primarily due to the Sarbanes-Oxley Act (see Chapter 1). Because of this, the budgeting process will begin with the CEO establishing financial goals for the company's profitability. From this, a company can develop a strategic plan to meet its mission and objectives, and the budget can serve as a link from the strategic plan to the company's financial goals. If a company's strategic plan and financial plan (budget) are in alignment, then the overall operation will be better prepared to achieve its mission.

At the middle levels of large hospitality companies, regional, district, area, and unit managers will be involved in the budgeting process because they will have access to the specific revenue and cost projections associated with the units for which they are responsible. In many cases, bonuses for these professionals will be directly tied to their ability to accurately forecast revenues and expenses in their units. If these managers seek to maximize their own incomes (through bonuses, raises, and promotions), they must plan (budget) carefully and then implement the management processes required to achieve their plans.

In addition, individual restaurant or hotel owners will want to know what they can expect to earn on their investments. A budget is necessary to project those earnings. Questions related to the amount of revenue that will likely be generated, the amount of cash that will be available for bill payment or distribution as earnings, and the proper timing of capital acquisitions are all questions that are of importance to organizations as small as a "mom and pop" restaurant and as large as a multi-national hotel company. As a result, in organizations of all sizes, proper budgeting is a process that is of critical importance, and it is equally critical that it is done well.

Types of Budgets

Experienced managerial accountants know that they may be responsible for helping to prepare not one, but several budgets at the same time. Budgets will need to be created with differing time frames and for very different purposes. "Length" and "purpose" are two of the most common methods of considering the different types of budgets managers prepare.

Length

One extremely helpful way to consider a budget is by its length or **horizon.** While a budget may be prepared for any time frame desired by a manager, budget lengths are typically considered to be one of three types, as follows:

1. Long-range budget
2. Annual budget
3. Achievement budget

Long-Range Budget

The **long-range budget** is typically prepared for a period of up to five years. While its detail is not great, it does provide a long-term financial view about where an operation should be going. It is also particularly useful in those cases where additional operational units may increase sales volume and accompanying expenses. For example, assume that you are preparing a budget for a business you own. Your company has entered into an agreement with an international franchise company to open 45 cinnamon bun kiosks in shopping malls across the United States and Canada. You will open a new store approximately every month for the next four years. To properly plan for your revenues and expenses in the coming four-year period, a long-range budget for your company will be much needed.

Annual Budget

The **annual budget**, or yearly budget, is the type many hospitality managers think of when the word budget is used. As it states, the annual budget is for a one-year period or, in some cases, one season. This would be true, for example, in the case of a religious summer camp that is open and serving meals only while school is out of session and campers are attending, or a ski resort that opens in late fall but closes when the snow melts.

It is important to remember that an annual budget need not follow a calendar year. In fact, the best time period for an annual budget is the one that makes sense for your own operation. A college food service director, for example, would want a budget that covers the time period of a school year, that is, from the fall of one year through the spring of the next. For a restaurant whose owners have a fiscal year different from a calendar year, the annual budget may coincide with either the fiscal year or the calendar, as the owners prefer.

It is also important to remember that an annual budget need not consist of 12, one-month periods. While many operators prefer one-month budgets, some prefer budgets consisting of 13, 28-day periods, while others use quarterly (three-month) or even weekly budgets to plan for revenues and costs throughout the budget year.

Achievement Budget

The **achievement budget**, or short-range budget, is always of a limited time period, often consisting of a month, a week, or even a day. It most often provides very current operating information and thus, greatly assists in making current operational decisions. A weekly achievement budget might, for example, be used to predict the number of gallons of milk needed for next week or the number of front office desk clerks to be scheduled on the next Tuesday night.

 *go figure!*

Assume that you are a manager for a casual dining restaurant in a midwestern city. You need to develop a labor budget for your servers during the dinner shifts for next week.

Each server can handle, on average, 20 covers per hour.
You pay your servers, on average, $4.00 per hour.

Your achievement budget for your servers for next week is as follows:

Day	Forecasted Covers	Total Number of Server Hours Needed	Total Labor Dollars Budgeted for Servers
Monday	200	10	40
Tuesday	240	12	48
Wednesday	260	13	52
Thursday	300	15	60
Friday	440	22	88
Saturday	500	25	100
Sunday	160	8	32
Total	2,100	105	$420

Purpose

While budgets can be classified based upon their length, they are also frequently classified based upon their specific purpose. This is easy to understand when you realize that the typical rationale for creating a budget is simply that of helping managers better plan for the operation of their businesses. As a result, budgets may be created for very specific purposes. For example, a front office manager in a hotel may want to create a monthly budget for the front desk's cost of labor, a restaurant manager may wish to budget for next week's cost of food, or a club manager may wish to create a budget designed to estimate the club's annual utility costs.

To consider yet another example, assume you are the director of operations for a hotel company that operates 15 franchised hotels. The franchisor has recently mandated that the bedding (mattresses, linen, and coverlets) in all of your properties must, within 12 months, be replaced with higher quality products. Your responsibility in this situation is to prepare a budget that would plan for the purchase of the upgraded bedding products.

As you have now seen, budgets can be created to serve a variety of identifiable purposes. For most hospitality managers, budgets can be created for use in one of three broad categories, which are:

- Operations budgets
- Cash budgets
- Capital budgets

Operations Budgets

Operations budgets are concerned with planning for the revenues, expenses, and profits associated with operating a business. For example, if Paige Vincent, the general manager of the Blue Lagoon Water Park Resort, asked each of her department managers to submit their own estimates of next year's departmental revenue, she would have begun the process of assembling the revenue portion of an operations budget. Similarly, if Paige asked Isabella Rosseta, her food and beverage director, to prepare an estimate of the labor cost required to operate the kitchen next month, that specific expense portion of the department's monthly operations budget would be developed.

One way to consider operational budgets is to compare them to the income statement you learned about in Chapter 3 (The Income Statement). The income statement details the actual revenue, expenses, and profits incurred in operating a business. The operations budget is simply management's estimate of all (or any portion of) the income statement. Operations budgets are so important to hospitality managers that this budget type will be the one most closely examined in this chapter.

Cash Budgets

In Chapter 5 (The Statement of Cash Flows), you learned that cash may be generated or expended by a business's operating activities, investing activities, and financing activities. **Cash budgets** are developed to estimate the actual impact on cash balances that will result from these activities.

The importance of cash budgeting can easily be seen by examining the case of Basil Bakal, who owns a 100-room, limited-service hotel. In his community, local property taxes are due and payable twice per year. As a result (because he uses an accrual accounting system), Basil's income statement lists, as a monthly operating expense, one-twelfth of his annual property tax bill. Payment of the tax, however, is made only twice per year. As a result, Basil must carefully budget (plan) for the significant cash outlay that he will encounter on the two months his property taxes are actually paid. If he does not, he may find that he has not reserved the cash needed to pay this expense when he is required to do so.

Proper cash budgeting, especially for those businesses whose revenues and expenses vary widely from month to month, or season to season, can be critically important. As a result, the cash budgeting process will be carefully examined in this chapter.

Capital Budgets

As you learned in Chapter 4 (The Balance Sheet), some expenses incurred by a business are not recorded on the income statement. **Capital expenditures** are those expenses associated with the purchase of land, property and equipment, and other fixed assets that are recorded on the balance sheet. In many cases, these expenses involve significant amounts of money or assumed liability, and as a result must be carefully planned.

The **capital budget** is the device used to plan for capital expenditures. Planning (budgeting) for capital expenditures is related to the investment goals of the business's owners, as well as their long-term business plans. Because the computation of the anticipated return on investment (ROI) related to such decisions is so critical, capital budgeting and capital budget decision making will be examined in depth in Chapter 12.

FIGURE 11.2 Budget Type and Purpose Summary

Budget Type	Purpose
Operations Budget	Estimates Income Statement Results
Cash Budget	Estimates Statement of Cash Flows Results
Capital Budget	Estimates Balance Sheet Results

As you have now learned, hospitality managers and managerial accountants utilize a variety of budget types to better operate their businesses. Figure 11.2 summarizes the three budget types and purposes most commonly utilized.

Operations Budget Essentials

An operations budget is simply a forecast of revenue, expenses, and resulting profits for a selected accounting period. Some managers think it is very difficult to establish an operations budget, and, thus, they simply do not take the time to do so. Creating an operations budget is not that complex. You can learn to do it and do it well.

Before managers can begin to develop an operations budget, they must understand the underpinning essentials required for its creation. If these essentials are not addressed prior to assembling the operations budget, the budgeting process which follows is not likely to yield a budget that is accurate or helpful in the operation of a business. Before you begin the process of assembling an operations budget you will need to have and understand the following information:

- Prior-period operating results (if an existing operation)
- Assumptions made about the next period's operations
- Knowledge of the organization's financial objectives

Prior-Period Operating Results

The task of budgeting becomes somewhat easier when you examine your operation's prior-period operating results. Experienced managerial accountants know that what has happened in the past is one of the best indicators of what is likely to happen in the future. The further back, and in more detail, you can track your operation's historical revenues and expenses, the better your budgets are likely to be. For example, if you know the revenues and expenses for the past 50 Saturdays, you are likely to be better able to forecast this coming Saturday's budget than if you have only the last two Saturdays' data available.

Historical data should always be considered in conjunction with the most recent data available. Assume for example, a restaurant manager knows that revenues have, on an annual average, increased 5% each month from the same period last year. However, in the last two months, the increase has been closer to zero. This may mean that the increase trend has slowed or stopped completely. Good managers always modify historical trends by closely examining current conditions.

Assumptions about the Next Period's Operations

Evaluating future conditions and activities are also necessary when developing an operations budget. Examples of this include the opening of new competitive restaurants or hotels, special scheduled occurrences including sporting events and concerts, or significant changes in your own operating hours resulting from these events. Local newspapers, trade or business associations, and Chambers of Commerce are possible sources of helpful information about changes in future demand for meals or rooms.

After demand factors have been considered, assumptions regarding revenues and expenses may be made. From these assumptions, projected percentages of increases or decreases in revenues and expenses may be made to develop the operations budget.

Knowledge of the Organization's Financial Objectives

An operation's financial objectives may consist of a given profit target defined as a percent of revenue or a total dollar amount, as well as specific financial and operational ratios that should be achieved by management (see Chapter 6). Many of these financial objectives will be determined by the company's owner(s) based on the desired return on investment. The operations budget must incorporate these goals.

Developing an Operations Budget

As you have seen, hospitality managers begin the budget development process by assembling needed information and then estimating their revenues and expenses based on that information. The operations budget is a detailed plan which can be simply expressed by the budget formula as follows:

> **Budgeted Revenue − Budgeted Expense = Budgeted Profit**

The budgeted profit level a manager seeks can be achieved when the operation realizes the budgeted revenue levels *and* expends only what has been budgeted to generate those revenues. If revenues fall short of forecast and/or if expenses are not reduced to match the shortfall, budgeted profit levels are not likely to be achieved. In a similar manner, if actual revenues exceed forecasted levels, expenses (variable and mixed) will also increase. If the increases are monitored carefully and are not excessive, increased profits should result. If, however, managers allow expenses to exceed the levels actually required by the additional revenue increase, budgeted profits again will not be achieved.

In order to illustrate the budget process, consider Joshua's Restaurant, which is located across the street from the Blue Lagoon Water Park Resort. Joshua is developing his operating budget for the year 2010, and he has determined his budget essentials as outlined below.

1. Joshua has gathered his prior-period operating results for the year 2009.
2. From information attained about the economic conditions of the area and competition, Joshua has made the following assumptions about his 2010 operations as follows:
   - Total revenues received will increase by 4% primarily due to a 4% price increase.
   - Food and beverage costs will increase by 4%. Targets are a 35% food cost and a 16% beverage cost.
   - Salaries, wages, and benefits have a target of 16% total labor cost. Although this might seem lower than average, Joshua's limited menu and relaxed service allows him to budget lower labor costs.
   - All other expenses (excluding income taxes) will total no more than 22.7% of sales.
3. Joshua's financial objectives for the organization are to earn profits (net income) of at least 18%.

In the next two sections, you will learn about budgeting revenues and expenses, and Joshua's Restaurant will be used to illustrate those concepts.

Budgeting Revenues

As you learned in Chapter 10, forecasting revenues is critical since all forecasted expenses and profits will be based on revenue forecasts. Effective managerial accountants know that, in most cases, revenues should be estimated on a monthly (or weekly) basis and then be combined to create the annual revenue budget. This is so because many hospitality operations have seasonal revenue variations. For example, a restaurant in a shopping mall may generate significantly higher revenues in November and December (because of holiday shoppers) than in March or April when shopping mall sales are generally lower. A ski resort hotel will, of course, be busier in the winter season than in the summer, and a large convention hotel in a downtown area may find that its group meetings business is greatly reduced during the December and New Year holiday periods because few groups wish to hold their conferences and meetings during that time.

Forecasting revenues is not an exact science. However, it can be made quite accurate if managers implement the following:

Review historical records. Review revenue records from previous years. When an operation has been open for a period of time equal in length to the budget period being developed, its revenue history is extremely helpful in predicting future revenue levels.

Consider internal factors affecting revenues. In this step, managers should consider any significant changes in the type, quantity, and direction of marketing efforts. Other internal activities that can impact future revenues include those related to facility renovation that may affect capacity and times when the operation may be disrupted because of the renovations. In restaurants, the number of hours to be opened may be changed. In hotels, significant increases or decreases in room rates to be charged will likely affect total revenues. In fact, any internal initiation or change that management believes will likely impact future revenues should be considered in this step.

Consider external factors affecting revenues. There are a variety of external issues that can affect an operation's revenue forecasts. These include new competitors' planned openings (or competitor closings) as well as other factors such as road improvements or construction that could disrupt normal traffic patterns, changes in local regulations regarding signage, and perhaps most important for many hospitality businesses, economic upturns or downturns that affect the willingness of potential guests to spend their discretionary income on hospitality services.

 *go figure!*

Returning to the example of Joshua's Restaurant, Joshua has looked at 2009 data for September and has found that his sales were $192,308, with a check average of $12.02.

He considers his internal and external factors affecting revenues, and he estimates a 4% increase in revenues for 2010. Using the sales forecast formula from Chapter 10, Joshua computes his sales forecast for September 2010 as follows:

> **Sales Last Year × (1 + % Increase Estimate) = Sales Forecast**
>
> or
>
> **$192,308 × (1 + 0.04) = $200,000**

Using historical data, he knows that approximately 80% of his sales are food and 20% of his sales are beverage. Thus, he estimates $160,000 ($200,000 × 0.80 = $160,000) for food sales and $40,000 ($200,000 × 0.20 = $40,000) for beverage sales.

Joshua's check average (including food and beverages) for 2009 was $12.02. With a forecasted increase of 4% in selling prices, his 2010 check average will be calculated as follows:

> **Selling Price Last Year × (1 + % Increase Estimate) = Selling Price Forecast (Check Average)**
>
> or
>
> **$12.02 × (1 + 0.04) = $12.50**

Thus, with forecasted sales of $200,000 and a forecasted check average of $12.50, his budgeted number of covers will be 16,000 ($200,000/$12.50 = 16,000 covers).

In most cases, it is not realistic to assume a manager can forecast a hospitality operation's exact revenues one year in advance. With practice, accurate historical sales data, and a realistic view of internal and external variables that will affect an operation's revenue generation, many managers can attain budget forecasts that are easily and routinely within 5 to 10% (plus or minus) of actual results for the forecast period.

Budgeting Expenses

Managers must budget for each fixed, variable, and mixed cost when addressing the individual **line items**, or expenses, found on the income statement. Fixed costs are simple to forecast because items such as rent, depreciation, and interest typically stay the same from month to month. Variable costs, however, are directly related to the amount of revenue produced by a business. Thus, for example, a restaurateur that forecasts the sale of 100 prime rib dinners on Friday night will likely have meat costs and server costs higher than the restaurateur in a similar facility that forecasts the sale of only 25 such dinners. Variable expenses such as food and beverages are affected by sales levels. Mixed costs, as you may remember from Chapter 9, contain both fixed and variable cost components. For example, a hotel located in an area with a warm climate will have substantial air-conditioning costs. The hotel must spend some money (fixed cost) to properly cool its public areas regardless of the number of guests staying in the hotel. However, as the number of rooms sold increases, the hotel is likely to spend additional dollars (variable costs) to maintain the appropriate temperatures in the occupied guest rooms. In this section of the chapter, you will learn how to budget for all three of these types of costs: fixed, variable, and mixed.

Fixed Costs

In most cases, budgeting fixed costs is quite easy. For example, Joshua knows his monthly rent (occupancy) payments are $10,000. Creating the annual budget for "rent" expense is a simple matter of multiplication: $10,000 a month for 12 months yields a total annual occupancy cost of $120,000 ($10,000 × 12 months = $120,000). In this situation, because rent is a fixed cost, it will remain unchanged regardless of the revenues generated by the restaurant. Of course, any anticipated increases in fixed costs for the year will have to be budgeted in each month.

Variable Costs

Variable costs, of course, increase or decrease as revenue volumes change. For example, consider the cost of napkins used at Joshua's Restaurant. As more guests are served, more napkins will be used, and more napkin expense will be incurred because of laundry charges. The laundry charges for napkins in this situation represent variable costs. The food Joshua will purchase, the beverages he will serve, and a variety of other expenses are all variable costs that will increase as number of covers increases.

Variable costs can be forecasted using targeted percentages or costs per unit (rooms or covers). For example, food costs might be forecasted at a targeted food cost % or food cost per cover. An executive housekeeper at a hotel might forecast cleaning solution as a percentage of total sales, or soaps at cost per room. When percentages are used, the sales forecast is simply multiplied by the target cost % to get the forecasted cost.

go figure!

In the case of Joshua's Restaurant, a targeted food cost percentage of 35% and $160,000 in food sales would yield the following food cost:

> **Sales Forecast × Targeted Cost % = Forecasted Cost**
>
> or
>
> **$160,000 × 0.35 = $56,000**

If Joshua wanted to forecast his costs using per-unit (cover) costs, he could first base his forecast using last year's cover costs plus his increase estimates. For example, Joshua estimated that his food costs will increase by 4%. If he knows that his food cost per cover in 2009 was $3.37, he could forecast his cost per cover as follows:

> **Cost per Cover Last Year × (1 + % Increase Estimate) = Cost per Cover Forecast**
>
> or
>
> **$3.37 × (1 + 0.04) = $3.50**

Joshua could then forecast his food costs using the following formula:

> **Cost per Cover Forecast × Forecasted Number of Covers = Forecasted Costs**
>
> or
>
> **$3.50 × 16,000 = $56,000**

Joshua can forecast all his variable costs for September 2010 using either targeted cost percentages or cost per cover.

Mixed Costs

Joshua must also remember to accurately forecast his mixed costs. One of the largest (if not the single largest!) line item costs in a hospitality operation is that of labor. Labor is a mixed cost because it includes hourly wages (variable costs), salaries (fixed costs), and employee benefits (mixed costs). Experienced managers know that, when labor costs are excessive, profits are reduced. As a result, this is an area of budgeting and cost control that is extremely important to hospitality managers. Accurate budgets used to help control future labor costs can be precisely calculated using a 3-step method.

Step 1. Determine Targeted Labor Dollars to be Spent

In most cases, the determination of labor costs is tied to the targeted or standard costs an operation seeks to achieve. These standards or goals may be established by considering the historical performance of an operation, by referring to industry segment or company averages, or by considering the profit level targets of the business. In most cases, the standard will be developed by a consideration of each of these important factors.

When all relevant labor-related information has, in fact, been considered, a labor standard is to be used when the operations budget is determined.

 *go figure!*

Joshua has set his labor standard to be 16% of total sales. Thus, with a $200,000 sales forecast for September, and a 16% labor cost percentage standard, the total amount to be budgeted for labor (salaries, wages, and employee benefits) would be calculated as:

> **Sales Forecast × Labor Cost % Standard = Forecasted Labor Cost**
>
> or
>
> **$200,000 × 0.16 = $32,000**

Step 2. Subtract Costs of Payroll Allocations

Payroll allocations consist of those costs associated with, or allocated to, payroll. These non-wage costs must be paid by employers and include items such as payroll taxes (for example, mandated contributions to Social Security and worker's compensation plans) as well as voluntary benefit programs that may be offered by the operation.

The cost of these mandatory (and voluntary) programs can be significant. Depending upon the restaurant or hotel, the cost of voluntary benefit programs that must be reduced from the total dollar amount available for labor include costs such as:

- Bonuses
- Health, dental, and vision insurance

- Life insurance
- Long-term disability insurance
- Employee meals
- Sick leave
- Paid holidays
- Paid vacation

Hospitality organizations may offer all, or some of these benefits; however, the applicable mandatory and voluntary payroll allocations must be subtracted from the labor dollars available to be spent when developing an accurate operations budget.

 *go figure!*

For Joshua's Restaurant, assume that mandatory and voluntary allocations account for 15.75% of the total labor costs incurred by the operation. Thus, the calculation required to determine the budgeted payroll allocation amount would be:

> Forecasted Labor Cost x Payroll Allocation % = Budgeted Payroll Allocation
>
> or
>
> $32,000 x 0.1575 = $5,040

In this example, the amount remaining for use in paying all operational salaries and hourly wages (budgeted payroll) would be computed as:

> Forecasted Labor Cost – Budgeted Payroll Allocation = Budgeted Payroll
>
> or
>
> $32,000 – $5,040 = $26,960

Step 3. Subtract Salaried (Fixed) Wages to Determine Variable Wages

In most cases, fixed payroll remains unchanged from one pay period to the next unless an individual receiving the pay separates employment from the organization. Variable payroll, on the other hand, consists of those dollars paid to hourly employees. Thus, variable payroll is the amount that "varies" with changes in sales volume. The distinction between fixed and variable labor is an important one, since managers may sometimes have little control over their fixed labor costs, while at the same time exerting nearly 100% control over variable labor costs.

 *go figure!*

To determine the amount of money to be budgeted for variable (hourly) workers, Joshua must first subtract the fixed portion of his labor costs. This fixed labor component consists of all the operational salaries he will pay. These fixed labor costs must be budgeted and subtracted from the total available for labor because the salary amounts will be paid regardless of sales volume. Assume Joshua pays $18,960 in salaries on a monthly basis. Thus, the amount to be budgeted for variable hourly payroll for September can be calculated as:

> **Budgeted Payroll − Salaries and Fixed Wages = Budgeted Hourly Payroll**
>
> or
>
> **$26,960 − $18,960 = $8,000**

Thus, $8,000 will be paid to front-of-house and back-of-house hourly employees.

In most restaurant operations, managers who successfully create an operations budget for food and labor will have accounted for more than 50% of their total costs. In a similar manner, hoteliers that have budgeted for their rooms-related expenses and labor costs are likely to have accounted for more than 50% of their total expenses.

All other expenses can be budgeted using the same methods for fixed, variable, and mixed costs. A successful manager will have separated all of the mixed costs into their fixed and variable components using the high/low method described in Chapter 9. This will make it easier to project changes in variable costs (and variable components of mixed costs) due to forecasted changes in sales.

By successfully forecasting sales and expenses, Joshua can develop the entire budget for his operations for September. Remember that Joshua's assumptions and financial objectives were as follows:

- Total revenues received will increase by 4% primarily due to a 4% price increase.
- Food and beverage costs will increase by 4%. Targets are a 35% food cost and a 16% beverage cost.
- Salaries, wages, and benefits have a target of 16% total labor cost.
- All other expenses (excluding income taxes) will total no more than 22.7% of sales.
- Profit (net income) will be at least 18% of revenues.

Based on this information, the resulting budget for Joshua's Restaurant for September 2010 is shown in Figure 11.3.

As can be seen in Figure 11.3, every additional fixed, variable, and mixed cost, considered individually, must be included in the operations budget. When that has been completed, the result will be an operations budget that:

FIGURE 11.3 Joshua's Restaurant Budget for September 2010

JOSHUA'S RESTAURANT
Budget for September 2010
Budgeted Number of Covers = 16,000

	Budget September 2010	%
SALES:		
Food	160,000	80.0
Beverage	40,000	20.0
Total Sales	**200,000**	**100.0**
COST OF SALES:		
Food	56,000	35.0
Beverage	6,400	16.0
Total Cost of Sales	**62,400**	**31.2**
GROSS PROFIT:		
Food	104,000	65.0
Beverage	33,600	84.0
Total Gross Profit	**137,600**	**68.8**
OPERATING EXPENSES:		
Salaries and Wages	26,960	13.5
Employee Benefits	5,040	2.5
Direct Operating Expenses	7,856	3.9
Music and Entertainment	1,070	0.5
Marketing	3,212	1.6
Utility Services	5,277	2.6
Repairs and Maintenance	1,810	0.9
Administrative and General	5,570	2.8
Occupancy	10,000	5.0
Depreciation	3,400	1.7
Total Operating Expenses	**70,195**	**35.1**
Operating Income	**67,405**	**33.7**
Interest	7,200	3.6
Income Before Income Taxes	**60,205**	**30.1**
Income Taxes	24,082	12.0
Net Income	**36,123**	**18.1**

1. Is based upon a realistic revenue estimate
2. Considers all known fixed, variable, and mixed costs
3. Is intended to achieve the financial goals of the organization
4. Can be monitored to ensure adherence to the budget's guidelines
5. May be modified when necessary

Because annual operations budgets are most typically the compilation of monthly operations budgets, managers may utilize their monthly operating budgets to create and monitor weekly (or even daily) versions of their overall operations budget.

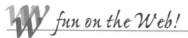
fun on the Web!

Today there are a variety of software programs available to help managers develop their operations budgets. To review one such program appropriate for restaurant and hotel use and designed for use with Microsoft Excel, go to:

www.outlooksoft.com

When you arrive, use the search field and enter "Budgeting" to try out the free demo that is provided.

Monitoring an Operations Budget

As you have learned, a budget is simply a plan for future financial activity. In many cases, a manager's view of the future will be quite accurate. In some other cases, it will not be accurate. For example, revenue may not reach forecasted levels, expenses may exceed estimates, and internal or external factors not considered when the operations budget was prepared may impact financial performance in negative or positive ways.

An operations budget has little value if management does not use it. In general, the operations budget should be regularly monitored in each of the following three areas:

- Revenues
- Expenses
- Profit

Revenues. If revenues should fall below projected levels, the impact on profit can be substantial. Simply put, if revenues fall far short of projections, it may be impossible to meet profit goals. If revenues consistently exceed projections, the overall budget must be modified or, ultimately, the expenses associated with these increased sales will soon exceed their budgeted amounts. Effective managers compare their actual revenue to that which they have projected on a regular basis.

Expenses. Effective food service managers are careful to monitor operational expenses because costs that are too high or too low may be cause for concern. Just as it is not possible to estimate future sales volume perfectly, it is also not possible to estimate future expenses perfectly, since some expenses will vary as sales volume increases or decreases.

As business conditions change, changes in the budget are to be expected. This is because budgets are based on a specific set of assumptions, and, as these assumptions change, so too does the budget that follows from the assumptions. Assume, for example, that you budgeted $1,000 in January for snow removal from the parking lot attached to the restaurant you own in New York State. If unusually severe weather causes you to spend $2,000 for snow removal in January instead, the assumption (normal levels of snowfall) was incorrect and the budget will be incorrect as well.

Profit.   In the final analysis, however, budgeted profit must be realized if the operation is to provide adequate returns for owner and investor risk. Consider the case of James, the operator of a food service establishment with excellent sales but below-budgeted profits. James budgeted a 5% profit on $2,000,000 of sales; thus, $100,000 profit ($2,000,000 × 0.05 = $100,000) was anticipated. In reality, at year's end, James achieved only $50,000 profit, or 2.5% of sales ($50,000/$2,000,000 = 2.5%). If the operation's owners feel that $50,000 is an adequate return for their risk, James' services may be retained. If they do not, he may lose his position, despite the fact that he operates a "profitable" restaurant. This is so because management's task is not merely to generate a profit, but rather to generate the budgeted profit!

Variances

One major role that is played by managers in all segments of the hospitality industry is that of ensuring operational profitability by analyzing the differences between budgeted (planned for) results and actual operating results. To do this effectively, managers must receive timely income statements that accurately detail actual operating results. When they do, these actual results can then be compared to the operations and/or achievement budgets from the same accounting period. The difference between planned results and actual results is called **variance**.

Variance may be expressed in either dollar or percentage terms and can be either positive (favorable) or negative (unfavorable). A **favorable variance** occurs when the variance is an improvement on the budget (revenues are higher or expenses are lower). An **unfavorable variance** occurs when actual results do not meet budget expectations (revenues are lower or expenses are higher).

 *go figure!*

For example, if the budget for snow removal services are $1,000 for a given month, but the actual expenditure for those services is $1,150, the variance is calculated as follows:

> **Actual Expense – Budgeted Expense = Variance**
>
> or
>
> **$1,150 – $1,000 = $150**

The variance may be expressed as a dollar amount ($150) or as a percentage of the original budget. The computation for percentage variance is:

$$\frac{Variance}{Budgeted\ Expense} = Percentage\ Variance$$

or

$$\frac{\$150}{\$1,000} = 0.15$$

Another way to compute the percentage variance is to use a math shortcut, as follows:

$$\left(\frac{Actual\ Expense}{Budgeted\ Expense}\right) - 1 = Percentage\ Variance$$

or

$$\left(\frac{\$1,150}{\$1,000}\right) - 1 = 0.15$$

The variance is unfavorable to the operation because the actual expense is higher than the budgeted expense. It is the manager's task to identify significant variances between budgeted and actual operating results. A significant variance may be defined in a variety of ways; however, a common definition is that a **significant variance** is any difference in dollars or percentage between budgeted and actual operating results that warrants further investigation. Significant variance is an important concept because not all variances should be investigated.

 *go figure!*

Assume, for example, that, in January, a hotel manager prepares an annual (12-month) operations budget with a December utility bill budgeted at $6,000. When, 12 months later, the December bill arrives, it actually totals $6,400.

Given the amount of the bill ($6,400) and the difficulty of estimating utility expenses one year in advance, a difference of only $400 or 7% ($400/$6,000 = 0.07) probably does *not* represent a significant variance from the operations budget estimate.

Alternatively, assume that the same manager had estimated office supplies usage at $100 for that same month, but the actual cost of supplies was $500. Again, the difference between the budgeted expense and actual expense is $400.

The office supplies variance, however, represents a very significant difference of 400% ($400/$100 = 4.00) between planned and actual results and should be thoroughly investigated.

Managerial accountants must decide what represents a significant variance based on their knowledge of their specific operations as well as their own company policies and procedures. Small percentage differences can be important if they represent large dollar amounts. Similarly, small dollar amounts can be significant if they represent large percentage differences from planned results. Variations from budgeted results can occur in revenues, expenses, and profits. Managers can monitor all of these areas using the following operations budget monitoring process.

Operations Budget Monitoring Process

Step 1 Compare actual results to the operations budget.
Step 2 Identify significant variances.
Step 3 Determine causes of variances.
Step 4 Take corrective action or modify the operations budget.

In Step 1, the manager studies income statement and operations budget data for a specified accounting period. In Steps 2 and 3, actual operating results are compared to the budget and significant variances, if any, are identified and analyzed. Finally, in Step 4, corrective action is taken to reduce or eliminate unfavorable variances, or if it is appropriate to do so, the budget is modified to reflect new realities faced by the business.

In most cases, managers will compare their actual results to operations budget results in each of the income statement's three major sections of revenue, expense, and profits. To illustrate the process, consider again the operations budget for Joshua's Restaurant. Figure 11.4 shows Joshua's original operations budget and his actual operating results for the month of September 2010.

Revenue Analysis

If Joshua is to properly monitor his budget, revenues are the first area he would examine when comparing his actual results to his budgeted results. This is true because if revenue falls significantly below projected levels, there will likely be a significant negative impact on profit goals. Secondly, when revenues vary from projections, variable costs will also fluctuate. In the case where revenues fall short of budget projections, variable costs should be less than budgeted. In addition, when actual revenues fall short of budgeted levels, those fixed and mixed expenses (such as rent and labor) incurred by the operation will represent a larger-than-budgeted percentage of total revenue. Alternatively, if actual revenues exceed the budget, total variable expenses will increase, while the fixed and mixed expenses incurred by the operation should, if properly managed, represent a smaller-than-budgeted percentage of total revenue.

A close examination of Figure 11.4 shows that Joshua has experienced a shortfall in both food and beverage revenue when compared to his operations budget. The main revenue problem Joshua faced in September is that he budgeted for 16,000 covers and only sold 15,000 covers. If revenues consistently fall short of forecasts, managers should evaluate all aspects of their entire operations, including their marketing efforts, to identify and correct the revenue shortfalls. Food service operations and hotels that consistently fall short of revenue projections must also evaluate the wisdom and validity of the primary assumptions used to produce the revenue portion of their operations budgets.

FIGURE 11.4   Joshua's Restaurant Budget versus Actual Comparison for September 2010

JOSHUA'S RESTAURANT
Budget versus Actual Comparison for September 2010

	Budgeted Number of Covers = 16,000		Actual Number of Covers = 15,000	
	Budget	%	Actual	%
SALES:				
Food	160,000	80.0	153,750	79.5
Beverage	40,000	20.0	39,750	20.5
Total Sales	**200,000**	**100.0**	**193,500**	**100.0**
COST OF SALES:				
Food	56,000	35.0	52,800	34.3
Beverage	6,400	16.0	5,500	13.8
Total Cost of Sales	**62,400**	**31.2**	**58,300**	**30.1**
GROSS PROFIT:				
Food	104,000	65.0	100,950	65.7
Beverage	33,600	84.0	34,250	86.2
Total Gross Profit	**137,600**	**68.8**	**135,200**	**69.9**
OPERATING EXPENSES:				
Salaries and Wages	26,960	13.5	27,960	14.4
Employee Benefits	5,040	2.5	5,321	2.7
Direct Operating Expenses	7,856	3.9	7,256	3.7
Music and Entertainment	1,070	0.5	1,070	0.6
Marketing	3,212	1.6	3,207	1.7
Utility Services	5,277	2.6	5,677	2.9
Repairs and Maintenance	1,810	0.9	1,839	1.0
Administrative and General	5,570	2.8	5,570	2.9
Occupancy	10,000	5.0	10,000	5.2
Depreciation	3,400	1.7	3,400	1.8
Total Operating Expenses	**70,195**	**35.1**	**71,300**	**36.8**
Operating Income	**67,405**	**33.7**	**63,900**	**33.0**
Interest	7,200	3.6	7,200	3.7
Income Before Income Taxes	**60,205**	**30.1**	**56,700**	**29.3**
Income Taxes	24,082	12.0	22,680	11.7
Net Income	**36,123**	**18.1**	**34,020**	**17.6**

Expense Analysis

Identifying significant variances in expenses is a critical part of the budget monitoring process as many types of operating expenses are controllable expenses (see Chapter 9). Some variation between budgeted and actual costs can be expected because most variable operating expenses do vary with revenue volumes and revenues are rarely predicted perfectly. The variances that occur can, however, tell managers a great deal about operational efficiencies, and experienced managers know that a key to ensuring profitability is to properly control their operating costs.

In Figure 11.4, Joshua's food costs in dollars were lower than budgeted and his food cost percentage was also lower than budgeted (34.3% actual food costs and 35% budgeted food costs). The lower food cost percentage might be viewed as favorable. However, Joshua might find it somewhat troubling that actual labor costs (salaries, wages, and employee benefits) were higher than budgeted. Note also that fixed costs (for example, occupancy, depreciation, and interest) did not vary in dollar amount, but, because revenues did not reach their budgeted levels, they represent a higher actual cost percentage because the fixed dollars were spread over a smaller revenue base. Note also that total operating expenses were budgeted at 35.1% of total revenue, yet the actual results were higher at 36.8%. These may not appear to be big variances, but when specific line item operating expenses vary significantly from the operations budget, those significant variances should be analyzed using the four-step budget "Operations Budget Monitoring Process" presented earlier in this chapter.

Profit (Net Income) Analysis

A hospitality operation's actual level of profit measured either in dollars, percentages, or both is simply the most critical number that most hospitality managers must evaluate. Returning to Figure 11.4, it is easy to see that Joshua's actual net income for the month was $34,020, or 17.6% of total revenues. This is less than the $36,123 (18.1% of revenues) which was forecast in the operations budget. This reduced profit level can be tied directly to Joshua's lower-than-expected revenues and, in some line item categories, higher-than-expected expenses. The inability of a business to meet its operational revenue budget typically means that the budget was ineffectively developed, internal/external conditions have changed, and/or that the operation's managers were not effective. Regardless of the cause, when revenues do not reach forecasted levels, corrective action is usually needed to prevent even more serious problems including profit erosion.

In the hospitality industry, profits are routinely reported in both percentages and dollars. In fact, many competent hospitality managers honestly disagree about the best way to evaluate operational profits. One frequently heard comment in the hospitality industry is, "You bank dollars, not percentages!" To better understand this statement, note in Figure 11.4 that Joshua achieved a profit that was a lower percentage than the operations budget forecast (17.6% actual versus 18.1% budgeted). However, what if Joshua's actual net income percentage had been 18.5%? This would have been a *higher* percentage than his operations budget predicted (18.5% actual versus 18.1% budgeted). However, the $35,798 total dollars of profit generated ($193,500 actual sales × 18.5% = $35,798) would still be *less* than the budgeted profit of $36,123. Thus, this is the reason for the statement, "You bank dollars, not percentages!"

The best managers learn to review *both* profit percentages and profit dollars when monitoring operations budgets. In most cases, their real interest is in learning how their operating results (profits generated) relate to the money initially invested to achieve those results. Profits generated relative to investment made is of critical importance to business owners and, as a result, this significant topic will be examined thoroughly in Chapter 12.

Budget Modifications

Experienced managers consider an operations budget to be an active and potentially evolving document. This should be regularly reviewed and modified as new and better information replaces the information that was available when the original operations budget was developed. This is especially true when the new information significantly and, perhaps permanently, affects the revenue and expense assumptions used to create the operations budget. The budget should be reviewed anytime it is believed that the assumptions upon which it is based are no longer sound.

For example, assume a hotel owner employs 50 full-time employees. Each employee is covered under the hotel's group health insurance policy. Last year, the hotel owner, who has agreed to pay 50% of each employee's insurance cost, paid $300 per month for every full-time employee. The total monthly cost of the insurance contribution was $15,000 (50 employees × $300 per employee = $15,000). When this year's budget was developed, the hotel owner assumed the hotel would be assessed a 10% increase in its health insurance premiums. If, later in the year, it was determined that the premiums actually will be increased by 20%, employee benefit costs will be much greater than projected in the original operations budget. This hotel owner now faces several choices, which are:

- Modify the budget.
- Reduce the amount contributed per employee to stay within the budget.
- Change (reduce) health insurance benefits/coverage to stay within the original costs allocated in the operations budget.

Regardless of this hotel owner's decision, the operations budget, if it is affected, should be modified. There are situations in which an operations budget should be legitimately modified; however, an operations budget should never be modified simply to compensate for management inefficiencies. To illustrate, assume, for example, that a labor cost percentage of 25% is realistic and achievable for a specific hospitality operation. The operation's management, however, consistently achieves its budgeted revenue levels but just as consistently greatly exceeds the labor cost percentage targets established by the operations budget. In this case, the labor cost portion of the operations budget should not be increased (nor should prices be increased!) simply to mask management's inefficiencies in this area. Instead, if the goal of a 25% labor cost is indeed reasonable and achievable, then that operation's managers must be challenged to correct the problem. Well-prepared operations budgets are designed to be achieved and managers must do their best to achieve them. There are cases, however, when operations budgets simply must be modified or they will lose their ability to assist managers in decision making. The following situations are examples of those that, if unknown and not considered at the time of the original budget development process, may legitimately require managers to contemplate a modification of their existing operations budget:

- Additions or subtractions from product offerings that materially affect revenue generation (for example, reduced or increased operating hours)
- The opening of a direct competitor
- The closing of a direct competitor
- A significant and long-term or permanent increase or decrease in the price of major cost items
- Franchisor-mandated operating standards changes that directly affect (increase) costs
- Significant and unanticipated increases in fixed expenses such as mortgage payments (for example, in the case of a loan repayment plan tied to a variable interest rate), insurance, or property taxes
- A management (or key employee) change that significantly alters the skill level of the facility's operating team
- Natural disasters such as floods, hurricanes, or severe weather that significantly affects forecasted revenues
- Changes in financial statement formats or expense coding policies
- Changes in the investment return expectations of the operation's owners

Flexible Budgets

As you have just learned, some budget modifications are necessary because assumptions have changed regarding the original budget. However, budget modifications can also be used to help managers better evaluate their performance based on varying levels of sales activity. These budget modifications result in the creation of flexible budgets. A **flexible budget** incorporates the assumptions of the original budget, such as fixed costs and target variable costs per unit or variable cost percentages, and then projects these costs based on varying levels of sales volume.

Using Joshua's Restaurant, for example, several flexible budgets could have been developed for September at 15,000 covers, 16,000 covers, and 17,000 covers. If you remember, the original budget was for 16,000 covers. By developing several budgets at varying levels of covers based on the same assumptions, Joshua could choose the budget with the number of covers closest to his actual sales activity (15,000 covers) to evaluate his performance.

As was stated earlier in this chapter, a successful manager will have separated all of the mixed costs into their fixed and variable components using the high/low method described in Chapter 9. Once this is done, it is easy to budget variable costs based on the budgeted sales activity (number of covers) and fixed costs separately.

Figure 11.5 shows the September 2010 flexible budget for Joshua's Restaurant. His flexible budget is divided into variable costs and fixed costs using the contribution margin income statement (see Chapter 9). In addition, the flexible budget is based on 15,000 covers, which are the actual covers Joshua sold in September. By modifying the original budget for the actual number of covers sold, Joshua can make a better comparison between budgeted sales and actual sales, and budgeted costs and actual costs.

FIGURE 11.5   Joshua's Flexible Budget for September 2010

JOSHUA'S RESTAURANT
FLEXIBLE BUDGET FOR SEPTEMBER 2010

Original budget number of covers = 16,000

	Variable Dollars per Cover	Flexible Budget	September Actual	Variance	Favorable or Unfavorable
NUMBER OF COVERS:		15,000	15,000		
SALES:					
Food	10.00	150,000	153,750	3,750	F
Beverage	2.50	37,500	39,750	2,250	F
Total Sales	**12.50**	**187,500**	**193,500**	**6,000**	**F**
LESS VARIABLE COSTS:					
Food Cost	3.50	52,500	52,800	300	U
Beverage Cost	0.40	6,000	5,500	−500	F
Salaries and Wages	0.50	7,500	9,000	1,500	U
Employee Benefits	0.02	300	396	96	U
Direct Operating Expenses	0.30	4,500	4,200	−300	F
Marketing	0.05	750	795	45	U
Utility Services	0.20	3,000	3,600	600	U
Repairs and Maintenance	0.03	450	509	59	U
Contribution Margin	**7.50**	**112,500**	**116,700**	**4,200**	**F**
LESS FIXED COSTS:					
Salaries and Wages		18,960	18,960	0	
Employee Benefits		4,925	4,925	0	
Direct Operating Expenses		3,056	3,056	0	
Music and Entertainment		1,070	1,070	0	
Marketing		2,412	2,412	0	
Utility Services		2,077	2,077	0	
Repairs and Maintenance		1,330	1,330	0	
Administrative and General		5,570	5,570	0	
Occupancy		10,000	10,000	0	
Depreciation		3,400	3,400	0	
Interest		7,200	7,200	0	
Income Before Taxes		**52,500**	**56,700**	**4,200**	**F**
Income Taxes		21,000	22,680	1,680	U
Net Income		**31,500**	**34,020**	**2,520**	**F**

The variable dollars per cover column shows the original budgeted variable sales and costs per unit (cover) based on the original assumptions. From earlier in this chapter, you may recall that the projected check average in the original budget was $12.50 and the projected food cost per cover was $3.50. These projections and the other variable cost projections in the column were based on the same assumptions used in the original budget. However, each of these sales and costs per cover are multiplied by 15,000 covers (not 16,000) in order to project the budget that reflects *actual* number of covers. Of course, fixed costs are the same as in the original budget since these do not vary with sales volume.

With both the flexible budget and actual results reflecting the same number of covers sold, realistic variances can be calculated. As you learned earlier, the variance is calculated by subtracting the budgeted sales or expenses from the actual sales or expenses. The final outcome is an analysis of favorable (F) or unfavorable (U) results.

By using flexible budgets, managers are not "stuck" with static budgets that do not accurately reflect their performance. When comparing the original budget to the actual results of Joshua's Restaurant in Figure 11.4, Joshua could see that his sales were lower than expected and some of his costs were higher or lower than expected. However, he was comparing sales and variable costs based on two different levels of sales activity.

Granted, Joshua did not achieve his desired sales level. But, as is shown in Figure 11.5, he did show a favorable variance in sales based on a flexible budget of 15,000 covers sold. This favorable variance was due to a higher check average than budgeted. His actual check average was $12.90 ($193,500/15,000 covers = $12.90)! Although he didn't achieve his target number of covers, he was able to increase his check average over the budgeted $12.50. By using a flexible budget, Joshua now knows that his servers are doing a good job of upselling his menu items to increase his check average, but he is not getting enough customers in his restaurant. This would help him to know that he should focus his efforts on marketing, not training his servers to upsell.

As with sales, Joshua can compare his variable costs in his flexible budget to his actual variable costs to get a better insight into his performance. Joshua still shows a problem with labor costs as they are still unfavorable when compared to the flexible budget. However, as can be seen at the bottom of Figure 11.5, his overall performance as a manager was favorable since he earned more net income than is indicated by his flexible budget. In other words, if Joshua had only achieved his target of 16,000 covers, he would have probably done well in meeting his original budget!

Cash Budgeting

In at least one way, hospitality businesses are like any other business ventures in that their primary objectives are to survive and grow. To survive and grow, a hospitality operation must provide excellent products and services, but that alone is not enough to ensure either survival or growth. To stay in business, a company simply must have access to enough cash to meet its obligations. If it does not, it will not survive. Securing sufficient cash to continue operations is not merely an important issue; it is every business's single most important issue.

A simple but realistic example can help to explain why this is so. Assume that a particular hotel does a fairly reasonable amount of business. The hotel regularly pays its employees, stays relatively current with its bills, and pays out to its manager a salary that provides for a comfortable, but not extravagant, lifestyle. Assume also that the hotel's bank balance is currently $10,000 and its accounts receivable balance is $40,000. As a result, the amount of "money" either currently held, or previously earned, by that hotel is $50,000 ($10,000 cash + $40,000 accounts receivable = $50,000). The actual cash on hand, however, is only $10,000.

Assume also that it is the 1st of the month and the hotel's $15,000 utility bill is now due. If this bill is not paid by the 10th, the utility company will disconnect the hotel's power supply, effectively closing the hotel. In this scenario, which of the following issues do you believe would be of utmost importance to the hotel's manager?

1. Resolving a guest complaint filed with the hotel two days ago?
2. Implementing a recently re-designed front desk agent training program?
3. Selecting new carpet colors for installation in the guest room corridors?
4. Considering the room rates to charge on a potentially sold-out weekend four months in the future?
5. Securing $5,000 in cash to pay the utility bill within the next 10 days.

If you answered 5 above, you understand the importance of ready cash to the survival of a business. Certainly, in the hospitality industry, prompt and professional responses to guest service shortcomings are important (1 above), so is employee training (2 above). As well, facility maintenance (3 above) and strategic pricing decisions (4 above) are critical to the long-term success of a business. For this manager, none of those issues will hold much importance if the utility bill is not paid on time. Managers of restaurants and hotels know that having sufficient cash and/or having ready access to sufficient cash are absolutely imperative if they are to be free to pay attention to other important aspects of operating their businesses.

For the purposes of this discussion, "cash" is considered to consist of all petty cash accounts held in an operation, all cashier bank balances, and all to-be-deposited, as well as previously deposited and unrestricted, cash receipts. As a practical matter, however, most hospitality operators must consider their cash balances to be the amount of money held in their unrestricted bank accounts. This is so because the cash amounts held in petty cash funds and cashier banks are actually needed to operate the business and are not generally considered available for bill payment.

In the hospitality industry, when business is good, cash needs are at their highest. This is so because most hospitality businesses find that their need for cash increases and decreases based upon their volume. Generally, more cash is required during high volume periods because payrolls are larger, more cash is tied up holding greater quantities of products in inventory, and in some restaurants as well as most hotels, accounts receivable amounts are higher in busy months. As a result, the need for cash planning is clearly evident to managers of all type businesses and at all times of the year.

Cash budgeting is the general term used by managerial accountants to identify a variety of cash monitoring and management activities. Cash budgeting is important because, many times, successful restaurants and hotels become increasingly insolvent (see Chapter 6) because they do not have enough cash to meet the needs of their increasing sales volume. The vexing result, as many ex-operators have discovered, can be stated simply as, "What good is additional sales volume if you're out of business?" Thus, effective cash budgeting is such a primary business objective that it often must override other objectives, such as increasing sales volume.

Sufficient cash is one of the keys to maintaining a successful business. Thus, it is critical that managerial accountants understand how cash moves or flows through their businesses and how planning can remove some of the uncertainties about their future cash requirements. In fact, the concept of total cash receipts (cash in) and cash disbursements (cash out) which occur in a business in a specific accounting period is called **cash flow**. As you learned in Chapter 5, this process is so important that it results in a financial summary (statement of cash flows) that is one of only three required to be prepared regularly by all businesses. In most businesses, cash flows, and thus changes in cash balances on hand, occur in a predictable cycle.

Typically, cash is used in the acquisition of materials and services to produce finished goods. Thus, restaurateurs buy food and beverages and hoteliers purchase room supplies that enable them to sell guest rooms. When the inventory is sold, these sales generate cash and accounts receivable (money owed from guests). When the guests actually pay, accounts receivable is reduced and the cash account increases. However, these cash flows "in" are not necessarily related to sales achieved in that accounting period because guests may pay their bills in the next accounting period or any of several alternative future periods. As a result, it is important to carefully monitor and forecast the timing of these cash flows.

Cash and Accounts Receivable Activities

After the determination has been made that credit terms will be extended, it is important to bill guests according to the policies established by the business. It is equally important to monitor accounts receivable (AR). This is done via the **accounts receivable aging report.** An accounts receivable aging report is used by management to monitor the average length of time money owed to the business has remained uncollected.

Figure 11.6 shows an example of an accounts receivable aging report for the Blue Lagoon Water Park Resort hotel with $100,000 in outstanding accounts receivable.

Figure 11.6 indicates that the total amount owed to the hotel is $100,000. This amount can be broken down into four distinct time periods. One-half of the total accounts receivable ($50,000) is owed to the hotel by guests who have received their bills 30 or fewer days ago, whereas 5% ($5,000) is due from guests who have had over 90 days to pay their bills. As a general rule, as the age of an accounts receivable increases, its likelihood of being collected decreases.

As a receivable account ages, an effective control system will direct the business to contact the affected guest to determine if there is a problem in billing, documentation, or some other item that is delaying payment. In severe cases of nonpayment, the guest could have their direct billing status revoked, and collection efforts could be undertaken.

FIGURE 11.6 Accounts Receivable Aging Report

BLUE LAGOON WATER PARK RESORT HOTEL
ACCOUNTS RECEIVABLE AGING REPORT FOR JANUARY, 2010

Total Amount Receivable = $100,000

	Number of Days Past Due			
	Less than 30	**30–60**	**60–90**	**90+**
	$50,000			
		$30,000		
			$15,000	
				$5,000
Total	**$50,000**	**$30,000**	**$15,000**	**$5,000**
% of Total	**50%**	**30%**	**15%**	**5%**

Effective managers "age" their accounts receivable to ensure that they understand fully the amount of money owed to their businesses and to ensure that their receivables are, in fact, collected in a timely manner. However, managers seeking to conserve or create cash may, in addition to stepping up collection efforts, also wish to re-evaluate their entire AR process. This includes considering the overall wisdom of extending credit to each customer. Before extending (or continuing to extend) credit terms to a specific customer or guest, managers should consider:

- The size of the customer's normal purchase and the potential for future business
- The length of time the customer (if a business) has been in business
- The status (age and balance) of the present account
- The amount of time until the sale will be made
- Where the customer falls on the operation's credit risk estimation (e.g., high, medium, or low risk)
- Whether a partial deposit should be required to extend credit

Credit sales, (if ultimately paid for by the guest!), are a positive occurrence for most businesses because these sales will eventually generate cash. **Write-offs**, which are in essence, official declarations that an account receivable is uncollectible, however, should be avoided whenever possible. Unfortunately, every business that extends credit, hoping to ultimately improve its profits (and thus its cash generating ability) will likely experience some bad debts and be forced to write them off. For that reason, when setting up each new credit account, a comprehensive credit application should be completed that allows the business considering offering credit access to financial and bank information about the entity seeking credit. Most banks are very cooperative in exchanging credit information, and they should be assured that the information obtained will be treated in the strictest confidence.

W *fun on the Web!*

Dun and Bradstreet offers credit reports on companies much the same way as credit bureaus offer reports on individuals. The reports are not free, but to enter a company name and see the type of information available, go to:

www.smallbusiness.dnb.com

When you arrive, use the search field and enter the name of any business with which you are familiar.

Logically, when cash is in short supply, managers most often move more aggressively on accounts receivable collections than when a cash shortage is not imminent. It is, of course, always important for managers to carefully monitor their accounts receivable. When a business faces the prospect of exhausting all of its cash, it is even more critical that managers truly maximize this critical source of potential cash.

Cash and Accounts Payable Activities

For many hospitality businesses, and especially for those who generate little or no credit sales (accounts receivable), the manipulation of accounts payable (AP) balances is the most commonly used method of managing temporary cash shortages. Simply put, when cash is in short supply and employees are at risk of not being able to cash their paychecks, the temporary postponement of normal bill paying may be necessary to ensure continued operations. As a result, it is not uncommon for restaurant and hotel operators (as well as those managers in many other businesses!) to delay bill payment to conserve cash. This strategy must be carefully implemented, however, because each of a hospitality business's creditors will also be evaluating the future credit worthiness of that business. Reliance on an untimely bill payment strategy to ease cash shortages is never a good long-term strategy and an over-reliance on it is a significant sign that the business is either unprofitable or **undercapitalized**, which means it is chronically short of the capital (money) it needs to sustain its operation.

Cash Receipts/Disbursements Approach to Cash Budgeting

When managers budget cash, they typically do so using the **cash receipts/disbursements approach to cash budgeting**, which requires managers to sum their cash receipts during a specific accounting period and then subtract the cash amounts they will spend. The remaining balance represents their forecasted cash excess or cash shortage.

To illustrate, consider the case of Joan Bott. Joan owns a large party planning and catering company. Joan wants to budget her business's cash usage for the months of July, August, and September (the third quarter of the year). To do so, she reviews her sales forecast, accounts receivable balances, and operational expense history to prepare the data found in Figure 11.7.

FIGURE 11.7   Cash Budget for the Third Quarter–Joan's Catering Company

Given Data:

	July	August	September
Revenues	247,000	227,500	208,000
Cost of Sales	74,100	68,250	62,400
Operating Expenses	86,450	79,626	72,800
Nonoperating Expenses			
Interest Expense	7,200	7,200	7,200
Insurance Premiums	10,000		

		Current Month	Second Month
Schedule of Receipts (AR)		30%	70%
AR from June (Received in July)	95,550		
Schedule of Payments (AP)			
Cost of Sales		60%	40%
Operating Expenses		50%	50%
Nonoperating Expenses		100%	
Cost of Sales from June (Paid in July)	31,200		
Operating Expenses from June (Paid in July)	45,500		

Cash Budget

		July	August	September
Receipts:				
Food Revenues				
Current Month	30%	74,100	68,250	62,400
Second Month	70%	95,550	172,900	159,250
Disbursements:				
Cost of Sales				
Current Month	60%	44,460	40,950	37,440
Second Month	40%	31,200	29,640	27,300
Operating Expenses				
Current Month	50%	43,225	39,813	36,400
Second Month	50%	45,500	43,225	39,813
Nonoperating Expenses	100%	17,200	7,200	7,200
Beginning Cash Balance		10,000	3,065	77,887
+ Cash Receipts		169,650	241,150	221,650
= Subtotal		179,650	244,215	299,537
− Cash Disbursements		181,585	160,828	148,153
= Subtotal		−1,935	83,387	151,384
+/− Short-Term Loans		5,000	−5,500	
= Ending Cash Balance		3,065	77,887	151,384

go figure!

In reviewing the data presented in Figure 11.7, there are several important points to note.

- She has budgeted her revenues, cost of sales, and operating expenses based on forecasts for the months of July, August, and September.
- She has interest expenses of $7,200 per month.
- She pays an insurance premium of $10,000 in the first month of every quarter.
- She expects to collect 30% of revenues in the month they are generated (current month) and the remaining 70% the next month as accounts receivable (AR) based on her aging of accounts receivable. The arrows show the placement of current and next-month revenues.
- She expects to collect in July $95,550 from accounts receivable from June.
- She expects to pay 60% of the cost of sales in the month they are incurred (current month) and the remaining 40% the next month as accounts payable (AP). The arrows show the placement of current and next-month cost of sales.
- She expects to pay 50% of her operating expenses in the month they are incurred (current month) and the remaining 50% the next month as accounts payable (AP). The arrows show the placement of current and next-month operating expenses.
- She expects to pay 100% of her nonoperating expenses in the month they are incurred.
- She expects to pay in July $31,200 from accounts payable for cost of sales from June.
- She expects to pay in July $45,500 from accounts payable for operating expenses from June.
- Her beginning cash balance in July will be $10,000.
- Ending cash balance for one month is the beginning cash balance of the next month.
- She requires a minimum cash balance of $3,000 at all times (for emergencies).
- Any shortages in cash will be covered with short-term loans of $5,000 with 10% interest.

Note that, in this example, despite projected July revenues that are higher than August or September, Joan is predicting a cash shortage for the month of −$1,935. She will have to borrow $5,000 in order to cover her shortage and provide a minimum cash balance of $3,000. She will have to pay back this loan with interest in August when her cash balance has a surplus. Joan's is a typical case of a business (operating on relatively small profit margins) that simply must be very careful in budgeting cash, despite the overall profitability of her business.

Of course Joan should ensure that all cash she receives as payment for services is immediately deposited (to reduce chances of theft or other loss) in her bank, and that all credit, debit, and bank card agreements should ensure that funds collected via these methods are deposited into her bank account in a timely manner. Many managers facing a cash shortage seek to manipulate the amount of cash available to them by emphasizing activities related to accounts receivable and accounts payable.

W fun on the Web!

Most everyone agrees that cash management is a challenge in the hospitality industry. This is especially so for seasonal businesses and those businesses for whom cash flows are irregular. Most would also agree that, given the number of business bankruptcies that occur, learning how to determine the creditworthiness of potential customers is also a crucial skill for all managerial accountants. As well, knowing how and when to pay the liabilities of a business is critical. Written in an easy-to-read style, H.A. Schaeffer, Jr.'s excellent book *Essentials of Cash Flow* is a resource that addresses all of these cash flow management issues and more. It should be read by all managers who now, or in the future, will be responsible for meeting payrolls, making mortgage payments, and planning for the long-term cash position of their operations. *Essentials of Cash Flow* can be found at:

www.amazon.com

When you arrive, enter *Essentials of Cash Flow* in the search line to view a copy of this book published by John Wiley & Sons.

Managing Budgets through Internal Controls

Operations budgets help managers plan for revenues, expenses, and profits, while cash budgets help managers plan for cash availability. All the planning in the world, however, does not ensure that these budgets are implemented properly. Many internal and external forces change the way operations are carried out. This portion of the chapter will show you some of the pitfalls and solutions to controlling the actual outcomes of careful budgeting.

It comes as a surprise to some managers that collecting revenue and recording the collection process do not ultimately ensure the continued security of that revenue. In many cases, the safekeeping of revenue earned is most threatened *after* it is collected. This is because the risk of **theft**, or the unlawful taking of a business's property and **fraud**, the intentional use of dishonest methods to take property, is actually greatest from a business's own employees. In fact, for most hospitality businesses the risk of losing assets like cash from **embezzlement** (employee theft) is actually much greater than the risk of **robbery** (theft using force).

In a similar manner, any employee responsible for paying the legitimate bills of a business may, like any other employee, occasionally make an honest mistake that results in overpayment of an invoice. In addition some vendors are unscrupulous and may attempt to defraud the business. The greatest risk of fraud related to payment of expenses, however, typically involves the business's own employees. For these reasons and more, it is very important for you to design and maintain control systems that ensure the security of your business's assets. In the hospitality industry, these revenue and expense controls may well mean the difference between you operating a business that makes a profit and one that actually loses money.

Internal controls can be of a variety of types, but the internal control system itself seeks to:

- Ensure accurate financial records keeping
- Restrict unnecessary and potentially detrimental access to the assets of the business
- Confirm, periodically, that those responsible for safeguarding assets can account for them
- Establish appropriate action steps for measuring and addressing variation between the expected and actual performance of those preserving the assets of the business

W fun on the Web!

Credit card merchants are an excellent source of free fraud reduction training procedures and materials. American Express has some of the best. To review them, go to:

www.americanexpress.com

When you arrive there, click on "Merchants." Then click "Fraud Prevention." Then click "Merchant Fraud Squad."

There are a variety of approaches that can be used to view management control systems for restaurants and hotels. In each case, however, an effective system will have five fundamental characteristics. These consist of:

- Management's concern for assets
- Accurate data collection and comparison to written standards
- Separation of responsibilities
- Cost effectiveness
- Regular external review

Management's Concern for Assets

Experienced hospitality managers know that they work in an industry in which their companies' assets are especially vulnerable to internal and external threats. As a result, a fundamental characteristic of any effective control system is its emphasis on protecting company assets. This characteristic encompasses a variety of related concerns including:

■ The documentation, collection, and preservation of sales revenues
■ The care and safeguarding of assets such as equipment and inventories that are owned by the business
■ The careful documentation and payment of the business's legitimate expenses

Unless management views its role as one of ensuring that adequate attention is paid to each of these concerns, adequate control systems will not likely be implemented. Consider, for example, the management team that does an excellent job ensuring that all revenue generated is collected and ultimately deposited in the business's bank account. Assume also that this management team very carefully has designed a system of bill payment that is highly efficient and accurate. If this same management team does not design systems to carefully safeguard the business's on-premise inventories and equipment, it is likely to be this area that is exploited by unscrupulous employees, vendors, and even guests.

Accurate Data Collection and Comparison to Written Standards

An effective control system is one in which financial data is carefully recorded and then compared to previously identified standards or expectations. For example, assume that a business seeks to control part of its revenue collection process by monitoring the amount of money its cashiers have in their cash drawers (banks) at the end of their shifts. If the cashier is **over** (has more money than anticipated in the cashier's bank) or **short** (has less money than anticipated in the cashier's bank) the amount of the variation from expectations is carefully recorded. In this example, it is easy to see that, if management is to make this process an effective part of the overall control system, the data recorded by the cashiers must, first and foremost, be accurate. It makes little sense to attempt to monitor over and shorts if these amounts cannot be accurately or fairly determined.

Secondly, in this example, knowing the size of an overage or shortage, may not, by itself, help managers better control their cash assets. If, for example, you learned that a specific cashier was $5.00 short at the end of his eight-hour shift, it would likely be helpful to also know if the total amount of money taken in on the shift was $50.00 or $500,000! Thus, the expectations of qualified managers will likely vary based upon the unique characteristics of their own operations. As a result, committing goals, standards, and expectations to writing is a critical part of an effective internal control system.

In each instance where management seeks to control or monitor revenues and expenses, the record keeping systems in place must be consistently accurate. If they are, the data collected in these systems can be legitimately compared to management's predetermined goals and expectations. The importance of committing these management standards to written policies is apparent, both for the sake of consistency (because the expectations of individual managers will frequently vary) and because it is important that employees fully understand the performance expectations by which they will be evaluated.

Separation of Responsibilities

Just as an effective restaurant requires skilled production personnel, servers, and managers, and hotels require talented housekeepers, front office staff, and maintenance professionals, so too do effective accounting systems require talented individuals who are responsible for very specific and separate tasks.

For example, in a restaurant, a server may place a guest's order for food and that order will be filled by a kitchen worker. If the same server was responsible, at the end of his or her shift, for reporting the number of items ordered, the number of items served, and the amount of money collected for those items, the potential for fraud will exist and it will be known to the server. If, however, the server reports the number of items ordered, a separate individual reports the number of items served, and yet a third individual (the manager) is responsible for tallying the actual amount of revenue collected, only in the case of **collusion** (the secret cooperation of two or more employees) could the potential for fraud exist.

It is, of course, impossible to ensure that all employees will be honest. However, with a clear separation of accounting duties, an internal system of checks and balances can be created that, when followed, can significantly reduce the chance of employee fraud and theft. In an effective internal control system, each involved employee is a member of a team. Because it is a team, each member helps reduce the theft opportunities of each team member. That is why, for example, a quality control system would assign one person to make bank deposits, but another person would be assigned the job of ensuring that the amount of money that was supposed to be deposited was, in fact, deposited in the proper account.

By separating component parts of the control process, even small restaurants and hotels can improve the quality of their control systems. Employee and management involvement and education is a key part of this process. When employees at any level fully understand that control systems have been developed that will expose dishonesty on their part, the temptation to commit theft is greatly reduced. Quality control systems separate control assignments and communicate that fact to affected staff.

Cost Effectiveness

Good control systems are also cost effective. Whenever you consider designing and implementing an internal control system, it is important to consider the system's total costs. It makes little sense, for example, to spend $100 per day of your business's assets to prevent the possible loss of an item whose cost cannot possibly exceed $1.00 per day. The costs incurred to design, implement, and maintain a control system must be considered at the same time the overall worthiness of the control system is evaluated.

For example, assume a new time-card system that eliminates employees punching in and out on paper time cards is available to hospitality operations for $50,000. The new system initially scans the retina of the eye of each employee, and then, when the employees "punch in and out," they do so using the scanner's ability to distinguish the individual employee retina pattern and color.

The system eliminates completely the possibility of **buddy punching**, the method by which an employee uses another's time card to punch that second employee in or out. While buddy punching is prohibited in nearly all businesses, it can sometimes be difficult for management to detect. To make a good decision about this purchase, a manager must determine:

- The potential magnitude of the operation's "buddy punching" problem
- The cost of using the retina scanner to address the problem

 *go figure!*

Situation A

To illustrate, assume that a small restaurant has five employees. The restaurant currently is equipped with a traditional paper/punch time-card system. At any one time, no more than three of the employees are working in the facility.

Each employee earns approximately $20,000 per year, thus the restaurant has a total hourly employee wages payroll of $20,000 × 5 employees = $100,000 per year.

The manager must weigh the cost of the $50,000 retina scanner in relation to the total cost of $100,000 in payroll for five employees. With only two or three employees working at one time, it would be relatively hard for management to be unaware of one employee's absence! Therefore, the cost of this solution is simply too high relative to the size of the potential buddy punching problem the restaurant likely faces.

Situation B

Consider now, however, the case of Luis Argote. Luis is the manager of a 1,000-room resort located on 150 beach-front acres.

The resort is staffed around the clock, seven days a week. It never closes. The resort employs nearly 1,500 full- and part-time staff members, many of whom are assigned to work in remote areas of the resort and at all hours of the day and night.

The payroll for Luis's resort exceeds $25,000,000 per year.

Luis must weigh the cost of the $50,000 retina scanner in relation to the total cost of $25,000,000 in payroll for 1,500 employees. For Luis, the retina scanning system may be an excellent purchase and may allow him to address some real issues related to potential buddy punching abuse at his resort.

Regular External Review

External review, or audit, is an important characteristic of all quality internal control systems. In Chapter 1 you learned that an audit is simply an independent verification of financial records and that an auditor is the individual or group of individuals that completes the verification. An external review of a business's internal control systems may be undertaken by an outside audit group, by upper management, or even by a team assembled by the business's own onsite managers and staff. The goal in all cases is to review the accounting, reporting, and control systems and procedures that have been established, and to make recommendations for future changes and enhancements that can lead to continuous improvement.

fun on the Web!

Many individuals responsible for the internal controls and audit functions of their businesses share challenges and concerns. In some cases, they get together to share information, tools, and ideas. One such gathering spot is the "ASK" (Auditors Sharing Knowledge) website. You can find it at:

www.auditnet.org/asapind.htm

The audit programs on AuditNet were contributed by auditors from around the world. Registration is required, but access to the information is free.

Thus far you have examined primarily how hospitality managers budget their operations' revenues, expenses, profits, and cash. You have also learned how managers can use internal controls to ensure the positive outcomes of those budgets. Depending upon the specific corporate form and the size of the company, methods of securing short- or long-term capital (money) to help meet budget requirements include:

- The sale of fixed assets
- The issuance of additional stock
- Borrowing from a short-term source
- Borrowing from a long-term source

The question of how much money an operation actually should keep readily on hand can be a vexing one. Certainly, this amount must be sufficient to operate the business, but an excessive amount of un-invested money creates a very small (if any) return on investment for its owners. The result is that managers and owners must carefully evaluate how they will secure the capital they need, as well as how the money they already have may best be invested in the short and long term. It is to the critical topic of capital investments and their rate of returns (ROI) that the next and final chapter of this text is directed.

 pply What You Have Learned

Jennifer Norton is the Registered Dietitian (R.D.) responsible for all dietary services at City Memorial Hospital. Her operation consists of two departments. The first, and largest, is patient feeding. It consists of the tray line staff and the majority of her food production staff. The second department is the public cafeteria, which includes special dining areas for staff and a large dining area for patient visitors. Annually on January 1, she submits to her supervisor an annual labor expense budget broken down by month for each department.

In June, and after four months of consideration and planning, Jennifer and her staff were excited to implement a new cafeteria menu. The response from the public was excellent. The dining room staff reported that there were many positive comments about the food selected for the new menu, and the production staff reported a 25% increase in the amount of food prepared for cafeteria service.

On July 7 when Jennifer's assistant, Joe, brought her the financial reports for the month of June, he was quite agitated. "I think we are in trouble Boss," he said. "As I read the reports, we were over our labor budget by more than $3,000 last month! How did that happen?"

Jennifer reviewed the labor portion of the budget and found the following:

	June Budget	June Actual
Patient Labor	$23,750	$23,824
Cafeteria Labor	$16,500	$19,850

1. What do you think is the cause of Jennifer's labor budget overages? How would you determine if you are correct?
2. Jennifer needs to supply her supervisor with an analysis of the labor budget variance she has incurred in each of her two operating units. Compute the variances from budget for her in both dollar amount and percentage. What other data might Jennifer wish to include in her report?

	June Budget	June Actual	Variance $	Variance %
Patient Labor	$23,750	$23,824		
Cafeteria Labor	$16,500	$19,850		

3. Assume that Jennifer came to you and asked how she could determine whether the increased dollars spent on labor in the public cafeteria were expended efficiently. What specific steps would you suggest she take to help find an accurate answer to that question?

Key Terms and Concepts

The following are terms and concepts discussed in the chapter that are important for you to know as a manager. To help you review, please define the following terms.

Budget	Payroll allocations	Cash receipts/disbursements
Chief Executive Officer	Variance	approach to cash
(CEO)	Favorable variance	budgeting
Horizon	Unfavorable variance	Theft
Long-range budget	Significant variance	Fraud
Annual budget	Flexible budget	Embezzlement
Achievement budget	Cash budgeting	Robbery
Operations budget	Cash flow	Over (cash bank)
Cash budget	Accounts receivable aging	Short (cash bank)
Capital expenditure	report	Collusion
Capital budget	Write-offs	Buddy punching
Line item	Undercapitalized	

Test Your Skills

Complete the Test Your Skills exercises by placing your answers in the shaded boxes.

1. Zheng Chung is the managing owner of the Stillwater Grill. This year, 2010, was a good year for him. Now he is preparing his 2011 budget. Using the information Zheng believes will be true, help him complete the dollar and percentage amounts in the budget worksheet that follows, then answer the questions he has about next year. Based upon his sales histories, sales projections, and cost records, Zheng predicts that in 2011 his operation will experience:

   ■ A 6% increase in food sales

   ■ A 4% increase in beverage sales

   ■ No change in food or beverage product cost percentage

   ■ Salaries and wages that will increase 3.5%

   ■ Benefits that will increase 10%

   ■ An increase in all other operating expenses (except depreciation) of 2%

   ■ A depreciation schedule that calls for a $750 per month entry

   ■ Interest payments for loans that will total $1,100 per month

   ■ Tax payments that are estimated to be 25% of income before income taxes

THE STILLWATER GRILL
BUDGET WORKSHEET FOR SEPTEMBER 2011

	2010 Actual	%	2011 Budget	%
SALES:				
Food	346,500	75.3%		
Beverage	113,500	24.7%		
Total Sales	**460,000**	100.0%		
COST OF SALES:				
Food	116,500	33.6%		
Beverage	18,750	16.5%		
Total Cost of Sales	**135,250**	29.4%		
GROSS PROFIT:				
Food	230,000	66.4%		
Beverage	94,750	83.5%		
Total Gross Profit	**324,750**	70.6%		
OPERATING EXPENSES:				
Salaries and Wages	72,500	15.8%		
Employee Benefits	12,400	2.7%		
Direct Operating Expenses	16,550	3.6%		
Music and Entertainment	3,200	0.7%		
Marketing	6,650	1.4%		
Utility Services	11,950	2.6%		
Repairs and Maintenance	3,500	0.8%		
Administrative and General	12,750	2.8%		
Occupancy	30,000	6.5%		
Depreciation	8,400	1.8%		
Total Operating Expenses	**177,900**	38.7%		
Operating Income	**146,850**	31.9%		
Interest	14,000	3.0%		
Income Before Income Taxes	**132,850**	28.9%		
Income Taxes	33,213	7.2%		
Net Income	**99,638**	21.7%		

a. What will be Zheng's total sales in 2011?

b. What will be Zheng's total cost of sales income 2011?

c. What will be the amount Zheng will spend on salaries, wages, and employee benefits in 2011?

   d. What is the estimated amount of income taxes Zheng will pay in 2011?

   e. What does Zheng estimate will be his operation's net income percentage (profit margin) in 2011? How will that compare to his 2010 percentage?

2. Dee Flowers owns the most successful catering business in town. December is her busiest month, and she has just completed it. Dee now has a chance to take a moment and evaluate the operations budget she has prepared for December, as well as the actual results achieved by her company. On the facing page are her original operations budget and her actual operating results for the month. Complete the sheet for her, providing variance dollars and variance percentages for each budgeted item, and then answer the questions that follow.

DEE'S CATERING
BUDGET VERSUS ACTUAL COMPARISON FOR DECEMBER 2010

	Budget	%	Actual	%	Variance	%
SALES:						
Food	185,200	73.9%	193,251	68.4%		
Beverage	65,250	26.1%	89,250	31.6%		
Total Sales	**250,450**	100.0%	**282,501**	100.0%		
COST OF SALES:						
Food	67,500	36.4%	68,925	35.7%		
Beverage	14,500	22.2%	20,415	22.9%		
Total Cost of Sales	**82,000**	32.7%	**89,340**	31.6%		
GROSS PROFIT:						
Food	117,700	63.6%	124,326	64.3%		
Beverage	50,750	77.8%	68,835	77.1%		
Total Gross Profit	**168,450**	67.3%	**193,161**	68.4%		
OPERATING EXPENSES:						
Salaries and Wages	38,750	15.5%	44,850	15.9%		
Employee Benefits	9,500	3.8%	11,203	4.0%		
Direct Operating Expenses	26,500	10.6%	27,210	9.6%		
Music and Entertainment	0	0.0%	0	0.0%		
Marketing	1,200	0.5%	150	0.1%		
Utility Services	3,250	1.3%	3,289	1.2%		
Repairs and Maintenance	3,500	1.4%	2,874	1.0%		
Administrative and General	24,750	9.9%	25,598	9.1%		
Occupancy	1,200	0.5%	1,200	0.4%		

Depreciation	2,200	0.9%	2,200	0.8%		
Total Operating Expenses	**110,850**	**44.3%**	**118,574**	**42.0%**		
Operating Income	**57,600**	**23.0%**	**74,587**	**26.4%**		
Interest	7,100	2.8%	7,100	2.5%		
Income Before Income Taxes	**50,500**	**20.2%**	**67,487**	**23.9%**		
Income Taxes	12,625	5.0%	16,872	6.0%		
Net Income	**37,875**	**15.1%**	**50,615**	**17.9%**		

a. What is the variance (dollar and percent) in Dee's total cost of sales for the month of December?

b. To what do you attribute the variance in Dee's total cost of sales for December?

c. What is the variance (dollar and percent) in Dee's salaries and wages for the month of December?

d. To what do you attribute the variance in Dee's salaries and wages for December?

e. What is the variance (dollar and percent) in Dee's marketing expenses for the month of December?

f. What advice would you give Dee regarding her marketing expense variance?

g. What is the variance (dollar and percent) in Dee's net income for the month of December?

h. To what do you attribute the variance in Dee's net income for December?

3. Watson Walbert has been the Executive Chef at the Altina Restaurant for five years. Altina Restaurant is located in a "dry" area (alcoholic beverage sales are illegal), so it only sells food. In the last five years, Watson has worked for several general managers. The new general manager, however, is a real stickler for staying in budget, and at the moment Watson is a bit worried. According to November's spreadsheet the general manager sent Watson, he had exceeded his food cost budget significantly. He felt his team had performed well, but according to the memo he got from the general manager, he still had to explain his department's "sub-par" performance to the general manager in person. Watson is confused, though. Although he spent more in food cost, he also sold more covers, so his food cost should be higher than originally budgeted! Watson decides to calculate a flexible budget based on his *actual* number of covers sold to see if he has, indeed, had cost control problems in any of his line items, especially food cost. Help him calculate his flexible budget, and then answer the questions that follow.

ALTINA RESTAURANT
FLEXIBLE BUDGET FOR NOVEMBER 2010

November 2010 original budget number of covers = 18,000
November 2010 actual covers sold = 21,000   Actual check average = [   ]

	Variable Dollars per Cover	Original Budget	Flexible Budget	Actual	Variance	F/U
NUMBER OF COVERS:		18,000	21,000	21,000		
SALES: FOOD	$9.00	$162,000	[ ]	$200,000	[ ]	[ ]
LESS VARIABLE COSTS:						
Food Cost	$3.12	56,160	[ ]	60,500	[ ]	[ ]
Salaries, Wages, and Benefits	$1.25	22,500	[ ]	22,000	[ ]	[ ]
Telephone	$0.02	360	[ ]	575	[ ]	[ ]
Marketing	$0.08	1,440	[ ]	1,750	[ ]	[ ]
Utilities	$0.14	2,520	[ ]	2,500	[ ]	[ ]
Repairs and Maintenance	$0.11	1,980	[ ]	2,600	[ ]	[ ]
Contribution Margin	$4.28	77,040	[ ]	110,075	[ ]	[ ]
LESS FIXED COSTS:						
Salaries, Wages, and Benefits		28,800	28,800	28,800	0	
Telephone		360	360	360	0	
Marketing		5,400	5,400	5,400	0	
Utilities		3,600	3,600	3,600	0	
Repairs and Maintenance		150	150	150	0	
Administrative and General		2,000	2,000	2,000	0	
Depreciation		1,000	1,000	1,000	0	
Occupancy Costs		5,000	5,000	5,000	0	
Income Before Taxes		30,730	[ ]	63,765	[ ]	[ ]
Taxes (40%)		12,292	[ ]	25,506	[ ]	[ ]
Net Income		18,438	[ ]	38,259	[ ]	[ ]

a. What was Watson's actual check average? Was this higher or lower than the original budget and flexible budget check average?

b. Were Watson's actual food sales higher or lower than the flexible budget? By how much? Was this favorable or unfavorable?

c. Was Watson's actual food cost higher or lower than the original budget? Why do you think this is so?

d. Was Watson's actual food cost higher or lower than the flexible budget? By how much? Was this favorable or unfavorable? How can Watson use this information in his report to his general manager?

e. Were Watson's variable salaries, wages, and benefits higher or lower than the original budget?

f. Were Watson's variable salaries, wages, and benefits higher or lower than the flexible budget? By looking at both the original budget and the flexible budget, what conclusion can you draw about Watson's ability to control his labor costs?

g. Was Watson's actual net income higher or lower than the flexible budget? By how much? Was this favorable or unfavorable?

h. Overall, how do you think Watson is doing at meeting the budget goals set by the general manager? How should he respond to his general manager's claim that his department is operating at a "sub-par" performance level?

4. Sithabiso's Wraps is an all-organic restaurant located near State University. It is managed by Eunice Ndlovu, and Eunice is preparing her first-quarter cash budget for 2010. It is important to her because of the variation in volume caused by the return of the university students. Help Eunice complete her cash budget and answer the questions that follow. Note the following forecast information and assumptions for Sithabiso's Wraps:

- Eunice has budgeted her revenues, cost of sales, and operating expenses based on forecasts for the months of January, February, and March.

- She expects to collect 80% of revenues in the month they are generated (current month) and the remaining 20% the next month as accounts receivable (AR) based on her aging of accounts receivable.

- She expects to collect in January $30,000 from accounts receivable from December.

- She expects to pay 60% of the cost of sales in the month they are incurred (current month) and the remaining 40% the next month as accounts payable (AP).

- She expects to pay in January $19,000 from accounts payable for cost of sales from December.

- She expects to pay 70% of her operating expenses in the month they are incurred (current month) and the remaining 30% the next month as accounts payable (AP).

- She expects to pay in January $21,000 from accounts payable for operating expenses from December.

- She expects to pay 100% of her nonoperating expenses in the month they are incurred.

- She has rent expense of $4,000 per month.

- She pays an insurance premium of $6,000 in the first month of every quarter.

- Her beginning cash balance in January will be $5,000.

- Ending cash balance for one month is the beginning cash balance of the next month.

■ She requires a minimum cash balance of $5,000 at all times (for emergencies).
■ Any shortages in cash will be covered with short-term loans of $5,000 with 10% interest.

SITHABISO'S WRAPS
CASH BUDGET FOR THE FIRST QUARTER OF 2010

Given Data:

	January	February	March
Revenues	60,000	132,000	96,000
Cost of Sales	21,000	46,200	33,600
Operating Expenses	28,000	36,000	32,000
Nonoperating Expenses			
Rent Expense	4,000	4,000	4,000
Insurance Premiums	6,000		

		Current Month	Second Month
Schedule of Receipts (AR)		80%	20%
AR from December (Received in January)	30,000		
Schedule of Payments (AP)			
Cost of Sales		60%	40%
Operating Expenses		70%	30%
Nonoperating Expenses		100%	
Cost of Sales from December (Paid in January)	19,000		
Operating Expenses from December (Paid in January)	21,000		

Cash Budget

		January	February	March
Receipts:				
Food Revenues:				
Current Month	80%			
Second Month	20%			
Disbursements:				
Cost of Sales:				
Current Month	60%			
Second Month	40%			

Operating Expenses				
Current Month	70%			
Second Month	30%			
Nonoperating Expenses	100%			
Beginning Cash Balance				
Cash Receipts				
Subtotal				
Cash Disbursements				
Subtotal				
Short-Term Loans				
Ending Cash Balance				

a. Will Eunice have to borrow any short-term loans to cover cash shortfalls in the first quarter of the year? If so, how much money will she have to borrow, and what do you think may have caused this?

b. If Eunice has to borrow a short-term loan to cover cash shortfalls in the first quarter of the year, will she be able to pay it back in a timely manner? If so, when?

c. By the end of the quarter, will Eunice have a surplus or deficit of cash? If she has a surplus, what should she do with the extra money?

d. Overall, how do you think Eunice is doing at planning her cash receipts and cash disbursements in order to keep enough cash on hand to pay her bills?

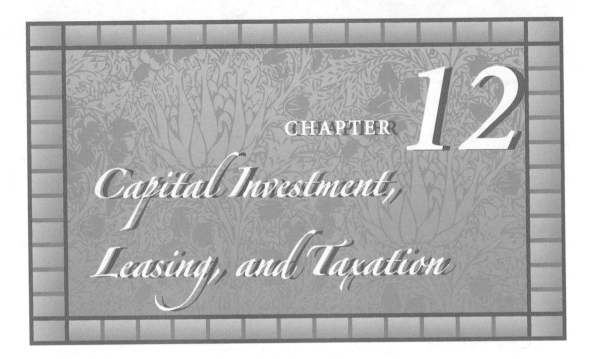

OVERVIEW

Many individuals, including experienced managerial accountants, aspire to own their own hospitality businesses. The ownership of a restaurant or hotel holds for many the promise of a greater sense of personal accomplishment, increased control over their own work lives, and most important for some, the promise of greater financial reward than that which could normally be achieved by managing a business for others.

As many current (as well as many former!) owners in the hospitality industry are well aware, however, the prospect of greater financial reward associated with ownership is also associated with greater financial risk. As a result, while many fortunes have been made in the hospitality industry, a good many fortunes have been lost as well. This is so because deciding to buy, build, or lease a restaurant or hotel most often places substantial amounts of the owner's capital (money) at risk of loss. Obviously, individuals or companies do not typically plan to lose money when they start a business, and if they are to maximize the chances for success, they must make good investment decisions.

In this chapter, you will learn how owners and investors determine which businesses are worthy of their capital investment. While it may not be possible to predict with 100% accuracy the chances of a specific business becoming a financial success, it is true that knowledge is power. Never has that been more true than in the area of capital investments. In this chapter, you will learn about key financial concepts such as the time value of money, how to compute rates of investment return, and the importance of proper capital budgeting.

As well, the concept of capitalization rates (cap rates), their calculation, and their application are examined carefully. Also, because investors often must make decisions about whether to borrow money to fund a business, consider whether to lease or buy equipment or land, and carefully consider whether to buy existing or build new facilities, each of these important concepts are presented and examined.

Finally, because government entities write tax codes that directly affect business investment, the tax considerations of economic decisions often determine to a great degree the wisdom of that decision. Taxes are not voluntary contributions. As a result, most people in business would agree that they should pay the taxes they owe, but most would also agree that they should not pay more than they owe. Thus, the chapter concludes with an examination of the legal strategies hospitality business owners can employ to help ensure they pay only the amount of taxes the law actually requires them to pay.

CHAPTER OUTLINE

- ■ Capital Budgeting
- ■ Capital Investment
- ■ Financing Alternatives
- ■ Taxation
- ■ Apply What You Have Learned
- ■ Key Terms and Concepts
- ■ Test Your Skills

LEARNING OUTCOMES

At the conclusion of this chapter, you will be able to:

- ✓ Identify the purpose of capital budgeting.
- ✓ Compute business owners' investment rates of return.
- ✓ Identify advantages and disadvantages of capital financing alternatives such as debt versus equity financing and lease versus buy decisions.
- ✓ Determine the effects of taxation on a hospitality business.

Capital Budgeting

In business, **capital** simply refers to money. Those who invest their capital are, not surprisingly, called **capitalists**, and the economic system that allows for the private ownership of property is called **capitalism**. As is the case in most industries, investing money in hospitality businesses can be risky. To achieve reasonable returns on their capital investment, owners must operate their businesses successfully; however, successful businesses are most often the end result of successful business planning.

In Chapter 11 you learned how managers prepare and monitor operations budgets. Operations budgets are concerned primarily with planning for the normal revenues and expenses associated with the day-to-day operating of a business. As such, operations budgets address estimated revenues as well as the purchase of labor, food, beverages, room supplies, routine business services such as trash removal and pest control, and professional services such as printing, marketing, and insurance.

In the hospitality industry, capital budgets are used to plan and evaluate purchases of fixed assets such land, property, and equipment. Purchases of this type are called **capital expenditures** and, as you learned previously, are recorded on a business's balance sheet (recall that operations budget expenses are normally recorded on the income statement). **Capital budgeting** is simply the management process of evaluating the wisdom of one or more capital expenditures. These capital expenditures typically are more costly than those related to daily operating expenses, and thus, the owners or directors of a business pay particularly close attention to them. In fact, because of their critical nature, in most cases only a company's owners will make capital budgeting decisions.

To better understand why this is so, consider the case of Guy Armstrong. Guy is an experienced restaurateur who would like to own his own business. He has saved some money through his career and now would like to open a restaurant featuring Argentinean-style roasted and served meats. His target market is the young professionals working in the financial district of the large city in which he lives.

Guy's restaurant concept is novel. He is convinced that his food and service will be excellent, and he also feels that the size of his target market is sufficient to support the operational volume he believes he needs to be successful. *Before* he can begin to create his operational budget, however, essential capital budgeting questions Guy must answer include:

- Should he use his own life savings to start the restaurant, or should he borrow some of the money needed to begin operating?
- Would it be best to buy the building that will house his restaurant, or should he rent the space?
- Should he purchase the equipment required to operate the business, or should it be leased?
- What will be his likely return on investment in this business?

- Would he achieve better investment returns by starting an alternative business?
- What net income levels must the restaurant attain if Guy is to achieve his desired return on investment goals?

Guy understands that the answers to questions of this type are critical because they establish the profit requirements of his business. Those profit requirements will, in turn, help determine the size restaurant he plans to open, the service levels he can provide, the menu prices he must charge, and the total volume he must achieve to become a successful restaurant. Techniques utilized in the capital budgeting process will help Guy address these questions and more. In fact, experienced managers know that capital budgeting is the essential process by which those in business evaluate which hospitality operations will be started, which will be expanded, and which will be closed.

It is important to realize that, in nearly all cases, business owners seek returns on their investments which are large enough to justify the continued investment of their capital. Capital budgeting allows owners to estimate the investment returns they will achieve if they follow a specific course of action. In general, capital budgeting techniques can be classified as those that are directed toward one or more of the following business activities:

- Establish a business
- Expand a business (increase revenues)
- Increase efficiency (reduce expenses)
- Comply with the law

Establish a business. Perhaps the most significant investment decision a person or a business entity can make is that of starting a new **venture** (new business). The investment risks are great, yet the investment returns can be great also. Making decisions related to supplying the capital to begin new ventures requires expertise so unique that those who specialize in doing so are called venture capitalists. **Venture capitalists** are individuals or companies that are willing to take risks by financing promising new businesses. Venture capital companies generally are private partnerships or closely held corporations funded by private and public pension funds, endowment funds, foundations, corporations, wealthy individuals, foreign investors, and the venture capitalists themselves. Technically, any person or entity who supplies the funding for a start-up business is a venture capitalist. Venture capitalists, in exchange for partial ownership in the business, assist entrepreneurs in securing the funding needed to begin operations.

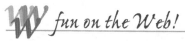 *fun on the Web!*

The number of venture capitalists operating today is so large that a specific trade association exists just for them. The National Venture Capitalists Association (NVCA) helps educate their members about new trends and techniques used to identify and provide start-up funding for promising new businesses. To view their member website, go to:

www.nvca.org

When you arrive, click on "Industry Overview."

Expand a business (increase revenues). Some of the most exciting types of capital budgeting decisions you will make relate to expanding a current business. Expansion may take the form of building additional restaurants or hotels, increasing the capacity of an existing restaurant or hotel, or simply funding the extension of a single property's additional hours or services. In most cases, a capital decision made regarding expansion of business should seek to increase the size, and thus the profits, of what is typically a successful business. Selecting new sites for buildings, working with architects to design new buildings, and planning for facility additions that will blend well with existing facilities are all specific examples of capital budgeting activities designed to expand an existing business.

Increase efficiency (reduce expenses). In many cases, a capital investment is made for the purpose of reducing expenses, and thus increasing profits. For example, assume that an upscale hotel offers guests limousine service as part of its "Anniversary package," which includes dinner in the hotel's restaurant, an overnight stay in one of the hotel's suites, and breakfast in bed the following morning. When the package was initiated, a local limousine service was retained to provide transportation to the hotel. Within weeks, the package had grown so successful that the hotel determined it would be less expensive to purchase its own limousine than it would be to continue the lease arrangement with the local limousine company.

In many other cases, capital budgeting decisions that result in updated facilities and/or equipment can significantly increase the productivity of a hospitality facility's workforce, thus reducing labor costs, and as a result, increasing profits. When capital can be utilized directly to increase operational efficiencies, returns on those investments can be immediate and substantial.

Comply with the law. In some cases, a business must make facility or operational investments regardless of their estimated rate of return. Mandated change may come from the passage of local, state, or federal regulations. When it does, a business must comply or face penalties and fines. Perhaps some of the most sweeping examples of significant capital budgeting decisions made in response to legislation are those related to the passage of the Americans with Disabilities Act (ADA) of 1990. The purpose of the legislation was to provide a national mandate for the elimination of discrimination against individuals with disabilities, and to invoke the powers of the federal government to ensure changes in the regulation of commerce (business) that would address the discrimination.

The ADA mandated many changes, including those related to the physical facilities of restaurants, hotels, and clubs. Title III of the ADA regulation covers public accommodations (i.e., private entities that own, operate, lease, or lease to places of public accommodation), such as restaurants, hotels, theaters, convention centers, retail stores, shopping centers, hospitals, zoos, amusement parks, private schools, day care centers, health spas, and bowling alleys. Because of the ADA, many hospitality operators found that capital investment in parking lots and spaces, entrance ways, and seating facilities were required. Careful capital budgeting decisions ensured that businesses complied with this law and maximized the societal good that could result from their investments.

fun on the Web!

Title III of the Americans with Disabilities Act was a significant piece of legislation for all disabled Americans as well as the restaurateurs and hoteliers who serve them. The impact of the law's requirements on capital budgeting in the hospitality industry has been significant. For a review of the requirements mandated by the ADA, go to:

www.ada.gov/t3hilght.htm

When you arrive, scroll down and examine, in particular, Section VII, "Existing Facilities: Removal of Barriers."

Learning capital budgeting skills, like learning skills related to operations budgeting, is important for all hospitality managers. It can be argued that both capital budgeting and operations budgeting are concerned with maximizing revenues and thus, the profits generated by a business. However, capital budgeting primarily addresses the funding of capital expenditures, while operations budgeting primarily addresses generating profits through operations.

Capital Investment

When a person or company makes a capital investment, they typically do so with the intention of increasing (not decreasing!) the monetary value of their investment. In most cases, investors can choose from a wide variety of investment options. In fact, in today's complex financial world, potential investors can choose from literally hundreds of investment options. In each case, the investor seeks to balance the concepts of **risk**, (the likelihood that the investment will decline in value) with that of **reward** (the likelihood that the investment will increase in value). The two concepts are highly correlated. That is, in most cases, as the amount of risk involved in an investment increases, the return on that investment also increases. In a similar manner, as the amount of investment risk decreases, the potential reward achieved by the investment will likely decrease as well.

FIGURE 12.1   Investment Risk and Reward

Investment Option	Risk	Reward
1. Home	Very Low	None
2. Bank savings account	Low	Low
3. Stock purchase	Moderate	Moderate to high
4. Entrepreneurship	High	Moderate to very high

To further illustrate the risk/reward relationship, assume, for example, that you had $1,000,000 to invest for one year. Assume also that you had identified four desirable investment options. The options are:

1. Keep the money in a very safe place at your home.
2. Deposit the money in a savings account at your local bank.
3. Purchase $1,000,000 worth of stock in a publicly traded restaurant or hotel company.
4. Invest the $1,000,000 to start your own restaurant or hotel.

Figure 12.1 summarizes what has historically been the long-term risk/reward relationship found in the four investment options you have selected.

 *go figure!*

To complete the illustration, consider that, in Option 1, at the end of your investment year, you would have $1,000,000. Your capital would be safely preserved, but would not grow.

If you select Option 2, at the end of the year you would likely have achieved a return on investment (ROI) of between 2 and 5% (based on current returns of savings accounts).

Assuming the return was 3%, at year end the total value of your $1,000,000 investment would be computed as:

> **Initial Investment + Return on Investment = Total Investment Value**
>
> or
>
> **$1,000,000 + ($1,000,000 × 0.03) = $1,030,000**

Option 3 in this example calls upon you to invest in company stock, that is, in a business operated by others. The value of an individual company's stock, and thus the value of your investment under this option would vary, of course, based upon the performance of the specific company stock you elected to purchase.

Historically, overall stock market returns have fluctuated greatly from year to year. In general, however, over the past 100 years, and despite its ups and downs, the U.S. stock market has rewarded investors with return on investment rates of approximately 5 to 7% above the country's then prevailing inflation rate. As a result, total stock market investment returns during the past 100 years have averaged just over 11% per year.

For purposes of this example, assume that your investment in the market yielded an 11% return. In this scenario, the value of your investment, at year end, would be computed as:

> **Initial Investment + Return on Investment = Total Investment Value**
>
> or
>
> **$1,000,000 + ($1,000,000 × 0.11) = $1,110,000**

Investment Option 4 in our example carries the greatest risk, as well as the greatest reward. If a new restaurant or hotel is successful, the investment returns can be outstanding. If the business fails, however, the investment loss may be 100%. Those who invest in their own businesses may literally stake their entire investment on their belief the business will succeed.

Which of the four investment options presented would be the best for you? The answer for you, as a wise investor, would likely be based upon a number of factors including the amount of the investment relative to all the money you have, the perceived investment risks, the perceived investment return, and even your own personality traits (high risk taker or high risk avoider).

In all cases, however, as an investor you would ultimately seek to compare the cost of making an investment today against the stream of income that the investment will generate in the future. To best make this "in the future" value comparison, it is important that you, and all investors, understand the **time value of money**, which is the concept that money has different values at different points in time.

Time Value of Money

When parents who graduated from college in the 1970s stare disbelievingly at their own children's college tuition bills, they are reacting to the fact that college tuition now costs almost three times as much as it did in the 70s (of course, entry-level wages for college graduates have also increased dramatically)! This typical example of how the passage of time truly does change people's view of the worth of a "dollar" is one key to understanding the time value of money, a concept that you already (and intuitively) understand.

To illustrate, assume that you have won $10,000 in the state lottery. Your options for collecting payment are:

- Receive $10,000 now, *or*
- Receive $10,000 in four years.

If you are like most people, you would choose to receive the $10,000 now. This is so because most people instinctively understand that it makes little sense to **defer** (delay) a cash flow into the future when they could have the exact same amount of money now. Thus, at the most basic level, the time value of money simply demonstrates that, all things being equal, it is better to have money now rather than later. From an investment perspective, those in business know you can do much more with money if you have it now because you can earn even more money through wise investments. Thus, as a general rule, "today" dollars are worth more than "tomorrow" dollars.

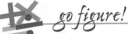 *go figure!*

To see why this is so, consider Rhonda and Ron. Both are owed $1,000. Rhonda collects the money owed to her on January 1, while Ron collects the $1,000 owed to him on December 31, of the same year.

After thoroughly evaluating her investment opportunities, Rhonda takes her money on January 1, and invests it in a company that will pay her a 10% annual rate of return. As a result, on December 31, Rhonda would have $1,100 as shown using the total investment value formula as follows:

> **Investment + Return on Investment = Total Investment Value**
>
> or
>
> **$1,000 + ($1,000 × 0.10) = $1,100**

As a result of her investment, at the end of the year, Rhonda's $1,000 is now worth $1,100, while Ron's $1,000 is, of course, still worth only $1,000.

Now, assume that Rhonda elects to re-invest her original $1,000 and all of her investment earnings. If she does so, Rhonda is poised to increase the future value of her money even further by earning investment returns over an even longer period of time. The value of the money that is invested now at a given rate of interest and grows over time is called the **future value** of money. The process of money earning interest and growing to a future value is called **compounding.**

If Rhonda maintained her investment for four years, it would grow as follows:

> Year 1 $1,000 + ($1,000 × 0.10) = $1,100
>
> Year 2 $1,100 + ($1,100 × 0.10) = $1,210
>
> Year 3 $1,210 + ($1,210 × 0.10) = $1,331
>
> Year 4 $1,331 + ($1,331 × 0.10) = $1,464

The effect of compound investment returns for Rhonda's investment is summarized in Figure 12.2.

Thus, in this example, the longer the investment is held, the more returns Rhonda receives.

FIGURE 12.2   Effect of Compound Investment Returns

Value	Year 1	Year 2	Year 3	Year 4
Beginning Value	$1,000	$1,100	$1,210	$1,331
Investment Earnings	100	110	121	133
Year End Total Investment Value	$1,100	$1,210	$1,331	$1,464

go figure!

The formula managerial accountants use to quickly compute the future value of an investment when the rate of return and length of the investment is known is as follows:

$$\text{Future Value} = \text{Investment Amount} \times (1 + \text{Investment Earnings \%})^n$$

or

$$FV_n = PV \times (1 + i)^n$$

Where FV equals the amount of the investment at the end of the investment period (future value), PV equals the present value of the investment, n equals the number of years the investment will be maintained, and i equals the interest rate percentage.

In the example of Rhonda's four-year investment, the future value formula would be computed as:

$$\$1,000 \times (1 + 0.10)^4 = \text{Future Value}$$

or

$$\$1,000 \times (1.464) = \$1,464$$

When a future value is known, then the **present value**, or the amount the future value of money is worth today, can be determined. The process of computing a present value is called **discounting**, or calculating the value of future money discounted to today's actual value. The formula managerial accountants use to quickly compute the present value of an investment when the rate of return and length of the investment is known is as follows:

$$\text{Present Value} = \frac{\text{Future Value}}{(1 + \text{Investment Earnings \%})^n}$$

or

$$PV = \frac{FV_n}{(1 + i)^n}$$

Where FV equals the amount of the investment at the end of the investment period (future value), PV equals the present value of the investment, n equals the number of years the investment will be maintained, and i equals the interest rate percentage.

In the example of Rhonda's four-year investment, the present value formula would be computed as:

$$\frac{\$1,464}{(1+0.10)^4} = \text{Present Value}$$

or

$$\frac{\$1,464}{1.464} = \$1,000$$

Put another way, Rhonda's $1,464 investment (received four years from now) would be worth $1,000 today.

Future values and present values can be calculated using the formulas stated in this chapter, time value of money tables, and/or financial calculators.

W fun on the Web!

A more in-depth explanation of the time value of money has been developed by Dr. Sharon Garrison at the University of Arizona. Time value of money tables and calculations can be found at:

www.studyfinance.com

When you arrive, click on "Time Value of Money" under "Overviews."

As you (and all savvy investors) now recognize, maximum returns on money invested (ROI) are achieved by utilizing one or both of the following investment strategies:

1. Increasing the length of time money is invested
2. Increasing the annual rate of return on the investment

The effect of these two variables on investment returns is shown graphically in Figure 12.3.

The number of years (or other defined investment period) an investment is held is, of course, very easy to establish. It is more complex, however, to fully understand the manner in which managerial accountants actually measure rates of return on investment (ROI).

FIGURE 12.3 Two Factors Affecting Return on Investment

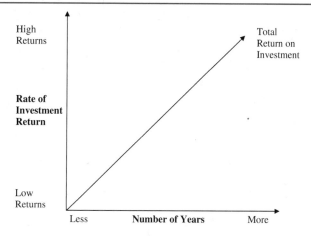

Rates of Return

Before closely examining rates of return, it is very important for those in the hospitality industry (as well as all other industries!) to understand that operating profits are not the same as return on investment.

Sometimes, a restaurant that achieves a very good profit (net income) is still not a good investment for the restaurant's owner. In other cases, a restaurant that achieves a less spectacular net income is a better investment.

 *go figure!*

For example, assume two restaurant owners have generated $200,000 in net income after a year of operating their respective restaurants. The first owner invested $2,000,000 in the operation, and the second owner invested $4,000,000.

Using the ROI formula you learned about in Chapter 3, the owners' ROIs can be calculated as follows:

$$\frac{\text{Money Earned on Funds Invested}}{\text{Funds Invested}} = \text{ROI}$$

or

First Owner:

$$\frac{\$200,000}{\$2,000,000} = 10\%$$

Second Owner:

$$\frac{\$200,000}{\$4,000,000} = 5\%$$

Actual returns on investment can vary greatly, but few, if any, investors will for a long period of time invest in a restaurant if the net income is less than what could be achieved in other investment opportunities with the same or lesser risks.

Sophisticated managerial accountants can utilize several variations of this basic ROI formula to help them make good decisions about investing their capital. For working managers interested in maximizing returns on investment, two of the most important of these formula variations are:

- Savings Rate of Return
- Payback Period

Savings Rate of Return

The **savings rate of return** is the relationship between the annual savings achieved by an investment and the initial capital invested. To illustrate this concept, consider the case of Amy Sessums. Amy is a country club manager who is contemplating the purchase of a new dish machine. To compute her estimated savings rate of return on this proposed capital expenditure, Amy must first collect some important information, which includes:

- The **book value** of the existing dish machine (the machine value as listed on the country club's balance sheet)
- The life expectancy of the current machine
- The value (if sold) of the existing machine
- The annual operating costs of the current machine

Similar information must be obtained for the new piece of equipment. Thus, Amy must determine:

- The purchase price (including installation) of the new machine
- The life expectancy of the new machine
- The value (when ultimately sold) of the new machine
- The annual operating costs of the new machine

Assume that, after investigating the situation, Amy determined the information presented in Figure 12.4.

FIGURE 12.4 Country Club Dish Machine Cost Analysis

Current Dish Machine	Proposed New Dish Machine
Book Value = $8,000	Cost is $22,000 installed
Expected machine life is 3 years	Expected machine life is 15 years
Current value (if sold) is $3,000	Value (if sold) in 15 years is $0
Annual operating costs are $41,200	Annual operating costs are $31,000, due to the machine's fewer labor hours required and increased energy efficiency

Based on the information Amy has gathered:

- The new machine costs $22,000 (installed) and the value of the old machine is $3,000.
- Thus, the new capital required to be invested in the machine would be $19,000 ($22,000 − $3,000 = $19,000).
- Amy will achieve cost savings of $10,200 per year ($41,200 to operate the old machine − $31,000 to operate the new machine = $10,200 annual savings).

She can compute her savings rate of return as follows:

$$\frac{\text{Annual Savings}}{\text{Capital Investment}} = \text{Savings Rate of Return}$$

or

$$\frac{\$10,200}{\$19,000} = 53.7\%$$

The question of whether or not Amy should consider this is a "good" or "acceptable" savings rate of return, will be based upon the capital return goals sought by the country club. In many cases, managerial accountants and/or the owners of a business will set an investment **return threshold** (minimum rate of return) that must be achieved prior to the approval of a capital expenditure. In this example, if the 53.7% return on investment exceeds the threshold established by the country club for its capital expenditures, Amy should purchase the dish machine.

Payback Period

Payback period refers to the length of time it will take to recover 100% of an amount invested. Typically, the shorter the time period required to recover all of the investment amount, the more desirable it is.

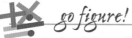

In the dish machine example cited in Figure 12.4, Amy would compute her payback period as:

$$\frac{\text{Capital Investment}}{\text{Annual Income (or Savings)}} = \text{Payback Period}$$

or

$$\frac{\$19,000}{\$10,200} = 1.86 \text{ years (approximately 1 year and 10 months)}$$

Managerial accountants often utilize the payback period formula to evaluate different investment alternatives. As was true with the savings rate of return, the question of the appropriate minimum length of payback period required to justify an investment is dependent upon the goals of the business.

Capitalization Rates

You have learned how business investors calculate their ROI when the amount earned on an investment is known. This is the case, for example, when money is invested (deposited) in a bank, which agrees to pay a predetermined annual percentage rate of return on the deposited funds. In most cases, however, business investors are not guaranteed a return on their investments. Rather, these investors must estimate the returns they will achieve prior to making their investment decisions. How then do managerial accountants and investors determine or estimate their anticipated rates of return for a specific investment? Considered a different way, the critical question is, "How do investors know when an investment will be a good one?"

Earlier in this chapter you learned that investment returns typically increase as an investment's risk level increases. Interestingly, "risk" is a relatively difficult concept to quantify in any segment of life. For example, would you consider it risky to go skydiving? Would skydiving be more or less risky than to go white water rafting on a rapidly moving river? Different individuals are likely to answer questions such as these in different ways. As you can easily see, the concept of risk and aversion to (or avoidance of) a specific risk level is a very personal one. Some businesses succeed when few believed they would, while other businesses seem poised for success and then fail. In the final analysis, all lenders or investors must be comfortable with the risk level of their investments and will want to see a realistic estimate of their return on investment (ROI) prior to investing. This is so because high levels of potential return may make an unacceptable risk level acceptable. For example, would you go skydiving just one time for $5.00? If not, would you go just one time for $50,000,000?

To fully appreciate how business investors estimate their ROIs and then consider risk levels, you must first understand capitalization rates. In the hospitality industry, **capitalization (cap) rates** are utilized to compare the price of entering a business (the investment) with the anticipated, but not guaranteed, returns from that investment (net operating income). The computation for a cap rate is:

$$\frac{\text{Net Operating Income}}{\text{Investment Amount}} = \text{Cap Rate \%}$$

This formula directly ties investment returns to:

- The size of the profits (net operating income) generated by the business
- The size of the investment in the business

Note that **net operating income (NOI)**, in general, is the income before interest and taxes you would find on a restaurant or hotel income statement (see Chapter 3). However, in many cases, the buyer will require potential sellers to calculate net operating income prior to debt service or depreciation, but inclusive of a reserve for replacement of assets, management fees, and franchise fees, with management fees and a reserve for equipment replacement each typically equal to 3 to 5% of the business's total revenue.

Investors generally do not want to pay more than the true value of any specific hospitality business or property they are considering purchasing.

 *go figure!*

To illustrate, consider the High Hills Hotel, which was offered for sale for $16,000,000. The hotel's net operating income for the past annual accounting period was $2,000,000. The cap rate % formula can be restated using the property value as the investment amount. The computation of the cap rate in this example would be:

$$\frac{\text{Net Operating Income}}{\text{Property Value}} = \text{Cap Rate \%}$$

or

$$\frac{\$2,000,000}{\$16,000,000} = 12.5\%$$

Cap rates that are *higher* tend to indicate a business is creating very favorable net operating incomes relative to the business's value (selling price). Cap rates that are *lower* indicate that the business is generating a smaller level of net operating income relative to the business's estimated value (selling price). Historically, hotel cap rates have averaged between 8 and 12%, reflecting differences in financial markets and investors' requirements when purchasing hotels. Cap rates in the restaurant industry also vary based upon the economy and the segment of the restaurant industry in which the business is located.

In general, cap rates are used to indicate the rate of return investors expect to achieve on a known level of investment. As well, by using the rules of algebra, investors can modify the formula to help them determine the value, or purchase price, of a specific hospitality business.

go figure!

Using the High Hills Hotel example, the property value estimate is calculated as follows:

$$\frac{\text{Net Operating Income}}{\text{Cap Rate \%}} = \text{Property Value Estimate}$$

or

$$\frac{\$2,000,000}{12.5\%} = \$16,000,000$$

Experienced investors and managerial accountants understand that there are two areas of common confusion when computing cap rates. The first difficult area is the definition of net operating income itself, and the second is the accounting period on which the net operating income is based. To illustrate, assume that two hotels are offered for sale at the same price and each seller states that their hotel yields a net operating income of $4,000,000. If you were considering the purchase of either hotel, it would be important for you to know exactly what expenses were and were not included in each seller's computation of net operating income. For example, were a reserve for equipment replacement, management fees, franchise fees, and depreciation deducted as expenses, or have they been included? Were GAAPs followed in reporting expenses? If not, in which areas were they not followed? The decision to include and how to include the actual expenses of the business will, of course, negatively or positively affect the overall net operating income achieved and, as a result, will directly affect the calculated cap rate.

In addition to net operating income, the accounting period analyzed will also significantly impact the cap rate computation, and as a result it is a very important factor to understand. Net operating income for a single (very good or very bad) year may or may not be a true reflection of a business's actual ability to create a consistent flow of operating income. Because this is true, it is usually best to analyze several years of net operating income when that is possible, with a particular concentration on whether net operating income is increasing, staying the same, or declining each year. The importance of doing so can be demonstrated by the data presented in Figure 12.5. It represents the financial performance of the Pickering Hotel for its first four years of operation. The owners of the Pickering now wish to **flip** (sell) the property, and they have created the advertisement in Figure 12.5.

FIGURE 12.5 "Hotel for Sale" Offering

The Pickering Hotel

Excellent, new property for sale. Only $7,000,000! Four years old and a real bargain at less than 2 times average rooms revenue! Strong average net operating income of over $650,000!

	Total Revenue	Net Operating Income	Operating Income %
This Year	$3,000,000	$480,000	16
Last Year	$3,500,000	$595,000	17
Two Years Ago	$3,750,000	$675,000	18
Three Years Ago	$4,000,000	$880,000	22
Average	**$3,562,500**	**$657,500**	**18.5**

go figure!

Utilizing the data from the seller's advertised (and technically accurate!) data, the cap rate would be computed as:

$$\frac{\text{Net Operating Income}}{\text{Property Value}} = \text{Cap Rate \%}$$

or

$$\frac{\$657,500}{\$7,000,000} = 9.39\%$$

This would be considered an acceptable risk/return for many hotel investors.

Considering only the Pickering Hotel's most recent year's performance, however, the property's cap rate would be computed as:

$$\frac{\text{Net Operating Income}}{\text{Property Value}} = \text{Cap Rate \%}$$

or

$$\frac{\$480,000}{\$7,000,000} = 6.86\%$$

This is a rate that few investors would find attractive, especially given the declining net operating income levels now achieved by this property! The importance of careful evaluation of net operating income and accounting period used is clear in this example.

While cap rates are a very critical element in understanding how an investment has performed in the past or will perform in the future, it is also important to very carefully interpret the two major business variables used to calculate them. This is so because, even for real estate experts, it has always been difficult to determine the true "value" of a business.

For example, assume a hotel is in a good location and is in good physical condition, but is poorly managed and thus does not generate an appropriate net operating income level. Should the selling price of such a hotel be based on its current net operating income or the profitability that it might achieve with better management? If you were the seller of the hotel, you would certainly take the position that the hotel has great **upside potential** (possible increased future value). That is, the property is more valuable than it first appears because, with proper management, its value would surely increase. As a potential investor (buyer), however, you would likely seek to purchase the hotel at the lowest possible price, and thus would take the position that improved management may indeed improve the hotel, but no guarantee exists that it would do so. Thus, significant price negotiation between buyer and seller is a common part of virtually every hospitality property sales transaction. While current profitability is often one important factor in establishing the value of a hotel, other factors assessed by investors include annual revenues achieved, physical condition and location of the property, and the quality and experience of management and staff.

In an effort to reduce risk, hospitality industry investors are careful to pay a fair price for the business they will own or operate. Traditionally, hospitality business values have been established through the use of one or more of the following evaluation methods.

Replacement approach. This approach assumes that a buyer would not be willing to pay more for a business than the amount required to build (replace) it with a similar business in a similar location. For example, if a buyer could build a restaurant for $275 per square foot of space, that buyer would be unlikely to pay the owner of an existing restaurant more than that amount. While this approach is useful for many new construction projects, it is less useful, for example, when attempting to estimate the value of a restaurant when no replacement restaurant has recently been (or even could have been) built in the area. This is often the case, for example, in high population density, high building density areas such as downtowns in metropolitan areas and interstate highway exits.

Revenue approach. This approach views a hospitality business primarily as a producer of revenue. Thus, a business's value is established as a multiple of its annual revenue. Using the logic of this approach, the more revenue produced, the more valuable the business. To illustrate, a hotel in good condition will generally sell for between 2 and 4 times its most recent annual rooms revenue. A hotel with rooms revenue of $5,000,000 per year would be valued at between $10,000,000 (2 times its annual revenues) and $20,000,000 (4 times its annual revenues), depending on other conditions affecting the hotel. Hotel owners often use this approach when quickly computing the estimated selling price of their properties and when developing advertisements offering businesses for sale.

Capitalization approach. As you have learned, the capitalization (cap rate) approach is the one most often used to establish a hospitality business's value. Essentially, as you have seen, this system seeks to develop a mathematical relationship (cap rate) between a business's projected net operating income and its market value. This approach, while often the most complex to employ, is also the most widely used.

W fun on the Web!

For those managers interested in better understanding hospitality investments (and especially hotel investments), the fourth edition of *Hotel Investments: Issues and Perspectives*, edited by Lori Raleigh and Rachel Roginsky, is truly outstanding. If you want to seriously investigate hospitality business ownership and investment issues, it is certainly worth reading! This book can be found at:

www.barnesandnoble.com

When you arrive, enter *Hotel Investments: Issues and Perspectives* in the search line to view a copy of this book.

Financing Alternatives

Most investors, of course, seek to maximize the returns on their investments. In the majority of cases, it is only after investors determine what it should actually cost them to secure an investment that they must determine the best way to finance the investment. For investors, **financing** simply refers to the method of securing (funding) the money needed to invest.

To illustrate the process, assume you are shopping for a new car. Your first task is to find the vehicle that suits your purpose offered for sale at a price you believe is reasonable. After you have done so, you would then determine the best manner in which to finance it. Theoretically, financing alternatives for your car purchase could range from paying cash for the full purchase price (100% equity financing) to borrowing the full purchase price (100% debt financing) and then agreeing to make regular payments to repay your loan. You could, in some cases, even elect to lease rather than purchase the car.

Because investments are typically financed with debt and/or equity funds, the precise manner in which financing is secured will have a major impact on the return on investment investors ultimately achieve. For a business, the decision to lease rather than purchase a capital asset greatly affects ROI as well as, in some cases, the taxes paid by the business. In this section of the chapter, you will learn about the impact of debt/equity financing decisions, as well as the impact of alternative lease/purchase decisions on ROI.

Debt versus Equity Financing

Investors seeking to fund their projects choose between debt and equity financing. With **debt financing,** the investor borrows money and must pay it back with interest within a certain timeframe. With **equity financing**, investors raise money by selling a portion of ownership in the company. If investors use their own money for equity financing, they are, in effect, selling the ownership in the business to themselves.

Common suppliers of debt financing include banks, finance companies, credit unions, credit card companies, and private corporations. Loans, for example, are a type of debt financing. Depending upon the creditworthiness of the investor, getting a business loan may be faster than searching out other investors. In fact, an advantage of debt financing is that, as investors pay down their loans, they also build creditworthiness. This makes them even more attractive to lenders and increases their chances of negotiating favorable loan terms in the future.

Equity financing typically means taking on investors and being accountable to them. Many small business investors secure equity funds from relatives, friends, colleagues, or customers who hope to see their businesses succeed and get a return on their investment. Other sources of equity financing can include venture capitalists, individuals with substantial net worth, corporations, and financial institutions. In many cases, equity investors do not expect an immediate return on investment during the first phase of a business enterprise. Rather, they count on the business being profitable in the near future (three to seven years). Equity investors can be passive or active. **Passive investors** are willing to give capital but will play little or no part in running the company, while **active investors** expect to be heavily involved in the company's operations.

It is critically important to understand that, regardless of whether an investor funds an investment with their own equity, with equity from passive investors, or with equity from active investors, an ROI on equity funds is achieved only *after* those who have supplied debt funding have earned their own ROIs. Stated another way, equity ROIs are subordinate to debt ROIs. Despite the fact that equity investors make returns on their investments only after debt repayments have been made, equity financing is not free. Equity investors typically are entitled to a share of the business's profits as long as they hold, or maintain, their investments.

The amount of ROI generated by an investment is greatly affected by the ratio of debt to equity financing in that investment. The debt to equity ratio in an investment will also directly affect the willingness of lenders to supply investment capital.

go figure!

To illustrate both of these concepts, consider the case of Paige Vincent, the general manager of the Blue Lagoon Water Park Resort. After a few successful years at the Blue Lagoon, Paige proposes to develop her own water park in which she would be the major investor.

The total project is estimated to cost $27,000,000.
The net operating income that the investment is estimated to achieve is $5,145,123 per year.

Assume Paige has the $27,000,000 needed to build the park. As you have learned earlier, if Paige invested all $27,000,000 of her own money, her ROI would be computed as follows:

$$\frac{\text{Money Earned on Funds Invested}}{\text{Funds Invested}} = \text{ROI}$$

or

$$\frac{\$5,145,123}{\$27,000,000} = 19\%$$

While many investors would consider 19% an excellent ROI, Paige desires more. In order to achieve this, Paige secures debt financing (one or more loans) at an annual percentage rate of 8%. Figure 12.6 illustrates the effect on her equity ROI of funding her investment with varying levels of debt and equity.

Essentially, it is true that for any investment, the greater the financial leverage (see Chapter 6) or funding supplied by debt, the greater the ROI achieved by the investor. As you can see from the data in Figure 12.6, if Paige elects to fund 50% (rather than 100%) of her project's cost with equity and 50% with debt, the ROI she would achieve is 30.1%, an ROI much higher than the 19% she could achieve if she did not leverage her investment at all. With even greater leverage (for example, 80% debt financing and 20% equity financing), Paige achieves even greater investment returns (63.3% ROI) on her equity investment.

Given the data presented in Figure 12.6, investors may ask, "Why not fund nearly 100% of every investment using debt?" The answer to this question lies in the column titled Debt Coverage Ratio. This is the same ratio as the Times Interest Earned ratio that you learned about in Chapter 6.

FIGURE 12.6 Effect of Debt on Equity Returns

Financing		Project Cost	Payment or Return	%	Net Operating Income	Debt Coverage Ratio
		27,000,000			5,145,123	
Debt	50%	−13,500,000	Interest Payment	8.0%	−1,080,000	4.8
Equity	50%	13,500,000	ROI	30.1%	4,065,123	
		27,000,000			5,145,123	
Debt	60%	−16,200,000	Interest Payment	8.0%	−1,296,000	4.0
Equity	40%	10,800,000	ROI	35.6%	3,849,123	
		27,000,000			5,145,123	
Debt	70%	−18,900,000	Interest Payment	8.0%	−1,512,000	3.4
Equity	30%	8,100,000	ROI	44.9%	3,633,123	
		27,000,000			5,145,123	
Debt	80%	−21,600,000	Interest Payment	8.0%	−1,728,000	3.0
Equity	20%	5,400,000	ROI	63.3%	3,417,123	

go figure!

The debt coverage ratio can be calculated for 50% debt and 50% equity financing from Figure 12.6 as follows:

$$\frac{\text{Net Operating Income}}{\text{Interest Payment}} = \text{Debt Coverage Ratio}$$

or

$$\frac{\$5,145,123}{\$1,080,000} = 4.8$$

Recall that an investment's debt funding entities must be repaid prior to those entities supplying equity funding. The **debt coverage ratio** then, is a measure of how likely the business is to actually have the funds necessary for loan repayment. Note in Figure 12.6, that as debt financing of the project increases, the debt coverage ratio declines from 4.8 (with 50% debt funding) to 3.0 (with 80% debt funding). Just as investors will maintain minimum ROI thresholds prior to considering an investment to be a "good" one, lenders will analyze debt coverage ratios and their own thresholds to determine the risk they are willing to assume when lending to an investor's project.

It is also important to recall that, as any investor's risk increases, the returns expected from that investment are expected to increase also. As a result, those who seek debt funding, but whose projects show lower than desirable debt coverage ratios will most often find that the only money lent to their project will come at a higher cost. The result, of course, is that the interest rates lenders will charge on loans they supply will be increased, and payback times may also be reduced. Because many lending institutions consider businesses in the hospitality industry to be high risk, some will provide debt financing for no more than 50 to 70% of a project's total cost. This creates a **loan to value (LTV) ratio**, a ratio of the outstanding debt on a property to the market value of that property, of 50 to 70%, while expecting the project's owner/investor(s) to secure the balance of the project's cost in equity funding.

Lease versus Buy Decisions

Leasing, (an agreement to **lease**) allows a business to control and use land, buildings, or equipment without buying them. Just as a business's decision to vary the debt/equity ratio funding of a project will directly affect its investors' ROI, so too will ROI be affected by a business entity's decision to lease rather than purchase capital assets. Leasing can provide distinct advantages for the **lessor** (the entity which owns the leased property) as well as for the **lessee** (the entity that leases the asset). In a lease arrangement, lessors gain immediate income while still maintaining ownership of their property. Lessees enjoy limited property

FIGURE 12.7   Select Legal Considerations of Buying versus Leasing Property

1. Right to Use the Property

Owner	Lessee
Property use is unlimited in any legal manner owner sees fit.	Property use is strictly limited to the terms of the lease.

2. Treatment of Cost

Owner	Lessee
Property is depreciable in accordance with federal and state income tax law.	Lease payments are deductible as a business expense, according to federal and state tax laws.

3. Ability to Finance

Owner	Lessee
The property can be used as collateral to secure a loan.	The property may not generally be used to secure a loan.

4. Termination

Owner	Lessee
Ownership passes to estate holders.	The right to possess the property concludes with the termination of the lease contract.

5. Non-Payment of Lease

Owner	Lessee
Owner retains the down payment and/or forecloses on the property.	Owner retains deposit and/or owner may evict lessee. For personal property, the owner may reclaim the leased item.

rights, distinct financial and tax advantages, as well as the right, in many cases, to buy the property at an agreed upon price at the end of the lease's term.

From a legal perspective, as well as a financial perspective, buying an asset is much different than leasing it. Figure 12.7 details some significant differences between the rights of property owners (lessors) and the lessee's of that same property.

Despite the significant differences in the legal treatment of owned versus leased property, in most cases, the decision to lease rather than purchase property is typically a financial rather than legal one. The most significant financial difference between buying and leasing is that payments for *owned* property are not listed as a business expense on the monthly income statement. Rather, the value of the asset is depreciated over a period of time appropriate for that specific asset. Payments for most (but not all) *leased* property, however, are considered an operating expense and thus are listed on the income statement. The financial and tax consequences of leasing assets rather than buying them are significant and, as a result, those managers considering such decisions should consult with their organization's tax advisors.

FIGURE 12.8 Advantages of Leasing

---

1. **Low Cost Tax Advantages.** One of the most popular reasons for leasing is its low cost. A lease can offer low cost financing because the lessor takes advantage of tax benefits that are passed to the lessee. If the lessee cannot currently use tax depreciation to offset taxable income due to current operating losses, depreciation benefits may be lost forever if the lessee purchases rather than leases.

2. **On or Off Balance Sheet Options.** In some cases, a lease can be structured to qualify as an operating lease, the expense for which is properly reported on the income statement, thus increasing the business's flexibility in financial reporting and directly affecting important financial ratios such as the operating profit percentage.

3. **Improved Return on Investment.** Many companies place a heavy emphasis on ROI for evaluating profitability and performance. Operating leases often have a positive effect on ROI because leasing typically requires less initial capital to secure an asset than does purchasing.

4. **100% Financing.** In many cases, leasing may allow the entire cost of securing an asset to be financed, while a typical purchase loan requires an initial down payment. Most costs incurred in acquiring equipment can be financed by the lease. These costs include delivery charges, interest charges on advance payments, sales or use taxes, and installation costs. Such costs are not usually financed under alternative methods of equipment financing.

5. **Budget Expansion.** The acquisition of equipment not included in a capital expenditure budget can sometimes be accomplished through use of a lease, with lease payments being classified as monthly operating expenses.

6. **Joint Ventures.** Leasing can be ideal for joint venture partnerships in which tax benefits are not available to one or more of the joint venture partners. This may be because of the way in which the partnership was structured, or because of the tax situation of one or more of the joint venture partners. In such cases, the lessor may utilize the tax benefits, which would otherwise be lost, and pass those benefits to the joint venture in the form of lower lease payments.

7. **Improved Cash Flow.** Lease payments may provide the lessee with improved cash flow compared to loan payments. As well, the overall cash flow on a present value basis is often more attractive in a lease.

Leasing capital equipment has become increasingly popular for a variety of reasons including advantages listed in Figure 12.8.

Despite their varied advantages, leases can have distinct disadvantages in some cases. These may include:

- Non-ownership of the leased item or property at the end of the lease.
- In situations where few lease options exist, the cost of leasing may ultimately be higher than the cost of buying.
- Changing technology may make leased equipment obsolete but the lease term is unexpired.
- Significant penalties may be incurred if the lessee seeks to terminate the lease before its original expiration date.

Perhaps the most significant decision to be made prior to obtaining a lease on a capital asset such as equipment is simply that of ultimate ownership. That is, does the organization seeking the lease want to ultimately own the leased item? If so, a purchase of the asset may be a better option. However, even if the organization does seek to own the item, a lease may be desirable because, in some cases, leases may lead to a purchase. To illustrate, consider the case of Elizabeth Pastera. Elizabeth is opening her own restaurant. She has saved her money and secured additional investors to raise the capital she needs, however, it will take all of the capital she has acquired to complete her dream and open the doors of her business. She has all of the equipment she needs *except* ice machines. She needs two, and these can be purchased for a total of $14,000, which she does not have! Alternatively, they can be leased for $300 per month on a 60 month lease. At the end of the lease's term, the lessor has agreed to sell the machines to Elizabeth for $1.00 each. In this scenario, because of a capital shortage and because her lease payments are ultimately helping her "buy" the ice machines, Elizabeth may well want to consider the lease arrangement. The $1.00 buy-out at the end of a lease's term is common with leased equipment, as is a buy-out based upon the leased item's fair market value (see Chapter 4) at the point in time at which a lease ends.

fun on the Web!

The decision of whether to invest capital by purchasing or leasing land, a building, or a piece of equipment can be complex. The final decision will most often be affected by a variety of factors. Some of these include the purchase price of the item, the credit-worthiness of the lessee, the length of the lease, and the treatment of the asset at the end of the lease period.

Managerial accountants considering the relative advantages and disadvantages of buying versus leasing a business asset should, of course, consult with their organization's tax advisor. However, it is easy to estimate the monthly amount it would cost to secure an asset via leasing by using a formula that calculates lease payments. Lease calculators are readily available online. To view one such calculator, go to:

www.ilslease.com/calculator.html

When you arrive, try out the "Lease Calculator."

The affect on an organization's balance sheet, income statement, and statement of cash flows of leasing capital assets can be significant and must be considered carefully. Sometimes, however, the decision to lease or not to lease equipment or space is a very simple one. For example, if a hotel operator wants to replace the air filters located in the ceiling of an atrium-style lobby four times a year, it makes little sense to purchase the mechanical lifts necessary to do the job. These pieces of equipment can be leased for a day and the task can be inexpensively completed. Also, if a restaurant operator seeks to develop a restaurant in a prime location in a mall's food court, that operator will likely have no option other than leasing. That is, the mall is not likely to sell the restaurateur the space needed to operate, but rather the operator will be required, if he or she really wants it, to lease the space.

Taxation

Benjamin Franklin once wrote, "But in this world nothing can be said to be certain, except death and taxes." This may be so, but managerial accountants who fully understand the very complex tax laws under which their businesses operate can help ensure that the taxes these businesses pay are exactly the amount owed by the business, and no more. This is important because when the correct amount of tax is paid, ROIs will be maximized and not wrongfully reduced. As you learned in Chapter 1, accounting for taxes is so complex in the United States (as well as many other parts of the world) that tax accounting is one of the five specialized branches of accounting.

Income Taxes

Taxing entities such as the federal, state, and local governments generally assess taxes to businesses based upon their own definitions of taxable income. It is important to understand that income taxes are not voluntary. Most U.S. citizens believe that every business should pay 100% of the taxes it legally owes. Most businesspersons would strongly agree. They would also agree, however, that no business should be required to pay *more* taxes than it actually owes. It is the job of the tax accountant to ensure that the businesses they advise do not overpay.

When a business computes the taxes it must pay, it is important to recognize the difference between tax avoidance and tax evasion. **Tax avoidance** is simply planning business transactions in such a way as to minimize or eliminate taxes owed. **Tax evasion**, on the other hand, is the act of reporting inaccurate financial information or concealing financial information in order to evade taxes by illegal means. Tax avoidance is legal and ethical, while tax evasion is not.

Taxable income is generally defined as gross income adjusted for various deductions allowable by law. However, there are regulations that must be followed in computing taxes, and it is important to understand that a company's taxable income will vary based upon a variety of factors, including a specific taxing authority's unique definition of taxable income. Because this is so, "true" taxable income can best be viewed as a legal concept, rather than an accounting concept. It is important for you to realize also that tax laws almost always are written to provide incentives to encourage companies to do certain things and discourage them from doing others. Accordingly, what is considered "income" to a tax agency may be far different from the accountant's measures of this same concept. Regardless of the taxing entity or its own goals, however, it is the purpose of professional tax accounting techniques and practices to ensure that businesses properly fulfill their legitimate tax obligations.

In Chapter 2 you learned about different types of business structures used to form businesses in the United States. In fact, one of the first questions asked by a **tax accountant**, a professional who assists businesses in paying their taxes using standard accounting practices and current tax laws, is that of organizational structure. This is so because different business structures are taxed differently. By far, the most popular form of business entity is the

FIGURE 12.9 Federal Corporate Income Tax Rates

Taxable Income Over	But Not Over	Tax rate
$0	50,000	15%
50,000	75,000	25%
75,000	100,000	34%
100,000	335,000	39%
335,000	10,000,000	34%
10,000,000	15,000,000	35%
15,000,000	18,333,333	38%
18,333,333+		35%

S corporation. There are about 3.3 million active S corporations in the United States, most of which are small businesses like restaurants and smaller hotels, usually with just one or two families as owners. Those who choose the S corporation typically make the decision to do so because it provides limited liability, fairly simple tax filings, possible tax advantages at the state level, and some ability to reduce Federal Insurance Contributions Act (FICA) taxation. Another popular form of business entity is the partnership. There are 2.5 million businesses in the United States taxed as partnerships. There are also about 2.1 million regular, or C corporations in the United States. The income tax rates (at the time of this book's publication) for C corporations are shown in Figure 12.9.

When most hospitality business owners and their tax accountants examine their taxes, the first tax to be considered is the income tax. It is important to understand that all business's net income is taxed at the federal level, but it most often also is taxed at the state and even local levels. Clearly, tax accountants at all levels do, and should, understand tax laws well to ensure that those they represent pay the proper tax amounts.

Capital Gains Taxes

Capital gains taxes are second only to income tax in the attention they receive from most hospitality business owners and their accountants. A **capital gain** is the surplus that results from the sale of an asset over its original purchase price adjusted for depreciation. A **capital loss** occurs when the price of the asset sold is less than the original purchase price adjusted for depreciation. Capital gains and losses occur with the sale of real assets, such as property, as well as financial assets, such as stocks and bonds. The federal government (and some states) imposes a tax on gains from the sale of assets. **Realized capital gains** occur when the actual sale of the asset is completed.

go figure!

To illustrate, assume that Joshua Richards, the owner of Joshua's Restaurant located across from the Blue Lagoon Water Park Resort, sells one of his fryers for $6,000.

The original purchase price of the fryer was $7,000 and it has depreciated by $2,000, resulting in the **asset's basis** (the purchase price minus depreciation) of $5,000.

Thus, Joshua realized a capital gain of $1,000 ($6,000 − $5,000 = $1,000) and would be taxed accordingly.

If, however, Joshua had sold the fryer for $4,000 instead of $6,000, he would incur a capital loss of $1,000 ($4,000 − $5,000 = −$1,000).

He could then use the capital loss to offset any capital gains he realized during the accounting period.

The manner in which the federal tax code treats capital gains income is in some ways more favorable than the way it treats income from other sources. For example, because of inflation, the difference between the sales price of an asset and its basis usually *overstates* the income that the asset holder earns. Because of the time value of money you learned about earlier, deferring payment of capital gains taxes is a powerful advantage. Also, capital gains taxes due on assets held for a long period of time (usually defined as longer than one year) are taxed at rates lower than those imposed on regular income.

Property Taxes

In addition to income and capital gains taxes, most hospitality businesses will be responsible for paying property taxes on the property owned by their businesses. These taxes are typically assessed by state and/or local entities (not federal) and may include a variety of assessments and credits. These assessments are determined through a **real estate appraisal**, which is an opinion of the value of a property, usually its market value, performed by a licensed appraiser. **Market value** is the price at which an asset would trade in a competitive setting. Figure 12.10 is a hypothetical example of a typical property tax bill for the Waxahachie Hotel, a business with total property valued at $1,000,000.

FIGURE 12.10   Sample Property Tax Bill for the Waxahachie Hotel

$1,000,000.00	Appraised Value of Property
× 0.40	Assessment Ratio (Assessed Value for Tax Purposes)
$400,000.00	Total Taxable Assessment
× 0.003483	Combined State Taxes Rate
$1,393.20	Total State Property Tax Due
+1,790.00	County Tax Due
+1,710.00	City Tax Due
−1,360.00	State Property Tax Relief (Reduction)
$3,533.20	Total Tax Due
+$890.00	Solid Waste Recycling and Disposal Fee
$4,423.20	Total Taxes and Fees Due

Property taxes vary widely by state as they are directly affected by the taxing strategy in place by each state legislature. As a result, property taxes in some states can be very low, while in others they can be very high. In some states, property taxes are paid annually, in others they may be paid semi-annually or quarterly. In all cases, those in the hospitality industry should be concerned, as is true with all taxes, in paying their fairly assessed amount, but no more than their fairly assessed amount. In many cases, legitimate initiated appeals of initial property tax assessments can result in substantial tax savings to a hospitality business.

Other Hospitality Industry Taxes

In addition to income taxes, capital gains taxes, and property taxes that apply to all businesses, hospitality managers and their tax accountants are responsible for reporting and paying a variety of hospitality industry taxes. Three of the most important of these taxes include:

Sales Tax In most cases, **sales taxes** are collected from guests by hospitality businesses for taxes assessed on the sale of food, beverages, rooms, and other hospitality services. Typically, the funds collected are then transferred (forwarded) to the appropriate taxing authority on a monthly or quarterly basis. While these collected taxes are in the possession of the business, the business is held strictly responsible for their safeguarding. Penalties for collecting but not ultimately forwarding these taxes to the appropriate taxing authority are significant, and a failure to forward them in a timely manner can even constitute a crime.

Occupancy (Bed) Tax As you learned in Chapter 1, occupancy (bed) taxes are a special assessment collected from guests and paid to a local taxing authority based upon the amount of revenue a hotel achieves when selling its guest rooms. This tax is typically due and payable each month for the room revenue the hotel achieved in the prior month. Failure to properly collect and pay this tax may subject the business to significant fines as well as criminal indictment.

Tipped Employee Tax. **Tipped employee taxes** are assessed on tips and gratuities given to employees by guests or the business as taxable income for those employees. As such, this income must be reported to the IRS, and taxes, if due, must be paid on that income. Despite a good deal of controversy within the hospitality industry about tipped employee taxes, employers are responsible for assisting the IRS in this reporting process by collecting tip reporting information and supplying it, when required, to the IRS.

Modified Accelerated Cost Recovery System

As you may recall from Chapter 2, depreciation is a method of allocating the cost of a fixed asset over the useful life of the asset. In Chapter 3, you learned that depreciation expense serves a very specific purpose. Depreciation is subtracted on the income statement primarily to lower income, thus lower taxes. The portion of assets depreciated each year is

FIGURE 12.11 MACRS Property Classes Table as Applied to Hospitality Businesses

Property Class	All Property Except Real Estate
3-Year Property	Special handling devices for food and beverage manufacture
5-Year Property	Computers and peripherals; automobiles
7-Year Property	All other property not assigned to another class including furniture, fixtures, and equipment

considered "tax deductible" because it is subtracted on the income statement before taxes are calculated.

The **Modified Accelerated Cost Recovery System (MACRS)** is the depreciation method required for equipment in the hospitality industry (and all industries). This depreciation method originated under the Economic Recovery Tax Act of 1981 with the development of the Accelerated Cost Recovery System (ACRS). The ACRS was replaced by the MACRS in the Tax Reform Act of 1986 and is still required today. MACRS was designed to accelerate depreciation in the first years of depreciating an asset in order to reduce the amount of taxes paid in those years. The legislation itself was designed to help start-up businesses reduce taxes in the first years of business when they may be struggling with generating profits and cash flows. Depreciation for real estate, however, follows **straight-line depreciation**, which is the cost of the asset divided evenly over the life of the asset.

MACRS establishes shorter recovery periods than in straight-line depreciation. Also, calculations are based on property class lives and an estimated **salvage value** (the estimated value of an asset at the end of its useful life) of zero. Property class lives as they are applied to hospitality businesses are shown in Figure 12.11.

Depreciation using MACRS is calculated using stated percentages for varying property classes as shown in Figure 12.12. You may notice that the number of **recovery years** (years of depreciation for the asset) include one more year than the years of the property class. Specifically, MACRS allows businesses to depreciate a 3-year property class for 4 years, a 5-year property class for 6 years, and a 7-year property class for 8 years. This is because of the half-year convention. The **half-year convention** allows for one-half of a year's depreciation

FIGURE 12.12 MACRS Percentages for Property Classes

Recovery Year	3-Year Property %	5-Year Property %	7-Year Property %
1	33.33	20.00	14.29
2	44.45	32.00	24.49
3	14.81	19.20	17.49
4	7.41	11.52	12.49
5		11.52	8.93
6		5.76	8.92
7			8.93
8			4.46

to be taken in the year of purchase and one-half in the year following the end of the class life. In effect, this allows for one more year of depreciation to occur.

To determine depreciation using MACRS, an asset is first classified in its appropriate property class life, for example, a 5-year property class for a computer. Then, each recovery year of the property class life is used to identify the appropriate percentage to be multiplied by the cost of the asset to calculate depreciation. For example, the first recovery year depreciation of a 5-year property class for a $1,000 computer would be $200 ($1,000 × 20% = $200).

If an asset has a known salvage value, then the salvage value would be subtracted from the original cost of the asset before depreciation is calculated.

 *go figure!*

To illustrate, consider again Joshua Richards, the owner of Joshua's Restaurant located across the street from the Blue Lagoon Water Park Resort. Assume that he wants to depreciate a fryer that he just purchased for $7,000.

Using a 7-year property class life from Figure 12.11 and the 7-year property MACRS percentages in Figure 12.12, Joshua can calculate his annual depreciation for the fryer by multiplying the cost of the fryer, $7,000, by the percentages for 7 recovery years to fully depreciate his fryer.

For example, Joshua's depreciation in recovery year 1 would be $1,000.30 ($7,000 × 14.29% = $1,000.30).

Joshua's calculations for all 7 years of depreciation are as follows:

Recovery Year	7-Year Property %	Depreciation $
1	14.29	$1,000.30
2	24.49	1,714.30
3	17.49	1,224.30
4	12.49	874.30
5	8.93	625.10
6	8.92	624.40
7	8.93	625.10
8	4.46	312.20
Total	100.00	$7,000.00

With literally thousands of federal, state, and local agencies, departments, offices, and individuals charged with setting or enforcing tax policy, it is simply not possible for a typical hospitality manager to be completely knowledgeable about all the tax requirements that could significantly affect their operations. It is for that reason that tax specialists are so important. While it is not reasonable for most hospitality managers to become tax experts, it is possible for them to:

1. Be aware of the major entities responsible for tax collection and enforcement.
2. Be aware of the specific tax deadlines for which they are responsible.
3. Stay abreast, to the greatest degree possible, of changes in tax laws that may directly affect their business.

The Internal Revenue Service (IRS) is the taxing authority with which hospitality managers are likely most familiar. The IRS is a division of the United States Department of Treasury. The stated mission of the IRS is to, "Provide America's taxpayers top quality service by helping them understand and meet their tax responsibilities and by applying the tax law with integrity and fairness to all." While it is unlikely that the agency responsible for collecting taxes will be popular in any country, the ability of the IRS to charge an individual with a criminal act makes it an agency that deserves a manager's thoughtful attention.

In the hospitality industry, managers interact with the IRS because of the manager's roles as both a taxpayer by paying income tax on the profits of a business and a tax collector by withholding individual employee taxes on income. Among other things, the IRS requires businesses to:

- File quarterly income tax returns and make payments on the profits earned from business operations.
- File an Income and Tax Statement with the Social Security Administration.
- Withhold income taxes from the wages of all employees and deposit these with the IRS at regular intervals.
- Report all employee income earned as tips and withhold taxes on the tipped income.
- Record the value of meals charged to employees when the meals are considered a portion of an employee's income.
- Furnish a record of withheld taxes to all employees on or before January 31 of each year (Form W-2).

As most managers are aware, the IRS ensures that businesses pay their taxes through periodic examinations and audits of the business's financial accounts and tax records. States and local governments also have, in many cases, the ability to monitor business records to ensure tax payments. Tax laws, like the people who make them, will change constantly. It is the role of hospitality managers to, among many other important tasks, stay abreast of significant changes in these laws and follow them to the letter.

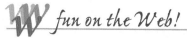

It is important for hospitality managers to fully understand their responsibilities in reporting tipped income of employees. To learn more about this important tax-reporting role go to:

www.irs.ustreas.gov

When you arrive, click on the following links in this order: Businesses, Employment Taxes, Forms and Publications, Publication Number, Publication 15 Circular E Employers Tax Guide. Then, read the section that refers to Tips.

It is the hope of the authors of this book that you use the managerial accounting information we have presented to better manage your business and thus contribute positively to the advancement of your industry, your family, and your own career.

Good Luck!

"I don't know, Bharath," said Arun Poddar, Bharath's close friend and business partner. "It looks risky to me."

Bharath Chaturvedi had just proposed that Arun go into business with him by purchasing the Carlton Hotel. The 400-room property was for sale and Bharath thought it would be a great investment. Bharath was an experienced hotel manager and would manage the hotel. His friend Arun had a financial net worth high enough that he certainly could, if he chose to do so, personally fund the purchase of the hotel.

"The owners only want $5,000,000 for the property. With just a few minor changes and better management," said Bharath, "I could easily get the net operating income (NOI) up to $700,000 per year. That's twice what it was last year!"

1. Based on the information provided by Bharath, compute the capitalization rate based on last year's NOI for the hotel. Next, compute the capitalization rate for the hotel assuming that Bharath is correct and that he can make the changes necessary to achieve his target NOI. What is your assessment of each cap rate?

2. Assuming you were Arun, what additional information would you want to see from the hotel's current owners before you would seriously consider making the investment suggested by Bharath?

3. Consider that Arun, if he decided to buy the property, could elect to fund the property himself or arrange with his bank for 50% debt financing. What factors would you advise him to assess before he decided which of these two funding options would best help him meet his own investment goals?

Key Terms and Concepts

The following are terms and concepts discussed in the chapter that are important for you to know as a manager. To help you review, please define the following terms.

Capital	Payback period	Tax accountant
Capitalist	Capitalization (cap) rates	Capital gain
Capitalism	Net operating income (NOI)	Capital loss
Capital expenditures	Flip	Realized capital gains
Capital budgeting	Upside potential	Asset's basis
Venture	Financing	Real estate appraisal
Venture capitalist	Debt financing	Market value
Risk	Equity financing	Sales taxes
Reward	Passive investors	Tipped employee taxes
Time value of money	Active investors	Modified Accelerated Cost
Defer	Debt coverage ratio	Recovery System
Future value	Loan to value (LTV) ratio	(MACRS)
Compounding	Lease	Straight-line depreciation
Present value	Lessor	Salvage value
Discounting	Lessee	Recovery years
Savings rate of return	Tax avoidance	Half-year convention
Book value	Tax evasion	
Return threshold	Taxable income	

Test Your Skills

Complete the Test Your Skills exercises by placing your answers in the shaded boxes

1. Scott Thatcher is the owner of the 50 Yard Line Lounge. He believes his business is good, and from what he reads, his profit margins are reasonable. But Scott wants to know more about the financial performance of his business.

   Help Scott complete and analyze the following income statement prepared at the end of last year, as well as the additional information provided, and then answer the questions Scott is pondering.

50 YARD LINE LOUNGE

Income Statement

For the Year Ended December 31, 2010

SALES:	
Food	102,556
Beverage	699,505
Total Sales	
COST OF SALES:	
Food	26,510
Beverage	151,000
Total Cost of Sales	
GROSS PROFIT:	
Food	76,046
Beverage	548,505
Total Gross Profit	
OPERATING EXPENSES:	
Salaries and Wages	161,500
Employee Benefits	3,500
Direct Operating Expenses	61,500
Music and Entertainment	7,624
Marketing	18,250
Utility Services	26,100
Repairs and Maintenance	5,325
Administrative and General	108,100
Occupancy	24,500
Depreciation	5,650
Total Operating Expenses	
Operating Income	
Interest	84,889
Income Before Income Taxes	
Income Taxes	47,000
Net Income	

a. What was Scott's before-tax income?

b. What was Scott's after-tax net income?

c. Assume Scott's investment in the Lounge was $750,000. Calculate Scott's before-tax ROI.

Money Earned on Funds Invested	
Funds Invested	
ROI	

d. Assume again Scott's investment in the Lounge was $750,000. Calculate his after-tax ROI.

Money Earned on Funds Invested	
Funds Invested	
ROI	

e. What before-tax income would Scott need to return a before-tax ROI of 17% on his invested funds of $750,000?

Money Earned on Funds Invested	
Funds Invested	
ROI	

2. Michele Austin knows that cap rates are a good way to estimate the value of a lodging property. She is considering the purchase of three different properties. The financial information she has about them is presented below. Using that information, help Michele calculate the answers needed to make a good purchase.

Property	Last Year Sales	Last Year Net Operating Income (NOI)
LaSalle Inn	$1,541,250	$373,450
The Breakers Lodge	$3,117,500	$623,750
The Waterford	$2,700,000	$541,200

a. If Michelle paid $3,000,000 for it, what would be the cap rate for the LaSalle Inn, based upon the NOI it achieved last year?

Net Operating Income	
Investment Amount	
Cap Rate %	

b. If Michelle paid $7,000,000 for it, what would be the cap rate for the Breakers Lodge, based upon the NOI it achieved last year?

Net Operating Income	
Investment Amount	
Cap Rate %	

c. If Michelle paid $6,000,000 for it, what would be the cap rate for the Waterford, based upon the NOI it achieved last year?

Net Operating Income	
Investment Amount	
Cap Rate %	

d. If Michele is satisfied with a hotel purchase returning a 10.5% cap rate:

At what price would she value the LaSalle Inn?

Net Operating Income	
Investment Amount	
Cap Rate %	

At what price would she value the Breakers Lodge?

Net Operating Income	
Investment Amount	
Cap Rate %	

At what price would she value the Waterford?

Net Operating Income	
Investment Amount	
Cap Rate %	

e. Based upon Michele's acceptable cap rate of 10.5%, which hotel do you think likely represents Michele's best investment option? Explain the reason for your answer.

3. Peggy Richards is considering purchasing the vacant lot adjacent to her current restaurant location. Peggy is convinced that by purchasing and paving it to make a parking lot, the additional net operating income (NOI) she would earn is $61,500 per year. The total project is estimated to cost $250,000. Peggy can borrow money at 8% interest. If she finances the purchase with 100% equity, she will earn a 24.6% return on her funds (if her projections are correct). Peggy thinks she can do better. Help her calculate the various returns on her money she could achieve with different debt/equity purchase strategies, then answer the questions she has about her project.

Financing		Project Cost	Payment or Return	%	Net Operating Income	Debt Coverage Ratio
		250,000			61,500	
Debt	50%		Interest Payment	8.00%		
Equity	50%		ROI			
		250,000			61,500	
Debt	60%		Interest Payment	8.00%		
Equity	40%		ROI			
		250,000			61,500	
Debt	70%		Interest Payment	8.00%		
Equity	30%		ROI			
		250,000			61,500	
Debt	80%		Interest Payment	8.00%		
Equity	20%		ROI			
Total	100%	250,000	ROI	24.60%	61,500	

a. What would be Peggy's rate of return on her own investment if she borrowed 50% of the money required for the lot's purchase and paving?
What would be her debt coverage ratio?

b. What would be Peggy's rate of return on her own investment if she borrowed 60% of the money required for the lot's purchase and paving?
What would be her debt coverage ratio?

c. What would be Peggy's rate of return on her own investment if she borrowed 70% of the money required for the lot's purchase and paving?
What would be her debt coverage ratio?

d. What would be Peggy's rate of return on her own investment if she borrowed 80% of the money required for the lot's purchase and paving?
What would be her debt coverage ratio?

e. List two potential disadvantages (to Peggy) of employing a highly leveraged strategy when making this purchase.

4. Jodi Jackson is the general manager of a student-operated public restaurant in a hospitality management program at a large state university. She used her old dish machine for as long as she could, but it is finally beyond repair! So, she has purchased a new dish machine for $21,400 that she will fully depreciate with no salvage value (according to state laws). According to the MACRS property class table, the dish machine has a 7-year class life.

Help Jodi complete her depreciation schedule for the dish machine using MACRS deprecation.

Recovery Year	7-Year Property %	Depreciation on Dish Machine
1	14.29%	
2	24.49%	
3	17.49%	
4	12.49%	
5	8.93%	
6	8.92%	
7	8.93%	
8	4.46%	
Total	100.00%	

a. Since the dish machine has a 7-year class life, why is it depreciated 8 years?

b. Why are the depreciation percentages more during the first 4 years than the last 4 years?

c. If Jodi was going to sell the dish machine for a salvage value instead of depreciating it fully, how would this change her depreciation calculations?

d. If Jodi sold the dish machine before it was fully depreciated for less than her purchase price, would this represent a capital gain or a capital loss? How would this affect her taxes?

Glossary

A

Account A record of increases or decreases in the assets, liabilities, or owners' equity of a business.

Accountant A person skilled in the recording and reporting of financial transactions.

Account balance The difference between a T account's total debits and total credits.

Account format A balance sheet format that lists the assets of a company on the left side of the report and the liabilities and owners' equity accounts on the right side of the report.

Accounting The process of recording financial transactions, summarizing them, and then accurately reporting them.

Accounting period The amount of time included in any summary of financial information.

Accounts payable The amount of money owed by the business to others, such as suppliers.

Accounts receivable The amount of money owed to a business by others, such as customers.

Accounts receivable aging report A report used by management to monitor the average length of time money owed to the business has remained uncollected.

Accrual accounting A system in which revenue is recorded when it is earned, regardless of when it is collected, and expenses are recorded when they are incurred, regardless of when they are paid.

Accumulated depreciation A record and accumulation of all depreciation expense charges that occur over the life of an asset.

Achievement budget A short-range budget consisting of a month, a week, or a day.

Acid-test ratio See *Quick ratio.*

Active investor Investor who expects to be heavily involved in the company's operations.

Activity-based costing A process that assigns each employee's time to different activities performed and then determines the cost spent on each activity as a percentage of each worker's time and pay.

Activity-based management Using activity-based costing to examine expenses.

Activity ratios Group of ratios that shows management's ability to effectively utilize the company's assets.

ADR See *Average daily rate.*

Amortized Systematically reduced in value.

Annual budget A budget prepared yearly.

Appreciation Increase in property value.

Assets   Those items owned by the business.

Asset's basis   The purchase price of an asset minus accumulated depreciation.

Audit   An independent verification of the financial records of a business.

Auditor   The individual or group of individuals that completes an independent verification of the financial records of a business.

Average cost per room   See *Cost per key*.

Average daily rate (ADR)   The price, on average, for which a hotel sells its rooms.

Average sales per guest   The average amount of money spent per customer during a given accounting period.

B

Balance sheet   An accounting summary that closely examines the financial condition, or health, of a business by reporting the value of a company's total assets, liabilities, and owners' equity on a specified date.

Baseline data   Known data used to predict trend lines.

Beginning inventory   The dollar value of all products on hand at the beginning of an accounting period.

Beverage cost percentage   The portion of beverage sales that was spent on beverage expenses.

Beverage inventory turnover   Ratio that shows the speed (number of times) that beverage inventory is replaced during a year.

Bookkeeper   Person who performs the task of initially recording financial transactions of a business.

Book value   The value of the existing piece of equipment as it is listed on the balance sheet.

Bottom line   Slang used to describe net income or profit and refers to the bottom line of the income statement.

Breakeven point   The point that operational expenses are exactly equal to sales revenue.

Buddy punching   The method by which an employee uses another's time card to punch that second employee in or out.

Budget   Financial plan.

Business dining   Food is provided as a service to the company's employees either as a no-cost (to the employee) benefit or at a greatly reduced price.

C

Calendar year   Twelve consecutive months beginning in January and ending in December.

Call accounting system   A system that generates hotel telephone toll charges based upon time of day, call length, call distance, and use or non-use of international service providers.

Call-around   A pricing method in which night auditors make decisions about their own room rates by asking other hotels' night auditors about their room rates.

Capital   A term used for money.

Capital budget   A budget used to plan for capital expenditures.

Capital budgeting   The management process of evaluating one or more capital expenditures.

Capital expenditure   The expense associated with the purchase of land, property and equipment, and other fixed assets that are recorded on the balance sheet.

Capital gain   The surplus that results from the sale of an asset over its original purchase price adjusted for depreciation.

Capitalism   An economic system that allows for the private ownership of property.

Capitalist   A person who invests money.

Capitalization (cap) rate   The rate utilized to compare the price of entering a business (the investment) with the anticipated, but not guaranteed, returns from that investment (net operating income).

Capital loss   The loss that results when the price of an asset sold is less than the original purchase price adjusted for depreciation.

Cap rate   See *Capitalization rate*.

Cash   The money held in cash banks, checking or savings accounts, electronic fund transfers from payment card companies, and certificates of deposit.

Cash accounting   A system that records revenue as being earned when it is actually received and expenditures when they are actually paid, regardless of when they were incurred.

Cash budget   A budget developed to estimate the actual impact on cash balances that will result from a business's operating activities, investing activities, and financing activities.

Cash budgeting   The general term used by managerial accountants to identify a variety of cash monitoring and management activities.

Cash equivalents   Short-term, temporary investments such as treasury bills, certificates of deposit, or commercial paper that can be quickly and easily converted to cash.

Cash flow   The concept of total cash receipts (cash in) and cash disbursements (cash out) which occurs in a business in a specific accounting period.

Cash flow from financing activities   The result of all the transactions and events involving buying or selling company stocks, payment of dividends, and borrowing and repayment of short- and long-term debt.

Cash flow from investing activities   The result of all the transactions and events involving the purchase and sale of marketable securities, investments, land, buildings, equipment, and other assets not generally purchased for resale.

Cash flow from operating activities   The result of all of the transactions and events that usually make up a business's day-to-day activities.

Cash receipts/disbursements approach to cash budgeting   A budgeting approach that sums the anticipated cash receipts and subtracts the anticipated cash payments during a specific accounting period to forecast cash excesses or cash shortages.

C corporation   See *Corporation*.

CD   See *Certificate of deposit*.

Central reservation system (CRS)   System used by companies to centrally book reservations.

CEO   See *Chief Executive Officer*.

Certificate of deposit (CD)   Financial instrument with a fixed term and interest rate and is considered cash because of its liquidity.

Certified Management Accountant (CMA) An individual recognized and certified as a highly competent professional who assists businesses by integrating accounting information into the business decision process.

Certified Public Accountant (CPA) An individual recognized and certified as highly competent and professional in one or more of the branches of accounting.

CFO See *Chief Financial Officer*.

Check average See *Average sales per guest*.

Chief Executive Officer (CEO) The highest-ranking officer in charge of the overall management of a company.

Chief Financial Officer (CFO) Corporate officer responsible for managing the financial operations of a company.

Classification Placement of expenses on the income statement.

Closed out The process of reducing temporary accounts (revenue and expense) to zero.

Closing inventory See *Ending inventory*.

CMA See *Certified Management Accountant*.

Collusion The secret cooperation of two or more employees to commit fraud.

Common-size analysis See *Vertical analysis*.

Common stock The balance sheet entry that represents the number of shares of stock issued (owned) multiplied by the value of each share.

Comp See *Complimentary*.

Comparative analysis See *Horizontal analysis*.

Competitive pricing A pricing method used to charge what the competition charges.

Competitive set (comp set) Group of hotels with whom a specific hotel competes and to which it compares its own operating performance.

Complimentary (comp) Term for a room that is provided free of charge.

Compounding The process of money earning interest and growing to a future value.

Comp set See *Competitive set*.

Condensed income statement A statement that reports the revenues, expenses, and profits in a summary format, absent of specific departmental and undistributed expense details.

Conservatism principle Requires the accountants of a business to be conservative when reporting its revenue (and thus not to report it until it is actually earned) and realistic when reporting its expenses and other liabilities.

Consistency principle A business must select and consistently report financial information under the rules of the specific system it elects to use.

Consolidated income statement A statement that combines the revenue, expense, and profit information from each individual sub-statement of a company.

Contra asset Represents deductions to a fixed asset and behaves *opposite* of all other asset accounts with regard to debits and credits.

Contribution margin The dollar amount, after subtracting variable costs from total sales, that contributes to covering fixed costs and providing for a profit.

Contribution margin income statement An income statement that shows items in terms of sales, variable costs, contribution margin, fixed costs, and profit.

Controllable cost   A cost over which a manager has primary control.

Controller   The person responsible for managing a hotel's accounting processes.

Corporate rate   The negotiated special rate offered by hotels for corporate guests.

Corporation (C corporation)   A legal entity that is separate and distinct from its owners and is allowed to own assets, can incur its own liabilities, and can sell shares of ownership.

Cost   Time or resources expended by the business. Also referred to as *expense*.

Cost accounting   The branch of accounting that is concerned with the classification, recording, and reporting of business expenses.

Cost allocation   A system used by management to assign portions of overhead costs among various profit centers.

Cost center   A unit that generates costs but no revenue or profits.

Cost of beverage sold (cost of sales: beverage)   The dollar amount of all beverage expenses incurred during an accounting period.

Cost of food consumed   The actual dollar value of all food used, or consumed, by an operation.

Cost of food sold (cost of sales: food)   The dollar amount of all food expenses incurred during an accounting period.

Cost of goods consumed   A general term for the cost of any products consumed by an operation.

Cost of goods sold   A general term for the cost of any products sold.

Cost of sales: beverage   See *Cost of beverage sold*.

Cost of sales: food   See *Cost of food sold*.

Cost per key   The average purchase price of a hotel's guest room calculated by dividing the purchase price of a hotel by the number of hotel rooms.

Cost per occupied room (CPOR)   Ratio that compares specific costs in relation to number of occupied rooms.

Cost principle   Requires accountants to record all business transactions at their cash cost.

Cost/volume/profit (CVP) analysis   The approach that predicts the sales dollars and volume required to achieve a breakeven point or desired profit based on known costs.

Covers   Term for number of guests in a food service establishment.

CPA   See *Certified Public Accountant*.

CPOR   See *Cost per occupied room*.

Credit   The right side of a T account.

Credit entry   A journal entry made on the right side of a T account.

Creditor   A company to whom a business owes money, such as a vendor.

Creditworthiness   The ability to pay bills promptly.

CRS   See *Central reservation system*.

Current asset   An asset which may reasonably be expected to be sold or turned into cash within one year (or one operating season).

Current dollar accounting   Accounting for inflation.

Current liabilities   Those obligations of a business that will be repaid within a year.

Current ratio   Ratio that shows the firm's ability to cover its current liabilities with its current assets.

CVP   See *Cost/volume/profit analysis*.

Cyclical trend   A data pattern that tends to be longer than a period of one year and might occur due to a product's life cycle.

D

Debit   The left side of a T account.

Debit entry   A journal entry made on the left side of a T account.

Debt   Funds lent to a business.

Debt coverage ratio   A measure of how likely a business is to have the funds necessary for loan repayment.

Debt financing   Funding an investment by borrowing money and paying it back with interest within a certain timeframe.

Debt to assets ratio   Ratio that compares total liabilities to total assets.

Debt to equity ratio   Ratio that compares total liabilities to owners' equity.

Default   Nonpayment of a loan.

Defer   To delay.

Deflation   The tendency for prices and costs to decrease.

Demand forecast   A prediction of periods in which demand will be generally high or low based on expected fluctuations in occupancy.

Departmental cost   An expense that is attributable to one department.

Depreciation   A method of allocating the cost of a fixed asset over the useful life of the asset.

Direct cost   A cost that can be directly attributed to a specific area or profit center within a business.

Direct operating expense   See *Departmental cost*.

Discounting   The process of computing a present value or calculating the value of future money discounted to today's actual value.

Discount pricing   A pricing method used to reduce rates below that of likely competitors.

Distinct business entity principle   The principle states that a business's financial transactions should be kept completely separate from those of its owners.

Dividend   Money paid out of net income to stockholders as a return on their investment in the company's stocks.

Dividend payout ratio   Ratio that shows the percentage of net income that is to be paid out in dividends.

Dividend yield ratio   Ratio that shows stockholders' return on investment paid in dividends.

Double entry accounting   Procedure requiring that a financial transaction has at least two separate accounting entries (changes to its accounts) every time a financial transaction modifies The Accounting Formula of a business.

Doubtful accounts   The amount of money that may not be collectable from receivables.

E

Early departure   A guest who checks out of the hotel before his or her originally scheduled check-out date.

Earnings before interest and taxes (EBIT)   The net operating income on the USALI.

Earnings per share (EPS)   Ratio that compares net income to common shares.

EBIT   See *Earnings before interest and taxes.*

Efficiency ratios   See *Turnover ratios.*

EFT   See *Electronic funds transfer.*

Electronic funds transfer (EFT)   Money that is paid or moved electronically from the business to the entity to which money is owed.

Embezzlement   Employee theft.

Employee meals   Employee benefit that is classified as a labor-related, not food-related, expense.

Ending inventory   The dollar value of all products on hand at the end of an accounting period.

EPS   See *Earnings per share.*

Equity   Funds supplied by its investors or owners.

Equity financing   Funding an investment by selling a portion of ownership in the company.

Ethics   The choices of proper conduct made by an individual in his or her relationships with others.

Expense   The cost of the items required to operate the business.

Expense classification   The process of carefully considering how a business's expenses will be detailed for reporting purposes.

External auditor   Individual or firm who is hired specifically to give an independent (external) assessment of a company's compliance with standardized accounting practices.

F

Fade rate   A reduced room rate authorized for use when a guest seeking a reservation is hesitant to make the reservation because the price is perceived as too high.

Fair market value   The price at which an item would change hands between a buyer and a seller without any compulsion to buy or sell, and with both having reasonable knowledge of the relevant facts.

FASB   See *Financial Accounting Standards Board.*

Favorable variance   The difference between planned and actual results that are an improvement on the budget (revenues are higher or expenses are lower).

Financial accounting   The branch of accounting that is concerned with recording, summarizing, and reporting financial transactions.

Financial Accounting Standards Board (FASB)   A private body whose mission is to establish and improve standards of financial accounting and reporting for the guidance and education of the public, including issuers, auditors, and users of financial information. The FASB publishes its recommendations known as generally accepted accounting principles.

Financial leverage   The use of debt to be reinvested to generate a higher return on investment than the cost of debt (interest).

Financing   The method of securing (funding) the money needed to invest.

Fiscal year   Twelve consecutive months not necessarily beginning in January and ending in December like a calendar year.

Fixed asset   An asset which management intends to keep for a period longer than one year including the property, building(s), and equipment owned by a business.

Fixed asset turnover ratio   See *Property and equipment turnover ratio.*

Fixed cost   A cost that remains constant despite increases or decreases in sales volume.

Flexible budget   A budget that incorporates the assumptions of the original budget, such as fixed costs and target variable costs per unit or variable cost percentages, and then projects these costs based on varying levels of sales volume.

Flip   A term meaning to sell.

Flow-through   A measure of the ability of a hotel to convert increased revenue dollars to increased gross operating profit dollars.

Folio   Individual bill for a hotel guest or room.

Follow the leader pricing   A pricing method used to charge what the dominant hotel in the area charges.

Food available for sale   The sum of the beginning inventory plus the value of all food purchases during an accounting period.

Food cost percentage   The portion of food sales that is spent on food expenses.

Food inventory turnover   Ratio that shows the speed (number of times) that food inventory is replaced during a year.

Fraud   The intentional use of dishonest methods to take property.

Free cash flow   The amount of cash a business generates from its operating activities *minus* the amount of cash it must spend on its investment activities and capital expenditures.

Full disclosure principle   Requires that any past or even future event which could materially affect the financial standing of the business and that cannot be easily discerned from reading the business's financial statements must be separately reported usually in the form of footnotes.

Future value   The value of money that is invested now at a given rate of interest and grows over time.

G

GAAP   See *Generally accepted accounting principles.*

GDS   See *Global distribution system.*

General ledger   A record of the up-to-date balances of all a business's individual asset, liability, and owners' equity, (as well as revenue and expense) accounts.

Generally accepted accounting principles (GAAP)   Standards used to develop financial statements that provide consistency and accuracy in reporting financial information.

Global distribution system (GDS)   System that books and sells rooms for multiple companies.

Goal value analysis   A menu pricing and analysis system that compares goals of the food service operation to performance of individual menu items.

Going concern principle   Assumption that the business will be ongoing (continue to exist) indefinitely and that there is no intention to liquidate all of the assets of the business.

Goodwill   The difference between the purchase price of an item and its fair market value.

GOPPAR   See *Gross operating profit per available room.*

Government rate   The negotiated special rate offered by hotels for government guests.

Gross operating profit margin   Ratio that shows management's ability to generate sales, control expenses, and provide a gross operating profit.

Gross operating profit per available room (GOPPAR)   A hotel's total revenue minus its management's controllable expenses per available room.

Gross profit section of the USAR   The first section of the USAR consisting of food and beverage sales, costs, and gross profits that can and should be controlled by the manager on a daily basis.

Group rate   The negotiated special rate offered by hotels for guests in a group.

H

Half-year convention   A MACRS depreciation method principle that allows for one-half of a year's depreciation to be taken in the year of purchase and one-half in the year following the end of the class life.

HFTP   See *Hospitality Financial and Technology Professionals*.

Horizon   Budget length into the future.

Horizontal analysis   An analytical approach used to evaluate the dollars or percentage change in revenues, expenses, and profits experienced by a business.

Hospitality   The friendly and charitable reception and entertainment of guests or strangers. Also refers to a specific segment of the travel and tourism industry.

Hospitality accounting   A very specialized area that focuses on those accounting techniques and practices used in restaurants, hotels, clubs, and other hospitality businesses.

Hospitality Financial and Technology Professionals (HFTP)   An organization that offers its own certifications and global network for hospitality professionals working in the accounting and technology areas.

Hotelier   Manager or owner of a hotel.

Hot spot   A Wi-Fi area that allows for high-speed wireless Internet access.

Hubbart formula   A bottom-up pricing formula used to determine what a hotel's average daily rate should be to reach the hotel owner(s)' financial goals.

I

Income statement   A report that details for a very specific time period, a business's revenue from all its revenue producing sources, the expenses required to generate those revenues, and the resulting profits or losses (net income).

Incremental cost   The increased cost of each additional unit.

Indirect cost   A cost that is not easily assigned to a specific operating unit or department.

Inflation   The tendency for prices and costs to increase.

In-line   A phrase used to describe being within reasonable limits or in compliance with the budget.

Intellectual capital assets   The resources of a company such as brand name, potential for growth, and intellectual or human capital when assessing a company's true worth.

Interest   The return on investment to a lender for funds lent (debt).

Interfaced   Electronically connected.

Internal auditor   An individual who is directly employed by a company to examine that company's own accounting procedures.

Internet travel site   Website for booking travel to end users.

Inventory   The value of the food, beverages, and supplies used by a restaurant, as well as sheets, towels, and in-room replacement items used by a hotel.

Inventory turnover   Ratio that shows the number of times the total value of inventory has been purchased and replaced in an accounting period.

Investment   An asset that is intended to be retained for a period of time longer than one year such as a security (stock or bond), asset owned by a business but not currently used by it, and a special fund such as a sinking fund.

Investor ratios   Group of ratios that shows the performance of earnings and stocks of a company.

Invoice   A bill from a vendor detailing the purchases made by a business.
Invoice credit. Refund on a bill.

Item contribution margin   The amount that remains after the food cost of a menu item is subtracted from that item's selling price.

Item gross profit margin   See *Item contribution margin.*

J

Joint cost   A cost that should be allocated to two (or more) departments or profit centers.

Journal   The written record of a specific business's financial transactions.

Journal entry   Record made to a specific account when changes to the Accounting Formula are documented.

L

Labor cost percentage   The portion of total sales that is spent on labor expenses.

Lease   An agreement that allows a business to control and use land, buildings, or equipment without buying them.

Lessee   The entity that leases an asset.

Lessor   The entity which owns a leased property.

Liabilities   The amount of money the business owes to others.

Lien   The legal right to hold another's property to satisfy a debt.

Limited Liability Corporation (LLC)   A special form of a corporation that limits the potential losses incurred by its owners only to what they have invested in the business and is typically regulated by the state in which the company is formed.

Limited Partnership (LP)   A business entity in which one or more general partners manage the business and are liable for its debts and one or more limited partners invest in the business but have limited personal liability for its debts.

Line item   Expense.

Liquidate   Sell assets of a business.

Liquidity   The ease with which current assets can be converted to cash in a short period of time (less than 12 months).

Liquidity ratios   Group of ratios that assesses how readily current assets could be converted to cash, as well as how much current liabilities those current assets could pay.

LLC   See *Limited Liability Corporation*.

Loan to value (LTV) ratio   A ratio of the outstanding debt on a property to the market value of that property.

Long-range budget   A budget prepared for a period of up to five years.

Long-term liabilities   Those obligations of a business that will not be completely paid within the current year.

Loss leader   A menu item that is priced very low, sometimes even below cost, for the purpose of drawing large numbers of guests to the operation.

Low-balling   The act of intentionally underestimating.

LP   See *Limited Partnership*.

LTV   See *Loan to value ratio*.

M

MACRS   See *Modified Accelerated Cost Recovery System*.

Managerial accounting   The system of recording and analyzing transactions for the purpose of making management decisions.

Margin of safety   The amount that shows how close a projected amount of sales will be to breakeven, and thus, how close an operation will be to incurring a loss.

Marketable security   An investment such as a stock or bond that can readily be bought or sold and thus is easily converted to cash.

Market value   The price at which an asset would trade in a competitive setting.

Matching principle   Closely matches expenses incurred to the actual revenue those expenses helped generate.

Materiality principle   If an item is deemed to be not significant (material), then other accounting principles may be ignored if it is not practical to use them.

Matrix analysis   A method used to make comparisons among menu items which places them into categories based on their unique characteristics such as food cost percentage, popularity, and contribution margin.

Menu engineering   A method in which the operator seeks to produce a menu that maximizes the menu's overall contribution margin.

Minimum operating cost   The total of food cost percentage plus variable cost percentage found in the denominator of the calculation for minimum sales point.

Minimum sales point (MSP)   The dollar sales volume required to justify staying open for a given period of time.

Mixed cost   A cost that contains a mixture of both fixed and variable cost characteristics.

Modified Accelerated Cost Recovery System (MACRS)   The depreciation method required for equipment which accelerates depreciation in the first years of depreciating an asset in order to reduce the amount of taxes paid in those years.

Monetary unit principle   To be understandable, financial statements must be prepared in an identifiable monetary unit (specific currency denomination).

MSP   See *Minimum sales point*.

N

Net ADR yield The percentage of average daily rate actually received by a hotel after subtracting the cost of fees and assessments associated with the room's sale.

Net changes in cash A representation of all cash inflows minus cash outflows from operating, investing, and financing activities.

Net operating income (NOI) The income before interest and taxes found on a restaurant or hotel income statement.

Net receivables Money owed by customers to a business calculated after subtracting any amounts that may not be collectable.

NOI See *Net operating income.*

Noncash transaction Nonmonetary exchange of the value of an investing or financing activity.

Non-controllable cost A cost which a manager cannot control in the short-term.

Noncurrent (fixed) asset See *Fixed asset.*

Nonoperating expenses section of the USALI The last section of the USALI, which is least controllable by the manager and includes items such as interest and taxes.

Nonoperating expenses section of the USAR The last section of the USAR, which is least controllable by the food service manager and includes items such as interest and taxes.

Non-room revenue Revenue generated by a hotel that is not specifically room sales.

No-show A guest who has a guaranteed reservation and neither cancels the reservation nor shows up at the hotel on their expected date of arrival.

No-show charge Fee assessed to guests when they have a guaranteed reservation and neither cancel the reservation nor show up at the hotel on their expected date of arrival.

O

Objectivity principle Financial transactions must have a confirmable (objective) basis in fact, and there must be a way to verify that a financial transaction actually occurred before it can be recorded in the business's financial records.

Occupancy percentage Ratio that shows the percentage of rooms sold in relation to rooms available for sale.

Occupancy tax The money paid to a local taxing authority based upon the amount of revenue a hotel achieves when selling its guest rooms.

On-change rooms Rooms that are vacant but not yet cleaned.

On-the-books The term hoteliers use to describe current data in reference to guest reservations.

OOO See *Out of order.*

Opening inventory See *Beginning inventory.*

Operated department income section of the USALI The first section of the USALI consisting of separate profit centers, which generate departmental income.

Operate in the black Slang term used to describe a business that is profitable.

Operate in the red Slang term used to describe a business that is not making a profit (losing money).

Operating cash flows to current liabilities ratio   Ratio that shows the firm's ability to cover its current liabilities with its operating cash flows.

Operating cash flows to total liabilities ratio   Ratio that shows the firm's ability to cover its total liabilities with its operating cash flows.

Operating efficiency ratio   See *Gross operating profit margin*.

Operating expenses section of the USAR   The second section of the USAR, which contains operating expenses controllable by the manager on a weekly or monthly basis (with the exception of wages, which can be controlled daily).

Operations budget   A budget concerned with planning for the revenues, expenses, and profits associated with operating a business.

Opportunity cost   The cost of foregoing the next best alternative when making a decision.

Other assets   Assets that are intended to be retained for a period of time longer than one year including items that are mostly intangible.

Out of order (OOO)   Term for a room that is not sellable because repairs, renovation, or construction is being done.

Over   Having more money than anticipated in the cashier's bank.

Overhead cost   See *Indirect cost*.

Overstay   A guest who checks out of the hotel after his or her originally scheduled check-out date.

Owners' equity   The residual claims owners have on their assets, or the amount left over in a business after subtracting its liabilities from its assets.

P

Package   A specially packaged collection of goods and services.

Package rate   A room rate charged by a hotel that combines the room rate with the prices of other hotel services or local area attractions.

Paid in capital   The portion of the balance sheet that reports any differences between the selling price and par value of stock.

Partnership   A business entity where two or more individuals agree to share ownership.

Par value   The value of stock recorded in the company's books.

Passive investor   Investor who is willing to give capital but will play little or no part in running the company.

Payback period   The length of time it will take to recover 100% of an amount invested.

Payroll allocation   The non-wage costs associated with, or allocated to, payroll.

Payroll tax   The money that a business must pay to taxing authorities on individuals employed by the business.

PE ratio   See *Price/earnings ratio*.

Percentage   A relationship between two numbers in which the numerator (top number) is divided by the denominator (bottom number).

Percentage variance   Percentage change in revenues, expenses, and profits from one time period to the next.

Permanent owners' equity accounts   These accounts include stock (or owner's investment) and retained earnings.

PMS   See *Property management system.*

Point of sales (POS) system   A computer system used for tracking sales data.

POS   See *Point of sales system.*

Preferred stock   Stock that provides a fixed dividend to stockholders.

Prepaid expense   Item that will be used within a year's time, but which must be completely paid for at the time of purchase.

Present value   The amount a future value of money is worth today.

Prestige pricing   A pricing method used to charge the highest rate in the area and justify it with better product and/or service levels.

Price/earnings (PE) ratio   Ratio that shows the perception of the firm in the market about future earnings growth of the company.

Price/value relationship   A reflection of guests' view of how much value they are receiving for the price they are paying.

Principal   The amount borrowed on a loan.

Profit   The dollars that remain after all expenses have been paid.

Profitability ratios   Group of ratios that measures how effectively management has generated profits for a company's owners.

Profit center   An area in a business that generates revenues, expenses, and profits.

Profit margin   The percentage of net income to revenues.

Property and equipment   Assets that are intended to be retained for a period of time longer than one year such as land, buildings, furnishings, and equipment.

Property and equipment (fixed asset) turnover ratio   Ratio that shows management's ability to effectively use net property and equipment to generate revenues.

Property management system (PMS)   A computer system used to manage guest bookings, online reservations, check-in/check-out, and guest purchases of amenities offered by a hotel.

Proprietorship   A business owned by a single individual.

Purchases   The sum costs of all products purchased during an accounting period.

Purchasing power   Amount of goods and services that can be bought.

Q

Quick ratio   Ratio that shows the firm's ability to cover its current liabilities with its *most liquid* current assets.

R

Rack rate   The price at which a hotel sells its rooms when no discounts of any kind are offered to the guests.

Random variation   A data variation that appears to occur on a totally unpredictable basis.

Real estate appraisal   An opinion of the value of a property, usually its market value, performed by a licensed appraiser.

Realized capital gain   The surplus that results from the sale of an asset over its original purchase price adjusted for depreciation when the actual sale of an asset is completed.

Reconcile   Compare and match accounting transactions.

Recovery years   Years of depreciation for an asset when using the MACRS depreciation method.

Regression analysis   An analysis that estimates an activity (dependent variable) based on other known activities (independent variables).

Report format   A balance sheet format that lists the assets of a company and the liabilities and owners' equity accounts (vertically), and presents the totals in such a manner as to prove to the reader that assets equal liabilities plus owners equity.

Reservation distribution channels   Sources of reservations.

Responsibility accounting   An approach to analyzing accounting information in which individual department managers are held responsible for their own efforts and results.

Restaurateur   Manager or owner of a restaurant.

Retained earnings   Accumulated account of profits over the life of the business that have not been distributed as dividends.

Return on assets (ROA)   Ratio that shows the firm's ability to use total assets to generate net income.

Return on equity (ROE)   Ratio that shows the firm's ability to use owners' equity to generate net income.

Return on investment (ROI)   A ratio of the money made compared to the money invested.

Returns   The original investment and profits paid back to owners.

Return threshold   The minimum rate of return that must be achieved on an investment.

Revenue   The term used to indicate the dollars taken in by the business in a defined period of time. Often referred to as sales.

Revenue management   A set of techniques and procedures that use hotel-specific data to manipulate occupancy, average daily rate, or both for the purpose of maximizing the revenue yield achieved by a hotel.

Revenue manager   Individual responsible for making decisions regarding the pricing and selling of guest rooms in order to maximize yield.

Revenue per available customer (RevPAC)   A measure of performance that identifies the amount of revenue generated by each customer.

Revenue per available room (RevPAR)   A measure of performance that combines occupancy percentage and average daily rate.

RevPAC   See *Revenue per available customer*.

RevPAR   See *Revenue per available room*.

Reward   The likelihood that an investment will increase in value.

Risk   The likelihood that an investment will decline in value.

ROA   See *Return on assets*.

Robbery   Theft using force.

ROE   See *Return on equity*.

ROI   See *Return on investment*.

Room mix   The variety of room types in a hotel.

Room rate economics   Economic tenet that states when the supply of hotel rooms is held constant, an increase in demand for those rooms will result in an increase in their selling price. Conversely, a decrease in demand leads to a decreased selling price.

Room types Rooms that usually sell at different nightly rates and may include standard sized rooms, upgraded rooms such as parlor or whirlpool suites, connecting rooms, or very large suites.

S

Sales forecast A prediction of the number of guests served and the revenues generated in a given future time period.

Sales history A systematic recording of all sales achieved during a predetermined time period.

Sales mix The frequency with which specific menu items are selected by guests.

Sales tax The money that a business must collect from customers and pay to taxing authorities as a result of realizing taxable sales.

Salvage value The estimated value of an asset at the end of its useful life.

Sarbanes-Oxley Act (SOX) Technically known as the Public Company Accounting Reform and Investor Protection Act, the law provides criminal penalties for those found to have committed accounting fraud.

Savings rate of return The relationship between the annual savings achieved by an investment and the initial capital invested.

SCF See *Statement of cash flows*.

Schedule A tool used by managerial accountants to provide statement readers with more in-depth information about important areas of revenues and expenses.

Seasonal rate A room rate that is higher or lower than the standard rack rate and that is offered during a hotel's highest volume season.

Seasonal trend A data pattern change due to seasonal fluctuations.

Seat turnover The number of times seats change from the current diner to the next diner in a given accounting period.

Security A stock or a bond.

Service charge A mandatory addition to a guest's food and beverage bill.

Short Having less money than anticipated in the cashier's bank.

Significant variance A difference in dollars or percentage between budgeted and actual operating results that warrants further investigation.

Simple average The value arrived at by adding the quantities in a series and dividing that sum by the number of items in the series.

Sinking fund Money that is reserved and invested for use in the future.

SMERF Social, Military, Education, Religious, and Fraternal segments used to classify guests and the revenues they generate.

Smith Travel Research (STR) A company that collects and distributes summaries of hotel financial and operational data related to historical performance and prepares industry averages and other hotel statistics that are readily available through companies.

Solvency The ability of a business to pay its debts as they become due.

Solvency ratio (as a single ratio) Ratio that shows the comparison of a business's total assets to its total liabilities.

Solvency ratios (as a group of ratios)   Group of ratios that assesses the firm's ability to cover its total liabilities with its total assets.

Solvent   The state of a business when its assets are greater than its liabilities.

Sources and uses of funds   Inflows and outflows of money affecting the cash position.

SOX   See *Sarbanes-Oxley Act*.

Special event rate   The room rate used when a hotel is assured of very high demand levels due to special holidays or events.

Stakeholders   Individuals or companies directly affected by a business's profitability including owners, investors, lenders, creditors, and managers.

Standard cost   The cost that should be incurred given a specific level of volume.

Star Reports   Statistical reports compiled by Smith Travel Research.

Statement of cash flows (SCF)   A statement that shows all sources and uses of funds from operating, investing, and financing activities of a business.

Statement of changes in financial position   A statement that intends to indicate how cash inflows and outflows affect the business during a specific accounting period.

Statement of retained earnings   A statement that reports the changes in the accumulated account of profits over the life of the business that have not been distributed as dividends from last year to this year.

Stayover   A guest that is not scheduled to check out of the hotel on the day his or her room status is assessed.

Step cost   A cost that increases as a range of activity increases or as a capacity limit is reached.

Stockholder   Owner who holds shares of stocks in a company.

STR   See *Smith Travel Research*.

Straight-line depreciation   A depreciation method in which the cost of the asset is divided evenly over the life of the asset.

Sub-S corporation   The distinctive type of corporation that is granted special status under U.S. tax laws which are very specific about how and when this type corporation can be formed and the number of stockholders it can have.

Sunk cost   A cost that has already been incurred and whose amount cannot now be altered.

Supplementary schedules   Additional information on the statement of cash flows that reports noncash investing and financing activities and cash paid for interest and income taxes.

Supply and demand   The economic law that states that, for most products purchased by consumers, as the price of an item increases, the number of those items sold will generally decrease. Conversely, as the price of an item decreases, the number of those items sold will generally increase.

𝒯

T account   Individual account shaped like a "T" used in a double entry accounting system.

Target turnover ratio   Ratio that shows the desired turnover rate for inventory.

Tax   A charge levied by a governmental unit on income, consumption, wealth, or other basis.

Taxable income   Gross income adjusted for various deductions allowable by law.

Tax accountant   A professional who assists businesses in paying their taxes using standard accounting practices and current tax laws.

Tax accounting   The branch of accounting that is concerned with the proper and timely filing of tax payments, forms, or other required documents with the governmental units that assess taxes.

Tax avoidance   The act of planning business transactions in such a way as to minimize or eliminate taxes owed.

Tax evasion   The act of reporting inaccurate financial information or concealing financial information in order to avoid taxes by illegal means.

Temporary owners' equity accounts   These accounts include revenue and expense accounts which can increase owners' equity (revenue accounts) or decrease owners' equity (expense accounts).

Terms   Conditions of a loan.

The $1.00 per $1,000 rule   A pricing formula that uses a rule of thumb that for every $1,000 invested in a hotel, the hotel should charge $1.00 in average daily rate.

The Accounting Formula   Assets = Liabilities + Owners' Equity.

Theft   The unlawful taking of a business's property.

Time period principle   Requires a business to clearly identify the time period for which its financial transactions are reported.

Times interest earned ratio   Ratio that shows the firm's ability to cover interest expenses with earnings before interest and taxes.

Time value of money   The concept that money has different values at difference points in time.

Timing   Decision made about how best to match revenues to expenses in an accounting period.

Tipped employee tax   Tax assessed on tips and gratuities given to employees by guests or the business as taxable income for those employees.

Total asset turnover ratio   Ratio that shows management's ability to effectively use total assets to generate revenues.

Transfers in   The value of items that have been transferred in to one unit from another.

Transfers out   The value of items that have been transferred out of one unit to another.

Trend   The directional movement of data over time.

Trend line   A graphical representation of trends in data that can be used to make predictions about the future.

Turnover ratios   Ratios that measure the number of times assets are replaced, thus assessing management's efficiency in handling inventories and long-term assets.

U

Undercapitalized   A term used to describe a business that is chronically short of the capital (money) it needs to sustain its operation.

Undistributed operating expense   An expense that cannot truly be assigned to one specific area within an operation.

Undistributed operating expenses section of the USALI   The second section of the USALI consisting of undistributed operating expenses, which are expenses that cannot truly be assigned to one specific department, and are thus, not distributed to the departments.

Unfavorable variance   The difference between planned and actual results when actual results do not meet budget expectations (revenues are lower or expenses are higher).

Uniform system of accounts   A series of suggested (uniform) accounting procedures which represent agreed upon methods of recording financial transactions within a specific industry segment.

Uniform System of Accounts for Restaurants (USAR)   The standardized accounting procedures for the restaurant industry.

Uniform System of Accounts for the Lodging Industry (USALI)   The standardized accounting procedures for the lodging industry.

Uniform System of Financial Reporting for Clubs (USFRC)   The standardized accounting procedures for the club industry.

Upside potential   The possible increased future value of an investment.

USALI   See *Uniform System of Accounts for the Lodging Industry.*

USAR   See *Uniform System of Accounts for Restaurants.*

USFRC   See *Uniform System of Financial Reporting for Clubs.*

Value pricing   An extremely low pricing strategy used to drive significant increases in guest counts.

Variable cost   A cost that increases as sales volume increases and decreases as sales volume decreases.

Variance   The difference between planned results and actual results.

Venture   A new business.

Venture capitalist   Individual or company that is willing to take risks by financing promising new businesses.

Vertical analysis   An analytical approach that uses percentages to compare all items on the income statement to revenues.

Voice over Internet protocol (VOIP)   A service that allows for "free" long-distance calls via computer.

VOIP   See *Voice over Internet protocol.*

Wealth   The current value of all a company's assets minus all of a company's obligations.

Weighted average sales per guest   The value arrived at by dividing the total amount guests spend by the total number of guests served.

Wi-fi   An abbreviation for Wireless Fidelity access.

Working capital   The difference between current assets and current liabilities.

Write-off   An official declaration that an account receivable is uncollectible.

Y

Yield   The percentage of total potential revenue that is actually realized.

Yield management   See *Revenue management.*

About the Authors

Lea R. Dopson is Chair and Associate Professor of the Hospitality Management program at the University of North Texas. Previously, she taught at Cal Poly Pomona, the University of Houston, and Texas Tech University. Lea holds an Ed.D. from the University of Houston, and an MBA and BS in Restaurant, Hotel, and Institutional Management from Texas Tech University. Her areas of teaching include hospitality managerial accounting, hospitality finance, and food and beverage cost controls. She is published in a variety of journals and has presented her research at numerous conferences. She has also co-authored with David Hayes, *Food and Beverage Cost Control*, published by John Wiley & Sons, which is presently in its fourth edition. Lea spent nine months in Zimbabwe, Africa, developing a degree program in international hospitality and tourism. In addition to her academic career, she has held various unit and corporate hospitality management positions with Texas Tech Foodservice, Sheraton Hotels, and Bristol Hotels.

David K. Hayes earned his Ph.D. in Education from Purdue University, as well as MS and BS degrees in Hotel/Restaurant Management. He held faculty positions at Purdue University and the University of Houston. At Texas Tech University he founded the Restaurant/Hotel program and served as Chair of the Department of Nutrition, Education and Restaurant/Hotel Management. Dr. Hayes was Vice President of the Educational Institute (E.I.) of the American Hotel and Lodging Association and was responsible for the development of training programs utilizing advanced technology delivery systems. An industry practitioner as well as academician, for six years he was the Owner/General Manager of the full-service Clarion Hotel and Conference Center in Lansing, Michigan. An accomplished author, his scholarly articles have appeared in *The Cornell Quarterly*. He has written 12 books, including texts translated into Spanish, Chinese, Portuguese, and Croatian. He is now a full-time author who divides his professional writing and industry advising activities between offices in Okemos, Michigan and Jamestown, Tennessee.

Index

A

Accountants, 6
  T accounts, usage, 37–38
Account format balance sheet, 120f
Accounting. *See* Hospitality industry
    accounting
  accuracy, importance, 6
  branches, 7–15
  concepts, 35f
  discipline, discussion, 6–7
  period, 48
    identification, 76–77
    usage, decision, 76
  process, 6
  relationship. *See* Bookkeeping
  term, origination, 6
Accounting formula, 31–32
  changes, recording, 32–43
    T accounts, usage, 37
  components, debit/credit entries (impact),
      38f
  equation, 31
  graphic representation, 33f
  revision, example, 43
  variations, 32f
Accounting fundamentals, 29
  learning application, 55–56
  skills test, 56–59
  terms/concepts, 56

Accounting Principles Board (APB), financial
    documents requirement, 146–147
Accounts, 31
  balance, 38
  increases/decreases, 39f
    hands, usage (representation), 40f
  uniform system. *See* Uniform system of
      accounts
Accounts payable (AP), 37
  activities, 410
  manipulation, 410
Accounts receivable (AR), 37
  accounts, managerial aging, 409
  activities, 408–410
  aging report, 408
    example, 409f
  monitoring, 408
Accrual accounting system, 49
Accumulated depreciation,
    record/accumulation, 37
Achievement budget, 384–385
  example, 385
Acid-test ratio. *See* Quick ratio
Active investors, 448
Activity-based costing (ABC), 316
Activity-based management, 316
Activity ratios, 197–201, 224f
Actual expenditures, budgeted expenditures
    (comparison formulas), 100, 102
ADR. *See* Average daily rate
After-tax profit goal, 339

Ambiance, impact, 240, 241
American Hotel & Lodging Association
(AH&LA), 17
American Institute of Certified Public
Accountants (AICPA), 13
funds statement recommendation,
145–146
Amortized asset, 126
Annual budget, 384
Appreciation. *See* Property appreciation
Assets, 123–127. *See also* Current assets;
Noncurrent assets
accounts, increase/decrease (direct effect),
148–150
amortization, 126
basis, 455–456
funds, sources/uses, 148f
inclusion, 8
liquidation, 46
management concern, 414–415
valuation, approaches, 118–119
worth, determination methods, 126
Audit, definition, 10
Auditing, 10–12
Auditor, definition, 10–11
Average cost per room, calculation, 284
Average daily rate (ADR), 210, 212, 224f
calculation, 284. *See also* Hotels
determination, Hubbart formula (usage),
277
reservation generation fees, subtraction,
295–296
rooms occupied approach, 293
usage, 292–293
yield. *See* Net ADR yield
Average sales per guest (check average),
222–223, 224f
income statement information, usage
(absence), 225

B

Balance sheet. *See* Account format balance
sheet; Creditors; Investors; Lenders;
Managers; Owners
accounting summary, 32
analysis, 129–136
balance, 122
components, 123–129
concept, 104
example, 186f
formats, 119–120
funds, sources/uses (inclusion), 164f
horizontal analysis, 130
example, 132f
learning application, 136
limitations, 118–119
overview, 112
paid in capital, 128
purpose, 113–119
skills test, 137–142
terms/concepts, 136–137
vertical analysis, 129–130
example, 131f
Baseline data, usage, 374
Bed tax. *See* Occupancy
Before-tax net income, calculation, 278, 280
Before-tax profit goal, 339
Beginning inventory, 217
accuracy, maintenance, 220
Beverage cost percentage, 220–221
Bill payments, reporting issue, 50
Blue Lagoon Water Park Resort, case study,
22–24
Bookkeepers, responsibility, 30
Bookkeeping, accounting (relationship),
30–31
Book value, 440

Bottom line, 90
Bottom-up format. *See* Hubbart room rate
    formula
Budgeted expenditures, comparison
    formulas. *See* Actual expenditures;
    In-line budget
Budgeted profit, calculation, 388
Budgeting controls
    learning application, 418–419
    overview, 380–381
    skills test, 420–426
    terms/concepts, 419–420
Budgets. *See* Achievement budget; Annual
        budget; Capital budgets; Cash; Flexible
        budgets; Long-range budget; Operations
        budgets
    expansion, 452f
    financial plan, 381–382
    importance, 381–383
    length/horizon, 383–385
    management, internal controls (usage),
        413–418
    modifications, 403–406
    preparation, 382
        advantages, 382f
    process, 388–389
    production, 382
    purpose, 385–387
        summary, 387f
    types, 383–387
        summary, 387f
    usage, advantages, 382f
    variation, 100
        percentage, 100
Business
    costs
        classification, 315–316
        guest incurrence, 333
    creditors, repayment consideration, 117
    dining situations, 65
    establishment, 431
    expansion, 432
    failures, impact, 11
    legal compliance, 432–433
    operations, consideration, 315
    values, approaches, 446
Buy decisions, contrast. *See* Leasing

C

Call accounting system, 303
    interfacing, 303
Call-around, usage, 286
Capital
    budgeting, 430–433
        management process, 430
    budgets, 386–387
    expenditures, 386, 430
    loss, occurrence, 455
    reference, 430
Capital gains, 455
    occurrence. *See* Realized capital gains
    taxes, 455–456
Capital investment, 433–435
    learning application, 461
    overview, 428–429
    skills test, 462–467
    terms/concepts, 461–462
Capitalism (property ownership), 430
Capitalists (investors), 430
Capitalization approach, 446
Capitalization rates (cap rates), 442–447
    computation, confusion, 444
    increase, 443
    percentage, formula, 445

Cash
  accounting system, 49
  activities, 408–410
  budgeting, 406–413
    importance, 386, 407–408
    receipts/disbursements approach,
      410–413
  budgets, 385, 386
    data, example, 412
    example, 411f
  consideration, 407
  equivalents, 147
  inflows/outflows, summary, 157f, 159f
  nearness, 147
  needs, 407
  net changes, 161–162
  reference, 123, 147
  sufficiency, 408
Cash flows. *See* Financing activities; Investing
    activities; Operating activities
  calculation/reporting methods, usage,
      157–158
  deference (delay), 435–436
  improvement, 452f
  statement. *See* Statement of cash flows
  summary
    comparisons, 168f
    dollar variances/percentage variances,
      169
  understanding, 144–145
C corporation, legal entity, 45
Central Reservation System (CRS), fees, 294
Certificates of deposit (CDs), 123
Certified Management Accountant (CMA),
    certification, 14
Certified Public Accountant (CPA),
    designation, 13
Check average. *See* Average sales per guest
Chief Executive Officer (CEO), responsibility,
    383
Chief Financial Officer (CFO), 167–168
Classification/placement. *See* Expense

Closed out temporary accounts, 32
Closing inventory, 217
Club Managers Association of America
    (CMAA), 18
Collusion (employee cooperation), 416
Common-size analysis, 92, 129
Common stock
  balance sheet entry, 127
  valuation, 127–128
Comparative analysis, 97, 129. *See also*
    Property operations/maintenance
    schedule
Competitive position, maintenance, 244
Competitive pricing, 285
Competitive set (comp set), 290–291
Complimentary (comp) basis, 211
Compounding, 436
Condensed F&B department schedule, 198f
Condensed income statement, 155
  example, 163f, 185f
Conservatism principle, 52–53
  requirements, 53
Consistency principle, 49–50
  statement, 50
Consolidated income statement, 146
Consumers, business transactions
    (interaction), 288–289
Contra asset, listing, 37
Contribution margin (CM), 250
  approach, criticism, 256
  criticism, 261
  dollar amount definition, 336
  income statement, 336
    example, 337f
    per-guest/percent calculations, example,
      337f
  matrix
    analysis, 259f
    development, 257–258
  popularity, comparison, 258
  selection, 258
  usage, 256–260

Controllable costs, 330–331
Controller, definition, 12
Control systems
    cost effectiveness, 416–417
    responsibilities, separation, 416
Corporate room rates, offering, 276
Corporations, types, 45
Cost, 9
    accountants
        discussion, 9–10
        issues, 316
    accounting, 9–10
    allocation system, usage, 327–328
    analysis, example, 441f
    center, operation, 65
    concept, 314–315
    identification, 323
    managerial accounting
        learning application, 343
        overview, 313
        skills test, 344–350
        terms/concepts, 343
    principle, 48–49
    reduction, 335
    types, 315, 331–335
Cost effectiveness. *See* Control systems
Cost of beverage sold, 218–220, 224f
    calculation, 219
Cost of food consumed, 217, 224f
Cost of food sold, 215–218, 224f
Cost of goods consumed, 217
Cost of goods sold (COGS), 215
Cost of sales: beverage, 218, 224f
Cost of sales: food, 215, 224f
Cost per Occupied Room (CPOR), 210,
    214–215, 224f
    usage, 215
Cost/volume/profit (CVP) analysis, 335–342
    computation, 336–340
Cost/volume/profit (CVP) relationship, 336f
Covers served, impact, 225

Covers sold per menu item, average
    popularity, 254
Creditors, 68–69
    balance sheet, 117
Credits, 34–43
    entry, 35
    right hand representation, 39f
Credit sales, occurrence, 409
Creditworthiness, 69
CRS. *See* Central Reservation System
Culinary, Hotel, and Restaurant
    Management, 4
Current assets, 123–125
    liquidity, order, 123f
        explanation, 124
Current data, usage, 369–373
Current dollar accounting, 135
Current liabilities, 127
    ratio, 191
Current ratio, 188–192
    desirability, 189
    summary, 189
Current value (replacement value) approach,
    119
CVP. *See* Cost/volume/profit

D

Debits, 34–43
    entry, 35
    left hand representation, 39f
Debt, impact. *See* Equity returns
Debt coverage ratio, 450
Debt financing, 68
    equity financing, contrast, 447–450
    suppliers, 448
Debt to assets ratio, 194–195
Debt to equity ratio, 194
Default risk, 68
Deflation, impact, 135
Demand forecasts, 366
Departmental cost, classification, 82

Depreciation
    determination, MACRS (usage),
        459–460
    expense, purpose, 74
    method, 37, 158
Direct costs, 327–330
Direct operating expense, 82
    schedule, example, 96f
Discounting, 437
Discount pricing, 285
Distinct business entity principle, 45–46
Dividend payout ratio, 208–209
Dividends, definition, 32
Dividend yield ratio, 209
Dollar change/variance, 97
    calculation, 99
    determination, 130–134
Dormitory, sales history (example), 359f
Double entry accounting, 33–34
Doubtful accounts, 124
Dr. Dopson's Stuff Theory, 122

E

Early departure, 368
Earnings, ratio, 66–67
Earnings before interest and taxes (EBIT), 196
Earnings per shares (EPS), 206–207
Educational Institute (EI), 17
Efficiency ratios, 197
Efficiency, increase, 432
Electronic fund transfers (ETFs),
    documentation, 52
Embezzlement (employee theft), 413
Employee meals, labor-related expense, 217
Ending inventory, 217
    accuracy, maintenance, 220
End-zone sales history, 358f
Enron Corporation, collapse, 11
Equipment purchase process, 440
Equity financing, 68
    contrast. See Debt financing

Equity funds, ROI, 448
Equity returns, debt (impact), 449f
Ethical analysis, 19–22
Ethical decision-making process, questions,
    19–21
Ethical guidelines, 20f
Ethics
    hospitality accounting, relationship,
      18–22
    reference, 19
Expense, 8, 9
    analysis, 88–89, 401–402
      methods, development, 104
    budgeting, 391–397
      methods, comparison, 396
    classification/placement, 78, 80–83
      process, 81
    control/monitoring, 415
    data, documentation, 78–83
    hospitality manager cost, 317–318
    rates, monitoring, 397–398
    reduction, 432
    timing, 78–80
External review (audit). See Internal controls

F

Fade rates, 276
Fair market value, 125
Favorable variance, 398
Federal Insurance Contributions Act (FICA)
    taxation, reduction, 455
Financial accounting, 8–9
Financial Accounting Standards Board
    (FASB)
    cash flows statement requirement, 146
    GAAP development, 44
Financial information, summary, 71f
Financial leverage, 184
    increase, 449
Financial objectives, knowledge, 387, 388
Financial position statement, changes, 145

Financial statements
  currency denomination, preparation, 47
  time period, reporting, 48
Financing activities
  cash flow, 160–161
  cash inflows/outflows summary, 161f
Financing alternatives, 447–461
Fiscal year, financial transactions (inclusion), 48
Fixed assets, 199. *See also* Noncurrent assets
  turnover, 199–200
Fixed costs, 316–319. *See also* Restaurants
  budgeting, 391
  determination, 323
  graph, example, 317f
  variation, 261
Flexible budgets, 404, 406
  development, 404
  example, 405f
  usage, 406
Flip (sell) process, 444–445
Flow-through, 296–298
Folios, maintenance, 43
Follow the leader pricing, 285
Food and beverage (F&B)
  department schedule. *See* Condensed F&B
    department schedule
  inventory turnover ratios, 197–198
  revenue, 300–302
  sales, denominator, 94
  services, 5
Food and beverage (F&B) pricing
  learning application, 268
  overview, 239
  skills test, 269–273
  terms/concepts, 268
Food available for sale, 217
Food cost matrix, analysis, 255f
Food cost percentage, 220, 245–247
  criticism, 261
  focus, 253–256
  formula, 245

item contribution margin, contrast, 248–249
  method, usage. *See* Menu evaluation
  popularity
    comparison, 254
    contrast, 255f
  selection, 258
  usage. *See* Predetermined food cost
    percentage
  variable, 253
Food costs forecast, example, 392
Forecasting
  illustration, 372–373
  learning application, 376
  overview, 353–354
  political aspects, 356
  skills test, 377–379
  terms/concepts, 376
  trend lines, usage, 374–375
Forecasts
  future, involvement, 355–356
  guide, utilization, 356
  historical data, reliance, 356
  importance, 354–356
  level, 366
  manager utilization, 355–356
  methodology, 357–373
Fraud, 413
Free cash flow, 170–171
Full disclosure principle, 53–54
Funds, sources/uses, 147–154. *See also* Assets;
    Liabilities; Owners
  advice, 153f
  calculation, 153
  comparison, 168f
  example, 154f
Future average sales per guest, forecasting, 364–365
Future data
  necessity, 370
  usage, 369–373
Future guest counts, forecasting, 363–364

Future revenues, forecasting, 361–363
Future value (FV). *See* Money
    approach, 119
    calculation, 438
    potential. *See* Upside potential

G

General ledger, 34
Generally accepted accounting principles
    (GAAP), 43–54
    usage, 444
Global Crossing, failure, 11
Global Distribution System (GDS), fees, 294
Glossary, 468–486
Goal value
    computation, 263
    formula, 262
    score, 265
    target, problem, 264–265
    unknowns, solutions (example), 266f
    variables, example, 266
Goal value analysis, 260–268
    accuracy, 264
    data, example, 263f
    purpose, 262
    results, example, 264f
    usefulness, 265–266
Going concern principle, 46
Goodwill, value, 126
GOPPAR. *See* Gross operating profit per
    available room
Government room rates, offering, 276
Gross operating profit (GOP)
    change, 296
    margin, 202–203
    value, 203
Gross operating profit per available room
    (GOPPAR), 298–300
    clarity, 299
    maximization, 372

Gross profit section, components, 71
Group room rates, offering, 276
Guest rooms, food/beverages (provision
    cost), 301
Guests
    cost, incurring, 88–89
    count forecast, calculation, 364
    count history, example, 363f, 364f
    forecasts, 365f
    organization, credit extension, 118
    types, impact, 240, 241

H

Half-year convention, 458–459
Hayes, David, 260
High/low method, usage. *See* Mixed costs
Historical approach, 118
Historical data, 368–369
    consideration, 387
    usage, 390
Historical records, review, 389
Historical room usage/current data, example,
    370f
Horizon. *See* Budgets
Horizontal analysis. *See* Balance sheet;
    Income statement
    calculations, importance, 134
Hospitality
    benefits, 393–394
    business cycle, 54–55
    flowchart, 54f
    lodging/food services definition, 5
    term, definition, 4
Hospitality accounting
    relationship. *See* Ethics
    specialization, 15
Hospitality Financial and Technology
    Professionals (HFTP), 14–15, 18
Hospitality industry
    aspects, 4–5
    performance measure, 298

sales, counting/defining methods, 355
segments, inclusion, 5
taxes, 457
Hospitality industry accounting
  case study, 22–24
  learning application, 25
  overview, 3
  purpose, 6–7
  skills test, 26–28
  terms/concepts, 26
Hospitality Management, 4
Hospitality managers
  action, ethical nature, 22
  managerial accounting, usage (reasons),
    15–16
Hospitality-specific ratios, 210–225
Hoteliers
  data, knowledge, 54
  financial management involvement, 286
  occupancy forecasts, 367
  sales volume, variation, 335
Hotel Management, 4
Hotel revenue management
  learning application, 305–306
  overview, 274
  skills test, 307–312
  terms/concepts, 306
Hotels
  ADR, calculation, 281–282
  financial statements, 84–85
  food services, restaurant food services
    (contrast), 302
  forecast types, 367f
  ratios, 210
  revenue, forecasting, 366–373
  rooms, perishability, 289
Hot spots, access, 305
Hubbart room rate formula, 277–283
  bottom-up approach, 277
  bottom-up format, 278f
  calculations, example, 282f
  computation, 283

normal format, 278f
usage. *See* Average daily rate
usefulness, 282
Huffmann, Lynn, 260

I

Income statement, 63. *See also* Condensed
    income statement
  accounting periods, example, 77f
  analysis, 86–104
  comparative analysis, example, 98f
  creation, decision, 76
  example, 72f, 279f. *See also* Vertical income
    statements
  format, 70–76
  horizontal analysis, 97–104
  horizontal format, 75f
  learning application, 105
  overview, 63
  physical layout, differences, 70
  preparation, 70–85
    principles, 85f
  purpose, 64–69
  report, 32
  revenue schedules, identification, 83f
  skills test, 106–111
  terms/concepts, 105–106
  time period, selection, 76–77
  vertical analysis
    approach, 90–97
    example, 91f–92f, 93f
  vertical format, 73f–74f
Income taxes, 454–455
Incremental costs, 332–333
Indirect costs (overhead costs), 327–330
  assignation, 327–329
Inflation
  accounting, 134–136
  adjustment, 135
In-line budget, 102–103
In-room safes, 305

Institutional Management, 4
Intellectual capital assets, 226–227
  importance, recognition, 227
  list, 227f
Interest, payment, 68
Interfacing. *See* Call accounting system
Internal controls
  learning application, 418–419
  overview, 380–381
  skills test, 420–427
  systems, external review, 417–418
  terms/concepts, 419–420
  types, 414
  usage. *See* Budgets
Internet
  access charges, 305
  impact, 373
  travel sites, fees, 294
Inventories. *See* Beginning inventory; Closing
    inventory; Ending inventory; Opening
    inventory
  inclusion, 124
  turnover, 197–199
    ratios. *See* Food and beverage
Invested funds, earning (computation), 67
Investing activities
  cash flow, 159–160
  cash inflows/outflows summary, 159f
Investments, 125
  objectives, 67
  return threshold, setting, 441
  risk, increase, 442
  risk/reward, 434f
Investors, 66–68
  balance sheet, 115
  information, example, 188f
  ratios, 206–209, 224f
Invoice
  credit, receiving, 79–80
  details, 69
Item contribution margin, 247–249
  contrast. *See* Food cost percentage

Item cost, comparison, 284
Item gross profit margin, 247–248

J

Joint costs, 331–332
Joint ventures, advantage, 452f
Journal
  entry, 34
    principles, 36f
  written record, 34

L

Labor cost
  control/evaluation, 222
  variation, 261–262
Labor cost percentage, 221–222
  ratio, computation, 222
Labor dollars, spending (determination), 393
Leased property, legal treatment, 451
Leases, disadvantages, 452
Leasing
  advantages, 452f
  decisions, buy decisions (contrast),
    450–453
  learning application, 461
  overview, 428–429
  skills test, 462–467
  terms/concepts, 461–462
Legal compliance. *See* Business
Lenders, 68
  balance sheet, 115–116
Lessor/lessee, 450–451
Liabilities, 8. *See also* Current liabilities;
    Long-term liabilities
  classification, 127
  funds, sources/uses, 151f
Lien, 115
Limited Liability Corporation (LLC), 45
Line items, consideration, 391

Liquidity
  order, 123. *See also* Current assets
  ratios, 188, 224f
Loans, consideration, 116
Loan to value (LTV) ratio, 450
Local competition, impact, 240
Location, impact, 240, 241
Lodging services, 5
Long-range budget, 384
Long-term liabilities, 127
Loss analysis, 89–90
Loss leader, 263–264
Low-balling, 366

M

MACRS. *See* Modified Accelerated Cost
    Recovery System
Managed properties, example, 328f
Management
  control systems, characteristics, 414
  role, 415
Managerial accountant analysis. *See* Revenue
Managerial accounting, 12–15
  definition, 13
  math, usage, 24–25
  usage, reasons. *See* Hospitality
Managerial accounts, 82
Managers, 69
  balance sheet, 117–118
  involvement, 383
Margin of safety, 340–341
  example, 340f
Marketable securities, 123
Marketing, sales approach, 244
Market value (asset price), 456
Matching principle, 50–51
Materiality principle, 51
Matrix analysis
  limitations, 259
  usage, 253
Meal period, impact, 240, 241

Menu analysis
  involvement, 249–250
  methods, 250f
  worksheet, example, 251f
Menu engineering, 256
Menu evaluation, food cost percentage
    method (usage), 256
Menu items
  characteristics, 255–256
  classification, 254, 258
  evaluation, goal value (impact), 267
  marketing strategy, 258
  matrix square, location, 258
  nonfood variable costs, assignation, 261
Menu prices
  analysis, 249–268
  assignation, 242–249
  average/weighted average, 252
  establishment, 248
  increase, results (alternative), 243f
  menu item, 250, 252
  totals, 252
Menu pricing, factors, 240–242
Minimum sales point (MSP), 341–342
Mixed costs, 319–321
  budgeting, 392–397
  fixed cost portion, determination, 322
  graph, example, 320f
  separation, high/low method (usage),
    322–323
  split, 321
  variable/fixed components, separation,
    321–326
Modified Accelerated Cost Recovery System
    (MACRS), 457–461
  classes table, hospitality business
    application, 458f
  depreciation method, 458
  percentages. *See* Property
  usage. *See* Depreciation
Monetary unit principle, 46–48
Monetary units, selection, 47f

Money
  future value, 436
  time value, 435–439
MSP. *See* Minimum sales point

N

National Restaurant Association (NRA), 17
National Venture Capitalists Association
    (NVCA), 431–432
Net ADR yield, 294–296
Net income analysis, 402–403
Net income/profit, 90
Net operating income (NOI), 443
  level, generation, 445–446
Net receivables, 124
New room revenue, 300–305
Noncash transaction, 162
Non-controllable costs, 330–331
Noncurrent assets (fixed assets),
    125–127
Nonfood variable costs, assignation. *See*
    Menu items
Nonoperating expenses, 71
  calculation, 280
  components, 74
Nonpayment risk, 68
No-show, 368
  charges, 305

O

Objectivity principle, 51–52
Occupancy
  forecasts. *See* Hoteliers
    example, 369f
  percentage, 210–212, 224f
    example, 225f, 226f
    usage, 291–292
  tax (bed tax), 457
    recording, 10

$1 per $1,000 rule, 283–285
  computation, 284
On-the-books, 370
Opening inventory, 217
Operated department
  income, 74
    calculation, 280–281
    payroll/expense summaries, 81f
    revenue, 304–305
Operated department income, separation,
    277
Operating activities
  cash flow, 156–159
    calculation, 158
  cash inflows/outflows summary, 157f
Operating activities,
    expenses, 156–157
Operating cash flows, 191
Operating cash flows to total liabilities ratio,
    195–196
Operating efficiency ratio, 202–203
Operating expenses, control, 71
Operational budgets, consideration, 386
Operations
  administration, example, 328f
  assumptions, 387, 388
Operations budgets, 385–386
  development, 388–397
  essentials, 387–388
  modification, 403–404
  monitoring, 397–406
    process, 400
  preparation, example, 399–400
Opportunity costs, 334–335
Other assets (noncurrent asset group), 126
Out of order (OOO), 211
Over. *See* Short
Overhead allocation
  annual revenue basis, 329f
  charges, 329
  room number basis, 329f
Overhead costs. *See* Indirect costs

Overstay, 368
Owned property, legal treatment, 451
Owners
    balance sheet, 114–115
    equity, 8, 127–129
        funds, sources/uses, 151f
        return, 205
        sole proprietorship, 128f

P

Package, 84
Package room rate, 276
Paid in capital. *See* Balance sheet
Partnerships, 45
Par value, 127
Passive investors, 448
Payback period, 441–442
Pay-per-play in-room games, 304–305
Pay-per-view movies, 304
Payroll allocations, costs (subtraction),
    393–394
Payroll taxes, 10
Percentage, 182
    change computation, help box, 134f
    fraction form, 182–183
Percentage variance, computation, 99, 362
    help box, example, 100f
Permanent owners' equity accounts, 31–32
PMS. *See* Property management system
Point of sale (POS) systems, 358
    programming, 223
Popularity (sales mix), 250
    variable, 253
Portion size, impact, 240, 241
Predetermined food cost percentage, usage,
    246
Preferred stock, issuance, 128
Prepaid expenses, 124
Present value (PV), 437
    calculation, 438
    computation process, 437–438

Prestige pricing, 285
Price/earnings (P/E) ratio, 207–208
    variation, 208
Price/value relationship, guest value
    perception, 243
Pricing. *See* Competitive pricing; Discount
    pricing; Follow the leader pricing;
    Prestige pricing
    cost approaches, 244–248
    factor table, 246f
    marketing approaches, 244
Principal, reduction, 160
Prior-period operating results, 387
Product quality, impact, 240, 241
Profit, 8
    achievement, 439–440
    analysis, 89–90, 402–403
        methods, development, 104
    center, 65
    factors, 89
    formula, 64, 314
    generation, 301–302
    manager responsibility, 330
    margin, 202. *See also* Gross operating profit
        margin; Item gross profit margin
        importance, 95
    percentage/dollar
        report, 402
        review, 402–403
    rates, monitoring, 397, 398
    representation, 64
Profitability ratios, 201–206, 224f
Property
    buying/leasing, contrast, 451f
    classes, MACRS percentages, 458f
    legal considerations, 451f
    tax bill, example, 456f
    taxes, 456–457
Property and equipment
    inclusion, 126
    turnover, 199–200
Property appreciation, 66

Property management system (PMS), 276
   dates, memorization, 290
   events, entry, 367
   historical data, 369
     absence, 372
   importance, 289–290
     reduction, 368
Property operations/maintenance schedule,
   comparative analysis, 101f
Proprietorships, 45
Public Company Accounting Reform and
   Investor Protection Act, 11
Purchases, 217
Purchasing power, 135

Q

Quick ratio (acid-test ratio), 190–191
Quick-service restaurant (QSR), 70

R

Rack rates
   price, 275
   room type basis, example, 276f
   variation, 275–276
Random variation, 357
Ratio analysis
   learning application, 228–229
   limitations, 226–228
   overview, 180
   skills test, 230–235
   terms/concepts, 229
Ratios
   comparative analysis, 225–226
   purpose/value, 181–184
   summary, 224f
   types, 185–225
   values. *See* Stakeholders
Real estate appraisal, 456
Realized capital gains, occurrence, 455
Receivable account, aging, 408

Recovery years, 458
Regression analysis, 374
Replacement approach, 446
Report format
   balance sheet, 121f
   usage, 120
Reservation distribution channels, 294
Responsibilities, separation. *See* Control
   systems
Responsibility accounting, 95
Restauranteurs, activity summaries, 54
Restaurant Management, 4
Restaurants
   budget
     comparison, 401f
     example, 396f
   costs, example, 321f
   fixed costs, 324
   income statement, example, 216f
   incremental costs, concern, 332–333
   ratios, 215
   revenues, forecasting, 358–365
   variable costs per guest, 324f
Retained earnings, 31–32. *See also* Statement
   of retained earnings
   reference, 128
Return on assets (ROA), 203–205
   ratio, 204
Return on equity (ROE), 205–206
Return on investment (ROI), 66
   achievement, 434
   computation, 67, 68
   estimation, 442
   factors, 439f
   improvement, 452f
   levels, demand, 147
   objectives, 67
   relationship, 386
   variation, 440
Returns, 203
   savings rate, 440–441
   threshold, setting. *See* Investments

Revenue
  analysis, 86–88, 400
    methods, development, 104
  approach, 446
  budgeting, 389–391
  changes, managerial accountant analysis,
    88
  collection process, recording, 413
  comparisons, 87f
  control/monitoring, 415
  data, documentation, 77–78
  decline, manager determination, 87
  definition, 8
  expense matching, decisions-80, 79
  external factors, consideration, 390
  increase, 432
  internal factors, consideration, 389–390
  levels, manager concern, 86–87
  management (yield management),
    287–300. See also Hotel revenue
    management
    mathematical programs, usage,
      289–290
    procedure, implementation, 289
    understanding, 288–289
  managers, responsibility, 288
  product, 288
  rates, monitoring, 397
  receiving, 64
  reconciliation, 12
  schedule, example, 84f
Revenue per Available Customer (RevPAC),
  210, 214, 224f
Revenue per Available Room (RevPAR), 210,
  212–213, 224f
  achievement, 290
  calculation, 213
  changes, evaluation, 290–291
  maximization, 372
    ability, 354
Reward. See Investments
  concepts, 433–434

Risk. See Investments
  concepts, 433–434
Robbery, risk, 413
Room rates
  creation. See Special event room rates
  economics, 275
  establishment, 275–287
  methodologies. See Web-influence room
    rate methodologies
    alternative, 285
  offering. See Corporate room rates;
    Government room rates; Group room
    rates; Package room rates; Seasonal
    room rate
  online discovery, 287
Rooms
  department revenues, calculation, 281
  inventories, managerial understanding, 275
  mix, basis, 275
  occupied approach. See Average daily rate
  revenue. See New room revenue
  statistics, example, 291f
  types, choice, 212

S

Salaried wages (fixed wages), subtraction,
  394–395
Sales
  data
    examples, 374f, 375f
    line graph/trend line, example, 375f
  increase, estimation, 363
  mix, impact, 240, 241–242
  offering, example, 445f
  records, accuracy (importance), 355
  taxes, 457
    payment, 10
Sales forecast
  calculation, 362f
  creation, 358

Sales history, 358, 365
  example, 360f, 361f
Salvage value, 37
  estimation, 458
Sarbanes-Oxley Act (SOX), 11
SCF. *See* Statement of cash flows
Schedules, 83–85. *See also* Supplementary
    schedules
  creation methods, 83
Seasonal room rate, offering, 276
Seasonal trend, data pattern change, 357
Seat turnover, 223–225
Securities, acquisition, 125
Selling price (SP), 250, 337
Semi-fixed costs (semi-variable costs), 319
Service charges, report, 302
Service levels, impact, 241
Service personnel, staffing implications, 359
Short (over), 415
Significant variance, 399
  identification, 401–402
Simple average, usage, 360
Sinking fund, purpose, 125
Smith Travel Research (STR), occupancy
    percentage statistics, 211
Sole proprietorship, 128f
Solvency, reference, 147
Solvency ratios, 192–196, 224f
  summary, 193
Special event room rates, creation, 266
Stakeholders
  profitability, impact, 65
  ratios, value, 183–184
Standard costs, 333–334
Statement of cash flows (SCF)
  additions/subtractions, 161f
  analysis, 167–171
  creation, 155–167
  example, 165f, 187f
  format, 156f
  funds sources, positive number, 160
  funds sources/uses, 146

learning application, 171
  overview, 143
  purpose, 145–147
  skills test, 172–179
  terms/concepts, 171–172
Statement of retained earnings, 155
  example, 163f, 188f
Stayover, 368
Step costs, 326–327
  example, 327f
Stockholders, impact, 45
Straight-line depreciation, 458
Stuff theory. *See* Dr. Dopson's Stuff Theory
Sub S corporation, special status, 45
Sunk costs, 334
Supplementary schedules, 162–167
Supply/demand, economic laws,
    242–243

T

T accounts, 34
  balances, 38f
  components, 35
  creation, 36
  establishment, example, 41–42
Target turnover ratios, 199
Taxable income (adjusted gross income), 454
Taxation, 454–461
  learning application, 461
  overview, 428–429
  skills test, 462–467
  terms/concepts, 461–462
Taxes
  accountant, questions, 454–455
  accounting, 10
  avoidance, 454
  control, 71–72
  definition, 10
  evasion, 454
Telecommunications revenue, 302–304

Telephone system, costs (association), 319–320
Temporary owners' equity accounts, inclusion, 32
   closeout, 32
Theft. *See* Embezzlement
   risk, 413
Time period principle, 48
Times interest earned ratio, 196
Time value of money. *See* Money
Timing. *See* Expense
Tipped employee tax, 457
Total asset turnover ratio, 200–201
   fixed asset turnover ratio, difference, 201
Total cost
   equation, 325–326
   substitution, 324
Total sales, increase, 222
Total sales, percentage (ratio calculations), 93–94
Total variable costs, determination, 322
Transaction recording/analysis, 30f
Transfers in/out, 218
Travel and Tourism Management, 4
Trend lines
   production, 374
   usage. *See* Forecasting
Turnover ratios, 197. *See also* Food and beverage; Target turnover ratios

U

Undistributed operating expenses, 74
   calculation, 280
   classification, 82
Unfavorable variance, 398
Uniform system of accounts, 16–18
Uniform System of Accounts for Restaurants (USAR), 17
   understanding, 71
   usage, 70–71

Uniform System of Accounts for the Lodging Industry (USALI), 17
   procedures recommendation, 77–78
   understanding, 74
Uniform System of Financial Reporting for Clubs (USFRC), 18
Upside potential (future value potential), 446

V

Value pricing, 260
Variable costs per guest. *See* Restaurants
   determination, 323
Variable costs (VC), 250, 316–318, 337
   budgeting, 391–392
   graph, example, 318f
   volume change, relationship, 261
Variable dollars per cover, 406
Variable wages, determination, 394–395
Variable workers (hourly workers), money budget (determination), 395
Variance, 398–403. *See also* Dollar change/variance; Favorable variance; Significant variance; Unfavorable variance
   cash calculation, 133
   determination, 130–134
Variation, occurrence, 357
Venture (new business), 431
Vertical analysis. *See* Balance sheet approach. *See* Income statement example, 96f. *See also* Income statement usage, 130
Vertical income statements, example, 297f
Voice Over Internet Protocol (VOIP), 303
Volume maximization, goal, 244
Voluntary benefit programs, cost, 393–394

W

Wealth, possession, 118
Web-influence room rate methodologies, 285–287

Weighted average sales per guest, usage, 360
Wireless fidelity (WiFi) access, 305
Working capital, 191–192
  summary, 192
WorldCom, failure, 11
Write-offs, 409

Y

Yield, 205
  description, 287–288
  management. *See* Revenue
  ratio. *See* Dividend yield ratio